MW00425815

4.4BSD
Programmer's
Reference Manual
(PRM)

CPCUG LIBRARY MATERIAL

AFTER USE PLEASE RETURN TO

Capital P C User Group Library
51 Monroe St., Plaza East Two
Rockville, MD 208⁻·

Now in its twentieth year, the USENIX Association, the UNIX and Advanced Computing Systems professional and technical organization, is a not-for-profit membership association of individuals and institutions with an interest in UNIX and UNIX-like systems, and, by extension, C++, X windows, and other advanced tools and technologies.

USENIX and its members are dedicated to:

- fostering innovation and communicating research and technological developments,
- sharing ideas and experience relevant to UNIX, UNIX-related, and advanced computing systems, and
- providing a neutral forum for the exercise of critical thought and airing of technical issues.

USENIX publishes a journal (**Computing Systems**), a newsletter (*;login:*), Proceedings from its frequent Conferences and Symposia, and a Book Series.

SAGE, The Systems Administrators Guild, a Special Technical Group with the USENIX Association, is dedicated to the advancement of system administration as a profession.

SAGE brings together systems managers and administrators to:

- propagate knowledge of good professional practice,
- recruit talented individuals to the profession,
- recognize individuals who attain professional excellence,
- foster technical development and share solutions to technical problems, and
- communicate in an organized voice with users, management, and vendors on system administration topics.

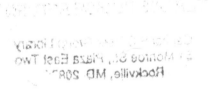

4.4BSD
Programmer's
Reference Manual
(PRM)

Berkeley Software Distribution

April, 1994

Computer Systems Research Group
University of California at Berkeley

CPCUG LIBRARY MATERIAL

AFTER USE PLEASE RETURN TO

Capital P C User Group Library
51 Monroe St., Plaza East Two
Rockville, MD 208⁻ ˙

A USENIX Association Book
O'Reilly & Associates, Inc.
103 Morris Street, Suite A
Sebastopol, CA 94572

First Printing, 1994

Copyright 1979, 1980, 1983, 1986, 1993, 1994 The Regents of the University of California. All rights reserved.

Other than the specific manual pages and documents listed below as copyrighted by AT&T, redistribution and use of this manual in source and binary forms, with or without modification, are permitted provided that the following conditions are met:

1) Redistributions of this manual must retain the copyright notices on this page, this list of conditions and the following disclaimer.

2) Software or documentation that incorporates part of this manual must reproduce the copyright notices on this page, this list of conditions and the following disclaimer in the documentation and/or other materials provided with the distribution.

3) All advertising materials mentioning features or use of this software must display the following acknowledgement: ''This product includes software developed by the University of California, Berkeley and its contributors.''

4) Neither the name of the University nor the names of its contributors may be used to endorse or promote products derived from this software without specific prior written permission.

THIS SOFTWARE IS PROVIDED BY THE REGENTS AND CONTRIBUTORS ''AS IS'' AND ANY EXPRESS OR IMPLIED WARRANTIES, INCLUDING, BUT NOT LIMITED TO, THE IMPLIED WARRANTIES OF MERCHANTABILITY AND FITNESS FOR A PARTICULAR PURPOSE ARE DISCLAIMED. IN NO EVENT SHALL THE REGENTS OR CONTRIBUTORS BE LIABLE FOR ANY DIRECT, INDIRECT, INCIDENTAL, SPECIAL, EXEMPLARY, OR CONSEQUENTIAL DAMAGES (INCLUDING, BUT NOT LIMITED TO, PROCUREMENT OF SUBSTITUTE GOODS OR SERVICES; LOSS OF USE, DATA, OR PROFITS; OR BUSINESS INTERRUPTION) HOWEVER CAUSED AND ON ANY THEORY OF LIABILITY, WHETHER IN CONTRACT, STRICT LIABILITY, OR TORT (INCLUDING NEGLIGENCE OR OTHERWISE) ARISING IN ANY WAY OUT OF THE USE OF THIS SOFTWARE, EVEN IF ADVISED OF THE POSSIBILITY OF SUCH DAMAGE.

The Institute of Electrical and Electronics Engineers and the American National Standards Committee X3, on Information Processing Systems have given us permission to reprint portions of their documentation.

In the following statement, the phrase ''this text'' refers to portions of the system documentation.

''Portions of this text are reprinted and reproduced in electronic form in 4.4BSD from IEEE Std 1003.1-1988, IEEE Standard Portable Operating System Interface for Computer Environments (POSIX), copyright 1988 by the Institute of Electrical and Electronics Engineers, Inc. In the event of any discrepancy between these versions and the original IEEE Standard, the original IEEE Standard is the referee document.''

In the following statement, the phrase ''This material'' refers to portions of the system documentation.

''This material is reproduced with permission from American National Standards Committee X3, on Information Processing Systems. Computer and Business Equipment Manufacturers Association (CBEMA), 311 First St., NW, Suite 500, Washington, DC 20001-2178. The developmental work of Programming Language C was completed by the X3J11 Technical Committee.''

Manual pages ptrace.2, ecvt.3, mp.3, plot.3, L-devices.5, L-dialcodes.5, L.aliases.5, L.cmds.5, L.sys.5, USERFILE.5, dump.5, and plot.5 are copyright 1979, AT&T Bell Laboratories, Incorporated. Holders of UNIX™/32V, System III, or System V software licenses are permitted to copy these documents, or any portion of them, as necessary for licensed use of the software, provided this copyright notice and statement of permission are included.

The views and conclusions contained in this manual are those of the authors and should not be interpreted as representing official policies, either expressed or implied, of the Regents of the University of California.

This book was printed and bound in the United States of America.
Distributed by O'Reilly & Associates, Inc.

[recycle logo] This book is printed on acid-free paper with 50% recycled content, 10-13% post-consumer waste. O'Reilly & Associates is committed to using paper with the highest recycled content available consistent with high quality.

ISBN: 1-56592-078-3

Contents

Introduction

The documentation for 4.4BSD is in a format similar to the one used for the 4.2BSD and 4.3BSD manuals. It is divided into three sets; each set consists of one or more volumes. The abbreviations for the volume names are listed in square brackets; the abbreviations for the manual sections are listed in parenthesis.

I. User's Documents
    User's Reference Manual [URM]
        Commands (1)
        Games (6)
        Macro packages and language conventions (7)
    User's Supplementary Documents [USD]
        Getting Started
        Basic Utilities
        Communicating with the World
        Text Editing
        Document Preparation
        Amusements

II. Programmer's Documents
    Programmer's Reference Manual [PRM]
        System calls (2)
        Subroutines (3)
        Special files (4)
        File formats and conventions (5)
    Programmer's Supplementary Documents [PSD]
        Documents of Historic Interest
        Languages in common use
        Programming Tools
        Programming Libraries
        General Reference

III. System Manager's Manual [SMM]
        Maintenance commands (8)
        System Installation and Administration

References to individual documents are given as "volume:document", thus USD:1 refers to the first document in the "User's Supplementary Documents". References to manual pages are given as "*name*(section)" thus *sh*(1) refers to the shell manual entry in section 1.

The manual pages give descriptions of the features of the 4.4BSD system, as developed at the University of California at Berkeley. They do not attempt to provide perspective or tutorial information about the 4.4BSD operating system, its facilities, or its implementation. Various documents on those topics are contained in the "UNIX User's Supplementary Documents" (USD), the "UNIX Programmer's Supplementary Documents" (PSD), and "UNIX System Manager's Manual" (SMM). In particular, for an overview see "The UNIX Time-Sharing System" (PSD:1) by Ritchie and Thompson; for a tutorial see "UNIX for Beginners" (USD:1) by Kernighan, and for an guide to the new features of this latest version, see "Berkeley Software Architecture Manual (4.4 Edition)" (PSD:5).

Within the area it surveys, this volume attempts to be timely, complete and concise. Where the latter two objectives conflict, the obvious is often left unsaid in favor of brevity. It is intended that each program be described as it is, not as it should be. Inevitably, this means that various sections will soon be out of date.

Commands are programs intended to be invoked directly by the user, in contrast to subroutines, that are intended to be called by the user's programs. User commands are described in URM section 1. Commands generally reside in directory /bin (for bin ary programs). Some programs also reside in /usr/ bin, to save space in /bin. These directories are searched automatically by the command interpreters. Additional directories that may be of interest include /usr/ contrib/ bin, which has contributed software /usr/ old/ bin, which has old but sometimes still useful software and /usr/ local/ bin, which contains software local to your site.

Games have been relegated to URM section 6 and /usr/ games, to keep them from contaminating the more staid information of URM section 1.

Miscellaneous collection of information necessary for writing in various specialized languages such as character codes, macro packages for typesetting, etc is contained in URM section 7.

System calls are entries into the BSD kernel. The system call interface is identical to a C language procedure call; the equivalent C procedures are described in PRM section 2.

An assortment of subroutines is available; they are described in PRM section 3. The primary libraries in which they are kept are described in *intro*(3). The functions are described in terms of C.

PRM section 4 discusses the characteristics of each system "file" that refers to an I/O device. The names in this section refer to the HP300 device names for the hardware, instead of the names of the special files themselves.

The file formats and conventions (PRM section 5) documents the structure of particular kinds of files; for example, the form of the output of the loader and assembler is given. Excluded are files used by only one command, for example the assembler's intermediate files.

Commands and procedures intended for use primarily by the system administrator are described in SMM section 8. The files described here are almost all kept in the directory /etc. The system administration binaries reside in /sbin, and /usr/ sbin.

Each section consists of independent entries of a page or so each. The name of the entry is in the upper corners of its pages, together with the section number. Entries within each section are alphabetized. The page numbers of each entry start at 1; it is infeasible to number consecutively the pages of a document like this that is republished in many variant forms.

All entries are based on a common format; not all subsections always appear.

> The *name* subsection lists the exact names of the commands and subroutines covered under the entry and gives a short description of their purpose.

> The *synopsis* summarizes the use of the program being described. A few conventions are used, particularly in the Commands subsection:

>> **Boldface** words are considered literals, and are typed just as they appear.

>> Square brackets [ ] around an argument show that the argument is optional. When an argument is given as "name", it always refers to a file name.

>> Ellipses "..." are used to show that the previous argument-prototype may be repeated.

>> A final convention is used by the commands themselves. An argument beginning with a minus sign "−" usually means that it is an option-specifying argument, even if it appears in a position where a file name could appear. Therefore, it is unwise to have files whose names begin with "−".

> The *description* subsection discusses in detail the subject at hand.

> The *files* subsection gives the names of files that are built into the program.

> A *see also* subsection gives pointers to related information.

> A *diagnostics* subsection discusses the diagnostic indications that may be produced. Messages that are intended to be self-explanatory are not listed.

> The *bugs* subsection gives known bugs and sometimes deficiencies. Occasionally the suggested fix is also described.

At the beginning of URM, PRM, and SSM is a List of Manual Pages, organized by section and alphabetically within each section, and a Permuted Index derived from that List. Within each index entry, the title of the writeup to which it refers is followed by the appropriate section number in parentheses. This fact is important because there is considerable name duplication among the sections, arising principally from commands that exist only to exercise a particular system call. Finally, there is a list of documents on the inside back cover of each volume.

List of Manual Pages

1. Commands and Application Programs

2. System Calls

3. C Library Subroutines

4. Special Files

5. File Formats

6. Games

7. Miscellaneous

8. System Maintenance

Permuted Index

Section 2
System
Calls

2

NAME

intro – introduction to system calls and error numbers

SYNOPSIS

`#include <sys/errno.h>`

DESCRIPTION

This section provides an overview of the system calls, their error returns, and other common definitions and concepts.

DIAGNOSTICS

Nearly all of the system calls provide an error number in the external variable *errno*, which is defined as:

```
extern int errno
```

When a system call detects an error, it returns an integer value indicating failure (usually -1) and sets the variable *errno* accordingly. <This allows interpretation of the failure on receiving a -1 and to take action accordingly.> Successful calls never set *errno*; once set, it remains until another error occurs. It should only be examined after an error. Note that a number of system calls overload the meanings of these error numbers, and that the meanings must be interpreted according to the type and circumstances of the call.

The following is a complete list of the errors and their names as given in <sys/errno.h>.

0 *Error 0*. Not used.

1 EPERM *Operation not permitted*. An attempt was made to perform an operation limited to processes with appropriate privileges or to the owner of a file or other resources.

2 ENOENT *No such file or directory*. A component of a specified pathname did not exist, or the pathname was an empty string.

3 ESRCH *No such process*. No process could be found corresponding to that specified by the given process ID.

4 EINTR *Interrupted function call*. An asynchronous signal (such as SIGINT or SIGQUIT) was caught by the process during the execution of an interruptible function. If the signal handler performs a normal return, the interrupted function call will seem to have returned the error condition.

5 EIO *Input/output error*. Some physical input or output error occurred. This error will not be reported until a subsequent operation on the same file descriptor and may be lost (over written) by any subsequent errors.

6 ENXIO *No such device or address*. Input or output on a special file referred to a device that did not exist, or made a request beyond the limits of the device. This error may also occur when, for example, a tape drive is not online or no disk pack is loaded on a drive.

7 E2BIG *Arg list too long*. The number of bytes used for the argument and environment list of the new process exceeded the current limit of 20480 bytes (NCARGS in <sys/param.h>).

8 ENOEXEC *Exec format error*. A request was made to execute a file that, although it has the appropriate permissions, was not in the format required for an executable file.

9 EBADF *Bad file descriptor*. A file descriptor argument was out of range, referred to no open file, or a read (write) request was made to a file that was only open for writing (reading).

2

10 ECHILD *No child processes.* A wait or waitpid function was executed by a process that had no existing or unwaited-for child processes.

11 EDEADLK *Resource deadlock avoided.* An attempt was made to lock a system resource that would have resulted in a deadlock situation.

12 ENOMEM *Cannot allocate memory.* The new process image required more memory than was allowed by the hardware or by system-imposed memory management constraints. A lack of swap space is normally temporary; however, a lack of core is not. Soft limits may be increased to their corresponding hard limits.

13 EACCES *Permission denied.* An attempt was made to access a file in a way forbidden by its file access permissions.

14 EFAULT *Bad address.* The system detected an invalid address in attempting to use an argument of a call.

15 ENOTBLK *Not a block device.* A block device operation was attempted on a non-block device or file.

16 EBUSY *Resource busy.* An attempt to use a system resource which was in use at the time in a manner which would have conflicted with the request.

17 EEXIST *File exists.* An existing file was mentioned in an inappropriate context, for instance, as the new link name in a link function.

18 EXDEV *Improper link.* A hard link to a file on another file system was attempted.

19 ENODEV *Operation not supported by device.* An attempt was made to apply an inappropriate function to a device, for example, trying to read a write-only device such as a printer.

20 ENOTDIR *Not a directory.* A component of the specified pathname existed, but it was not a directory, when a directory was expected.

21 EISDIR *Is a directory.* An attempt was made to open a directory with write mode specified.

22 EINVAL *Invalid argument.* Some invalid argument was supplied. (For example, specifying an undefined signal to a signal or kill function).

23 ENFILE *Too many open files in system.* Maximum number of file descriptors allowable on the system has been reached and a requests for an open cannot be satisfied until at least one has been closed.

24 EMFILE *Too many open files.* <As released, the limit on the number of open files per process is 64.> Getdtablesize(2) will obtain the current limit.

25 ENOTTY *Inappropriate ioctl for device.* A control function (see ioctl(2)) was attempted for a file or special device for which the operation was inappropriate.

26 ETXTBSY *Text file busy.* The new process was a pure procedure (shared text) file which was open for writing by another process, or while the pure procedure file was being executed an open call requested write access.

27 EFBIG *File too large.* The size of a file exceeded the maximum (about 2^{31} bytes).

28 ENOSPC *Device out of space.* A write to an ordinary file, the creation of a directory or symbolic link, or the creation of a directory entry failed because no more disk blocks were available on the file system, or the allocation of an inode for a newly created file failed because no more inodes were available on the file system.

2

29 ESPIPE *Illegal seek.* An lseek function was issued on a socket, pipe or FIFO.

30 EROFS *Read-only file system.* An attempt was made to modify a file or directory was made on a file system that was read-only at the time.

31 EMLINK *Too many links.* Maximum allowable hard links to a single file has been exceeded (limit of 32767 hard links per file).

32 EPIPE *Broken pipe.* A write on a pipe, socket or FIFO for which there is no process to read the data.

33 EDOM *Numerical argument out of domain.* A numerical input argument was outside the defined domain of the mathematical function.

34 ERANGE *Numerical result out of range.* A numerical result of the function was too large to fit in the available space (perhaps exceeded precision).

35 EAGAIN *Resource temporarily unavailable.* This is a temporary condition and later calls to the same routine may complete normally.

36 EINPROGRESS *Operation now in progress.* An operation that takes a long time to complete (such as a connect(2)) was attempted on a non-blocking object (see fcntl(2)).

37 EALREADY *Operation already in progress.* An operation was attempted on a non-blocking object that already had an operation in progress.

38 ENOTSOCK *Socket operation on non-socket.* Self-explanatory.

39 EDESTADDRREQ *Destination address required.* A required address was omitted from an operation on a socket.

40 EMSGSIZE *Message too long.* A message sent on a socket was larger than the internal message buffer or some other network limit.

41 EPROTOTYPE *Protocol wrong type for socket.* A protocol was specified that does not support the semantics of the socket type requested. For example, you cannot use the ARPA Internet UDP protocol with type SOCK_STREAM.

42 ENOPROTOOPT *Protocol not available.* A bad option or level was specified in a getsockopt(2) or setsockopt(2) call.

43 EPROTONOSUPPORT *Protocol not supported.* The protocol has not been configured into the system or no implementation for it exists.

44 ESOCKTNOSUPPORT *Socket type not supported.* The support for the socket type has not been configured into the system or no implementation for it exists.

45 EOPNOTSUPP *Operation not supported.* The attempted operation is not supported for the type of object referenced. Usually this occurs when a file descriptor refers to a file or socket that cannot support this operation, for example, trying to *accept* a connection on a datagram socket.

46 EPFNOSUPPORT *Protocol family not supported.* The protocol family has not been configured into the system or no implementation for it exists.

47 EAFNOSUPPORT *Address family not supported by protocol family.* An address incompatible with the requested protocol was used. For example, you shouldn't necessarily expect to be able to use NS addresses with ARPA Internet protocols.

48 EADDRINUSE *Address already in use.* Only one usage of each address is normally permitted.

49 EADDRNOTAVAIL *Cannot assign requested address.* Normally results from an attempt to create a socket with an address not on this machine.

50 ENETDOWN *Network is down.* A socket operation encountered a dead network.

51 ENETUNREACH *Network is unreachable.* A socket operation was attempted to an unreachable network.

52 ENETRESET *Network dropped connection on reset.* The host you were connected to crashed and rebooted.

53 ECONNABORTED *Software caused connection abort.* A connection abort was caused internal to your host machine.

54 ECONNRESET *Connection reset by peer.* A connection was forcibly closed by a peer. This normally results from a loss of the connection on the remote socket due to a timeout or a reboot.

55 ENOBUFS *No buffer space available.* An operation on a socket or pipe was not performed because the system lacked sufficient buffer space or because a queue was full.

56 EISCONN *Socket is already connected.* A `connect` request was made on an already connected socket; or, a `sendto` or `sendmsg` request on a connected socket specified a destination when already connected.

57 ENOTCONN *Socket is not connected.* An request to send or receive data was disallowed because the socket was not connected and (when sending on a datagram socket) no address was supplied.

58 ESHUTDOWN *Cannot send after socket shutdown.* A request to send data was disallowed because the socket had already been shut down with a previous `shutdown(2)` call.

60 ETIMEDOUT *Operation timed out.* A `connect` or `send` request failed because the connected party did not properly respond after a period of time. (The timeout period is dependent on the communication protocol.)

61 ECONNREFUSED *Connection refused.* No connection could be made because the target machine actively refused it. This usually results from trying to connect to a service that is inactive on the foreign host.

62 ELOOP *Too many levels of symbolic links.* A path name lookup involved more than 8 symbolic links.

63 ENAMETOOLONG *File name too long.* A component of a path name exceeded 255 (MAXNAMELEN) characters, or an entire path name exceeded 1023 (MAXPATHLEN-1) characters.

64 EHOSTDOWN *Host is down.* A socket operation failed because the destination host was down.

65 EHOSTUNREACH *No route to host.* A socket operation was attempted to an unreachable host.

66 ENOTEMPTY *Directory not empty.* A directory with entries other than '.' and '..' was supplied to a remove directory or rename call.

67 EPROCLIM *Too many processes.*

68 EUSERS *Too many users.* The quota system ran out of table entries.

69 EDQUOT *Disc quota exceeded.* A `write` to an ordinary file, the creation of a directory or symbolic link, or the creation of a directory entry failed because the user's quota of disk blocks was exhausted, or the allocation of an inode for a newly created file failed because the user's quota of inodes was exhausted.

70 ESTALE *Stale NFS file handle.* An attempt was made to access an open file (on an NFS filesystem) which is now unavailable as referenced by the file descriptor. This may indicate the file was deleted on the NFS server or some other catastrophic event occurred.

72 EBADRPC *RPC struct is bad.* Exchange of RPC information was unsuccessful.

73 ERPCMISMATCH *RPC version wrong.* The version of RPC on the remote peer is not compatible with the local version.

74 EPROGUNAVAIL *RPC prog. not avail.* The requested program is not registered on the remote host.

75 EPROGMISMATCH *Program version wrong.* The requested version of the program is not available on the remote host (RPC).

76 EPROCUNAVAIL *Bad procedure for program.* An RPC call was attempted for a procedure which doesn't exist in the remote program.

77 ENOLCK *No locks available.* A system-imposed limit on the number of simultaneous file locks was reached.

78 ENOSYS *Function not implemented.* Attempted a system call that is not available on this system.

DEFINITIONS

Process ID.

Each active process in the system is uniquely identified by a non-negative integer called a process ID. The range of this ID is from 0 to 30000.

Parent process ID

A new process is created by a currently active process; (see fork(2)). The parent process ID of a process is initially the process ID of its creator. If the creating process exits, the parent process ID of each child is set to the ID of a system process, init.

Process Group

Each active process is a member of a process group that is identified by a non-negative integer called the process group ID. This is the process ID of the group leader. This grouping permits the signaling of related processes (see termios(4)) and the job control mechanisms of csh(1).

Session

A session is a set of one or more process groups. A session is created by a successful call to setsid(2), which causes the caller to become the only member of the only process group in the new session.

Session leader

A process that has created a new session by a successful call to setsid(2), is known as a session leader. Only a session leader may acquire a terminal as its controlling terminal (see termios(4)).

Controlling process

A session leader with a controlling terminal is a controlling process.

Controlling terminal

A terminal that is associated with a session is known as the controlling terminal for that session and its members.

Terminal Process Group ID
> A terminal may be acquired by a session leader as its controlling terminal. Once a terminal is associated with a session, any of the process groups within the session may be placed into the foreground by setting the terminal process group ID to the ID of the process group. This facility is used to arbitrate between multiple jobs contending for the same terminal; (see csh(1) and tty(4)).

Orphaned Process Group
> A process group is considered to be *orphaned* if it is not under the control of a job control shell. More precisely, a process group is orphaned when none of its members has a parent process that is in the same session as the group, but is in a different process group. Note that when a process exits, the parent process for its children is changed to be init, which is in a separate session. Not all members of an orphaned process group are necessarily orphaned processes (those whose creating process has exited). The process group of a session leader is orphaned by definition.

Real User ID and Real Group ID
> Each user on the system is identified by a positive integer termed the real user ID.

> Each user is also a member of one or more groups. One of these groups is distinguished from others and used in implementing accounting facilities. The positive integer corresponding to this distinguished group is termed the real group ID.

> All processes have a real user ID and real group ID. These are initialized from the equivalent attributes of the process that created it.

Effective User Id, Effective Group Id, and Group Access List
> Access to system resources is governed by two values: the effective user ID, and the group access list. The first member of the group access list is also known as the effective group ID. (In POSIX.1, the group access list is known as the set of supplementary group IDs, and it is unspecified whether the effective group ID is a member of the list.)

> The effective user ID and effective group ID are initially the process's real user ID and real group ID respectively. Either may be modified through execution of a set-user-ID or set-group-ID file (possibly by one its ancestors) (see execve(2)). By convention, the effective group ID (the first member of the group access list) is duplicated, so that the execution of a set-group-ID program does not result in the loss of the original (real) group ID.

> The group access list is a set of group IDs used only in determining resource accessibility. Access checks are performed as described below in ''File Access Permissions''.

Saved Set User ID and Saved Set Group ID
> When a process executes a new file, the effective user ID is set to the owner of the file if the file is set-user-ID, and the effective group ID (first element of the group access list) is set to the group of the file if the file is set-group-ID. The effective user ID of the process is then recorded as the saved set-user-ID, and the effective group ID of the process is recorded as the saved set-group-ID. These values may be used to regain those values as the effective user or group ID after reverting to the real ID (see setuid(2)). (In POSIX.1, the saved set-user-ID and saved set-group-ID are optional, and are used in setuid and setgid, but this does not work as desired for the super-user.)

Super-user
> A process is recognized as a *super-user* process and is granted special privileges if its effective user ID is 0.

Special Processes

The processes with process IDs of 0, 1, and 2 are special. Process 0 is the scheduler. Process 1 is the initialization process `init`, and is the ancestor of every other process in the system. It is used to control the process structure. Process 2 is the paging daemon.

Descriptor

An integer assigned by the system when a file is referenced by open(2) or dup(2), or when a socket is created by `pipe(2)`, `socket(2)` or `socketpair(2)`, which uniquely identifies an access path to that file or socket from a given process or any of its children.

File Name

Names consisting of up to 255 (`MAXNAMELEN`) characters may be used to name an ordinary file, special file, or directory.

These characters may be selected from the set of all ASCII character excluding 0 (NUL) and the ASCII code for '`/`' (slash). (The parity bit, bit 7, must be 0.)

Note that it is generally unwise to use '`*`', '`?`', '`[`' or '`]`' as part of file names because of the special meaning attached to these characters by the shell.

Path Name

A path name is a NUL-terminated character string starting with an optional slash '`/`', followed by zero or more directory names separated by slashes, optionally followed by a file name. The total length of a path name must be less than 1024 (`MAXPATHLEN`) characters.

If a path name begins with a slash, the path search begins at the *root* directory. Otherwise, the search begins from the current working directory. A slash by itself names the root directory. An empty pathname refers to the current directory.

Directory

A directory is a special type of file that contains entries that are references to other files. Directory entries are called links. By convention, a directory contains at least two links, '`.`' and '`..`', referred to as *dot* and *dot-dot* respectively. Dot refers to the directory itself and dot-dot refers to its parent directory.

Root Directory and Current Working Directory

Each process has associated with it a concept of a root directory and a current working directory for the purpose of resolving path name searches. A process's root directory need not be the root directory of the root file system.

File Access Permissions

Every file in the file system has a set of access permissions. These permissions are used in determining whether a process may perform a requested operation on the file (such as opening a file for writing). Access permissions are established at the time a file is created. They may be changed at some later time through the chmod(2) call.

File access is broken down according to whether a file may be: read, written, or executed. Directory files use the execute permission to control if the directory may be searched.

File access permissions are interpreted by the system as they apply to three different classes of users: the owner of the file, those users in the file's group, anyone else. Every file has an independent set of access permissions for each of these classes. When an access check is made, the system decides if permission should be granted by checking the access information applicable to the caller.

Read, write, and execute/search permissions on a file are granted to a process if:

The process's effective user ID is that of the super-user. (Note: even the super-user cannot execute a non-executable file.)

The process's effective user ID matches the user ID of the owner of the file and the owner permissions allow the access.

The process's effective user ID does not match the user ID of the owner of the file, and either the process's effective group ID matches the group ID of the file, or the group ID of the file is in the process's group access list, and the group permissions allow the access.

Neither the effective user ID nor effective group ID and group access list of the process match the corresponding user ID and group ID of the file, but the permissions for ''other users'' allow access.

Otherwise, permission is denied.

Sockets and Address Families

A socket is an endpoint for communication between processes. Each socket has queues for sending and receiving data.

Sockets are typed according to their communications properties. These properties include whether messages sent and received at a socket require the name of the partner, whether communication is reliable, the format used in naming message recipients, etc.

Each instance of the system supports some collection of socket types; consult socket(2) for more information about the types available and their properties.

Each instance of the system supports some number of sets of communications protocols. Each protocol set supports addresses of a certain format. An Address Family is the set of addresses for a specific group of protocols. Each socket has an address chosen from the address family in which the socket was created.

SEE ALSO

intro(3), perror(3)

2

NAME

accept – accept a connection on a socket

SYNOPSIS

```
#include <sys/types.h>
#include <sys/socket.h>

int
accept(int s, struct sockaddr *addr, int *addrlen);
```

DESCRIPTION

The argument s is a socket that has been created with socket(2), bound to an address with bind(2), and is listening for connections after a listen(2). The **accept()** argument extracts the first connection request on the queue of pending connections, creates a new socket with the same properties of s and allocates a new file descriptor for the socket. If no pending connections are present on the queue, and the socket is not marked as non-blocking, **accept()** blocks the caller until a connection is present. If the socket is marked non-blocking and no pending connections are present on the queue, **accept()** returns an error as described below. The accepted socket may not be used to accept more connections. The original socket s remains open.

The argument addr is a result parameter that is filled in with the address of the connecting entity, as known to the communications layer. The exact format of the addr parameter is determined by the domain in which the communication is occurring. The addrlen is a value-result parameter; it should initially contain the amount of space pointed to by addr; on return it will contain the actual length (in bytes) of the address returned. This call is used with connection-based socket types, currently with SOCK_STREAM.

It is possible to select(2) a socket for the purposes of doing an **accept()** by selecting it for read.

For certain protocols which require an explicit confirmation, such as ISO or DATAKIT, **accept()** can be thought of as merely dequeueing the next connection request and not implying confirmation. Confirmation can be implied by a normal read or write on the new file descriptor, and rejection can be implied by closing the new socket.

One can obtain user connection request data without confirming the connection by issuing a recvmsg(2) call with an msg_iovlen of 0 and a non-zero msg_controllen, or by issuing a getsockopt(2) request. Similarly, one can provide user connection rejection information by issuing a sendmsg(2) call with providing only the control information, or by calling setsockopt(2).

RETURN VALUES

The call returns −1 on error. If it succeeds, it returns a non-negative integer that is a descriptor for the accepted socket.

ERRORS

The **accept()** will fail if:

[EBADF]   The descriptor is invalid.

[ENOTSOCK]   The descriptor references a file, not a socket.

[EOPNOTSUPP]
                 The referenced socket is not of type SOCK_STREAM.

[EFAULT]   The addr parameter is not in a writable part of the user address space.

[EWOULDBLOCK]
> The socket is marked non-blocking and no connections are present to be accepted.

SEE ALSO

bind(2), connect(2), listen(2), select(2), socket(2)

HISTORY

The accept function appeared in 4.2BSD.

2

NAME

`access` – check access permissions of a file or pathname

SYNOPSIS

`#include <unistd.h>`

`int`
`access(const char *path, int mode);`

DESCRIPTION

The `access()` function checks the accessibility of the file named by *path* for the access permissions indicated by *mode*. The value of *mode* is the bitwise inclusive OR of the access permissions to be checked (R_OK for read permission, W_OK for write permission and X_OK for execute/search permission) or the existence test, F_OK. All components of the pathname *path* are checked for access permissions (including F_OK).

The real user ID is used in place of the effective user ID and the real group access list (including the real group ID) are used in place of the effective ID for verifying permission.

Even if a process has appropriate privileges and indicates success for X_OK, the file may not actually have execute permission bits set. Likewise for R_OK and W_OK.

RETURN VALUES

If *path* cannot be found or if any of the desired access modes would not be granted, then a -1 value is returned; otherwise a 0 value is returned.

ERRORS

Access to the file is denied if:

[ENOTDIR]   A component of the path prefix is not a directory.

[EINVAL]   The pathname contains a character with the high-order bit set.

[ENAMETOOLONG]
                 A component of a pathname exceeded 255 characters, or an entire path name exceeded 1023 characters.

[ENOENT]   The named file does not exist.

[ELOOP]   Too many symbolic links were encountered in translating the pathname.

[EROFS]   Write access is requested for a file on a read-only file system.

[ETXTBSY]   Write access is requested for a pure procedure (shared text) file presently being executed.

[EACCES]   Permission bits of the file mode do not permit the requested access, or search permission is denied on a component of the path prefix. The owner of a file has permission checked with respect to the ''owner'' read, write, and execute mode bits, members of the file's group other than the owner have permission checked with respect to the ''group'' mode bits, and all others have permissions checked with respect to the ''other'' mode bits.

[EFAULT]   *Path* points outside the process's allocated address space.

[EIO]   An I/O error occurred while reading from or writing to the file system.

SEE ALSO
    chmod(2), stat(2)

STANDARDS
    Access( ) conforms to IEEE Std 1003.1-1988 ("POSIX").

CAVEAT
    Access( ) is a potential security hole and should never be used.

2

2

NAME
acct – enable or disable process accounting

SYNOPSIS
`#include <unistd.h>`

int
`acct(`*const char *file*`)`;

DESCRIPTION
The **acct()** call enables or disables the collection of system accounting records. If the argument *file* is a nil pointer, accounting is disabled. If *file* is an *existing* pathname (null-terminated), record collection is enabled and for every process initiated which terminates under normal conditions an accounting record is appended to *file*. Abnormal conditions of termination are reboots or other fatal system problems. Records for processes which never terminate can not be produced by **acct()**.

For more information on the record structure used by **acct()**, see /usr/include/sys/acct.h and acct(5).

This call is permitted only to the super-user.

NOTES
Accounting is automatically disabled when the file system the accounting file resides on runs out of space; it is enabled when space once again becomes available.

RETURN VALUES
On error -1 is returned. The file must exist and the call may be exercised only by the super-user.

ERRORS
Acct() will fail if one of the following is true:

[EPERM]   The caller is not the super-user.

[ENOTDIR]   A component of the path prefix is not a directory.

[EINVAL]   The pathname contains a character with the high-order bit set.

[ENAMETOOLONG]
                A component of a pathname exceeded 255 characters, or an entire path name exceeded 1023 characters.

[ENOENT]   The named file does not exist.

[EACCES]   Search permission is denied for a component of the path prefix, or the path name is not a regular file.

[ELOOP]   Too many symbolic links were encountered in translating the pathname.

[EROFS]   The named file resides on a read-only file system.

[EFAULT]   *File* points outside the process's allocated address space.

[EIO]   An I/O error occurred while reading from or writing to the file system.

SEE ALSO
acct(5), sa(8)

HISTORY

An `acct` function call appeared in Version 7 AT&T UNIX.

2

2

NAME
adjtime – correct the time to allow synchronization of the system clock

SYNOPSIS
`#include <sys/time.h>`

`int`
`adjtime(struct timeval *delta, struct timeval *olddelta);`

DESCRIPTION
Adjtime() makes small adjustments to the system time, as returned by gettimeofday(2), advancing or retarding it by the time specified by the timeval *delta*. If *delta* is negative, the clock is slowed down by incrementing it more slowly than normal until the correction is complete. If *delta* is positive, a larger increment than normal is used. The skew used to perform the correction is generally a fraction of one percent. Thus, the time is always a monotonically increasing function. A time correction from an earlier call to **adjtime**() may not be finished when **adjtime**() is called again. If *olddelta* is non-nil, the structure pointed to will contain, upon return, the number of microseconds still to be corrected from the earlier call.

This call may be used by time servers that synchronize the clocks of computers in a local area network. Such time servers would slow down the clocks of some machines and speed up the clocks of others to bring them to the average network time.

The call **adjtime**() is restricted to the super-user.

RETURN VALUES
A return value of 0 indicates that the call succeeded. A return value of -1 indicates that an error occurred, and in this case an error code is stored in the global variable *errno*.

ERRORS
Adjtime() will fail if:

[EFAULT]   An argument points outside the process's allocated address space.

[EPERM]   The process's effective user ID is not that of the super-user.

SEE ALSO
date(1), gettimeofday(2), timed(8), timedc(8),

R. Gusella, and S. Zatti, *TSP: The Time Synchronization Protocol for UNIX 4.3BSD*.

HISTORY
The adjtime function call appeared in 4.3BSD.

NAME

bind – bind a name to a socket

SYNOPSIS

```
#include <sys/types.h>
#include <sys/socket.h>

int
bind(int s, struct sockaddr *name, int namelen);
```

DESCRIPTION

Bind() assigns a name to an unnamed socket. When a socket is created with socket(2) it exists in a name space (address family) but has no name assigned. **Bind**() requests that *name* be assigned to the socket.

NOTES

Binding a name in the UNIX domain creates a socket in the file system that must be deleted by the caller when it is no longer needed (using unlink(2)).

The rules used in name binding vary between communication domains. Consult the manual entries in section 4 for detailed information.

RETURN VALUES

If the bind is successful, a 0 value is returned. A return value of -1 indicates an error, which is further specified in the global *errno*.

ERRORS

The **bind**() call will fail if:

[EBADF]　　　　　*S* is not a valid descriptor.

[ENOTSOCK]　　　*S* is not a socket.

[EADDRNOTAVAIL]
　　　　　　　　The specified address is not available from the local machine.

[EADDRINUSE]
　　　　　　　　The specified address is already in use.

[EINVAL]　　　　The socket is already bound to an address.

[EACCES]　　　　The requested address is protected, and the current user has inadequate permission to access it.

[EFAULT]　　　　The *name* parameter is not in a valid part of the user address space.

The following errors are specific to binding names in the UNIX domain.

[ENOTDIR]　　　　A component of the path prefix is not a directory.

[EINVAL]　　　　The pathname contains a character with the high-order bit set.

[ENAMETOOLONG]
　　　　　　　　A component of a pathname exceeded 255 characters, or an entire path name exceeded 1023 characters.

2

[ENOENT]	A prefix component of the path name does not exist.
[ELOOP]	Too many symbolic links were encountered in translating the pathname.
[EIO]	An I/O error occurred while making the directory entry or allocating the inode.
[EROFS]	The name would reside on a read-only file system.
[EISDIR]	An empty pathname was specified.

SEE ALSO

connect(2), listen(2), socket(2), getsockname(2)

HISTORY

The bind function call appeared in 4.2BSD.

NAME
brk, sbrk – change data segment size

SYNOPSIS
```
#include <sys/types.h>
```

```
char
*brk(const char *addr);
```

```
char *
*sbrk(int incr);
```

DESCRIPTION
The brk and sbrk functions are historical curiosities left over from earlier days before the advent of virtual memory management. The `brk()` function sets the break or lowest address of a process's data segment (uninitialized data) to *addr* (immediately above bss). Data addressing is restricted between *addr* and the lowest stack pointer to the stack segment. Memory is allocated by *brk* in page size pieces; if *addr* is not evenly divisible by the system page size, it is increased to the next page boundary.

The current value of the program break is reliably returned by "`sbrk(0)`" (see also end(3)). The `getrlimit(2)` system call may be used to determine the maximum permissible size of the *data* segment; it will not be possible to set the break beyond the *rlim_max* value returned from a call to `getrlimit`, e.g. "qetext + rlp→rlim_max." (see end(3) for the definition of *etext*).

RETURN VALUES
Brk returns 0 if successful; otherwise -1 with *errno* set to indicate why the allocation failed. Sbrk returns a pointer to the base of the new storage if successful; otherwise -1 with *errno* set to indicate why the allocation failed.

ERRORS
Brk or sbrk will fail and no additional memory will be allocated if one of the following are true:

[ENOMEM] The limit, as set by `setrlimit(2)`, was exceeded.

[ENOMEM] The maximum possible size of a data segment (compiled into the system) was exceeded.

[ENOMEM] Insufficient space existed in the swap area to support the expansion.

SEE ALSO
execve(2), getrlimit(2), malloc(3), end(3)

BUGS
Setting the break may fail due to a temporary lack of swap space. It is not possible to distinguish this from a failure caused by exceeding the maximum size of the data segment without consulting `getrlimit`.

HISTORY
A **brk** function call appeared in Version 7 AT&T UNIX.

2

NAME
chdir, fchdir – change current working directory

SYNOPSIS
`#include <unistd.h>`

`int`
`chdir(const char *path);`

`int`
`fchdir(int fd);`

DESCRIPTION
The *path* argument points to the pathname of a directory. The **chdir**( ) function causes the named directory to become the current working directory, that is, the starting point for path searches of pathnames not beginning with a slash, '/'.

The **fchdir**( ) function causes the directory referenced by *fd* to become the current working directory, the starting point for path searches of pathnames not beginning with a slash, '/'.

In order for a directory to become the current directory, a process must have execute (search) access to the directory.

RETURN VALUES
Upon successful completion, a value of 0 is returned. Otherwise, a value of -1 is returned and *errno* is set to indicate the error.

ERRORS
Chdir( ) will fail and the current working directory will be unchanged if one or more of the following are true:

[ENOTDIR]   A component of the path prefix is not a directory.

[EINVAL]   The pathname contains a character with the high-order bit set.

[ENAMETOOLONG]
                A component of a pathname exceeded 255 characters, or an entire path name exceeded 1023 characters.

[ENOENT]   The named directory does not exist.

[ELOOP]   Too many symbolic links were encountered in translating the pathname.

[EACCES]   Search permission is denied for any component of the path name.

[EFAULT]   *Path* points outside the process's allocated address space.

[EIO]   An I/O error occurred while reading from or writing to the file system.

Fchdir( ) will fail and the current working directory will be unchanged if one or more of the following are true:

[EACCES]   Search permission is denied for the directory referenced by the file descriptor.

[ENOTDIR]   The file descriptor does not reference a directory.

[EBADF]   The argument *fd* is not a valid file descriptor.

SEE ALSO
　　chroot(2)

STANDARDS
　　Chdir( ) is expected to conform to IEEE Std 1003.1-1988 (''POSIX'') .

HISTORY
　　The **fchdir**( ) function call appeared in 4.2BSD.

2

2

NAME

chflags, fchflags – set file flags

SYNOPSIS

```
#include <sys/stat.h>
#include <unistd.h>

int
chflags(const char *path, u_long flags);

int
fchflags(int fd, u_long flags);
```

DESCRIPTION

The file whose name is given by *path* or referenced by the descriptor *fd* has its flags changed to *flags*.

The flags specified are formed by *or*'ing the following values

UF_NODUMP	Do not dump the file.
UF_IMMUTABLE	
	The file may not be changed.
UF_APPEND	The file may only be appended to.
SF_IMMUTABLE	
	The file may not be changed.
SF_APPEND	The file may only be appended to.

The ''UF_IMMUTABLE'' and ''UF_APPEND'' flags may be set or unset by either the owner of a file or the super-user.

The ''SF_IMMUTABLE'' and ''SF_APPEND'' flags may only be set or unset by the super-user. They may be set at any time, but normally may only be unset when the system is in single-user mode. (See init(8) for details.)

RETURN VALUES

Upon successful completion, a value of 0 is returned. Otherwise, -1 is returned and the global variable *errno* is set to indicate the error.

ERRORS

Chflags( ) will fail it:

[ENOTDIR]　　A component of the path prefix is not a directory.

[EINVAL]　　The pathname contains a character with the high-order bit set.

[ENAMETOOLONG]
　　　　　　　A component of a pathname exceeded 255 characters, or an entire path name exceeded 1023 characters.

[ENOENT]　　The named file does not exist.

[EACCES]　　Search permission is denied for a component of the path prefix.

[ELOOP]　　Too many symbolic links were encountered in translating the pathname.

2

[EPERM]   The effective user ID does not match the owner of the file and the effective user ID is not the super-user.

[EROFS]   The named file resides on a read-only file system.

[EFAULT]   *Path* points outside the process's allocated address space.

[EIO]   An I/O error occurred while reading from or writing to the file system.

Fchflags() will fail if:

[EBADF]   The descriptor is not valid.

[EINVAL]   *Fd* refers to a socket, not to a file.

[EPERM]   The effective user ID does not match the owner of the file and the effective user ID is not the super-user.

[EROFS]   The file resides on a read-only file system.

[EIO]   An I/O error occurred while reading from or writing to the file system.

SEE ALSO

chflags(1,) init(8)

HISTORY

The **chflags** and **fchflags** functions first appeared in 4.4BSD.

2

NAME
chmod, fchmod – change mode of file

SYNOPSIS
#include ⟨sys/stat.h⟩

int
chmod(*const char *path*, *mode_t mode*);

int
fchmod(*int fd*, *mode_t mode*);

DESCRIPTION
The function **chmod**( ) sets the file permission bits of the file specified by the pathname *path* to *mode*. **Fchmod**( ) sets the permission bits of the specified file descriptor *fd*. **Chmod**( ) verifies that the process owner (user) either owns the file specified by *path* (or *fd*), or is the super-user. A mode is created from *or'd* permission bit masks defined in <sys/stat.h>:

```
#define S_IRWXU 0000700      /* RWX mask for owner */
#define S_IRUSR 0000400      /* R for owner */
#define S_IWUSR 0000200      /* W for owner */
#define S_IXUSR 0000100      /* X for owner */

#define S_IRWXG 0000070      /* RWX mask for group */
#define S_IRGRP 0000040      /* R for group */
#define S_IWGRP 0000020      /* W for group */
#define S_IXGRP 0000010      /* X for group */

#define S_IRWXO 0000007      /* RWX mask for other */
#define S_IROTH 0000004      /* R for other */
#define S_IWOTH 0000002      /* W for other */
#define S_IXOTH 0000001      /* X for other */

#define S_ISUID 0004000      /* set user id on execution */
#define S_ISGID 0002000      /* set group id on execution */
#define S_ISVTX 0001000      /* save swapped text even after use */
```

The ISVTX (the *sticky bit*) indicates to the system which executable files are shareable (the default) and the system maintains the program text of the files in the swap area. The sticky bit may only be set by the super user on shareable executable files.

If mode ISVTX (the 'sticky bit') is set on a directory, an unprivileged user may not delete or rename files of other users in that directory. The sticky bit may be set by any user on a directory which the user owns or has appropriate permissions. For more details of the properties of the sticky bit, see sticky(8).

Writing or changing the owner of a file turns off the set-user-id and set-group-id bits unless the user is the super-user. This makes the system somewhat more secure by protecting set-user-id (set-group-id) files from remaining set-user-id (set-group-id) if they are modified, at the expense of a degree of compatibility.

RETURN VALUES
Upon successful completion, a value of 0 is returned. Otherwise, a value of -1 is returned and *errno* is set to indicate the error.

ERRORS

Chmod( ) will fail and the file mode will be unchanged if:

[ENOTDIR]   A component of the path prefix is not a directory.

[EINVAL]   The pathname contains a character with the high-order bit set.

[ENAMETOOLONG]
              A component of a pathname exceeded 255 characters, or an entire path name exceeded 1023 characters.

[ENOENT]   The named file does not exist.

[EACCES]   Search permission is denied for a component of the path prefix.

[ELOOP]   Too many symbolic links were encountered in translating the pathname.

[EPERM]   The effective user ID does not match the owner of the file and the effective user ID is not the super-user.

[EROFS]   The named file resides on a read-only file system.

[EFAULT]   *Path* points outside the process's allocated address space.

[EIO]   An I/O error occurred while reading from or writing to the file system.

Fchmod( ) will fail if:

[EBADF]   The descriptor is not valid.

[EINVAL]   *Fd* refers to a socket, not to a file.

[EROFS]   The file resides on a read-only file system.

[EIO]   An I/O error occurred while reading from or writing to the file system.

SEE ALSO

chmod(1), open(2), chown(2), stat(2), sticky(8)

STANDARDS

Chmod( ) is expected to conform to IEEE Std 1003.1-1988 (''POSIX'').

HISTORY

The fchmod( ) function call appeared in 4.2BSD.

2

NAME
chown, fchown – change owner and group of a file

SYNOPSIS
`#include <unistd.h>`

int
chown(*const char *path, uid_t owner, gid_t group*);

int
fchown(*int fd, uid_t owner, uid_t group*);

DESCRIPTION
The owner ID and group ID of the file named by *path* or referenced by *fd* is changed as specified by the arguments *owner* and *group*. The owner of a file may change the *group* to a group of which he or she is a member, but the change *owner* capability is restricted to the super-user.

Chown( ) clears the set-user-id and set-group-id bits on the file to prevent accidental or mischievous creation of set-user-id and set-group-id programs.

Fchown( ) is particularly useful when used in conjunction with the file locking primitives (see flock(2)).

One of the owner or group id's may be left unchanged by specifying it as -1.

RETURN VALUES
Zero is returned if the operation was successful; -1 is returned if an error occurs, with a more specific error code being placed in the global variable *errno*.

ERRORS
Chown( ) will fail and the file will be unchanged if:

[ENOTDIR]   A component of the path prefix is not a directory.

[EINVAL]   The pathname contains a character with the high-order bit set.

[ENAMETOOLONG]
              A component of a pathname exceeded 255 characters, or an entire path name exceeded 1023 characters.

[ENOENT]   The named file does not exist.

[EACCES]   Search permission is denied for a component of the path prefix.

[ELOOP]   Too many symbolic links were encountered in translating the pathname.

[EPERM]   The effective user ID is not the super-user.

[EROFS]   The named file resides on a read-only file system.

[EFAULT]   *Path* points outside the process's allocated address space.

[EIO]   An I/O error occurred while reading from or writing to the file system.

Fchown( ) will fail if:

[EBADF]   *Fd* does not refer to a valid descriptor.

[EINVAL]	*Fd* refers to a socket, not a file.
[EPERM]	The effective user ID is not the super-user.
[EROFS]	The named file resides on a read-only file system.
[EIO]	An I/O error occurred while reading from or writing to the file system.

SEE ALSO

chown(8), chgrp(1), chmod(2), flock(2)

STANDARDS

Chown( ) is expected to conform to IEEE Std 1003.1-1988 (''POSIX'').

HISTORY

The **fchown**( ) function call appeared in 4.2BSD.

The **chown**( ) and **fchown**( ) functions were changed to follow symbolic links in 4.4BSD.

2

NAME

chroot – change root directory

SYNOPSIS

```
#include <unistd.h>
```

int
chroot(*const char *dirname*);

DESCRIPTION

Dirname is the address of the pathname of a directory, terminated by an ASCII NUL. Chroot() causes *dirname* to become the root directory, that is, the starting point for path searches of pathnames beginning with '/'.

In order for a directory to become the root directory a process must have execute (search) access for that directory.

It should be noted that chroot() has no effect on the process's current directory.

This call is restricted to the super-user.

RETURN VALUES

Upon successful completion, a value of 0 is returned. Otherwise, a value of -1 is returned and *errno* is set to indicate an error.

ERRORS

Chroot() will fail and the root directory will be unchanged if:

[ENOTDIR]   A component of the path name is not a directory.

[EINVAL]   The pathname contains a character with the high-order bit set.

[ENAMETOOLONG]
              A component of a pathname exceeded 255 characters, or an entire path name exceeded 1023 characters.

[ENOENT]   The named directory does not exist.

[EACCES]   Search permission is denied for any component of the path name.

[ELOOP]   Too many symbolic links were encountered in translating the pathname.

[EFAULT]   *Path* points outside the process's allocated address space.

[EIO]   An I/O error occurred while reading from or writing to the file system.

SEE ALSO

chdir(2)

HISTORY

The chroot function call appeared in 4.2BSD.

NAME

close – delete a descriptor

SYNOPSIS

```
#include <unistd.h>
```

int
close(*int* *d*);

DESCRIPTION

The **close()** call deletes a descriptor from the per-process object reference table. If this is the last reference to the underlying object, the object will be deactivated. For example, on the last close of a file the current *seek* pointer associated with the file is lost; on the last close of a socket(2) associated naming information and queued data are discarded; on the last close of a file holding an advisory lock the lock is released (see further flock(2)).

When a process exits, all associated file descriptors are freed, but since there is a limit on active descriptors per processes, the **close()** function call is useful when a large quantity of file descriptors are being handled.

When a process forks (see fork(2)), all descriptors for the new child process reference the same objects as they did in the parent before the fork. If a new process is then to be run using execve(2), the process would normally inherit these descriptors. Most of the descriptors can be rearranged with dup2(2) or deleted with **close()** before the execve is attempted, but if some of these descriptors will still be needed if the execve fails, it is necessary to arrange for them to be closed if the execve succeeds. For this reason, the call "fcntl(d, F_SETFD, 1)" is provided, which arranges that a descriptor will be closed after a successful execve; the call "fcntl(d, F_SETFD, 0)" restores the default, which is to not close the descriptor.

RETURN VALUES

Upon successful completion, a value of 0 is returned. Otherwise, a value of -1 is returned and the global integer variable *errno* is set to indicate the error.

ERRORS

Close() will fail if:

[EBADF]   *D* is not an active descriptor.

[EINTR]   An interrupt was received.

SEE ALSO

accept(2), flock(2), open(2), pipe(2), socket(2), socketpair(2), execve(2), fcntl(2)

STANDARDS

Close() conforms to IEEE Std 1003.1-1988 ("POSIX").

2

NAME

connect – initiate a connection on a socket

SYNOPSIS

```
#include <sys/types.h>
#include <sys/socket.h>

int
connect(int s, struct sockaddr *name, int namelen);
```

DESCRIPTION

The parameter s is a socket. If it is of type SOCK_DGRAM, this call specifies the peer with which the socket is to be associated; this address is that to which datagrams are to be sent, and the only address from which datagrams are to be received. If the socket is of type SOCK_STREAM, this call attempts to make a connection to another socket. The other socket is specified by name, which is an address in the communications space of the socket. Each communications space interprets the name parameter in its own way. Generally, stream sockets may successfully connect() only once; datagram sockets may use connect() multiple times to change their association. Datagram sockets may dissolve the association by connecting to an invalid address, such as a null address.

RETURN VALUES

If the connection or binding succeeds, 0 is returned. Otherwise a -1 is returned, and a more specific error code is stored in *errno*.

ERRORS

The connect() call fails if:

[EBADF]	S is not a valid descriptor.
[ENOTSOCK]	S is a descriptor for a file, not a socket.
[EADDRNOTAVAIL]	The specified address is not available on this machine.
[EAFNOSUPPORT]	Addresses in the specified address family cannot be used with this socket.
[EISCONN]	The socket is already connected.
[ETIMEDOUT]	Connection establishment timed out without establishing a connection.
[ECONNREFUSED]	The attempt to connect was forcefully rejected.
[ENETUNREACH]	The network isn't reachable from this host.
[EADDRINUSE]	The address is already in use.
[EFAULT]	The name parameter specifies an area outside the process address space.
[EINPROGRESS]	The socket is non-blocking and the connection cannot be completed immediately. It is possible to select(2) for completion by selecting the socket for writing.
[EALREADY]	The socket is non-blocking and a previous connection attempt has not yet been completed.

The following errors are specific to connecting names in the UNIX domain. These errors may not apply in future versions of the UNIX IPC domain.

2

[ENOTDIR]	A component of the path prefix is not a directory.
[EINVAL]	The pathname contains a character with the high-order bit set.
[ENAMETOOLONG]	A component of a pathname exceeded 255 characters, or an entire path name exceeded 1023 characters.
[ENOENT]	The named socket does not exist.
[EACCES]	Search permission is denied for a component of the path prefix.
[EACCES]	Write access to the named socket is denied.
[ELOOP]	Too many symbolic links were encountered in translating the pathname.

SEE ALSO

accept(2), select(2), socket(2), getsockname(2)

HISTORY

The **connect** function call appeared in 4.2BSD.

2

NAME
     creat – create a new file

SYNOPSIS
     #include <fcntl.h>

     int
     creat(*char *path*, *mode_t mode*);

DESCRIPTION
     This interface is made obsolete by: open(2).

     Creat() is the same as:

          open(path, O_CREAT | O_TRUNC | O_WRONLY, mode);

SEE ALSO
     open(2)

HISTORY
     The creat function call appeared in Version 6 AT&T UNIX.

NAME

　　dup, dup2 – duplicate an existing file descriptor

SYNOPSIS

　　`#include <unistd.h>`

　　int
　　dup(*int oldd*);

　　int
　　dup2(*int oldd, int newd*);

DESCRIPTION

　　Dup() duplicates an existing object descriptor and returns its value to the calling process (*newd* = dup(*oldd*)). The argument *oldd* is a small non-negative integer index in the per-process descriptor table. The value must be less than the size of the table, which is returned by getdtablesize(2). The new descriptor returned by the call is the lowest numbered descriptor currently not in use by the process.

　　The object referenced by the descriptor does not distinguish between *oldd* and *newd* in any way. Thus if *newd* and *oldd* are duplicate references to an open file, read(2), write(2) and lseek(2) calls all move a single pointer into the file, and append mode, non-blocking I/O and asynchronous I/O options are shared between the references. If a separate pointer into the file is desired, a different object reference to the file must be obtained by issuing an additional open(2) call. The close-on-exec flag on the new file descriptor is unset.

　　In **dup2**(), the value of the new descriptor *newd* is specified. If this descriptor is already in use, the descriptor is first deallocated as if a close(2) call had been done first.

RETURN VALUES

　　The value -1 is returned if an error occurs in either call. The external variable *errno* indicates the cause of the error.

ERRORS

　　Dup( ) and dup2( ) fail if:

　　[EBADF]　　　　*Oldd* or *newd* is not a valid active descriptor

　　[EMFILE]　　　　Too many descriptors are active.

SEE ALSO

　　accept(2), open(2), close(2), fcntl(2), pipe(2), socket(2), socketpair(2), getdtablesize(2)

STANDARDS

　　Dup( ) and dup2( ) are expected to conform to IEEE Std 1003.1-1988 (''POSIX'').

NAME

execve – execute a file

SYNOPSIS

```
#include <unistd.h>
```

int
execve(*const char *path, char *const argv[ ], char *const envp[ ]*);

DESCRIPTION

Execve( ) transforms the calling process into a new process. The new process is constructed from an ordinary file, whose name is pointed to by *path*, called the *new process file*. This file is either an executable object file, or a file of data for an interpreter. An executable object file consists of an identifying header, followed by pages of data representing the initial program (text) and initialized data pages. Additional pages may be specified by the header to be initialized with zero data; see a.out(5).

An interpreter file begins with a line of the form:

> #! *interpreter* [*arg*]

When an interpreter file is **execve**'d, the system **execve**'s runs the specified *interpreter*. If the optional *arg* is specified, it becomes the first argument to the *interpreter*, and the name of the originally **execve**'d file becomes the second argument; otherwise, the name of the originally **execve**'d file becomes the first argument. The original arguments are shifted over to become the subsequent arguments. The zeroth argument, normally the name of the **execve**'d file, is left unchanged.

The argument *argv* is a pointer to a null-terminated array of character pointers to null-terminated character strings. These strings construct the argument list to be made available to the new process. At least one argument must be present in the array; by custom, the first element should be the name of the executed program (for example, the last component of *path*).

The argument *envp* is also a pointer to a null-terminated array of character pointers to null-terminated strings. A pointer to this array is normally stored in the global variable *environ*. These strings pass information to the new process that is not directly an argument to the command (see environ(7)).

File descriptors open in the calling process image remain open in the new process image, except for those for which the close-on-exec flag is set (see close(2) and fcntl(2)). Descriptors that remain open are unaffected by **execve**().

Signals set to be ignored in the calling process are set to be ignored in the new process. Signals which are set to be caught in the calling process image are set to default action in the new process image. Blocked signals remain blocked regardless of changes to the signal action. The signal stack is reset to be undefined (see sigaction(2) for more information).

If the set-user-ID mode bit of the new process image file is set (see chmod(2)), the effective user ID of the new process image is set to the owner ID of the new process image file. If the set-group-ID mode bit of the new process image file is set, the effective group ID of the new process image is set to the group ID of the new process image file. (The effective group ID is the first element of the group list.) The real user ID, real group ID and other group IDs of the new process image remain the same as the calling process image. After any set-user-ID and set-group-ID processing, the effective user ID is recorded as the saved set-user-ID, and the effective group ID is recorded as the saved set-group-ID. These values may be used in changing the effective IDs later (see setuid(2)).

The new process also inherits the following attributes from the calling process:

process ID	see getpid(2)
parent process ID	see getppid(2)
process group ID	see getpgrp(2)
access groups	see getgroups(2)
working directory	see chdir(2)
root directory	see chroot(2)
control terminal	see termios(4)
resource usages	see getrusage(2)
interval timers	see getitimer(2)
resource limits	see getrlimit(2)
file mode mask	see umask(2)
signal mask	see sigvec(2), sigsetmask(2)

When a program is executed as a result of an **execve**( ) call, it is entered as follows:

```
main(argc, argv, envp)
int argc;
char **argv, **envp;
```

where *argc* is the number of elements in *argv* (the "arg count") and *argv* points to the array of character pointers to the arguments themselves.

RETURN VALUES

As the **execve**( ) function overlays the current process image with a new process image the successful call has no process to return to. If **execve**( ) does return to the calling process an error has occurred; the return value will be -1 and the global variable *errno* is set to indicate the error.

ERRORS

Execve( ) will fail and return to the calling process if:

[ENOTDIR]	A component of the path prefix is not a directory.
[EINVAL]	The pathname contains a character with the high-order bit set.
[ENAMETOOLONG]	A component of a pathname exceeded 255 characters, or an entire path name exceeded 1023 characters.
[ENOENT]	The new process file does not exist.
[ELOOP]	Too many symbolic links were encountered in translating the pathname.
[EACCES]	Search permission is denied for a component of the path prefix.
[EACCES]	The new process file is not an ordinary file.
[EACCES]	The new process file mode denies execute permission.
[ENOEXEC]	The new process file has the appropriate access permission, but has an invalid magic number in its header.
[ETXTBSY]	The new process file is a pure procedure (shared text) file that is currently open for writing or reading by some process.

[ENOMEM]　　　　　The new process requires more virtual memory than is allowed by the imposed maximum (getrlimit(2)).

[E2BIG]　　　　　The number of bytes in the new process's argument list is larger than the system-imposed limit. The limit in the system as released is 20480 bytes (NCARGS in <sys/param.h>.

[EFAULT]　　　　　The new process file is not as long as indicated by the size values in its header.

[EFAULT]　　　　　*Path*, *argv*, or *envp* point to an illegal address.

[EIO]　　　　　An I/O error occurred while reading from the file system.

CAVEAT

If a program is *setuid* to a non-super-user, but is executed when the real *uid* is "root", then the program has some of the powers of a super-user as well.

SEE ALSO

exit(2), fork(2), execl(3), environ(7)

HISTORY

The **execve** function call appeared in 4.2BSD.

2

NAME

_exit – terminate the calling process

SYNOPSIS

```
#include <unistd.h>
```

void
_exit(*int status*);

DESCRIPTION

The **_exit**( ) function terminates a process with the following consequences:

- All of the descriptors open in the calling process are closed. This may entail delays, for example, waiting for output to drain; a process in this state may not be killed, as it is already dying.

- If the parent process of the calling process has an outstanding wait call or catches the SIGCHLD signal, it is notified of the calling process's termination and the *status* is set as defined by wait(2).

- The parent process-ID of all of the calling process's existing child processes are set to 1; the initialization process (see the DEFINITIONS section of intro(2)) inherits each of these processes.

- If the termination of the process causes any process group to become orphaned (usually because the parents of all members of the group have now exited; see "orphaned process group" in intro(2)), and if any member of the orphaned group is stopped, the SIGHUP signal and the SIGCONT signal are sent to all members of the newly-orphaned process group.

- If the process is a controlling process (see intro(2)), the SIGHUP signal is sent to the foreground process group of the controlling terminal, and all current access to the controlling terminal is revoked.

Most C programs call the library routine exit(3), which flushes buffers, closes streams, unlinks temporary files, etc., before calling **_exit**().

RETURN VALUE

_exit( ) can never return.

SEE ALSO

fork(2), sigvec(2), wait(2), exit(3)

STANDARDS

The **_exit** function is defined by IEEE Std1003.1-1988 ("POSIX").

NAME

    fcntl – file control

SYNOPSIS

    #include ⟨fcntl.h⟩

    int
    fcntl(*int fd, int cmd, int arg*);

DESCRIPTION

    Fcntl( ) provides for control over descriptors. The argument *fd* is a descriptor to be operated on by *cmd* as follows:

    F_DUPFD   Return a new descriptor as follows:

- Lowest numbered available descriptor greater than or equal to *arg*.
- Same object references as the original descriptor.
- New descriptor shares the same file offset if the object was a file.
- Same access mode (read, write or read/write).
- Same file status flags (i.e., both file descriptors share the same file status flags).
- The close-on-exec flag associated with the new file descriptor is set to remain open across execv(2) system calls.

    F_GETFD   Get the close-on-exec flag associated with the file descriptor *fd*. If the low-order bit of the returned value is 0, the file will remain open across **exec**(), otherwise the file will be closed upon execution of **exec**( ) (*arg* is ignored).

    F_SETFD   Set the close-on-exec flag associated with *fd* to the low order bit of *arg* (0 or 1 as above).

    F_GETFL   Get descriptor status flags, as described below (*arg* is ignored).

    F_SETFL   Set descriptor status flags to *arg*.

    F_GETOWN   Get the process ID or process group currently receiving SIGIO and SIGURG signals; process groups are returned as negative values (*arg* is ignored).

    F_SETOWN   Set the process or process group to receive SIGIO and SIGURG signals; process groups are specified by supplying *arg* as negative, otherwise *arg* is interpreted as a process ID.

    The flags for the F_GETFL and F_SETFL flags are as follows:

    O_NONBLOCK   Non-blocking I/O; if no data is available to a read call, or if a write operation would block, the read or write call returns -1 with the error EAGAIN.

    O_APPEND   Force each write to append at the end of file; corresponds to the O_APPEND flag of open(2).

    O_ASYNC   Enable the SIGIO signal to be sent to the process group when I/O is possible, e.g., upon availability of data to be read.

    Several commands are available for doing advisory file locking; they all operate on the following structure:

```
struct flock {
        off_t   l_start;        /* starting offset */
        off_t   l_len;          /* len = 0 means until end of file */
        pid_t   l_pid;          /* lock owner */
```

```
        short   l_type;         /* lock type: read/write, etc. */
        short   l_whence;       /* type of l_start */
};
```
The commands available for advisory record locking are as follows:

F_GETLK   Get the first lock that blocks the lock description pointed to by the third argument, *arg*, taken
           as a pointer to a *struct flock* (see above). The information retrieved overwrites the in-
           formation passed to **fcntl** in the *flock* structure. If no lock is found that would prevent
           this lock from being created, the structure is left unchanged by this function call except for the
           lock type which is set to F_UNLCK.

F_SETLK   Set or clear a file segment lock according to the lock description pointed to by the third argu-
           ment, *arg*, taken as a pointer to a *struct flock* (see above). F_SETLK is used to estab-
           lish shared (or read) locks (F_RDLCK) or exclusive (or write) locks, (F_WRLCK), as well
           as remove either type of lock (F_UNLCK). If a shared or exclusive lock cannot be set,
           fcntl returns immediately with EACCES.

F_SETLKW   This command is the same as F_SETLK except that if a shared or exclusive lock is blocked
           by other locks, the process waits until the request can be satisfied. If a signal that is to be
           caught is received while **fcntl** is waiting for a region, the **fcntl** will be interrupted if the
           signal handler has not specified the SA_RESTART (see sigaction(2)).

When a shared lock has been set on a segment of a file, other processes can set shared locks on that segment
or a portion of it. A shared lock prevents any other process from setting an exclusive lock on any portion of
the protected area. A request for a shared lock fails if the file descriptor was not opened with read access.

An exclusive lock prevents any other process from setting a shared lock or an exclusive lock on any portion
of the protected area. A request for an exclusive lock fails if the file was not opened with write access.

The value of *l_whence* is SEEK_SET, SEEK_CUR, or SEEK_END to indicate that the relative offset,
l_start bytes, will be measured from the start of the file, current position, or end of the file, respectively.
The value of *l_len* is the number of consecutive bytes to be locked. If *l_len* is negative, the result is
undefined. The *l_pid* field is only used with F_GETLK to return the process ID of the process holding a
blocking lock. After a successful F_GETLK request, the value of *l_whence* is SEEK_SET.

Locks may start and extend beyond the current end of a file, but may not start or extend before the beginning
of the file. A lock is set to extend to the largest possible value of the file offset for that file if *l_len* is set to
zero. If *l_whence* and *l_start* point to the beginning of the file, and *l_len* is zero, the entire file is
locked. If an application wishes only to do entire file locking, the flock(2) system call is much more
efficient.

There is at most one type of lock set for each byte in the file. Before a successful return from an F_SETLK
or an F_SETLKW request when the calling process has previously existing locks on bytes in the region
specified by the request, the previous lock type for each byte in the specified region is replaced by the new
lock type. As specified above under the descriptions of shared locks and exclusive locks, an F_SETLK or an
F_SETLKW request fails or blocks respectively when another process has existing locks on bytes in the
specified region and the type of any of those locks conflicts with the type specified in the request.

This interface follows the completely stupid semantics of System V and IEEE Std1003.1-1988 (''POSIX'')
that require that all locks associated with a file for a given process are removed when *any* file descriptor for
that file is closed by that process. This semantic means that applications must be aware of any files that a
subroutine library may access. For example if an application for updating the password file locks the password file database while making the update, and then calls getpwname(3) to retrieve a record, the lock will
be lost because getpwname(3) opens, reads, and closes the password database. The database close will
release all locks that the process has associated with the database, even if the library routine never requested
a lock on the database. Another minor semantic problem with this interface is that locks are not inherited by

2

a child process created using the fork(2) function. The flock(2) interface has much more rational last close semantics and allows locks to be inherited by child processes. Flock(2) is recommended for applications that want to ensure the integrity of their locks when using library routines or wish to pass locks to their children. Note that flock(2) and fcntl(2) locks may be safely used concurrently.

All locks associated with a file for a given process are removed when the process terminates.

A potential for deadlock occurs if a process controlling a locked region is put to sleep by attempting to lock the locked region of another process. This implementation detects that sleeping until a locked region is unlocked would cause a deadlock and fails with an EDEADLK error.

RETURN VALUES

Upon successful completion, the value returned depends on *cmd* as follows:

F_DUPFD   A new file descriptor.

F_GETFD   Value of flag (only the low-order bit is defined).

F_GETFL   Value of flags.

F_GETOWN   Value of file descriptor owner.

other   Value other than -1.

Otherwise, a value of -1 is returned and *errno* is set to indicate the error.

ERRORS

Fcntl() will fail if:

[EACCES]   The argument *arg* is F_SETLK, the type of lock *(l_type)* is a shared lock (F_RDLCK) or exclusive lock (F_WRLCK), and the segment of a file to be locked is already exclusive-locked by another process; or the type is an exclusive lock and some portion of the segment of a file to be locked is already shared-locked or exclusive-locked by another process.

[EBADF]   *Fildes* is not a valid open file descriptor.

The argument *cmd* is F_SETLK or F_SETLKW, the type of lock *(l_type)* is a shared lock (F_RDLCK), and *fildes* is not a valid file descriptor open for reading.

The argument *cmd* is F_SETLK or F_SETLKW, the type of lock *(l_type)* is an exclusive lock (F_WRLCK), and *fildes* is not a valid file descriptor open for writing.

[EMFILE]   *Cmd* is F_DUPFD and the maximum allowed number of file descriptors are currently open.

[EDEADLK]   The argument *cmd* is F_SETLKW, and a deadlock condition was detected.

[EINTR]   The argument *cmd* is F_SETLKW, and the function was interrupted by a signal.

[EINVAL]   *Cmd* is F_DUPFD and *arg* is negative or greater than the maximum allowable number (see getdtablesize(2)).

The argument *cmd* is F_GETLK, F_SETLK, or F_SETLKW and the data to which *arg* points is not valid, or *fildes* refers to a file that does not support locking.

[EMFILE]   The argument *cmd* is F_DUPED and the maximum number of file descriptors permitted for the process are already in use, or no file descriptors greater than or equal to *arg* are available.

[ENOLCK]   The argument *cmd* is F_SETLK or F_SETLKW, and satisfying the lock or unlock request would result in the number of locked regions in the system exceeding a system-imposed limit.

[ESRCH]   *Cmd* is F_SETOWN and the process ID given as argument is not in use.

SEE ALSO

close(2), execve(2), flock(2), getdtablesize(2), open(2), sigvec(2)

HISTORY

The **fcntl** function call appeared in 4.2BSD.

2

NAME
flock – apply or remove an advisory lock on an open file

SYNOPSIS
```
#include <sys/file.h>
#define     LOCK_SH    1     /* shared lock */
#define     LOCK_EX    2     /* exclusive lock */
#define     LOCK_NB    4     /* don't block when locking */
#define     LOCK_UN    8     /* unlock */

int
flock(int fd, int operation);
```

DESCRIPTION
Flock() applies or removes an *advisory* lock on the file associated with the file descriptor *fd*. A lock is applied by specifying an *operation* parameter that is one of LOCK_SH or LOCK_EX with the optional addition of LOCK_NB. To unlock an existing lock *operation* should be LOCK_UN.

Advisory locks allow cooperating processes to perform consistent operations on files, but do not guarantee consistency (i.e., processes may still access files without using advisory locks possibly resulting in inconsistencies).

The locking mechanism allows two types of locks: *shared* locks and *exclusive* locks. At any time multiple shared locks may be applied to a file, but at no time are multiple exclusive, or both shared and exclusive, locks allowed simultaneously on a file.

A shared lock may be *upgraded* to an exclusive lock, and vice versa, simply by specifying the appropriate lock type; this results in the previous lock being released and the new lock applied (possibly after other processes have gained and released the lock).

Requesting a lock on an object that is already locked normally causes the caller to be blocked until the lock may be acquired. If LOCK_NB is included in *operation*, then this will not happen; instead the call will fail and the error EWOULDBLOCK will be returned.

NOTES
Locks are on files, not file descriptors. That is, file descriptors duplicated through dup(2) or fork(2) do not result in multiple instances of a lock, but rather multiple references to a single lock. If a process holding a lock on a file forks and the child explicitly unlocks the file, the parent will lose its lock.

Processes blocked awaiting a lock may be awakened by signals.

RETURN VALUES
Zero is returned if the operation was successful; on an error a -1 is returned and an error code is left in the global location *errno*.

ERRORS
The flock() call fails if:

[EWOULDBLOCK]   The file is locked and the LOCK_NB option was specified.

[EBADF]   The argument *fd* is an invalid descriptor.

[EINVAL]   The argument *fd* refers to an object other than a file.

SEE ALSO
open(2), close(2), dup(2), execve(2), fork(2)

HISTORY
The **flock** function call appeared in 4.2BSD.

2

NAME
fork – create a new process

SYNOPSIS
#include <unistd.h>

pid_t
fork(*void*);

DESCRIPTION
Fork() causes creation of a new process. The new process (child process) is an exact copy of the calling process (parent process) except for the following:

- The child process has a unique process ID.

- The child process has a different parent process ID (i.e., the process ID of the parent process).

- The child process has its own copy of the parent's descriptors. These descriptors reference the same underlying objects, so that, for instance, file pointers in file objects are shared between the child and the parent, so that an lseek(2) on a descriptor in the child process can affect a subsequent read or write by the parent. This descriptor copying is also used by the shell to establish standard input and output for newly created processes as well as to set up pipes.

- The child processes resource utilizations are set to 0; see setrlimit(2).

RETURN VALUES
Upon successful completion, fork() returns a value of 0 to the child process and returns the process ID of the child process to the parent process. Otherwise, a value of -1 is returned to the parent process, no child process is created, and the global variable *errno* is set to indicate the error.

ERRORS
Fork() will fail and no child process will be created if:

[EAGAIN]   The system-imposed limit on the total number of processes under execution would be exceeded. This limit is configuration-dependent.

[EAGAIN]   The system-imposed limit MAXUPRC (<sys/param.h>) on the total number of processes under execution by a single user would be exceeded.

[ENOMEM]   There is insufficient swap space for the new process.

SEE ALSO
execve(2), wait(2)

HISTORY
A fork(*2*) function call appeared in Version 6 AT&T UNIX.

2

NAME

fsync – synchronize a file's in-core state with that on disk

SYNOPSIS

```
#include <unistd.h>
```

int
fsync(*int fd*);

DESCRIPTION

Fsync() causes all modified data and attributes of *fd* to be moved to a permanent storage device. This normally results in all in-core modified copies of buffers for the associated file to be written to a disk.

Fsync() should be used by programs that require a file to be in a known state, for example, in building a simple transaction facility.

RETURN VALUES

A 0 value is returned on success. A -1 value indicates an error.

ERRORS

The **fsync**() fails if:

[EBADF]   *Fd* is not a valid descriptor.

[EINVAL]   *Fd* refers to a socket, not to a file.

[EIO]   An I/O error occurred while reading from or writing to the file system.

SEE ALSO

sync(2), sync(8), update(8)

HISTORY

The **fsync** function call appeared in 4.2BSD.

2

NAME

getdirentries – get directory entries in a filesystem independent format

SYNOPSIS

```
#include <sys/dirent.h>

int
getdirentries(int fd, char *buf, int nbytes, long *basep);
```

DESCRIPTION

Getdirentries() reads directory entries from the directory referenced by the file descriptor *fd* into the buffer pointed to by *buf*, in a filesystem independent format. Up to *nbytes* of data will be transferred. *Nbytes* must be greater than or equal to the block size associated with the file, see stat(2). Some filesystems may not support getdirentries() with buffers smaller than this size.

The data in the buffer is a series of *dirent* structures each containing the following entries:

```
unsigned long   d_fileno;
unsigned short  d_reclen;
unsigned short  d_namlen;
char            d_name[MAXNAMELEN + 1]; /* see below */
```

The *d_fileno* entry is a number which is unique for each distinct file in the filesystem. Files that are linked by hard links (see link(2)) have the same *d_fileno*. The *d_reclen* entry is the length, in bytes, of the directory record. The *d_name* entry contains a null terminated file name. The *d_namlen* entry specifies the length of the file name excluding the null byte. Thus the actual size of *d_name* may vary from 1 to MAXNAMELEN + 1.

Entries may be separated by extra space. The *d_reclen* entry may be used as an offset from the start of a *dirent* structure to the next structure, if any.

The actual number of bytes transferred is returned. The current position pointer associated with *fd* is set to point to the next block of entries. The pointer may not advance by the number of bytes returned by **getdirentries**(). A value of zero is returned when the end of the directory has been reached.

Getdirentries() writes the position of the block read into the location pointed to by *basep*. Alternatively, the current position pointer may be set and retrieved by lseek(2). The current position pointer should only be set to a value returned by lseek(2), a value returned in the location pointed to by *basep*, or zero.

RETURN VALUES

If successful, the number of bytes actually transferred is returned. Otherwise, -1 is returned and the global variable *errno* is set to indicate the error.

ERRORS

Getdirentries() will fail if:

EBADF   *fd* is not a valid file descriptor open for reading.

EFAULT   Either *buf* or *basep* point outside the allocated address space.

EIO   An I/O error occurred while reading from or writing to the file system.

SEE ALSO
open(2), lseek(2)

HISTORY
The **getdirentries** function first appeared in 4.4BSD.

2

NAME
getdtablesize – get descriptor table size

SYNOPSIS
`#include <unistd.h>`

int
getdtablesize(*void*);

DESCRIPTION
Each process has a fixed size descriptor table, which is guaranteed to have at least 20 slots. The entries in the descriptor table are numbered with small integers starting at 0. The call **getdtablesize**( ) returns the size of this table.

SEE ALSO
close(2), dup(2), open(2), select(2)

HISTORY
The **getdtablesize** function call appeared in 4.2BSD.

2

NAME
getfh – get file handle

SYNOPSIS
```
#include <sys/types.h>
#include <sys/mount.h>

int
getfh(char *path, fhandle_t *fhp);
```

DESCRIPTION
Getfh() returns a file handle for the specified file or directory in the file handle pointed to by *fhp*. This system call is restricted to the superuser.

RETURN VALUES
Upon successful completion, a value of 0 is returned. Otherwise, -1 is returned and the global variable *errno* is set to indicate the error.

ERRORS
Getfh( ) fails if one or more of the following are true:

[ENOTDIR]   A component of the path prefix of *path* is not a directory.

[EINVAL]   *path* contains a character with the high-order bit set.

[ENAMETOOLONG]
              The length of a component of *path* exceeds 255 characters, or the length of *path* exceeds 1023 characters.

[ENOENT]   The file referred to by *path* does not exist.

[EACCES]   Search permission is denied for a component of the path prefix of *path*.

[ELOOP]   Too many symbolic links were encountered in translating *path*.

[EFAULT]   *Fhp* points to an invalid address.

[EIO]   An I/O error occurred while reading from or writing to the file system.

HISTORY
The **getfh** function first appeared in 4.4BSD.

NAME

    getfsstat – get list of all mounted filesystems

SYNOPSIS

    `#include <sys/param.h>`
    `#include <sys/ucred.h>`
    `#include <sys/mount.h>`

    int
    getfsstat(*struct statfs *buf, long bufsize, int flags*);

DESCRIPTION

    Getfsstat() returns information about all mounted filesystems. *Buf* is a pointer to statfs structures defined as follows:

```
typedef quad fsid_t;

#define MNAMELEN 32    /* length of buffer for returned name */

struct statfs {
    short   f_type;    /* type of filesystem (see below) */
    short   f_flags;   /* copy of mount flags */
    long    f_bsize;   /* fundamental filesystem block size */
    long    f_iosize;  /* optimal transfer block size */
    long    f_blocks;  /* total data blocks in filesystem */
    long    f_bfree;   /* free blocks in fs */
    long    f_bavail;  /* free blocks avail to non-superuser */
    long    f_files;   /* total file nodes in filesystem */
    long    f_ffree;   /* free file nodes in fs */
    fsid_t  f_fsid;    /* filesystem id */
    long    f_spare[6];        /* spare for later */
    char    f_mntonname[MNAMELEN]; /* directory on which mounted */
    char    f_mntfromname[MNAMELEN]; /* mounted filesystem */
};
/*
 * File system types.
 */
#define MOUNT_UFS    1
#define MOUNT_NFS    2
#define MOUNT_PC     3
```

    Fields that are undefined for a particular filesystem are set to -1. The buffer is filled with an array of *fsstat* structures, one for each mounted filesystem up to the size specified by *bufsize*.

    If *buf* is given as NULL, getfsstat() returns just the number of mounted filesystems.

    Normally *flags* should be specified as MNT_WAIT. If *flags* is set to MNT_NOWAIT, getfsstat() will return the information it has available without requesting an update from each filesystem. Thus, some of the information will be out of date, but getfsstat() will not block waiting for information from a filesystem that is unable to respond.

2

RETURN VALUES

Upon successful completion, the number of *fsstat* structures is returned. Otherwise, -1 is returned and the global variable *errno* is set to indicate the error.

ERRORS

Getfsstat() fails if one or more of the following are true:

EFAULT   *Buf* points to an invalid address.

EIO   An I/O error occurred while reading from or writing to the filesystem.

SEE ALSO

statfs(2), fstab(5), mount(8)

HISTORY

The getfsstat function first appeared in 4.4BSD.

2

NAME
getgid, getegid – get group process identification

SYNOPSIS
`#include <sys/types.h>`

gid_t
getgid(*void*);

gid_t
getegid(*void*);

DESCRIPTION
The **getgid**( ) function returns the real group ID of the calling process, **getegid**( ) returns the effective group ID of the calling process.

The real group ID is specified at login time.

The real group ID is the group of the user who invoked the program. As the effective group ID gives the process additional permissions during the execution of *"set-group-ID"* mode processes, **getgid**( ) is used to determine the real-user-id of the calling process.

ERRORS
The **getgid**( ) and **getegid**( ) functions are always successful, and no return value is reserved to indicate an error.

SEE ALSO
getuid(2), setregid(2), setgid(3)

STANDARDS
Getgid( ) and **getegid**( ) conform to IEEE Std 1003.1-1988 (''POSIX'').

NAME

getgroups – get group access list

SYNOPSIS

```
#include <sys/param.h>
#include <unistd.h>
```

int
getgroups(*int gidsetlen, gid_t *gidset*);

DESCRIPTION

Getgroups() gets the current group access list of the user process and stores it in the array *gidset*. The parameter *gidsetlen* indicates the number of entries that may be placed in *gidset*. Getgroups() returns the actual number of groups returned in *gidset*. No more than NGROUPS, as defined in <sys/param.h>, will ever be returned.

RETURN VALUES

A successful call returns the number of groups in the group set. A value of -1 indicates that an error occurred, and the error code is stored in the global variable *errno*.

ERRORS

The possible errors for **getgroups**() are:

[EINVAL]　　　　The argument *gidsetlen* is smaller than the number of groups in the group set.

[EFAULT]　　　　The argument *gidset* specifies an invalid address.

SEE ALSO

setgroups(2), initgroups(3)

HISTORY

The **getgroups** function call appeared in 4.2BSD.

2

NAME
getitimer, setitimer – get/set value of interval timer

SYNOPSIS
```
#include <sys/time.h>
#define ITIMER_REAL          0
#define ITIMER_VIRTUAL    1
#define ITIMER_PROF          2

int
getitimer(int which, struct itimerval *value);

int
setitimer(int which, struct itimerval *value, struct itimerval *ovalue);
```

DESCRIPTION
The system provides each process with three interval timers, defined in <sys/time.h>. The **getiti-mer**( ) call returns the current value for the timer specified in *which* in the structure at *value*. The **seti-timer**( ) call sets a timer to the specified *value* (returning the previous value of the timer if *ovalue* is non-nil).

A timer value is defined by the *itimerval* structure:

```
struct itimerval {
        struct  timeval it_interval;    /* timer interval */
        struct  timeval it_value;       /* current value */
};
```

If *it_value* is non-zero, it indicates the time to the next timer expiration. If *it_interval* is non-zero, it specifies a value to be used in reloading *it_value* when the timer expires. Setting *it_value* to 0 disables a timer. Setting *it_interval* to 0 causes a timer to be disabled after its next expiration (assuming *it_value* is non-zero).

Time values smaller than the resolution of the system clock are rounded up to this resolution (typically 10 milliseconds).

The ITIMER_REAL timer decrements in real time. A SIGALRM signal is delivered when this timer expires.

The ITIMER_VIRTUAL timer decrements in process virtual time. It runs only when the process is executing. A SIGVTALRM signal is delivered when it expires.

The ITIMER_PROF timer decrements both in process virtual time and when the system is running on behalf of the process. It is designed to be used by interpreters in statistically profiling the execution of interpreted programs. Each time the ITIMER_PROF timer expires, the SIGPROF signal is delivered. Because this signal may interrupt in-progress system calls, programs using this timer must be prepared to restart interrupted system calls.

NOTES
Three macros for manipulating time values are defined in <sys/time.h>. *Timerclear* sets a time value to zero, *timerisset* tests if a time value is non-zero, and *timercmp* compares two time values (beware that >= and <= do not work with this macro).

RETURN VALUES
If the calls succeed, a value of 0 is returned. If an error occurs, the value -1 is returned, and a more precise error code is placed in the global variable *errno*.

2

ERRORS

Getitimer( ) and **setitimer**( ) will fail if:

[EFAULT]   The *value* parameter specified a bad address.

[EINVAL]   A *value* parameter specified a time that was too large to be handled.

SEE ALSO

select(2), sigvec(2), gettimeofday(2)

HISTORY

The **getitimer** function call appeared in 4.2BSD.

2

NAME
getlogin, setlogin – get/set login name

SYNOPSIS
```
#include <unistd.h>
```
char *
getlogin(*void*);

int
setlogin(*const char *name*);

DESCRIPTION
The getlogin() routine returns the login name of the user associated with the current session, as previously set by setlogin(). The name is normally associated with a login shell at the time a session is created, and is inherited by all processes descended from the login shell. (This is true even if some of those processes assume another user ID, for example when su(1) is used.)

Setlogin() sets the login name of the user associated with the current session to *name*. This call is restricted to the super-user, and is normally used only when a new session is being created on behalf of the named user (for example, at login time, or when a remote shell is invoked).

RETURN VALUES
If a call to getlogin() succeeds, it returns a pointer to a null-terminated string in a static buffer. If the name has not been set, it returns NULL. If a call to setlogin() succeeds, a value of 0 is returned. If setlogin() fails, a value of -1 is returned and an error code is placed in the global location *errno*.

ERRORS
The following errors may be returned by these calls:

[EFAULT]   The *name* parameter gave an invalid address.

[EINVAL]   The *name* parameter pointed to a string that was too long. Login names are limited to MAXLOGNAME (from <sys/param.h>) characters, currently 12.

[EPERM]   The caller tried to set the login name and was not the super-user.

SEE ALSO
setsid(2)

BUGS
Login names are limited in length by setlogin(). However, lower limits are placed on login names elsewhere in the system (UT_NAMESIZE in <utmp.h>).

In earlier versions of the system, getlogin() failed unless the process was associated with a login terminal. The current implementation (using setlogin()) allows getlogin to succeed even when the process has no controlling terminal. In earlier versions of the system, the value returned by getlogin() could not be trusted without checking the user ID. Portable programs should probably still make this check.

HISTORY
The getlogin() function first appeared in 4.4BSD.

NAME

getpeername – get name of connected peer

SYNOPSIS

int

getpeername(*int s, struct sockaddr *name, int *namelen*);

DESCRIPTION

Getpeername() returns the name of the peer connected to socket *s*. The *namelen* parameter should be initialized to indicate the amount of space pointed to by *name*. On return it contains the actual size of the name returned (in bytes). The name is truncated if the buffer provided is too small.

DIAGNOSTICS

A 0 is returned if the call succeeds, -1 if it fails.

ERRORS

The call succeeds unless:

[EBADF]   The argument *s* is not a valid descriptor.

[ENOTSOCK] The argument *s* is a file, not a socket.

[ENOTCONN] The socket is not connected.

[ENOBUFS]   Insufficient resources were available in the system to perform the operation.

[EFAULT]   The *name* parameter points to memory not in a valid part of the process address space.

SEE ALSO

accept(2), bind(2), socket(2), getsockname(2)

HISTORY

The **getpeername** function call appeared in 4.2BSD.

2

NAME
getpgrp – get process group

SYNOPSIS
#include <unistd.h>

pid_t
getpgrp(*void*);

DESCRIPTION
The process group of the current process is returned by getpgrp().

Process groups are used for distribution of signals, and by terminals to arbitrate requests for their input: processes that have the same process group as the terminal are foreground and may read, while others will block with a signal if they attempt to read.

This call is thus used by programs such as csh(1) to create process groups in implementing job control. The tcgetpgrp() and tcsetpgrp() calls are used to get/set the process group of the control terminal.

SEE ALSO
setpgid(2), termios(4)

HISTORY
The getpgrp function call appeared in 4.0BSD.

STANDARDS
The getpgrp() function conforms to IEEE Std 1003.1-1988 (''POSIX'').

COMPATABILITY
This version of getpgrp() differs from past Berkeley versions by not taking a *pid_t pid* argument. This incompatibility is required by IEEE Std1003.1-1988 (''POSIX'').

From the IEEE Std1003.1-1988 (''POSIX'') Rationale:

4.3BSD provides a getpgrp() function that returns the process group ID for a specified process. Although this function is used to support job control, all known job-control shells always specify the calling process with this function. Thus, the simpler System V getpgrp() suffices, and the added complexity of the 4.3BSD getpgrp() has been omitted from POSIX.1.

2

NAME
getpid, getppid – get parent or calling process identification

SYNOPSIS
```
#include <unistd.h>
```

pid_t
getpid(*void*);

pid_t
getppid(*void*);

DESCRIPTION
Getpid() returns the process ID of the calling process. The ID is guaranteed to be unique and is useful for constructing temporary file names.

Getppid() returns the process ID of the parent of the calling process.

ERRORS
The getpid() and getppid() functions are always successful, and no return value is reserved to indicate an error.

SEE ALSO
gethostid(2)

STANDARDS
Getpid() and getppid() conform to IEEE Std 1003.1-1988 (''POSIX'').

NAME

getpriority, setpriority – get/set program scheduling priority

SYNOPSIS

#include ⟨sys/time.h⟩
#include ⟨sys/resource.h⟩

int
getpriority(int which, int who);

int
setpriority(int which, int who, int prio);

DESCRIPTION

The scheduling priority of the process, process group, or user, as indicated by *which* and *who* is obtained with the getpriority() call and set with the setpriority() call. *Which* is one of PRIO_PROCESS, PRIO_PGRP, or PRIO_USER, and *who* is interpreted relative to *which* (a process identifier for PRIO_PROCESS, process group identifier for PRIO_PGRP, and a user ID for PRIO_USER). A zero value of *who* denotes the current process, process group, or user. *Prio* is a value in the range -20 to 20. The default priority is 0; lower priorities cause more favorable scheduling.

The getpriority() call returns the highest priority (lowest numerical value) enjoyed by any of the specified processes. The setpriority() call sets the priorities of all of the specified processes to the specified value. Only the super-user may lower priorities.

RETURN VALUES

Since getpriority() can legitimately return the value -1, it is necessary to clear the external variable *errno* prior to the call, then check it afterward to determine if a -1 is an error or a legitimate value. The setpriority() call returns 0 if there is no error, or -1 if there is.

ERRORS

Getpriority() and setpriority() will fail if:

[ESRCH]   No process was located using the *which* and *who* values specified.

[EINVAL]   *Which* was not one of PRIO_PROCESS, PRIO_PGRP, or PRIO_USER.

In addition to the errors indicated above, setpriority() will fail if:

[EPERM]   A process was located, but neither its effective nor real user ID matched the effective user ID of the caller.

[EACCES]   A non super-user attempted to lower a process priority.

SEE ALSO

nice(1), fork(2), renice(8)

HISTORY

The getpriority function call appeared in 4.2BSD.

2

NAME
getrlimit, setrlimit – control maximum system resource consumption

SYNOPSIS
```
#include <sys/types.h>
#include <sys/time.h>
#include <sys/resource.h>

int
getrlimit(int resource, struct rlimit *rlp);

int
setrlimit(int resource, struct rlimit *rlp);
```

DESCRIPTION
Limits on the consumption of system resources by the current process and each process it creates may be obtained with the getrlimit() call, and set with the setrlimit() call.

The *resource* parameter is one of the following:

RLIMIT_CORE   The largest size (in bytes) core file that may be created.

RLIMIT_CPU   The maximum amount of cpu time (in seconds) to be used by each process.

RLIMIT_DATA   The maximum size (in bytes) of the data segment for a process; this defines how far a program may extend its break with the sbrk(2) system call.

RLIMIT_FSIZE   The largest size (in bytes) file that may be created.

RLIMIT_MEMLOCK   The maximum size (in bytes) which a process may lock into memory using the mlock(2) function.

RLIMIT_NOFILE   The maximum number of open files for this process.

RLIMIT_NPROC   The maximum number of simultaneous processes for this user id.

RLIMIT_RSS   The maximum size (in bytes) to which a process's resident set size may grow. This imposes a limit on the amount of physical memory to be given to a process; if memory is tight, the system will prefer to take memory from processes that are exceeding their declared resident set size.

RLIMIT_STACK   The maximum size (in bytes) of the stack segment for a process; this defines how far a program's stack segment may be extended. Stack extension is performed automatically by the system.

A resource limit is specified as a soft limit and a hard limit. When a soft limit is exceeded a process may receive a signal (for example, if the cpu time or file size is exceeded), but it will be allowed to continue execution until it reaches the hard limit (or modifies its resource limit). The *rlimit* structure is used to specify the hard and soft limits on a resource,

```
struct rlimit {
        quad_t rlim_cur;        /* current (soft) limit */
        quad_t rlim_max;        /* hard limit */
};
```

Only the super-user may raise the maximum limits. Other users may only alter *rlim_cur* within the range from 0 to *rlim_max* or (irreversibly) lower *rlim_max*.

An "infinite" value for a limit is defined as RLIM_INFINITY.

Because this information is stored in the per-process information, this system call must be executed directly by the shell if it is to affect all future processes created by the shell; **limit** is thus a built-in command to csh(1).

The system refuses to extend the data or stack space when the limits would be exceeded in the normal way: a break call fails if the data space limit is reached. When the stack limit is reached, the process receives a segmentation fault (SIGSEGV); if this signal is not caught by a handler using the signal stack, this signal will kill the process.

A file I/O operation that would create a file larger that the process' soft limit will cause the write to fail and a signal SIGXFSZ to be generated; this normally terminates the process, but may be caught. When the soft cpu time limit is exceeded, a signal SIGXCPU is sent to the offending process.

RETURN VALUES

A 0 return value indicates that the call succeeded, changing or returning the resource limit. A return value of -1 indicates that an error occurred, and an error code is stored in the global location *errno*.

ERRORS

Getrlimit() and setrlimit() will fail if:

[EFAULT]   The address specified for *rlp* is invalid.

[EPERM]   The limit specified to setrlimit() would have raised the maximum limit value, and the caller is not the super-user.

SEE ALSO

csh(1), quota(2), sigaltstack(2), sigvec(2), sysctl(3)

BUGS

There should be **limit** and **unlimit** commands in sh(1) as well as in csh.

HISTORY

The getrlimit function call appeared in 4.2BSD.

2

NAME
getrusage – get information about resource utilization

SYNOPSIS
```
#include <sys/time.h>
#include <sys/resource.h>
#define      RUSAGE_SELF   0
#define      RUSAGE_CHILDREN    -1

int
getrusage(int who, struct rusage *rusage);
```

DESCRIPTION
Getrusage() returns information describing the resources utilized by the current process, or all its terminated child processes. The who parameter is either RUSAGE_SELF or RUSAGE_CHILDREN. The buffer to which rusage points will be filled in with the following structure:

```
struct rusage {
        struct timeval ru_utime;    /* user time used */
        struct timeval ru_stime;    /* system time used */
        long ru_maxrss;             /* integral max resident set size */
        long ru_ixrss;              /* integral shared text memory size */
        long ru_idrss;              /* integral unshared data size */
        long ru_isrss;              /* integral unshared stack size */
        long ru_minflt;             /* page reclaims */
        long ru_majflt;             /* page faults */
        long ru_nswap;              /* swaps */
        long ru_inblock;            /* block input operations */
        long ru_oublock;            /* block output operations */
        long ru_msgsnd;             /* messages sent */
        long ru_msgrcv;             /* messages received */
        long ru_nsignals;           /* signals received */
        long ru_nvcsw;              /* voluntary context switches */
        long ru_nivcsw;             /* involuntary context switches */
};
```

The fields are interpreted as follows:

ru_utime   the total amount of time spent executing in user mode.

ru_stime   the total amount of time spent in the system executing on behalf of the process(es).

ru_maxrss   the maximum resident set size utilized (in kilobytes).

ru_ixrss   an integral value indicating the amount of memory used by the text segment that was also shared among other processes. This value is expressed in units of kilobytes * ticks-of-execution.

ru_idrss   an integral value of the amount of unshared memory residing in the data segment of a process (expressed in units of kilobytes * ticks-of-execution).

ru_isrss   an integral value of the amount of unshared memory residing in the stack segment of a process (expressed in units of kilobytes * ticks-of-execution).

2

ru_minflt	the number of page faults serviced without any I/O activity; here I/O activity is avoided by reclaiming a page frame from the list of pages awaiting reallocation.
ru_majflt	the number of page faults serviced that required I/O activity.
ru_nswap	the number of times a process was swapped out of main memory.
ru_inblock	the number of times the file system had to perform input.
ru_oublock	the number of times the file system had to perform output.
ru_msgsnd	the number of IPC messages sent.
ru_msgrcv	the number of IPC messages received.
ru_nsignals	the number of signals delivered.
ru_nvcsw	the number of times a context switch resulted due to a process voluntarily giving up the processor before its time slice was completed (usually to await availability of a resource).
ru_nivcsw	the number of times a context switch resulted due to a higher priority process becoming runnable or because the current process exceeded its time slice.

NOTES

The numbers *ru_inblock* and *ru_oublock* account only for real I/O; data supplied by the caching mechanism is charged only to the first process to read or write the data.

ERRORS

`Getrusage()` returns -1 on error. The possible errors are:

[EINVAL]   The *who* parameter is not a valid value.

[EFAULT]   The address specified by the *rusage* parameter is not in a valid part of the process address space.

SEE ALSO

gettimeofday(2), wait(2)

BUGS

There is no way to obtain information about a child process that has not yet terminated.

HISTORY

The getrusage function call appeared in 4.2BSD.

2

NAME
getsockname – get socket name

SYNOPSIS
int
getsockname(*int s, struct sockaddr *name, int *namelen*);

DESCRIPTION
`Getsockname`() returns the current *name* for the specified socket. The *namelen* parameter should be initialized to indicate the amount of space pointed to by *name*. On return it contains the actual size of the name returned (in bytes).

DIAGNOSTICS
A 0 is returned if the call succeeds, -1 if it fails.

ERRORS
The call succeeds unless:

[EBADF]   The argument *s* is not a valid descriptor.

[ENOTSOCK]   The argument *s* is a file, not a socket.

[ENOBUFS]   Insufficient resources were available in the system to perform the operation.

[EFAULT]   The *name* parameter points to memory not in a valid part of the process address space.

SEE ALSO
bind(2), socket(2)

BUGS
Names bound to sockets in the UNIX domain are inaccessible; getsockname returns a zero length name.

HISTORY
The **getsockname** function call appeared in 4.2BSD.

2

NAME

`getsockopt`, `setsockopt` – get and set options on sockets

SYNOPSIS

```
#include <sys/types.h>
#include <sys/socket.h>
```

int
`getsockopt`(*int s*, *int level*, *int optname*, *void *optval*, *int *optlen*);

int
`setsockopt`(*int s*, *int level*, *int optname*, *const void *optval*, *int optlen*);

DESCRIPTION

`Getsockopt`( ) and `setsockopt`( ) manipulate the *options* associated with a socket. Options may exist at multiple protocol levels; they are always present at the uppermost "socket" level.

When manipulating socket options the level at which the option resides and the name of the option must be specified. To manipulate options at the socket level, *level* is specified as SOL_SOCKET. To manipulate options at any other level the protocol number of the appropriate protocol controlling the option is supplied. For example, to indicate that an option is to be interpreted by the TCP protocol, *level* should be set to the protocol number of TCP; see getprotoent(3).

The parameters *optval* and *optlen* are used to access option values for `setsockopt`(). For **getsockopt**() they identify a buffer in which the value for the requested option(s) are to be returned. For `getsockopt`(), *optlen* is a value-result parameter, initially containing the size of the buffer pointed to by *optval*, and modified on return to indicate the actual size of the value returned. If no option value is to be supplied or returned, *optval* may be NULL.

Optname and any specified options are passed uninterpreted to the appropriate protocol module for interpretation. The include file <sys/socket.h> contains definitions for socket level options, described below. Options at other protocol levels vary in format and name; consult the appropriate entries in section 4 of the manual.

Most socket-level options utilize an *int* parameter for *optval*. For **setsockopt**(), the parameter should be non-zero to enable a boolean option, or zero if the option is to be disabled. SO_LINGER uses a *struct linger* parameter, defined in <sys/socket.h>, which specifies the desired state of the option and the linger interval (see below). SO_SNDTIMEO and SO_RCVTIMEO use a *struct timeval* parameter, defined in <sys/time.h>.

The following options are recognized at the socket level. Except as noted, each may be examined with **getsockopt**() and set with **setsockopt**().

SO_DEBUG	enables recording of debugging information
SO_REUSEADDR	enables local address reuse
SO_REUSEPORT	enables duplicate address and port bindings
SO_KEEPALIVE	enables keep connections alive
SO_DONTROUTE	enables routing bypass for outgoing messages
SO_LINGER	linger on close if data present
SO_BROADCAST	enables permission to transmit broadcast messages
SO_OOBINLINE	enables reception of out-of-band data in band
SO_SNDBUF	set buffer size for output

2

SO_RCVBUF	set buffer size for input
SO_SNDLOWAT	set minimum count for output
SO_RCVLOWAT	set minimum count for input
SO_SNDTIMEO	set timeout value for output
SO_RCVTIMEO	set timeout value for input
SO_TYPE	get the type of the socket (get only)
SO_ERROR	get and clear error on the socket (get only)

SO_DEBUG enables debugging in the underlying protocol modules. SO_REUSEADDR indicates that the rules used in validating addresses supplied in a bind(2) call should allow reuse of local addresses. SO_REUSEPORT allows completely duplicate bindings by multiple processes if they all set SO_REUSEPORT before binding the port. This option permits multiple instances of a program to each receive UDP/IP multicast or broadcast datagrams destined for the bound port. SO_KEEPALIVE enables the periodic transmission of messages on a connected socket. Should the connected party fail to respond to these messages, the connection is considered broken and processes using the socket are notified via a SIGPIPE signal when attempting to send data. SO_DONTROUTE indicates that outgoing messages should bypass the standard routing facilities. Instead, messages are directed to the appropriate network interface according to the network portion of the destination address.

SO_LINGER controls the action taken when unsent messages are queued on socket and a close(2) is performed. If the socket promises reliable delivery of data and SO_LINGER is set, the system will block the process on the close attempt until it is able to transmit the data or until it decides it is unable to deliver the information (a timeout period, termed the linger interval, is specified in the setsockopt() call when SO_LINGER is requested). If SO_LINGER is disabled and a close is issued, the system will process the close in a manner that allows the process to continue as quickly as possible.

The option SO_BROADCAST requests permission to send broadcast datagrams on the socket. Broadcast was a privileged operation in earlier versions of the system. With protocols that support out-of-band data, the SO_OOBINLINE option requests that out-of-band data be placed in the normal data input queue as received; it will then be accessible with recv or read calls without the MSG_OOB flag. Some protocols always behave as if this option is set. SO_SNDBUF and SO_RCVBUF are options to adjust the normal buffer sizes allocated for output and input buffers, respectively. The buffer size may be increased for high-volume connections, or may be decreased to limit the possible backlog of incoming data. The system places an absolute limit on these values.

SO_SNDLOWAT is an option to set the minimum count for output operations. Most output operations process all of the data supplied by the call, delivering data to the protocol for transmission and blocking as necessary for flow control. Nonblocking output operations will process as much data as permitted subject to flow control without blocking, but will process no data if flow control does not allow the smaller of the low water mark value or the entire request to be processed. A select(2) operation testing the ability to write to a socket will return true only if the low water mark amount could be processed. The default value for SO_SNDLOWAT is set to a convenient size for network efficiency, often 1024. SO_RCVLOWAT is an option to set the minimum count for input operations. In general, receive calls will block until any (non-zero) amount of data is received, then return with the smaller of the amount available or the amount requested. The default value for SO_RCVLOWAT is 1. If SO_RCVLOWAT is set to a larger value, blocking receive calls normally wait until they have received the smaller of the low water mark value or the requested amount. Receive calls may still return less than the low water mark if an error occurs, a signal is caught, or the type of data next in the receive queue is different than that returned.

SO_SNDTIMEO is an option to set a timeout value for output operations. It accepts a struct timeval parameter with the number of seconds and microseconds used to limit waits for output operations to complete. If a send operation has blocked for this much time, it returns with a partial count or with the error EWOULDBLOCK if no data were sent. In the current implementation, this timer is restarted each time additional data are delivered to the protocol, implying that the limit applies to output portions ranging in size

2

from the low water mark to the high water mark for output. SO_RCVTIMEO is an option to set a timeout value for input operations. It accepts a *struct timeval* parameter with the number of seconds and microseconds used to limit waits for input operations to complete. In the current implementation, this timer is restarted each time additional data are received by the protocol, and thus the limit is in effect an inactivity timer. If a receive operation has been blocked for this much time without receiving additional data, it returns with a short count or with the error EWOULDBLOCK if no data were received.

Finally, SO_TYPE and SO_ERROR are options used only with **getsockopt**(). SO_TYPE returns the type of the socket, such as SOCK_STREAM; it is useful for servers that inherit sockets on startup. SO_ERROR returns any pending error on the socket and clears the error status. It may be used to check for asynchronous errors on connected datagram sockets or for other asynchronous errors.

RETURN VALUES
A 0 is returned if the call succeeds, -1 if it fails.

ERRORS
The call succeeds unless:

[EBADF]   The argument *s* is not a valid descriptor.

[ENOTSOCK]   The argument *s* is a file, not a socket.

[ENOPROTOOPT]   The option is unknown at the level indicated.

[EFAULT]   The address pointed to by *optval* is not in a valid part of the process address space. For **getsockopt**(), this error may also be returned if *optlen* is not in a valid part of the process address space.

SEE ALSO
ioctl(2), socket(2), getprotoent(3) protocols(5)

BUGS
Several of the socket options should be handled at lower levels of the system.

HISTORY
The **getsockopt** system call appeared in 4.2BSD.

NAME

  gettimeofday, **settimeofday** – get/set date and time

SYNOPSIS

  #include <sys/time.h>

  int
  gettimeofday(*struct timeval *tp, struct timezone *tzp*);

  int
  settimeofday(*struct timeval *tp, struct timezone *tzp*);

DESCRIPTION

  Note: timezone is no longer used; this information is kept outside the kernel. The system's notion of the current Greenwich time and the current time zone is obtained with the **gettimeofday**( ) call, and set with the **settimeofday**( ) call. The time is expressed in seconds and microseconds since midnight (0 hour), January 1, 1970. The resolution of the system clock is hardware dependent, and the time may be updated continuously or in "ticks." If *tp* or *tzp* is NULL, the associated time information will not be returned or set.

  The structures pointed to by *tp* and *tzp* are defined in <sys/time.h> as:

```
struct timeval {
        long    tv_sec;         /* seconds since Jan. 1, 1970 */
        long    tv_usec;        /* and microseconds */
};

struct timezone {
        int     tz_minuteswest; /* of Greenwich */
        int     tz_dsttime;     /* type of dst correction to apply */
};
```

  The *timezone* structure indicates the local time zone (measured in minutes of time westward from Greenwich), and a flag that, if nonzero, indicates that Daylight Saving time applies locally during the appropriate part of the year.

  Only the super-user may set the time of day or time zone.

RETURN

  A 0 return value indicates that the call succeeded. A -1 return value indicates an error occurred, and in this case an error code is stored into the global variable *errno*.

ERRORS

  The following error codes may be set in *errno*:

  [EFAULT] An argument address referenced invalid memory.

  [EPERM] A user other than the super-user attempted to set the time.

SEE ALSO

  date(1), adjtime(2), ctime(3), timed(8)

HISTORY

The `gettimeofday` function call appeared in 4.2BSD.

2

NAME
getuid, geteuid – get user identification

SYNOPSIS
```
#include <unistd.h>
#include <sys/types.h>
```
uid_t
getuid(*void*);

uid_t
geteuid(*void*);

DESCRIPTION
The **getuid**( ) function returns the real user ID of the calling process. The **geteuid**( ) function returns the effective user ID of the calling process.

The real user ID is that of the user who has invoked the program. As the effective user ID gives the process additional permissions during execution of *"set-user-ID"* mode processes, **getuid**( ) is used to determine the real-user-id of the calling process.

ERRORS
The **getuid**( ) and **geteuid**( ) functions are always successful, and no return value is reserved to indicate an error.

SEE ALSO
getgid(2), setreuid(2)

STANDARDS
Geteuid( ) and **getuid**( ) conform to IEEE Std 1003.1-1988 ("POSIX").

2

NAME
    `ioctl` – control device

SYNOPSIS
    `#include <sys/ioctl.h>`

    `int`
    `ioctl(int d, unsigned long request, char *argp);`

DESCRIPTION
    The `ioctl()` function manipulates the underlying device parameters of special files. In particular, many operating characteristics of character special files (e.g. terminals) may be controlled with `ioctl()` requests. The argument d must be an open file descriptor.

    An ioctl `request` has encoded in it whether the argument is an "in" parameter or "out" parameter, and the size of the argument `argp` in bytes. Macros and defines used in specifying an ioctl `request` are located in the file `<sys/ioctl.h>`.

RETURN VALUES
    If an error has occurred, a value of -1 is returned and *errno* is set to indicate the error.

ERRORS
    `Ioctl()` will fail if:

    `[EBADF]` d is not a valid descriptor.

    `[ENOTTY]` d is not associated with a character special device.

    `[ENOTTY]`   The specified request does not apply to the kind of object that the descriptor d references.

    `[EINVAL]`   *Request* or `argp` is not valid.

SEE ALSO
    mt(1), execve(2), fcntl(2), tty(4), intro(4)

HISTORY
    An `ioctl` function call appeared in Version 7 AT&T UNIX.

2

NAME
kill – send signal to a process

SYNOPSIS
```
#include <signal.h>

int
kill(pid_t pid, int sig);
```

DESCRIPTION
The **kill**() function sends the signal given by *sig* to *pid*, a process or a group of processes. *Sig* may be one of the signals specified in sigaction(2) or it may be 0, in which case error checking is performed but no signal is actually sent. This can be used to check the validity of *pid*.

For a process to have permission to send a signal to a process designated by *pid*, the real or effective user ID of the receiving process must match that of the sending process or the user must have appropriate privileges (such as given by a set-user-ID program or the user is the super-user). A single exception is the signal SIGCONT, which may always be sent to any descendant of the current process.

If *pid* is greater than zero:
>   *Sig* is sent to the process whose ID is equal to *pid*.

If *pid* is zero:
>   *Sig* is sent to all processes whose group ID is equal to the process group ID of the sender, and for which the process has permission; this is a variant of killpg(2).

If *pid* is -1:
>   If the user has super-user privileges, the signal is sent to all processes excluding system processes and the process sending the signal. If the user is not the super user, the signal is sent to all processes with the same uid as the user excluding the process sending the signal. No error is returned if any process could be signaled.

For compatibility with System V, if the process number is negative but not -1, the signal is sent to all processes whose process group ID is equal to the absolute value of the process number. This is a variant of killpg(2).

RETURN VALUES
Upon successful completion, a value of 0 is returned. Otherwise, a value of -1 is returned and *errno* is set to indicate the error.

ERRORS
Kill() will fail and no signal will be sent if:

[EINVAL] *Sig* is not a valid signal number.

[ESRCH]   No process can be found corresponding to that specified by *pid*.

[ESRCH]   The process id was given as 0 but the sending process does not have a process group.

[EPERM]   The sending process is not the super-user and its effective user id does not match the effective user-id of the receiving process. When signaling a process group, this error is returned if any members of the group could not be signaled.

SEE ALSO

    getpid(2), getpgrp(2), killpg(2), sigaction(2)

STANDARDS

    The kill( ) function is expected to conform to IEEE Std 1003.1-1988 ("POSIX").

2

NAME
killpg – send signal to a process group

SYNOPSIS
#include ⟨signal.h⟩

int
killpg(*pid_t pgrp*, *int sig*);

DESCRIPTION
Killpg( ) sends the signal *sig* to the process group *pgrp*. See sigaction(2) for a list of signals. If *pgrp* is 0, killpg( ) sends the signal to the sending process's process group.

The sending process and members of the process group must have the same effective user ID, or the sender must be the super-user. As a single special case the continue signal SIGCONT may be sent to any process that is a descendant of the current process.

RETURN VALUES
Upon successful completion, a value of 0 is returned. Otherwise, a value of -1 is returned and the global variable *errno* is set to indicate the error.

ERRORS
Killpg( ) will fail and no signal will be sent if:

[EINVAL]   *Sig* is not a valid signal number.

[ESRCH]   No process can be found in the process group specified by *pgrp*.

[ESRCH]   The process group was given as 0 but the sending process does not have a process group.

[EPERM]   The sending process is not the super-user and one or more of the target processes has an effective user ID different from that of the sending process.

SEE ALSO
kill(2), getpgrp(2), sigaction(2)

HISTORY
The killpg function call appeared in 4.0BSD.

2

NAME
　　　ktrace – process tracing

SYNOPSIS
　　　`#include <sys/types.h>`
　　　`#include <sys/ktrace.h>`

　　　int
　　　ktrace(*const char *tracefile, int ops, int trpoints, int pid*);

DESCRIPTION
　　　The **ktrace**( ) function enables or disables tracing of one or more processes. Users may only trace their
　　　own processes. Only the super-user can trace setuid or setgid programs.

　　　The *tracefile* gives the pathname of the file to be used for tracing. The file must exist and be writable
　　　by the calling process. All trace records are always appended to the file, so the file must be truncated to zero
　　　length to discard previous trace data. If tracing points are being disabled (see KTROP_CLEAR below),
　　　tracefile may be NULL.

　　　The **ops** parameter specifies the requested ktrace operation. The defined operations are:

KTROP_SET	Enable trace points specified in *trpoints*.
KTROP_CLEAR	Disable trace points specified in *trpoints*.
KTROP_CLEARFILE	Stop all tracing.
KTRFLAG_DESCEND	The tracing change should apply to the specified process and all its current children.

　　　The **trpoints** parameter specifies the trace points of interest. The defined trace points are:

KTRFAC_SYSCALL	Trace system calls.
KTRFAC_SYSRET	Trace return values from system calls.
KTRFAC_NAMEI	Trace name lookup operations.
KTRFAC_GENIO	Trace all I/O (note that this option can generate much output).
KTRFAC_PSIG	Trace posted signals.
KTRFAC_CSW	Trace context switch points.
KTRFAC_INHERIT	Inherit tracing to future children.

　　　Each tracing event outputs a record composed of a generic header followed by a trace point specific struc-
　　　ture. The generic header is:

```
struct ktr_header {
        int     ktr_len;                 /* length of buf */
        short   ktr_type;                /* trace record type */
        pid_t   ktr_pid;                 /* process id */
        char    ktr_comm[MAXCOMLEN+1];   /* command name */
        struct timeval ktr_time;         /* timestamp */
        caddr_t ktr_buf;
};
```

　　　The **ktr_len** field specifies the length of the **ktr_type** data that follows this header. The **ktr_pid** and
　　　ktr_comm fields specify the process and command generating the record. The **ktr_time** field gives the
　　　time (with microsecond resolution) that the record was generated. The **ktr_buf** is an internal kernel
　　　pointer and is not useful.

The generic header is followed by **ktr_len** bytes of a **ktr_type** record. The type specific records are defined in the <sys/ktrace.h> include file.

RETURN VALUES

On successful completion a value of 0 is returned. Otherwise, a value of -1 is returned and *errno* is set to show the error.

ERRORS

Ktrace( ) will fail if:

[ENOTDIR]	A component of the path prefix is not a directory.
[EINVAL]	The pathname contains a character with the high-order bit set.
[ENAMETOOLONG]	A component of a pathname exceeded 255 characters, or an entire path name exceeded 1023 characters.
[ENOENT]	The named tracefile does not exist.
[EACCES]	Search permission is denied for a component of the path prefix.
[ELOOP]	Too many symbolic links were encountered in translating the pathname.
[EIO]	An I/O error occurred while reading from or writing to the file system.

SEE ALSO

ktrace(1), kdump(1)

HISTORY

A **ktrace** function call first appeared in 4.4BSD.

NAME

link – make a hard file link

SYNOPSIS

```
#include <unistd.h>

int
link(const char *name1, const char *name2);
```

DESCRIPTION

The link() function call atomically creates the specified directory entry (hard link) *name2* with the attributes of the underlying object pointed at by *name1* If the link is successful: the link count of the underlying object is incremented; *name1* and *name2* share equal access and rights to the underlying object.

If *name1* is removed, the file *name2* is not deleted and the link count of the underlying object is decremented.

Name1 must exist for the hard link to succeed and both *name1* and *name2* must be in the same file system. Unless the caller is the super-user, *name1* may not be a directory.

RETURN VALUES

Upon successful completion, a value of 0 is returned. Otherwise, a value of -1 is returned and *errno* is set to indicate the error.

ERRORS

Link( ) will fail and no link will be created if:

[ENOTDIR]   A component of either path prefix is not a directory.

[EINVAL]   Either pathname contains a character with the high-order bit set.

[ENAMETOOLONG]
               A component of either pathname exceeded 255 characters, or entire length of either path name exceeded 1023 characters.

[ENOENT]   A component of either path prefix does not exist.

[EACCES]   A component of either path prefix denies search permission.

[EACCES]   The requested link requires writing in a directory with a mode that denies write permission.

[ELOOP]   Too many symbolic links were encountered in translating one of the pathnames.

[ENOENT]   The file named by *name1* does not exist.

[EEXIST]   The link named by *name2* does exist.

[EPERM]   The file named by *name1* is a directory and the effective user ID is not super-user.

[EXDEV]   The link named by *name2* and the file named by *name1* are on different file systems.

[ENOSPC]   The directory in which the entry for the new link is being placed cannot be extended because there is no space left on the file system containing the directory.

[EDQUOT]	The directory in which the entry for the new link is being placed cannot be extended because the user's quota of disk blocks on the file system containing the directory has been exhausted.
[EIO]	An I/O error occurred while reading from or writing to the file system to make the directory entry.
[EROFS]	The requested link requires writing in a directory on a read-only file system.
[EFAULT]	One of the pathnames specified is outside the process's allocated address space.

SEE ALSO
symlink(2), unlink(2)

STANDARDS
Link() is expected to conform to IEEE Std 1003.1-1988 (''POSIX'').

2

NAME

`listen` – listen for connections on a socket

SYNOPSIS

`#include <sys/socket.h>`

`int`
`listen(int s, int backlog);`

DESCRIPTION

To accept connections, a socket is first created with `socket(2)`, a willingness to accept incoming connections and a queue limit for incoming connections are specified with `listen()`, and then the connections are accepted with `accept(2)`. The `listen()` call applies only to sockets of type SOCK_STREAM or SOCK_SEQPACKET.

The `backlog` parameter defines the maximum length the queue of pending connections may grow to. If a connection request arrives with the queue full the client may receive an error with an indication of ECONNREFUSED, or, if the underlying protocol supports retransmission, the request may be ignored so that retries may succeed.

RETURN VALUES

A 0 return value indicates success; -1 indicates an error.

ERRORS

`Listen()` will fail if:

[EBADF]   The argument *s* is not a valid descriptor.

[ENOTSOCK]   The argument *s* is not a socket.

[EOPNOTSUPP] The socket is not of a type that supports the operation `listen()`.

SEE ALSO

`accept(2)`, `connect(2)`, `socket(2)`

BUGS

The `backlog` is currently limited (silently) to 5.

HISTORY

The `listen` function call appeared in 4.2BSD.

2

NAME
lseek – reposition read/write file offset

SYNOPSIS
`#include <unistd.h>`

`off_t`
`lseek(int fildes, off_t offset, int whence);`

DESCRIPTION
The lseek( ) function repositions the offset of the file descriptor *fildes* to the argument *offset* according to the directive *whence*. The argument *fildes* must be an open file descriptor. Lseek( ) repositions the file pointer *fildes* as follows:

If *whence* is SEEK_SET, the offset is set to *offset* bytes.

If *whence* is SEEK_CUR, the offset is set to its current location plus *offset* bytes.

If *whence* is SEEK_END, the offset is set to the size of the file plus *offset* bytes.

The lseek( ) function allows the file offset to be set beyond the end of the existing end-of-file of the file. If data is later written at this point, subsequent reads of the data in the gap return bytes of zeros (until data is actually written into the gap).

Some devices are incapable of seeking. The value of the pointer associated with such a device is undefined.

RETURN VALUES
Upon successful completion, lseek( ) returns the resulting offset location as measured in bytes from the beginning of the file. Otherwise, a value of -1 is returned and *errno* is set to indicate the error.

ERRORS
Lseek( ) will fail and the file pointer will remain unchanged if:

[EBADF]   *Fildes* is not an open file descriptor.

[ESPIPE]   *Fildes* is associated with a pipe, socket, or FIFO.

[EINVAL]   *Whence* is not a proper value.

SEE ALSO
dup(2), open(2)

BUGS
This document's use of *whence* is incorrect English, but is maintained for historical reasons.

STANDARDS
The lseek( ) function conforms to IEEE Std 1003.1-1988 (''POSIX'').

2

NAME

madvise – give advise about use of memory

SYNOPSIS

madvise(*caddr_t addr*, *int len*, *int behav*);

DESCRIPTION

The **madvise**() system call allows a process that has knowledge of its memory behavior to describe it to the system. The known behaviors are given in <sys/mman.h>:

```
#define MADV_NORMAL      0        /* no further special treatment */
#define MADV_RANDOM      1        /* expect random page references */
#define MADV_SEQUENTIAL          2        /* expect sequential references */
#define MADV_WILLNEED    3        /* will need these pages */
#define MADV_DONTNEED    4        /* don't need these pages */
#define MADV_SPACEAVAIL          5        /* insure that resources are reserved */
```

SEE ALSO

msync(2), munmap(2), mprotect(2), mincore(2)

HISTORY

The **madvise** function first appeared in 4.4BSD.

2

NAME

mincore – get advise about use of memory

SYNOPSIS

mincore(*caddr_t addr*, *int len*, *char *vec*);

DESCRIPTION

The **mincore**( ) system call allows a process to obtain information about whether pages are core resident. Here the current core residency of the pages is returned in the character array *vec*, with a value of 1 meaning that the page is in-core.

SEE ALSO

msync(2), munmap(2), mprotect(2), madvise(2),

HISTORY

The **mincore**( ) function first appeared in 4.4BSD.

2

NAME

mkdir – make a directory file

SYNOPSIS

`#include <sys/stat.h>`

`int`
`mkdir(const char *path, mode_t mode);`

DESCRIPTION

The directory *path* is created with the access permissions specified by *mode* and restricted by the the umask(2) of the calling process.

The directory's owner ID is set to the process's effective user ID. The directory's group ID is set to that of the parent directory in which it is created.

RETURN VALUES

A 0 return value indicates success. A -1 return value indicates an error, and an error code is stored in *errno*.

ERRORS

Mkdir( ) will fail and no directory will be created if:

[ENOTDIR]   A component of the path prefix is not a directory.

[EINVAL]   The pathname contains a character with the high-order bit set.

[ENAMETOOLONG]
          A component of a pathname exceeded 255 characters, or an entire path name exceeded 1023 characters.

[ENOENT]   A component of the path prefix does not exist.

[EACCES]   Search permission is denied for a component of the path prefix.

[ELOOP]   Too many symbolic links were encountered in translating the pathname.

[EPERM]   The *path* argument contains a byte with the high-order bit set.

[EROFS]   The named file resides on a read-only file system.

[EEXIST]   The named file exists.

[ENOSPC]   The new directory cannot be created because there is no space left on the file system that will contain the directory.

[ENOSPC]   There are no free inodes on the file system on which the directory is being created.

[EDQUOT]   The new directory cannot be created because the user's quota of disk blocks on the file system that will contain the directory has been exhausted.

[EDQUOT]   The user's quota of inodes on the file system on which the directory is being created has been exhausted.

[EIO]   An I/O error occurred while making the directory entry or allocating the inode.

[EIO]   An I/O error occurred while reading from or writing to the file system.

[EFAULT]   *Path* points outside the process's allocated address space.

SEE ALSO
    chmod(2), stat(2), umask(2)

STANDARDS
    Mkdir() conforms to IEEE Std 1003.1-1988 (''POSIX'').

2

2

NAME
mkfifo – make a fifo file

SYNOPSIS
`#include ⟨sys/stat.h⟩`

`int`
`mkfifo(const char *path, mode_t mode);`

DESCRIPTION
Mkfifo() creates a new fifo file with name *path*. The access permissions are specified by *mode* and restricted by the umask(2) of the calling process.

The fifo's owner ID is set to the process's effective user ID. The fifo's group ID is set to that of the parent directory in which it is created.

RETURN VALUES
A 0 return value indicates success. A -1 return value indicates an error, and an error code is stored in *errno*.

ERRORS
Mkfifo() will fail and no fifo will be created if:

[ENOTSUPP]   The kernel has not been configured to support fifo's.

[ENOTDIR]   A component of the path prefix is not a directory.

[EINVAL]   The pathname contains a character with the high-order bit set.

[ENAMETOOLONG]
　　　　　　A component of a pathname exceeded 255 characters, or an entire path name exceeded 1023 characters.

[ENOENT]   A component of the path prefix does not exist.

[EACCES]   Search permission is denied for a component of the path prefix.

[ELOOP]   Too many symbolic links were encountered in translating the pathname.

[EPERM]   The *path* argument contains a byte with the high-order bit set.

[EROFS]   The named file resides on a read-only file system.

[EEXIST]   The named file exists.

[ENOSPC]   The directory in which the entry for the new fifo is being placed cannot be extended because there is no space left on the file system containing the directory.

[ENOSPC]   There are no free inodes on the file system on which the fifo is being created.

[EDQUOT]   The directory in which the entry for the new fifo is being placed cannot be extended because the user's quota of disk blocks on the file system containing the directory has been exhausted.

[EDQUOT]   The user's quota of inodes on the file system on which the fifo is being created has been exhausted.

[EIO]   An I/O error occurred while making the directory entry or allocating the inode.

2

[EIO]   An I/O error occurred while reading from or writing to the file system.

[EFAULT]   *Path* points outside the process's allocated address space.

SEE ALSO

chmod(2), stat(2), umask(2)

STANDARDS

The **mkfifo** function call conforms to IEEE Std1003.1-1988 (''POSIX'').

NAME
    mknod – make a special file node

SYNOPSIS
    #include <unistd.h>

    int
    mknod(*const char *path, mode_t mode, dev_t dev*);

DESCRIPTION
    The device special file *path* is created with the major and minor device numbers extracted from *mode*. The access permissions of *path* are descendant from the umask(2) of the parent process.

    If *mode* indicates a block or character special file, *dev* is a configuration dependent specification of a character or block I/O device and the superblock of the device. If *mode* does not indicate a block special or character special device, *dev* is ignored.

    Mknod( ) requires super-user privileges.

RETURN VALUES
    Upon successful completion a value of 0 is returned. Otherwise, a value of -1 is returned and *errno* is set to indicate the error.

ERRORS
    Mknod( ) will fail and the file will be not created if:

    [ENOTDIR]   A component of the path prefix is not a directory.

    [EINVAL]   The pathname contains a character with the high-order bit set.

    [ENAMETOOLONG]
                 A component of a pathname exceeded 255 characters, or an entire path name exceeded 1023 characters.

    [ENOENT]   A component of the path prefix does not exist.

    [EACCES]   Search permission is denied for a component of the path prefix.

    [ELOOP]   Too many symbolic links were encountered in translating the pathname.

    [EPERM]   The process's effective user ID is not super-user.

    [EPERM]   The pathname contains a character with the high-order bit set.

    [EIO]   An I/O error occurred while making the directory entry or allocating the inode.

    [ENOSPC]   The directory in which the entry for the new node is being placed cannot be extended because there is no space left on the file system containing the directory.

    [ENOSPC]   There are no free inodes on the file system on which the node is being created.

[EDQUOT]	The directory in which the entry for the new node is being placed cannot be extended because the user's quota of disk blocks on the file system containing the directory has been exhausted.
[EDQUOT]	The user's quota of inodes on the file system on which the node is being created has been exhausted.
[EROFS]	The named file resides on a read-only file system.
[EEXIST]	The named file exists.
[EFAULT]	*Path* points outside the process's allocated address space.

SEE ALSO

chmod(2), stat(2), umask(2)

HISTORY

A **mknod** function call appeared in Version 6 AT&T UNIX.

2

NAME

mlock, munlock – lock (unlock) physical pages in memory

SYNOPSIS

```
#include <sys/types.h>
#include <sys/mman.h>

int
mlock(caddr_t addr, size_t len);

int
munlock(caddr_t addr, size_t len);
```

DESCRIPTION

The mlock system call locks into memory the physical pages associated with the virtual address range starting at *addr* for *len* bytes. The munlock call unlocks pages previously locked by one or more mlock calls. For both, the *addr* parameter should be aligned to a multiple of the page size. If the *len* parameter is not a multiple of the page size, it will be rounded up to be so. The entire range must be allocated.

After an mlock call, the indicated pages will cause neither a non-resident page nor address-translation fault until they are unlocked. They may still cause protection-violation faults or TLB-miss faults on architectures with software-managed TLBs. The physical pages remain in memory until all locked mappings for the pages are removed. Multiple processes may have the same physical pages locked via their own virtual address mappings. A single process may likewise have pages multiply-locked via different virtual mappings of the same pages or via nested mlock calls on the same address range. Unlocking is performed explicitly by munlock or implicitly by a call to munmap which deallocates the unmapped address range. Locked mappings are not inherited by the child process after a fork(2).

Since physical memory is a potentially scarce resource, processes are limited in how much they can lock down. A single process can mlock the minimum of a system-wide ''wired pages'' limit and the per-process RLIMIT_MEMLOCK resource limit.

RETURN VALUES

A return value of 0 indicates that the call succeeded and all pages in the range have either been locked or unlocked. A return value of -1 indicates an error occurred and the locked status of all pages in the range remains unchanged. In this case, the global location *errno* is set to indicate the error.

ERRORS

Mlock( ) will fail if:

[EINVAL]   The address given is not page aligned or the length is negative.

[EAGAIN]   Locking the indicated range would exceed either the system or per-process limit for locked memory.

[ENOMEM]   Some portion of the indicated address range is not allocated. There was an error faulting/mapping a page.

Munlock( ) will fail if:

[EINVAL]   The address given is not page aligned or the length is negative.

[ENOMEM]   Some portion of the indicated address range is not allocated. Some portion of the indicated address range is not locked.

SEE ALSO

fork(2), mmap(2), munmap(2), setrlimit(2), getpagesize(3)

BUGS

Unlike The Sun implementation, multiple **mlock** calls on the same address range require the corresponding number of **munlock** calls to actually unlock the pages, i.e. **mlock** nests. This should be considered a consequence of the implementation and not a feature.

The per-process resource limit is a limit on the amount of virtual memory locked, while the system-wide limit is for the number of locked physical pages. Hence a process with two distinct locked mappings of the same physical page counts as 2 pages against the per-process limit and as only a single page in the system limit.

HISTORY

The **mlock**( ) and **munlock**( ) functions first appeared in 4.4BSD.

2

NAME
mmap – map files or devices into memory

SYNOPSIS
```
#include <sys/types.h>
#include <sys/mman.h>

caddr_t
mmap(caddr_t addr, size_t len, int prot, int flags, int fd, off_t offset);
```

DESCRIPTION
The **mmap** function causes the pages starting at *addr* and continuing for at most *len* bytes to be mapped from the object described by *fd*, starting at byte offset *offset*. If *offset* or *len* is not a multiple of the pagesize, the mapped region may extend past the specified range.

If *addr* is non-zero, it is used as a hint to the system. (As a convenience to the system, the actual address of the region may differ from the address supplied.) If *addr* is zero, an address will be selected by the system. The actual starting address of the region is returned. A successful *mmap* deletes any previous mapping in the allocated address range.

The protections (region accessibility) are specified in the *prot* argument by *or*'ing the following values:

PROT_EXEC   Pages may be executed.

PROT_READ   Pages may be read.

PROT_WRITE Pages may be written.

The *flags* parameter specifies the type of the mapped object, mapping options and whether modifications made to the mapped copy of the page are private to the process or are to be shared with other references. Sharing, mapping type and options are specified in the *flags* argument by *or*'ing the following values:

MAP_ANON   Map anonymous memory not associated with any specific file. The file descriptor used for creating MAP_ANON regions is used only for naming, and may be specified as −1 if no name is associated with the region.

MAP_FIXED   Do not permit the system to select a different address than the one specified. If the specified address cannot be used, **mmap** will fail. If MAP_FIXED is specified, *addr* must be a multiple of the pagesize. Use of this option is discouraged.

MAP_HASSEMAPHORE
                Notify the kernel that the region may contain semaphores and that special handling may be necessary.

MAP_INHERIT
                Permit regions to be inherited across exec(2) system calls.

MAP_PRIVATE
                Modifications are private.

MAP_SHARED Modifications are shared.

The close(2) function does not unmap pages, see munmap(2) for further information.

The current design does not allow a process to specify the location of swap space. In the future we may define an additional mapping type, MAP_SWAP, in which the file descriptor argument specifies a file or device to which swapping should be done.

RETURN VALUES

Upon successful completion, **mmap** returns a pointer to the mapped region. Otherwise, a value of -1 is returned and *errno* is set to indicate the error.

ERRORS

Mmap( ) will fail if:

[EACCES]   The flag PROT_READ was specified as part of the *prot* parameter and *fd* was not open for reading. The flags PROT_WRITE, MAP_SHARED and MAP_WRITE were specified as part of the *flags* and *prot* parameters and *fd* was not open for writing.

[EBADF]   *Fd* is not a valid open file descriptor. MAP_FIXED was specified and the parameter was not page aligned. *Fd* did not reference a regular or character special file.

[ENOMEM]   MAP_FIXED was specified and the *addr* parameter wasn't available. MAP_ANON was specified and insufficient memory was available.

SEE ALSO

getpagesize(2), msync(2), munmap(2), mprotect(2), madvise(2), mincore(2)

2

NAME
mount, unmount – mount or dismount a filesystem

SYNOPSIS
```
#include <sys/param.h>
#include <sys/mount.h>

int
mount(int type, const char *dir, int flags, caddr_t data);

int
unmount(const char *dir, int flags);
```

DESCRIPTION
The mount() function grafts a filesystem object onto the system file tree at the point *dir*. The argument *data* describes the filesystem object to be mounted. The argument *type* tells the kernel how to interpret *data* (See *type* below). The contents of the filesystem become available through the new mount point *dir*. Any files in *dir* at the time of a successful mount are swept under the carpet so to speak, and are unavailable until the filesystem is unmounted.

The following *flags* may be specified to suppress default semantics which affect filesystem access.

MNT_RDONLY   The filesystem should be treated as read-only; Even the super-user may not write on it.

MNT_NOEXEC   Do not allow files to be executed from the filesystem.

MNT_NOSUID   Do not honor setuid or setgid bits on files when executing them.

MNT_NODEV   Do not interpret special files on the filesystem.

MNT_SYNCHRONOUS All I/O to the filesystem should be done synchronously.

The flag MNT_UPDATE indicates that the mount command is being applied to an already mounted filesystem. This allows the mount flags to be changed without requiring that the filesystem be unmounted and remounted. Some filesystems may not allow all flags to be changed. For example, most filesystems will not allow a change from read-write to read-only.

The *type* argument defines the type of the filesystem. The types of filesystems known to the system are defined in <sys/mount.h>. *Data* is a pointer to a structure that contains the type specific arguments to mount. The currently supported types of filesystems and their type specific data are:

```
MOUNT_UFS
    struct ufs_args {
            char    *fspec;  /* Block special file to mount */
            int     exflags; /* export related flags */
            uid_t   exroot;  /* mapping for root uid */
    };

MOUNT_NFS
    struct nfs_args {
            struct sockaddr_in *addr; /* file server address */
            nfsv2fh_t *fh;        /* File handle to be mounted */
            int     flags;        /* flags */
            int     wsize;        /* write size in bytes */
            int     rsize;        /* read size in bytes */
            int     timeo;        /* initial timeout 0.1 secs */
```

```
        int      retrans;   /* times to retry send */
        char     *hostname; /* server's name */
};
```

MOUNT_MFS

```
    struct mfs_args {
        char    *name;  /* name of backing process */
        caddr_t base;   /* base address of the filesystem */
        u_long  size;   /* size of the filesystem */
    };
```

The **umount**( ) function call disassociates the filesystem from the specified mount point *dir*.

The *flags* argument may specify MNT_FORCE to specify that the filesystem should be forcibly unmounted even if files are still active. Active special devices continue to work, but any further accesses to any other active files result in errors even if the filesystem is later remounted.

RETURN VALUES

The **mount**( ) returns the value 0 if the mount was successful, otherwise -1 is returned and the variable *errno* is set to indicate the error.

Umount returns the value 0 if the umount succeeded; otherwise -1 is returned and the variable *errno* is set to indicate the error.

ERRORS

Mount( ) will fail when one of the following occurs:

[EPERM]   The caller is not the super-user.

[ENAMETOOLONG]

               A component of a pathname exceeded 255 characters, or the entire length of a path name exceeded 1023 characters.

[ELOOP]   Too many symbolic links were encountered in translating a pathname.

[ENOENT]   A component of *dir* does not exist.

[ENOTDIR] A component of *name* is not a directory, or a path prefix of *special* is not a directory.

[EINVAL]   A pathname contains a character with the high-order bit set.

[EBUSY]   Another process currently holds a reference to *dir*.

[EFAULT]   *Dir* points outside the process's allocated address space.

The following errors can occur for a *ufs* filesystem mount:

[ENODEV]   A component of ufs_args *fspec* does not exist.

[ENOTBLK] *Fspec* is not a block device.

[ENXIO]   The major device number of *fspec* is out of range (this indicates no device driver exists for the associated hardware).

[EBUSY]   *Fspec* is already mounted.

[EMFILE]   No space remains in the mount table.

[EINVAL]   The super block for the filesystem had a bad magic number or an out of range block size.

[ENOMEM]   Not enough memory was available to read the cylinder group information for the filesystem.

[EIO]   An I/O error occurred while reading the super block or cylinder group information.

[EFAULT]   *Fspec* points outside the process's allocated address space.

The following errors can occur for a *nfs* filesystem mount:

[ETIMEDOUT]
             Nfs timed out trying to contact the server.

[EFAULT]   Some part of the information described by nfs_args points outside the process's allocated address space.

The following errors can occur for a *mfs* filesystem mount:

[EMFILE]   No space remains in the mount table.

[EINVAL]   The super block for the filesystem had a bad magic number or an out of range block size.

[ENOMEM]   Not enough memory was available to read the cylinder group information for the filesystem.

[EIO]   A paging error occurred while reading the super block or cylinder group information.

[EFAULT]   *Name* points outside the process's allocated address space.

Umount may fail with one of the following errors:

[EPERM]   The caller is not the super-user.

[ENOTDIR]   A component of the path is not a directory.

[EINVAL]   The pathname contains a character with the high-order bit set.

[ENAMETOOLONG]
             A component of a pathname exceeded 255 characters, or an entire path name exceeded 1023 characters.

[ELOOP]   Too many symbolic links were encountered in translating the pathname.

[EINVAL]   The requested directory is not in the mount table.

[EBUSY]   A process is holding a reference to a file located on the filesystem.

[EIO]   An I/O error occurred while writing cached filesystem information.

[EFAULT]   *Dir* points outside the process's allocated address space.

A *ufs* or *mfs* mount can also fail if the maximum number of filesystems are currently mounted.

SEE ALSO
mount(8), umount(8), mfs(8)

BUGS
Some of the error codes need translation to more obvious messages.

HISTORY
Mount( ) and **umount**( ) function calls appeared in Version 6 AT&T UNIX.

2

NAME
`mprotect` – control the protection of pages

SYNOPSIS
`mprotect(`*caddr_t addr*`, `*int len*`, `*int prot*`)`;

DESCRIPTION
The `mprotect()` system call changes the specified pages to have protection *prot*. Not all implementations will guarantee protection on a page basis; the granularity of protection changes may be as large as an entire region.

SEE ALSO
`msync(2)`, `munmap(2)`, `madvise(2)`, `mincore(2)`

HISTORY
The `mprotect()` function first appeared in 4.4BSD.

2

NAME

msync – synchronize a mapped region

SYNOPSIS

msync(*caddr_t addr*, *int len*);

DESCRIPTION

The msync() system call writes any modified pages back to the filesystem and updates the file modification time. If *len* is 0, all modified pages within the region containing *addr* will be flushed; if *len* is non-zero, only the pages containing *addr* and *len* succeeding locations will be examined. Any required synchronization of memory caches will also take place at this time. Filesystem operations on a file that is mapped for shared modifications are unpredictable except after an msync().

SEE ALSO

madvise(2), munmap(2), mprotect(2), mincore(2)

HISTORY

The msync() function first appeared in 4.4BSD.

NAME

munmap – remove a mapping

SYNOPSIS

munmap(*caddr_t addr*, *size_t len*);

DESCRIPTION

The munmap( ) system call deletes the mappings for the specified address range, and causes further references to addresses within the range to generate invalid memory references.

RETURN VALUES

Upon successful completion, munmap returns zero. Otherwise, a value of -1 is returned and *errno* is set to indicate the error.

ERRORS

Munmap( ) will fail if:

[EINVAL]   The *addr* parameter was not page aligned, the *len* parameter was negative, or some part of the region being unmapped is not part of the currently valid address space.

SEE ALSO

getpagesize(2), msync(2), munmap(2), mprotect(2), madvise(2), mincore(2)

HISTORY

The munmap( ) function first appeared in 4.4BSD.

2

NAME
nfssvc – NFS services

SYNOPSIS
```
#include <unistd.h>
#include <nfs/nfs.h>

int
nfssvc(int flags, void *argstructp);
```

DESCRIPTION
The **nfssvc()** function is used by the NFS daemons to pass information into and out of the kernel and also to enter the kernel as a server daemon. The *flags* argument consists of several bits that show what action is to be taken once in the kernel and the *argstructp* points to one of three structures depending on which bits are set in flags.

On the client side, nfsiod(8) calls **nfssvc()** with the *flags* argument set to NFSSVC_BIOD and *argstructp* set to NULL to enter the kernel as a block I/O server daemon. For **NQNFS**, mount_nfs(8) calls **nfssvc()** with the NFSSVC_MNTD flag, optionally or'd with the flags NFSSVC_GOTAUTH and NFSSVC_AUTHINFAIL along with a pointer to a

```
struct nfsd_cargs {
        char            *ncd_dirp;      /* Mount dir path */
        uid_t           ncd_authuid;    /* Effective uid */
        int             ncd_authtype;   /* Type of authenticator */
        int             ncd_authlen;    /* Length of authenticator string */
        char            *ncd_authstr;   /* Authenticator string */
};
```

structure. The initial call has only the NFSSVC_MNTD flag set to specify service for the mount point. If the mount point is using Kerberos, then the mount_nfs(8) daemon will return from **nfssvc()** with errno == ENEEDAUTH whenever the client side requires an "rcmd" authentication ticket for the user. Mount_nfs(8) will attempt to get the Kerberos ticket, and if successful will call **nfssvc()** with the flags NFSSVC_MNTD and NFSSVC_GOTAUTH after filling the ticket into the ncd_authstr field and setting the ncd_authlen and ncd_authtype fields of the nfsd_cargs structure. If mount_nfs(8) failed to get the ticket, **nfssvc()** will be called with the flags NFSSVC_MNTD, NFSSVC_GOTAUTH and NFSSVC_AUTHINFAIL to denote a failed authentication attempt.

On the server side, **nfssvc()** is called with the flag NFSSVC_NFSD and a pointer to a

```
struct nfsd_srvargs {
        struct nfsd     *nsd_nfsd;      /* Pointer to in kernel nfsd struct */
        uid_t           nsd_uid;        /* Effective uid mapped to cred */
        u_long          nsd_haddr;      /* Ip address of client */
        struct ucred    nsd_cr;         /* Cred. uid maps to */
        int             nsd_authlen;    /* Length of auth string (ret) */
        char            *nsd_authstr;   /* Auth string (ret) */
};
```

to enter the kernel as an nfsd(8) daemon. Whenever an nfsd(8) daemon receives a Kerberos authentication ticket, it will return from **nfssvc()** with errno == ENEEDAUTH. The nfsd(8) will attempt to authenticate the ticket and generate a set of credentials on the server for the "user id" specified in the field nsd_uid. This is done by first authenticating the Kerberos ticket and then mapping the Kerberos principal to a local name and getting a set of credentials for that user via. getpwnam(3) and getgrouplist(3). If successful, the nfsd(8) will call **nfssvc**( ) with the NFSSVC_NFSD and NFSSVC_AUTHIN flags set to pass the credential mapping in nsd_cr into the kernel to be cached on the server socket for that client. If the authentication failed, nfsd(8) calls **nfssvc**( ) with the flags NFSSVC_NFSD and NFSSVC_AUTHINFAIL to denote an authentication failure.

The master nfsd(8) server daemon calls **nfssvc**( ) with the flag NFSSVC_ADDSOCK and a pointer to a

```
struct nfsd_args {
        int     sock;          /* Socket to serve */
        caddr_t name;          /* Client address for connection based sockets */
        int     namelen;       /* Length of name */
};
```

to pass a server side NFS socket into the kernel for servicing by the nfsd(8) daemons.

RETURN VALUES

Normally **nfssvc** does not return unless the server is terminated by a signal when a value of 0 is returned. Otherwise, -1 is returned and the global variable *errno* is set to specify the error.

ERRORS

[ENEEDAUTH]   This special error value is really used for authentication support, particularly Kerberos, as explained above.

[EPERM]   The caller is not the super-user.

SEE ALSO

nfsd(8), mount_nfs(8), nfsiod(8)

HISTORY

The **nfssvc** function first appeared in 4.4BSD.

BUGS

The **nfssvc** system call is designed specifically for the NFS support daemons and as such is specific to their requirements. It should really return values to indicate the need for authentication support, since ENEEDAUTH is not really an error. Several fields of the argument structures are assumed to be valid and sometimes to be unchanged from a previous call, such that **nfssvc** must be used with extreme care.

2

NAME
open – open or create a file for reading or writing

SYNOPSIS
```
#include <fcntl.h>
```

int
open(*const char *path, int flags, mode_t mode*);

DESCRIPTION
The file name specified by *path* is opened for reading and/or writing as specified by the argument *flags* and the file descriptor returned to the calling process. The *flags* argument may indicate the file is to be created if it does not exist (by specifying the O_CREAT flag), in which case the file is created with mode *mode* as described in chmod(2) and modified by the process' umask value (see umask(2)).

The flags specified are formed by *or*'ing the following values

O_RDONLY	open for reading only
O_WRONLY	open for writing only
O_RDWR	open for reading and writing
O_NONBLOCK	do not block on open
O_APPEND	append on each write
O_CREAT	create file if it does not exist
O_TRUNC	truncate size to 0
O_EXCL	error if create and file exists
O_SHLOCK	atomically obtain a shared lock
O_EXLOCK	atomically obtain an exclusive lock

Opening a file with O_APPEND set causes each write on the file to be appended to the end. If O_TRUNC is specified and the file exists, the file is truncated to zero length. If O_EXCL is set with O_CREAT and the file already exists, **open**( ) returns an error. This may be used to implement a simple exclusive access locking mechanism. If O_EXCL is set and the last component of the pathname is a symbolic link, **open**( ) will fail even if the symbolic link points to a non-existent name. If the O_NONBLOCK flag is specified and the **open**( ) call would result in the process being blocked for some reason (e.g., waiting for carrier on a dialup line), **open**( ) returns immediately. The first time the process attempts to perform I/O on the open file it will block (not currently implemented).

When opening a file, a lock with flock(2) semantics can be obtained by setting O_SHLOCK for a shared lock, or O_EXLOCK for an exclusive lock. If creating a file with O_CREAT, the request for the lock will never fail (provided that the underlying filesystem supports locking).

If successful, **open**( ) returns a non-negative integer, termed a file descriptor. It returns -1 on failure. The file pointer used to mark the current position within the file is set to the beginning of the file.

When a new file is created it is given the group of the directory which contains it.

The new descriptor is set to remain open across execve system calls; see close(2) and fcntl(2).

The system imposes a limit on the number of file descriptors open simultaneously by one process. Getdtablesize(2) returns the current system limit.

ERRORS

The named file is opened unless:

[ENOTDIR]   A component of the path prefix is not a directory.

[ENAMETOOLONG]

              A component of a pathname exceeded 255 characters, or an entire path name exceeded 1023 characters.

[ENOENT]   O_CREAT is not set and the named file does not exist.

[ENOENT]   A component of the path name that must exist does not exist.

[EACCES]   Search permission is denied for a component of the path prefix.

[EACCES]   The required permissions (for reading and/or writing) are denied for the given flags.

[EACCES]   O_CREAT is specified, the file does not exist, and the directory in which it is to be created does not permit writing.

[ELOOP]   Too many symbolic links were encountered in translating the pathname.

[EISDIR]   The named file is a directory, and the arguments specify it is to be opened for writing.

[EROFS]   The named file resides on a read-only file system, and the file is to be modified.

[EMFILE]   The process has already reached its limit for open file descriptors.

[ENFILE]   The system file table is full.

[ENXIO]   The named file is a character special or block special file, and the device associated with this special file does not exist.

[EINTR]   The **open** operation was interrupted by a signal.

[EOPNOTSUPP]

              O_SHLOCK or O_EXLOCK is specified but the underlying filesystem does not support locking.

[ENOSPC]   O_CREAT is specified, the file does not exist, and the directory in which the entry for the new file is being placed cannot be extended because there is no space left on the file system containing the directory.

[ENOSPC]   O_CREAT is specified, the file does not exist, and there are no free inodes on the file system on which the file is being created.

[EDQUOT]   O_CREAT is specified, the file does not exist, and the directory in which the entry for the new file is being placed cannot be extended because the user's quota of disk blocks on the file system containing the directory has been exhausted.

[EDQUOT]   O_CREAT is specified, the file does not exist, and the user's quota of inodes on the file system on which the file is being created has been exhausted.

[EIO]   An I/O error occurred while making the directory entry or allocating the inode for O_CREAT.

[ETXTBSY]   The file is a pure procedure (shared text) file that is being executed and the **open**( ) requests write access.

2

[EFAULT]　　　*Path* points outside the process's allocated address space.

[EEXIST]　　　O_CREAT and O_EXCL were specified and the file exists.

[EOPNOTSUPP]
　　　　　　　An attempt was made to open a socket (not currently implemented).

SEE ALSO
chmod(2), close(2), dup(2), getdtablesize(2), lseek(2), read(2), write(2), umask(2)

HISTORY
An **open** function call appeared in Version 6 AT&T UNIX.

2

NAME
pathconf, fpathconf – get configurable pathname variables

SYNOPSIS
`#include <unistd.h>`

long
pathconf(*const char *path, int name*);

long
fpathconf(*int fd, int name*);

DESCRIPTION
The **pathconf()** and **fpathconf()** functions provides a method for applications to determine the current value of a configurable system limit or option variable associated with a pathname or file descriptor.

For **pathconf**, the *path* argument is the name of a file or directory. For **fpathconf**, the *fd* argument is an open file descriptor. The *name* argument specifies the system variable to be queried. Symbolic constants for each name value are found in the include file `<unistd.h>`.

The available values are as follows:

_PC_LINK_MAX
> The maximum file link count.

_PC_MAX_CANON
> The maximum number of bytes in terminal canonical input line.

_PC_MAX_INPUT
> The minimum maximum number of bytes for which space is available in a terminal input queue.

_PC_NAME_MAX
> The maximum number of bytes in a file name.

_PC_PATH_MAX
> The maximum number of bytes in a pathname.

_PC_PIPE_BUF
> The maximum number of bytes which will be written atomically to a pipe.

_PC_CHOWN_RESTRICTED
> Return 1 if appropriate privileges are required for the chown(2) system call, otherwise 0.

_PC_NO_TRUNC
> Return 1 if file names longer than KERN_NAME_MAX are truncated.

_PC_VDISABLE
> Returns the terminal character disabling value.

RETURN VALUES
If the call to **pathconf** or **fpathconf** is not successful, −1 is returned and *errno* is set appropriately. Otherwise, if the variable is associated with functionality that does not have a limit in the system, −1 is returned and *errno* is not modified. Otherwise, the current variable value is returned.

2

ERRORS

If any of the following conditions occur, the `pathconf` and `fpathconf` functions shall return -1 and set *errno* to the corresponding value.

[EINVAL]   The value of the *name* argument is invalid.

[EINVAL]   The implementation does not support an association of the variable name with the associated file.

`Pathconf`( ) will fail if:

[ENOTDIR]   A component of the path prefix is not a directory.

[ENAMETOOLONG]   A component of a pathname exceeded 255 characters, or an entire path name exceeded 1023 characters.

[ENOENT]   The named file does not exist.

[EACCES]   Search permission is denied for a component of the path prefix.

[ELOOP]   Too many symbolic links were encountered in translating the pathname.

[EIO]   An I/O error occurred while reading from or writing to the file system.

`Fpathconf`( ) will fail if:

[EBADF]   *fd* is not a valid open file descriptor.

[EIO]   An I/O error occurred while reading from or writing to the file system.

SEE ALSO

sysctl(3)

HISTORY

The `pathconf` and `fpathconf` functions first appeared in 4.4BSD.

2

NAME
pipe – create descriptor pair for interprocess communication

SYNOPSIS
```
#include <unistd.h>

int
pipe(int *fildes);
```

DESCRIPTION
The **pipe**() function creates a *pipe*, which is an object allowing unidirectional data flow, and allocates a pair of file descriptors. The first descriptor connects to the *read end* of the pipe, and the second connects to the *write end*, so that data written to *fildes[1]* appears on (i.e., can be read from) *fildes[0]*. This allows the output of one program to be sent to another program: the source's standard output is set up to be the write end of the pipe, and the sink's standard input is set up to be the read end of the pipe. The pipe itself persists until all its associated descriptors are closed.

A pipe whose read or write end has been closed is considered *widowed*. Writing on such a pipe causes the writing process to receive a SIGPIPE signal. Widowing a pipe is the only way to deliver end-of-file to a reader: after the reader consumes any buffered data, reading a widowed pipe returns a zero count.

Pipes are really a special case of the socketpair(2) call and, in fact, are implemented as such in the system.

RETURN VALUES
On successful creation of the pipe, zero is returned. Otherwise, a value of -1 is returned and the variable *errno* set to indicate the error.

ERRORS
The **pipe**() call will fail if:

[EMFILE]   Too many descriptors are active.

[ENFILE]   The system file table is full.

[EFAULT]   The *fildes* buffer is in an invalid area of the process's address space.

SEE ALSO
sh(1), read(2), write(2), fork(2), socketpair(2)

HISTORY
A **pipe** function call appeared in Version 6 AT&T UNIX.

2

NAME
profil – control process profiling

SYNOPSIS
int
profil(char *samples, int size, int offset, int scale);

DESCRIPTION
The **profil()** function enables or disables program counter profiling of the current process. If profiling is enabled, then at every clock tick, the kernel updates an appropriate count in the *samples* buffer.

The buffer *samples* contains *size* bytes and is divided into a series of 16-bit bins. Each bin counts the number of times the program counter was in a particular address range in the process when a clock tick occurred while profiling was enabled. For a given program counter address, the number of the corresponding bin is given by the relation:

[(pc - offset) / 2] * scale / 65536

The *offset* parameter is the lowest address at which the kernel takes program counter samples. The *scale* parameter ranges from 1 to 65536 and can be used to change the span of the bins. A scale of 65536 maps each bin to 2 bytes of address range; a scale of 32768 gives 4 bytes, 16384 gives 8 bytes and so on. Intermediate values provide approximate intermediate ranges. A *scale* value of 0 disables profiling.

RETURN VALUES
If the *scale* value is nonzero and the buffer *samples* contains an illegal address, **profil()** returns −1, profiling is terminated and *errno* is set appropriately. Otherwise **profil()** returns 0.

FILES
/usr/lib/gcrt0.o profiling C run-time startup file
gmon.out   conventional name for profiling output file

ERRORS
The following error may be reported:

[EFAULT]   The buffer *samples* contains an invalid address.

SEE ALSO
gprof(1)

BUGS
This routine should be named **profile()**.

The *samples* argument should really be a vector of type *unsigned short*.

The format of the gmon.out file is undocumented.

NAME

    ptrace – process trace

SYNOPSIS

    #include <sys/param.h>
    #include <sys/ptrace.h>
    #include <signal.h>

    ptrace(request, pid, addr, data)
    int request, pid, *addr, data;

DESCRIPTION

    Ptrace provides a means by which a parent process may control the execution of a child process, and examine and change its core image. Its primary use is for the implementation of breakpoint debugging. There are four arguments whose interpretation depends on a *request* argument. Generally, *pid* is the process ID of the traced process, which must be a child (no more distant descendant) of the tracing process. A process being traced behaves normally until it encounters some signal whether internally generated like "illegal instruction" or externally generated like "interrupt". See *sigvec*(2) for the list. Then the traced process enters a stopped state and its parent is notified via *wait*(2). When the child is in the stopped state, its core image can be examined and modified using *ptrace*. If desired, another *ptrace* request can then cause the child either to terminate or to continue, possibly ignoring the signal.

    The value of the *request* argument determines the precise action of the call:

PT_TRACE_ME

    This request is the only one used by the child process; it declares that the process is to be traced by its parent. All the other arguments are ignored. Peculiar results will ensue if the parent does not expect to trace the child.

PT_READ_I, PT_READ_D

    The word in the child process's address space at *addr* is returned. If I and D space are separated (e.g. historically on a pdp-11), request PT_READ_I indicates I space, PT_READ_D D space. *Addr* must be even on some machines. The child must be stopped. The input *data* is ignored.

PT_READ_U

    The word of the system's per-process data area corresponding to *addr* is returned. *Addr* must be even on some machines and less than 512. This space contains the registers and other information about the process; its layout corresponds to the *user* structure in the system.

PT_WRITE_I, PT_WRITE_D

    The given *data* is written at the word in the process's address space corresponding to *addr,* which must be even on some machines. No useful value is returned. If I and D space are separated, request PT_WRITE_I indicates I space, PT_WRITE_D D space. Attempts to write in pure procedure fail if another process is executing the same file.

PT_WRITE_U

    The process's system data is written, as it is read with request PT_READ_U. Only a few locations can be written in this way: the general registers, the floating point status and registers, and certain bits of the processor status word.

PT_CONTINUE

    The *data* argument is taken as a signal number and the child's execution continues at location *addr* as if it had incurred that signal. Normally the signal number will be either 0 to indicate that the signal that caused the stop should be ignored, or that value fetched out of the process's image indicating which signal caused the stop. If *addr* is (int *)1 then execution continues from where it stopped.

PT_KILL

    The traced process terminates.

PT_STEP

    Execution continues as in request PT_CONTINUE; however, as soon as possible after execution of at least one instruction, execution stops again. The signal number from the stop is SIGTRAP. (On the VAX-11 the T-bit is used and just one instruction is executed.) This is part of the mechanism for implementing breakpoints.

PT_ATTACH

The process indicated by *pid* is re-parented to the calling process and delivered a SIGSTOP signal. The child process may then be traced by the parent, as in PT_TRACE_ME. A process already being traced cannot be attached to.

If the calling process is not owned by root, it must have the same real user ID as the target process and not have used set user or group privileges.

PT_DETACH

The process indicated by *pid* is detached from tracing and continues its execution. The process, which must be a traced child of the caller, is re-parented with the parent it had before tracing began. The *data* and *addr* arguments behave as in PT_CONTINUE.

As indicated, these calls (except for request PT_TRACE_ME) can be used only when the subject process has stopped. The *wait* call is used to determine when a process stops; in such a case the "termination" status returned by *wait* has the value 0177 to indicate stoppage rather than genuine termination.

To forestall possible fraud, *ptrace* inhibits the set-user-id and set-group-id facilities on subsequent *execve*(2) calls. If a traced process calls *execve*, it will stop before executing the first instruction of the new image showing signal SIGTRAP.

On a VAX-11, "word" also means a 32-bit integer, but the "even" restriction does not apply.

RETURN VALUE

A 0 value is returned if the call succeeds. If the call fails then a −1 is returned and the global variable *errno* is set to indicate the error.

ERRORS

[EIO]	The request code is invalid.
[ESRCH]	The specified process does not exist.
[EIO]	The given signal number is invalid.
[EIO]	The specified address is out of bounds.
[EPERM]	The specified process cannot be traced.

SEE ALSO

wait(2), sigvec(2), adb(1)

BUGS

Ptrace is unique and arcane; it should be replaced with a special file that can be opened and read and written. The control functions could then be implemented with *ioctl*(2) calls on this file. This would be simpler to understand and have much better performance.

The request PT_TRACE_ME call should be able to specify signals that are to be treated normally and not cause a stop. In this way, for example, programs with simulated floating point (which use "illegal instruction" signals at a very high rate) could be efficiently debugged.

The error indication, −1, is a legitimate function value; *errno,* (see *intro*(2)), can be used to disambiguate.

It should be possible to stop a process on occurrence of a system call; in this way a completely controlled environment could be provided.

PT_STEP is not supported on all architectures. For example, the SPARC architecture does not have a trace bit, which complicates single instruction stepping. Debuggers and the like can emulate PT_STEP by placing breakpoints at all possible locations of the next instruction.

NAME

　　`quotactl` – manipulate filesystem quotas

SYNOPSIS

　　`#include <ufs/quota.h>　/* for ufs quotas */ int`
　　`quotactl(const char *path, int cmd, int id, char *addr);`

DESCRIPTION

　　The `quotactl()` call enables, disables and manipulates filesystem quotas. A quota control command given by `cmd` operates on the given filename `path` for the given user `id`. The address of an optional command specific data structure, `addr`, may be given; its interpretation is discussed below with each command.

　　Currently quotas are supported only for the "ufs" filesystem. For "ufs", a command is composed of a primary command (see below) and a command type used to interpret the `id`. Types are supported for interpretation of user identifiers and group identifiers. The "ufs" specific commands are:

Q_QUOTAON　　Enable disk quotas for the filesystem specified by `path`. The command type specifies the type of the quotas being enabled. The `addr` argument specifies a file from which to take the quotas. The quota file must exist; it is normally created with the quotacheck(8) program. The `id` argument is unused. Only the super-user may turn quotas on.

Q_QUOTAOFF

　　　　　　　Disable disk quotas for the filesystem specified by `path`. The command type specifies the type of the quotas being disabled. The `addr` and `id` arguments are unused. Only the super-user may turn quotas off.

Q_GETQUOTA

　　　　　　　Get disk quota limits and current usage for the user or group (as determined by the command type) with identifier `id`. `Addr` is a pointer to a `struct dqblk` structure (defined in `<ufs/quota.h>`).

Q_SETQUOTA

　　　　　　　Set disk quota limits for the user or group (as determined by the command type) with identifier `id`. `Addr` is a pointer to a `struct dqblk` structure (defined in `<ufs/quota.h>`). The usage fields of the `dqblk` structure are ignored. This call is restricted to the super-user.

Q_SETUSE　　Set disk usage limits for the user or group (as determined by the command type) with identifier `id`. `Addr` is a pointer to a `struct dqblk` structure (defined in `<ufs/quota.h>`). Only the usage fields are used. This call is restricted to the super-user.

Q_SYNC　　　Update the on-disk copy of quota usages. The command type specifies which type of quotas are to be updated. The `id` and `addr` parameters are ignored.

RETURN VALUES

　　A successful call returns 0, otherwise the value -1 is returned and the global variable *errno* indicates the reason for the failure.

ERRORS

　　A `quotactl()` call will fail if:

[EOPNOTSUPP]　　The kernel has not been compiled with the QUOTA option.

[EUSERS]	The quota table cannot be expanded.
[EINVAL]	*Cmd* or the command type is invalid.
[EINVAL]	A pathname contains a character with the high-order bit set.
[EACCES]	In Q_QUOTAON, the quota file is not a plain file.
[EACCES]	Search permission is denied for a component of a path prefix.
[ENOTDIR]	A component of a path prefix was not a directory.
[ENAMETOOLONG]	A component of either pathname exceeded 255 characters, or the entire length of either path name exceeded 1023 characters.
[ENOENT]	A filename does not exist.
[ELOOP]	Too many symbolic links were encountered in translating a pathname.
[EROFS]	In Q_QUOTAON, the quota file resides on a read-only filesystem.
[EIO]	An I/O error occurred while reading from or writing to a file containing quotas.
[EFAULT]	An invalid *addr* was supplied; the associated structure could not be copied in or out of the kernel.
[EFAULT]	*Path* points outside the process's allocated address space.
[EPERM]	The call was privileged and the caller was not the super-user.

SEE ALSO

quota(1), fstab(5), edquota(8), quotacheck(8), quotaon(8), repquota(8)

BUGS

There should be some way to integrate this call with the resource limit interface provided by setrlimit(2) and getrlimit(2).

HISTORY

The quotactl function call appeared in 4.3BSD–Reno.

NAME
read, readv – read input

SYNOPSIS
```
#include <sys/types.h>
#include <sys/uio.h>
#include <unistd.h>
```

```
ssize_t
read(int d, void *buf, size_t nbytes);
```

```
ssize_t
readv(int d, const struct iovec *iov, int iovcnt);
```

DESCRIPTION
Read() attempts to read *nbytes* of data from the object referenced by the descriptor *d* into the buffer pointed to by *buf*. Readv() performs the same action, but scatters the input data into the *iovcnt* buffers specified by the members of the *iov* array: iov[0], iov[1], ..., iov[iovcnt − 1].

For readv(), the *iovec* structure is defined as:

```
struct iovec {
        void *iov_base;
        size_t iov_len;
};
```

Each *iovec* entry specifies the base address and length of an area in memory where data should be placed. Readv() will always fill an area completely before proceeding to the next.

On objects capable of seeking, the read() starts at a position given by the pointer associated with *d* (see lseek(2)). Upon return from read(), the pointer is incremented by the number of bytes actually read.

Objects that are not capable of seeking always read from the current position. The value of the pointer associated with such an object is undefined.

Upon successful completion, read() and readv() return the number of bytes actually read and placed in the buffer. The system guarantees to read the number of bytes requested if the descriptor references a normal file that has that many bytes left before the end-of-file, but in no other case.

RETURN VALUES
If successful, the number of bytes actually read is returned. Upon reading end-of-file, zero is returned. Otherwise, a -1 is returned and the global variable *errno* is set to indicate the error.

ERRORS
Read() and readv() will succeed unless:

[EBADF]   *D* is not a valid file or socket descriptor open for reading.

[EFAULT]   *Buf* points outside the allocated address space.

[EIO]   An I/O error occurred while reading from the file system.

[EINTR]   A read from a slow device was interrupted before any data arrived by the delivery of a signal.

2

[EINVAL]   The pointer associated with *d* was negative.

[EAGAIN]   The file was marked for non-blocking I/O, and no data were ready to be read.

In addition, **readv**( ) may return one of the following errors:

[EINVAL]   *Iovcnt* was less than or equal to 0, or greater than 16.

[EINVAL]   One of the *iov_len* values in the *iov* array was negative.

[EINVAL]   The sum of the *iov_len* values in the *iov* array overflowed a 32-bit integer.

[EFAULT]   Part of the *iov* points outside the process's allocated address space.

SEE ALSO
dup(2), fcntl(2), open(2), pipe(2), select(2), socket(2), socketpair(2)

STANDARDS
Read( ) is expected to conform to IEEE Std 1003.1-1988 (''POSIX'').

HISTORY
The **readv**( ) function call appeared in 4.2BSD. A **read** function call appeared in Version 6 AT&T UNIX.

2

NAME

readlink – read value of a symbolic link

SYNOPSIS

```
#include <unistd.h>
```

int
readlink(*const char *path, char *buf, int bufsiz*);

DESCRIPTION

Readlink() places the contents of the symbolic link *path* in the buffer *buf*, which has size *bufsiz*. Readlink does not append a NUL character to *buf*.

RETURN VALUES

The call returns the count of characters placed in the buffer if it succeeds, or a -1 if an error occurs, placing the error code in the global variable *errno*.

ERRORS

Readlink( ) will fail if:

[ENOTDIR]   A component of the path prefix is not a directory.

[EINVAL]   The pathname contains a character with the high-order bit set.

[ENAMETOOLONG]
              A component of a pathname exceeded 255 characters, or an entire path name exceeded 1023 characters.

[ENOENT]   The named file does not exist.

[EACCES]   Search permission is denied for a component of the path prefix.

[ELOOP]   Too many symbolic links were encountered in translating the pathname.

[EINVAL]   The named file is not a symbolic link.

[EIO]   An I/O error occurred while reading from the file system.

[EFAULT]   *Buf* extends outside the process's allocated address space.

SEE ALSO

stat(2), lstat(2), symlink(2) symlink(7),

HISTORY

The readlink function call appeared in 4.2BSD.

2

NAME
`reboot` – reboot system or halt processor

SYNOPSIS
```
#include <unistd.h>
#include <sys/reboot.h>

int
reboot(int howto);
```

DESCRIPTION
`Reboot()` reboots the system. Only the super-user may reboot a machine on demand. However, a reboot is invoked automatically in the event of unrecoverable system failures.

Howto is a mask of options; the system call interface allows the following options, defined in the include file <sys/reboot.h>, to be passed to the new kernel or the new bootstrap and init programs.

RB_AUTOBOOT   The default, causing the system to reboot in its usual fashion.

RB_ASKNAME   Interpreted by the bootstrap program itself, causing it to prompt on the console as to what file should be booted. Normally, the system is booted from the file "*xx*(0,0)vmunix", where *xx* is the default disk name, without prompting for the file name.

RB_DFLTROOT   Use the compiled in root device. Normally, the system uses the device from which it was booted as the root device if possible. (The default behavior is dependent on the ability of the bootstrap program to determine the drive from which it was loaded, which is not possible on all systems.)

RB_DUMP   Dump kernel memory before rebooting; see `savecore`(8) for more information.

RB_HALT   the processor is simply halted; no reboot takes place. This option should be used with caution.

RB_INITNAME   An option allowing the specification of an init program (see `init`(8)) other than /sbin/init to be run when the system reboots. This switch is not currently available.

RB_KDB   Load the symbol table and enable a built-in debugger in the system. This option will have no useful function if the kernel is not configured for debugging. Several other options have different meaning if combined with this option, although their use may not be possible via the `reboot`() call. See `kadb`(4) for more information.

RB_NOSYNC   Normally, the disks are sync'd (see `sync`(8)) before the processor is halted or rebooted. This option may be useful if file system changes have been made manually or if the processor is on fire.

RB_RDONLY   Initially mount the root file system read-only. This is currently the default, and this option has been deprecated.

RB_SINGLE   Normally, the reboot procedure involves an automatic disk consistency check and then multi-user operations. RB_SINGLE prevents this, booting the system with a single-user shell on the console. RB_SINGLE is actually interpreted by the `init`(8) program in the newly booted system.

When no options are given (i.e., RB_AUTOBOOT is used), the system is rebooted from file "vmunix" in the root file system of unit 0 of a disk chosen in a processor specific way. An automatic consistency check of the disks is normally performed (see `fsck`(8)).

RETURN VALUES

If successful, this call never returns. Otherwise, a -1 is returned and an error is returned in the global variable *errno*.

ERRORS

[EPERM]   The caller is not the super-user.

SEE ALSO

kadb(4), crash(8), halt(8), init(8), reboot(8), savecore(8)

BUGS

The HP300 implementation supports neither RB_DFLTROOT nor RB_KDB.

HISTORY

The **reboot** function call appeared in 4.0BSD.

2

NAME

recv, recvfrom, recvmsg – receive a message from a socket

SYNOPSIS

```
#include <sys/types.h>
#include <sys/socket.h>
```

ssize_t
recv(int s, void *buf, size_t len, int flags);

ssize_t
recvfrom(int s, void *buf, size_t len, int flags, struct sockaddr *from,
        int *fromlen);

ssize_t
recvmsg(int s, struct msghdr *msg, int flags);

DESCRIPTION

Recvfrom() and recvmsg() are used to receive messages from a socket, and may be used to receive data on a socket whether or not it is connection-oriented.

If *from* is non-nil, and the socket is not connection-oriented, the source address of the message is filled in. *Fromlen* is a value-result parameter, initialized to the size of the buffer associated with *from*, and modified on return to indicate the actual size of the address stored there.

The recv() call is normally used only on a *connected* socket (see connect(2)) and is identical to recvfrom() with a nil *from* parameter. As it is redundant, it may not be supported in future releases.

All three routines return the length of the message on successful completion. If a message is too long to fit in the supplied buffer, excess bytes may be discarded depending on the type of socket the message is received from (see socket(2)).

If no messages are available at the socket, the receive call waits for a message to arrive, unless the socket is nonblocking (see fcntl(2)) in which case the value -1 is returned and the external variable *errno* set to EAGAIN. The receive calls normally return any data available, up to the requested amount, rather than waiting for receipt of the full amount requested; this behavior is affected by the socket-level options SO_RCVLOWAT and SO_RCVTIMEO described in getsockopt(2).

The select(2) call may be used to determine when more data arrive.

The *flags* argument to a recv call is formed by *or Ap ing* one or more of the values:

MSG_OOB	process out-of-band data
MSG_PEEK	peek at incoming message
MSG_WAITALL	wait for full request or error

The MSG_OOB flag requests receipt of out-of-band data that would not be received in the normal data stream. Some protocols place expedited data at the head of the normal data queue, and thus this flag cannot be used with such protocols. The MSG_PEEK flag causes the receive operation to return data from the beginning of the receive queue without removing that data from the queue. Thus, a subsequent receive call will return the same data. The MSG_WAITALL flag requests that the operation block until the full request is satisfied. However, the call may still return less data than requested if a signal is caught, an error or disconnect occurs, or the next data to be received is of a different type than that returned.

The recvmsg() call uses a *msghdr* structure to minimize the number of directly supplied parameters. This structure has the following form, as defined in <sys/socket.h>:

```
struct msghdr {
        caddr_t msg_name;        /* optional address */
        u_int   msg_namelen;     /* size of address */
        struct  iovec *msg_iov;  /* scatter/gather array */
        u_int   msg_iovlen;      /* # elements in msg_iov */
        caddr_t msg_control;     /* ancillary data, see below */
        u_int   msg_controllen;  /* ancillary data buffer len */
        int     msg_flags;       /* flags on received message */
};
```

Here *msg_name* and *msg_namelen* specify the destination address if the socket is unconnected; *msg_name* may be given as a null pointer if no names are desired or required. *Msg_iov* and *msg_iovlen* describe scatter gather locations, as discussed in read(2). *Msg_control*, which has length *msg_controllen*, points to a buffer for other protocol control related messages or other miscellaneous ancillary data. The messages are of the form:

```
struct cmsghdr {
        u_int   cmsg_len;        /* data byte count, including hdr */
        int     cmsg_level;      /* originating protocol */
        int     cmsg_type;       /* protocol-specific type */
/* followed by
        u_char  cmsg_data[]; */
};
```

As an example, one could use this to learn of changes in the data-stream in XNS/SPP, or in ISO, to obtain user-connection-request data by requesting a recvmsg with no data buffer provided immediately after an **accept( )** call.

Open file descriptors are now passed as ancillary data for AF_UNIX domain sockets, with *cmsg_level* set to SOL_SOCKET and *cmsg_type* set to SCM_RIGHTS.

The *msg_flags* field is set on return according to the message received. MSG_EOR indicates end-of-record; the data returned completed a record (generally used with sockets of type SOCK_SEQPACKET). MSG_TRUNC indicates that the trailing portion of a datagram was discarded because the datagram was larger than the buffer supplied. MSG_CTRUNC indicates that some control data were discarded due to lack of space in the buffer for ancillary data. MSG_OOB is returned to indicate that expedited or out-of-band data were received.

RETURN VALUES

These calls return the number of bytes received, or -1 if an error occurred.

ERRORS

The calls fail if:

[EBADF] The argument *s* is an invalid descriptor.

[ENOTCONN] The socket is associated with a connection-oriented protocol and has not been connected (see connect(2) and accept(2)).

[ENOTSOCK] The argument *s* does not refer to a socket.

[EAGAIN] The socket is marked non-blocking, and the receive operation would block, or a receive timeout had been set, and the timeout expired before data were received.

2

[EINTR]   The receive was interrupted by delivery of a signal before any data were available.

[EFAULT]   The receive buffer pointer(s) point outside the process's address space.

SEE ALSO
fcntl(2), read(2), select(2), getsockopt(2), socket(2)

HISTORY
The **recv** function call appeared in 4.2BSD.

2

NAME
rename – change the name of a file

SYNOPSIS
```
#include <stdio.h>

int
rename(const char *from, const char *to);
```

DESCRIPTION
Rename() causes the link named *from* to be renamed as *to*. If *to* exists, it is first removed. Both *from* and *to* must be of the same type (that is, both directories or both non-directories), and must reside on the same file system.

Rename() guarantees that an instance of *to* will always exist, even if the system should crash in the middle of the operation.

If the final component of *from* is a symbolic link, the symbolic link is renamed, not the file or directory to which it points.

CAVEAT
The system can deadlock if a loop in the file system graph is present. This loop takes the form of an entry in directory 'a', say 'a/foo', being a hard link to directory 'b', and an entry in directory 'b', say 'b/bar', being a hard link to directory 'a'. When such a loop exists and two separate processes attempt to perform rename a/foo b/bar and rename b/bar a/foo, respectively, the system may deadlock attempting to lock both directories for modification. Hard links to directories should be replaced by symbolic links by the system administrator.

RETURN VALUES
A 0 value is returned if the operation succeeds, otherwise **rename()** returns -1 and the global variable *errno* indicates the reason for the failure.

ERRORS
Rename() will fail and neither of the argument files will be affected if:

[EINVAL]   Either pathname contains a character with the high-order bit set.

[ENAMETOOLONG]
                 A component of either pathname exceeded 255 characters, or the entire length of either path name exceeded 1023 characters.

[ENOENT]   A component of the *from* path does not exist, or a path prefix of *to* does not exist.

[EACCES]   A component of either path prefix denies search permission.

[EACCES]   The requested link requires writing in a directory with a mode that denies write permission.

[EPERM]   The directory containing *from* is marked sticky, and neither the containing directory nor *from* are owned by the effective user ID.

[EPERM]   The *to* file exists, the directory containing *to* is marked sticky, and neither the containing directory nor *to* are owned by the effective user ID.

2

[ELOOP]   Too many symbolic links were encountered in translating either pathname.

[ENOTDIR]   A component of either path prefix is not a directory.

[ENOTDIR]   *from* is a directory, but *to* is not a directory.

[EISDIR]   *to* is a directory, but *from* is not a directory.

[EXDEV]   The link named by *to* and the file named by *from* are on different logical devices (file systems). Note that this error code will not be returned if the implementation permits cross-device links.

[ENOSPC]   The directory in which the entry for the new name is being placed cannot be extended because there is no space left on the file system containing the directory.

[EDQUOT]   The directory in which the entry for the new name is being placed cannot be extended because the user's quota of disk blocks on the file system containing the directory has been exhausted.

[EIO]   An I/O error occurred while making or updating a directory entry.

[EROFS]   The requested link requires writing in a directory on a read-only file system.

[EFAULT]   *Path* points outside the process's allocated address space.

[EINVAL]   *From* is a parent directory of *to*, or an attempt is made to rename '.' or '..'.

[ENOTEMPTY]   *To* is a directory and is not empty.

SEE ALSO
open(2) symlink(7)

STANDARDS
Rename( ) conforms to IEEE Std 1003.1-1988 (''POSIX'').

2

NAME
revoke – revoke file access

SYNOPSIS
int
revoke(*char *path*);

DESCRIPTION
The **revoke** function invalidates all current open file descriptors in the system for the file named by *path*. Subsequent operations on any such descriptors fail, with the exceptions that a **read**( ) from a character device file which has been revoked returns a count of zero (end of file), and a **close**( ) call will succeed. If the file is a special file for a device which is open, the device close function is called as if all open references to the file had been closed.

Access to a file may be revoked only by its owner or the super user. The **revoke** function is currently supported only for block and character special device files. It is normally used to prepare a terminal device for a new login session, preventing any access by a previous user of the terminal.

RETURN VALUES
A 0 value indicated that the call succeeded. A −1 return value indicates an error occurred and *errno* is set to indicated the reason.

ERRORS
Access to the named file is revoked unless one of the following:

[ENOTDIR]   A component of the path prefix is not a directory.

[ENAMETOOLONG]
            A component of a pathname exceeded 255 characters, or an entire path name exceeded 1024 characters.

[ENOENT]   The named file or a component of the path name does not exist.

[EACCES]   Search permission is denied for a component of the path prefix.

[ELOOP]   Too many symbolic links were encountered in translating the pathname.

[EFAULT]   *Path* points outside the process's allocated address space.

[EINVAL]   The named file is neither a character special or block special file.

[EPERM]   The caller is neither the owner of the file nor the super user.

SEE ALSO
close(2)

HISTORY
The **revoke** function was introduced in 4.3BSD–Reno.

2

NAME
rmdir – remove a directory file

SYNOPSIS
`#include <unistd.h>`

int
`rmdir(const char *path);`

DESCRIPTION
Rmdir() removes a directory file whose name is given by *path*. The directory must not have any entries
other than '.' and '..'.

RETURN VALUES
A 0 is returned if the remove succeeds; otherwise a -1 is returned and an error code is stored in the global location *errno*.

ERRORS
The named file is removed unless:

[ENOTDIR]	A component of the path is not a directory.
[EINVAL]	The pathname contains a character with the high-order bit set.
[ENAMETOOLONG]	A component of a pathname exceeded 255 characters, or an entire path name exceed-ed 1023 characters.
[ENOENT]	The named directory does not exist.
[ELOOP]	Too many symbolic links were encountered in translating the pathname.
[ENOTEMPTY]	The named directory contains files other than '.' and '..' in it.
[EACCES]	Search permission is denied for a component of the path prefix.
[EACCES]	Write permission is denied on the directory containing the link to be removed.
[EPERM]	The directory containing the directory to be removed is marked sticky, and neither the containing directory nor the directory to be removed are owned by the effective user ID.
[EBUSY]	The directory to be removed is the mount point for a mounted file system.
[EIO]	An I/O error occurred while deleting the directory entry or deallocating the inode.
[EROFS]	The directory entry to be removed resides on a read-only file system.
[EFAULT]	*Path* points outside the process's allocated address space.

SEE ALSO
mkdir(2), unlink(2)

HISTORY
The rmdir function call appeared in 4.2BSD.

2

NAME
select – synchronous I/O multiplexing

SYNOPSIS
```
#include <sys/types.h>
#include <sys/time.h>
#include <unistd.h>

int
select(int nfds, fd_set *readfds, fd_set *writefds, fd_set *exceptfds,
        struct timeval *timeout);

FD_SET(fd, &fdset);

FD_CLR(fd, &fdset);

FD_ISSET(fd, &fdset);

FD_ZERO(&fdset);
```

DESCRIPTION
Select() examines the I/O descriptor sets whose addresses are passed in *readfds*, *writefds*, and *exceptfds* to see if some of their descriptors are ready for reading, are ready for writing, or have an exceptional condition pending, respectively. The first *nfds* descriptors are checked in each set; i.e., the descriptors from 0 through *nfds*-1 in the descriptor sets are examined. On return, select() replaces the given descriptor sets with subsets consisting of those descriptors that are ready for the requested operation. Select() returns the total number of ready descriptors in all the sets.

The descriptor sets are stored as bit fields in arrays of integers. The following macros are provided for manipulating such descriptor sets: FD_ZERO(&*fdsetx*) initializes a descriptor set *fdset* to the null set. FD_SET(*fd*, &*fdset*) includes a particular descriptor *fd* in *fdset*. FD_CLR(*fd*, &*fdset*) removes *fd* from *fdset*. FD_ISSET(*fd*, &*fdset*) is non-zero if *fd* is a member of *fdset*, zero otherwise. The behavior of these macros is undefined if a descriptor value is less than zero or greater than or equal to FD_SETSIZE, which is normally at least equal to the maximum number of descriptors supported by the system.

If *timeout* is a non-nil pointer, it specifies a maximum interval to wait for the selection to complete. If *timeout* is a nil pointer, the select blocks indefinitely. To affect a poll, the *timeout* argument should be non-nil, pointing to a zero-valued timeval structure.

Any of *readfds*, *writefds*, and *exceptfds* may be given as nil pointers if no descriptors are of interest.

RETURN VALUES
Select() returns the number of ready descriptors that are contained in the descriptor sets, or -1 if an error occurred. If the time limit expires, select() returns 0. If select() returns with an error, including one due to an interrupted call, the descriptor sets will be unmodified.

ERRORS
An error return from select() indicates:

[EBADF]   One of the descriptor sets specified an invalid descriptor.

2

[EINTR]   A signal was delivered before the time limit expired and before any of the selected events occurred.

[EINVAL]   The specified time limit is invalid. One of its components is negative or too large.

SEE ALSO

accept(2), connect(2), getdtablesize(2), gettimeofday(2), read(2), recv(2), send(2), write(2)

BUGS

Although the provision of getdtablesize(2) was intended to allow user programs to be written independent of the kernel limit on the number of open files, the dimension of a sufficiently large bit field for select remains a problem. The default size FD_SETSIZE (currently 256) is somewhat larger than the current kernel limit to the number of open files. However, in order to accommodate programs which might potentially use a larger number of open files with select, it is possible to increase this size within a program by providing a larger definition of FD_SETSIZE before the inclusion of <sys/types.h>.

Select() should probably return the time remaining from the original timeout, if any, by modifying the time value in place. This may be implemented in future versions of the system. Thus, it is unwise to assume that the timeout value will be unmodified by the select() call.

HISTORY

The select function call appeared in 4.2BSD.

NAME
send, sendto, sendmsg – send a message from a socket

SYNOPSIS
```
#include <sys/types.h>
#include <sys/socket.h>
```

ssize_t
send(*int s, const void *msg, size_t len, int flags*);

ssize_t
sendto(*int s, const void *msg, size_t len, int flags,*
        *const struct sockaddr *to, int tolen*);

ssize_t
sendmsg(*int s, const struct msghdr *msg, int flags*);

DESCRIPTION
Send(), **sendto**(), and **sendmsg**() are used to transmit a message to another socket. **Send**() may be used only when the socket is in a *connected* state, while **sendto**() and **sendmsg**() may be used at any time.

The address of the target is given by *to* with *tolen* specifying its size. The length of the message is given by *len*. If the message is too long to pass atomically through the underlying protocol, the error EMSGSIZE is returned, and the message is not transmitted.

No indication of failure to deliver is implicit in a **send**(). Locally detected errors are indicated by a return value of -1.

If no messages space is available at the socket to hold the message to be transmitted, then **send**() normally blocks, unless the socket has been placed in non-blocking I/O mode. The select(2) call may be used to determine when it is possible to send more data.

The *flags* parameter may include one or more of the following:

```
#define MSG_OOB        0x1   /* process out-of-band data */
#define MSG_DONTROUTE  0x4   /* bypass routing, use direct interface */
```

The flag MSG_OOB is used to send "out-of-band" data on sockets that support this notion (e.g. SOCK_STREAM); the underlying protocol must also support "out-of-band" data. MSG_DONTROUTE is usually used only by diagnostic or routing programs.

See recv(2) for a description of the *msghdr* structure.

RETURN VALUES
The call returns the number of characters sent, or -1 if an error occurred.

ERRORS
Send(), **sendto**(), and **sendmsg**() fail if:

[EBADF]   An invalid descriptor was specified.

[ENOTSOCK]   The argument *s* is not a socket.

[EFAULT]   An invalid user space address was specified for a parameter.

2

[EMSGSIZE]   The socket requires that message be sent atomically, and the size of the message to be sent made this impossible.

[EAGAIN]   The socket is marked non-blocking and the requested operation would block.

[ENOBUFS]   The system was unable to allocate an internal buffer. The operation may succeed when buffers become available.

[ENOBUFS]   The output queue for a network interface was full. This generally indicates that the interface has stopped sending, but may be caused by transient congestion.

SEE ALSO
fcntl(2), recv(2), select(2), getsockopt(2), socket(2), write(2)

HISTORY
The send function call appeared in 4.2BSD.

2

NAME
    setgroups – set group access list

SYNOPSIS
    #include <sys/param.h>
    #include <unistd.h>

    int
    setgroups(int ngroups, const gid_t *gidset);

DESCRIPTION
Setgroups() sets the group access list of the current user process according to the array *gidset*. The parameter *ngroups* indicates the number of entries in the array and must be no more than NGROUPS, as defined in <sys/param.h>.

Only the super-user may set new groups.

RETURN VALUES
A 0 value is returned on success, -1 on error, with an error code stored in *errno*.

ERRORS
The setgroups() call will fail if:

[EPERM]   The caller is not the super-user.

[EFAULT]   The address specified for *gidset* is outside the process address space.

SEE ALSO
    getgroups(2), initgroups(3)

HISTORY
The setgroups function call appeared in 4.2BSD.

2

NAME
setpgid, setpgrp – set process group

SYNOPSIS
`#include <unistd.h>`

`int`
`setpgid(`*pid_tpid*`, `*pid_tpgrp*`);`

`int`
`setpgrp(`*pid_tpid*`, `*pid_tpgrp*`);`

DESCRIPTION
Setpgid( ) sets the process group of the specified process *pid* to the specified *pgrp*. If *pid* is zero, then the call applies to the current process.

If the invoker is not the super-user, then the affected process must have the same effective user-id as the invoker or be a descendant of the invoking process.

RETURN VALUES
Setpgid( ) returns 0 when the operation was successful. If the request failed, -1 is returned and the global variable *errno* indicates the reason.

ERRORS
Setpgid( ) will fail and the process group will not be altered if:

[ESRCH]
The requested process does not exist.

[EPERM]
The effective user ID of the requested process is different from that of the caller and the process is not a descendent of the calling process.

SEE ALSO
getpgrp(2)

STANDARDS
Setpgid( ) conforms to IEEE Std 1003.1-1988 (''POSIX'').

COMPATIBILITY
Setpgrp( ) is identical to setpgid(), and is retained for calling convention compatibility with historical versions of BSD.

2

NAME
setregid – set real and effective group ID

SYNOPSIS
`#include <unistd.h>`

`int`
`setregid(gid_t rgid, gid_t egid);`

DESCRIPTION
The real and effective group ID's of the current process are set to the arguments. Unprivileged users may change the real group ID to the effective group ID and vice-versa; only the super-user may make other changes.

Supplying a value of -1 for either the real or effective group ID forces the system to substitute the current ID in place of the -1 parameter.

The `setregid()` function was intended to allow swapping the real and effective group IDs in set-group-ID programs to temporarily relinquish the set-group-ID value. This function did not work correctly, and its purpose is now better served by the use of the `setegid()` function (see setuid(2)).

When setting the real and effective group IDs to the same value, the standard `setgid()` function is preferred.

RETURN VALUES
Upon successful completion, a value of 0 is returned. Otherwise, a value of -1 is returned and *errno* is set to indicate the error.

ERRORS
[EPERM]   The current process is not the super-user and a change other than changing the effective group-id to the real group-id was specified.

SEE ALSO
getgid(2), setegid(2), setgid(2), setuid(2)

HISTORY
The `setregid` function call appeared in 4.2BSD and was dropped in 4.4BSD.

NAME

    `setreuid` – set real and effective user ID's

SYNOPSIS

    `#include <unistd.h>`

    `int`
    `setreuid(uid_t ruid, uid_t euid);`

DESCRIPTION

    The real and effective user IDs of the current process are set according to the arguments. If `ruid` or `euid` is -1, the current uid is filled in by the system. Unprivileged users may change the real user ID to the effective user ID and vice-versa; only the super-user may make other changes.

    The `setreuid()` function has been used to swap the real and effective user IDs in set-user-ID programs to temporarily relinquish the set-user-ID value. This purpose is now better served by the use of the `seteuid()` function (see `setuid(2)`).

    When setting the real and effective user IDs to the same value, the standard `setuid()` function is preferred.

RETURN VALUES

    Upon successful completion, a value of 0 is returned. Otherwise, a value of -1 is returned and *errno* is set to indicate the error.

ERRORS

    [EPERM] The current process is not the super-user and a change other than changing the effective user-id to the real user-id was specified.

SEE ALSO

    getuid(2), seteuid(2), setuid(2)

HISTORY

    The `setreuid` function call appeared in 4.2BSD and was dropped in 4.4BSD.

NAME
　　　　setsid – create session and set process group ID

SYNOPSIS
　　　　#include <sys/types.h>

　　　　pid_t
　　　　setsid(*void*);

DESCRIPTION
　　　　The **setsid** function creates a new session. The calling process is the session leader of the new session, is the process group leader of a new process group and has no controlling terminal. The calling process is the only process in either the session or the process group.

　　　　Upon successful completion, the **setsid** function returns the value of the process group ID of the new process group, which is the same as the process ID of the calling process.

ERRORS
　　　　If an error occurs, **setsid** returns -1 and the global variable *errno* is set to indicate the error, as follows:

　　　　[EPERM]　　　　The calling process is already a process group leader, or the process group ID of a process other than the calling process matches the process ID of the calling process.

SEE ALSO
　　　　setpgid(3), tcgetpgrp(3), tcsetpgrp(3)

STANDARDS
　　　　The **setsid** function is expected to be compliant with the IEEE Std1003.1-1988 (''POSIX'') specification.

2

NAME
setuid, seteuid, setgid, setegid, – set user and group ID

SYNOPSIS
```
#include <sys/types.h>
#include <unistd.h>
```

int
setuid(*uid_t uid*);

int
seteuid(*uid_t euid*);

int
setgid(*gid_t gid*);

int
setegid(*gid_t egid*);

DESCRIPTION
The **setuid**( ) function sets the real and effective user IDs and the saved set-user-ID of the current process to the specified value. The **setuid**( ) function is permitted if the specified ID is equal to the real user ID of the process, or if the effective user ID is that of the super user.

The **setgid**( ) function sets the real and effective group IDs and the saved set-group-ID of the current process to the specified value. The **setgid**( ) function is permitted if the specified ID is equal to the real group ID of the process, or if the effective user ID is that of the super user.

The **seteuid**( ) function (**setegid**( )) sets the effective user ID (group ID) of the current process. The effective user ID may be set to the value of the real user ID or the saved set-user-ID (see intro(2) and execve(2)); in this way, the effective user ID of a set-user-ID executable may be toggled by switching to the real user ID, then re-enabled by reverting to the set-user-ID value. Similarly, the effective group ID may be set to the value of the real group ID or the saved set-user-ID.

RETURN VALUES
Upon success, these functions return 0; otherwise −1 is returned.

If the user is not the super user, or the uid specified is not the real, effective ID, or saved ID, these functions return −1.

SEE ALSO
getuid(2), getgid(2)

STANDARDS
The **setuid**( ) and **setgid**( ) functions are compliant with the IEEE Std1003.1-1988 (''POSIX'') specification with _POSIX_SAVED_IDS not defined. The **seteuid**( ) and **setegid**( ) functions are extensions based on the POSIX concept of _POSIX_SAVED_IDS, and have been proposed for a future revision of the standard.

2

NAME

shutdown – shut down part of a full-duplex connection

SYNOPSIS

```
#include <sys/socket.h>
```

int
shutdown(*int s*, *int how*);

DESCRIPTION

The **shutdown**( ) call causes all or part of a full-duplex connection on the socket associated with *s* to be shut down. If *how* is 0, further receives will be disallowed. If *how* is 1, further sends will be disallowed. If *how* is 2, further sends and receives will be disallowed.

DIAGNOSTICS

A 0 is returned if the call succeeds, -1 if it fails.

ERRORS

The call succeeds unless:

[EBADF]   *S* is not a valid descriptor.

[ENOTSOCK]   *S* is a file, not a socket.

[ENOTCONN] The specified socket is not connected.

SEE ALSO

connect(2), socket(2)

HISTORY

The **shutdown** function call appeared in 4.2BSD.

2

NAME
`sigaction` – software signal facilities

SYNOPSIS
```
#include <signal.h>

struct sigaction {
        void     (*sa_handler)();
        sigset_t sa_mask;
        int      sa_flags;
};

sigaction(int sig, struct sigaction *act, struct sigaction *oact);
```

DESCRIPTION
The system defines a set of signals that may be delivered to a process. Signal delivery resembles the occurrence of a hardware interrupt: the signal is blocked from further occurrence, the current process context is saved, and a new one is built. A process may specify a *handler* to which a signal is delivered, or specify that a signal is to be *ignored*. A process may also specify that a default action is to be taken by the system when a signal occurs. A signal may also be *blocked*, in which case its delivery is postponed until it is *unblocked*. The action to be taken on delivery is determined at the time of delivery. Normally, signal handlers execute on the current stack of the process. This may be changed, on a per-handler basis, so that signals are taken on a special *signal stack*.

Signal routines execute with the signal that caused their invocation *blocked*, but other signals may yet occur. A global *signal mask* defines the set of signals currently blocked from delivery to a process. The signal mask for a process is initialized from that of its parent (normally empty). It may be changed with a `sigprocmask(2)` call, or when a signal is delivered to the process.

When a signal condition arises for a process, the signal is added to a set of signals pending for the process. If the signal is not currently *blocked* by the process then it is delivered to the process. Signals may be delivered any time a process enters the operating system (e.g., during a system call, page fault or trap, or clock interrupt). If multiple signals are ready to be delivered at the same time, any signals that could be caused by traps are delivered first. Additional signals may be processed at the same time, with each appearing to interrupt the handlers for the previous signals before their first instructions. The set of pending signals is returned by the `sigpending(2)` function. When a caught signal is delivered, the current state of the process is saved, a new signal mask is calculated (as described below), and the signal handler is invoked. The call to the handler is arranged so that if the signal handling routine returns normally the process will resume execution in the context from before the signal's delivery. If the process wishes to resume in a different context, then it must arrange to restore the previous context itself.

When a signal is delivered to a process a new signal mask is installed for the duration of the process' signal handler (or until a `sigprocmask` call is made). This mask is formed by taking the union of the current signal mask set, the signal to be delivered, and the signal mask associated with the handler to be invoked.

`Sigaction()` assigns an action for a specific signal. If `act` is non-zero, it specifies an action (SIG_DFL, SIG_IGN, or a handler routine) and mask to be used when delivering the specified signal. If `oact` is non-zero, the previous handling information for the signal is returned to the user.

Once a signal handler is installed, it remains installed until another `sigaction()` call is made, or an `execve(2)` is performed. A signal-specific default action may be reset by setting `sa_handler` to SIG_DFL. The defaults are process termination, possibly with core dump; no action; stopping the process; or continuing the process. See the signal list below for each signal's default action. If `sa_handler` is SIG_DFL, the default action for the signal is to discard the signal, and if a signal is pending, the pending signal is discarded even if the signal is masked. If *sa_handler* is set to SIG_IGN current and pending instances of the signal are ignored and discarded.

Options may be specified by setting *sa_flags*. If the SA_NOCLDSTOP bit is set when installing a catching function for the SIGCHLD signal, the SIGCHLD signal will be generated only when a child process exits, not when a child process stops. Further, if the SA_ONSTACK bit is set in *sa_flags*, the system will deliver the signal to the process on a *signal stack*, specified with sigstack(2).

If a signal is caught during the system calls listed below, the call may be forced to terminate with the error EINTR, the call may return with a data transfer shorter than requested, or the call may be restarted. Restart of pending calls is requested by setting the SA_RESTART bit in *sa_flags*. The affected system calls include open(2), read(2), write(2), sendto(2), recvfrom(2), sendmsg(2) and recvmsg(2) on a communications channel or a slow device (such as a terminal, but not a regular file) and during a wait(2) or ioctl(2). However, calls that have already committed are not restarted, but instead return a partial success (for example, a short read count).

After a fork(2) or vfork(2) all signals, the signal mask, the signal stack, and the restart/interrupt flags are inherited by the child.

Execve(2) reinstates the default action for all signals which were caught and resets all signals to be caught on the user stack. Ignored signals remain ignored; the signal mask remains the same; signals that restart pending system calls continue to do so.

The following is a list of all signals with names as in the include file <signal.h>:

NAME	Default Action	Description
SIGHUP	terminate process	terminal line hangup
SIGINT	terminate process	interrupt program
SIGQUIT	create core image	quit program
SIGILL	create core image	illegal instruction
SIGTRAP	create core image	trace trap
SIGABRT	create core image	abort(2) call (formerly SIGIOT)
SIGEMT	create core image	emulate instruction executed
SIGFPE	create core image	floating-point exception
SIGKILL	terminate process	kill program
SIGBUS	create core image	bus error
SIGSEGV	create core image	segmentation violation
SIGSYS	create core image	system call given invalid argument
SIGPIPE	terminate process	write on a pipe with no reader
SIGALRM	terminate process	real-time timer expired
SIGTERM	terminate process	software termination signal
SIGURG	discard signal	urgent condition present on socket
SIGSTOP	stop process	stop (cannot be caught or ignored)
SIGTSTP	stop process	stop signal generated from keyboard
SIGCONT	discard signal	continue after stop
SIGCHLD	discard signal	child status has changed
SIGTTIN	stop process	background read attempted from control terminal
SIGTTOU	stop process	background write attempted to control terminal
SIGIO	discard signal	I/O is possible on a descriptor (see fcntl(2))
SIGXCPU	terminate process	cpu time limit exceeded (see setrlimit(2))
SIGXFSZ	terminate process	file size limit exceeded (see setrlimit(2))
SIGVTALRM	terminate process	virtual time alarm (see setitimer(2))

SIGPROF	terminate process	profiling timer alarm (see setitimer(2))
SIGWINCH	discard signal	Window size change
SIGINFO	discard signal	status request from keyboard
SIGUSR1	terminate process	User defined signal 1
SIGUSR2	terminate process	User defined signal 2

NOTE

The mask specified in *act* is not allowed to block SIGKILL or SIGSTOP. This is done silently by the system.

RETURN VALUES

A 0 value indicated that the call succeeded. A −1 return value indicates an error occurred and *errno* is set to indicated the reason.

EXAMPLE

The handler routine can be declared:

```
void handler(sig, code, scp)
int sig, code;
struct sigcontext *scp;
```

Here *sig* is the signal number, into which the hardware faults and traps are mapped. *Code* is a parameter that is either a constant or the code provided by the hardware. *Scp* is a pointer to the *sigcontext* structure (defined in <signal.h>), used to restore the context from before the signal.

ERRORS

Sigaction() will fail and no new signal handler will be installed if one of the following occurs:

[EFAULT]   Either *act* or *oact* points to memory that is not a valid part of the process address space.

[EINVAL]   *Sig* is not a valid signal number.

[EINVAL]   An attempt is made to ignore or supply a handler for SIGKILL or SIGSTOP.

STANDARDS

The **sigaction** function is defined by IEEE Std1003.1-1988 (''POSIX''). The SA_ONSTACK and SA_RESTART flags are Berkeley extensions, as are the signals, SIGTRAP, SIGEMT, SIGBUS, SIGSYS, SIGURG, SIGIO, SIGXCPU, SIGXFSZ, SIGVTALRM, SIGPROF, SIGWINCH, and SIGINFO. Those signals are available on most BSD–derived systems.

SEE ALSO

kill(1), ptrace(2), kill(2), sigaction(2), sigprocmask(2), sigsuspend(2), sigblock(2), sigsetmask(2), sigpause(2), sigstack(2), sigvec(2), setjmp(3), siginterrupt(3), sigsetops(3), tty(4)

NAME

  sigaltstack – set and/or get signal stack context

SYNOPSIS

```
#include <sys/types.h>
#include <signal.h>

struct sigaltstack {
        caddr_t ss_sp;
        long    ss_size;
        int     ss_flags;
};

int
sigaltstack(const struct sigaltstack *ss, struct sigaltstack *oss);
```

DESCRIPTION

  Sigaltstack() allows users to define an alternate stack on which signals are to be processed. If *ss* is non-zero, it specifies a pointer to and the size of a *signal stack* on which to deliver signals, and tells the system if the process is currently executing on that stack. When a signal's action indicates its handler should execute on the signal stack (specified with a sigaction(2) call), the system checks to see if the process is currently executing on that stack. If the process is not currently executing on the signal stack, the system arranges a switch to the signal stack for the duration of the signal handler's execution.

  If SA_DISABLE is set in *ss_flags*, *ss_sp* and *ss_size* are ignored and the signal stack will be disabled. Trying to disable an active stack will cause **sigaltstack** to return -1 with *errno* set to EINVAL. A disabled stack will cause all signals to be taken on the regular user stack. If the stack is later re-enabled then all signals that were specified to be processed on an alternate stack will resume doing so.

  If *oss* is non-zero, the current signal stack state is returned. The *ss_flags* field will contain the value SA_ONSTACK if the process is currently on a signal stack and SA_DISABLE if the signal stack is currently disabled.

NOTES

  The value SIGSTKSZ is defined to be the number of bytes/chars that would be used to cover the usual case when allocating an alternate stack area. The following code fragment is typically used to allocate an alternate stack.

```
      if ((sigstk.ss_sp = malloc(SIGSTKSZ)) == NULL)
              /* error return */
      sigstk.ss_size = SIGSTKSZ;
      sigstk.ss_flags = 0;
      if (sigaltstack(&sigstk,0) < 0)
              perror("sigaltstack");
```

An alternative approach is provided for programs with signal handlers that require a specific amount of stack space other than the default size. The value MINSIGSTKSZ is defined to be the number of bytes/chars that is required by the operating system to implement the alternate stack feature. In computing an alternate stack size, programs should add MINSIGSTKSZ to their stack requirements to allow for the operating system overhead.

  Signal stacks are automatically adjusted for the direction of stack growth and alignment requirements. Signal stacks may or may not be protected by the hardware and are not ''grown'' automatically as is done for the normal stack. If the stack overflows and this space is not protected unpredictable results may occur.

RETURN VALUES

Upon successful completion, a value of 0 is returned. Otherwise, a value of -1 is returned and *errno* is set to indicate the error.

ERRORS

`Sigstack()` will fail and the signal stack context will remain unchanged if one of the following occurs.

[EFAULT] Either *ss* or *oss* points to memory that is not a valid part of the process address space.

[EINVAL] An attempt was made to disable an active stack.

[ENOMEM] Size of alternate stack area is less than or equal to MINSIGSTKSZ.

SEE ALSO

sigaction(2), setjmp(3)

HISTORY

The predecessor to `sigaltstack`, the `sigstack()` system call, appeared in 4.2BSD.

NAME
sigblock – block signals

SYNOPSIS
`#include <signal.h>`

int
`sigblock(int mask)`;

int
`sigmask(signum)`;

DESCRIPTION
This interface is made obsolete by: sigprocmask(2).

Sigblock( ) adds the signals specified in *mask* to the set of signals currently being blocked from delivery. Signals are blocked if the corresponding bit in *mask* is a 1; the macro **sigmask**( ) is provided to construct the mask for a given *signum*.

It is not possible to block SIGKILL or SIGSTOP; this restriction is silently imposed by the system.

RETURN VALUES
The previous set of masked signals is returned.

SEE ALSO
kill(2), sigprocmask(2), sigaction(2), sigsetmask(2), sigsetops(3)

HISTORY
The **sigblock** function call appeared in 4.2BSD and has been deprecated.

2

NAME
sigpause – atomically release blocked signals and wait for interrupt

SYNOPSIS
#include <signal.h>

int
sigpause(int sigmask);

DESCRIPTION
This interface is made obsolete by sigsuspend(2).

Sigpause() assigns *sigmask* to the set of masked signals and then waits for a signal to arrive; on return the set of masked signals is restored. *Sigmask* is usually 0 to indicate that no signals are to be blocked. Sigpause() always terminates by being interrupted, returning -1 with *errno* set to EINTR

SEE ALSO
sigsuspend(2), kill(2), sigaction(2), sigprocmask(2), sigblock(2), sigvec(2)

HISTORY
The **sigpause** function call appeared in 4.2BSD and has been deprecated.

2

NAME
　　sigpending – get pending signals

SYNOPSIS
　　#include <signal.h>

　　int
　　sigpending(*sigset_t *set*);

DESCRIPTION
　　The **sigpending** function returns a mask of the signals pending for delivery to the calling process in the location indicated by *set*. Signals may be pending because they are currently masked, or transiently before delivery (although the latter case is not normally detectable).

RETURN VALUES
　　A 0 value indicated that the call succeeded. A −1 return value indicates an error occurred and *errno* is set to indicated the reason.

ERRORS
　　The **sigpending** function does not currently detect any errors.

SEE ALSO
　　sigaction(2), sigprocmask(2)

STANDARDS
　　The **sigpending** function is defined by IEEE Std1003.1-1988 (''POSIX'').

NAME

`sigprocmask` – manipulate current signal mask

SYNOPSIS

`#include <signal.h>`

int
`sigprocmask(`*int how, const sigset_t *set, sigset_t *oset*`)`;

`sigmask(`*signum*`)`;

DESCRIPTION

The `sigprocmask()` function examines and/or changes the current signal mask (those signals that are blocked from delivery). Signals are blocked if they are members of the current signal mask set.

If *set* is not null, the action of `sigprocmask()` depends on the value of the parameter *how*. The signal mask is changed as a function of the specified *set* and the current mask. The function is specified by *how* using one of the following values from <signal.h>:

SIG_BLOCK   The new mask is the union of the current mask and the specified *set*.

SIG_UNBLOCK The new mask is the intersection of the current mask and the complement of the specified *set*.

SIG_SETMASK The current mask is replaced by the specified *set*.

If *oset* is not null, it is set to the previous value of the signal mask. When *set* is null, the value of *how* is insignificant and the mask remains unset providing a way to examine the signal mask without modification.

The system quietly disallows SIGKILL or SIGSTOP to be blocked.

RETURN VALUES

A 0 value indicated that the call succeeded. A -1 return value indicates an error occurred and *errno* is set to indicated the reason.

ERRORS

The `sigprocmask()` call will fail and the signal mask will be unchanged if one of the following occurs:

[EINVAL]   *how* has a value other than those listed here.

SEE ALSO

kill(2), sigaction(2), sigsetops(3), sigsuspend(2)

STANDARDS

The `sigprocmask` function call is expected to conform to IEEE Std1003.1-1988 (''POSIX'').

2

NAME
    sigreturn – return from signal

SYNOPSIS
    #include <signal.h>

    struct sigcontext {
            int sc_onstack;
            int sc_mask;
            int sc_sp;
            int sc_fp;
            int sc_ap;
            int sc_pc;
            int sc_ps;
    };

    int
    sigreturn(*struct sigcontext *scp*);

DESCRIPTION
    Sigreturn( ) allows users to atomically unmask, switch stacks, and return from a signal context. The processes signal mask and stack status are restored from the context. The system call does not return; the users stack pointer, frame pointer, argument pointer, and processor status longword are restored from the context. Execution resumes at the specified pc. This system call is used by the trampoline code and longjmp(3) when returning from a signal to the previously executing program.

NOTES
    This system call is not available in 4.2 BSD hence it should not be used if backward compatibility is needed.

RETURN VALUES
    If successful, the system call does not return. Otherwise, a value of -1 is returned and *errno* is set to indicate the error.

ERRORS
    Sigreturn( ) will fail and the process context will remain unchanged if one of the following occurs.

    [EFAULT]   *Scp* points to memory that is not a valid part of the process address space.

    [EINVAL]   The process status longword is invalid or would improperly raise the privilege level of the process.

SEE ALSO
    sigvec(2), setjmp(3)

HISTORY
    The **sigreturn** function call appeared in 4.3BSD.

2

NAME
sigsetmask – set current signal mask

SYNOPSIS
#include ⟨signal.h⟩

int
sigsetmask(*int mask*);

sigmask(*signum*);

DESCRIPTION
This interface is made obsoleted by: sigprocmask(2).

Sigsetmask( ) sets the current signal mask Signals are blocked from delivery if the corresponding bit in *mask* is a 1; the macro **sigmask**( ) is provided to construct the mask for a given *signum*.

The system quietly disallows SIGKILL or SIGSTOP to be blocked.

RETURN VALUES
The previous set of masked signals is returned.

SEE ALSO
sigprocmask(2), kill(2), sigaction(2), sigsuspend(2), sigvec(2), sigblock(2), sigsetops(3)

HISTORY
The **sigsetmask** function call appeared in 4.2BSD and has been deprecated.

NAME

   sigstack – set and/or get signal stack context

DESCRIPTION

   The **sigstack**( ) function has been deprecated in favor of the interface described in sigaltstack(2).

SEE ALSO

   sigaltstack(2)

HISTORY

   The **sigstack** function call appeared in 4.2BSD.

NAME

　　sigsuspend – atomically release blocked signals and wait for interrupt

SYNOPSIS

```
#include <signal.h>

int
sigsuspend(const sigset_t *sigmask);
```

DESCRIPTION

　　Sigsuspend() temporarily changes the blocked signal mask to the set to which *sigmask* points, and then waits for a signal to arrive; on return the previous set of masked signals is restored. The signal mask set is usually empty to indicate that all signals are to be unblocked for the duration of the call.

　　In normal usage, a signal is blocked using sigprocmask(2) to begin a critical section, variables modified on the occurrence of the signal are examined to determine that there is no work to be done, and the process pauses awaiting work by using **sigsuspend**() with the previous mask returned by sigprocmask.

RETURN VALUES

　　The sigsuspend() function always terminates by being interrupted, returning -1 with *errno* set to EINTR.

SEE ALSO

　　sigprocmask(2), sigaction(2), sigsetops(3)

STANDARDS

　　The **sigsupend** function call conforms to IEEE Std1003.1-1988 ("POSIX").

NAME

sigvec – software signal facilities

SYNOPSIS

```
#include <signal.h>
```

```
struct sigvec {
        void      (*sv_handler)();
        sigset_t sv_mask;
        int       sv_flags;
};
```

sigvec(*int sig*, *struct sigvec *vec*, *struct sigvec *ovec*);

DESCRIPTION

This interface is made obsolete by sigaction(2).

The system defines a set of signals that may be delivered to a process. Signal delivery resembles the occurrence of a hardware interrupt: the signal is blocked from further occurrence, the current process context is saved, and a new one is built. A process may specify a *handler* to which a signal is delivered, or specify that a signal is to be *blocked* or *ignored*. A process may also specify that a default action is to be taken by the system when a signal occurs. Normally, signal handlers execute on the current stack of the process. This may be changed, on a per-handler basis, so that signals are taken on a special *signal stack*.

All signals have the same *priority*. Signal routines execute with the signal that caused their invocation *blocked*, but other signals may yet occur. A global *signal mask* defines the set of signals currently blocked from delivery to a process. The signal mask for a process is initialized from that of its parent (normally 0). It may be changed with a sigblock(2) or sigsetmask(2) call, or when a signal is delivered to the process.

When a signal condition arises for a process, the signal is added to a set of signals pending for the process. If the signal is not currently *blocked* by the process then it is delivered to the process. When a signal is delivered, the current state of the process is saved, a new signal mask is calculated (as described below), and the signal handler is invoked. The call to the handler is arranged so that if the signal handling routine returns normally the process will resume execution in the context from before the signal's delivery. If the process wishes to resume in a different context, then it must arrange to restore the previous context itself.

When a signal is delivered to a process a new signal mask is installed for the duration of the process' signal handler (or until a sigblock or sigsetmask call is made). This mask is formed by taking the current signal mask, adding the signal to be delivered, and *or*'ing in the signal mask associated with the handler to be invoked.

Sigvec( ) assigns a handler for a specific signal. If *vec* is non-zero, it specifies a handler routine and mask to be used when delivering the specified signal. Further, if the SV_ONSTACK bit is set in *sv_flags*, the system will deliver the signal to the process on a *signal stack*, specified with sigaltstack(2). If *ovec* is non-zero, the previous handling information for the signal is returned to the user.

The following is a list of all signals with names as in the include file <signal.h>:

NAME	Default Action	Description
SIGHUP	terminate process	terminal line hangup
SIGINT	terminate process	interrupt program

2

SIGQUIT	create core image	quit program
SIGILL	create core image	illegal instruction
SIGTRAP	create core image	trace trap
SIGABRT	create core image	abort(2) call (formerly SIGIOT)
SIGEMT	create core image	emulate instruction executed
SIGFPE	create core image	floating-point exception
SIGKILL	terminate process	kill program
SIGBUS	create core image	bus error
SIGSEGV	create core image	segmentation violation
SIGSYS	create core image	system call given invalid argument
SIGPIPE	terminate process	write on a pipe with no reader
SIGALRM	terminate process	real-time timer expired
SIGTERM	terminate process	software termination signal
SIGURG	discard signal	urgent condition present on socket
SIGSTOP	stop process	stop (cannot be caught or ignored)
SIGTSTP	stop process	stop signal generated from keyboard
SIGCONT	discard signal	continue after stop
SIGCHLD	discard signal	child status has changed
SIGTTIN	stop process	background read attempted from control terminal
SIGTTOU	stop process	background write attempted to control terminal
SIGIO	discard signal	I/O is possible on a descriptor (see fcntl(2))
SIGXCPU	terminate process	cpu time limit exceeded (see setrlimit(2))
SIGXFSZ	terminate process	file size limit exceeded (see setrlimit(2))
SIGVTALRM	terminate process	virtual time alarm (see setitimer(2))
SIGPROF	terminate process	profiling timer alarm (see setitimer(2))
SIGWINCH	discard signal	Window size change
SIGINFO	discard signal	status request from keyboard
SIGUSR1	terminate process	User defined signal 1
SIGUSR2	terminate process	User defined signal 2

Once a signal handler is installed, it remains installed until another **sigvec**() call is made, or an execve(2) is performed. A signal-specific default action may be reset by setting *sv_handler* to SIG_DFL. The defaults are process termination, possibly with core dump; no action; stopping the process; or continuing the process. See the above signal list for each signal's default action. If *sv_handler* is SIG_IGN current and pending instances of the signal are ignored and discarded.

If a signal is caught during the system calls listed below, the call is normally restarted. The call can be forced to terminate prematurely with an EINTR error return by setting the SV_INTERRUPT bit in *sv_flags*. The affected system calls include read(2), write(2), sendto(2), recvfrom(2), sendmsg(2) and recvmsg(2) on a communications channel or a slow device (such as a terminal, but not a regular file) and during a wait(2) or ioctl(2). However, calls that have already committed are not restarted, but instead return a partial success (for example, a short read count).

After a fork(2) or vfork(2) all signals, the signal mask, the signal stack, and the restart/interrupt flags are inherited by the child.

Execve(2) reinstates the default action for all signals which were caught and resets all signals to be caught on the user stack. Ignored signals remain ignored; the signal mask remains the same; signals that interrupt system calls continue to do so.

NOTES

The mask specified in *vec* is not allowed to block SIGKILL or SIGSTOP. This is done silently by the system.

The SV_INTERRUPT flag is not available in 4.2BSD, hence it should not be used if backward compatibility is needed.

RETURN VALUES

A 0 value indicated that the call succeeded. A −1 return value indicates an error occurred and *errno* is set to indicated the reason.

ERRORS

Sigvec( ) will fail and no new signal handler will be installed if one of the following occurs:

[EFAULT]   Either *vec* or *ovec* points to memory that is not a valid part of the process address space.

[EINVAL]   *Sig* is not a valid signal number.

[EINVAL]   An attempt is made to ignore or supply a handler for SIGKILL or SIGSTOP.

SEE ALSO

kill(1), kill(2), ptrace(2), sigaction(2), sigaltstack(2), sigblock(2), sigpause(2), sigprocmask(2), sigsetmask(2), sigsuspend(2), setjmp(3), siginterrupt(3), signal(3,) sigsetops(3), tty(4)

EXAMPLE

On the VAX–11 The handler routine can be declared:

```
void handler(sig, code, scp)
int sig, code;
struct sigcontext *scp;
```

Here *sig* is the signal number, into which the hardware faults and traps are mapped as defined below. *Code* is a parameter that is either a constant as given below or, for compatibility mode faults, the code provided by the hardware (Compatibility mode faults are distinguished from the other SIGILL traps by having PSL_CM set in the psl). *Scp* is a pointer to the *sigcontext* structure (defined in <signal.h>), used to restore the context from before the signal.

BUGS

This manual page is still confusing.

2

NAME
    socket – create an endpoint for communication

SYNOPSIS
    #include <sys/types.h>
    #include <sys/socket.h>

    int
    socket(int domain, int type, int protocol);

DESCRIPTION
Socket() creates an endpoint for communication and returns a descriptor.

The *domain* parameter specifies a communications domain within which communication will take place; this selects the protocol family which should be used. These families are defined in the include file <sys/socket.h>. The currently understood formats are

AF_UNIX	(UNIX internal protocols),
AF_INET	(ARPA Internet protocols),
AF_ISO	(ISO protocols),
AF_NS	(Xerox Network Systems protocols), and
AF_IMPLINK	(IMP host at IMP link layer).

The socket has the indicated *type*, which specifies the semantics of communication. Currently defined types are:

    SOCK_STREAM
    SOCK_DGRAM
    SOCK_RAW
    SOCK_SEQPACKET
    SOCK_RDM

A SOCK_STREAM type provides sequenced, reliable, two-way connection based byte streams. An out-of-band data transmission mechanism may be supported. A SOCK_DGRAM socket supports datagrams (connectionless, unreliable messages of a fixed (typically small) maximum length). A SOCK_SEQPACKET socket may provide a sequenced, reliable, two-way connection-based data transmission path for datagrams of fixed maximum length; a consumer may be required to read an entire packet with each read system call. This facility is protocol specific, and presently implemented only for PF_NS. SOCK_RAW sockets provide access to internal network protocols and interfaces. The types SOCK_RAW, which is available only to the super-user, and SOCK_RDM, which is planned, but not yet implemented, are not described here.

The *protocol* specifies a particular protocol to be used with the socket. Normally only a single protocol exists to support a particular socket type within a given protocol family. However, it is possible that many protocols may exist, in which case a particular protocol must be specified in this manner. The protocol number to use is particular to the communication domain in which communication is to take place; see protocols(5).

Sockets of type SOCK_STREAM are full-duplex byte streams, similar to pipes. A stream socket must be in a *connected* state before any data may be sent or received on it. A connection to another socket is created with a connect(2) call. Once connected, data may be transferred using read(2) and write(2) calls or some variant of the send(2) and recv(2) calls. When a session has been completed a close(2) may be performed. Out-of-band data may also be transmitted as described in send(2) and received as described in recv(2).

The communications protocols used to implement a SOCK_STREAM insure that data is not lost or duplicated. If a piece of data for which the peer protocol has buffer space cannot be successfully transmitted within a reasonable length of time, then the connection is considered broken and calls will indicate an error with -1 returns and with ETIMEDOUT as the specific code in the global variable *errno*. The protocols optionally keep sockets "warm" by forcing transmissions roughly every minute in the absence of other activity. An error is then indicated if no response can be elicited on an otherwise idle connection for a extended period (e.g. 5 minutes). A SIGPIPE signal is raised if a process sends on a broken stream; this causes naive processes, which do not handle the signal, to exit.

SOCK_SEQPACKET sockets employ the same system calls as SOCK_STREAM sockets. The only difference is that read(2) calls will return only the amount of data requested, and any remaining in the arriving packet will be discarded.

SOCK_DGRAM and SOCK_RAW sockets allow sending of datagrams to correspondents named in send(2) calls. Datagrams are generally received with recvfrom(2), which returns the next datagram with its return address.

An fcntl(2) call can be used to specify a process group to receive a SIGURG signal when the out-of-band data arrives. It may also enable non-blocking I/O and asynchronous notification of I/O events via SIGIO.

The operation of sockets is controlled by socket level *options*. These options are defined in the file <sys/socket.h>. Setsockopt(2) and getsockopt(2) are used to set and get options, respectively.

RETURN VALUES
A -1 is returned if an error occurs, otherwise the return value is a descriptor referencing the socket.

ERRORS
The **socket( )** call fails if:

[EPROTONOSUPPORT]	The protocol type or the specified protocol is not supported within this domain.
[EMFILE]	The per-process descriptor table is full.
[ENFILE]	The system file table is full.
[EACCESS]	Permission to create a socket of the specified type and/or protocol is denied.
[ENOBUFS]	Insufficient buffer space is available. The socket cannot be created until sufficient resources are freed.

SEE ALSO
accept(2), bind(2), connect(2), getprotoent(3), getsockname(2), getsockopt(2), ioctl(2), listen(2), read(2), recv(2), select(2), send(2), shutdown(2), socketpair(2), write(2)

An Introductory 4.3 BSD Interprocess Communication Tutorial, reprinted in UNIX Programmer's Supplementary Documents Volume 1.

BSD Interprocess Communication Tutorial, reprinted in UNIX Programmer's Supplementary Documents Volume 1.

HISTORY
The **socket** function call appeared in 4.2BSD.

2

NAME

    `socketpair` – create a pair of connected sockets

SYNOPSIS

    `#include <sys/types.h>`
    `#include <sys/socket.h>`

    int
    `socketpair(`*int d, int type, int protocol, int *sv*`);`

DESCRIPTION

    The `socketpair()` call creates an unnamed pair of connected sockets in the specified domain *d*, of the specified *type*, and using the optionally specified *protocol*. The descriptors used in referencing the new sockets are returned in *sv*[0] and *sv*[1]. The two sockets are indistinguishable.

DIAGNOSTICS

    A 0 is returned if the call succeeds, -1 if it fails.

ERRORS

    The call succeeds unless:

    [EMFILE]   Too many descriptors are in use by this process.

    [EAFNOSUPPORT]   The specified address family is not supported on this machine.

    [EPROTONOSUPPORT]
                  The specified protocol is not supported on this machine.

    [EOPNOSUPPORT]   The specified protocol does not support creation of socket pairs.

    [EFAULT]   The address *sv* does not specify a valid part of the process address space.

SEE ALSO

    read(2), write(2), pipe(2)

BUGS

    This call is currently implemented only for the UNIX domain.

HISTORY

    The `socketpair` function call appeared in 4.2BSD.

2

NAME
stat, lstat, fstat – get file status

SYNOPSIS
```
#include <sys/types.h>
#include <sys/stat.h>

int
stat(const char *path, struct stat *sb);

int
lstat(const char *path, struct stat *sb);

int
fstat(int fd, struct stat *sb);
```

DESCRIPTION
The **stat()** function obtains information about the file pointed to by *path*. Read, write or execute permission of the named file is not required, but all directories listed in the path name leading to the file must be searchable.

Lstat() is like **stat()** except in the case where the named file is a symbolic link, in which case lstat() returns information about the link, while **stat()** returns information about the file the link references. Unlike other filesystem objects, symbolic links do not have an owner, group, access mode, times, etc. Instead, these attributes are taken from the directory that contains the link. The only attributes returned from an lstat() that refer to the symbolic link itself are the file type (S_IFLNK), size, blocks, and link count (always 1).

The **fstat()** obtains the same information about an open file known by the file descriptor *fd*.

The *sb* argument is a pointer to a **stat()** structure as defined by <sys/stat.h> (shown below) and into which information is placed concerning the file.

```
struct stat {
    dev_t    st_dev;     /* device inode resides on */
    ino_t    st_ino;     /* inode's number */
    mode_t   st_mode;    /* inode protection mode */
    nlink_t  st_nlink;   /* number or hard links to the file */
    uid_t    st_uid;     /* user-id of owner */
    gid_t    st_gid;     /* group-id of owner */
    dev_t    st_rdev;    /* device type, for special file inode */
    struct timespec st_atimespec;  /* time of last access */
    struct timespec st_mtimespec;  /* time of last data modification */
    struct timespec st_ctimespec;  /* time of last file status change */
    off_t    st_size;    /* file size, in bytes */
    quad_t   st_blocks;  /* blocks allocated for file */
    u_long   st_blksize; /* optimal file sys I/O ops blocksize */
    u_long   st_flags;   /* user defined flags for file */
    u_long   st_gen;     /* file generation number */
};
```

2

The time-related fields of *struct stat* are as follows:

st_atime   Time when file data last accessed. Changed by the mknod(2), utimes(2) and read(2) system calls.

st_mtime   Time when file data last modified. Changed by the mknod(2), utimes(2) and write(2) system calls.

st_ctime   Time when file status was last changed (inode data modification). Changed by the chmod(2), chown(2), link(2), mknod(2), rename(2), unlink(2), utimes(2) and write(2) system calls.

The size-related fields of the *struct stat* are as follows:

st_blksize   The optimal I/O block size for the file.

st_blocks   The actual number of blocks allocated for the file in 512-byte units. As short symbolic links are stored in the inode, this number may be zero.

The status information word *st_mode* has the following bits:

```
#define S_IFMT 0170000              /* type of file */
#define        S_IFIFO  0010000     /* named pipe (fifo) */
#define        S_IFCHR  0020000     /* character special */
#define        S_IFDIR  0040000     /* directory */
#define        S_IFBLK  0060000     /* block special */
#define        S_IFREG  0100000     /* regular */
#define        S_IFLNK  0120000     /* symbolic link */
#define        S_IFSOCK 0140000     /* socket */
#define S_ISUID 0004000  /* set user id on execution */
#define S_ISGID 0002000  /* set group id on execution */
#define S_ISVTX 0001000  /* save swapped text even after use */
#define S_IRUSR 0000400  /* read permission, owner */
#define S_IWUSR 0000200  /* write permission, owner */
#define S_IXUSR 0000100  /* execute/search permission, owner */
```

For a list of access modes, see <sys/stat.h>, access(2) and chmod(2).

RETURN VALUES

Upon successful completion a value of 0 is returned. Otherwise, a value of -1 is returned and *errno* is set to indicate the error.

COMPATIBILITY

Previous versions of the system used different types for the st_dev, st_uid, st_gid, st_rdev, st_size, st_blksize and st_blocks fields.

ERRORS

stat() and lstat() will fail if:

[ENOTDIR]   A component of the path prefix is not a directory.

[EINVAL]   The pathname contains a character with the high-order bit set.

[ENAMETOOLONG] A component of a pathname exceeded 255 characters, or an entire path name exceeded 1023 characters.

[ENOENT]	The named file does not exist.
[EACCES]	Search permission is denied for a component of the path prefix.
[ELOOP]	Too many symbolic links were encountered in translating the pathname.
[EFAULT]	*Sb* or *name* points to an invalid address.
[EIO]	An I/O error occurred while reading from or writing to the file system.

Fstat( ) will fail if:

[EBADF]	*fd* is not a valid open file descriptor.
[EFAULT]	*Sb* points to an invalid address.
[EIO]	An I/O error occurred while reading from or writing to the file system.

CAVEAT

The fields in the stat structure currently marked *st_spare1*, *st_spare2*, and *st_spare3* are present in preparation for inode time stamps expanding to 64 bits. This, however, can break certain programs that depend on the time stamps being contiguous (in calls to utimes(2)).

SEE ALSO

chmod(2), chown(2), utimes(2) symlink(7)

BUGS

Applying fstat to a socket (and thus to a pipe) returns a zero'd buffer, except for the blocksize field, and a unique device and inode number.

STANDARDS

The **stat**( ) and **fstat**( ) function calls are expected to conform to IEEE Std 1003.1-1988 (''POSIX'').

HISTORY

A **lstat** function call appeared in 4.2BSD.

2

NAME
   statfs – get file system statistics

SYNOPSIS
   #include <sys/param.h>
   #include <sys/mount.h>

   int
   statfs(*const char *path, struct statfs *buf*);

   int
   fstatfs(*int fd, struct statfs *buf*);

DESCRIPTION
   Statfs() returns information about a mounted file system. *Path* is the path name of any file within the mounted filesystem. *Buf* is a pointer to a **statfs**() structure defined as follows:

```
typedef quad fsid_t;

#define MNAMELEN 90    /* length of buffer for returned name */

struct statfs {
short   f_type;         /* type of filesystem (see below) */
short   f_flags;        /* copy of mount flags */
long    f_bsize;        /* fundamental file system block size */
long    f_iosize;       /* optimal transfer block size */
long    f_blocks;       /* total data blocks in file system */
long    f_bfree;        /* free blocks in fs */
long    f_bavail;       /* free blocks avail to non-superuser */
long    f_files;        /* total file nodes in file system */
long    f_ffree;        /* free file nodes in fs */
fsid_t  f_fsid;         /* file system id */
long    f_spare[9];     /* spare for later */
char    f_mntonname[MNAMELEN];   /* mount point */
char    f_mntfromname[MNAMELEN]; /* mounted filesystem */
};
/*
 * File system types.
 */
#define MOUNT_UFS     1       /* Fast Filesystem */
#define MOUNT_NFS     2       /* Sun-compatible Network Filesystem */
#define MOUNT_MFS     3       /* Memory-based Filesystem */
#define MOUNT_MSDOS   4       /* MS/DOS Filesystem */
#define MOUNT_LFS     5       /* Log-based Filesystem */
#define MOUNT_LOFS    6       /* Loopback Filesystem */
#define MOUNT_FDESC   7       /* File Descriptor Filesystem */
#define MOUNT_PORTAL  8       /* Portal Filesystem */
#define MOUNT_NULL    9       /* Minimal Filesystem Layer */
#define MOUNT_UMAP    10      /* Uid/Gid Remapping Filesystem */
#define MOUNT_KERNFS  11      /* Kernel Information Filesystem */
#define MOUNT_PROCFS  12      /* /proc Filesystem */
#define MOUNT_AFS     13      /* Andrew Filesystem */
```

```
#define MOUNT_CD9660   14      /* ISO9660 (aka CDROM) Filesystem */
#define MOUNT_UNION    15      /* Union (translucent) Filesystem */
```

Fields that are undefined for a particular file system are set to -1. **Fstatfs**() returns the same information about an open file referenced by descriptor *fd*.

RETURN VALUES

Upon successful completion, a value of 0 is returned. Otherwise, -1 is returned and the global variable *errno* is set to indicate the error.

ERRORS

Statfs() fails if one or more of the following are true:

[ENOTDIR]   A component of the path prefix of *Path* is not a directory.

[EINVAL]   *path* contains a character with the high-order bit set.

[ENAMETOOLONG]
                   The length of a component of *path* exceeds 255 characters, or the length of *path* exceeds 1023 characters.

[ENOENT]   The file referred to by *path* does not exist.

[EACCES]   Search permission is denied for a component of the path prefix of *path*.

[ELOOP]   Too many symbolic links were encountered in translating *path*.

[EFAULT]   *Buf* or *path* points to an invalid address.

[EIO]   An I/O error occurred while reading from or writing to the file system.

Fstatfs() fails if one or more of the following are true:

[EBADF]   *Fd* is not a valid open file descriptor.

[EFAULT]   *Buf* points to an invalid address.

[EIO]   An I/O error occurred while reading from or writing to the file system.

HISTORY

The **statfs** function first appeared in 4.4BSD.

2

NAME
swapon – add a swap device for interleaved paging/swapping

SYNOPSIS
```
#include <unistd.h>

int
swapon(const char *special);
```

DESCRIPTION
Swapon() makes the block device *special* available to the system for allocation for paging and swap-ping. The names of potentially available devices are known to the system and defined at system configuration time. The size of the swap area on *special* is calculated at the time the device is first made available for swapping.

RETURN VALUES
If an error has occurred, a value of -1 is returned and *errno* is set to indicate the error.

ERRORS
Swapon() succeeds unless:

[ENOTDIR]   A component of the path prefix is not a directory.

[EINVAL]   The pathname contains a character with the high-order bit set.

[ENAMETOOLONG]
                 A component of a pathname exceeded 255 characters, or an entire path name exceeded 1023 characters.

[ENOENT]   The named device does not exist.

[EACCES]   Search permission is denied for a component of the path prefix.

[ELOOP]   Too many symbolic links were encountered in translating the pathname.

[EPERM]   The caller is not the super-user.

[ENOTBLK]   *Special* is not a block device.

[EBUSY]   The device specified by *special* has already been made available for swapping

[EINVAL]   The device configured by *special* was not configured into the system as a swap device.

[ENXIO]   The major device number of *special* is out of range (this indicates no device driver ex-ists for the associated hardware).

[EIO]   An I/O error occurred while opening the swap device.

[EFAULT]   *Special* points outside the process's allocated address space.

SEE ALSO
swapon(8), config(8)

BUGS
There is no way to stop swapping on a disk so that the pack may be dismounted.

This call will be upgraded in future versions of the system.

HISTORY

The **swapon** function call appeared in 4.0BSD.

2

NAME

`symlink` – make symbolic link to a file

SYNOPSIS

`#include <unistd.h>`

int
`symlink`(*const char *name1, const char *name2*);

DESCRIPTION

A symbolic link *name2* is created to *name1* (*name2* is the name of the file created, *name1* is the string used in creating the symbolic link). Either name may be an arbitrary path name; the files need not be on the same file system.

RETURN VALUES

Upon successful completion, a zero value is returned. If an error occurs, the error code is stored in *errno* and a -1 value is returned.

ERRORS

The symbolic link succeeds unless:

[ENOTDIR]
> A component of the *name2* prefix is not a directory.

[EINVAL] Either *name1* or *name2* contains a character with the high-order bit set.

[ENAMETOOLONG]
> A component of either pathname exceeded 255 characters, or the entire length of either path name exceeded 1023 characters.

[ENOENT] The named file does not exist.

[EACCES] A component of the *name2* path prefix denies search permission.

[ELOOP] Too many symbolic links were encountered in translating the pathname.

[EEXIST] *Name2* already exists.

[EIO] An I/O error occurred while making the directory entry for *name2*, or allocating the inode for *name2*, or writing out the link contents of *name2*.

[EROFS] The file *name2* would reside on a read-only file system.

[ENOSPC] The directory in which the entry for the new symbolic link is being placed cannot be extended because there is no space left on the file system containing the directory.

[ENOSPC] The new symbolic link cannot be created because there there is no space left on the file system that will contain the symbolic link.

[ENOSPC] There are no free inodes on the file system on which the symbolic link is being created.

[EDQUOT] The directory in which the entry for the new symbolic link is being placed cannot be extended because the user's quota of disk blocks on the file system containing the directory has been exhausted.

[EDQUOT]　The new symbolic link cannot be created because the user's quota of disk blocks on the file system that will contain the symbolic link has been exhausted.

[EDQUOT]　The user's quota of inodes on the file system on which the symbolic link is being created has been exhausted.

[EIO]　　　An I/O error occurred while making the directory entry or allocating the inode.

[EFAULT]　*Name1* or *name2* points outside the process's allocated address space.

SEE ALSO

link(2), ln(1), unlink(2)

HISTORY

The **symlink** function call appeared in 4.2BSD.

2

NAME
`sync` – synchronize disk block in-core status with that on disk

SYNOPSIS
`#include <unistd.h>`

void
`sync(`*void*`)`;

DESCRIPTION
The `sync()` function forces a write of dirty (modified) buffers in the block buffer cache out to disk. The kernel keeps this information in core to reduce the number of disk I/O transfers required by the system. As information in the cache is lost after a system crash a `sync()` call is issued frequently by the user process update(8) (about every 30 seconds).

The function `fsync(2)` may be used to synchronize individual file descriptor attributes.

SEE ALSO
`fsync(2)`, `sync(8)`, `update(8)`

BUGS
`Sync()` may return before the buffers are completely flushed.

HISTORY
A `sync` function call appeared in Version 6 AT&T UNIX.

NAME

syscall, __syscall – indirect system call

SYNOPSIS

```
#include <sys/syscall.h>
#include <unistd.h>

int
syscall(int number, ...);

int
__syscall(quad_t number, ...);
```

DESCRIPTION

Syscall() performs the system call whose assembly language interface has the specified *number* with the specified arguments. Symbolic constants for system calls can be found in the header file <sys/syscall.h>. The __syscall form should be used when one or more of the parameters is a 64-bit argument to ensure that argument alignment is correct. This system call is useful for testing new system calls that do not have entries in the C library.

RETURN VALUES

The return values are defined by the system call being invoked. In general, a 0 return value indicates success. A -1 return value indicates an error, and an error code is stored in *errno*.

BUGS

There is no way to simulate system calls that have multiple return values such as pipe(2).

HISTORY

The syscall function call appeared in 4.0BSD.

2

NAME
truncate, ftruncate – truncate a file to a specified length

SYNOPSIS
```
#include <unistd.h>

int
truncate(const char *path, off_t length);

int
ftruncate(int fd, off_t length);
```

DESCRIPTION
Truncate() causes the file named by *path* or referenced by *fd* to be truncated to at most *length* bytes in size. If the file previously was larger than this size, the extra data is lost. With **ftruncate**(), the file must be open for writing.

RETURN VALUES
A value of 0 is returned if the call succeeds. If the call fails a -1 is returned, and the global variable *errno* specifies the error.

ERRORS
Truncate() succeeds unless:

[ENOTDIR]   A component of the path prefix is not a directory.

[EINVAL]   The pathname contains a character with the high-order bit set.

[ENAMETOOLONG]
            A component of a pathname exceeded 255 characters, or an entire path name exceeded 1023 characters.

[ENOENT]   The named file does not exist.

[EACCES]   Search permission is denied for a component of the path prefix.

[EACCES]   The named file is not writable by the user.

[ELOOP]   Too many symbolic links were encountered in translating the pathname.

[EISDIR]   The named file is a directory.

[EROFS]   The named file resides on a read-only file system.

[ETXTBSY]   The file is a pure procedure (shared text) file that is being executed.

[EIO]   An I/O error occurred updating the inode.

[EFAULT]   *Path* points outside the process's allocated address space.

Ftruncate() succeeds unless:

[EBADF]   The *fd* is not a valid descriptor.

[EINVAL]   The *fd* references a socket, not a file.

[EINVAL]   The *fd* is not open for writing.

SEE ALSO

    open(2)

BUGS

    These calls should be generalized to allow ranges of bytes in a file to be discarded.

HISTORY

    The `truncate` function call appeared in 4.2BSD.

2

NAME
umask – set file creation mode mask

SYNOPSIS
`#include <sys/stat.h>`

`mode_t`
`umask(mode_t numask);`

DESCRIPTION
The umask() routine sets the process's file mode creation mask to *numask* and returns the previous value of the mask. The 9 low-order access permission bits of *numask* are used by system calls, including open(2), mkdir(2), and mkfifo(2), to turn off corresponding bits requested in file mode. (See chmod(2)). This clearing allows each user to restrict the default access to his files.

The default mask value is S_IWGRP|S_IWOTH (022, write access for the owner only). Child processes inherit the mask of the calling process.

RETURN VALUES
The previous value of the file mode mask is returned by the call.

ERRORS
The umask() function is always successful.

SEE ALSO
chmod(2), mknod(2), open(2)

STANDARDS
The umask() function call is expected to conform to IEEE Std 1003.1-1988 (''POSIX'').

2

NAME
unlink – remove directory entry

SYNOPSIS
`#include <unistd.h>`

int
unlink(*const char *path*);

DESCRIPTION
The **unlink**( ) function removes the link named by *path* from its directory and decrements the link count of the file which was referenced by the link. If that decrement reduces the link count of the file to zero, and no process has the file open, then all resources associated with the file are reclaimed. If one or more process have the file open when the last link is removed, the link is removed, but the removal of the file is delayed until all references to it have been closed.

RETURN VALUES
Upon successful completion, a value of 0 is returned. Otherwise, a value of -1 is returned and *errno* is set to indicate the error.

ERRORS
The **unlink**( ) succeeds unless:

[ENOTDIR]	A component of the path prefix is not a directory.
[EINVAL]	The pathname contains a character with the high-order bit set.
[ENAMETOOLONG]	A component of a pathname exceeded 255 characters, or an entire path name exceeded 1023 characters.
[ENOENT]	The named file does not exist.
[EACCES]	Search permission is denied for a component of the path prefix.
[EACCES]	Write permission is denied on the directory containing the link to be removed.
[ELOOP]	Too many symbolic links were encountered in translating the pathname.
[EPERM]	The named file is a directory and the effective user ID of the process is not the super-user.
[EPERM]	The directory containing the file is marked sticky, and neither the containing directory nor the file to be removed are owned by the effective user ID.
[EBUSY]	The entry to be unlinked is the mount point for a mounted file system.
[EIO]	An I/O error occurred while deleting the directory entry or deallocating the inode.
[EROFS]	The named file resides on a read-only file system.
[EFAULT]	*Path* points outside the process's allocated address space.

SEE ALSO
close(2), link(2), rmdir(2) symlink(7)

HISTORY
     An `unlink` function call appeared in Version 6 AT&T UNIX.

NAME

utimes – set file access and modification times

SYNOPSIS

`#include <sys/time.h>`

int
utimes(*const char *file, const struct timeval *times*);

DESCRIPTION

The **utimes**( ) function sets the access and modification times of the named file from the structures in the argument array *times*.

The first structure is the access time, and the second is the modification time.

If the times are specified (the *times* argument is non-NULL) the caller must be the owner of the file or be the super-user.

If the times are not specified (the *times* argument is NULL) the caller must be the owner of the file, have permission to write the file, or be the super-user.

RETURN VALUES

Upon successful completion, a value of 0 is returned. Otherwise, a value of -1 is returned and *errno* is set to indicate the error.

ERRORS

Utimes( ) will fail if:

[EACCES]   Search permission is denied for a component of the path prefix; or the *times* argument is NULL and the effective user ID of the process does not match the owner of the file, and is not the super-user, and write access is denied.

[EFAULT]   File or *times* points outside the process's allocated address space.

[EINVAL]   The pathname contains a character with the high-order bit set.

[EIO]   An I/O error occurred while reading or writing the affected inode.

[ELOOP]   Too many symbolic links were encountered in translating the pathname.

[ENAMETOOLONG]
             A component of a pathname exceeded 255 characters, or an entire path name exceeded 1023 characters.

[ENOENT]   The named file does not exist.

[ENOTDIR]   A component of the path prefix is not a directory.

[EPERM]   The *times* argument is not NULL and the calling process's effective user ID does not match the owner of the file and is not the super-user.

[EROFS]   The file system containing the file is mounted read-only.

SEE ALSO

stat(2)

2

HISTORY
The `utimes` function call appeared in 4.2BSD.

NAME
`vfork` – spawn new process in a virtual memory efficient way

SYNOPSIS
`#include <unistd.h>`

int
vfork(*void*);

DESCRIPTION
Vfork( ) can be used to create new processes without fully copying the address space of the old process, which is horrendously inefficient in a paged environment. It is useful when the purpose of `fork`(2) would have been to create a new system context for an `execve`. **Vfork**( ) differs from `fork` in that the child borrows the parent's memory and thread of control until a call to `execve`(2) or an exit (either by a call to `exit`(2) or abnormally.) The parent process is suspended while the child is using its resources.

Vfork( ) returns 0 in the child's context and (later) the pid of the child in the parent's context.

Vfork( ) can normally be used just like `fork`. It does not work, however, to return while running in the childs context from the procedure that called **vfork**( ) since the eventual return from **vfork**( ) would then return to a no longer existent stack frame. Be careful, also, to call `_exit` rather than `exit` if you can't `execve`, since `exit` will flush and close standard I/O channels, and thereby mess up the parent processes standard I/O data structures. (Even with `fork` it is wrong to call `exit` since buffered data would then be flushed twice.)

SEE ALSO
`fork`(2), `execve`(2), `sigvec`(2), `wait`(2),

DIAGNOSTICS
Same as for `fork`.

BUGS
This system call will be eliminated when proper system sharing mechanisms are implemented. Users should not depend on the memory sharing semantics of `vfork` as it will, in that case, be made synonymous to `fork`.

To avoid a possible deadlock situation, processes that are children in the middle of a **vfork**( ) are never sent `SIGTTOU` or `SIGTTIN` signals; rather, output or `ioctl`(2) calls are allowed and input attempts result in an end-of-file indication.

HISTORY
The **vfork** function call appeared in 3.0BSD.

2

NAME
wait, waitpid, wait4, wait3 – wait for process termination

SYNOPSIS
```
#include <sys/types.h>
#include <sys/wait.h>
```
pid_t
wait(*int *status*);

```
#include <sys/time.h>
#include <sys/resource.h>
```
pid_t
waitpid(*pid_t wpid, int *status, int options*);

pid_t
wait3(*int *status, int options, struct rusage *rusage*);

pid_t
wait4(*pid_t wpid, int *status, int options, struct rusage *rusage*);

DESCRIPTION
The **wait**( ) function suspends execution of its calling process until *status* information is available for a terminated child process, or a signal is received. On return from a successful **wait**( ) call, the *status* area contains termination information about the process that exited as defined below.

The **wait4**( ) call provides a more general interface for programs that need to wait for certain child processes, that need resource utilization statistics accumulated by child processes, or that require options. The other wait functions are implemented using **wait4**().

The *wpid* parameter specifies the set of child processes for which to wait. If *wpid* is -1, the call waits for any child process. If *wpid* is 0, the call waits for any child process in the process group of the caller. If *wpid* is greater than zero, the call waits for the process with process id *wpid*. If *wpid* is less than -1, the call waits for any process whose process group id equals the absolute value of *wpid*.

The *status* parameter is defined below. The *options* parameter contains the bitwise OR of any of the following options. The WNOHANG option is used to indicate that the call should not block if there are no processes that wish to report status. If the WUNTRACED option is set, children of the current process that are stopped due to a SIGTTIN, SIGTTOU, SIGTSTP, or SIGSTOP signal also have their status reported.

If *rusage* is non-zero, a summary of the resources used by the terminated process and all its children is returned (this information is currently not available for stopped processes).

When the WNOHANG option is specified and no processes wish to report status, **wait4**( ) returns a process id of 0.

The **waitpid**( ) call is identical to **wait4**( ) with an *rusage* value of zero. The older **wait3**( ) call is the same as **wait4**( ) with a *wpid* value of -1.

The following macros may be used to test the manner of exit of the process. One of the first three macros will evaluate to a non-zero (true) value:

WIFEXITED(*status*)
> True if the process terminated normally by a call to _exit(2) or exit(2).

2

WIFSIGNALED(*status*)
>   True if the process terminated due to receipt of a signal.

WIFSTOPPED(*status*)
>   True if the process has not terminated, but has stopped and can be restarted. This macro can be true only if the wait call specified the WUNTRACED option or if the child process is being traced (see ptrace(2)).

Depending on the values of those macros, the following macros produce the remaining status information about the child process:

WEXITSTATUS(*status*)
>   If **WIFEXITED**(*status*) is true, evaluates to the low-order 8 bits of the argument passed to _exit(2) or exit(2) by the child.

WTERMSIG(*status*)
>   If **WIFSIGNALED**(*status*) is true, evaluates to the number of the signal that caused the termination of the process.

WCOREDUMP(*status*)
>   If **WIFSIGNALED**(*status*) is true, evaluates as true if the termination of the process was accompanied by the creation of a core file containing an image of the process when the signal was received.

WSTOPSIG(*status*)
>   If **WIFSTOPPED**(*status*) is true, evaluates to the number of the signal that caused the process to stop.

NOTES

See sigaction(2) for a list of termination signals. A status of 0 indicates normal termination.

If a parent process terminates without waiting for all of its child processes to terminate, the remaining child processes are assigned the parent process 1 ID (the init process ID).

If a signal is caught while any of the **wait**( ) calls is pending, the call may be interrupted or restarted when the signal-catching routine returns, depending on the options in effect for the signal; see intro(2), System call restart.

RETURN VALUES

If **wait**( ) returns due to a stopped or terminated child process, the process ID of the child is returned to the calling process. Otherwise, a value of -1 is returned and *errno* is set to indicate the error.

If **wait4**(), **wait3**( ) or **waitpid**( ) returns due to a stopped or terminated child process, the process ID of the child is returned to the calling process. If there are no children not previously awaited, -1 is returned with *errno* set to [ECHILD]. Otherwise, if WNOHANG is specified and there are no stopped or exited children, 0 is returned. If an error is detected or a caught signal aborts the call, a value of -1 is returned and *errno* is set to indicate the error.

ERRORS

Wait( ) will fail and return immediately if:

[ECHILD]   The calling process has no existing unwaited-for child processes.

[EFAULT]   The *status* or *rusage* arguments point to an illegal address. (May not be detected before exit of a child process.)

2

[EINTR]   The call was interrupted by a caught signal, or the signal did not have the SA_RESTART flag set.

STANDARDS

The wait() and waitpid() functions are defined by POSIX; wait4() and wait3() are not specified by POSIX. The WCOREDUMP() macro and the ability to restart a pending wait() call are extensions to the POSIX interface.

SEE ALSO

exit(2), sigaction(2)

HISTORY

A wait function call appeared in Version 6 AT&T UNIX.

2

NAME
write, writev – write output

SYNOPSIS
```
#include <sys/types.h>
#include <sys/uio.h>
#include <unistd.h>
```

ssize_t
write(*int d, const void *buf, size_t nbytes*);

ssize_t
writev(*int d, const struct iovec *iov, int iovcnt*);

DESCRIPTION
Write( ) attempts to write *nbytes* of data to the object referenced by the descriptor *d* from the buffer pointed to by *buf*. **Writev**( ) performs the same action, but gathers the output data from the *iovcnt* buffers specified by the members of the *iov* array: iov[0], iov[1], ..., iov[iovcnt‑1].

For **writev**(), the *iovec* structure is defined as:

```
struct iovec {
        void *iov_base;
        size_t iov_len;
};
```

Each *iovec* entry specifies the base address and length of an area in memory from which data should be written. **Writev**( ) will always write a complete area before proceeding to the next.

On objects capable of seeking, the **write**( ) starts at a position given by the pointer associated with *d*, see lseek(2). Upon return from **write**(), the pointer is incremented by the number of bytes which were written.

Objects that are not capable of seeking always write from the current position. The value of the pointer associated with such an object is undefined.

If the real user is not the super-user, then **write**( ) clears the set-user-id bit on a file. This prevents penetration of system security by a user who "captures" a writable set-user-id file owned by the super-user.

When using non-blocking I/O on objects such as sockets that are subject to flow control, **write**( ) and **writev**( ) may write fewer bytes than requested; the return value must be noted, and the remainder of the operation should be retried when possible.

RETURN VALUES
Upon successful completion the number of bytes which were written is returned. Otherwise a -1 is returned and the global variable *errno* is set to indicate the error.

ERRORS
Write( ) and **writev**( ) will fail and the file pointer will remain unchanged if:

[EBADF]   *D* is not a valid descriptor open for writing.

[EPIPE]   An attempt is made to write to a pipe that is not open for reading by any process.

2

[EPIPE]   An attempt is made to write to a socket of type that is not connected to a peer socket.

[EFBIG]   An attempt was made to write a file that exceeds the process's file size limit or the maximum file size.

[EFAULT]   Part of *iov* or data to be written to the file points outside the process's allocated address space.

[EINVAL]   The pointer associated with *d* was negative.

[ENOSPC]   There is no free space remaining on the file system containing the file.

[EDQUOT]   The user's quota of disk blocks on the file system containing the file has been exhausted.

[EIO]   An I/O error occurred while reading from or writing to the file system.

[EAGAIN]   The file was marked for non-blocking I/O, and no data could be written immediately.

In addition, **writev**( ) may return one of the following errors:

[EINVAL]   *Iovcnt* was less than or equal to 0, or greater than UIO_MAXIOV.

[EINVAL]   One of the *iov_len* values in the *iov* array was negative.

[EINVAL]   The sum of the *iov_len* values in the *iov* array overflowed a 32-bit integer.

SEE ALSO
fcntl(2), lseek(2), open(2), pipe(2), select(2)

STANDARDS
Write( ) is expected to conform to IEEE Std 1003.1-1988 (''POSIX'').

HISTORY
The **writev**( ) function call appeared in 4.2BSD. A **write** function call appeared in Version 6 AT&T UNIX.

Section 3

C-Library
Subroutines

NAME
intro – introduction to the C libraries

DESCRIPTION
This section provides an overview of the C library functions, their error returns and other common definitions and concepts. Most of these functions are available from the C library, *libc* (see libc(3)). Other libraries, such as the math library, *libm*, must be indicated at compile time with the −1 option of the compiler.

A subset of the libc(functions) are available from Fortran; they are described separately in intro(3f).

The various libraries (followed by the loader flag):

libc(−lc)　　　Standard C library functions. (See libc(3).) When using the C compiler cc(1), it is not necessary to supply the loader flag −lc for these functions. There are several 'libraries' or groups of functions included inside of libc: the standard I/O routines, database routines, bit operators, string operators, character tests and character operators, des encryption routines, storage allocation, time functions, signal handling and more.

libcurses(−lcurses −ltermcap)
　　　　　　Terminal independent screen management routines for two dimensional non-bitmap display terminals. (See curses(3).)

libcompat(−lcompat)
　　　　　　Functions which are obsolete but are available for compatibility with 4.3BSD. In particular, a number of system call interfaces provided in previous releases of BSD have been included for source code compatibility. Use of these routines should, for the most part, be avoided. The manual page entry for each compatibility routine indicates the proper interface to use.

libl(−ll)　　The library for lex(1).

libm(−lm)　　The math library, *libm*. The math library is loaded as needed by the Pascal compiler pc(1), but not by the C compiler which requires the −lm flag. (See math(3).)

libmp(−lmp)

libplot(−lplot)
　　　　　　Device independent plotting functions. (See plot(3).)

libplotf77(−lplotf77)
　　　　　　The device independent plotting functions for fortran. (See plot(3).)

libtermcap−ltermcap
　　　　　　The terminal independent operation library package. (See termcap(3).)

liby(−ly)　　The library for yacc(1).

FILES
/usr/lib/libc.a　　the C library
/usr/lib/libm.a　　the math library
/usr/lib/libc_p.a the C library compiled for profiling
/usr/lib/libm_p.a the math library compiled for profiling

SEE ALSO
stdio(3), math(3), intro(2), cc(1), ld(1), nm(1)

HISTORY
　　　　An `intro` manual appeared in Version 7 AT&T UNIX.

3

NAME

abort – cause abnormal program termination

SYNOPSIS

#include <stdlib.h>

void
abort(void);

DESCRIPTION

The abort() function causes abnormal program termination to occur, unless the signal SIGABRT is being caught and the signal handler does not return.

No open streams are closed or flushed.

RETURN VALUES

The abort function never returns.

SEE ALSO

sigaction(2), exit(2)

STANDARDS

The abort() function conforms to ANSI C X3.159-1989 (''ANSI C '').

NAME

abs – integer absolute value function

SYNOPSIS

`#include <stdlib.h>`

int
abs(*int j*);

DESCRIPTION

The **abs**( ) function computes the absolute value of the integer *j*.

RETURN VALUES

The **abs**( ) function returns the absolute value.

SEE ALSO

floor(3), labs(3) cabs(3) hypot(3) math(3)

STANDARDS

The **abs**( ) function conforms to ANSI C X3.159-1989 (''ANSI C '').

BUGS

The absolute value of the most negative integer remains negative.

3

NAME

    acl_canonicalize_principal, acl_check, acl_exact_match, acl_add, acl_delete, acl_initialize – access control list routines

SYNOPSIS

    cc <files> –lacl –lkrb

    #include <krb.h>

    acl_canonicalize_principal(principal, buf)
    char ∗principal;
    char ∗buf;

    acl_check(acl, principal)
    char ∗acl;
    char ∗principal;

    acl_exact_match(acl, principal)
    char ∗acl;
    char ∗principal;

    acl_add(acl, principal)
    char ∗acl;
    char ∗principal;

    acl_delete(acl, principal)
    char ∗acl;
    char ∗principal;

    acl_initialize(acl_file, mode)
    char ∗acl_file;
    int mode;

DESCRIPTION

    Introduction

    An access control list (ACL) is a list of principals, where each principal is represented by a text string which cannot contain whitespace. The library allows application programs to refer to named access control lists to test membership and to atomically add and delete principals using a natural and intuitive interface. At present, the names of access control lists are required to be Unix filenames, and refer to human-readable Unix files; in the future, when a networked ACL server is implemented, the names may refer to a different namespace specific to the ACL service.

    Principal Names

    Principal names have the form
        <name>[.<instance>][@<realm>]
    e.g.:

        asp
        asp.root
        asp@ATHENA.MIT.EDU
        asp.@ATHENA.MIT.EDU
        asp.root@ATHENA.MIT.EDU

    It is possible for principals to be underspecified. If an instance is missing, it is assumed to be "". If realm is missing, it is assumed to be the local realm as determined by *krb_get_lrealm*(3). The canonical form contains all of name, instance, and realm; the acl_add and acl_delete routines will always leave the file in that form. Note that the canonical form of asp@ATHENA.MIT.EDU is actually asp.@ATHENA.MIT.EDU.

Routines

acl_canonicalize_principal stores the canonical form of *principal* in *buf*. *Buf* must contain enough space to store a principal, given the limits on the sizes of name, instance, and realm specified as ANAME_SZ, INST_SZ, and REALM_SZ, respectively, in */usr/include/krb.h*.

acl_check returns nonzero if *principal* appears in *acl*. Returns 0 if principal does not appear in acl, or if an error occurs. Canonicalizes principal before checking, and allows the ACL to contain wildcards. The only supported wildcards are entries of the form name.*@realm, *.*@realm, and *.*@*. An asterisk matches any value for its component field. For example, "jtkohl.*@*" would match principal jtkohl, with any instance and any realm.

acl_exact_match performs like *acl_check*, but does no canonicalization or wildcard matching.

acl_add atomically adds *principal* to *acl*. Returns 0 if successful, nonzero otherwise. It is considered a failure if *principal* is already in *acl*. This routine will canonicalize *principal*, but will treat wildcards literally.

acl_delete atomically deletes *principal* from *acl*. Returns 0 if successful, nonzero otherwise. It is considered a failure if *principal* is not already in *acl*. This routine will canonicalize *principal*, but will treat wildcards literally.

acl_initialize initializes *acl_file*. If the file *acl_file* does not exist, *acl_initialize* creates it with mode *mode*. If the file *acl_file* exists, *acl_initialize* removes all members. Returns 0 if successful, nonzero otherwise. WARNING: Mode argument is likely to change with the eventual introduction of an ACL service.

NOTES

In the presence of concurrency, there is a very small chance that *acl_add* or *acl_delete* could report success even though it would have had no effect. This is a necessary side effect of using lock files for concurrency control rather than flock(2), which is not supported by NFS.

The current implementation caches ACLs in memory in a hash-table format for increased efficiency in checking membership; one effect of the caching scheme is that one file descriptor will be kept open for each ACL cached, up to a maximum of 8.

SEE ALSO

kerberos(3), krb_get_lrealm(3)

AUTHOR

James Aspnes (MIT Project Athena)

NAME

acos – arc cosine function

SYNOPSIS

```
#include <math.h>
```

double
acos(*double x*);

DESCRIPTION

The **acos**() function computes the principal value of the arc cosine of *x*. A domain error occurs for arguments not in the range [-1, +1]. For a discussion of error due to roundoff, see math(3).

RETURN VALUES

The **acos**() function returns the arc cosine in the range $[0, \pi]$ radians. On the VAX and Tahoe, if:

$|x| > 1,$

acos(*x*) sets the global variable *errno* to EDOM and a reserved operand fault is generated.

SEE ALSO

sin(3), cos(3), tan(3), asin(3), atan(3), atan2(3), sinh(3), cosh(3), tanh(3), math(3),

STANDARDS

The **acos**() function conforms to ANSI C X3.159-1989 (''ANSI C '').

NAME

acosh – inverse hyperbolic cosine function

SYNOPSIS

`#include <math.h>`

double
`acosh(`*double x*`)`;

DESCRIPTION

The `acosh()` function computes the inverse hyperbolic cosine of the real argument x. For a discussion of error due to roundoff, see `math(3)`.

RETURN VALUES

The `acosh()` function returns the inverse hyperbolic cosine of x. On the VAX and Tahoe, if the argument is less than one `acosh()` sets the global variable *errno* to EDOM and causes a reserved operand fault.

SEE ALSO

asinh(3), atanh(3), exp(3), infnan(3) math(3),

HISTORY

The `acosh()` function appeared in 4.3BSD.

NAME

alarm – set signal timer alarm

SYNOPSIS

```
#include <unistd.h>

u_int
alarm(u_int seconds);
```

DESCRIPTION

This interface is made obsolete by setitimer(2).

The alarm() function waits a count of *seconds* before asserting the terminating signal SIGALRM. When the signal has successfully been caught, alarm() returns the amount of time left on the clock. The maximum number of *seconds* allowed is 2147483647.

If an alarm has been set with alarm(), another call to alarm() will supersede the prior call. The request alarm(*0*) voids the current alarm.

SEE ALSO

sigaction(2), setitimer(2), sigpause(2), sigvec(2), signal(3), sleep(3), ualarm(3), usleep(3)

HISTORY

An alarm() function appeared in Version 7 AT&T UNIX.

NAME

    alloca – memory allocator

SYNOPSIS

    #include <stdlib.h>

    void *

    alloca(*size_t size*);

DESCRIPTION

    The alloca() function allocates *size* bytes of space in the stack frame of the caller. This temporary space is automatically freed on return.

RETURN VALUES

    The alloca() function returns a pointer to the beginning of the allocated space. If the allocation failed, a NULL pointer is returned.

SEE ALSO

    brk(2), pagesize(2) calloc(3), malloc(3), realloc(3),

BUGS

    The alloca() function is machine dependent; its use is discouraged.

NAME

`asin` – arc sine function

SYNOPSIS

`#include <math.h>`

double
`asin(`*double x*`);`

DESCRIPTION

The `asin()` function computes the principal value of the arc sine of *x*. A domain error occurs for arguments not in the range [-1, +1]. For a discussion of error due to roundoff, see `math(3)`.

RETURN VALUES

The `asin()` function returns the arc sine in the range [-π/2, +π/2] radians. On the VAX, and Tahoe , if:

$|x| > 1$

the global variable *errno* is set to EDOM and a reserved operand fault generated.

SEE ALSO

acos(3), atan(3), atan2(3), cos(3), cosh(3), sin(3), sinh(3), tan(3), tanh(3), math(3),

STANDARDS

The `asin()` function conforms to ANSI C X3.159-1989 (''ANSI C '').

NAME
asinh – inverse hyperbolic sine function

SYNOPSIS
`#include <math.h>`

double
`asinh`(*double x*);

DESCRIPTION
The `asinh`( ) function computes the inverse hyperbolic sine of the real argument x. For a discussion of error due to roundoff, see math(3).

RETURN VALUES
The `asinh`( ) function returns the inverse hyperbolic sine of x.

SEE ALSO
acosh(3), atanh(3), exp(3), infnan(3) math(3),

HISTORY
The `asinh`( ) function appeared in 4.3BSD.

NAME

　　　assert – expression verification macro

SYNOPSIS

　　　#include ⟨assert.h⟩

　　　assert(*expression*);

DESCRIPTION

　　　The assert( ) macro tests the given *expression* and if it is false, the calling process is terminated. A diagnostic message is written to the *stderr* and the function _exit(2) is called effectively terminating the program.

　　　If *expression* is true, the assert( ) macro does nothing.

　　　The assert( ) macro may be removed at compile time with the −**NDEBUG** option, see cc(1).

DIAGNOSTICS

　　　The following diagnostic message is written to *stderr* if *expression* is false:

```
"assertion \"%s\" failed: file \"%s\", line %d0, \
                "expression", __FILE__, __LINE__);
```

HISTORY

　　　A assert macro appeared in Version 6 AT&T UNIX.

NAME

`atan` – arc tangent function of one variable

SYNOPSIS

`#include <math.h>`

double
`atan(`*double x*`);`

DESCRIPTION

The `atan()` function computes the principal value of the arc tangent of *x*. For a discussion of error due to roundoff, see `math`(3).

RETURN VALUES

The `atan()` function returns the arc tangent in the range [-π/2, +π/2] radians.

SEE ALSO

`acos`(3), `asin`(3), `atan2`(3), `cos`(3), `cosh`(3), `sin`(3), `sinh`(3), `tan`(3), `tanh`(3), `math`(3),

STANDARDS

The `atan()` function conforms to ANSI C X3.159-1989 (''ANSI C '').

NAME

atan2 – arc tangent function of two variables

SYNOPSIS

```
#include <math.h>
```

double
atan2(*double y, double x*);

DESCRIPTION

The atan2 function computes the principal value of the arc tangent of y/x, using the signs of both arguments to determine the quadrant of the return value.

RETURN VALUES

The atan2 function, if successful, returns the arc tangent of y/x in the range $[-\pi, +\pi]$ radians. If both x and y are zero, the global variable *errno* is set to EDOM. On the VAX:

$$atan2(y, x) := \begin{cases} atan(y/x) & \text{if } x > 0, \\ sign(y)*(\pi - atan(|y/x|)) & \text{if } x < 0, \\ 0 & \text{if } x = y = 0, \text{ or} \\ sign(y)*\pi/2 & \text{if } x = 0 \ y. \end{cases}$$

NOTES

The function **atan2()** defines "if x > 0," **atan2**($0, 0$) = 0 on a VAX despite that previously **atan2**($0, 0$) may have generated an error message. The reasons for assigning a value to **atan2**($0, 0$) are these:

1. Programs that test arguments to avoid computing **atan2**($0, 0$) must be indifferent to its value. Programs that require it to be invalid are vulnerable to diverse reactions to that invalidity on diverse computer systems.

2. The **atan2()** function is used mostly to convert from rectangular (x,y) to polar (r,θ) coordinates that must satisfy x = r*cosθ and y = r*sinθ. These equations are satisfied when (x=0,y=0) is mapped to (r=0,θ=0) on a VAX. In general, conversions to polar coordinates should be computed thus:

    r   := hypot(x,y); ... := $\sqrt{(x^2+y^2)}$
    θ   := atan2(y,x).

3. The foregoing formulas need not be altered to cope in a reasonable way with signed zeros and infinities on a machine that conforms to IEEE 754; the versions of hypot(3) and **atan2()** provided for such a machine are designed to handle all cases. That is why **atan2**($\pm0, -0$) = $\pm\pi$ for instance. In general the formulas above are equivalent to these:

    r := $\sqrt{(x*x+y*y)}$;   if r = 0 then x := copysign(1,x);

SEE ALSO

acos(3), asin(3), atan(3), cos(3), cosh(3), sin(3), sinh(3), tan(3), tanh(3), math(3),

STANDARDS

The **atan2()** function conforms to ANSI C X3.159-1989 (''ANSI C '').

NAME
atanh – inverse hyperbolic tangent function

SYNOPSIS
`#include <math.h>`

double
atanh(*double x*);

DESCRIPTION
The **atanh**( ) function computes the inverse hyperbolic tangent of the real argument *x*. For a discussion of error due to roundoff, see `math`(3).

RETURN VALUES
The **atanh**( ) function returns the inverse hyperbolic tangent of *x* if successful. On the VAX and Tahoe, if the argument has absolute value bigger than or equal to 1, **atanh**( ) sets the global variable *errno* to EDOM and a reserved operand fault is generated.

SEE ALSO
`acosh`(3), `asinh`(3), `exp`(3), `infnan`(3) `math`(3),

HISTORY
The **atanh**( ) function appeared in 4.3BSD.

NAME
atexit – register a function to be called on exit

SYNOPSIS
`#include <stdlib.h>`

int
`atexit(`*void (*function)(void)*`)`;

DESCRIPTION
The `atexit()` function registers the given *function* to be called at program exit, whether via exit(3) or via return from the program's *main*. Functions so registered are called in reverse order; no arguments are passed. At least 32 functions can always be registered, and more are allowed as long as sufficient memory can be allocated.

RETURN VALUES
The `atexit()` function returns the value 0 if successful; otherwise the value -1 is returned and the global variable *errno* is set to indicate the error.

ERRORS
[ENOMEM]　No memory was available to add the function to the list. The existing list of functions is unmodified.

SEE ALSO
exit(3)

STANDARDS
The `atexit()` function conforms to ANSI C X3.159-1989 (''ANSI C '').

NAME
　　　atof – convert ASCII string to double

SYNOPSIS
　　　#include ⟨stdlib.h⟩

　　　double
　　　atof(*const char *nptr*);

DESCRIPTION
　　　The **atof**( ) function converts the initial portion of the string pointed to by *nptr* to *double* representation.

　　　It is equivalent to:

　　　　　strtod(nptr, (char **)NULL);

SEE ALSO
　　　atoi(3), atol(3), strtod(3), strtol(3), strtoul(3)

STANDARDS
　　　The **atof**( ) function conforms to ANSI C X3.159-1989 (''ANSI C '').

BUGS
　　　This manual page represents intent instead of actual practice. While it is intended that **atof**( ) be imple-
　　　mented using strtod(3), this has not yet happened. In the current system, **atof**( ) translates a string in
　　　the following form to a double: a string of leading white space, possibly followed by a sign (''+'' or ''-''),
　　　followed by a digit string which may contain one decimal point (''.''), which may be followed by either of
　　　the exponent flags (''E'' or ''e''), and lastly, followed by a signed or unsigned integer.

NAME
atoi – convert ASCII string to integer

SYNOPSIS
`#include <stdlib.h>`

int
`atoi(`*const char *nptr*`)`;

DESCRIPTION
The `atoi`() function converts the initial portion of the string pointed to by *nptr* to *integer* representation.

It is equivalent to:

```
(int)strtol(nptr, (char **)NULL, 10);
```

SEE ALSO
atof(3), atol(3), strtod(3), strtol(3), strtoul(3)

STANDARDS
The `atoi`() function conforms to ANSI C X3.159-1989 (''ANSI C '').

NAME

`atol` – convert ASCII string to long integer

SYNOPSIS

`#include <stdlib.h>`

long
`atol(const char *nptr)`;

DESCRIPTION

The `atol()` function converts the initial portion of the string pointed to by *nptr* to *long integer* representation.

It is equivalent to:

```
strtol(nptr, (char **)NULL, 10);
```

SEE ALSO

`atof`(3), `atoi`(3), `strtod`(3), `strtol`(3), `strtoul`(3)

STANDARDS

The `atol()` function conforms to ANSI C X3.159-1989 (''ANSI C '').

NAME

    bcmp – compare byte string

SYNOPSIS

    `#include <string.h>`

    int
    bcmp(*const void *b1, const void *b2, size_t len*);

DESCRIPTION

    The **bcmp**( ) function compares byte string *b1* against byte string *b2*, returning zero if they are identical, non-zero otherwise. Both strings are assumed to be *len* bytes long. Zero-length strings are always identical.

    The strings may overlap.

SEE ALSO

    bcmp(3), memcmp(3), strcasecmp(3), strcmp(3), strcoll(3), strxfrm(3)

HISTORY

    A **bcmp**( ) function first appeared in 4.2BSD.

NAME
bcopy – copy byte string

SYNOPSIS
`#include <string.h>`

void
bcopy(*const void *src*, *void *dst*, *size_t len*);

DESCRIPTION
The **bcopy**( ) function copies *len* bytes from string *src* to string *dst*. The two strings may overlap. If *len* is zero, no bytes are copied.

SEE ALSO
memccpy(3), memcpy(3), memmove(3), strcpy(3), strncpy(3)

HISTORY
A **bcopy**( ) function appeared in 4.2BSD.

NAME

bit_alloc, bit_clear, bit_decl, bit_ffs, bit_nclear, bit_nset, bit_set, bitstr_size, bit_test – bit-string manipulation macros

SYNOPSIS

```
#include <bitstring.h>
```

```
bitstr_t *
bit_alloc(int nbits);
```

```
bit_decl(bit_str name, int nbits);
```

```
bit_clear(bit_str name, int bit);
```

```
bit_ffc(bit_str name, int nbits, int *value);
```

```
bit_ffs(bit_str name, int nbits, int *value);
```

```
bit_nclear(bit_str name, int start, int stop);
```

```
bit_nset(bit_str name, int start, int stop);
```

```
bit_set(bit_str name, int bit);
```

```
bitstr_size(int nbits);
```

```
bit_test(bit_str name, int bit);
```

DESCRIPTION

These macros operate on strings of bits.

The macro bit_alloc() returns a pointer of type "bitstr_t *" to sufficient space to store nbits bits, or NULL if no space is available.

The macro bit_decl() allocates sufficient space to store nbits bits on the stack.

The macro bitstr_size() returns the number of elements of type bitstr_t necessary to store nbits bits. This is useful for copying bit strings.

The macros bit_clear() and bit_set() clear or set the zero-based numbered bit bit, in the bit string name.

The bit_nset() and bit_nclear() macros set or clear the zero-based numbered bits from start to stop in the bit string name.

The bit_test() macro evaluates to non-zero if the zero-based numbered bit bit of bit string name is set, and zero otherwise.

The bit_ffs() macro stores in the location referenced by value the zero-based number of the first bit set in the array of nbits bits referenced by name. If no bits are set, the location referenced by value is set to −1.

The macro bit_ffc() stores in the location referenced by value the zero-based number of the first bit not set in the array of nbits bits referenced by name. If all bits are set, the location referenced by value is set to −1.

The arguments to these macros are evaluated only once and may safely have side effects.

EXAMPLE

```
#include <limits.h>
#include <bitstring.h>

#define LPR_BUSY_BIT          0
#define LPR_FORMAT_BIT        1
#define LPR_DOWNLOAD_BIT      2
#define LPR_AVAILABLE_BIT     9
#define LPR_MAX_BITS          10

make_lpr_available()
{
        bitstr_t bit_decl(bitlist, LPR_MAX_BITS);
        ...
        bit_nclear(bitlist, 0, LPR_MAX_BITS - 1);
        ...
        if (!bit_test(bitlist, LPR_BUSY_BIT)) {
                bit_clear(bitlist, LPR_FORMAT_BIT);
                bit_clear(bitlist, LPR_DOWNLOAD_BIT);
                bit_set(bitlist, LPR_AVAILABLE_BIT);
        }
}
```

SEE ALSO

malloc(3)

HISTORY

The **bitstring** functions first appeared in 4.4BSD.

3

NAME

bsearch – binary search of a sorted table

SYNOPSIS

```
#include <stdlib.h>
```

void *
bsearch(*const void *key, const void *base, size_t nmemb, size_t size,*
        int (*compar) (const void *, const void *));

DESCRIPTION

The **bsearch**() function searches an array of *nmemb* objects, the initial member of which is pointed to by *base*, for a member that matches the object pointed to by *key*. The size of each member of the array is specified by *size*.

The contents of the array should be in ascending sorted order according to the comparison function referenced by *compar*. The *compar* routine is expected to have two arguments which point to the *key* object and to an array member, in that order, and should return an integer less than, equal to, or greater than zero if the *key* object is found, respectively, to be less than, to match, or be greater than the array member.

RETURN VALUES

The **bsearch**() function returns a pointer to a matching member of the array, or a null pointer if no match is found. If two members compare as equal, which member is matched is unspecified.

SEE ALSO

db(3), lsearch(3), qsort(3),

STANDARDS

The **bsearch**() function conforms to ANSI C X3.159-1989 (''ANSI C '').

NAME
bcmp, bcopy, bzero, memccpy, memchr, memcmp, memcpy, memmove, memset – byte string operations

SYNOPSIS
#include <string.h>

int
bcmp(*const void *b1, const void *b2, size_t len*);

void
bcopy(*const void *src, void *dst, size_t len*);

void
bzero(*void *b, size_t len*);

*void **
memchr(*const void *b, int c, size_t len*);

int
memcmp(*const void *b1, const void *b2, size_t len*);

*void **
memccpy(*void *dst, const void *src, int c, size_t len*);

*void **
memcpy(*void *dst, const void *src, size_t len*);

*void **
memmove(*void *dst, const void *src, size_t len*);

*void **
memset(*void *b, int c, size_t len*);

DESCRIPTION
These functions operate on variable length strings of bytes. They do not check for terminating null bytes as the routines listed in string(3) do.

See the specific manual pages for more information.

SEE ALSO
bcmp(3), bcopy(3), bzero(3), memccpy(3), memchr(3), memcmp(3), memcpy(3), memmove(3), memset(3)

STANDARDS
The functions **memchr**(), **memcmp**(), **memcpy**(), **memmove**(), and **memset**() conform to ANSI C X3.159-1989 (''ANSI C '').

HISTORY
The functions **bzero**() and **memccpy**() appeared in 4.3BSD; the functions **bcmp**(), **bcopy**(), appeared in 4.2BSD.

NAME

    btree – btree database access method

SYNOPSIS

    #include <sys/types.h>
    #include <db.h>

DESCRIPTION

The routine *dbopen* is the library interface to database files. One of the supported file formats is btree files. The general description of the database access methods is in *dbopen*(3), this manual page describes only the btree specific information.

The btree data structure is a sorted, balanced tree structure storing associated key/data pairs.

The btree access method specific data structure provided to *dbopen* is defined in the <db.h> include file as follows:

```
typedef struct {
        u_long flags;
        u_int cachesize;
        int maxkeypage;
        int minkeypage;
        u_int psize;
        int (*compare)(const DBT *key1, const DBT *key2);
        size_t (*prefix)(const DBT *key1, const DBT *key2);
        int lorder;
} BTREEINFO;
```

The elements of this structure are as follows:

flags   The flag value is specified by *or*'ing any of the following values:

    R_DUP Permit duplicate keys in the tree, i.e. permit insertion if the key to be inserted already exists in the tree. The default behavior, as described in *dbopen*(3), is to overwrite a matching key when inserting a new key or to fail if the R_NOOVERWRITE flag is specified. The R_DUP flag is overridden by the R_NOOVERWRITE flag, and if the R_NOOVERWRITE flag is specified, attempts to insert duplicate keys into the tree will fail.

        If the database contains duplicate keys, the order of retrieval of key/data pairs is undefined if the *get* routine is used, however, *seq* routine calls with the R_CURSOR flag set will always return the logical ''first'' of any group of duplicate keys.

cachesize

    A suggested maximum size (in bytes) of the memory cache. This value is **only** advisory, and the access method will allocate more memory rather than fail. Since every search examines the root page of the tree, caching the most recently used pages substantially improves access time. In addition, physical writes are delayed as long as possible, so a moderate cache can reduce the number of I/O operations significantly. Obviously, using a cache increases (but only increases) the likelihood of corruption or lost data if the system crashes while a tree is being modified. If *cachesize* is 0 (no size is specified) a default cache is used.

maxkeypage

    The maximum number of keys which will be stored on any single page. Not currently implemented.

minkeypage

    The minimum number of keys which will be stored on any single page. This value is used to determine which keys will be stored on overflow pages, i.e. if a key or data item is longer than the pagesize divided by the minkeypage value, it will be stored on overflow pages instead of in the page itself. If *minkeypage* is 0 (no minimum number of keys is specified) a value of 2 is used.

psize   Page size is the size (in bytes) of the pages used for nodes in the tree. The minimum page size is 512 bytes and the maximum page size is 64K. If *psize* is 0 (no page size is specified) a page size is chosen based on the underlying file system I/O block size.

compare
         Compare is the key comparison function. It must return an integer less than, equal to, or greater than zero if the first key argument is considered to be respectively less than, equal to, or greater than the second key argument. The same comparison function must be used on a given tree every time it is opened. If *compare* is NULL (no comparison function is specified), the keys are compared lexically, with shorter keys considered less than longer keys.

prefix   Prefix is the prefix comparison function. If specified, this routine must return the number of bytes of the second key argument which are necessary to determine that it is greater than the first key argument. If the keys are equal, the key length should be returned. Note, the usefulness of this routine is very data dependent, but, in some data sets can produce significantly reduced tree sizes and search times. If *prefix* is NULL (no prefix function is specified), **and** no comparison function is specified, a default lexical comparison routine is used. If *prefix* is NULL and a comparison routine is specified, no prefix comparison is done.

lorder   The byte order for integers in the stored database metadata. The number should represent the order as an integer; for example, big endian order would be the number 4,321. If *lorder* is 0 (no order is specified) the current host order is used.

If the file already exists (and the O_TRUNC flag is not specified), the values specified for the parameters flags, lorder and psize are ignored in favor of the values used when the tree was created.

Forward sequential scans of a tree are from the least key to the greatest.

Space freed up by deleting key/data pairs from the tree is never reclaimed, although it is normally made available for reuse. This means that the btree storage structure is grow-only. The only solutions are to avoid excessive deletions, or to create a fresh tree periodically from a scan of an existing one.

Searches, insertions, and deletions in a btree will all complete in O lg base N where base is the average fill factor. Often, inserting ordered data into btrees results in a low fill factor. This implementation has been modified to make ordered insertion the best case, resulting in a much better than normal page fill factor.

SEE ALSO
dbopen(3), *hash*(3), *mpool*(3), *recno*(3)

The Ubiquitous B-tree, Douglas Comer, ACM Comput. Surv. 11, 2 (June 1979), 121-138.

Prefix B-trees, Bayer and Unterauer, ACM Transactions on Database Systems, Vol. 2, 1 (March 1977), 11-26.

The Art of Computer Programming Vol. 3: Sorting and Searching, D.E. Knuth, 1968, pp 471-480.

BUGS
Only big and little endian byte order is supported.

NAME
　　　htonl, htons, ntohl, ntohs – convert values between host and network byte order

SYNOPSIS
　　　#include ⟨sys/param.h⟩

　　　u_long
　　　htonl(*u_long hostlong*);

　　　u_short
　　　htons(*u_short hostshort*);

　　　u_long
　　　ntohl(*u_long netlong*);

　　　u_short
　　　ntohs(*u_short netshort*);

DESCRIPTION
　　　These routines convert 16 and 32 bit quantities between network byte order and host byte order. On machines which have a byte order which is the same as the network order, routines are defined as null macros.

　　　These routines are most often used in conjunction with Internet addresses and ports as returned by gethostbyname(3) and getservent(3).

SEE ALSO
　　　gethostbyname(3), getservent(3)

HISTORY
　　　The **byteorder** functions appeared in 4.2BSD.

BUGS
　　　On the VAX bytes are handled backwards from most everyone else in the world. This is not expected to be fixed in the near future.

NAME

bzero – write zeroes to a byte string

SYNOPSIS

`#include <string.h>`

void
bzero(*void *b, size_t len*);

DESCRIPTION

The **bzero**( ) function writes *len* zero bytes to the string *b*. If *len* is zero, **bzero**( ) does nothing.

SEE ALSO

memset(3), swab(3)

HISTORY

A **bzero**( ) function appeared in 4.3BSD.

3

NAME
calloc – allocate clean memory (zero initialized space)

SYNOPSIS
`#include <stdlib.h>`

void *
`calloc(`*size_t nmemb*, *size_t size*`);`

DESCRIPTION
The `calloc()` function allocates space for an array of *nmemb* objects, each of whose size is *size*. The space is initialized to all bits zero.

RETURN VALUES
The `calloc()` function returns a pointer to the the allocated space if successful; otherwise a null pointer is returned.

SEE ALSO
`malloc(3)`, `realloc(3)`, `free(3)`,

STANDARDS
The `calloc()` function conforms to ANSI C X3.159-1989 (''ANSI C '').

NAME

`ceil` – smallest integral value not greater than x

SYNOPSIS

`#include <math.h>`

double
`ceil(`*double x*`)`;

DESCRIPTION

The `ceil( )` function computes the smallest integral value not less than x.

RETURN VALUES

The `ceil( )` function returns the smallest integral value expressed as a double.

SEE ALSO

`abs(3)`, `fabs(3)`, `floor(3)`, `rint(3)`, `ieee(3)`, `math.3`

STANDARDS

The `ceil( )` function conforms to ANSI C X3.159-1989 (''ANSI C '').

3

NAME
clock – determine processor time used

SYNOPSIS
```
#include <sys/types.h>
```

clock_t
clock(*void*);

DESCRIPTION
The clock( ) function determines the amount of processor time used since the invocation of the calling process, measured in CLK_TCKs.

RETURN VALUES
The clock( ) function returns the amount of time used unless an error occurs, in which case the return value is −1.

SEE ALSO
getrusage(2)

STANDARDS
The clock( ) function conforms to ANSI C X3.159-1989 ("ANSI C ").

NAME

confstr – get string-valued configurable variables

SYNOPSIS

```
#include <unistd.h>
```

size_t
confstr(int name, char *buf, size_t len);

DESCRIPTION

This interface is obsoleted by sysctl(3).

The confstr( ) function provides a method for applications to get configuration defined string values.

The *name* argument specifies the system variable to be queried. Symbolic constants for each name value are found in the include file <unistd.h>. The *len* argument specifies the size of the buffer referenced by the argument *buf*. If *len* is non-zero, *buf* is a non-null pointer, and *name* has a value, up to *len* − 1 bytes of the value are copied into the buffer *buf*. The copied value is always null terminated.

The available values are as follows:

_CS_PATH
　　　　Return a value for the PATH environment variable that finds all the standard utilities.

RETURN VALUES

If the call to confstr is not successful, −1 is returned and *errno* is set appropriately. Otherwise, if the variable does not have a configuration defined value, 0 is returned and *errno* is not modified. Otherwise, the buffer size needed to hold the entire configuration-defined value is returned. If this size is greater than the argument *len*, the string in *buf* was truncated.

ERRORS

The confstr function may fail and set *error* for any of the errors specified for the library functions malloc(3) and sysctl(3).

In addition, the following errors may be reported:

[EINVAL]　　　The value of the *name* argument is invalid.

SEE ALSO

sysctl(3)

HISTORY

The confstr function first appeared in 4.4BSD.

NAME

    cos – cosine function

SYNOPSIS

    `#include <math.h>`

    double
    `cos(`*double x*`)`;

DESCRIPTION

    The `cos()` function computes the cosine of x (measured in radians). A large magnitude argument may yield a result with little or no significance. For a discussion of error due to roundoff, see `math(3)`.

RETURN VALUES

    The `cos()` function returns the cosine value.

SEE ALSO

    `sin(3)`, `tan(3)`, `asin(3)`, `acos(3)`, `atan(3)`, `atan2(3)`, `sinh(3)`, `cosh(3)`, `tanh(3)`, `math(3)`,

STANDARDS

    The `acos()` function conforms to ANSI C X3.159-1989 (''ANSI C '').

NAME

cosh – hyperbolic cosine function

SYNOPSIS

`#include <math.h>`

double
cosh(*double x*);

DESCRIPTION

The **cosh**( ) function computes the hyperbolic cosine of x.

RETURN VALUES

The **cosh**( ) function returns the hyperbolic cosine unless the magnitude of x is too large; in this event, the global variable *errno* is set to ERANGE.

SEE ALSO

acos(3), asin(3), atan(3), atan2(3), cos(3), sin(3), sinh(3), tan(3), tanh(3), math(3),

STANDARDS

The **cosh**( ) function conforms to ANSI C X3.159-1989 (''ANSI C '').

NAME
crypt, setkey, encrypt, des_setkey, des_cipher – DES encryption

SYNOPSIS
char
*crypt(*const char *key, const char *setting*);

int
setkey(*char *key*);

int
encrypt(*char *block, int flag*);

int
des_setkey(*const char *key*);

int
des_cipher(*const char *in, char *out, long salt, int count*);

DESCRIPTION
The crypt function performs password encryption. It is derived from the NBS Data Encryption Standard. Additional code has been added to deter key search attempts. The first argument to **crypt** is a NUL-terminated string (normally a password typed by a user). The second is a character array, 9 bytes in length, consisting of an underscore ("_") followed by 4 bytes of iteration count and 4 bytes of salt. Both the iteration *count* and the *salt* are encoded with 6 bits per character, least significant bits first. The values 0 to 63 are encoded by the characters "./0-9A-Za-z", respectively.

The *salt* is used to induce disorder in to the DES algorithm in one of 16777216 possible ways (specifically, if bit *i* of the *salt* is set then bits *i* and *i+24* are swapped in the DES "E" box output). The *key* is divided into groups of 8 characters (a short final group is null-padded) and the low-order 7 bits of each character (56 bits per group) are used to form the DES key as follows: the first group of 56 bits becomes the initial DES key. For each additional group, the XOR of the group bits and the encryption of the DES key with itself becomes the next DES key. Then the final DES key is used to perform *count* cumulative encryptions of a 64-bit constant. The value returned is a NUL-terminated string, 20 bytes in length, consisting of the *setting* followed by the encoded 64-bit encryption.

For compatibility with historical versions of crypt(3), the *setting* may consist of 2 bytes of salt, encoded as above, in which case an iteration *count* of 25 is used, fewer perturbations of DES are available, at most 8 characters of *key* are used, and the returned value is a NUL-terminated string 13 bytes in length.

The functions, **encrypt()**, **setkey()**, **des_setkey()** and **des_cipher()** allow limited access to the DES algorithm itself. The *key* argument to **setkey()** is a 64 character array of binary values (numeric 0 or 1). A 56-bit key is derived from this array by dividing the array into groups of 8 and ignoring the last bit in each group.

The **encrypt()** argument *block* is also a 64 character array of binary values. If the value of *flag* is 0, the argument *block* is encrypted, otherwise it is decrypted. The encryption or decryption is returned in the original array *block* after using the key specified by **setkey()** to process it.

The **des_setkey()** and **des_cipher()** functions are faster but less portable than **setkey()** and **encrypt()**. The argument to **des_setkey()** is a character array of length 8. The *least* significant bit in each character is ignored and the next 7 bits of each character are concatenated to yield a 56-bit key. The function **des_cipher()** encrypts (or decrypts if *count* is negative) the 64-bits stored in the 8 characters at *in* using abs(3) of *count* iterations of DES and stores the 64-bit result in the 8 characters at *out*. The *salt* specifies perturbations to DES as described above.

The function `crypt()` returns a pointer to the encrypted value on success and NULL on failure. The functions `setkey()`, `encrypt()`, `des_setkey()`, and `des_cipher()` return 0 on success and 1 on failure. Historically, the functions `setkey()` and `encrypt()` did not return any value. They have been provided return values primarily to distinguish implementations where hardware support is provided but not available or where the DES encryption is not available due to the usual political silliness.

SEE ALSO
login(1), passwd(1), getpass(3), passwd(5)

Wayne Patterson, *Mathematical Cryptology for Computer Scientists and Mathematicians*, ISBN 0-8476-7438-X, 1987.

R. Morris, and Ken Thompson, "Password Security: A Case History", *Communications of the ACM*, vol. 22, pp. 594-597, Nov. 1979.

M.E. Hellman, "DES will be Totally Insecure within Ten Years", *IEEE Spectrum*, vol. 16, pp. 32-39, July 1979.

HISTORY
A rotor-based `crypt()` function appeared in Version 6 AT&T UNIX. The current style `crypt()` first appeared in Version 7 AT&T UNIX.

BUGS
Dropping the *least* significant bit in each character of the argument to `des_setkey()` is ridiculous.

The `crypt()` function leaves its result in an internal static object and returns a pointer to that object. Subsequent calls to `crypt()` will modify the same object.

NAME
ctermid – generate terminal pathname

SYNOPSIS
`#include <stdio.h>`

char *
`ctermid(char *buf);`

DESCRIPTION
The `ctermid()` function generates a string, that, when used as a pathname, refers to the current controlling terminal of the calling process.

If *buf* is the NULL pointer, a pointer to a static area is returned. Otherwise, the pathname is copied into the memory referenced by *buf*. The argument *buf* is assumed to be at least L_ctermid (as defined in the include file `<stdio.h>`) bytes long.

The current implementation simply returns `/dev/tty`.

RETURN VALUES
Upon successful completion, a non-NULL pointer is returned. Otherwise, a NULL pointer is returned and the global variable *errno* is set to indicate the error.

ERRORS
The current implementation detects no error conditions.

SEE ALSO
`ttyname`(3)

STANDARDS
The `ctermid` function conforms to IEEE Std1003.1-1988 ("POSIX").

BUGS
By default the `ctermid()` function writes all information to an internal static object. Subsequent calls to `ctermid()` will modify the same object.

NAME

  `asctime`, `ctime`, `difftime`, `gmtime`, `localtime`, `mktime` – transform binary date and time value to ASCII

SYNOPSIS

```
#include <sys/types.h>
#include <time.h>
```

`extern char *tzname[2];`

`char *`
`ctime`(*const time_t *clock*);

`double`
`difftime`(*time_t time1, time_t time0*);

`char *`
`asctime`(*const struct tm *tm*);

`struct tm *`
`localtime`(*const time_t *clock*);

`struct tm *`
`gmtime`(*const time_t *clock*);

`time_t`
`mktime`(*struct tm *tm*);

DESCRIPTION

The functions `ctime()`, `gmtime()` and `localtime()` all take as an argument a time value representing the time in seconds since the Epoch (00:00:00 UTC, January 1, 1970; see `time(3)`).

The function `localtime()` converts the time value pointed at by *clock*, and returns a pointer to a "*struct tm*" (described below) which contains the broken-out time information for the value after adjusting for the current time zone (and any other factors such as Daylight Saving Time). Time zone adjustments are performed as specified by the TZ environmental variable (see `tzset(3)`). The function `localtime()` uses `tzset` to initialize time conversion information if `tzset` has not already been called by the process.

After filling in the tm structure, `localtime()` sets the *tm_isdst*'th element of *tzname* to a pointer to an ASCII string that's the time zone abbreviation to be used with `localtime()`'s return value.

The function `gmtime()` similarly converts the time value, but without any time zone adjustment, and returns a pointer to a tm structure (described below).

The `ctime()` function adjusts the time value for the current time zone in the same manner as `localtime()`, and returns a pointer to a 26-character string of the form:

  `Thu Nov 24 18:22:48 1986\n\0`

All the fields have constant width.

The `asctime()` function converts the broken down time in the structure *tm* pointed at by **tm* to the form shown in the example above.

The function `mktime()` converts the broken-down time, expressed as local time, in the structure pointed to by tm into a time value with the same encoding as that of the values returned by the `time(3)` function, that is, seconds from the Epoch, UTC.

The original values of the *tm_wday* and *tm_yday* components of the structure are ignored, and the original values of the other components are not restricted to their normal ranges. (A positive or zero value for *tm_isdst* causes **mktime**( ) to presume initially that summer time (for example, Daylight Saving Time) is or is not in effect for the specified time, respectively. A negative value for *tm_isdst* causes the **mktime**( ) function to attempt to divine whether summer time is in effect for the specified time.)

On successful completion, the values of the *tm_wday* and *tm_yday* components of the structure are set appropriately, and the other components are set to represent the specified calendar time, but with their values forced to their normal ranges; the final value of *tm_mday* is not set until *tm_mon* and *tm_year* are determined. **Mktime**( ) returns the specified calendar time; if the calendar time cannot be represented, it returns −1;

The **difftime**( ) function returns the difference between two calendar times, (*time1* - *time0*), expressed in seconds.

External declarations as well as the tm structure definition are in the <time.h> include file. The tm structure includes at least the following fields:

```
int tm_sec;      /* seconds (0 - 60) */
int tm_min;      /* minutes (0 - 59) */
int tm_hour;     /* hours (0 - 23) */
int tm_mday;     /* day of month (1 - 31) */
int tm_mon;      /* month of year (0 - 11) */
int tm_year;     /* year - 1900 */
int tm_wday;     /* day of week (Sunday = 0) */
int tm_yday;     /* day of year (0 - 365) */
int tm_isdst;    /* is summer time in effect? */
char *tm_zone;   /* abbreviation of timezone name */
long tm_gmtoff;       /* offset from UTC in seconds */
```

The field *tm_isdst* is non-zero if summer time is in effect.

The field *tm_gmtoff* is the offset (in seconds) of the time represented from UTC, with positive values indicating east of the Prime Meridian.

SEE ALSO
date(1), gettimeofday(2), getenv(3), time(3), tzset(3), tzfile(5)

HISTORY
This manual page is derived from the time package contributed to Berkeley by Arthur Olsen and which appeared in 4.3BSD.

BUGS
Except for **difftime**( ) and **mktime**(), these functions leaves their result in an internal static object and return a pointer to that object. Subsequent calls to these function will modify the same object.

The *tm_zone* field of a returned tm structure points to a static array of characters, which will also be overwritten by any subsequent calls (as well as by subsequent calls to tzset(3) and tzsetwall(3)).

Use of the external variable *tzname* is discouraged; the *tm_zone* entry in the tm structure is preferred.

Avoid using out-of-range values with **mktime**( ) when setting up lunch with promptness sticklers in Riyadh.

NAME

isalnum, isalpha, isascii, isblank, iscntrl, isdigit, isgraph, islower, isprint, ispunct, isspace, isupper, isxdigit, toascii tolower, toupper, – character classification macros

SYNOPSIS

```
#include <ctype.h>
```
int c

isalnum(*int c*);

isalpha(*int c*);

isascii(*int c*);

iscntrl(*int c*);

isdigit(*int c*);

isgraph(*int c*);

islower(*int c*);

isprint(*int c*);

ispunct(*int c*);

isspace(*int c*);

isupper(*int c*);

isxdigit(*int c*);

toascii(*int c*);

tolower(*int c*);

toupper(*int c*);

DESCRIPTION

The above functions perform character tests and conversions on the integer *c*. They are available as macros, defined in the include file <ctype.h>, or as true functions in the C library. See the specific manual pages for more information.

SEE ALSO

isalnum(3), isalpha(3), isascii(3), isblank(3), iscntrl(3), isdigit(3), isgraph(3), islower(3), isprint(3), ispunct(3), isspace(3), isupper(3), isxdigit(3), toascii(3), tolower(3), toupper(3), ascii(7)

STANDARDS

These functions, except for **isblank**(), **toupper**(), **tolower**() and **toascii**(), conform to ANSI C X3.159-1989 ("ANSI C").

NAME

curses – screen functions with "optimal" cursor motion

SYNOPSIS

cc [*flags*] *files* **–lcurses** **–ltermcap** [*libraries*]

DESCRIPTION

These routines give the user a method of updating screens with reasonable optimization. They keep an image of the current screen, and the user sets up an image of a new one. Then the **refresh**( ) tells the routines to make the current screen look like the new one. In order to initialize the routines, the routine **initscr**( ) must be called before any of the other routines that deal with windows and screens are used. The routine **endwin**( ) should be called before exiting.

SEE ALSO

ioctl(2), getenv(3), tty(4), termcap(5)

Ken Arnold, *Screen Updating and Cursor Movement Optimization: A Library Package.*

AUTHOR

Ken Arnold

FUNCTIONS

addch(ch)	add a character to *stdscr*
addstr(str)	add a string to *stdscr*
box(win,vert,hor)	draw a box around a window
cbreak()	set cbreak mode
clear()	clear *stdscr*
clearok(scr,boolf)	set clear flag for *scr*
clrtobot()	clear to bottom on *stdscr*
clrtoeol()	clear to end of line on *stdscr*
delch()	delete a character
deleteln()	delete a line
delwin(win)	delete *stdscr*
echo()	set echo mode
endwin()	end window modes
erase()	erase *stdscr*
flusok(win,boolf)	set flush-on-refresh flag for *win*
getch()	get a char through *stdscr*
getcap(name)	get terminal capability *name*
getstr(str)	get a string through *stdscr*
gettmode()	get tty modes
getyx(win,y,x)	get (y,x) co-ordinates
inch()	get char at current (y,x) co-ordinates
initscr()	initialize screens
insch(c)	insert a char
insertln()	insert a line
leaveok(win,boolf)	set leave flag for *stdscr*
longname(termbuf,name)	get long name from *termbuf*
move(y,x)	move to (y,x) on *stdscr*

mvcur(lasty,lastx,newy,newx)	actually move cursor
newwin(lines,cols,begin_y,begin_x)	create a new window
nl()	set newline mapping
nocbreak()	unset cbreak mode
noecho()	unset echo mode
nonl()	unset newline mapping
noraw()	unset raw mode
overlay(win1,win2)	overlay win1 on win2
overwrite(win1,win2)	overwrite win1 on top of win2
printw(fmt,arg1,arg2,...)	printf on *stdscr*
raw()	set raw mode
refresh()	make current screen look like *stdscr*
resetty()	reset tty flags to stored value
savetty()	stored current tty flags
scanw(fmt,arg1,arg2,...)	scanf through *stdscr*
scroll(win)	scroll *win* one line
scrollok(win,boolf)	set scroll flag
setterm(name)	set term variables for name
standend()	end standout mode
standout()	start standout mode
subwin(win,lines,cols,begin_y,begin_x)	create a subwindow
touchline(win,y,sx,ex)	mark line *y sx* through *sy* as changed
touchoverlap(win1,win2)	mark overlap of *win1* on *win2* as changed
touchwin(win)	change all of *win*
unctrl(ch)	printable version of *ch*
waddch(win,ch)	add char to *win*
waddstr(win,str)	add string to *win*
wclear(win)	clear *win*
wclrtobot(win)	clear to bottom of *win*
wclrtoeol(win)	clear to end of line on *win*
wdelch(win,c)	delete char from *win*
wdeleteln(win)	delete line from *win*
werase(win)	erase *win*
wgetch(win)	get a char through *win*
wgetstr(win,str)	get a string through *win*
winch(win)	get char at current (y,x) in *win*
winsch(win,c)	insert char into *win*
winsertln(win)	insert line into *win*
wmove(win,y,x)	set current (y,x) co-ordinates on *win*
wprintw(win,fmt,arg1,arg2,...)	printf on *win*
wrefresh(win)	make screen look like *win*
wscanw(win,fmt,arg1,arg2,...)	scanf through *win*
wstandend(win)	end standout mode on *win*
wstandout(win)	start standout mode on *win*

HISTORY

The curses package appeared in 4.0BSD.

NAME

     daemon – run in the background

SYNOPSIS

     daemon(*int nochdir, int noclose*);

DESCRIPTION

     The **daemon()** function is for programs wishing to detach themselves from the controlling terminal and run
     in the background as system daemons.

     Unless the argument *nochdir* is non-zero, **daemon()** changes the current working directory to the root
     ("/").

     Unless the argument *noclose* is non-zero, **daemon()** will redirect standard input, standard output and
     standard error to "/dev/null".

ERRORS

     The function **daemon()** may fail and set *errno* for any of the errors specified for the library functions
     fork(2) and setsid(2).

SEE ALSO

     setsid(2)

HISTORY

     The **daemon()** function first appeared in 4.4BSD.

NAME

dbopen – database access methods

SYNOPSIS

#include <sys/types.h>
#include <limits.h>
#include <db.h>

DB *
dbopen(const char *file, int flags, int mode, DBTYPE type,
        const void *openinfo);

DESCRIPTION

Dbopen is the library interface to database files. The supported file formats are btree, hashed and UNIX file oriented. The btree format is a representation of a sorted, balanced tree structure. The hashed format is an extensible, dynamic hashing scheme. The flat-file format is a byte stream file with fixed or variable length records. The formats and file format specific information are described in detail in their respective manual pages *btree*(3), *hash*(3) and *recno*(3).

Dbopen opens *file* for reading and/or writing. Files never intended to be preserved on disk may be created by setting the file parameter to NULL.

The *flags* and *mode arguments* are as specified to the *open*(2) routine, however, only the O_CREAT, O_EXCL, O_EXLOCK, O_NONBLOCK, O_RDONLY, O_RDWR, O_SHLOCK and O_TRUNC flags are meaningful. (Note, opening a database file O_WRONLY is not possible.)

The *type* argument is of type DBTYPE (as defined in the <db.h> include file) and may be set to DB_BTREE, DB_HASH or DB_RECNO.

The *openinfo* argument is a pointer to an access method specific structure described in the access method's manual page. If *openinfo* is NULL, each access method will use defaults appropriate for the system and the access method.

Dbopen returns a pointer to a DB structure on success and NULL on error. The DB structure is defined in the <db.h> include file, and contains at least the following fields:

```
typedef struct {
        DBTYPE type;
        int (*close)(const DB *db);
        int (*del)(const DB *db, const DBT *key, u_int flags);
        int (*fd)(const DB *db);
        int (*get)(const DB *db, DBT *key, DBT *data, u_int flags);
        int (*put)(const DB *db, DBT *key, const DBT *data,
                        u_int flags);
        int (*sync)(const DB *db, u_int flags);
        int (*seq)(const DB *db, DBT *key, DBT *data, u_int flags);
} DB;
```

These elements describe a database type and a set of functions performing various actions. These functions take a pointer to a structure as returned by *dbopen*, and sometimes one or more pointers to key/data structures and a flag value.

type   The type of the underlying access method (and file format).

close   A pointer to a routine to flush any cached information to disk, free any allocated resources, and close the underlying file(s). Since key/data pairs may be cached in memory, failing to sync the file with a *close* or *sync* function may result in inconsistent or lost information. *Close* routines return -1 on error (setting *errno*) and 0 on success.

del   A pointer to a routine to remove key/data pairs from the database.

The parameter *flag* may be set to the following value:

R_CURSOR
> Delete the record referenced by the cursor. The cursor must have previously been initialized.

Delete routines return -1 on error (setting *errno*), 0 on success, and 1 if the specified *key* was not in the file.

fd   A pointer to a routine which returns a file descriptor representative of the underlying database. A file descriptor referencing the same file will be returned to all processes which call *dbopen* with the same *file* name. This file descriptor may be safely used as an argument to the *fcntl*(2) and *flock*(2) locking functions. The file descriptor is not necessarily associated with any of the underlying files used by the access method. No file descriptor is available for in memory databases. *Fd* routines return -1 on error (setting *errno*), and the file descriptor on success.

get   A pointer to a routine which is the interface for keyed retrieval from the database. The address and length of the data associated with the specified *key* are returned in the structure referenced by *data*. *Get* routines return -1 on error (setting *errno*), 0 on success, and 1 if the *key* was not in the file.

put   A pointer to a routine to store key/data pairs in the database.

The parameter *flag* may be set to one of the following values:

R_CURSOR
> Replace the key/data pair referenced by the cursor. The cursor must have previously been initialized.

R_IAFTER
> Append the data immediately after the data referenced by *key*, creating a new key/data pair. The record number of the appended key/data pair is returned in the *key* structure. (Applicable only to the DB_RECNO access method.)

R_IBEFORE
> Insert the data immediately before the data referenced by *key*, creating a new key/data pair. The record number of the inserted key/data pair is returned in the *key* structure. (Applicable only to the DB_RECNO access method.)

R_NOOVERWRITE
> Enter the new key/data pair only if the key does not previously exist.

R_SETCURSOR
> Store the key/data pair, setting or initializing the position of the cursor to reference it. (Applicable only to the DB_BTREE and DB_RECNO access methods.)

R_SETCURSOR is available only for the DB_BTREE and DB_RECNO access methods because it implies that the keys have an inherent order which does not change.

R_IAFTER and R_IBEFORE are available only for the DB_RECNO access method because they each imply that the access method is able to create new keys. This is only true if the keys are ordered and independent, record numbers for example.

The default behavior of the *put* routines is to enter the new key/data pair, replacing any previously existing key.

Put routines return -1 on error (setting *errno*), 0 on success, and 1 if the R_NOOVERWRITE *flag* was set and the key already exists in the file.

seq   A pointer to a routine which is the interface for sequential retrieval from the database. The address and length of the key are returned in the structure referenced by *key*, and the address and length of the data are returned in the structure referenced by *data*.

Sequential key/data pair retrieval may begin at any time, and the position of the ''cursor'' is not affected by calls to the *del*, *get*, *put*, or *sync* routines. Modifications to the database during a sequential scan will be reflected in the scan, i.e. records inserted behind the cursor will not be returned while records inserted in front of the cursor will be returned.

The flag value **must** be set to one of the following values:

R_CURSOR
> The data associated with the specified key is returned. This differs from the *get* routines in that it sets or initializes the cursor to the location of the key as well. (Note, for the DB_BTREE access method, the returned key is not necessarily an exact match for the specified key. The returned key is the smallest key greater than or equal to the specified key, permitting partial key matches and range searches.)

R_FIRST
> The first key/data pair of the database is returned, and the cursor is set or initialized to reference it.

R_LAST
> The last key/data pair of the database is returned, and the cursor is set or initialized to reference it. (Applicable only to the DB_BTREE and DB_RECNO access methods.)

R_NEXT
> Retrieve the key/data pair immediately after the cursor. If the cursor is not yet set, this is the same as the R_FIRST flag.

R_PREV
> Retrieve the key/data pair immediately before the cursor. If the cursor is not yet set, this is the same as the R_LAST flag. (Applicable only to the DB_BTREE and DB_RECNO access methods.)

R_LAST and R_PREV are available only for the DB_BTREE and DB_RECNO access methods because they each imply that the keys have an inherent order which does not change.

Seq routines return -1 on error (setting *errno*), 0 on success and 1 if there are no key/data pairs less than or greater than the specified or current key. If the DB_RECNO access method is being used, and if the database file is a character special file and no complete key/data pairs are currently available, the *seq* routines return 2.

sync   A pointer to a routine to flush any cached information to disk. If the database is in memory only, the *sync* routine has no effect and will always succeed.

The flag value may be set to the following value:

R_RECNOSYNC
> If the DB_RECNO access method is being used, this flag causes the sync routine to apply to the btree file which underlies the recno file, not the recno file itself. (See the *bfname* field of the *recno*(3) manual page for more information.)

Sync routines return -1 on error (setting *errno*) and 0 on success.

KEY/DATA PAIRS

Access to all file types is based on key/data pairs. Both keys and data are represented by the following data structure:

```
typedef struct {
        void *data;
        size_t size;
} DBT;
```

The elements of the DBT structure are defined as follows:

data   A pointer to a byte string.

size   The length of the byte string.

Key and data byte strings may reference strings of essentially unlimited length although any two of them must fit into available memory at the same time. It should be noted that the access methods provide no guarantees about byte string alignment.

ERRORS

The *dbopen* routine may fail and set *errno* for any of the errors specified for the library routines *open*(2) and *malloc*(3) or the following:

[EFTYPE]
A file is incorrectly formatted.

[EINVAL]
A parameter has been specified (hash function, pad byte etc.) that is incompatible with the current file specification or which is not meaningful for the function (for example, use of the cursor without prior initialization) or there is a mismatch between the version number of file and the software.

The *close* routines may fail and set *errno* for any of the errors specified for the library routines *close*(2), *read*(2), *write*(2), *free*(3), or *fsync*(2).

The *del*, *get*, *put* and *seq* routines may fail and set *errno* for any of the errors specified for the library routines *read*(2), *write*(2), *free*(3) or *malloc*(3).

The *fd* routines will fail and set *errno* to ENOENT for in memory databases.

The *sync* routines may fail and set *errno* for any of the errors specified for the library routine *fsync*(2).

SEE ALSO

btree(3), *hash*(3), *mpool*(3), *recno*(3)

LIBTP: Portable, Modular Transactions for UNIX, Margo Seltzer, Michael Olson, USENIX proceedings, Winter 1992.

BUGS

The typedef DBT is a mnemonic for "data base thang", and was used because noone could think of a reasonable name that wasn't already used.

The file descriptor interface is a kluge and will be deleted in a future version of the interface.

None of the access methods provide any form of concurrent access, locking, or transactions.

NAME

des_read_password, des_string_to_key, des_random_key, des_set_key, des_ecb_encrypt, des_cbc_encrypt, des_pcbc_encrypt, des_cbc_cksum, des_quad_cksum, – (new) DES encryption

SYNOPSIS

#include <kerberosIV/des.h>

int des_read_password(key,prompt,verify)
des_cblock *key;
char *prompt;
int verify;

int des_string_to_key(str,key)
char *str;
des_cblock key;

int des_random_key(key)
des_cblock *key;

int des_set_key(key,schedule)
des_cblock *key;
des_key_schedule schedule;

int des_ecb_encrypt(input,output,schedule,encrypt)
des_cblock *input;
des_cblock *output;
des_key_schedule schedule;
int encrypt;

int des_cbc_encrypt(input,output,length,schedule,ivec,encrypt)
des_cblock *input;
des_cblock *output;
long length;
des_key_schedule schedule;
des_cblock *ivec;
int encrypt;

int des_pcbc_encrypt(input,output,length,schedule,ivec,encrypt)
des_cblock *input;
des_cblock *output;
long length;
des_key_schedule schedule;
des_cblock *ivec;
int encrypt;

unsigned long des_cbc_cksum(input,output,length,schedule,ivec)
des_cblock *input;
des_cblock *output;
long length;
des_key_schedule schedule;
des_cblock *ivec;

unsigned long quad_cksum(input,output,length,out_count,seed)
des_cblock *input;
des_cblock *output;
long length;
int out_count;
des_cblock *seed;

DESCRIPTION

This library supports various DES encryption related operations. It differs from the *crypt, setkey, and encrypt* library routines in that it provides a true DES encryption, without modifying the algorithm, and executes much faster.

For each key that may be simultaneously active, create a **des_key_schedule** struct, defined in "des.h". Next, create key schedules (from the 8-byte keys) as needed, via *des_set_key*, prior to using the encryption or checksum routines. Then setup the input and output areas. Make sure to note the restrictions on lengths being multiples of eight bytes. Finally, invoke the encryption/decryption routines, *des_ecb_encrypt* or *des_cbc_encrypt* or *des_pcbc_encrypt*, or, to generate a cryptographic checksum, use *quad_cksum* (fast) or *des_cbc_cksum* (slow).

A *des_cblock* struct is an 8 byte block used as the fundamental unit for DES data and keys, and is defined as:

> **typedef unsigned char des_cblock[8];**

and a *des_key_schedule*, is defined as:

> **typedef struct des_ks_struct {des_cblock _;} des_key_schedule[16];**

des_read_password writes the string specified by *prompt* to the standard output, turns off echo (if possible) and reads an input string from standard input until terminated with a newline. If *verify* is non-zero, it prompts and reads input again, for use in applications such as changing a password; both versions are compared, and the input is requested repeatedly until they match. Then *des_read_password* converts the input string into a valid DES key, internally using the *des_string_to_key* routine. The newly created key is copied to the area pointed to by the *key* argument. *des_read_password* returns a zero if no errors occurred, or a -1 indicating that an error occurred trying to manipulate the terminal echo.

des_string_to_key converts an arbitrary length null-terminated string to an 8 byte DES key, with odd byte parity, per FIPS specification. A one-way function is used to convert the string to a key, making it very difficult to reconstruct the string from the key. The *str* argument is a pointer to the string, and *key* should point to a *des_cblock* supplied by the caller to receive the generated key. No meaningful value is returned. Void is not used for compatibility with other compilers.

des_random_key generates a random DES encryption key (eight bytes), set to odd parity per FIPS specifications. This routine uses the current time, process id, and a counter as a seed for the random number generator. The caller must supply space for the output key, pointed to by argument *key*, then after calling *des_random_key* should call the *des_set_key* routine when needed. No meaningful value is returned. Void is not used for compatibility with other compilers.

des_set_key calculates a key schedule from all eight bytes of the input key, pointed to by the *key* argument, and outputs the schedule into the *des_key_schedule* indicated by the *schedule* argument. Make sure to pass a valid eight byte key; no padding is done. The key schedule may then be used in subsequent encryption/decryption/checksum operations. Many key schedules may be cached for later use. The user is responsible to clear keys and schedules as soon as no longer needed, to prevent their disclosure. The routine also checks the key parity, and returns a zero if the key parity is correct (odd), a -1 indicating a key parity error, or a -2 indicating use of an illegal weak key. If an error is returned, the key schedule was not created.

des_ecb_encrypt is the basic DES encryption routine that encrypts or decrypts a single 8-byte block in **electronic code book** mode. It always transforms the input data, pointed to by *input*, into the output data, pointed to by the *output* argument.

If the *encrypt* argument is non-zero, the *input* (cleartext) is encrypted into the *output* (ciphertext) using the key_schedule specified by the *schedule* argument, previously set via *des_set_key*

If encrypt is zero, the *input* (now ciphertext) is decrypted into the *output* (now cleartext).

Input and output may overlap.

No meaningful value is returned. Void is not used for compatibility with other compilers.

des_cbc_encrypt encrypts/decrypts using the **cipher-block-chaining mode of DES.** If the *encrypt* argument is non-zero, the routine cipher-block-chain encrypts the cleartext data pointed to by the *input* argument into the ciphertext pointed to by the *output* argument, using the key schedule provided by the *schedule* argument, and initialization vector provided by the *ivec* argument. If the *length* argument is not an integral multiple of eight bytes, the last block is copied to a temp and zero filled (highest addresses). The output is ALWAYS an integral multiple of eight bytes.

If *encrypt* is zero, the routine cipher-block chain decrypts the (now) ciphertext data pointed to by the *input* argument into (now) cleartext pointed to by the *output* argument using the key schedule provided by the *schedule* argument, and initialization vector provided by the *ivec* argument. Decryption ALWAYS operates on integral multiples of 8 bytes, so it will round the *length* provided up to the appropriate multiple. Consequently, it will always produce the rounded-up number of bytes of output cleartext. The application must determine if the output cleartext was zero-padded due to original cleartext lengths that were not integral multiples of 8.

No errors or meaningful values are returned. Void is not used for compatibility with other compilers.

A characteristic of cbc mode is that changing a single bit of the cleartext, then encrypting using cbc mode, affects ALL the subsequent ciphertext. This makes cryptanalysis much more difficult. However, modifying a single bit of the ciphertext, then decrypting, only affects the resulting cleartext from the modified block and the succeeding block. Therefore, *des_pcbc_encrypt* is STRONGLY recommended for applications where indefinite propagation of errors is required in order to detect modifications.

des_pcbc_encrypt encrypts/decrypts using a modified block chaining mode. Its calling sequence is identical to *des_cbc_encrypt*. It differs in its error propagation characteristics.

des_pcbc_encrypt is highly recommended for most encryption purposes, in that modification of a single bit of the ciphertext will affect ALL the subsequent (decrypted) cleartext. Similarly, modifying a single bit of the cleartext will affect ALL the subsequent (encrypted) ciphertext. "PCBC" mode, on encryption, "xors" both the cleartext of block N and the ciphertext resulting from block N with the cleartext for block N+1 prior to encrypting block N+1.

des_cbc_cksum produces an 8 byte cryptographic checksum by cipher-block-chain encrypting the cleartext data pointed to by the *input* argument. All of the ciphertext output is discarded, except the last 8-byte ciphertext block, which is written into the area pointed to by the *output* argument. It uses the key schedule, provided by the *schedule* argument and initialization vector provided by the *ivec* argument. If the *length* argument is not an integral multiple of eight bytes, the last cleartext block is copied to a temp and zero filled (highest addresses). The output is ALWAYS eight bytes.

The routine also returns an unsigned long, which is the last (highest address) half of the 8 byte checksum computed.

quad_cksum produces a checksum by chaining quadratic operations on the cleartext data pointed to by the *input* argument. The *length* argument specifies the length of the input -- only exactly that many bytes are included for the checksum, without any padding.

The algorithm may be iterated over the same input data, if the *out_count* argument is 2, 3 or 4, and the optional *output* argument is a non-null pointer . The default is one iteration, and it will not run more than 4 times. Multiple iterations run slower, but provide a longer checksum if desired. The *seed* argument provides an 8-byte seed for the first iteration. If multiple iterations are requested, the results of one iteration are automatically used as the seed for the next iteration.

It returns both an unsigned long checksum value, and if the *output* argument is not a null pointer, up to 16 bytes of the computed checksum are written into the output.

FILES

/usr/include/kerberosIV/des.h
/usr/lib/libdes.a

SEE ALSO
DIAGNOSTICS
BUGS

This software has not yet been compiled or tested on machines other than the VAX and the IBM PC.

AUTHORS

Steve Miller, MIT Project Athena/Digital Equipment Corporation

RESTRICTIONS

COPYRIGHT 1985,1986 Massachusetts Institute of Technology

This software may not be exported outside of the US without a special license from the US Dept of Commerce. It may be replaced by any secret key block cipher with block length and key length of 8 bytes, as long as the interface is the same as described here.

NAME

devname – get device name

SYNOPSIS

```
#include <stdlib.h>
```

*char ***
devname(*dev_t dev*, *mode_t type*);

DESCRIPTION

The **devname()** function returns a pointer to the name of the block or character device in "/dev" with a device number of *dev*, and a file type matching the one encoded in *type* which must be one of S_IFBLK or S_IFCHR. If no device matches the specified values, or no information is available, the string "??" is returned.

SEE ALSO

stat(2), dev_mkdb(8)

HISTORY

The **devname** function call appeared in 4.4BSD.

NAME
opendir, readdir, telldir, seekdir, rewinddir, closedir, dirfd – directory operations

SYNOPSIS
```
#include <sys/types.h>
#include <dirent.h>

DIR *
opendir(const char *filename);

struct dirent *
readdir(DIR *dirp);

long
telldir(const DIR *dirp);

void
seekdir(DIR *dirp, long loc);

void
rewinddir(DIR *dirp);

int
closedir(DIR *dirp);

int
dirfd(DIR *dirp);
```

DESCRIPTION
The opendir() function opens the directory named by filename, associates a *directory stream* with it and returns a pointer to be used to identify the *directory stream* in subsequent operations. The pointer NULL is returned if filename cannot be accessed, or if it cannot malloc(3) enough memory to hold the whole thing.

The readdir() function returns a pointer to the next directory entry. It returns NULL upon reaching the end of the directory or detecting an invalid seekdir() operation.

The telldir() function returns the current location associated with the named *directory stream*.

The seekdir() function sets the position of the next readdir() operation on the *directory stream*. The new position reverts to the one associated with the *directory stream* when the telldir() operation was performed. Values returned by telldir() are good only for the lifetime of the DIR pointer, dirp, from which they are derived. If the directory is closed and then reopened, the telldir() value may be invalidated due to undetected directory compaction. It is safe to use a previous telldir() value immediately after a call to opendir() and before any calls to readdir().

The rewinddir() function resets the position of the named *directory stream* to the beginning of the directory.

The closedir() function closes the named *directory stream* and frees the structure associated with the dirp pointer, returning 0 on success. On failure, −1 is returned and the global variable *errno* is set to indicate the error.

The dirfd() function returns the integer file descriptor associated with the named *directory stream*, see open(2).

Sample code which searchs a directory for entry ''name'' is:

```
len = strlen(name);
dirp = opendir(".");
while ((dp = readdir(dirp)) != NULL)
        if (dp->d_namlen == len && !strcmp(dp->d_name, name)) {
                (void)closedir(dirp);
                return FOUND;
        }
(void)closedir(dirp);
return NOT_FOUND;
```

SEE ALSO

open(2), close(2), read(2), lseek(2), dir(5)

HISTORY

The **opendir**(), **readdir**(), **telldir**(), **seekdir**(), **rewinddir**(), **closedir**(), and **dirfd**() functions appeared in 4.2BSD.

3

NAME
div – return quotient and remainder from division

SYNOPSIS
`#include <stdlib.h>`

div_t
div(*int num, int denom*);

DESCRIPTION
The **div**( ) function computes the value *num/denom* and returns the quotient and remainder in a structure named *div_t* that contains two *int* members named *quot* and *rem*.

SEE ALSO
ldiv(3)

STANDARDS
The **div**( ) function conforms to ANSI C X3.159-1989 (''ANSI C '').

NAME

ecvt, fcvt, gcvt – output conversion

SYNOPSIS

char *ecvt(value, ndigit, decpt, sign)
double value;
int ndigit, *decpt, *sign;

char *fcvt(value, ndigit, decpt, sign)
double value;
int ndigit, *decpt, *sign;

char *gcvt(value, ndigit, buf)
double value;
char *buf;

DESCRIPTION

These interfaces are obsoleted by printf(3).
They are available from the compatibility library, libcompat.

Ecvt converts the *value* to a null-terminated string of *ndigit* ASCII digits and returns a pointer thereto. The position of the decimal point relative to the beginning of the string is stored indirectly through *decpt* (negative means to the left of the returned digits). If the sign of the result is negative, the word pointed to by *sign* is non-zero, otherwise it is zero. The low-order digit is rounded.

Fcvt is identical to *ecvt*, except that the correct digit has been rounded for Fortran F-format output of the number of digits specified by *ndigits*.

Gcvt converts the *value* to a null-terminated ASCII string in *buf* and returns a pointer to *buf*. It attempts to produce *ndigit* significant digits in Fortran F format if possible, otherwise E format, ready for printing. Trailing zeros may be suppressed.

SEE ALSO

printf(3)

BUGS

The return values point to static data whose content is overwritten by each call.

NAME

end, etext, edata – end boundaries of image segments

SYNOPSIS

```
extern end;
extern etext;
extern edata;
```

DESCRIPTION

The global variables *end*, *extext* and *edata* correspond to the the next address following the end of the text segment, the initialized data segment and the end of the data segment (BSS). These values are initially set at execution time by brk(2).

SEE ALSO

brk(2), malloc(3)

HISTORY

A end manual appeared in Version 6 AT&T UNIX.

3

NAME
erf, erfc – error function operators

SYNOPSIS
`#include <math.h>`

double
`erf(double x);`

double
`erfc(double x);`

DESCRIPTION
These functions calculate the error function of x.

The `erf()` calculates the error function of x; where

$$\text{erf}(x) := (2/\sqrt{\pi}) \int_0^x \exp(-t^2)\, dt.$$

The `erfc()` function calculates the complementary error function of x; that is `erfc()` subtracts the result of the error function `erf`(x) from 1.0. This is useful, since for large x places disappear.

SEE ALSO
math(3)

HISTORY
The `erf()` and `erfc()` functions appeared in 4.3BSD.

NAME

err, verr, errx, verrx, warn, vwarn, warnx, vwarnx – formatted error messages

SYNOPSIS

```
#include <err.h>
```

void
err(*int eval, const char *fmt, . . .*);

void
verr(*int eval, const char *fmt, va_list args*);

void
errx(*int eval, const char *fmt, . . .*);

void
verrx(*int eval, const char *fmt, va_list args*);

void
warn(*const char *fmt, . . .*);

void
vwarn(*const char *fmt, va_list args*);

void
warnx(*const char *fmt, . . .*);

void
vwarnx(*const char *fmt, va_list args*);

DESCRIPTION

The **err( )** and **warn( )** family of functions display a formatted error message on the standard error output. In all cases, the last component of the program name, a colon character, and a space are output. If the *fmt* argument is not NULL, the formatted error message, a colon character, and a space are output. In the case of the **err()**, **verr()**, **warn()**, and **vwarn( )** functions, the error message string affiliated with the current value of the global variable *errno* is output. In all cases, the output is followed by a newline character.

The **err()**, **verr()**, **errx()**, and **verrx( )** functions do not return, but exit with the value of the argument *eval*.

EXAMPLES

Display the current errno information string and exit:

```
if ((p = malloc(size)) == NULL)
        err(1, NULL);
if ((fd = open(file_name, O_RDONLY, 0)) == -1)
        err(1, "%s", file_name);
```

Display an error message and exit:

```
if (tm.tm_hour < START_TIME)
        errx(1, "too early, wait until %s", start_time_string);
```

Warn of an error:

```
if ((fd = open(raw_device, O_RDONLY, 0)) == -1)
        warnx("%s: %s: trying the block device",
            raw_device, strerror(errno));
```

```
        if ((fd = open(block_device, O_RDONLY, 0)) == -1)
                err(1, "%s", block_device);
```

SEE ALSO
   strerror(3)

HISTORY
   The **err**( ) and **warn**( ) functions first appeared in 4.4BSD.

3

NAME

execl, **execlp**, **execle**, **exect**, **execv**, **execvp** – execute a file

SYNOPSIS

```
#include <unistd.h>
```

*extern char **environ;*

int
execl(*const char *path, const char *arg, ...*);

int
execlp(*const char *file, const char *arg, ...*);

int
execle(*const char *path, const char *arg, ..., char *const envp[]*);

int
exect(*const char *path, char *const argv[], char *const envp[]*);

int
execv(*const char *path, char *const argv[]*);

int
execvp(*const char *file, char *const argv[]*);

DESCRIPTION

The **exec** family of functions replaces the current process image with a new process image. The functions described in this manual page are front-ends for the function execve(2). (See the manual page for execve for detailed information about the replacement of the current process.)

The initial argument for these functions is the pathname of a file which is to be executed.

The *const char *arg* and subsequent ellipses in the **execl**(), **execlp**(), and **execle**() functions can be thought of as *arg0*, *arg1*, ..., *argn*. Together they describe a list of one or more pointers to null-terminated strings that represent the argument list available to the executed program. The first argument, by convention, should point to the file name associated with the file being executed. The list of arguments *must* be terminated by a NULL pointer.

The **exect**(), **execv**(), and **execvp**() functions provide an array of pointers to null-terminated strings that represent the argument list available to the new program. The first argument, by convention, should point to the file name associated with the file begin executed. The array of pointers **must** be terminated by a NULL pointer.

The **execle**() and **exect**() functions also specify the environment of the executed process by following the NULL pointer that terminates the list of arguments in the parameter list or the pointer to the argv array with an additional parameter. This additional parameter is an array of pointers to null-terminated strings and *must* be terminated by a NULL pointer. The other functions take the environment for the new process image from the external variable *environ* in the current process.

Some of these functions have special semantics.

The functions **execlp**() and **execvp**() will duplicate the actions of the shell in searching for an executable file if the specified file name does not contain a slash "/" character. The search path is the path specified in the environment by "PATH" variable. If this variable isn't specified, the default path "/bin:/usr/bin:" is used. In addition, certain errors are treated specially.

If permission is denied for a file (the attempted `execve` returned EACCES), these functions will continue searching the rest of the search path. If no other file is found, however, they will return with the global variable *errno* set to EACCES.

If the header of a file isn't recognized (the attempted `execve` returned ENOEXEC), these functions will execute the shell with the path of the file as its first argument. (If this attempt fails, no further searching is done.)

If the file is currently busy (the attempted `execve` returned ETXTBUSY), these functions will sleep for several seconds, periodically re-attempting to execute the file.

The function **exect**( ) executes a file with the program tracing facilities enabled (see `ptrace`(2)).

RETURN VALUES

If any of the `exec` functions returns, an error will have occurred. The return value is −1, and the global variable *errno* will be set to indicate the error.

FILES

`/bin/sh` The shell.

ERRORS

Execl(), **execle**(), **execlp**( ) and **execvp**( ) may fail and set *errno* for any of the errors specified for the library functions `execve`(2) and `malloc`(3).

Exect( ) and **execv**( ) may fail and set *errno* for any of the errors specified for the library function `execve`(2).

SEE ALSO

`sh`(1), `execve`(2), `fork`(2), `trace`(2), `environ`(7), `ptrace`(2), `environ`(7),

COMPATIBILITY

Historically, the default path for the **execlp**( ) and **execvp**( ) functions was ``:/bin:/usr/bin''. This was changed to place the current directory last to enhance system security.

The behavior of **execlp**( ) and **execvp**( ) when errors occur while attempting to execute the file is historic practice, but has not traditionally been documented and is not specified by the POSIX standard.

Traditionally, the functions **execlp**( ) and **execvp**( ) ignored all errors except for the ones described above and ENOMEM and E2BIG, upon which they returned. They now return if any error other than the ones described above occurs.

STANDARDS

Execl(), **execv**(), **execle**(), **execlp**( ) and **execvp**( ) conform to IEEE Std1003.1-1988 (``POSIX'').

NAME

　　　exit – perform normal program termination

SYNOPSIS

　　　`#include <stdlib.h>`

　　　void
　　　exit(*int status*);

DESCRIPTION

　　　Exit( ) terminates a process.

　　　Before termination it performs the following functions in the order listed:

　　　　1.　Call the functions registered with the `atexit`(3) function, in the reverse order of their registration.

　　　　2.　Flush all open output streams.

　　　　3.　Close all open streams.

　　　　4.　Unlink all files created with the `tmpfile`(3) function.

RETURN VALUES

　　　The **exit**( ) function never returns.

SEE ALSO

　　　`_exit`(2), `atexit`(3), `intro`(3), `tmpfile`(3)

STANDARDS

　　　The **exit**( ) function conforms to ANSI C X3.159-1989 (''ANSI C '').

NAME

exp, **expml**, **log**, **log10**, **log1p**, **pow** – exponential, logarithm, power functions

SYNOPSIS

```
#include <math.h>
```

double
exp(*double x*);

double
expml(*double x*);

double
log(*double x*);

double
log10(*double x*);

double
log1p(*double x*);

double
pow(*double x, double y*);

DESCRIPTION

The **exp**( ) function computes the exponential value of the given argument *x*.

The **expml**( ) function computes the value exp(x)–1 accurately even for tiny argument *x*.

The **log**( ) function computes the value for the natural logarithm of the argument x.

The **log10**( ) function computes the value for the logarithm of argument *x* to base 10.

The **log1p**( ) function computes the value of log(1+x) accurately even for tiny argument *x*.

The **pow**( ) computes the value of *x* to the exponent *y*.

ERROR (due to Roundoff etc.)

exp(x), log(x), expml(x) and log1p(x) are accurate to within an *up*, and log10(x) to within about 2 *ups*; an *up* is one *Unit* in the *Last Place*. The error in **pow**(*x*, *y*) is below about 2 *ups* when its magnitude is moderate, but increases as **pow**(*x*, *y*) approaches the over/underflow thresholds until almost as many bits could be lost as are occupied by the floating–point format's exponent field; that is 8 bits for VAX D and 11 bits for IEEE 754 Double. No such drastic loss has been exposed by testing; the worst errors observed have been below 20 *ups* for VAX D, 300 *ups* for IEEE 754 Double. Moderate values of **pow**( ) are accurate enough that **pow**(*integer, integer*) is exact until it is bigger than 2**56 on a VAX, 2**53 for IEEE 754.

RETURN VALUES

These functions will return the appropriate computation unless an error occurs or an argument is out of range. The functions **exp**(), **expml**( ) and **pow**( ) detect if the computed value will overflow, set the global variable *errno to* RANGE and cause a reserved operand fault on a VAX or Tahoe. The function **pow**(*x*, *y*) checks to see if *x* < 0 and *y* is not an integer, in the event this is true, the global variable *errno* is set to EDOM and on the VAX and Tahoe generate a reserved operand fault. On a VAX and Tahoe, *errno* is set to EDOM and the reserved operand is returned by log unless *x* > 0, by **log1p**( ) unless *x* > –1.

NOTES

The functions exp(x)−1 and log(1+x) are called expm1 and logp1 in BASIC on the Hewlett–Packard HP–71B and APPLE Macintosh, EXP1 and LN1 in Pascal, exp1 and log1 in C on APPLE Macintoshes, where they have been provided to make sure financial calculations of ((1+x)**n−1)/x, namely expm1(n*log1p(x))/x, will be accurate when x is tiny. They also provide accurate inverse hyperbolic functions.

The function **pow**(x, 0) returns x**0 = 1 for all x including x = 0, ∞ (not found on a VAX), and *NaN* (the reserved operand on a VAX). Previous implementations of pow may have defined x**0 to be undefined in some or all of these cases. Here are reasons for returning x**0 = 1 always:

1.   Any program that already tests whether x is zero (or infinite or *NaN*) before computing x**0 cannot care whether 0**0 = 1 or not. Any program that depends upon 0**0 to be invalid is dubious anyway since that expression's meaning and, if invalid, its consequences vary from one computer system to another.

2.   Some Algebra texts (e.g. Sigler's) define x**0 = 1 for all x, including x = 0. This is compatible with the convention that accepts a[0] as the value of polynomial

$$p(x) = a[0]*x**0 + a[1]*x**1 + a[2]*x**2 +...+ a[n]*x**n$$

at x = 0 rather than reject a[0]*0**0 as invalid.

3.   Analysts will accept 0**0 = 1 despite that x**y can approach anything or nothing as x and y approach 0 independently. The reason for setting 0**0 = 1 anyway is this:

If x(z) and y(z) are *any* functions analytic (expandable in power series) in z around z = 0, and if there x(0) = y(0) = 0, then x(z)**y(z) → 1 as z → 0.

4.   If 0**0 = 1, then ∞**0 = 1/0**0 = 1 too; and then *NaN***0 = 1 too because x**0 = 1 for all finite and infinite x, i.e., independently of x.

SEE ALSO

math(3), infnan(3)

HISTORY

A **exp**(), **log**() and **pow**() function appeared in Version 6 AT&T UNIX. A **log10**() function appeared in Version 7 AT&T UNIX. The **log1p**() and **expm1**() functions appeared in 4.3BSD.

NAME
　　　fabs – floating-point absolute value function

SYNOPSIS
　　　#include <math.h>

　　　double
　　　fabs(*double x*);

DESCRIPTION
　　　The **fabs**( ) function computes the absolute value of a floating-point number *x*.

RETURN VALUES
　　　The **fabs**( ) function returns the absolute value of *x*.

SEE ALSO
　　　abs(3), ceil(3), floor(3), rint(3), ieee(3), math.3

STANDARDS
　　　The **fabs**( ) function conforms to ANSI C X3.159-1989 ("ANSI C ").

3

NAME

      fclose – close a stream

SYNOPSIS

      #include <stdio.h>

      int
      fclose(*FILE *stream*);

DESCRIPTION

      The **fclose()** function dissociates the named *stream* from its underlying file or set of functions. If the stream was being used for output, any buffered data is written first, using fflush(3).

RETURN VALUES

      Upon successful completion 0 is returned. Otherwise, EOF is returned and the global variable *errno* is set to indicate the error. In either case no further access to the stream is possible.

ERRORS

      [EBADF] The argument *stream* is not an open stream.

      The **fclose()** function may also fail and set *errno* for any of the errors specified for the routines close(2) or fflush(3).

SEE ALSO

      close(2), fflush(3), fopen(3), setbuf(3)

STANDARDS

      The **fclose()** function conforms to ANSI C X3.159-1989 (''ANSI C '').

3

NAME
clearerr, feof, ferror, fileno – check and reset stream status

SYNOPSIS
#include <stdio.h>

void
clearerr(*FILE *stream*);

int
feof(*FILE *stream*);

int
ferror(*FILE *stream*);

int
fileno(*FILE *stream*);

DESCRIPTION
The function clearerr() clears the end-of-file and error indicators for the stream pointed to by *stream*.

The function feof() tests the end-of-file indicator for the stream pointed to by *stream*, returning non-zero if it is set. The end-of-file indicator can only be cleared by the function clearerr().

The function ferror() tests the error indicator for the stream pointed to by *stream*, returning non-zero if it is set. The error indicator can only be reset by the clearerr() function.

The function fileno() examines the argument *stream* and returns its integer descriptor.

ERRORS
These functions should not fail and do not set the external variable *errno*.

SEE ALSO
open(2), stdio(3)

STANDARDS
The functions clearerr(), feof(), and ferror() conform to ANSI C X3.159-1989 (''ANSI C '').

3

NAME
fflush, fpurge – flush a stream

SYNOPSIS
```
#include <stdio.h>
```

```
int
fflush(FILE *stream);
```

```
int
fpurge(FILE *stream);
```

DESCRIPTION
The function **fflush()** forces a write of all buffered data for the given output or update *stream* via the stream's underlying write function. The open status of the stream is unaffected.

If the *stream* argument is NULL, **fflush()** flushes *all* open output streams.

The function **fpurge()** erases any input or output buffered in the given *stream*. For output streams this discards any unwritten output. For input streams this discards any input read from the underlying object but not yet obtained via getc(3); this includes any text pushed back via ungetc.

RETURN VALUES
Upon successful completion 0 is returned. Otherwise, EOF is returned and the global variable *errno* is set to indicate the error.

ERRORS
[EBADF] *Stream* is not an open stream, or, in the case of **fflush()**, not a stream open for writing.

The function **fflush()** may also fail and set *errno* for any of the errors specified for the routine write(2).

SEE ALSO
write(2), fopen(3), fclose(3), setbuf(3)

STANDARDS
The **fflush()** function conforms to ANSI C X3.159-1989 (''ANSI C '').

NAME

ffs – find first bit set in a bit string

SYNOPSIS

#include <string.h>

int
ffs(*int value*);

DESCRIPTION

The **ffs**( ) function finds the first bit set in *value* and returns the index of that bit. Bits are numbered starting from 1, starting at the right-most bit. A return value of 0 means that the argument was zero.

SEE ALSO

bitstring(3)

HISTORY

The **ffs**( ) function appeared in 4.3BSD.

3

NAME
     fgetln – get a line from a stream

SYNOPSIS
     #include <stdio.h>

     *char ***
     fgetln(*FILE *stream, size_t *len*);

DESCRIPTION
     The **fgetln**( ) function returns a pointer to the next line from the stream referenced by *stream*. This line
     is *not* a C string as it does not end with a terminating NUL character. The length of the line, including the
     final newline, is stored in the memory location to which *len* points. (Note, however, that if the line is the
     last in a file that does not end in a newline, the returned text will not contain a newline.)

RETURN VALUES
     Upon successful completion a pointer is returned; this pointer becomes invalid after the next I/O operation on
     stream (whether successful or not) or as soon as the stream is closed. Otherwise, NULL is returned. The
     fgetln( ) function does not distinguish between end-of-file and error; the routines feof(3) and fer-
     ror(3) must be used to determine which occurred. If an error occurs, the global variable *errno* is set to indi-
     cate the error. The end-of-file condition is remembered, even on a terminal, and all subsequent attempts to
     read will return NULL until the condition is cleared with clearerr(3).

     The text to which the returned pointer points may be modified, provided that no changes are made beyond
     the returned size. These changes are lost as soon as the pointer becomes invalid.

ERRORS
     [EBADF] The argument *stream* is not a stream open for reading.

     The **fgetln**( ) function may also fail and set *errno* for any of the errors specified for the routines
     fflush(3), malloc(3), read(2), stat(2), or realloc(3).

SEE ALSO
     ferror(3), fgets(3), fopen(3), putc(3)

HISTORY
     The **fgetln**( ) function first appeared in 4.4BSD.

NAME

fgets, **gets** – get a line from a stream

SYNOPSIS

```
#include <stdio.h>
```

*char ***
fgets(*char *str*, *size_t size*, *FILE *stream*);

*char ***
gets(*char *str*);

DESCRIPTION

The **fgets**() function reads at most one less than the number of characters specified by `size` from the given *stream* and stores them in the string *str*. Reading stops when a newline character is found, at end-of-file or error. The newline, if any, is retained. In any case a '`\0`' character is appended to end the string.

The **gets**() function is equivalent to **fgets**() with an infinite `size` and a *stream* of *stdin*, except that the newline character (if any) is not stored in the string. It is the caller's responsibility to ensure that the input line, if any, is sufficiently short to fit in the string.

RETURN VALUES

Upon successful completion, **fgets**() and **gets**() return a pointer to the string. If end-of-file or an error occurs before any characters are read, they return `NULL`. The **fgets**() and functions **gets**() do not distinguish between end-of-file and error, and callers must use `feof(3)` and `ferror(3)` to determine which occurred.

ERRORS

[`EBADF`]　The given *stream* is not a readable stream.

The function **fgets**() may also fail and set *errno* for any of the errors specified for the routines `fflush(3)`, `fstat(2)`, `read(2)`, or `malloc(3)`.

The function **gets**() may also fail and set *errno* for any of the errors specified for the routine `getchar(3)`.

SEE ALSO

`feof(3)`, `ferror(3)`, `fgetline(3)`

STANDARDS

The functions **fgets**() and **gets**() conform to ANSI C X3.159-1989 (''ANSI C '').

BUGS

Since it is usually impossible to ensure that the next input line is less than some arbitrary length, and because overflowing the input buffer is almost invariably a security violation, programs should *NEVER* use **gets**(). The **gets**() function exists purely to conform to ANSI C X3.159-1989 (''ANSI C '').

NAME
floor – largest integral value not greater than x

SYNOPSIS
`#include <math.h>`

double
`floor`(*double x*);

DESCRIPTION
The `floor()` function computes the largest integral value not greater than *x*.

RETURN VALUES
The `floor()` function returns the largest integral value expressed as a double.

SEE ALSO
abs(3), ieee(3), fabs(3), floor(3), rint(3), math(3)

STANDARDS
The `floor()` function conforms to ANSI C X3.159-1989 (''ANSI C '').

NAME
fmod – floating-point remainder function

SYNOPSIS
`#include <math.h>`

double
fmod(*double x, double y*);

DESCRIPTION
The **fmod**( ) function computes the floating-point remainder of x/y.

RETURN VALUES
The **fmod**( ) function returns the value $x-i*y$, for some integer i such that, if y is non-zero, the result has the same sign as x and magnitude less than the magnitude of y. If y is zero, whether a domain error occurs or the **fmod**( ) function returns zero is implementation-defined.

SEE ALSO
math(3)

STANDARDS
The **fmod**( ) function conforms to ANSI C X3.159-1989 (''ANSI C '').

NAME
fnmatch – match filename or pathname

SYNOPSIS
`#include <fnmatch.h>`

int
fnmatch(*const char *pattern, const char *string, int flags*);

DESCRIPTION
The fnmatch() function matches patterns according to the rules used by the shell. It checks the string specified by the *string* argument to see if it matches the pattern specified by the *pattern* argument.

The *flags* argument modifies the interpretation of *pattern* and *string*. The value of *flags* is the bit-wise inclusive OR of any of the following constants, which are defined in the include file fnmatch.h.

FNM_NOESCAPE Normally, every occurrence of a backslash ('\') followed by a character in *pattern* is replaced by that character. This is done to negate any special meaning for the character. If the FNM_NOESCAPE flag is set, a backslash character is treated as an ordinary character.

FNM_PATHNAME Slash characters in *string* must be explicitly matched by slashes in *pattern*. If this flag is not set, then slashes are treated as regular characters.

FNM_PERIOD Leading periods in strings match periods in patterns. The definition of ''leading'' is related to the specification of FNM_PATHNAME. A period is always ''leading'' if it is the first character in *string*. Additionally, if FNM_PATHNAME is set, a period is ''leading'' if it immediately follows a slash.

RETURN VALUES
The fnmatch() function returns zero if *string* matches the pattern specified by *pattern*, otherwise, it returns the value FNM_NOMATCH.

SEE ALSO
sh(1), glob(3), regex(3), wordexp(3)

STANDARDS
The fnmatch() function conforms to IEEE Std1003.2 (''POSIX'').

HISTORY
The fnmatch() function first appeared in 4.4BSD.

BUGS
The pattern '*' matches the empty string, even if FNM_PATHNAME is specified.

NAME

fopen, fdopen, freopen – stream open functions

SYNOPSIS

```
#include <stdio.h>
```

FILE *
fopen(*char *path, char *mode*);

FILE *
fdopen(*int fildes, char *mode*);

FILE *
freopen(*char *path, char *mode, FILE *stream*);

DESCRIPTION

The **fopen( )** function opens the file whose name is the string pointed to by *path* and associates a stream with it.

The argument *mode* points to a string beginning with one of the following sequences (Additional characters may follow these sequences.):

"r"   Open text file for reading. The stream is positioned at the beginning of the file.

"r+"   Open for reading and writing. The stream is positioned at the beginning of the file.

"w"   Truncate file to zero length or create text file for writing. The stream is positioned at the beginning of the file. It "w+" Open for reading and writing. The file is created if it does not exist, otherwise it is truncated. The stream is positioned at the beginning of the file.

"a"   Open for writing. The file is created if it does not exist. The stream is positioned at the end of the file.

"a+"   Open for reading and writing. The file is created if it does not exist. The stream is positioned at the end of the file.

The *mode* string can also include the letter "b" either as a third character or as a character between the characters in any of the two-character strings described above. This is strictly for compatibility with ANSI C X3.159-1989 ("ANSI C ") and has no effect; the "b" is ignored.

Any created files will have mode "S_IRUSR | S_IWUSR | S_IRGRP | S_IWGRP | S_IROTH | S_IWOTH" (0666), as modified by the process' umask value (see umask(2)).

Reads and writes may be intermixed on read/write streams in any order, and do not require an intermediate seek as in previous versions of *stdio*. This is not portable to other systems, however; ANSI C requires that a file positioning function intervene between output and input, unless an input operation encounters end-of-file.

The **fdopen( )** function associates a stream with the existing file descriptor, *fildes*. The *mode* of the stream must be compatible with the mode of the file descriptor.

The **freopen( )** function opens the file whose name is the string pointed to by *path* and associates the stream pointed to by *stream* with it. The original stream (if it exists) is closed. The *mode* argument is used just as in the **fopen** function. The primary use of the **freopen( )** function is to change the file associated with a standard text stream (*stderr*, *stdin*, or *stdout*).

RETURN VALUES

Upon successful completion **fopen**(), **fdopen**( ) and **freopen**( ) return a FILE pointer. Otherwise, NULL is returned and the global variable *errno* is set to indicate the error.

ERRORS

[EINVAL] The *mode* provided to **fopen**(), **fdopen**(), or **freopen**( ) was invalid.

The **fopen**(), **fdopen**( ) and **freopen**( ) functions may also fail and set *errno* for any of the errors specified for the routine malloc(3).

The **fopen**( ) function may also fail and set *errno* for any of the errors specified for the routine open(2).

The **fdopen**( ) function may also fail and set *errno* for any of the errors specified for the routine fcntl(2).

The **freopen**( ) function may also fail and set *errno* for any of the errors specified for the routines open(2), fclose(3) and fflush(3).

SEE ALSO

open(2), fclose(3), fseek(3), funopen(3)

STANDARDS

The **fopen**( ) and **freopen**( ) functions conform to ANSI C X3.159-1989 (''ANSI C ''). The **fdopen**( ) function conforms to IEEE Std1003.1-1988 (''POSIX'').

NAME
fputs, **puts** – output a line to a stream

SYNOPSIS
#include <stdio.h>

int
fputs(*const char *str, FILE *stream*);

int
puts(*const char *str*);

DESCRIPTION
The function **fputs**() writes the string pointed to by *str* to the stream pointed to by *stream*.

The function **puts**() writes the string *str*, and a terminating newline character, to the stream *stdout*.

RETURN VALUES
The **fputs**() function returns 0 on success and EOF on error; **puts**() returns a nonnegative integer on success and EOF on error.

ERRORS
[EBADF]   The *stream* supplied is not a writable stream.

The functions **fputs**() and **puts**() may also fail and set *errno* for any of the errors specified for the routines write(2).

SEE ALSO
putc(3), ferror(3), stdio(3)

STANDARDS
The functions **fputs**() and **puts**() conform to ANSI C X3.159-1989 (''ANSI C '').

NAME
fread, fwrite – binary stream input/output

SYNOPSIS
`#include <stdio.h>`

int
`fread(`*void *ptr, size_t size, size_t nmemb, FILE *stream*`)`;

int
`fwrite(`*const void *ptr, size_t size, size_t nmemb, FILE *stream*`)`;

DESCRIPTION
The function **fread()** reads *nmemb* objects, each `size` bytes long, from the stream pointed to by *stream*, storing them at the location given by *ptr*.

The function **fwrite()** writes *nmemb* objects, each *size* bytes long, to the stream pointed to by *stream*, obtaining them from the location given by *ptr*.

RETURN VALUES
The functions **fread()** and **fwrite()** advance the file position indicator for the stream by the number of bytes read or written. They return the number of objects read or written. If an error occurs, or the end-of-file is reached, the return value is a short object count (or zero).

The function **fread()** does not distinguish between end-of-file and error, and callers must use `feof(3)` and `ferror(3)` to determine which occurred. The function **fwrite()** returns a value less than *nmemb* only if a write error has occurred.

SEE ALSO
`read(2)`, `write(2)`

STANDARDS
The functions **fread()** and **fwrite()** conform to ANSI C X3.159-1989 ("ANSI C ").

NAME

free – free up memory allocated with malloc, calloc or realloc

SYNOPSIS

#include <stdlib.h>

void
free(*void *ptr*);

DESCRIPTION

The **free**() function causes the space pointed to by *ptr* to be deallocated, that is, made available for further allocation. If *ptr* is a null pointer, no action occurs. Otherwise, if the argument does not match a pointer earlier returned by the `calloc`, `malloc`, or `realloc` function, or if the space has been deallocated by a call to **free**() or `realloc`, general havoc may occur.

RETURN VALUES

The **free**() function returns no value.

SEE ALSO

`calloc`(3), `malloc`(3), `realloc`(3)

STANDARDS

The **free**() function conforms to ANSI C X3.159-1989 (''ANSI C '').

3

NAME
frexp – convert floating-point number to fractional and integral components

SYNOPSIS
```
#include <math.h>
```
double
frexp(*double value, int *exp*);

DESCRIPTION
The **frexp**() function breaks a floating-point number into a normalized fraction and an integral power of 2. It stores the integer in the *int* object pointed to by *exp*.

RETURN VALUES
The **frexp**() function returns the value x, such that x is a *double* with magnitude in the interval [1/2, 1] or zero, and *value* equals x times 2 raised to the power *exp*. If *value* is zero, both parts of the result are zero.

SEE ALSO
ldexp(3), modf(3), math(3)

STANDARDS
The **frexp**() function conforms to ANSI C X3.159-1989 (''ANSI C '').

3

NAME

fgetpos, fseek, fsetpos, ftell, rewind – reposition a stream

SYNOPSIS

```
#include <stdio.h>

int
fseek(FILE *stream, long offset, int whence);

long
ftell(FILE *stream);

void
rewind(FILE *stream);

int
fgetpos(FILE *stream, fpos_t *pos);

int
fsetpos(FILE *stream, fpos_t *pos);
```

DESCRIPTION

The **fseek**( ) function sets the file position indicator for the stream pointed to by *stream*. The new position, measured in bytes, is obtained by adding *offset* bytes to the position specified by *whence*. If *whence* is set to SEEK_SET, SEEK_CUR, or SEEK_END, the offset is relative to the start of the file, the current position indicator, or end-of-file, respectively. A successful call to the **fseek**( ) function clears the end-of-file indicator for the stream and undoes any effects of the ungetc(3) function on the same stream.

The **ftell**( ) function obtains the current value of the file position indicator for the stream pointed to by *stream*.

The **rewind**( ) function sets the file position indicator for the stream pointed to by *stream* to the beginning of the file. It is equivalent to:

```
(void)fseek(stream, 0L, SEEK_SET)
```

except that the error indicator for the stream is also cleared (see clearerr(3)).

The **fgetpos**( ) and **fsetpos**( ) functions are alternate interfaces equivalent to **ftell**( ) and **fseek**( ) (with whence set to SEEK_SET), setting and storing the current value of the file offset into or from the object referenced by *pos*. On some (non-UNIX) systems an ‘‘*fpos_t*’’ object may be a complex object and these routines may be the only way to portably reposition a text stream.

RETURN VALUES

The **rewind**( ) function returns no value. Upon successful completion, **fgetpos**( ), **fseek**( ), **fsetpos**( ) return 0, and **ftell**( ) returns the current offset. Otherwise, −1 is returned and the global variable errno is set to indicate the error.

ERRORS

[EBADF]　　The *stream* specified is not a seekable stream.

[EINVAL]　 The *whence* argument to **fseek**( ) was not SEEK_SET, SEEK_END, or SEEK_CUR.

The function **fgetpos**( ), **fseek**( ), **fsetpos**( ), and **ftell**( ) may also fail and set *errno* for any of the errors specified for the routines fflush(3), fstat(2), lseek(2), and malloc(3).

SEE ALSO
　　　lseek(2)

STANDARDS
　　　The **fgetpos**(), **fsetpos**(), **fseek**(), **ftell**(), and **rewind**( ) functions conform to ANSI C X3.159-1989 (''ANSI C '').

3

NAME

ftime – get date and time

SYNOPSIS

```
#include <sys/types.h>
#include <sys/timeb.h>

struct timeb *
ftime(struct timeb *tp);
```

DESCRIPTION

This interface is obsoleted by gettimeofday(2).

It is available from the compatibility library, libcompat.

The **ftime( )** routine fills in a structure pointed to by its argument, as defined by <sys/timeb.h>:

```
/*
 * Structure returned by ftime system call
 */
struct timeb
{
        time_t  time;
        unsigned short millitm;
        short   timezone;
        short   dstflag;
};
```

The structure contains the time since the epoch in seconds, up to 1000 milliseconds of more-precise interval, the local time zone (measured in minutes of time westward from Greenwich), and a flag that, if nonzero, indicates that Daylight Saving time applies locally during the appropriate part of the year.

SEE ALSO

gettimeofday(2), settimeofday(2), time(2), ctime(3)

HISTORY

The **ftime** function appeared in 4.2BSD.

NAME

     fts – traverse a file hierarchy

SYNOPSIS

     #include ⟨sys/types.h⟩
     #include ⟨sys/stat.h⟩
     #include ⟨fts.h⟩

     *FTS ***
     fts_open(*char * const *path_argv, int options,*
             *int *compar(const FTSENT **, const FTSENT **)*);

     *FTSENT ***
     fts_read(*FTS *ftsp*);

     *FTSENT ***
     fts_children(*FTS *ftsp, int options*);

     int
     fts_set(*FTS ftsp, FTSENT *f, int options*);

     int
     fts_close(*FTS *ftsp*);

DESCRIPTION

     The **fts** functions are provided for traversing UNIX file hierarchies. A simple overview is that the
     fts_open( ) function returns a "handle" on a file hierarchy, which is then supplied to the other **fts** func-
     tions. The function **fts_read**( ) returns a pointer to a structure describing one of the files in the file hierar-
     chy. The function **fts_children**( ) returns a pointer to a linked list of structures, each of which describes
     one of the files contained in a directory in the hierarchy. In general, directories are visited two distinguish-
     able times; in pre-order (before any of their descendants are visited) and in post-order (after all of their des-
     cendants have been visited). Files are visited once. It is possible to walk the hierarchy "logically" (ignor-
     ing symbolic links) or physically (visiting symbolic links), order the walk of the hierarchy or prune and/or
     re-visit portions of the hierarchy.

     Two structures are defined (and typedef'd) in the include file <fts.h>. The first is *FTS*, the structure that
     represents the file hierarchy itself. The second is *FTSENT*, the structure that represents a file in the file
     hierarchy. Normally, an *FTSENT* structure is returned for every file in the file hierarchy. In this manual
     page, "file" and "*FTSENT* structure" are generally interchangeable. The *FTSENT* structure contains at
     least the following fields, which are described in greater detail below:

     ```
     typedef struct _ftsent {
             u_short fts_info;              /* flags for FTSENT structure */
             char *fts_accpath;             /* access path */
             char *fts_path;                /* root path */
             short fts_pathlen;             /* strlen(fts_path) */
             char *fts_name;                /* file name */
             short fts_namelen;             /* strlen(fts_name) */
             short fts_level;               /* depth (−1 to N) */
             int fts_errno;                 /* file errno */
             long fts_number;               /* local numeric value */
             void *fts_pointer;             /* local address value */
             struct ftsent *fts_parent;     /* parent directory */
             struct ftsent *fts_link;       /* next file structure */
     ```

```
        struct ftsent *fts_cycle;       /* cycle structure */
        struct stat *fts_statp;                 /* stat(2) information */
} FTSENT;
```

These fields are defined as follows:

fts_info   One of the following flags describing the returned *FTSENT* structure and the file it
                represents. With the exception of directories without errors (FTS_D), all of these entries
                are terminal, that is, they will not be revisited, nor will any of their descendants be visited.

                FTS_D   A directory being visited in pre-order.

                FTS_DC   A directory that causes a cycle in the tree. (The *fts_cycle* field of the
                               FTSENT structure will be filled in as well.)

                FTS_DEFAULT   Any *FTSENT* structure that represents a file type not explicitly described
                               by one of the other *fts_info* values.

                FTS_DNR   A directory which cannot be read. This is an error return, and the
                               fts_errno field will be set to indicate what caused the error.

                FTS_DOT   A file named '.' or '..' which was not specified as a file name to
                               fts_open() (see FTS_SEEDOT).

                FTS_DP   A directory being visited in post-order. The contents of the *FTSENT*
                               structure will be unchanged from when it was returned in pre-order, i.e.
                               with the *fts_info* field set to FTS_D.

                FTS_ERR   This is an error return, and the *fts_errno* field will be set to indicate
                               what caused the error.

                FTS_F   A regular file.

                FTS_NS   A file for which no stat(2) information was available. The contents of
                               the *fts_statp* field are undefined. This is an error return, and the
                               fts_errno field will be set to indicate what caused the error.

                FTS_NSOK   A file for which no stat(2) information was requested. The contents of
                               the *fts_statp* field are undefined.

                FTS_SL   A symbolic link.

                FTS_SLNONE   A symbolic link with a non-existent target. The contents of the
                               fts_statp field reference the file characteristic information for the
                               symbolic link itself.

fts_accpath A path for accessing the file from the current directory.

fts_path   The path for the file relative to the root of the traversal. This path contains the path
               specified to **fts_open**() as a prefix.

fts_pathlen The length of the string referenced by *fts_path*.

fts_name   The name of the file.

fts_namelen The length of the string referenced by *fts_name*.

fts_level   The depth of the traversal, numbered from −1 to N, where this file was found. The
               FTSENT structure representing the parent of the starting point (or root) of the traversal is

numbered −1, and the *FTSENT* structure for the root itself is numbered 0.

fts_errno   Upon return of a *FTSENT* structure from the **fts_children**() or **fts_read**() functions, with its *fts_info* field set to FTS_DNR, FTS_ERR or FTS_NS, the *fts_errno* field contains the value of the external variable *errno* specifying the cause of the error. Otherwise, the contents of the *fts_errno* field are undefined.

fts_number This field is provided for the use of the application program and is not modified by the **fts** functions. It is initialized to 0.

fts_pointer This field is provided for the use of the application program and is not modified by the **fts** functions. It is initialized to NULL.

fts_parent A pointer to the *FTSENT* structure referencing the file in the hierarchy immediately above the current file, i.e. the directory of which this file is a member. A parent structure for the initial entry point is provided as well, however, only the *fts_level*, *fts_number* and *fts_pointer* fields are guaranteed to be initialized.

fts_link   Upon return from the **fts_children**() function, the *fts_link* field points to the next structure in the NULL-terminated linked list of directory members. Otherwise, the contents of the *fts_link* field are undefined.

fts_cycle   If a directory causes a cycle in the hierarchy (see FTS_DC), either because of a hard link between two directories, or a symbolic link pointing to a directory, the *fts_cycle* field of the structure will point to the *FTSENT* structure in the hierarchy that references the same file as the current *FTSENT* structure. Otherwise, the contents of the *fts_cycle* field are undefined.

fts_statp   A pointer to stat(2) information for the file.

A single buffer is used for all of the paths of all of the files in the file hierarchy. Therefore, the *fts_path* and *fts_accpath* fields are guaranteed to be NULL-terminated *only* for the file most recently returned by **fts_read**(). To use these fields to reference any files represented by other *FTSENT* structures will require that the path buffer be modified using the information contained in that *FTSENT* structure's *fts_pathlen* field. Any such modifications should be undone before further calls to **fts_read**() are attempted. The *fts_name* field is always NULL-terminated.

FTS_OPEN

The **fts_open**() function takes a pointer to an array of character pointers naming one or more paths which make up a logical file hierarchy to be traversed. The array must be terminated by a NULL pointer.

There are a number of options, at least one of which (either FTS_LOGICAL or FTS_PHYSICAL) must be specified. The options are selected by *or*'ing the following values:

FTS_COMFOLLOW
          This option causes any symbolic link specified as a root path to be followed immediately whether or not FTS_LOGICAL is also specified.

FTS_LOGICAL This option causes the **fts** routines to return *FTSENT* structures for the targets of symbolic links instead of the symbolic links themselves. If this option is set, the only symbolic links for which *FTSENT* structures are returned to the application are those referencing non-existent files. Either FTS_LOGICAL or FTS_PHYSICAL *must* be provided to the **fts_open**() function.

FTS_NOCHDIR As a performance optimization, the **fts** functions change directories as they walk the file hierarchy. This has the side-effect that an application cannot rely on being in any particular directory during the traversal. The FTS_NOCHDIR option turns off this optimization, and the **fts** functions will not change the current directory. Note that applications should not themselves change their current directory and try to access files unless FTS_NOCHDIR is specified and absolute pathnames were provided as arguments to **fts_open**().

FTS_NOSTAT   By default, returned *FTSENT* structures reference file characteristic information (the *statp* field) for each file visited. This option relaxes that requirement as a performance optimization, allowing the **fts** functions to set the *fts_info* field to FTS_NSOK and leave the contents of the *statp* field undefined.

FTS_PHYSICAL   This option causes the **fts** routines to return *FTSENT* structures for symbolic links themselves instead of the target files they point to. If this option is set, *FTSENT* structures for all symbolic links in the hierarchy are returned to the application. Either FTS_LOGICAL or FTS_PHYSICAL *must* be provided to the **fts_open**() function.

FTS_SEEDOT   By default, unless they are specified as path arguments to **fts_open**(), any files named '.' or '..' encountered in the file hierarchy are ignored. This option causes the **fts** routines to return *FTSENT* structures for them.

FTS_XDEV   This option prevents **fts** from descending into directories that have a different device number than the file from which the descent began.

The argument **compar**() specifies a user-defined function which may be used to order the traversal of the hierarchy. It takes two pointers to pointers to *FTSENT* structures as arguments and should return a negative value, zero, or a positive value to indicate if the file referenced by its first argument comes before, in any order with respect to, or after, the file referenced by its second argument. The *fts_accpath*, *fts_path* and *fts_pathlen* fields of the *FTSENT* structures may *never* be used in this comparison. If the *fts_info* field is set to FTS_NS or FTS_NSOK, the *fts_statp* field may not either. If the **compar**() argument is NULL, the directory traversal order is in the order listed in *path_argv* for the root paths, and in the order listed in the directory for everything else.

FTS_READ

The **fts_read**() function returns a pointer to an *FTSENT* structure describing a file in the hierarchy. Directories (that are readable and do not cause cycles) are visited at least twice, once in pre-order and once in post-order. All other files are visited at least once. (Hard links between directories that do not cause cycles or symbolic links to symbolic links may cause files to be visited more than once, or directories more than twice.)

If all the members of the hierarchy have been returned, **fts_read**() returns NULL and sets the external variable *errno* to 0. If an error unrelated to a file in the hierarchy occurs, **fts_read**() returns NULL and sets *errno* appropriately. If an error related to a returned file occurs, a pointer to an *FTSENT* structure is returned, and *errno* may or may not have been set (see *fts_info*).

The *FTSENT* structures returned by **fts_read**() may be overwritten after a call to **fts_close**() on the same file hierarchy stream, or, after a call to **fts_read**() on the same file hierarchy stream unless they represent a file of type directory, in which case they will not be overwritten until after a call to **fts_read**() after the *FTSENT* structure has been returned by the function **fts_read**() in post-order.

FTS_CHILDREN

The **fts_children**() function returns a pointer to an *FTSENT* structure describing the first entry in a NULL-terminated linked list of the files in the directory represented by the *FTSENT* structure most recently returned by **fts_read**(). The list is linked through the *fts_link* field of the *FTSENT* structure, and is ordered by the user-specified comparison function, if any. Repeated calls to **fts_children**() will recreate this linked list.

As a special case, if **fts_read**() has not yet been called for a hierarchy, **fts_children**() will return a pointer to the files in the logical directory specified to **fts_open**(), i.e. the arguments specified to **fts_open**(). Otherwise, if the *FTSENT* structure most recently returned by **fts_read**() is not a directory being visited in pre-order, or the directory does not contain any files, **fts_children**() returns NULL and sets *errno* to zero. If an error occurs, **fts_children**() returns NULL and sets *errno* appropriately.

The *FTSENT* structures returned by **fts_children**() may be overwritten after a call to **fts_children**(), **fts_close**() or **fts_read**() on the same file hierarchy stream.

Option may be set to the following value:

FTS_NAMEONLY Only the names of the files are needed. The contents of all the fields in the returned linked list of structures are undefined with the exception of the *fts_name* and *fts_namelen* fields.

FTS_SET

The function **fts_set**() allows the user application to determine further processing for the file *f* of the stream *ftsp*. The **fts_set**() function returns 0 on success, and −1 if an error occurs. *Option* must be set to one of the following values:

FTS_AGAIN Re-visit the file; any file type may be re-visited. The next call to **fts_read**() will return the referenced file. The *fts_stat* and *fts_info* fields of the structure will be reinitialized at that time, but no other fields will have been changed. This option is meaningful only for the most recently returned file from **fts_read**(). Normal use is for post-order directory visits, where it causes the directory to be re-visited (in both pre and post-order) as well as all of its descendants.

FTS_FOLLOW The referenced file must be a symbolic link. If the referenced file is the one most recently returned by **fts_read**(), the next call to **fts_read**() returns the file with the *fts_info* and *fts_statp* fields reinitialized to reflect the target of the symbolic link instead of the symbolic link itself. If the file is one of those most recently returned by **fts_children**(), the *fts_info* and *fts_statp* fields of the structure, when returned by **fts_read**(), will reflect the target of the symbolic link instead of the symbolic link itself. In either case, if the target of the symbolic link does not exist the fields of the returned structure will be unchanged and the *fts_info* field will be set to FTS_SLNONE.

If the target of the link is a directory, the pre-order return, followed by the return of all of its descendants, followed by a post-order return, is done.

FTS_SKIP No descendants of this file are visited. The file may be one of those most recently returned by either **fts_children**() or **fts_read**().

FTS_CLOSE

The **fts_close**() function closes a file hierarchy stream *ftsp* and restores the current directory to the directory from which **fts_open**() was called to open *ftsp*. The **fts_close**() function returns 0 on success, and −1 if an error occurs.

ERRORS

The function **fts_open**() may fail and set *errno* for any of the errors specified for the library functions open(2) and malloc(3).

The function **fts_close**() may fail and set *errno* for any of the errors specified for the library functions chdir(2) and close(2).

The functions **fts_read**( ) and **fts_children**( ) may fail and set *errno* for any of the errors specified for the library functions chdir(2), malloc(3), opendir(3), readdir(3) and stat(2).

In addition, **fts_children**(), **fts_open**( ) and **fts_set**( ) may fail and set *errno* as follows:

[EINVAL]   The options were invalid.

SEE ALSO
find(1), chdir(2), stat(2), qsort(3)

STANDARDS
The **fts** utility is expected to be included in a future IEEE Std1003.1-1988 (''POSIX'') revision.

3

NAME

funopen, fropen, fwopen – open a stream

SYNOPSIS

```
#include <stdio.h>
```

```
FILE *
funopen(void *cookie, int (*readfn)(void *, char *, int),
        int (writefn*)(void *, const char *, int),
        fpos_t (seekfn*)(void *, fpos_t, int), int (closefn*)(void *));
```

```
FILE *
fropen(void *cookie, int (*readfn)(void *, char *, int));
```

```
FILE *
fwopen(void *cookie, int (*writefn)(void *, char *, int));
```

DESCRIPTION

The **funopen**() function associates a stream with up to four "I/O functions". Either *readfn* or *writefn* must be specified; the others can be given as an appropriately-typed NULL pointer. These I/O functions will be used to read, write, seek and close the new stream.

In general, omitting a function means that any attempt to perform the associated operation on the resulting stream will fail. If the close function is omitted, closing the stream will flush any buffered output and then succeed.

The calling conventions of *readfn*, *writefn*, *seekfn* and *closefn* must match those, respectively, of read(2), write(2), seek(2), and close(2) with the single exception that they are passed the *cookie* argument specified to **funopen**() in place of the traditional file descriptor argument.

Read and write I/O functions are allowed to change the underlying buffer on fully buffered or line buffered streams by calling setvbuf(3). They are also not required to completely fill or empty the buffer. They are not, however, allowed to change streams from unbuffered to buffered or to change the state of the line buffering flag. They must also be prepared to have read or write calls occur on buffers other than the one most recently specified.

All user I/O functions can report an error by returning −1. Additionally, all of the functions should set the external variable *errno* appropriately if an error occurs.

An error on **closefn**() does not keep the stream open.

As a convenience, the include file <stdio.h> defines the macros **fropen**() and **fwopen**() as calls to **funopen**() with only a read or write function specified.

RETURN VALUES

Upon successful completion, **funopen**() returns a FILE pointer. Otherwise, NULL is returned and the global variable *errno* is set to indicate the error.

ERRORS

[EINVAL]　The **funopen**() function was called without either a read or write function. The **funopen**() function may also fail and set *errno* for any of the errors specified for the routine malloc(3).

SEE ALSO

fcntl(2), open(2), fclose(3), fopen(3), fseek(3), setbuf(3)

HISTORY

The **funopen**( ) functions first appeared in 4.4BSD.

BUGS

The **funopen**( ) function may not be portable to systems other than BSD.

3

NAME

    getbsize – get user block size

SYNOPSIS

    #include <stdlib.h>

    char *
    getbsize(*int *headerlenp, long *blocksizep*);

DESCRIPTION

    The getbsize function determines the user's preferred block size based on the value of the ''BLOCKSIZE'' environment variable; see environ(7) for details on its use and format.

    The getbsize function returns a pointer to a null-terminated string describing the block size, something like ''1K-blocks''. The memory referenced by *headerlenp* is filled in with the length of the string (not including the terminating null). The memory referenced by *blocksizep* is filled in with block size, in bytes.

    If the user's block size is unreasonable, a warning message is written to standard error and the returned information reflects a block size of 512 bytes.

SEE ALSO

    df(1), du(1), ls(1), systat(1), environ(7)

HISTORY

    The getbsize function call appeared in 4.4BSD.

NAME

fgetc, getc, getchar, getw – get next character or word from input stream

SYNOPSIS

#include ⟨stdio.h⟩

int
fgetc(*FILE *stream*);

int
getc(*FILE *stream*);

int
getchar( );

int
getw(*FILE *stream*);

DESCRIPTION

The **fgetc**( ) function obtains the next input character (if present) from the stream pointed at by *stream*, or the next character pushed back on the stream via ungetc.

The **getc**( ) function acts essentially identically to **fgetc**(), but is a macro that expands in-line.

The **getchar**( ) function is equivalent to: getc with the argument stdin.

The **getw**( ) function obtains the next *int* (if present) from the stream pointed at by *stream*.

RETURN VALUES

If successful, these routines return the next requested object from the *stream*. If the stream is at end-of-file or a read error occurs, the routines return EOF. The routines feof(3) and ferror(3) must be used to distinguish between end-of-file and error. If an error occurs, the global variable *errno* is set to indicate the error. The end-of-file condition is remembered, even on a terminal, and all subsequent attempts to read will return EOF until the condition is cleared with clearerr.

SEE ALSO

ferror(3), fread(3), fopen(3), putc(3), ungetc(3)

STANDARDS

The **fgetc**(), **getc**( ) and **getchar**( ) functions conform to ANSI C X3.159-1989 (''ANSI C '').

BUGS

Since EOF is a valid integer value, feof and ferror must be used to check for failure after calling **getw**(). The size and byte order of an *int* varies from one machine to another, and **getw**( ) is not recommended for portable applications.

NAME

cgetent, cgetset, cgetmatch, cgetcap, cgetnum, cgetstr, cgetustr, cgetfirst, cgetnext, cgetclose – capability database access routines

SYNOPSIS

#include ⟨stdlib.h⟩

int
cgetent(*char **buf, char **db_array, char *name*);

int
cgetset(*char *ent*);

int
cgetmatch(*char *buf, char *name*);

char ∗
cgetcap(*char *buf, char *cap, char type*);

int
cgetnum(*char *buf, char *cap, long *num*);

int
cgetstr(*char *buf, char *cap, char **str*);

int
cgetustr(*char *buf, char *cap, char **str*);

int
cgetfirst(*char **buf, char **db_array*);

int
cgetnext(*char **buf, char **db_array*);

int
cgetclose(*void*);

DESCRIPTION

Cgetent( ) extracts the capability rec *name* from the database specified by the NULL terminated file array *db_array* and returns a pointer to a malloc'd copy of it in *buf*. **Cgetent** will first look for files ending in **.db** (see cap_mkdb(1)) before accessing the ASCII file. *Buf* must be retained through all subsequent calls to **cgetmatch**(), **cgetcap**(), **cgetnum**(), **cgetstr**(), and **cgetustr**(), but may then be free'd. On success 0 is returned, 1 if the returned record contains an unresolved **tc** expansion, −1 if the requested record couldn't be found, −2 if a system error was encountered (couldn't open/read a file, etc.) also setting *errno*, and −3 if a potential reference loop is detected (see **tc=** comments below).

Cgetset enables the addition of a character buffer containing a single capability record entry to the capability database. Conceptually, the entry is added as the first "file" in the database, and is therefore searched first on the call to **cgetent**. The entry is passed in *ent*. If *ent* is NULL, the current entry is removed from the database. **Cgetset** must precede the database traversal. It must be called before the **cgetent** call. If a sequential access is being performed (see below), it must be called before the first sequential access call (**cgetfirst** or **cgetnext**), or be directly preceded by a **cgetclose** call. On success 0 is returned and −1 on failure.

Cgetmatch will return 0 if *name* is one of the names of the capability record *buf*, −1 if not.

Cgetcap searches the capability record *buf* for the capability *cap* with type *type*. A *type* is specified using any single character. If a colon (':') is used, an untyped capability will be searched for (see below for explanation of types). A pointer to the value of *cap* in *buf* is returned on success, NULL if the requested capability couldn't be found. The end of the capability value is signaled by a ':' or ASCII NUL (see below for capability database syntax).

Cgetnum retrieves the value of the numeric capability *cap* from the capability record pointed to by *buf*. The numeric value is returned in the *long* pointed to by *num*. 0 is returned on success, −1 if the requested numeric capability couldn't be found.

Cgetstr retrieves the value of the string capability *cap* from the capability record pointed to by *buf*. A pointer to a decoded, NUL terminated, malloc'd copy of the string is returned in the *char* * pointed to by *str*. The number of characters in the decoded string not including the trailing NUL is returned on success, −1 if the requested string capability couldn't be found, −2 if a system error was encountered (storage allocation failure).

Cgetustr is identical to **cgetstr** except that it does not expand special characters, but rather returns each character of the capability string literally.

Cgetfirst, cgetnext, comprise a function group that provides for sequential access of the NULL pointer terminated array of file names, *db_array*. **Cgetfirst** returns the first record in the database and resets the access to the first record. **Cgetnext** returns the next record in the database with respect to the record returned by the previous **cgetfirst** or **cgetnext** call. If there is no such previous call, the first record in the database is returned. Each record is returned in a malloc'd copy pointed to by *buf*. Tc expansion is done (see **tc=** comments below). Upon completion of the database 0 is returned, 1 is returned upon successful return of record with possibly more remaining (we haven't reached the end of the database yet), 2 is returned if the record contains an unresolved **tc** expansion, −1 is returned if an system error occurred, and −2 is returned if a potential reference loop is detected (see **tc=** comments below). Upon completion of database (0 return) the database is closed.

Cgetclose closes the sequential access and frees any memory and file descriptors being used. Note that it does not erase the buffer pushed by a call to **cgetset**.

CAPABILITY DATABASE SYNTAX

Capability databases are normally ASCII and may be edited with standard text editors. Blank lines and lines beginning with a '#' are comments and are ignored. Lines ending with a '\' indicate that the next line is a continuation of the current line; the '\' and following newline are ignored. Long lines are usually continued onto several physical lines by ending each line except the last with a '\'.

Capability databases consist of a series of records, one per logical line. Each record contains a variable number of ':'-separated fields (capabilities). Empty fields consisting entirely of white space characters (spaces and tabs) are ignored.

The first capability of each record specifies its names, separated by 'l' characters. These names are used to reference records in the database. By convention, the last name is usually a comment and is not intended as a lookup tag. For example, the *vt100* record from the **termcap** database begins:

      d0 | vt100 | vt100-am | vt100am | dec vt100 :

giving four names that can be used to access the record.

The remaining non-empty capabilities describe a set of (name, value) bindings, consisting of a names optionally followed by a typed values:

name   typeless [boolean] capability *name* is present [true]

name*T*value	capability (*name*, *T*) has value *value*
name@	no capability *name* exists
name*T*@	capability (*name*, *T*) does not exist

Names consist of one or more characters. Names may contain any character except ':', but it's usually best to restrict them to the printable characters and avoid use of graphics like '#', '=', '%', '@', etc. Types are single characters used to separate capability names from their associated typed values. Types may be any character except a ':'. Typically, graphics like '#', '=', '%', etc. are used. Values may be any number of characters and may contain any character except ':'.

CAPABILITY DATABASE SEMANTICS

Capability records describe a set of (name, value) bindings. Names may have multiple values bound to them. Different values for a name are distinguished by their *types*. Cgetcap will return a pointer to a value of a name given the capability name and the type of the value.

The types '#' and '=' are conventionally used to denote numeric and string typed values, but no restriction on those types is enforced. The functions cgetnum and cgetstr can be used to implement the traditional syntax and semantics of '#' and '='. Typeless capabilities are typically used to denote boolean objects with presence or absence indicating truth and false values respectively. This interpretation is conveniently represented by:

```
(getcap(buf, name, ':') != NULL)
```

A special capability, tc= *name*, is used to indicate that the record specified by *name* should be substituted for the tc capability. Tc capabilities may interpolate records which also contain tc capabilities and more than one tc capability may be used in a record. A tc expansion scope (i.e., where the argument is searched for) contains the file in which the tc is declared and all subsequent files in the file array.

When a database is searched for a capability record, the first matching record in the search is returned. When a record is scanned for a capability, the first matching capability is returned; the capability :name*T*@: will hide any following definition of a value of type *T* for *name*; and the capability :name@: will prevent any following values of *name* from being seen.

These features combined with tc capabilities can be used to generate variations of other databases and records by either adding new capabilities, overriding definitions with new definitions, or hiding following definitions via '@' capabilities.

EXAMPLES

example l an example of binding multiple values to names:\
     :foo%bar:foo^blah:foo@:\
     :abc%xyz:abc^frap:abc$@:\
     :tc=more:

The capability foo has two values bound to it (bar of type '%' and blah of type '^') and any other value bindings are hidden. The capability abc also has two values bound but only a value of type '$' is prevented from being defined in the capability record more.

file1:
     new l new_record l a modification of "old":\
          :fript=bar:who-cares@:tc=old:blah:tc=extensions:
file2:
     old l old_record l an old database record:\
          :fript=foo:who-cares:glork#200:

The records are extracted by calling cgetent with file1 preceding file2. In the capability record new in file1, fript=bar overrides the definition of fript=foo interpolated from the capability record old in file2, who-cares@ prevents the definition of any who-cares definitions in old from being seen, glork#200 is inherited from old, and blah and anything defined by the record extensions is added to those definitions in old. Note that the position of the fript=bar and who-cares@ definitions before tc=old is important here. If they were after, the definitions in old would take precedence.

CGETNUM AND CGETSTR SYNTAX AND SEMANTICS

Two types are predefined by **cgetnum** and **cgetstr**:

name#number	numeric capability *name* has value *number*
name=string	string capability *name* has value *string*
name#@	the numeric capability *name* does not exist
name=@	the string capability *name* does not exist

Numeric capability values may be given in one of three numeric bases. If the number starts with either '0x' or '0X' it is interpreted as a hexadecimal number (both upper and lower case a-f may be used to denote the extended hexadecimal digits). Otherwise, if the number starts with a '0' it is interpreted as an octal number. Otherwise the number is interpreted as a decimal number.

String capability values may contain any character. Non-printable ASCII codes, new lines, and colons may be conveniently represented by the use of escape sequences:

^X	('X' & 037)	control-X
\b, \B	(ASCII 010)	backspace
\t, \T	(ASCII 011)	tab
\n, \N	(ASCII 012)	line feed (newline)
\f, \F	(ASCII 014)	form feed
\r, \R	(ASCII 015)	carriage return
\e, \E	(ASCII 027)	escape
\c, \C	(:)	colon
\\	(\)	back slash
\^	(^)	caret
\nnn	(ASCII octal *nnn*)	

A '\' may be followed by up to three octal digits directly specifies the numeric code for a character. The use of ASCII NULs, while easily encoded, causes all sorts of problems and must be used with care since NULs are typically used to denote the end of strings; many applications use '\200' to represent a NUL.

DIAGNOSTICS

Cgetent, cgetset, cgetmatch, cgetnum, cgetstr, cgetustr, cgetfirst, and **cgetnext** return a value greater than or equal to 0 on success and a value less than 0 on failure. **Cgetcap** returns a character pointer on success and a NULL on failure.

Cgetent, and **cgetseq** may fail and set *errno* for any of the errors specified for the library functions: fopen(2), fclose(2), open(2), and close(2).

Cgetent, cgetset, cgetstr, and **cgetustr** may fail and set *errno* as follows:

[ENOMEM]   No memory to allocate.

SEE ALSO

cap_mkdb(1), malloc(3)

BUGS

Colons (':') can't be used in names, types, or values.

There are no checks for `tc=name` loops in **cgetent**.

The buffer added to the database by a call to **cgetset** is not unique to the database but is rather prepended to any database used.

NAME

getcwd – get working directory pathname

SYNOPSIS

`#include <stdio.h>`

char *
getcwd(*char *buf*, *size_t size*);

char *
getwd(*char *buf*);

DESCRIPTION

The **getcwd**( ) function copies the absolute pathname of the current working directory into the memory referenced by *buf* and returns a pointer to *buf*. The *size* argument is the size, in bytes, of the array referenced by *buf*.

If *buf* is NULL, space is allocated as necessary to store the pathname. This space may later be free(3)'d.

The function **getwd**( ) is a compatibility routine which calls **getcwd**( ) with its *buf* argument and a size of MAXPATHLEN (as defined in the include file <sys/param.h>). Obviously, *buf* should be at least MAXPATHLEN bytes in length.

These routines have traditionally been used by programs to save the name of a working directory for the purpose of returning to it. A much faster and less error-prone method of accomplishing this is to open the current directory ('.') and use the fchdir(2) function to return.

RETURN VALUES

Upon successful completion, a pointer to the pathname is returned. Otherwise a NULL pointer is returned and the global variable *errno* is set to indicate the error. In addition, **getwd**( ) copies the error message associated with *errno* into the memory referenced by *buf*.

ERRORS

The **getcwd**( ) function will fail if:

[EACCESS]   Read or search permission was denied for a component of the pathname.

[EINVAL]   The *size* argument is zero.

[ENOENT]   A component of the pathname no longer exists.

[ENOMEM]   Insufficient memory is available.

[ERANGE]   The *size* argument is greater than zero but smaller than the length of the pathname plus 1.

SEE ALSO

chdir(2), fchdir(2), malloc(3), strerror(3)

STANDARDS

The **getcwd**( ) function conforms to ANSI C X3.159-1989 (''ANSI C ''). The ability to specify a NULL pointer and have **getcwd**( ) allocate memory as necessary is an extension.

HISTORY

The **getwd**( ) function appeared in 4.0BSD.

BUGS

      The `getwd()` function does not do sufficient error checking and is not able to return very long, but valid, paths. It is provided for compatibility.

NAME

getdiskbyname – get generic disk description by its name

SYNOPSIS

#include <sys/disklabel.h>

struct disklabel *
getdiskbyname(*const char *name*);

DESCRIPTION

The **getdiskbyname**() function takes a disk name (e.g. rm03) and returns a prototype disk label describing its geometry information and the standard disk partition tables. All information is obtained from the disktab(5) file.

SEE ALSO

disklabel(5), disktab(5), disklabel(8)

HISTORY

The **getdiskbyname**() function appeared in 4.3BSD.

NAME

getenv, putenv, setenv, unsetenv – environment variable functions

SYNOPSIS

```
#include <stdlib.h>

char *
getenv(const char *name);

int
setenv(const char *name, const char *value, int overwrite);

int
putenv(const char *string);

void
unsetenv(const char *name);
```

DESCRIPTION

These functions set, unset and fetch environment variables from the host *environment list*. For compatibility with differing environment conventions, the given arguments *name* and *value* may be appended and prepended, respectively, with an equal sign "=".

The getenv( ) function obtains the current value of the environment variable, *name*. If the variable *name* is not in the current environment, a null pointer is returned.

The setenv( ) function inserts or resets the environment variable *name* in the current environment list. If the variable *name* does not exist in the list, it is inserted with the given *value*. If the variable does exist, the argument *overwrite* is tested; if *overwrite is* zero, the variable is not reset, otherwise it is reset to the given *value*.

The putenv( ) function takes an argument of the form "name=value" and is equivalent to:

```
setenv(name, value, 1);
```

The unsetenv( ) function deletes all instances of the variable name pointed to by *name* from the list.

RETURN VALUES

The functions setenv( ) and putenv( ) return zero if successful; otherwise the global variable *errno* is set to indicate the error and a –1 is returned.

ERRORS

[ENOMEM]   The function setenv( ) or putenv( ) failed because they were unable to allocate memory for the environment.

SEE ALSO

csh(1), sh(1), execve(2), environ(7)

STANDARDS

The getenv( ) function conforms to ANSI C X3.159-1989 ("ANSI C ").

HISTORY

The functions setenv( ) and unsetenv( ) appeared in Version 7 AT&T UNIX. The putenv( ) function appeared in 4.3BSD–Reno.

NAME

getfsent, getfsspec, getfsfile, setfsent, endfsent – get file system descriptor file entry

SYNOPSIS

```
#include <fstab.h>
```

fstab *
getfsent(*void*);

struct fstab *
getfsspec(*const char *spec*);

struct fstab *
getfsfile(*const char *file*);

int
setfsent(*void*);

void
endfsent(*void*);

DESCRIPTION

The getfsent(), getfsspec(), and getfsfile( ) functions each return a pointer to an object with the following structure containing the broken-out fields of a line in the file system description file, <fstab.h>.

```
struct fstab {
        char    *fs_spec;       /* block special device name */
        char    *fs_file;       /* file system path prefix */
        char    *fs_vfstype;    /* type of file system */
        char    *fs_mntops;     /* comma separated mount options */
        char    *fs_type;       /* rw, ro, sw, or xx */
        int     fs_freq;        /* dump frequency, in days */
        int     fs_passno;      /* pass number on parallel dump */
};
```

The fields have meanings described in fstab(5).

The setfsent( ) function opens the file (closing any previously opened file) or rewinds it if it is already open.

The endfsent( ) function closes the file.

The getfsspec( ) and getfsfile( ) functions search the entire file (opening it if necessary) for a matching special file name or file system file name.

For programs wishing to read the entire database, getfsent( ) reads the next entry (opening the file if necessary).

All entries in the file with a type field equivalent to FSTAB_XX are ignored.

RETURN VALUES

The getfsent(), getfsspec(), and getfsfile( ) functions return a null pointer (0) on EOF or error. The setfsent( ) function returns 0 on failure, 1 on success. The endfsent( ) function returns nothing.

FILES

    `/etc/fstab`

SEE ALSO

    fstab(5)

HISTORY

    The `getfsent()` function appeared in 4.0BSD; the **endfsent()**, **getfsfile()**, **getfsspec()**, and **setfsent()** functions appeared in 4.3BSD.

BUGS

    These functions use static data storage; if the data is needed for future use, it should be copied before any subsequent calls overwrite it.

NAME

getgrent, getgrnam, getgrgid, setgroupent, setgrent, endgrent – group database operations

SYNOPSIS

#include <grp.h>

*struct group *
getgrent(*void*);

*struct group *
getgrnam(*const char *name*);

*struct group *
getgrgid(*gid_t gid*);

*struct group *
setgroupent(*int stayopen*);

int
setgrent(*void*);

void
endgrent(*void*);

DESCRIPTION

These functions operate on the group database file /etc/group which is described in group(5). Each
line of the database is defined by the structure *group* found in the include file <grp.h>:

```
struct group {
        char    *gr_name;       /* group name */
        char    *gr_passwd;     /* group password */
        gid_t   gr_gid;         /* group id */
        char    **gr_mem;       /* group members */
};
```

The functions **getgrnam**( ) and **getgrgid**( ) search the group database for the given group name pointed
to by *name* or the group id pointed to by *gid*, respectively, returning the first one encountered. Identical
group names or group gids may result in undefined behavior.

The **getgrent**( ) function sequentially reads the group database and is intended for programs that wish to
step through the complete list of groups.

All three routines will open the group file for reading, if necessary.

The **setgroupent**( ) function opens the file, or rewinds it if it is already open. If *stayopen* is non-zero,
file descriptors are left open, significantly speeding functions subsequent calls. This functionality is unnecessary for **getgrent**( ) as it doesn't close its file descriptors by default. It should also be noted that it is
dangerous for long-running programs to use this functionality as the group file may be updated.

The **setgrent**( ) function is identical to **setgroupent**( ) with an argument of zero.

The **endgrent**( ) function closes any open files.

RETURN VALUES

The functions **getgrent**(), **getgrnam**(), and **getgrgid**(), return a pointer to the group entry if successful; if end-of-file is reached or an error occurs a null pointer is returned. The functions **setgroupent**( )

and `setgrent()` return the value 1 if successful, otherwise the value 0 is returned. The functions `endgrent()` and `setgrfile()` have no return value.

FILES
　　`/etc/group` group database file

SEE ALSO
　　getpwent(*3*), `group`(*5*)

HISTORY
　　The functions `endgrent()`, `getgrent()`, `getgrnam()`, `getgrgid()`, and `setgrent()` appeared in Version 7 AT&T UNIX. The functions `setgrfile()` and `setgroupent()` appeared in 4.3BSD–Reno.

COMPATIBILITY
　　The historic function `setgrfile()`, which allowed the specification of alternate password databases, has been deprecated and is no longer available.

BUGS
　　The functions `getgrent()`, `getgrnam()`, `getgrgid()`, `setgroupent()` and `setgrent()` leave their results in an internal static object and return a pointer to that object. Subsequent calls to the same function will modify the same object.

　　The functions `getgrent()`, `endgrent()`, `setgroupent()`, and `setgrent()` are fairly useless in a networked environment and should be avoided, if possible.

NAME
getgrouplist – calculate group access list

SYNOPSIS
```
#include <unistd.h>

int
getgrouplist(const char *name, int basegid, int *groups, int *ngroups);
```

DESCRIPTION
The getgrouplist() function reads through the group file and calculates the group access list for the user specified in *name*. The *basegid* is automatically included in the groups list. Typically this value is given as the group number from the password file.

The resulting group list is returned in the integer array pointed to by *groups*. The caller specifies the size of the *groups* array in the integer pointed to by *ngroups*; the actual number of groups found is returned in *ngroups*.

RETURN VALUES
The getgrouplist() function returns −1 if the size of the group list is too small to hold all the user's groups. Here, the group array will be filled with as many groups as will fit.

FILES
/etc/group group membership list

SEE ALSO
setgroups(2), initgroups(3)

HISTORY
The getgrouplist() function first appeared in 4.4BSD.

BUGS
The getgrouplist() function uses the routines based on getgrent(3). If the invoking program uses any of these routines, the group structure will be overwritten in the call to getgrouplist().

NAME

gethostbyname, gethostbyaddr, gethostent, sethostent, endhostent, herror – get network host entry

SYNOPSIS

```
#include <netdb.h>
extern struct h_errno;
```

struct hostent *
gethostbyname(*char *name*);

struct hostent *
gethostbyaddr(*char *addr, int len, int type*);

struct hostent *
gethostent(*void*);

sethostent(*int stayopen*);

endhostent(*void*);

herror(*char *string*);

DESCRIPTION

The **gethostbyname**( ) and **gethostbyaddr**( ) functions each return a pointer to an object with the following structure describing an internet host referenced by name or by address, respectively. This structure contains either the information obtained from the name server, named(8), or broken-out fields from a line in /etc/hosts. If the local name server is not running these routines do a lookup in /etc/hosts.

```
struct  hostent {
        char    *h_name;        /* official name of host */
        char    **h_aliases;    /* alias list */
        int     h_addrtype;     /* host address type */
        int     h_length;       /* length of address */
        char    **h_addr_list;  /* list of addresses from name server */
};
#define h_addr  h_addr_list[0] /* address, for backward compatibility */
```

The members of this structure are:

h_name   Official name of the host.

h_aliases   A zero terminated array of alternate names for the host.

h_addrtype The type of address being returned; currently always AF_INET.

h_length   The length, in bytes, of the address.

h_addr_list A zero terminated array of network addresses for the host. Host addresses are returned in network byte order.

h_addr   The first address in *h_addr_list*; this is for backward compatibility.

When using the nameserver, **gethostbyname**( ) will search for the named host in the current domain and its parents unless the name ends in a dot. If the name contains no dot, and if the environment variable ''HOSTALIASES'' contains the name of an alias file, the alias file will first be searched for an alias matching the input name. See hostname(7) for the domain search procedure and the alias file format.

The **sethostent**( ) function may be used to request the use of a connected TCP socket for queries. If the *stayopen* flag is non-zero, this sets the option to send all queries to the name server using TCP and to retain the connection after each call to **gethostbyname**() or **gethostbyaddr**(). Otherwise, queries are performed using UDP datagrams.

The **endhostent**( ) function closes the TCP connection.

FILES
    /etc/hosts

DIAGNOSTICS
Error return status from **gethostbyname**( ) and **gethostbyaddr**( ) is indicated by return of a null pointer. The external integer *h_errno* may then be checked to see whether this is a temporary failure or an invalid or unknown host. The routine **herror**( ) can be used to print an error message describing the failure. If its argument *string* is non-NULL, it is printed, followed by a colon and a space. The error message is printed with a trailing newline.

The variable *h_errno* can have the following values:

HOST_NOT_FOUND No such host is known.

TRY_AGAIN   This is usually a temporary error and means that the local server did not receive a response from an authoritative server. A retry at some later time may succeed.

NO_RECOVERY   Some unexpected server failure was encountered. This is a non-recoverable error.

NO_DATA   The requested name is valid but does not have an IP address; this is not a temporary error. This means that the name is known to the name server but there is no address associated with this name. Another type of request to the name server using this domain name will result in an answer; for example, a mail-forwarder may be registered for this domain.

SEE ALSO
    resolver(3), hosts(5), hostname(7), named(8)

CAVEAT
The **gethostent**( ) function is defined, and **sethostent**( ) and **endhostent**( ) are redefined, when libc(3) is built to use only the routines to lookup in /etc/hosts and not the name server.

The **gethostent**( ) function reads the next line of /etc/hosts, opening the file if necessary.

The **sethostent**( ) function opens and/or rewinds the file /etc/hosts. If the *stayopen* argument is non-zero, the file will not be closed after each call to **gethostbyname**( ) or **gethostbyaddr**( ).

The **endhostent**( ) function closes the file.

HISTORY
The **herror**( ) function appeared in 4.3BSD. The **endhostent**(), **gethostbyaddr**(), **gethostbyname**(), **gethostent**(), and **sethostent**( ) functions appeared in 4.2BSD.

BUGS
These functions use static data storage; if the data is needed for future use, it should be copied before any subsequent calls overwrite it. Only the Internet address format is currently understood.

NAME

gethostid, sethostid – get/set unique identifier of current host

SYNOPSIS

#include ⟨unistd.h⟩

long
gethostid(*void*);

int
sethostid(*long hostid*);

DESCRIPTION

Sethostid( ) establishes a 32-bit identifier for the current processor that is intended to be unique among all UNIX systems in existence. This is normally a DARPA Internet address for the local machine. This call is allowed only to the super-user and is normally performed at boot time.

Gethostid( ) returns the 32-bit identifier for the current processor.

This function has been deprecated. The hostid should be set or retrieved by use of sysctl(2).

SEE ALSO

sysctl(2), gethostname(3), sysctl(8).

BUGS

32 bits for the identifier is too small.

HISTORY

The gethostid( ) and sethostid( ) syscalls appeared in 4.2BSD and were dropped in 4.4BSD.

NAME

gethostname, sethostname – get/set name of current host

SYNOPSIS

```
#include <unistd.h>
```

int
gethostname(*char *name, int namelen*);

int
sethostname(*const char *name, int namelen*);

DESCRIPTION

Gethostname( ) returns the standard host name for the current processor, as previously set by **sethostname**(). The parameter *namelen* specifies the size of the *name* array. The returned name is null-terminated unless insufficient space is provided.

Sethostname( ) sets the name of the host machine to be *name*, which has length *namelen*. This call is restricted to the super-user and is normally used only when the system is bootstrapped.

RETURN VALUES

If the call succeeds a value of 0 is returned. If the call fails, a value of -1 is returned and an error code is placed in the global location *errno*.

ERRORS

The following errors may be returned by these calls:

[EFAULT]　　　The *name* or *namelen* parameter gave an invalid address.

[EPERM]　　　The caller tried to set the hostname and was not the super-user.

SEE ALSO

sysctl(2) gethostid(3)

BUGS

Host names are limited to MAXHOSTNAMELEN (from <sys/param.h>) characters, currently 256.

HISTORY

The **gethostname** function call appeared in 4.2BSD.

NAME

  getloadavg – get system load averages

SYNOPSIS

  getloadavg(*double loadavg[]*, *int nelem*);

DESCRIPTION

  The **getloadavg( )** function returns the number of processes in the system run queue averaged over various periods of time. Up to *nelem* samples are retrieved and assigned to successive elements of
  loadavg[ ]. The system imposes a maximum of 3 samples, representing averages over the last 1, 5, and 15
  minutes, respectively.

DIAGNOSTICS

  If the load average was unobtainable, −1 is returned; otherwise, the number of samples actually retrieved is
  returned.

SEE ALSO

  uptime(1), sysctl(2), kvm_getloadavg(3)

HISTORY

  The **getloadavg( )** function appeared in 4.3BSD–Reno.

NAME
getmntinfo – get information about mounted file systems

SYNOPSIS
```
#include <sys/param.h>
#include <sys/ucred.h>
#include <sys/mount.h>

int
getmntinfo(struct statfs **mntbufp, int flags);
```

DESCRIPTION
The **getmntinfo()** function returns an array of statfs structures describing each currently mounted file system (see statfs(2)).

The **getmntinfo()** function passes its *flags* parameter transparently to getfsstat(2).

RETURN VALUES
On successful completion, **getmntinfo()** returns a count of the number of elements in the array. The pointer to the array is stored into *mntbufp*.

If an error occurs, zero is returned and the external variable *errno* is set to indicate the error. Although the pointer *mntbufp* will be unmodified, any information previously returned by **getmntinfo()** will be lost.

ERRORS
The **getmntinfo()** function may fail and set errno for any of the errors specified for the library routines getfsstat(2) or malloc(3).

SEE ALSO
getfsstat(2), statfs(2), mount(2), mount(8)

HISTORY
The **getmntinfo()** function first appeared in 4.4BSD.

BUGS
The **getmntinfo()** function writes the array of structures to an internal static object and returns a pointer to that object. Subsequent calls to **getmntinfo()** will modify the same object.

The memory allocated by **getmntinfo()** cannot be free(2)'d by the application.

NAME

getmntopts – scan mount options

SYNOPSIS

`#include <mntopts.h>`

void
getmntopts(*char *options, struct mntopt *mopts, int *flagp*);

DESCRIPTION

The **getmntopts** function takes a comma separated option list and a list of valid option names, and computes the bitmask corresponding to the requested set of options.

The string options is broken down into a sequence of comma separated tokens. Each token is looked up in the table described by mopts and the bits in the word referenced by flagp are updated. The flag word is not initialized by **getmntopt**. The table, mopts, has the following format:

```
struct mntopt {
        char *m_option;          /* option name */
        int m_inverse;           /* is this a negative option, eg "dev" */
        int m_flag;              /* bit to set, eg MNT_RDONLY */
};
```

The members of this structure are:

m_option   the option name, for example ''suid''.

m_inverse tells **getmntopts** that the name has the inverse meaning of the bit. For example, ''suid'' is the string, whereas the mount flag is MNT_NOSUID. In this case, the sense of the string and the flag are inverted, so the m_inverse flag should be set.

m_flag   the value of the bit to be set or cleared in the flag word when the option is recognized. The bit is set when the option is discovered, but cleared if the option name was preceded by the letters ''no''. The m_inverse flag causes these two operations to be reversed.

Each of the user visible MNT_ flags has a corresponding MOPT_ macro which defines an appropriate struct mntopt entry. To simplify the program interface and ensure consistency across all programs, a general purpose macro, MOPT_STDOPTS, is defined which contains an entry for all the generic VFS options. In addition, the macros MOPT_FORCE and MOPT_UPDATE exist to enable the MNT_FORCE and MNT_UPDATE flags to be set. Finally, the table must be terminated by an entry with a NULL first element.

EXAMPLES

Most commands will use the standard option set. Local filesystems which support the MNT_UPDATE flag, would also have an MOPT_UPDATE entry. This can be declared and used as follows:

```
#include "mntopts.h"

struct mntopt mopts[] = {
        MOPT_STDOPTS,
        MOPT_UPDATE,
        { NULL }
};


        ...
        mntflags = 0;
```

```
...
    getmntopts(options, mopts, &mntflags)
...
```

DIAGNOSTICS

The **getmntopts** function displays an error message and exits if an unrecognized option is encountered.

SEE ALSO

err(3), mount(8)

HISTORY

The **getmntopts**( ) function appeared in 4.4BSD.

3

NAME

getnetent, getnetbyaddr, getnetbyname, setnetent, endnetent – get network entry

SYNOPSIS

```
#include <netdb.h>
```

struct netent *
getnetent();

struct netent *
getnetbyname(*char *name*);

struct netent *
getnetbyaddr(*long net, int type*);

setnetent(*int stayopen*);

endnetent();

DESCRIPTION

The **getnetent**(), **getnetbyname**(), and **getnetbyaddr**() functions each return a pointer to an object with the following structure containing the broken-out fields of a line in the network data base, /etc/networks.

```
struct netent {
        char        *n_name;        /* official name of net */
        char        **n_aliases;    /* alias list */
        int         n_addrtype;     /* net number type */
        unsigned long  n_net;       /* net number */
};
```

The members of this structure are:

n_name   The official name of the network.

n_aliases A zero terminated list of alternate names for the network.

n_addrtype The type of the network number returned; currently only AF_INET.

n_net   The network number. Network numbers are returned in machine byte order.

The **getnetent**() function reads the next line of the file, opening the file if necessary.

The **setnetent**() function opens and rewinds the file. If the *stayopen* flag is non-zero, the net data base will not be closed after each call to **getnetbyname**() or **getnetbyaddr**().

The **endnetent**() function closes the file.

The **getnetbyname**() function and **getnetbyaddr**() sequentially search from the beginning of the file until a matching net name or net address and type is found, or until EOF is encountered. Network numbers are supplied in host order.

FILES

/etc/networks

DIAGNOSTICS

Null pointer (0) returned on EOF or error.

SEE ALSO

networks(5)

HISTORY

The **getnetent**(), **getnetbyaddr**(), **getnetbyname**(), **setnetent**(), and **endnetent**() functions appeared in 4.2BSD.

BUGS

The data space used by these functions is static; if future use requires the data, it should be copied before any subsequent calls to these functions overwrite it. Only Internet network numbers are currently understood. Expecting network numbers to fit in no more than 32 bits is probably naive.

3

NAME

getnetgrent, innetgr, setnetgrent, endnetgrent – netgroup database operations

SYNOPSIS

```
int
getnetgrent(char **host, char **user, char **domain);

int
innetgr(const char *netgroup, const char *host, const char *user, const
        char *domain);

void
setnetgrent(const char *netgroup);

void
endnetgrent(void);
```

DESCRIPTION

These functions operate on the netgroup database file /etc/netgroup which is described in netgroup(5). The database defines a set of netgroups, each made up of one or more triples:

```
(host, user, domain)
```

that defines a combination of host, user and domain. Any of the three fields may be specified as "wildcards" that match any string.

The function getnetgrent( ) sets the three pointer arguments to the strings of the next member of the current netgroup. If any of the string pointers are (char *)0 that field is considered a wildcard.

The functions setnetgrent( ) and endnetgrent( ) set the current netgroup and terminate the current netgroup respectively. If setnetgrent( ) is called with a different netgroup than the previous call, an implicit endnetgrent( ) is implied. Setnetgrent( ) also sets the offset to the first member of the netgroup.

The function innetgr( ) searches for a match of all fields within the specified group. If any of the **host**, **user**, or **domain** arguments are (**char** *)0 those fields will match any string value in the netgroup member.

RETURN VALUES

The function getnetgrent( ) returns 0 for "no more netgroup members" and 1 otherwise. The function innetgr( ) returns 1 for a successful match and 0 otherwise. The functions setnetgrent( ) and endnetgrent( ) have no return value.

FILES

/etc/netgroup netgroup database file

SEE ALSO

netgroup(5)

COMPATIBILITY

The netgroup members have three string fields to maintain compatibility with other vendor implementations, however it is not obvious what use the **domain** string has within BSD.

BUGS

The function getnetgrent( ) returns pointers to dynamically allocated data areas that are free'd when the function endnetgrent( ) is called.

3

NAME
   getopt – get option character from command line argument list

SYNOPSIS
   #include <stdlib.h>

   extern char *optarg;
   extern int optind;
   extern int optopt;
   extern int opterr;
   extern int optreset;

   int
   getopt(*int argc,* char * const *argv, *const char *optstring*);

DESCRIPTION
   The **getopt**( ) function incrementally parses a command line argument list *argv* and returns the next *known* option character. An option character is *known* if it has been specified in the string of accepted option characters, *optstring*.

   The option string *optstring* may contain the following elements: individual characters, and characters followed by a colon to indicate an option argument is to follow. For example, an option string "x" recognizes an option ''−x'', and an option string "x:" recognizes an option and argument ''−x argument''. It does not matter to **getopt**( ) if a following argument has leading white space.

   On return from **getopt**(), *optarg* points to an option argument, if it is anticipated, and the variable *optind* contains the index to the next *argv* argument for a subsequent call to **getopt**(). The variable *optopt* saves the last *known* option character returned by **getopt**().

   The variable *opterr* and *optind* are both initialized to 1. The *optind* variable may be set to another value before a set of calls to **getopt**( ) in order to skip over more or less argv entries.

   In order to use **getopt**( ) to evaluate multiple sets of arguments, or to evaluate a single set of arguments multiple times, the variable *optreset* must be set to 1 before the second and each additional set of calls to **getopt**(), and the variable *optind* must be reinitialized.

   The **getopt**( ) function returns an EOF when the argument list is exhausted, or a non-recognized option is encountered. The interpretation of options in the argument list may be cancelled by the option '− −' (double dash) which causes **getopt**( ) to signal the end of argument processing and return an EOF. When all options have been processed (i.e., up to the first non-option argument), **getopt**( ) returns EOF.

DIAGNOSTICS
   If the **getopt**( ) function encounters a character not found in the string *optarg* or detects a missing option argument it writes an error message and returns '?' to the *stderr*. Setting *opterr* to a zero will disable these error messages. If *optstring* has a leading ':' then a missing option argument causes a ':' to be returned in addition to suppressing any error messages.

   Option arguments are allowed to begin with ''−''; this is reasonable but reduces the amount of error checking possible.

EXTENSIONS
   The *optreset* variable was added to make it possible to call the **getopt**( ) function multiple times. This is an extension to the IEEE Std1003.2 (''POSIX'') specification.

EXAMPLE

```
extern char *optarg;
extern int optind;
int bflag, ch, fd;

bflag = 0;
while ((ch = getopt(argc, argv, "bf:")) != EOF)
        switch(ch) {
        case 'b':
                bflag = 1;
                break;
        case 'f':
                if ((fd = open(optarg, O_RDONLY, 0)) < 0) {
                        (void)fprintf(stderr,
                                "myname: %s: %s\n", optarg, strerror(errno));
                        exit(1);
                }
                break;
        case '?':
        default:
                usage();
}
argc -= optind;
argv += optind;
```

HISTORY

The **getopt**( ) function appeared 4.3BSD.

BUGS

A single dash "-" may be specified as an character in *optstring*, however it should *never* have an argument associated with it. This allows **getopt**( ) to be used with programs that expect "-" as an option flag. This practice is wrong, and should not be used in any current development. It is provided for backward compatibility *only*. By default, a single dash causes **getopt**( ) to return EOF. This is, we believe, compatible with System V.

It is also possible to handle digits as option letters. This allows **getopt**( ) to be used with programs that expect a number ("-3") as an option. This practice is wrong, and should not be used in any current development. It is provided for backward compatibility *only*. The following code fragment works in most cases.

```
int length;
char *p;
```

```
while ((c = getopt(argc, argv, "0123456789")) != EOF)
        switch (c) {
        case '0': case '1': case '2': case '3': case '4':
        case '5': case '6': case '7': case '8': case '9':
                p = argv[optind - 1];
                if (p[0] == '-' && p[1] == ch && !p[2])
                        length = atoi(++p);
                else
                        length = atoi(argv[optind] + 1);
                break;
        }
}
```

3

NAME

    getpagesize – get system page size

SYNOPSIS

    #include <unistd.h>

    int
    getpagesize(*void*);

DESCRIPTION

    Getpagesize() returns the number of bytes in a page. Page granularity is the granularity of many of the memory management calls.

    The page size is a system page size and may not be the same as the underlying hardware page size.

SEE ALSO

    sbrk(2), pagesize(1)

HISTORY

    The getpagesize function call appeared in 4.2BSD.

NAME
getpass – get a password

SYNOPSIS
```
#include <pwd.h>
#include <unistd.h>

char *
getpass(const char *prompt);
```

DESCRIPTION
The `getpass()` function displays a prompt to, and reads in a password from, `/dev/tty`. If this file is not accessible, `getpass` displays the prompt on the standard error output and reads from the standard input.

The password may be up to _PASSWORD_LEN (currently 128) characters in length. Any additional characters and the terminating newline character are discarded.

`Getpass` turns off character echoing while reading the password.

RETURN VALUES
`Getpass` returns a pointer to the null terminated password.

FILES
`/dev/tty`

SEE ALSO
crypt(3)

HISTORY
A `getpass` function appeared in Version 7 AT&T UNIX.

BUGS
The `getpass` function leaves its result in an internal static object and returns a pointer to that object. Subsequent calls to `getpass` will modify the same object.

The calling process should zero the password as soon as possible to avoid leaving the cleartext password visible in the process's address space.

3

NAME
getprotoent, getprotobynumber, getprotobyname, setprotoent, endprotoent – get
protocol entry

SYNOPSIS
`#include <netdb.h>`

struct protoent *
`getprotoent();`

struct protoent *
`getprotobyname(`*char *name*`);`

struct protoent *
`getprotobynumber(`*int proto*`);`

`setprotoent(`*int stayopen*`);`

`endprotoent();`

DESCRIPTION
The **getprotoent()**, **getprotobyname()**, and **getprotobynumber()** functions each return a
pointer to an object with the following structure containing the broken-out fields of a line in the network protocol data base, `/etc/protocols`.

```
struct protoent {
        char    *p_name;        /* official name of protocol */
        char    **p_aliases;    /* alias list */
        int     p_proto;        /* protocol number */
};
```

The members of this structure are:

p_name   The official name of the protocol.

p_aliases A zero terminated list of alternate names for the protocol.

p_proto   The protocol number.

The **getprotoent()** function reads the next line of the file, opening the file if necessary.

The **setprotoent()** function opens and rewinds the file. If the *stayopen* flag is non-zero, the net data base will not be closed after each call to **getprotobyname()** or **getprotobynumber()**.

The **endprotoent()** function closes the file.

The **getprotobyname()** function and **getprotobynumber()** sequentially search from the beginning of the file until a matching protocol name or protocol number is found, or until EOF is encountered.

RETURN VALUES
Null pointer (0) returned on EOF or error.

FILES
`/etc/protocols`

SEE ALSO

protocols(5)

HISTORY

The **getprotoent**(), **getprotobynumber**(), **getprotobyname**(), **setprotoent**(), and **endprotoent**( ) functions appeared in 4.2BSD.

BUGS

These functions use a static data space; if the data is needed for future use, it should be copied before any subsequent calls overwrite it. Only the Internet protocols are currently understood.

3

NAME

getpw – get name from uid

SYNOPSIS

getpw(*uid*, *char *buf*);

DESCRIPTION

The getpw function is made obsolete by getpwuid(3).
It is available from the compatibility library, libcompat.

The getpw( ) function reads the file /etc/passwd, and if it finds the specified *uid*, copies the password entry line into the string pointed to by *buf*. the null terminated entry line from the password database, and appends the NUL character.

RETURN VALUES

The getpw( ) function returns the zero if successful, otherwise a non-zero if the entry does not exist.

FILES

/etc/passwd

SEE ALSO

getpwent(3), passwd(5)

HISTORY

A getpw( ) function appeared in Version 6 AT&T UNIX.

NAME

getpwent, getpwnam, getpwuid, setpassent, setpwent, endpwent – password database operations

SYNOPSIS

```
#include <sys/types.h>
#include <pwd.h>
```

struct passwd *
getpwent(*void*);

struct passwd *
getpwnam(*const char *login*);

struct passwd *
getpwuid(*uid_t uid*);

int
setpassent(*int stayopen*);

int
setpwent(*void*);

void
endpwent(*void*);

DESCRIPTION

These functions operate on the password database file which is described in passwd(5). Each entry in the database is defined by the structure *passwd* found in the include file <pwd.h>:

```
struct passwd {
        char    *pw_name;       /* user name */
        char    *pw_passwd;     /* encrypted password */
        uid_t   pw_uid;         /* user uid */
        gid_t   pw_gid;         /* user gid */
        time_t  pw_change;      /* password change time */
        char    *pw_class;      /* user access class */
        char    *pw_gecos;      /* Honeywell login info */
        char    *pw_dir;        /* home directory */
        char    *pw_shell;      /* default shell */
        time_t  pw_expire;      /* account expiration */
};
```

The functions **getpwnam**( ) and **getpwuid**( ) search the password database for the given login name or user uid, respectively, always returning the first one encountered.

The **getpwent**( ) function sequentially reads the password database and is intended for programs that wish to process the complete list of users.

The **setpassent**( ) function accomplishes two purposes. First, it causes **getpwent**( ) to "rewind" to the beginning of the database. Additionally, if *stayopen* is non-zero, file descriptors are left open, significantly speeding up subsequent accesses for all of the routines. (This latter functionality is unnecessary for **getpwent**( ) as it doesn't close its file descriptors by default.)

It is dangerous for long-running programs to keep the file descriptors open as the database will become out of date if it is updated while the program is running.

The `setpwent( )` function is identical to **setpassent( )** with an argument of zero.

The `endpwent( )` function closes any open files.

These routines have been written to ''shadow'' the password file, e.g. allow only certain programs to have access to the encrypted password. If the process which calls them has an effective uid of 0, the encrypted password will be returned, otherwise, the password field of the returned structure will point to the string '*'.

RETURN VALUES

The functions `getpwent()`, `getpwnam()`, and `getpwuid()`, return a valid pointer to a passwd structure on success and a null pointer if end-of-file is reached or an error occurs. The functions **setpassent( )** and `setpwent( )` return 0 on failure and 1 on success. The **endpwent( )** function has no return value.

FILES

/var/db/pwd.db	The insecure password database file
/var/db/spwd.db	The secure password database file
/etc/master.passwd	The current password file
/etc/passwd	A Version 7 format password file

SEE ALSO

getlogin(3), getgrent(3), passwd(5), pwd_mkdb(8), vipw(8)

HISTORY

The `getpwent`, `getpwnam`, `getpwuid`, `setpwent,` and **endpwent** functions appeared in Version 7 AT&T UNIX. The **setpassent** function appeared in 4.3BSD–Reno.

BUGS

The functions `getpwent()`, `getpwnam()`, and `getpwuid()`, leave their results in an internal static object and return a pointer to that object. Subsequent calls to the same function will modify the same object.

The routines `getpwent()`, `endpwent()`, `setpassent()`, and `setpwent()` are fairly useless in a networked environment and should be avoided, if possible.

COMPATIBILITY

The historic function setpwfile(3), which allowed the specification of alternate password databases, has been deprecated and is no longer available.

NAME

getservent, getservbyport, getservbyname, setservent, endservent – get service entry

SYNOPSIS

```
#include <netdb.h>
```

struct servent *
getservent( );

struct servent *
getservbyname(*char *name, char *proto*);

struct servent *
getservbyport(*int port, proto*);

void
setservent(*int stayopen*);

void
endservent(*void*);

DESCRIPTION

The **getservent**(), **getservbyname**(), and **getservbyport**( ) functions each return a pointer to an object with the following structure containing the broken-out fields of a line in the network services data base, /etc/services.

```
struct servent {
        char    *s_name;        /* official name of service */
        char    **s_aliases;    /* alias list */
        int     s_port;         /* port service resides at */
        char    *s_proto;       /* protocol to use */
};
```

The members of this structure are:

s_name   The official name of the service.

s_aliases A zero terminated list of alternate names for the service.

s_port   The port number at which the service resides. Port numbers are returned in network byte order.

s_proto   The name of the protocol to use when contacting the service.

The **getservent**( ) function reads the next line of the file, opening the file if necessary.

The **setservent**( ) function opens and rewinds the file. If the *stayopen* flag is non-zero, the net data base will not be closed after each call to **getservbyname**( ) or **getservbyport**().

The **endservent**( ) function closes the file.

The **getservbyname**( ) and **getservbyport**( ) functions sequentially search from the beginning of the file until a matching protocol name or port number is found, or until EOF is encountered. If a protocol name is also supplied (non- NULL), searches must also match the protocol.

FILES
  /etc/services

DIAGNOSTICS
  Null pointer (0) returned on EOF or error.

SEE ALSO
  getprotoent(3), services(5)

HISTORY
  The `getservent()`, `getservbyport()`, `getservbyname()`, `setservent()`, and `endservent()` functions appeared in 4.2BSD.

BUGS
  These functions use static data storage; if the data is needed for future use, it should be copied before any subsequent calls overwrite it. Expecting port numbers to fit in a 32 bit quantity is probably naive.

NAME

    getsubopt – get sub options from an argument

SYNOPSIS

    #include <stdlib.h>

    *extern char *suboptarg*

    int
    getsubopt(*char **optionp, char * const *tokens, char **valuep*);

DESCRIPTION

    The **getsubopt**( ) function parses a string containing tokens delimited by one or more tab, space or comma (',') characters. It is intended for use in parsing groups of option arguments provided as part of a utility command line.

    The argument *optionp* is a pointer to a pointer to the string. The argument *tokens* is a pointer to a NULL-terminated array of pointers to strings.

    The **getsubopt**( ) function returns the zero-based offset of the pointer in the *tokens* array referencing a string which matches the first token in the string, or, −1 if the string contains no tokens or *tokens* does not contain a matching string.

    If the token is of the form ''name=value'', the location referenced by *valuep* will be set to point to the start of the ''value'' portion of the token.

    On return from **getsubopt**(), *optionp* will be set to point to the start of the next token in the string, or the null at the end of the string if no more tokens are present. The external variable *suboptarg* will be set to point to the start of the current token, or NULL if no tokens were present. The argument *valuep* will be set to point to the ''value'' portion of the token, or NULL if no ''value'' portion was present.

EXAMPLE

```
char *tokens[] = {
        #define ONE     0
                "one",
        #define TWO     1
                "two",
        NULL
};

...

extern char *optarg, *suboptarg;
char *options, *value;

while ((ch = getopt(argc, argv, "ab:")) != −1) {
        switch(ch) {
        case 'a':
                /* process ''a'' option */
                break;
        case 'b':
                options = optarg;
                while (*options) {
```

3

```
switch(getsubopt(&options, tokens, &value)) {
case ONE:
        /* process ''one'' sub option */
        break;
case TWO:
        /* process ''two'' sub option */
        if (!value)
                error("no value for two");
        i = atoi(value);
        break;
case -1:
        if (suboptarg)
                error("illegal sub option %s",
                    suboptarg);
        else
                error("missing sub option");
        break;
    }
    break;
}
```

SEE ALSO

getopt(3), strsep(3)

HISTORY

The **getsubopt**( ) function first appeared in 4.4BSD.

NAME

getttyent, getttynam, setttyent, endttyent – get ttys file entry

SYNOPSIS

#include ⟨ttyent.h⟩

struct ttyent *
getttyent();

struct ttyent *
getttynam(*char *name*);

int
setttyent(*void*);

int
endttyent(*void*);

DESCRIPTION

The **getttyent**(), and **getttynam**( ) functions each return a pointer to an object, with the following
structure, containing the broken-out fields of a line from the tty description file.

```
struct ttyent {
        char    *ty_name;       /* terminal device name */
        char    *ty_getty;      /* command to execute */
        char    *ty_type;       /* terminal type */
#define TTY_ON          0x01    /* enable logins */
#define TTY_SECURE      0x02    /* allow uid of 0 to login */
        int     ty_status;      /* flag values */
        char    *ty_window;     /* command for window manager */
        char    *ty_comment;    /* comment field */
};
```

The fields are as follows:

ty_name   The name of the character-special file.

ty_getty   The name of the command invoked by init(8) to initialize tty line characteristics.

ty_type   The name of the default terminal type connected to this tty line.

ty_status   A mask of bit fields which indicate various actions allowed on this tty line. The possible
flags are as follows:

        TTY_ON   Enables logins (i.e., init(8) will start the command referenced by
ty_getty on this entry).

        TTY_SECURE Allow users with a uid of 0 to login on this terminal.

ty_window   The command to execute for a window system associated with the line.

ty_comment Any trailing comment field, with any leading hash marks (''#'') or whitespace removed.

If any of the fields pointing to character strings are unspecified, they are returned as null pointers. The field
ty_status will be zero if no flag values are specified.

See ttys(5) for a more complete discussion of the meaning and usage of the fields.

The `getttyent`( ) function reads the next line from the ttys file, opening the file if necessary. The **setttyent**( ) function rewinds the file if open, or opens the file if it is unopened. The **endttyent**( ) function closes any open files.

The `getttynam`( ) function searches from the beginning of the file until a matching *name* is found (or until EOF is encountered).

RETURN VALUES

The routines `getttyent`( ) and `getttynam`( ) return a null pointer on EOF or error. The **setttyent**( ) function and **endttyent**( ) return 0 on failure and 1 on success.

FILES

/etc/ttys

SEE ALSO

login(1), ttyslot(3), gettytab(5), termcap(5), ttys(5), getty(8), init(8)

HISTORY

The **getttyent**(), **getttynam**(), **setttyent**(), and **endttyent**( ) functions appeared in 4.3BSD.

BUGS

These functions use static data storage; if the data is needed for future use, it should be copied before any subsequent calls overwrite it.

NAME
getusershell, setusershell, endusershell – get legal user shells

SYNOPSIS
char *
getusershell(*void*);

void
setusershell(*void*);

void
endusershell(*void*);

DESCRIPTION
The **getusershell**( ) function returns a pointer to a legal user shell as defined by the system manager in the file /etc/shells. If /etc/shells is unreadable or does not exist, **getusershell**( ) behaves as if /bin/sh and /bin/csh were listed in the file.

The **getusershell**( ) function reads the next line (opening the file if necessary); **setusershell**( ) rewinds the file; **endusershell**( ) closes it.

FILES
/etc/shells

DIAGNOSTICS
The routine **getusershell**( ) returns a null pointer (0) on EOF.

SEE ALSO
shells(5)

HISTORY
The **getusershell**( ) function appeared in 4.3BSD.

BUGS
The **getusershell**( ) function leaves its result in an internal static object and returns a pointer to that object. Subsequent calls to **getusershell**( ) will modify the same object.

3

NAME
glob, globfree – generate pathnames matching a pattern

SYNOPSIS
`#include <glob.h>`

```
int
glob(const char *pattern, int flags,
        const int (*errfunc)(const char *, int), glob_t *pglob);

void
globfree(glob_t *pglob);
```

DESCRIPTION
The glob() function is a pathname generator that implements the rules for file name pattern matching used by the shell.

The include file glob.h defines the structure type glob_t, which contains at least the following fields:

```
typedef struct {
        int gl_pathc;           /* count of total paths so far */
        int gl_matchc;          /* count of paths matching pattern */
        int gl_offs;            /* reserved at beginning of gl_pathv */
        int gl_flags;           /* returned flags */
        char **gl_pathv;        /* list of paths matching pattern */
} glob_t;
```

The argument *pattern* is a pointer to a pathname pattern to be expanded. The glob() argument matches all accessible pathnames against the pattern and creates a list of the pathnames that match. In order to have access to a pathname, glob() requires search permission on every component of a path except the last and read permission on each directory of any filename component of *pattern* that contains any of the special characters '*', '?' or '['.

The glob() argument stores the number of matched pathnames into the *gl_pathc* field, and a pointer to a list of pointers to pathnames into the *gl_pathv* field. The first pointer after the last pathname is NULL. If the pattern does not match any pathnames, the returned number of matched paths is set to zero.

It is the caller's responsibility to create the structure pointed to by *pglob*. The glob() function allocates other space as needed, including the memory pointed to by *gl_pathv*.

The argument *flags* is used to modify the behavior of glob(). The value of *flags* is the bitwise inclusive OR of any of the following values defined in glob.h:

GLOB_APPEND   Append pathnames generated to the ones from a previous call (or calls) to glob(). The value of *gl_pathc* will be the total matches found by this call and the previous call(s). The pathnames are appended to, not merged with the pathnames returned by the previous call(s). Between calls, the caller must not change the setting of the GLOB_DOOFFS flag, nor change the value of *gl_offs* when GLOB_DOOFFS is set, nor (obviously) call globfree() for *pglob*.

GLOB_DOOFFS   Make use of the gl_offs field. If this flag is set, gl_offs is used to specify how many NULL pointers to prepend to the beginning of the gl_pathv field. In other words, gl_pathv will point to gl_offs NULL pointers, followed by gl_pathc pathname pointers, followed by a NULL pointer.

GLOB_ERR   Causes **glob**( ) to return when it encounters a directory that it cannot open or read. Ordinarily, **glob**( ) continues to find matches.

GLOB_MARK   Each pathname that is a directory that matches *pattern* has a slash appended.

GLOB_NOCHECK   If *pattern* does not match any pathname, then **glob**( ) returns a list consisting of only *pattern*, with the number of total pathnames is set to 1, and the number of matched pathnames set to 0. If GLOB_QUOTE is set, its effect is present in the pattern returned.

GLOB_NOSORT   By default, the pathnames are sorted in ascending ASCII order; this flag prevents that sorting (speeding up **glob**()).

The following values may also be included in *flags*, however, they are non-standard extensions to IEEE Std1003.2 ("POSIX").

GLOB_ALTDIRFUNC The following additional fields in the pglob structure have been initialized with alternate functions for glob to use to open, read, and close directories and to get stat information on names found in those directories.

```
void *(*gl_opendir)(const char * name);
struct dirent *(*gl_readdir)(void *);
void (*gl_closedir)(void *);
int (*gl_lstat)(const char *name, struct stat *st);
int (*gl_stat)(const char *name, struct stat *st);
```

This extension is provided to allow programs such as restore(8) to provide globbing from directories stored on tape.

GLOB_BRACE   Pre-process the pattern string to expand {pat,pat,...} strings like csh(1.)The pattern '{}' is left unexpanded for historical reasons (Csh(1) does the same thing to ease typing of find(1) patterns).

GLOB_MAGCHAR   Set by the **glob**( ) function if the pattern included globbing characters. See the description of the usage of the gl_matchc structure member for more details.

GLOB_NOMAGIC   Is the same as GLOB_NOCHECK but it only appends the *pattern* if it does not contain any of the special characters "*", "?" or "[". GLOB_NOMAGIC is provided to simplify implementing the historic csh(1) globbing behavior and should probably not be used anywhere else.

GLOB_QUOTE   Use the backslash ('\') character for quoting: every occurrence of a backslash followed by a character in the pattern is replaced by that character, avoiding any special interpretation of the character.

GLOB_TILDE   Expand patterns that start with '~' to user name home directories.

If, during the search, a directory is encountered that cannot be opened or read and *errfunc* is non-NULL, **glob**( ) calls *(*errfunc)(path, errno)*. This may be unintuitive: a pattern like */Makefile will try to stat(2) foo/Makefile even if foo is not a directory, resulting in a call to *errfunc*. The error routine can suppress this action by testing for ENOENT and ENOTDIR; however, the GLOB_ERR flag will still cause an immediate return when this happens.

If *errfunc* returns non-zero, **glob**( ) stops the scan and returns GLOB_ABEND after setting *gl_pathc* and *gl_pathv* to reflect any paths already matched. This also happens if an error is encountered and GLOB_ERR is set in *flags*, regardless of the return value of *errfunc*, if called. If GLOB_ERR is not set and either *errfunc* is NULL or *errfunc* returns zero, the error is ignored.

The **globfree**( ) function frees any space associated with *pglob* from a previous call(s) to **glob**().

RETURN VALUES

On successful completion, **glob**( ) returns zero. In addition the fields of *pglob* contain the values described below:

gl_pathc   contains the total number of matched pathnames so far. This includes other matches from previous invocations of **glob**( ) if GLOB_APPEND was specified.

gl_matchc   contains the number of matched pathnames in the current invocation of **glob**().

gl_flags   contains a copy of the *flags* parameter with the bit GLOB_MAGCHAR set if *pattern* contained any of the special characters "*", "?" or "[", cleared if not.

gl_pathv   contains a pointer to a NULL-terminated list of matched pathnames. However, if *gl_pathc* is zero, the contents of *gl_pathv* are undefined.

If **glob**( ) terminates due to an error, it sets errno and returns one of the following non-zero constants, which are defined in the include file <glob.h>:

GLOB_NOSPACE An attempt to allocate memory failed.

GLOB_ABEND   The scan was stopped because an error was encountered and either GLOB_ERR was set or *(*errfunc)( )* returned non-zero.

The arguments *pglob->gl_pathc* and *pglob->gl_pathv* are still set as specified above.

EXAMPLE

A rough equivalent of ls -l *.c *.h can be obtained with the following code:

```
glob_t g;

g.gl_offs = 2;
glob("*.c", GLOB_DOOFFS, NULL, &g);
glob("*.h", GLOB_DOOFFS | GLOB_APPEND, NULL, &g);
g.gl_pathv[0] = "ls";
g.gl_pathv[1] = "-l";
execvp("ls", g.gl_pathv);
```

SEE ALSO

sh(1), fnmatch(3), regexp(3)

STANDARDS

The **glob**( ) function is expected to be IEEE Std1003.2 ("POSIX") compatible with the exception that the flags GLOB_ALTDIRFUNC, GLOB_BRACE GLOB_MAGCHAR, GLOB_NOMAGIC, GLOB_QUOTE, and GLOB_TILDE, and the fields *gl_matchc* and *gl_flags* should not be used by applications striving for strict POSIX conformance.

HISTORY

The **glob**( ) and **globfree**( ) functions first appeared in 4.4BSD.

BUGS

Patterns longer than MAXPATHLEN may cause unchecked errors.

The **glob**( ) argument may fail and set errno for any of the errors specified for the library routines stat(2), closedir(3), opendir(3), readdir(3), malloc(3), and free(3).

NAME

    hash – hash database access method

SYNOPSIS

    #include <sys/types.h>
    #include <db.h>

DESCRIPTION

    The routine *dbopen* is the library interface to database files. One of the supported file formats is hash files. The general description of the database access methods is in *dbopen*(3), this manual page describes only the hash specific information.

    The hash data structure is an extensible, dynamic hashing scheme.

    The access method specific data structure provided to *dbopen* is defined in the <db.h> include file as follows:

```
typedef struct {
        u_int bsize;
        u_int ffactor;
        u_int nelem;
        u_int cachesize;
        u_int32_t (*hash)(const void *, size_t);
        int lorder;
} HASHINFO;
```

    The elements of this structure are as follows:

bsize   *Bsize* defines the hash table bucket size, and is, by default, 256 bytes. It may be preferable to increase the page size for disk-resident tables and tables with large data items.

ffactor   *Ffactor* indicates a desired density within the hash table. It is an approximation of the number of keys allowed to accumulate in any one bucket, determining when the hash table grows or shrinks. The default value is 8.

nelem   *Nelem* is an estimate of the final size of the hash table. If not set or set too low, hash tables will expand gracefully as keys are entered, although a slight performance degradation may be noticed. The default value is 1.

cachesize

    A suggested maximum size, in bytes, of the memory cache. This value is **only** advisory, and the access method will allocate more memory rather than fail.

hash   *Hash* is a user defined hash function. Since no hash function performs equally well on all possible data, the user may find that the built-in hash function does poorly on a particular data set. User specified hash functions must take two arguments (a pointer to a byte string and a length) and return a 32-bit quantity to be used as the hash value.

lorder   The byte order for integers in the stored database metadata. The number should represent the order as an integer; for example, big endian order would be the number 4,321. If *lorder* is 0 (no order is specified) the current host order is used. If the file already exists, the specified value is ignored and the value specified when the tree was created is used.

    If the file already exists (and the O_TRUNC flag is not specified), the values specified for the parameters bsize, ffactor, lorder and nelem are ignored and the values specified when the tree was created are used.

    If a hash function is specified, *hash_open* will attempt to determine if the hash function specified is the same as the one with which the database was created, and will fail if it is not.

    Backward compatible interfaces to the routines described in *dbm*(3), and *ndbm*(3) are provided, however these interfaces are not compatible with previous file formats.

SEE ALSO

btree(3), *dbopen*(3), *mpool*(3), *recno*(3)

Dynamic Hash Tables, Per-Ake Larson, Communications of the ACM, April 1988.

A New Hash Package for UNIX, Margo Seltzer, USENIX Proceedings, Winter 1991.

BUGS

Only big and little endian byte order is supported.

NAME
hypot, cabs – euclidean distance and complex absolute value functions

SYNOPSIS
```
#include <math.h>
```

double
hypot(*double x*, *double y*);

struct {double x, y;} z;

double
cabs(*z*);

DESCRIPTION
The **hypot()** and **cabs()** functions computes the sqrt(x*x+y*y) in such a way that underflow will not happen, and overflow occurs only if the final result deserves it.

hypot(∞, v) = **hypot**(v, ∞) = $+\infty$ for all v, including *NaN*.

ERROR (due to Roundoff, etc.)
Below 0.97 *ulps*. Consequently **hypot**(*5.0*, *12.0*) = 13.0 exactly; in general, hypot and cabs return an integer whenever an integer might be expected.

The same cannot be said for the shorter and faster version of hypot and cabs that is provided in the comments in cabs.c; its error can exceed 1.2 *ulps*.

NOTES
As might be expected, **hypot**(v, *NaN*) and **hypot**(*NaN*, v) are *NaN* for all *finite* v; with "reserved operand" in place of "*NaN*", the same is true on a VAX. But programmers on machines other than a VAX (if has no ∞) might be surprised at first to discover that **hypot**($\pm\infty$, *NaN*) = $+\infty$. This is intentional; it happens because **hypot**(∞, v) = $+\infty$ for *all* v, finite or infinite. Hence **hypot**(∞, v) is independent of v. Unlike the reserved operand fault on a VAX, the IEEE *NaN* is designed to disappear when it turns out to be irrelevant, as it does in **hypot**(∞, *NaN*).

SEE ALSO
math(3), sqrt(3)

HISTORY
Both a **hypot()** function and a **cabs()** function appeared in Version 7 AT&T UNIX.

3

NAME

copysign, drem, finite, logb, scalb – IEEE 754 floating point support

SYNOPSIS

```
#include <math.h>
```

double
copysign(*double* x, *double* y);

double
drem(*double* x, *double* y);

int
finite(*double* x);

double
logb(*double* x);

double
scalb(*double* x, *int* n);

DESCRIPTION

These functions are required for, or recommended by the IEEE standard 754 for floating–point arithmetic.

The **copysign**( ) function returns x with its sign changed to y's.

The **drem**( ) function returns the remainder $r := x - n*y$ where n is the integer nearest the exact value of x/y; moreover if $|n - x/y| = 1/2$ then n is even. Consequently the remainder is computed exactly and $|r| \le |y|/2$. But **drem**(x, 0) is exceptional. (See below under DIAGNOSTICS.)

The **finite**( ) function returns the value 1 just when $-\infty < x < +\infty$; otherwise a zero is returned (when $|x| = \infty$ or x is *NaN* or is the VAX's reserved operand).

The **logb**( ) function returns x's exponent n, a signed integer converted to double–precision floating–point and so chosen that $1 (<= |x|2**n < 2$ unless $x = 0$ or (only on machines that conform to IEEE 754) $|x| = \infty$ or x lies between 0 and the Underflow Threshold. (See below under BUGS.)

The **scalb**( ) function returns $x*(2**n)$ computed, for integer n, without first computing $2*n$.

RETURN VALUES

The IEEE standard 754 defines **drem**(x, 0) and **drem**(∞, y) to be invalid operations that produce a *NaN*. On the VAX, **drem**(x, 0) generates a reserved operand fault. No ∞ exists on a VAX.

IEEE 754 defines $= \infty$ and **logb**(0) $= -\infty$, and requires the latter to signal Division–by–Zero. But on a VAX, **logb**(0) $= 1.0 - 2.0**31 = -2,147,483,647.0$. And if the correct value of **scalb**( ) would overflow on a VAX, it generates a reserved operand fault and sets the global variable *errno* to ERANGE.

SEE ALSO

floor(3), math(3), infnan(3)

HISTORY

The **ieee** functions appeared in 4.3BSD.

BUGS

Should **drem**(x, 0) and **logb**(0) on a VAX signal invalidity by setting *errno* = EDOM ? Should **logb**(0) return $-1.7e38$?

IEEE 754 currently specifies that $\texttt{logb}(denormalized\ no.) = \texttt{logb}(tiniest\ normalized\ no.$ $> 0)$ but the consensus has changed to the specification in the new proposed IEEE standard p854, namely that $\texttt{logb}(x)$ satisfy

$$1 \le \texttt{scalb}(|x|, -logb(x)) < \text{Radix} \ \ ... = 2 \text{ for IEEE 754}$$

for every x except 0, ∞ and *NaN*. Almost every program that assumes 754's specification will work correctly if $\texttt{logb}()$ follows 854's specification instead.

IEEE 754 requires $\texttt{copysign}(x,\ NaN)) = \pm x$ but says nothing else about the sign of a *NaN*. A *NaN (Not a Number)* is similar in spirit to the VAX's reserved operand, but very different in important details. Since the sign bit of a reserved operand makes it look negative,

$$\texttt{copysign}(x,\ reserved\ operand) = -x;$$

should this return the reserved operand instead?

NAME
index – locate character in string

SYNOPSIS
    #include <string.h>

    char *
    index(const char *s, int c);

DESCRIPTION
The **index()** function locates the first character matching c (converted to a *char*) in the null-terminated string *s*.

RETURN VALUES
A pointer to the character is returned if it is found; otherwise NULL is returned. If c is '\0', **index()** locates the terminating '\0'.

SEE ALSO
memchr(3), rindex(3), strchr(3), strcspn(3), strpbrk(3), strrchr(3), strsep(3), strspn(3), strstr(3), strtok(3)

HISTORY
A **index()** function appeared in Version 6 AT&T UNIX.

NAME

inet_aton, inet_addr, inet_network, inet_ntoa, inet_makeaddr, inet_lnaof, inet_netof – Internet address manipulation routines

SYNOPSIS

```
#include <sys/socket.h>
#include <netinet/in.h>
#include <arpa/inet.h>

int
inet_aton(char *cp, struct in_addr *pin);

unsigned long
inet_addr(char *cp);

unsigned long
inet_network(char *cp);

char *
inet_ntoa(struct in_addr in);

struct in_addr
inet_makeaddr(int net, int lna);

unsigned long
inet_lnaof(struct in_addr in);

unsigned long
inet_netof(struct in_addr in);
```

DESCRIPTION

The routines **inet_aton()**, **inet_addr()** and **inet_network()** interpret character strings representing numbers expressed in the Internet standard '.' notation. The **inet_aton()** routine interprets the specified character string as an Internet address, placing the address into the structure provided. It returns 1 if the string was successfully interpreted, or 0 if the string is invalid. The **inet_addr()** and **inet_network()** functions return numbers suitable for use as Internet addresses and Internet network numbers, respectively. The routine **inet_ntoa()** takes an Internet address and returns an ASCII string representing the address in '.' notation. The routine **inet_makeaddr()** takes an Internet network number and a local network address and constructs an Internet address from it. The routines **inet_netof()** and **inet_lnaof()** break apart Internet host addresses, returning the network number and local network address part, respectively.

All Internet addresses are returned in network order (bytes ordered from left to right). All network numbers and local address parts are returned as machine format integer values.

INTERNET ADDRESSES

Values specified using the '.' notation take one of the following forms:

```
a.b.c.d
a.b.c
a.b
a
```

When four parts are specified, each is interpreted as a byte of data and assigned, from left to right, to the four bytes of an Internet address. Note that when an Internet address is viewed as a 32-bit integer quantity on the VAX the bytes referred to above appear as "d.c.b.a". That is, VAX bytes are ordered from right to left.

When a three part address is specified, the last part is interpreted as a 16-bit quantity and placed in the right-most two bytes of the network address. This makes the three part address format convenient for specifying Class B network addresses as "`128.net.host`".

When a two part address is supplied, the last part is interpreted as a 24-bit quantity and placed in the right most three bytes of the network address. This makes the two part address format convenient for specifying Class A network addresses as "`net.host`".

When only one part is given, the value is stored directly in the network address without any byte rearrangement.

All numbers supplied as "parts" in a '.' notation may be decimal, octal, or hexadecimal, as specified in the C language (i.e., a leading 0x or 0X implies hexadecimal; otherwise, a leading 0 implies octal; otherwise, the number is interpreted as decimal).

DIAGNOSTICS

The constant INADDR_NONE is returned by **inet_addr**() and **inet_network**() for malformed requests.

SEE ALSO

gethostbyname(3), getnetent(3), hosts(5), networks(5),

HISTORY

These functions appeared in 4.2BSD.

BUGS

The value INADDR_NONE (0xffffffff) is a valid broadcast address, but **inet_addr**() cannot return that value without indicating failure. The newer **inet_aton**() function does not share this problem. The problem of host byte ordering versus network byte ordering is confusing. The string returned by inet_ntoa() resides in a static memory area.

Inet_addr should return a *struct in_addr*.

3

NAME

infnan – signals invalid floating–point operations on a VAX (temporary)

SYNOPSIS

```
#include <math.h>
```

double
infnan(*int iarg*);

DESCRIPTION

At some time in the future, some of the useful properties of the Infinities and *NaN*s in the IEEE standard 754 for Binary Floating–Point Arithmetic will be simulated in UNIX on the DEC VAX by using its Reserved Operands. Meanwhile, the Invalid, Overflow and Divide–by–Zero exceptions of the IEEE standard are being approximated on a VAX by calls to a procedure **infnan()** in appropriate places in libm(3). When better exception–handling is implemented in UNIX, only **infnan()** among the codes in libm will have to be changed. And users of libm can design their own **infnan()** now to insulate themselves from future changes.

Whenever an elementary function code in libm has to simulate one of the aforementioned IEEE exceptions, it calls **infnan(*iarg*)** with an appropriate value of *iarg*. Then a reserved operand fault stops computation. But **infnan()** could be replaced by a function with the same name that returns some plausible value, assigns an apt value to the global variable *errno*, and allows computation to resume. Alternatively, the Reserved Operand Fault Handler could be changed to respond by returning that plausible value, etc. instead of aborting.

In the table below, the first two columns show various exceptions signaled by the IEEE standard, and the default result it prescribes. The third column shows what value is given to *iarg* by functions in libm when they invoke **infnan(*iarg*)** under analogous circumstances on a VAX. Currently **infnan()** stops computation under all those circumstances. The last two columns offer an alternative; they suggest a setting for *errno* and a value for a revised **infnan()** to return. And a C program to implement that suggestion follows.

IEEE Signal	IEEE Default	*iarg*	*errno*	infnan()	
Invalid	*NaN*	EDOM	EDOM	0	
Overflow	±∞	ERANGE	ERANGE	HUGE	
Div–by–0	±Infinity	±ERANGE	ERANGE or EDOM	±HUGE	
	(HUGE = 1.7e38 ... nearly 2.0**127)				

ALTERNATIVE **infnan()**:

```
#include      <math.h>
#include      <errno.h>
extern int    errno ;
double infnan(iarg)
int    iarg ;
{
      switch(iarg) {
      case    ERANGE:      errno = ERANGE; return(HUGE);
      case   -ERANGE:      errno = EDOM;   return(-HUGE);
      default:             errno = EDOM;   return(0);
      }
}
```

SEE ALSO

math(3), intro(2), signal(3).

ERANGE and EDOM are defined in <errno.h>. (See intro(2) for explanation of EDOM and ERANGE.)

HISTORY

The **infnan**( ) function appeared in 4.3BSD.

NAME

    `initgroups` – initialize group access list

SYNOPSIS

    `#include <unistd.h>`

    int
    `initgroups(`*const char *name, int basegid*`)`;

DESCRIPTION

    The `initgroups()` function uses the `getgrouplist`(3) function to calculate the group access list for the user specified in *name*. This group list is then setup for the current process using `setgroups`(2). The *basegid* is automatically included in the groups list. Typically this value is given as the group number from the password file.

RETURN VALUES

    The `initgroups()` function returns −1 if it was not invoked by the super-user.

SEE ALSO

    `setgroups`(2), `getgrouplist`(3)

HISTORY

    The `initgroups` function appeared in 4.2BSD.

BUGS

    The `getgrouplist()` function called by `initgroups` uses the routines based on `getgrent`(3). If the invoking program uses any of these routines, the group structure will be overwritten in the call to `initgroups()`.

NAME
insque, remque – insert/remove element from a queue

SYNOPSIS

```
struct qelem {
        struct  qelem *q_forw;
        struct  qelem *q_back;
        char    q_data[];
};
```

insque(*(caddr_t) struct qelem *elem*, *(caddr_t) struct qelem *pred*);

remque(*(caddr_t) struct qelem *elem*);

DESCRIPTION
The insque() and remque() functions manipulate queues built from doubly linked lists. Each element in the queue must be in the form of "struct qelem". The function insque() inserts *elem* in a queue immediately after *pred*; remque() removes an entry *elem* from a queue.

SEE ALSO
VAX Architecture Handbook, pp. 228-235.

HISTORY
The insque() and remque() functions appeared in 4.2BSD.

3

NAME

isalnum – alphanumeric character test

SYNOPSIS

```
#include <ctype.h>
```

int
isalnum(*int c*);

DESCRIPTION

The isalnum() function tests for any character for which isalpha(3) or isdigit(3) is true. In the ASCII character set, this includes the following characters:

060 "0"	061 "1"	062 "2"	063 "3"	064 "4"
065 "5"	066 "6"	067 "7"	070 "8"	071 "9"
101 "A"	102 "B"	103 "C"	104 "D"	105 "E"
106 "F"	107 "G"	110 "H"	111 "I"	112 "J"
113 "K"	114 "L"	115 "M"	116 "N"	117 "O"
120 "P"	121 "Q"	122 "R"	123 "S"	124 "T"
125 "U"	126 "V"	127 "W"	130 "X"	131 "Y"
132 "Z"	141 "a"	142 "b"	143 "c"	144 "d"
145 "e"	146 "f"	147 "g"	150 "h"	151 "i"
152 "j"	153 "k"	154 "l"	155 "m"	156 "n"
157 "o"	160 "p"	161 "q"	162 "r"	163 "s"
164 "t"	165 "u"	166 "v"	167 "w"	170 "x"
171 "y"	172 "z"			

RETURN VALUES

The isalnum() function returns zero if the character tests false and returns non-zero if the character tests true.

SEE ALSO

ctype(3), ascii(7)

STANDARDS

The isalnum() function conforms to ANSI C X3.159-1989 ("ANSI C ").

3

NAME

isalpha – alphabetic character test

SYNOPSIS

`#include <ctype.h>`

int
`isalpha(`*int c*`);`

DESCRIPTION

The `isalpha()` function tests for any character for which `isupper`(3) or `islower`(3) is true. In the ASCII character set, this includes the following characters:

101 "A"	102 "B"	103 "C"	104 "D"	105 "E"
106 "F"	107 "G"	110 "H"	111 "I"	112 "J"
113 "K"	114 "L"	115 "M"	116 "N"	117 "O"
120 "P"	121 "Q"	122 "R"	123 "S"	124 "T"
125 "U"	126 "V"	127 "W"	130 "X"	131 "Y"
132 "Z"	141 "a"	142 "b"	143 "c"	144 "d"
145 "e"	146 "f"	147 "g"	150 "h"	151 "i"
152 "j"	153 "k"	154 "l"	155 "m"	156 "n"
157 "o"	160 "p"	161 "q"	162 "r"	163 "s"
164 "t"	165 "u"	166 "v"	167 "w"	170 "x"
171 "y"	172 "z"			

RETURN VALUES

The `isalpha()` function returns zero if the character tests false and returns non-zero if the character tests true.

SEE ALSO

`ctype`(3), `ascii`(7)

STANDARDS

The `isalpha()` function conforms to ANSI C X3.159-1989 ("ANSI C ").

NAME

isascii – test for ASCII character

SYNOPSIS

`#include <ctype.h>`

int
`isascii(int c);`

3

DESCRIPTION

The `isascii()` function tests for an ASCII character, which is any character with a value less than or equal to 0177.

SEE ALSO

`ctype`(3), `ascii`(7)

STANDARDS

The `isascii()` function conforms to ANSI C X3.159-1989 (''ANSI C '').

NAME
isblank – space or tab character test

SYNOPSIS
#include <ctype.h>

int
isblank(*int c*);

DESCRIPTION
The **isblank**( ) function tests for a space or tab character.

RETURN VALUES
The **isblank**( ) function returns zero if the character tests false and returns non-zero if the character tests true.

SEE ALSO
ctype(3), ascii(7)

3

NAME
iscntrl – control character test

SYNOPSIS
#include <ctype.h>

int
iscntrl(*int c*);

DESCRIPTION
The iscntrl() function tests for any control character. In the ASCII character set, this includes the following characters:

000 nul	001 soh	002 stx	003 etx	004 eot
005 enq	006 ack	007 bel	010 bs	011 ht
012 nl	013 vt	014 np	015 cr	016 so
017 si	020 dle	021 dc1	022 dc2	023 dc3
024 dc4	025 nak	026 syn	027 etb	030 can
031 em	032 sub	033 esc	034 fs	035 gs
036 rs	037 us	177 del		

RETURN VALUES
The iscntrl() function returns zero if the character tests false and returns non-zero if the character tests true.

SEE ALSO
ctype(3), ascii(7)

STANDARDS
The iscntrl() function conforms to ANSI C X3.159-1989 (''ANSI C '').

NAME

isdigit – decimal-digit character test

SYNOPSIS

```
#include <ctype.h>

int
isdigit(int c);
```

DESCRIPTION

The isdigit() function tests for any decimal-digit character. In the ASCII character set, this includes the following characters:

060 "0"	061 "1"	062 "2"	063 "3"	064 "4"
065 "5"	066 "6"	067 "7"	070 "8"	071 "9"

RETURN VALUES

The isdigit() function returns zero if the character tests false and returns non-zero if the character tests true.

SEE ALSO

ctype(3), ascii(7)

STANDARDS

The isdigit() function conforms to ANSI C X3.159-1989 ("ANSI C ").

3

NAME
isgraph – printing character test (space character exclusive)

SYNOPSIS
`#include <ctype.h>`

int
`isgraph(int c);`

DESCRIPTION
The `isgraph()` function tests for any printing character except space. In the ASCII character set, this includes the following characters:

041 "!"	042 "'"	043 "#"	044 "$"	045 "%"
046 "&"	047 "'"	050 "("	051 ")"	052 "*"
053 "+"	054 ","	055 "-"	056 "."	057 "/"
060 "0"	061 "1"	062 "2"	063 "3"	064 "4"
065 "5"	066 "6"	067 "7"	070 "8"	071 "9"
072 ":"	073 ";"	074 "<"	075 "="	076 ">"
077 "?"	100 "@"	101 "A"	102 "B"	103 "C"
104 "D"	105 "E"	106 "F"	107 "G"	110 "H"
111 "I"	112 "J"	113 "K"	114 "L"	115 "M"
116 "N"	117 "O"	120 "P"	121 "Q"	122 "R"
123 "S"	124 "T"	125 "U"	126 "V"	127 "W"
130 "X"	131 "Y"	132 "Z"	133 "["	134 ""
135 "]"	136 "^"	137 "_"	140 "'"	141 "a"
142 "b"	143 "c"	144 "d"	145 "e"	146 "f"
147 "g"	150 "h"	151 "i"	152 "j"	153 "k"
154 "l"	155 "m"	156 "n"	157 "o"	160 "p"
161 "q"	162 "r"	163 "s"	164 "t"	165 "u"
166 "v"	167 "w"	170 "x"	171 "y"	172 "z"
173 "{"	174 "l"	175 "}"	176 "~"	

RETURN VALUES
The `isgraph()` function returns zero if the character tests false and returns non-zero if the character tests true.

SEE ALSO
`ctype(3), ascii(7)`

STANDARDS
The `isgraph()` function conforms to ANSI C X3.159-1989 (''ANSI C '').

NAME

isinf, isnan – test for infinity or not-a-number

SYNOPSIS

int
isinf(*double*);

int
isnan(*double*);

DESCRIPTION

The **isninf**( ) function returns 1 if the number is "∞", otherwise 0.

The **isnan**( ) function returns 1 if the number is "not-a-number", otherwise 0.

SEE ALSO

math(3)

IEEE Standard for Binary Floating-Point Arithmetic, Std 754-1985, ANSI.

BUGS

Neither the VAX nor the Tahoe floating point have distinguished values for either infinity or not-a-number. These routines always return 0 on those architectures.

NAME

islower – lower-case character test

SYNOPSIS

`#include <ctype.h>`

int
`islower(int c);`

DESCRIPTION

The `islower()` function tests for any lower-case letters. In the ASCII character set, this includes the following characters:

141 "a"	142 "b"	143 "c"	144 "d"	145 "e"
146 "f"	147 "g"	150 "h"	151 "i"	152 "j"
153 "k"	154 "l"	155 "m"	156 "n"	157 "o"
160 "p"	161 "q"	162 "r"	163 "s"	164 "t"
165 "u"	166 "v"	167 "w"	170 "x"	171 "y"
172 "z"				

RETURN VALUES

The `islower()` function returns zero if the character tests false and returns non-zero if the character tests true.

SEE ALSO

`ctype`(3), `ascii`(7)

STANDARDS

The `islower()` function conforms to ANSI C X3.159-1989 ("ANSI C ").

NAME

iso_addr, iso_ntoa – elementary network address conversion routines for Open System Interconnection

SYNOPSIS

```
#include <sys/types.h>
#include <netiso/iso.h>
```

*struct iso_addr ***
iso_addr(*char *cp*);

*char ***
iso_ntoa(*struct iso_addr *isoa*);

DESCRIPTION

The routine iso_addr() interprets character strings representing OSI addresses, returning binary information suitable for use in system calls. The routine iso_ntoa() takes OSI addresses and returns ASCII strings representing NSAPs (network service access points) in a notation inverse to that accepted by iso_addr().

Unfortunately, no universal standard exists for representing OSI network addresses.

The format employed by iso_addr() is a sequence of hexadecimal ''digits'' (optionally separated by periods), of the form:

<hex digits>.<hex digits>.<hex digits>

Each pair of hexadecimal digits represents a byte with the leading digit indicating the higher-ordered bits. A period following an even number of bytes has no effect (but may be used to increase legibility). A period following an odd number of bytes has the effect of causing the byte of address being translated to have its higher order bits filled with zeros.

RETURN VALUES

iso_ntoa() always returns a null terminated string. iso_addr() always returns a pointer to a struct iso_addr. (See BUGS.)

SEE ALSO

iso(4)

HISTORY

The iso_addr() and iso_ntoa() functions appeared in 4.3BSD–Reno.

BUGS

The returned values reside in a static memory area.

The function iso_addr() should diagnose improperly formed input, and there should be an unambiguous way to recognize this.

NAME
isprint – printing character test (space character inclusive)

SYNOPSIS
`#include <ctype.h>`

int
isprint(*int c*);

DESCRIPTION
The isprint() function tests for any printing character including space (' '). In the ASCII character set, this includes the following characters:

040 sp	041 "!"	042 "″"	043 "#"	044 "$"
045 "%"	046 "&"	047 "′"	050 "("	051 ")"
052 "*"	053 "+"	054 ","	055 "-"	056 "."
057 "/"	060 "0"	061 "1"	062 "2"	063 "3"
064 "4"	065 "5"	066 "6"	067 "7"	070 "8"
071 "9"	072 ":"	073 ";"	074 "<"	075 "="
076 ">"	077 "?"	100 "@"	101 "A"	102 "B"
103 "C"	104 "D"	105 "E"	106 "F"	107 "G"
110 "H"	111 "I"	112 "J"	113 "K"	114 "L"
115 "M"	116 "N"	117 "O"	120 "P"	121 "Q"
122 "R"	123 "S"	124 "T"	125 "U"	126 "V"
127 "W"	130 "X"	131 "Y"	132 "Z"	133 "["
134 "∖"	135 "]"	136 "^"	137 "_"	140 "`"
141 "a"	142 "b"	143 "c"	144 "d"	145 "e"
146 "f"	147 "g"	150 "h"	151 "i"	152 "j"
153 "k"	154 "l"	155 "m"	156 "n"	157 "o"
160 "p"	161 "q"	162 "r"	163 "s"	164 "t"
165 "u"	166 "v"	167 "w"	170 "x"	171 "y"
172 "z"	173 "{"	174 "|"	175 "}"	176 "~"

RETURN VALUES
The isprint() function returns zero if the character tests false and returns non-zero if the character tests true.

SEE ALSO
ctype(3), ascii(7)

STANDARDS
The isprint() function conforms to ANSI C X3.159-1989 ("ANSI C").

NAME
ispunct – punctuation character test

SYNOPSIS
```
#include <ctype.h>
```
int
ispunct(*int c*);

DESCRIPTION
The ispunct() function tests for any printing character except for space (' ') or a character for which isalnum(3) is true. In the ASCII character set, this includes the following characters:

041 "!"	042 """	043 "#"	044 "$"	045 "%"
046 "&"	047 "'"	050 "("	051 ")"	052 "*"
053 "+"	054 ","	055 "-"	056 "."	057 "/"
072 ":"	073 ";"	074 "<"	075 "="	076 ">"
077 "?"	100 "@"	133 "["	134 "\"	135 "]"
136 "^"	137 "_"	140 "`"	173 "{"	174 "|"
175 "}"	176 "~"			

RETURN VALUES
The ispunct() function returns zero if the character tests false and returns non-zero if the character tests true.

SEE ALSO
ctype(3), ascii(7)

STANDARDS
The ispunct() function conforms to ANSI C X3.159-1989 ("ANSI C ").

3

NAME
isspace – white-space character test

SYNOPSIS
#include <ctype.h>

int
isspace(*int c*);

DESCRIPTION
The isspace() function tests for the standard white-space characters. In the ASCII character set, this includes the following characters:

011 ht	012 nl	013 vt	014 np	015 cr
040 sp				

RETURN VALUES
The isspace() function returns zero if the character tests false and returns non-zero if the character tests true.

SEE ALSO
ctype(3), ascii(7)

STANDARDS
The isspace() function conforms to ANSI C X3.159-1989 (''ANSI C '').

NAME

isupper – upper-case character test

SYNOPSIS

#include ⟨ctype.h⟩

int
isupper(*int c*);

DESCRIPTION

The isupper() function tests for any upper-case letter. In the ASCII character set, this includes the following characters:

101 "A"	102 "B"	103 "C"	104 "D"	105 "E"
106 "F"	107 "G"	110 "H"	111 "I"	112 "J"
113 "K"	114 "L"	115 "M"	116 "N"	117 "O"
120 "P"	121 "Q"	122 "R"	123 "S"	124 "T"
125 "U"	126 "V"	127 "W"	130 "X"	131 "Y"
132 "Z"				

RETURN VALUES

The isupper() function returns zero if the character tests false and returns non-zero if the character tests true.

SEE ALSO

ctype(3), ascii(7)

STANDARDS

The isupper function conforms to ANSI C X3.159-1989 ("ANSI C ").

NAME

isxdigit – hexadecimal-digit character test

SYNOPSIS

```
#include <ctype.h>
```

int
isxdigit(*int c*);

DESCRIPTION

The isxdigit() function tests for any hexadecimal-digit character. In the ASCII character set, this includes the following characters:

060 "0"	061 "1"	062 "2"	063 "3"	064 "4"
065 "5"	066 "6"	067 "7"	070 "8"	071 "9"
101 "A"	102 "B"	103 "C"	104 "D"	105 "E"
106 "F"	141 "a"	142 "b"	143 "c"	144 "d"
145 "e"	146 "f"			

RETURN VALUES

The isxdigit() function returns zero if the character tests false and returns non-zero if the character tests true.

SEE ALSO

ctype(3), ascii(7)

STANDARDS

The isxdigit() function conforms to ANSI C X3.159-1989 (''ANSI C '').

3

NAME

j0, j1, jn, y0, y1, yn – bessel functions of first and second kind

SYNOPSIS

```
#include <math.h>
```

double
j0(*double x*);

double
j1(*double x*);

double
jn(*int n, double x*);

double
y0(*double x*);

double
y1(*double x*);

double
yn(*int n, double x*);

DESCRIPTION

The functions j0( ) and j1( ) compute the *Bessel function of the first kind of the order* 1, respectively, for the real value x; the function jn( ) computes the *Bessel function of the first kind of the integer n* for the real value x.

The functions y0( ) and y1( ) compute the linearly independent *Bessel function of the second kind of the order* 0 and the *order* 1, respectively, for the positive *integer* value x (expressed as a double); the function yn( ) computes the *Bessel function of the second kind for the integer n* for the positive *integer* value x (expressed as a double).

RETURN VALUES

If these functions are successful, the computed value is returned. On the VAX and Tahoe architectures, a negative x value results in an error; the global variable *errno* is set to EDOM and a reserve operand fault is generated.

SEE ALSO

math(3), infnan(3)

HISTORY

A set of these functions function appeared in Version 7 AT&T UNIX.

NAME

        krb_mk_req, krb_rd_req, krb_kntoln, krb_set_key, krb_get_cred, krb_mk_priv, krb_rd_priv, krb_mk_safe, krb_rd_safe, krb_mk_err, krb_rd_err, krb_ck_repl – Kerberos authentication library

SYNOPSIS

        #include <kerberosIV/des.h>
        #include <kerberosIV/krb.h>

        extern char *krb_err_txt[];

        int krb_mk_req(authent,service,instance,realm,checksum)
        KTEXT authent;
        char *service;
        char *instance;
        char *realm;
        u_long checksum;

        int krb_rd_req(authent,service,instance,from_addr,ad,fn)
        KTEXT authent;
        char *service;
        char *instance;
        u_long from_addr;
        AUTH_DAT *ad;
        char *fn;

        int krb_kntoln(ad,lname)
        AUTH_DAT *ad;
        char *lname;

        int krb_set_key(key,cvt)
        char *key;
        int cvt;

        int krb_get_cred(service,instance,realm,c)
        char *service;
        char *instance;
        char *realm;
        CREDENTIALS *c;

        long krb_mk_priv(in,out,in_length,schedule,key,sender,receiver)
        u_char *in;
        u_char *out;
        u_long in_length;
        des_cblock key;
        des_key_schedule schedule;
        struct sockaddr_in *sender;
        struct sockaddr_in *receiver;

        long krb_rd_priv(in,in_length,schedule,key,sender,receiver,msg_data)
        u_char *in;
        u_long in_length;
        Key_schedule schedule;
        des_cblock key;
        struct sockaddr_in *sender;
        struct sockaddr_in *receiver;
        MSG_DAT *msg_data;

        long krb_mk_safe(in,out,in_length,key,sender,receiver)
        u_char *in;
        u_char *out;

u_long in_length;
des_cblock key;
struct sockaddr_in *sender;
struct sockaddr_in *receiver;

long krb_rd_safe(in,length,key,sender,receiver,msg_data)
u_char *in;
u_long length;
des_cblock key;
struct sockaddr_in *sender;
struct sockaddr_in *receiver;
MSG_DAT *msg_data;

long krb_mk_err(out,code,string)
u_char *out;
long code;
char *string;

long krb_rd_err(in,length,code,msg_data)
u_char *in;
u_long length;
long code;
MSG_DAT *msg_data;

DESCRIPTION

This library supports network authentication and various related operations. The library contains many routines beyond those described in this man page, but they are not intended to be used directly. Instead, they are called by the routines that are described, the authentication server and the login program.

krb_err_txt[] contains text string descriptions of various Kerberos error codes returned by some of the routines below.

krb_mk_req takes a pointer to a text structure in which an authenticator is to be built. It also takes the name, instance, and realm of the service to be used and an optional checksum. It is up to the application to decide how to generate the checksum. *krb_mk_req* then retrieves a ticket for the desired service and creates an authenticator. The authenticator is built in *authent* and is accessible to the calling procedure.

It is up to the application to get the authenticator to the service where it will be read by *krb_rd_req*. Unless an attacker possesses the session key contained in the ticket, it will be unable to modify the authenticator. Thus, the checksum can be used to verify the authenticity of the other data that will pass through a connection.

krb_rd_req takes an authenticator of type **KTEXT**, a service name, an instance, the address of the host originating the request, and a pointer to a structure of type **AUTH_DAT** which is filled in with information obtained from the authenticator. It also optionally takes the name of the file in which it will find the secret key(s) for the service. If the supplied *instance* contains "*", then the first service key with the same service name found in the service key file will be used, and the *instance* argument will be filled in with the chosen instance. This means that the caller must provide space for such an instance name.

It is used to find out information about the principal when a request has been made to a service. It is up to the application protocol to get the authenticator from the client to the service. The authenticator is then passed to *krb_rd_req* to extract the desired information.

krb_rd_req returns zero (RD_AP_OK) upon successful authentication. If a packet was forged, modified, or replayed, authentication will fail. If the authentication fails, a non-zero value is returned indicating the particular problem encountered. See *krb.h* for the list of error codes.

If the last argument is the null string (""), krb_rd_req will use the file /etc/srvtab to find its keys. If the last argument is NULL, it will assume that the key has been set by *krb_set_key* and will not bother looking further.

krb_kntoln converts a Kerberos name to a local name. It takes a structure of type AUTH_DAT and uses the name and instance to look in the database /etc/aname to find the corresponding local name. The local name is returned and can be used by an application to change uids, directories, or other parameters. It is not an integral part of Kerberos, but is instead provided to support the use of Kerberos in existing utilities.

krb_set_key takes as an argument a des key. It then creates a key schedule from it and saves the original key to be used as an initialization vector. It is used to set the server's key which must be used to decrypt tickets.

If called with a non-zero second argument, *krb_set_key* will first convert the input from a string of arbitrary length to a DES key by encrypting it with a one-way function.

In most cases it should not be necessary to call *krb_set_key*. The necessary keys will usually be obtained and set inside *krb_rd_req*. *krb_set_key* is provided for those applications that do not wish to place the application keys on disk.

krb_get_cred searches the caller's ticket file for a ticket for the given service, instance, and realm; and, if a ticket is found, fills in the given CREDENTIALS structure with the ticket information.

If the ticket was found, *krb_get_cred* returns GC_OK. If the ticket file can't be found, can't be read, doesn't belong to the user (other than root), isn't a regular file, or is in the wrong mode, the error GC_TKFIL is returned.

krb_mk_priv creates an encrypted, authenticated message from any arbitrary application data, pointed to by *in* and *in_length* bytes long. The private session key, pointed to by *key* and the key schedule, *schedule*, are used to encrypt the data and some header information using *pcbc_encrypt. sender* and *receiver* point to the Internet address of the two parties. In addition to providing privacy, this protocol message protects against modifications, insertions or replays. The encapsulated message and header are placed in the area pointed to by *out* and the routine returns the length of the output, or -1 indicating an error.

krb_rd_priv decrypts and authenticates a received *krb_mk_priv* message. *in* points to the beginning of the received message, whose length is specified in *in_length*. The private session key, pointed to by *key*, and the key schedule, *schedule*, are used to decrypt and verify the received message. *msg_data* is a pointer to a *MSG_DAT* struct, defined in *krb.h*. The routine fills in the *app_data* field with a pointer to the decrypted application data, *app_length* with the length of the *app_data* field, *time_sec* and *time_5ms* with the timestamps in the message, and *swap* with a 1 if the byte order of the receiver is different than that of the sender. (The application must still determine if it is appropriate to byte-swap application data; the Kerberos protocol fields are already taken care of). The *hash* field returns a value useful as input to the *krb_ck_repl* routine.

The routine returns zero if ok, or a Kerberos error code. Modified messages and old messages cause errors, but it is up to the caller to check the time sequence of messages, and to check against recently replayed messages using *krb_ck_repl* if so desired.

krb_mk_safe creates an authenticated, but unencrypted message from any arbitrary application data, pointed to by *in* and *in_length* bytes long. The private session key, pointed to by *key*, is used to seed the *quad_cksum()* checksum algorithm used as part of the authentication. *sender* and *receiver* point to the Internet address of the two parties. This message does not provide privacy, but does protect (via detection) against modifications, insertions or replays. The encapsulated message and header are placed in the area pointed to by *out* and the routine returns the length of the output, or -1 indicating an error. The authentication provided by this routine is not as strong as that provided by *krb_mk_priv* or by computing the checksum using *cbc_cksum* instead, both of which authenticate via DES.

krb_rd_safe authenticates a received *krb_mk_safe* message. *in* points to the beginning of the received message, whose length is specified in *in_length*. The private session key, pointed to by *key*, is used to seed the quad_cksum() routine as part of the authentication. *msg_data* is a pointer to a *MSG_DAT* struct, defined in *krb.h* . The routine fills in these *MSG_DAT* fields: the *app_data* field with a pointer to the application data, *app_length* with the length of the *app_data* field, *time_sec* and *time_5ms* with the timestamps in the message, and *swap* with a 1 if the byte order of the receiver is different than that of the sender. (The application must still determine if it is appropriate to byte-swap application data; the Kerberos protocol fields are already taken care of). The *hash* field returns a value useful as input to the *krb_ck_repl* routine.

The routine returns zero if ok, or a Kerberos error code. Modified messages and old messages cause errors, but it is up to the caller to check the time sequence of messages, and to check against recently replayed messages using *krb_ck_repl* if so desired.

krb_mk_err constructs an application level error message that may be used along with *krb_mk_priv* or *krb_mk_safe*. *out* is a pointer to the output buffer, *code* is an application specific error code, and *string* is an application specific error string.

krb_rd_err unpacks a received *krb_mk_err* message. *in* points to the beginning of the received message, whose length is specified in *in_length*. *code* is a pointer to a value to be filled in with the error value provided by the application. *msg_data* is a pointer to a *MSG_DAT* struct, defined in *krb.h* . The routine fills in these *MSG_DAT* fields: the *app_data* field with a pointer to the application error text, *app_length* with the length of the *app_data* field, and *swap* with a 1 if the byte order of the receiver is different than that of the sender. (The application must still determine if it is appropriate to byte-swap application data; the Kerberos protocol fields are already taken care of).

The routine returns zero if the error message has been successfully received, or a Kerberos error code.

The *KTEXT* structure is used to pass around text of varying lengths. It consists of a buffer for the data, and a length. krb_rd_req takes an argument of this type containing the authenticator, and krb_mk_req returns the authenticator in a structure of this type. KTEXT itself is really a pointer to the structure. The actual structure is of type KTEXT_ST.

The *AUTH_DAT* structure is filled in by krb_rd_req. It must be allocated before calling krb_rd_req, and a pointer to it is passed. The structure is filled in with data obtained from Kerberos. *MSG_DAT* structure is filled in by either krb_rd_priv, krb_rd_safe, or krb_rd_err. It must be allocated before the call and a pointer to it is passed. The structure is filled in with data obtained from Kerberos.

FILES

        /usr/include/kerberosIV/krb.h
        /usr/lib/libkrb.a
        /usr/include/kerberosIV/des.h
        /usr/lib/libdes.a
        /etc/kerberosIV/aname
        /etc/kerberosIV/srvtab
        /tmp/tkt[uid]

SEE ALSO

        kerberos(1), des_crypt(3)

DIAGNOSTICS

BUGS

        The caller of *krb_rd_req, krb_rd_priv, and krb_rd_safe* must check time order and for replay attempts. *krb_ck_repl* is not implemented yet.

AUTHORS

        Clifford Neuman, MIT Project Athena
        Steve Miller, MIT Project Athena/Digital Equipment Corporation

RESTRICTIONS

        COPYRIGHT 1985,1986,1989 Massachusetts Institute of Technology

3

NAME

krb_realmofhost, krb_get_phost, krb_get_krbhst, krb_get_admhst, krb_get_lrealm – additional Kerberos utility routines

SYNOPSIS

#include <kerberosIV/krb.h>
#include <kerberosIV/des.h>
#include <netinet/in.h>

char *krb_realmofhost(host)
char *host;

char *krb_get_phost(alias)
char *alias;

krb_get_krbhst(host,realm,n)
char *host;
char *realm;
int n;

krb_get_admhst(host,realm,n)
char *host;
char *realm;
int n;

krb_get_lrealm(realm,n)
char *realm;
int n;

DESCRIPTION

krb_realmofhost returns the Kerberos realm of the host *host*, as determined by the translation table */etc/kerberosIV/krb.realms*. *host* should be the fully-qualified domain-style primary host name of the host in question. In order to prevent certain security attacks, this routine must either have *a priori* knowledge of a host's realm, or obtain such information securely.

The format of the translation file is described by *krb.realms*(5). If *host* exactly matches a host_name line, the corresponding realm is returned. Otherwise, if the domain portion of *host* matches a domain_name line, the corresponding realm is returned. If *host* contains a domain, but no translation is found, *host*'s domain is converted to upper-case and returned. If *host* contains no discernible domain, or an error occurs, the local realm name, as supplied by *krb_get_lrealm*(3), is returned.

krb_get_phost converts the hostname *alias* (which can be either an official name or an alias) into the instance name to be used in obtaining Kerberos tickets for most services, including the Berkeley rcmd suite (rlogin, rcp, rsh).
The current convention is to return the first segment of the official domain-style name after conversion to lower case.

krb_get_krbhst fills in *host* with the hostname of the *n*th host running a Kerberos key distribution center (KDC) for realm *realm*, as specified in the configuration file (*/etc/kerberosIV/krb.conf*). The configuration file is described by *krb.conf*(5). If the host is successfully filled in, the routine returns KSUCCESS. If the file cannot be opened, and *n* equals 1, then the value of KRB_HOST as defined in *<krb.h>* is filled in, and KSUCCESS is returned. If there are fewer than *n* hosts running a Kerberos KDC for the requested realm, or the configuration file is malformed, the routine returns KFAILURE.

krb_get_admhst fills in *host* with the hostname of the *n*th host running a Kerberos KDC database administration server for realm *realm*, as specified in the configuration file (*/etc/kerberosIV/krb.conf*). If the file cannot be opened or is malformed, or there are fewer than *n* hosts running a Kerberos KDC database administration server, the routine returns KFAILURE.

The character arrays used as return values for *krb_get_krbhst*, *krb_get_admhst*, should be large enough to hold any hostname (MAXHOSTNAMELEN from <sys/param.h>).

krb_get_lrealm fills in *realm* with the *n*th realm of the local host, as specified in the configuration file. *realm* should be at least REALM_SZ (from *<krb.h>)*characters*long*.

SEE ALSO

kerberos(3), krb.conf(5), krb.realms(5)

FILES

/etc/kerberosIV/krb.realms

    translation file for host-to-realm mapping.

/etc/kerberosIV/krb.conf

    local realm-name and realm/server configuration file.

BUGS

The current convention for instance names is too limited; the full domain name should be used.

krb_get_lrealm currently only supports *n* = 1. It should really consult the user's ticket cache to determine the user's current realm, rather than consulting a file on the host.

3

NAME

krb_sendauth, krb_recvauth, krb_net_write, krb_net_read – Kerberos routines for sending authentication via network stream sockets

SYNOPSIS

#include <kerberosIV/krb.h>
#include <kerberosIV/des.h>
#include <netinet/in.h>

int krb_sendauth(options, fd, ktext, service, inst, realm, checksum, msg_data, cred, schedule, laddr,
               faddr, version)
long options;
int fd;
KTEXT ktext;
char *service, *inst, *realm;
u_long checksum;
MSG_DAT *msg_data;
CREDENTIALS *cred;
Key_schedule schedule;
struct sockaddr_in *laddr, *faddr;
char *version;

int krb_recvauth(options, fd, ktext, service, inst, faddr, laddr, auth_data, filename, schedule, version)
long options;
int fd;
KTEXT ktext;
char *service, *inst;
struct sockaddr_in *faddr, *laddr;
AUTH_DAT *auth_data;
char *filename;
Key_schedule schedule;
char *version;

int krb_net_write(fd, buf, len)
int fd;
char *buf;
int len;

int krb_net_read(fd, buf, len)
int fd;
char *buf;
int len;

DESCRIPTION

These functions, which are built on top of the core Kerberos library, provide a convenient means for client and server programs to send authentication messages to one another through network connections. The *krb_sendauth* function sends an authenticated ticket from the client program to the server program by writing the ticket to a network socket. The *krb_recvauth* function receives the ticket from the client by reading from a network socket.

KRB_SENDAUTH

This function writes the ticket to the network socket specified by the file descriptor *fd*, returning KSUCCESS if the write proceeds successfully, and an error code if it does not.

The *ktext* argument should point to an allocated KTEXT_ST structure. The *service*, *inst*, and *realm* arguments specify the server program's Kerberos principal name, instance, and realm. If you are writing a client that uses the local realm exclusively, you can set the *realm* argument to NULL.

The *version* argument allows the client program to pass an application-specific version string that the server program can then match against its own version string. The *version* string can be up to KSEND_VNO_LEN (see *<krb.h>*) characters in length.

The *checksum* argument can be used to pass checksum information to the server program. The client program is responsible for specifying this information. This checksum information is difficult to corrupt because *krb_sendauth* passes it over the network in encrypted form. The *checksum* argument is passed as the checksum argument to *krb_mk_req*.

You can set *krb_sendauth's* other arguments to NULL unless you want the client and server programs to mutually authenticate themselves. In the case of mutual authentication, the client authenticates itself to the server program, and demands that the server in turn authenticate itself to the client.

KRB_SENDAUTH AND MUTUAL AUTHENTICATION

If you want mutual authentication, make sure that you read all pending data from the local socket before calling *krb_sendauth*. Set *krb_sendauth's* *options* argument to **KOPT_DO_MUTUAL** (this macro is defined in the *krb.h* file); make sure that the *laddr* argument points to the address of the local socket, and that *faddr* points to the foreign socket's network address.

Krb_sendauth fills in the other arguments-- *msg_data*, *cred*, and *schedule*--before sending the ticket to the server program. You must, however, allocate space for these arguments before calling the function.

Krb_sendauth supports two other options: **KOPT_DONT_MK_REQ,** and **KOPT_DONT_CANON.** If called with *options* set as KOPT_DONT_MK_REQ, *krb_sendauth* will not use the *krb_mk_req* function to retrieve the ticket from the Kerberos server. The *ktext* argument must point to an existing ticket and authenticator (such as would be created by *krb_mk_req*), and the *service*, *inst*, and *realm* arguments can be set to NULL.

If called with *options* set as KOPT_DONT_CANON, *krb_sendauth* will not convert the service's instance to canonical form using *krb_get_phost*(3).

If you want to call *krb_sendauth* with a multiple *options* specification, construct *options* as a bitwise-OR of the options you want to specify.

KRB_RECVAUTH

The *krb_recvauth* function reads a ticket/authenticator pair from the socket pointed to by the *fd* argument. Set the *options* argument as a bitwise-OR of the options desired. Currently only KOPT_DO_MUTUAL is useful to the receiver.

The *ktext* argument should point to an allocated KTEXT_ST structure. *Krb_recvauth* fills *ktext* with the ticket/authenticator pair read from *fd*, then passes it to *krb_rd_req*.

The *service* and *inst* arguments specify the expected service and instance for which the ticket was generated. They are also passed to *krb_rd_req*. The *inst* argument may be set to "*" if the caller wishes *krb_mk_req* to fill in the instance used (note that there must be space in the *inst* argument to hold a full instance name, see *krb_mk_req*(3)).

The *faddr* argument should point to the address of the peer which is presenting the ticket. It is also passed to *krb_rd_req*.

If the client and server plan to mutually authenticate one another, the *laddr* argument should point to the local address of the file descriptor. Otherwise you can set this argument to NULL.

The *auth_data* argument should point to an allocated AUTH_DAT area. It is passed to and filled in by *krb_rd_req*. The checksum passed to the corresponding *krb_sendauth* is available as part of the filled-in AUTH_DAT area.

The *filename* argument specifies the filename which the service program should use to obtain its service key. *Krb_recvauth* passes *filename* to the *krb_rd_req* function. If you set this argument to "", *krb_rd_req* looks for the service key in the file */etc/kerberosIV/srvtab*.

If the client and server are performing mutual authentication, the *schedule* argument should point to an allocated Key_schedule. Otherwise it is ignored and may be NULL.

The *version* argument should point to a character array of at least KSEND_VNO_LEN characters. It is filled in with the version string passed by the client to *krb_sendauth*.

KRB_NET_WRITE AND KRB_NET_READ

The *krb_net_write* function emulates the write(2) system call, but guarantees that all data specified is written to *fd* before returning, unless an error condition occurs.

The *krb_net_read* function emulates the read(2) system call, but guarantees that the requested amount of data is read from *fd* before returning, unless an error condition occurs.

BUGS

krb_sendauth, krb_recvauth, krb_net_write, and *krb_net_read* will not work properly on sockets set to non-blocking I/O mode.

SEE ALSO

krb_mk_req(3), krb_rd_req(3), krb_get_phost(3)

AUTHOR

John T. Kohl, MIT Project Athena

RESTRICTIONS

Copyright 1988, Massachusetts Instititute of Technology. For copying and distribution information, please see the file <mit-copyright.h>.

NAME

krb_set_tkt_string – set Kerberos ticket cache file name

SYNOPSIS

#include <kerberosIV/krb.h>

void krb_set_tkt_string(filename)
char *filename;

DESCRIPTION

krb_set_tkt_string sets the name of the file that holds the user's cache of Kerberos server tickets and associated session keys.

The string *filename* passed in is copied into local storage. Only MAXPATHLEN-1 (see <sys/param.h>) characters of the filename are copied in for use as the cache file name.

This routine should be called during initialization, before other Kerberos routines are called; otherwise the routines which fetch the ticket cache file name may be called and return an undesired ticket file name until this routine is called.

FILES

/tmp/tkt[uid]   default ticket file name, unless the environment variable KRBTKFILE is set. [uid] denotes the user's uid, in decimal.

SEE ALSO

kerberos(3), setenv(3)

3

NAME

kuserok – Kerberos version of ruserok

SYNOPSIS

#include <kerberosIV/krb.h>

kuserok(kdata, localuser)
AUTH_DAT *auth_data;
char   *localuser;

DESCRIPTION

kuserok determines whether a Kerberos principal described by the structure *auth_data* is authorized to login as user *localuser* according to the authorization file ("*localuser*/.klogin" by default). It returns 0 (zero) if authorized, 1 (one) if not authorized.

If there is no account for *localuser* on the local machine, authorization is not granted. If there is no authorization file, and the Kerberos principal described by *auth_data* translates to *localuser* (using *krb_kntoln*(3)), authorization is granted. If the authorization file can't be accessed, or the file is not owned by *localuser*, authorization is denied. Otherwise, the file is searched for a matching principal name, instance, and realm. If a match is found, authorization is granted, else authorization is denied.

The file entries are in the format:
                    name.instance@realm
with one entry per line.

SEE ALSO

kerberos(3), ruserok(3), krb_kntoln(3)

FILES

~*localuser*/.klogin   authorization list

NAME
kvm – kernel memory interface

DESCRIPTION
The kvm(3) library provides a uniform interface for accessing kernel virtual memory images, including live systems and crashdumps. Access to live systems is via /dev/mem while crashdumps can be examined via the core file generated by savecore(8). The interface behaves identically in both cases. Memory can be read and written, kernel symbol addresses can be looked up efficiently, and information about user processes can be gathered.

kvm_open( ) is first called to obtain a descriptor for all subsequent calls.

COMPATIBILITY
The kvm interface was first introduced in SunOS. A considerable number of programs have been developed that use this interface, making backward compatibility highly desirable. In most respects, the Sun kvm interface is consistent and clean. Accordingly, the generic portion of the interface (i.e., kvm_open(), kvm_close(), kvm_read(), kvm_write(), and kvm_nlist()) has been incorporated into the BSD interface. Indeed, many kvm applications (i.e., debuggers and statistical monitors) use only this subset of the interface.

The process interface was not kept. This is not a portability issue since any code that manipulates processes is inherently machine dependent.

Finally, the Sun kvm error reporting semantics are poorly defined. The library can be configured either to print errors to stderr automatically, or to print no error messages at all. In the latter case, the nature of the error cannot be determined. To overcome this, the BSD interface includes a routine, kvm_geterr(3), to return (not print out) the error message corresponding to the most recent error condition on the given descriptor.

SEE ALSO
kvm_close(3), kvm_getargv(3), kvm_getenvv(3), kvm_geterr(3), kvm_getloadavg(3), kvm_getprocs(3), kvm_nlist(3), kvm_open(3), kvm_openfiles(3), kvm_read(3), kvm_write(3)

NAME

kvm_geterr – get error message on kvm descriptor

SYNOPSIS

#include ⟨kvm.h⟩

char *
kvm_geterr(kvm_t *kd);

DESCRIPTION

This function returns a string describing the most recent error condition on the descriptor kd. The results are undefined if the most recent kvm(3) library call did not produce an error. The string returned is stored in memory owned by kvm(3) so the message should be copied out and saved elsewhere if necessary.

BUGS

This routine cannot be used to access error conditions due to a failed **kvm_openfiles()** call, since failure is indicated by returning a NULL descriptor. Therefore, errors on open are output to the special error buffer passed to **kvm_openfiles()**. This option is not available to **kvm_open()**.

SEE ALSO

kvm(3), kvm_close(3), kvm_getargv(3), kvm_getenvv(3), kvm_getprocs(3), kvm_nlist(3), kvm_open(3), kvm_openfiles(3), kvm_read(3), kvm_write(3)

NAME

kvm_getfiles – survey open files

SYNOPSIS

#include ⟨kvm.h⟩
#include ⟨sys/kinfo.h⟩
#define KERNEL
#include ⟨sys/file.h⟩
#undef KERNEL

char *
kvm_getfiles(*kvm_t *kd, int op, int arg, int *cnt*);

DESCRIPTION

kvm_getfiles( ) returns a (sub-)set of the open files in the kernel indicated by *kd*. The *op* and *arg* arguments constitute a predicate which limits the set of files returned. No predicates are currently defined.

The number of processes found is returned in the reference parameter *cnt*. The files are returned as a contiguous array of file structures, preceded by the address of the first file entry in the kernel. This memory is owned by kvm and is not guaranteed to be persistent across subsequent kvm library calls. Data should be copied out if it needs to be saved.

RETURN VALUES

kvm_getfiles( ) will return NULL on failure.

BUGS

This routine does not belong in the kvm interface.

SEE ALSO

kvm(3), kvm_open(3), kvm_openfiles(3), kvm_close(3), kvm_read(3), kvm_write(3), kvm_nlist(3), kvm_geterr(3)

3

NAME

kvm_getloadavg – get error message on kvm descriptor

SYNOPSIS

```
#include <sys/resource.h>
#include <kvm.h>

int
kvm_getloadavg(kvm_t *kd, double loadavg[], int nelem);
```

DESCRIPTION

The **kvm_getloadavg**( ) function returns the number of processes in the system run queue of the kernel indicated by *kd*, averaged over various periods of time. Up to *nelem* samples are retrieved and assigned to successive elements of *loadavg*[ ]. The system imposes a maximum of 3 samples, representing averages over the last 1, 5, and 15 minutes, respectively.

DIAGNOSTICS

If the load average was unobtainable, −1 is returned; otherwise, the number of samples actually retrieved is returned.

SEE ALSO

uptime(1), kvm(3), getloadavg(3)

NAME

kvm_getprocs, kvm_getargv, kvm_getenvv – access user process state

SYNOPSIS

```
#include <kvm.h>
#include <sys/kinfo.h>
#include <sys/kinfo_proc.h>
```

```
struct kinfo_proc *
kvm_getprocs(kvm_t *kd, int op, int arg, int *cnt);
```

```
char **
kvm_getargv(kvm_t *kd, const struct kinfo_proc *p, int nchr);
```

```
char **
kvm_getenvv(kvm_t *kd, const struct kinfo_proc *p, int nchr);
```

DESCRIPTION

kvm_getprocs( ) returns a (sub-)set of active processes in the kernel indicated by *kd*. The *op* and *arg* arguments constitute a predicate which limits the set of processes returned. The value of *op* describes the filtering predicate as follows:

KINFO_PROC_ALL	all processes
KINFO_PROC_PID	processes with process id *arg*
KINFO_PROC_PGRP	processes with process group *arg*
KINFO_PROC_SESSION	
	processes with session *arg*
KINFO_PROC_TTY	processes with tty *arg*
KINFO_PROC_UID	processes with effective user id *arg*
KINFO_PROC_RUID	processes with real user id *arg*

The number of processes found is returned in the reference parameter *cnt*. The processes are returned as a contiguous array of kinfo_proc structures. This memory is locally allocated, and subsequent calls to **kvm_getprocs( )** and **kvm_close( )** will overwrite this storage.

kvm_getargv( ) returns a null-terminated argument vector that corresponds to the command line arguments passed to process indicated by *p*. Most likely, these arguments correspond to the values passed to exec(3) on process creation. This information is, however, deliberately under control of the process itself. Note that the original command name can be found, unaltered, in the p_comm field of the process structure returned by **kvm_getprocs()**.

The *nchr* argument indicates the maximum number of characters, including null bytes, to use in building the strings. If this amount is exceeded, the string causing the overflow is truncated and the partial result is returned. This is handy for programs like ps(1) and w(1) that print only a one line summary of a command and should not copy out large amounts of text only to ignore it. If *nchr* is zero, no limit is imposed and all argument strings are returned in their entirety.

The memory allocated to the argv pointers and string storage is owned by the kvm library. Subsequent **kvm_getprocs( )** and kvm_close(3) calls will clobber this storage.

The **kvm_getenvv( )** function is similar to **kvm_getargv( )** but returns the vector of environment strings. This data is also alterable by the process.

RETURN VALUES

kvm_getprocs(), kvm_getargv(), and kvm_getenvv(), all return NULL on failure.

BUGS

These routines do not belong in the kvm interface.

SEE ALSO

kvm(3), kvm_close(3), kvm_geterr(3), kvm_nlist(3), kvm_open(3), kvm_openfiles(3), kvm_read(3), kvm_write(3)

NAME

kvm_nlist – retrieve symbol table names from a kernel image

SYNOPSIS

```
#include <kvm.h>
#include <nlist.h>

int
kvm_nlist(kvm_t *kd, struct nlist *nl);
```

DESCRIPTION

kvm_nlist() retrieves the symbol table entries indicated by the name list argument *nl*. This argument points to an array of nlist structures, terminated by an entry whose n_name field is NULL (see nlist(3)). Each symbol is looked up using the n_name field, and if found, the corresponding n_type and n_value fields are filled in. These fields are set to 0 if the symbol is not found.

The program kvm_mkdb(8) builds a database from the running kernel's namelist. If the database matches the opened kernel, **kvm_nlist**() uses it to speed lookups.

RETURN VALUES

The **kvm_nlist**() function returns the number of invalid entries found. If the kernel symbol table was unreadable, -1 is returned.

FILES

/var/db/kvm_vmunix.db

SEE ALSO

kvm(3), kvm_close(3), kvm_getargv(3), kvm_getenvv(3), kvm_geterr(3), kvm_getprocs(3), kvm_open(3), kvm_openfiles(3), kvm_read(3), kvm_write(3), kvm_mkdb(8)

NAME

kvm_open, kvm_openfiles, kvm_close – initialize kernel virtual memory access

SYNOPSIS

```
#include <fcntl.h>
#include <kvm.h>

kvm_t *
kvm_open(const char *execfile, const char *corefile, char *swapfile,
        int flags, const char *errstr);

kvm_t *
kvm_openfiles(const char *execfile, const char *corefile, char *swapfile,
        int flags, char *errbuf);

int
kvm_close(kvm_t *kd);
```

DESCRIPTION

The functions **kvm_open()** and **kvm_openfiles()** return a descriptor used to access kernel virtual memory via the kvm(3) library routines. Both active kernels and crash dumps are accessible through this interface.

execfile is the executable image of the kernel being examined. This file must contain a symbol table. If this argument is NULL, the currently running system is assumed, which is indicated by _PATH_UNIX in <paths.h>.

corefile is the kernel memory device file. It can be either /dev/mem or a crash dump core generated by savecore(8). If *corefile* is NULL, the default indicated by _PATH_MEM from <paths.h> is used.

swapfile should indicate the swap device. If NULL, _PATH_DRUM from <paths.h> is used.

The *flags* argument indicates read/write access as in open(2) and applies only to the core file. Only O_RDONLY, O_WRONLY, and O_RDWR are permitted.

There are two open routines which differ only with respect to the error mechanism. One provides backward compatibility with the SunOS kvm library, while the other provides an improved error reporting framework.

The **kvm_open()** function is the Sun kvm compatible open call. Here, the *errstr* argument indicates how errors should be handled. If it is NULL, no errors are reported and the application cannot know the specific nature of the failed kvm call. If it is not NULL, errors are printed to stderr with *errstr* prepended to the message, as in perror(3). Normally, the name of the program is used here. The string is assumed to persist at least until the corresponding **kvm_close()** call.

The **kvm_openfiles()** function provides BSD style error reporting. Here, error messages are not printed out by the library. Instead, the application obtains the error message corresponding to the most recent kvm library call using **kvm_geterr()** (see kvm_geterr(3)). The results are undefined if the most recent kvm call did not produce an error. Since **kvm_geterr()** requires a kvm descriptor, but the open routines return NULL on failure, **kvm_geterr()** cannot be used to get the error message if open fails. Thus, **kvm_openfiles()** will place any error message in the *errbuf* argument. This buffer should be _POSIX2_LINE_MAX characters large (from <limits.h>).

RETURN VALUES

The **kvm_open()** and **kvm_openfiles()** functions both return a descriptor to be used in all subsequent kvm library calls. The library is fully re-entrant. On failure, NULL is returned, in which case **kvm_openfiles()** writes the error message into *errbuf*.

The `kvm_close()` function returns 0 on success and -1 on failure.

BUGS

There should not be two open calls. The ill-defined error semantics of the Sun library and the desire to have a backward-compatible library for BSD left little choice.

SEE ALSO

open(2), kvm(3), kvm_getargv(3), kvm_getenvv(3), kvm_geterr(3), kvm_getprocs(3), kvm_nlist(3), kvm_read(3), kvm_write(3)

3

3

NAME
kvm_read, kvm_write – read or write kernel virtual memory

SYNOPSIS
#include ⟨kvm.h⟩

ssize_t
kvm_read(*kvm_t *kd, u_long addr, void *buf, size_t nbytes*);

ssize_t
kvm_write(*kvm_t *kd, u_long addr, const void *buf, size_t nbytes*);

DESCRIPTION
The **kvm_read**() and **kvm_write**() functions are used to read and write kernel virtual memory (or a crash dump file). See **kvm_open**(*3*) or **kvm_openfiles**(*3*) for information regarding opening kernel virtual memory and crash dumps.

The **kvm_read**() function transfers *nbytes* bytes of data from the kernel space address *addr* to *buf*. Conversely, **kvm_write**() transfers data from *buf* to *addr*. Unlike their SunOS counterparts, these functions cannot be used to read or write process address spaces.

RETURN VALUES
Upon success, the number of bytes actually transferred is returned. Otherwise, -1 is returned.

SEE ALSO
kvm(3), kvm_close(3), kvm_getargv(3), kvm_getenvv(3), kvm_geterr(3), kvm_getprocs(3), kvm_nlist(3), kvm_open(3), kvm_openfiles(3)

NAME

labs – return the absolute value of a long integer

SYNOPSIS

#include <stdlib.h>

long
labs(*long j*);

DESCRIPTION

The **labs**( ) function returns the absolute value of the long integer *j*.

SEE ALSO

abs(3), floor(3), cabs(3), math(3)

STANDARDS

The **labs**( ) function conforms to ANSI C X3.159-1989 (''ANSI C '').

BUGS

The absolute value of the most negative integer remains negative.

NAME
  ldexp – multiply floating-point number by integral power of 2

SYNOPSIS
  `#include <math.h>`

  double
  `ldexp(double x, int exp);`

DESCRIPTION
  The **ldexp**( ) function multiplies a floating-point number by an integral power of 2.

RETURN VALUES
  The **ldexp**( ) function returns the value of x times 2 raised to the power *exp*.

  If the resultant value would cause an overflow, the global variable *errno* is set to ERANGE and the value HUGE is returned.

SEE ALSO
  frexp(3), modf(3), math(3)

STANDARDS
  The **ldexp**( ) function conforms ANSI C X3.159-1989 (''ANSI C '').

NAME

ldiv – return quotient and remainder from division

SYNOPSIS

```
#include <stdlib.h>
```

ldiv_t
ldiv(*int num, int denom*);

DESCRIPTION

The **ldiv**( ) function computes the value *num/denom* and returns the quotient and remainder in a structure named *ldiv_t* that contains two *long integer* members named *quot* and *rem*.

SEE ALSO

div(3), math(3)

STANDARDS

The **ldiv**( ) function conforms to ANSI C X3.159-1989 ("ANSI C ").

NAME

lgamma gamma – log gamma function, gamma function

SYNOPSIS

```
#include <math.h>
```

extern int signgam;

double
lgamma(*double x*);

double
gamma(*double x*);

DESCRIPTION

Lgamma(*x*) returns ln $|\Gamma(x)|$ where

$$\Gamma(x) = \int_0^\infty t^{x-1} e^{-t} dt \qquad \text{for x > 0 and}$$
$$\Gamma(x) = \pi/(\Gamma(1-x) \sin(\pi x)) \quad \text{for x < 1.}$$

The external integer *signgam* returns the sign of $\Gamma(x)$.

Gamma(*x*) returns $\Gamma(x)$, with no effect on *signgam*.

IDIOSYNCRASIES

Do not use the expression ``signgam*exp(lgamma(x))'' to compute g := $\Gamma(x)$. Instead use a program like this (in C):

```
lg = lgamma(x); g = signgam*exp(lg);
```

Only after **lgamma**( ) has returned can signgam be correct.

For arguments in its range, **gamma**( ) is preferred, as for positive arguments it is accurate to within one unit in the last place. Exponentiation of **lgamma**( ) will lose up to 10 significant bits.

RETURN VALUES

Gamma( ) and **lgamma**( ) return appropriate values unless an argument is out of range. Overflow will occur for sufficiently large positive values, and non-positive integers. On the VAX, the reserved operator is returned, and *errno* is set to ERANGE For large non-integer negative values, **gamma**( ) will underflow.

SEE ALSO

math(3), infnan(3)

HISTORY

The **lgamma** function appeared in 4.3BSD. The **gamma** function appeared in 4.4BSD. The name **gamma**( ) was originally dedicated to the **lgamma**( ) function, so some old code may no longer be compatible.

NAME

　　　link_addr, link_ntoa – elementary address specification routines for link level access

SYNOPSIS

```
#include <sys/types.h>
#include <sys/socket.h>
#include <net/if_dl.h>

void
link_addr(const char *addr, struct sockaddr_dl *sdl);

char *
link_ntoa(const struct sockaddr_dl *sdl);
```

DESCRIPTION

　　　The routine link_addr() interprets character strings representing link-level addresses, returning binary information suitable for use in system calls. The routine link_ntoa() takes a link-level address and returns an ASCII string representing some of the information present, including the link level address itself, and the interface name or number, if present. This facility is experimental and is still subject to change.

　　　For link_addr(), the string addr may contain an optional network interface identifier of the form "name unit-number", suitable for the first argument to ifconfig(4), followed in all cases by a colon and an interface address in the form of groups of hexadecimal digits separated by periods. Each group represents a byte of address; address bytes are filled left to right from low order bytes through high order bytes.

　　　Thus le0:8.0.9.13.d.30 represents an ethernet address to be transmitted on the first Lance ethernet interface.

RETURN VALUES

　　　link_ntoa() always returns a null terminated string. link_addr() has no return value. (See BUGS.)

SEE ALSO

　　　iso(4),

HISTORY

　　　The link_addr() and link_ntoa() functions appeared in 4.3BSD–Reno.

BUGS

　　　The returned values for link_ntoa reside in a static memory area.

　　　The function link_addr() should diagnose improperly formed input, and there should be an unambiguous way to recognize this.

　　　If the *sdl_len* field of the link socket address *sdl* is 0, link_ntoa() will not insert a colon before the interface address bytes. If this translated address is given to link_addr() without inserting an initial colon, the latter will not interpret it correctly.

NAME

lsearch, lfind, – linear searching routines

SYNOPSIS

```
char *
lsearch(const void *key, const void *base, size_t *nelp, size_t width,
        int (*compar)(void *, void *));

char *
lfind(const void *key, const void *base, size_t *nelp, size_t width,
        int (*compar)(void *, void *));
```

DESCRIPTION

This interface was obsolete before it was written. It is available from the compatibility library, libcompat.

The functions lsearch(), and lfind() provide basic linear searching functionality.

Base is the pointer to the beginning of an array. The argument *nelp* is the current number of elements in the array, where each element is *width* bytes long. The *compar* function is a comparison routine which is used to compare two elements. It takes two arguments which point to the *key* object and to an array member, in that order, and must return an integer less than, equivalent to, or greater than zero if the *key* object is considered, respectively, to be less than, equal to, or greater than the array member.

The lsearch() and lfind() functions return a pointer into the array referenced by *base* where *key* is located. If *key* does not exist, lfind() will return a null pointer and lsearch() will add it to the array. When an element is added to the array by lsearch() the location referenced by the argument *nelp* is incremented by one.

SEE ALSO

bsearch(3), db(3)

NAME

malloc, – general memory allocation function

SYNOPSIS

```
#include <stdlib.h>
```

void *
malloc(*size_t size*);

DESCRIPTION

The **malloc**( ) function allocates uninitialized space for an object whose size is specified by *size*. The **malloc**( ) function maintains multiple lists of free blocks according to size, allocating space from the appropriate list.

The allocated space is suitably aligned (after possible pointer coercion) for storage of any type of object. If the space is of *pagesize* or larger, the memory returned will be page-aligned.

RETURN VALUES

The **malloc**( ) function returns a pointer to the allocated space if successful; otherwise a null pointer is returned.

SEE ALSO

brk(2), pagesize(2), free(3), calloc(3), alloca(3), realloc(3), memory(3)

STANDARDS

The **malloc**( ) function conforms to ANSI C X3.159-1989 (''ANSI C '').

BUGS

The current implementation of malloc does not always fail gracefully when system memory limits are approached. It may fail to allocate memory when larger free blocks could be broken up, or when limits are exceeded because the size is rounded up. It is optimized for sizes that are powers of two.

NAME

math – introduction to mathematical library functions

DESCRIPTION

These functions constitute the C math library, *libm*. The link editor searches this library under the ''–lm'' option. Declarations for these functions may be obtained from the include file *<math.h>*. The Fortran math library is described in ''man 3f intro''.

LIST OF FUNCTIONS

Name	Appears on Page	Description	Error Bound (ULPs)
acos	sin.3m	inverse trigonometric function	3
acosh	asinh.3m	inverse hyperbolic function	3
asin	sin.3m	inverse trigonometric function	3
asinh	asinh.3m	inverse hyperbolic function	3
atan	sin.3m	inverse trigonometric function	1
atanh	asinh.3m	inverse hyperbolic function	3
atan2	sin.3m	inverse trigonometric function	2
cabs	hypot.3m	complex absolute value	1
cbrt	sqrt.3m	cube root	1
ceil	floor.3m	integer no less than	0
copysign	ieee.3m	copy sign bit	0
cos	sin.3m	trigonometric function	1
cosh	sinh.3m	hyperbolic function	3
drem	ieee.3m	remainder	0
erf	erf.3m	error function	???
erfc	erf.3m	complementary error function	???
exp	exp.3m	exponential	1
expm1	exp.3m	exp(x)–1	1
fabs	floor.3m	absolute value	0
floor	floor.3m	integer no greater than	0
hypot	hypot.3m	Euclidean distance	1
infnan	infnan.3m	signals exceptions	
j0	j0.3m	bessel function	???
j1	j0.3m	bessel function	???
jn	j0.3m	bessel function	???
lgamma	lgamma.3m	log gamma function; (formerly gamma.3m)	
log	exp.3m	natural logarithm	1
logb	ieee.3m	exponent extraction	0
log10	exp.3m	logarithm to base 10	3
log1p	exp.3m	log(1+x)	1
pow	exp.3m	exponential x**y	60–500
rint	floor.3m	round to nearest integer	0
scalb	ieee.3m	exponent adjustment	0
sin	sin.3m	trigonometric function	1
sinh	sinh.3m	hyperbolic function	3
sqrt	sqrt.3m	square root	1
tan	sin.3m	trigonometric function	3
tanh	sinh.3m	hyperbolic function	3
y0	j0.3m	bessel function	???
y1	j0.3m	bessel function	???
yn	j0.3m	bessel function	???

NOTES

In 4.3 BSD, distributed from the University of California in late 1985, most of the foregoing functions come in two versions, one for the double–precision "D" format in the DEC VAX–11 family of computers, another for double–precision arithmetic conforming to the IEEE Standard 754 for Binary Floating–Point Arithmetic. The two versions behave very similarly, as should be expected from programs more accurate and robust than was the norm when UNIX was born. For instance, the programs are accurate to within the numbers of *ulps* tabulated above; an *ulp* is one *Unit* in the *Last Place*. And the programs have been cured of anomalies that afflicted the older math library *libm* in which incidents like the following had been reported:

sqrt(−1.0) = 0.0 and log(−1.0) = −1.7e38.
cos(1.0e−11) > cos(0.0) > 1.0.
pow(x,1.0) ≠ x when x = 2.0, 3.0, 4.0, ..., 9.0.
pow(−1.0,1.0e10) trapped on Integer Overflow.
sqrt(1.0e30) and sqrt(1.0e−30) were very slow.

However the two versions do differ in ways that have to be explained, to which end the following notes are provided.

DEC VAX–11 D_floating–point:

This is the format for which the original math library *libm* was developed, and to which this manual is still principally dedicated. It is *the* double–precision format for the PDP–11 and the earlier VAX–11 machines; VAX–11s after 1983 were provided with an optional "G" format closer to the IEEE double–precision format. The earlier DEC MicroVAXs have no D format, only G double–precision. (Why? Why not?)

Properties of D_floating–point:

Wordsize: 64 bits, 8 bytes. Radix: Binary.

Precision: 56 significant bits, roughly like 17 significant decimals.

If x and x' are consecutive positive D_floating–point numbers (they differ by 1 *ulp*), then
1.3e–17 < 0.5**56 < (x'–x)/x ≤ 0.5**55 < 2.8e–17.

Range: Overflow threshold = 2.0**127 = 1.7e38.

Underflow threshold = 0.5**128 = 2.9e–39.

NOTE: THIS RANGE IS COMPARATIVELY NARROW.

Overflow customarily stops computation.

Underflow is customarily flushed quietly to zero.

CAUTION:

It is possible to have x ≠ y and yet x–y = 0 because of underflow. Similarly x > y > 0 cannot prevent either x*y = 0 or y/x = 0 from happening without warning.

Zero is represented ambiguously.

Although 2**55 different representations of zero are accepted by the hardware, only the obvious representation is ever produced. There is no –0 on a VAX.

∞ is not part of the VAX architecture.

Reserved operands:

of the 2**55 that the hardware recognizes, only one of them is ever produced. Any floating–point operation upon a reserved operand, even a MOVF or MOVD, customarily stops computation, so they are not much used.

Exceptions:

Divisions by zero and operations that overflow are invalid operations that customarily stop computation or, in earlier machines, produce reserved operands that will stop computation.

Rounding:

Every rational operation (+, –, *, /) on a VAX (but not necessarily on a PDP–11), if not an over/underflow nor division by zero, is rounded to within half an *ulp*, and when the rounding error is exactly half an *ulp* then rounding is away from 0.

Except for its narrow range, D_floating–point is one of the better computer arithmetics designed in the 1960's. Its properties are reflected fairly faithfully in the elementary functions for a VAX distributed in 4.3 BSD. They over/underflow only if their results have to lie out of range or very nearly so, and then they behave much as any rational arithmetic operation that over/underflowed would behave. Similarly, expressions like log(0) and atanh(1) behave like 1/0; and sqrt(−3) and acos(3) behave like 0/0; they all produce reserved operands and/or stop computation! The situation is described in more detail in manual pages. *This response seems excessively punitive, so it is destined to be replaced at some time in the foreseeable future by a more flexible but still uniform scheme being developed to handle all floating–point arithmetic exceptions neatly. See infnan(3M) for the present state of affairs.*

How do the functions in 4.3 BSD's new *libm* for UNIX compare with their counterparts in DEC's VAX/VMS library? Some of the VMS functions are a little faster, some are a little more accurate, some are more puritanical about exceptions (like pow(0.0,0.0) and atan2(0.0,0.0)), and most occupy much more memory than their counterparts in *libm*. The VMS codes interpolate in large table to achieve speed and accuracy; the *libm* codes use tricky formulas compact enough that all of them may some day fit into a ROM.

More important, DEC regards the VMS codes as proprietary and guards them zealously against unauthorized use. But the *libm* codes in 4.3 BSD are intended for the public domain; they may be copied freely provided their provenance is always acknowledged, and provided users assist the authors in their researches by reporting experience with the codes. Therefore no user of UNIX on a machine whose arithmetic resembles VAX D_floating–point need use anything worse than the new *libm*.

IEEE STANDARD 754 Floating–Point Arithmetic:

This standard is on its way to becoming more widely adopted than any other design for computer arithmetic. VLSI chips that conform to some version of that standard have been produced by a host of manufacturers, among them ...

Intel i8087, i80287	National Semiconductor 32081
Motorola 68881	Weitek WTL-1032, ... , -1165
Zilog Z8070	Western Electric (AT&T) WE32106.

Other implementations range from software, done thoroughly in the Apple Macintosh, through VLSI in the Hewlett–Packard 9000 series, to the ELXSI 6400 running ECL at 3 Megaflops. Several other companies have adopted the formats of IEEE 754 without, alas, adhering to the standard's way of handling rounding and exceptions like over/underflow. The DEC VAX G_floating–point format is very similar to the IEEE 754 Double format, so similar that the C programs for the IEEE versions of most of the elementary functions listed above could easily be converted to run on a MicroVAX, though nobody has volunteered to do that yet.

The codes in 4.3 BSD's *libm* for machines that conform to IEEE 754 are intended primarily for the National Semi. 32081 and WTL 1164/65. To use these codes with the Intel or Zilog chips, or with the Apple Macintosh or ELXSI 6400, is to forego the use of better codes provided (perhaps freely) by those companies and designed by some of the authors of the codes above. Except for *atan*, *cabs*, *cbrt*, *erf*, *erfc*, *hypot*, *j0–jn*, *lgamma*, *pow* and *y0–yn*, the Motorola 68881 has all the functions in *libm* on chip, and faster and more accurate; it, Apple, the i8087, Z8070 and WE32106 all use 64 significant bits. The main virtue of 4.3 BSD's *libm* codes is that they are intended for the public domain; they may be copied freely provided their provenance is always acknowledged, and provided users assist the authors in their researches by reporting experience with the codes. Therefore no user of UNIX on a machine that conforms to IEEE 754 need use anything worse than the new *libm*.

Properties of IEEE 754 Double–Precision:
        Wordsize: 64 bits, 8 bytes. Radix: Binary.
        Precision: 53 significant bits, roughly like 16 significant decimals.
                If x and x' are consecutive positive Double–Precision numbers (they differ by 1 *ulp*), then
                $1.1e{-}16 < 0.5{*}{*}53 < (x'{-}x)/x \leq 0.5{*}{*}52 < 2.3e{-}16.$
        Range: Overflow threshold　= $2.0{*}{*}1024$ = 1.8e308
                Underflow threshold = $0.5{*}{*}1022$ = 2.2e–308
                Overflow goes by default to a signed ∞.
                Underflow is *Gradual,* rounding to the nearest integer multiple of $0.5{*}{*}1074$ = 4.9e–324.

Zero is represented ambiguously as +0 or −0.

Its sign transforms correctly through multiplication or division, and is preserved by addition of zeros with like signs; but x−x yields +0 for every finite x. The only operations that reveal zero's sign are division by zero and copysign(x,±0). In particular, comparison (x > y, x ≥ y, etc.) cannot be affected by the sign of zero; but if finite x = y then ∞ = 1/(x−y) ≠ −1/(y−x) = −∞.

∞ is signed.

it persists when added to itself or to any finite number. Its sign transforms correctly through multiplication and division, and (finite)/±∞ = ±0 (nonzero)/0 = ±∞. But ∞−∞, ∞*0 and ∞/∞ are, like 0/0 and sqrt(−3), invalid operations that produce *NaN*. ...

Reserved operands:

there are 2**53−2 of them, all called *NaN* (*Not a N*umber). Some, called Signaling *NaN*s, trap any floating−point operation performed upon them; they are used to mark missing or uninitialized values, or nonexistent elements of arrays. The rest are Quiet *NaN*s; they are the default results of Invalid Operations, and propagate through subsequent arithmetic operations. If x ≠ x then x is *NaN*; every other predicate (x > y, x = y, x < y, ...) is FALSE if *NaN* is involved.

NOTE: Trichotomy is violated by *NaN*.

Besides being FALSE, predicates that entail ordered comparison, rather than mere (in)equality, signal Invalid Operation when *NaN* is involved.

Rounding:

Every algebraic operation (+, −, *, /, √) is rounded by default to within half an *ulp*, and when the rounding error is exactly half an *ulp* then the rounded value's least significant bit is zero. This kind of rounding is usually the best kind, sometimes provably so; for instance, for every x = 1.0, 2.0, 3.0, 4.0, ..., 2.0**52, we find (x/3.0)*3.0 == x and (x/10.0)*10.0 == x and ... despite that both the quotients and the products have been rounded. Only rounding like IEEE 754 can do that. But no single kind of rounding can be proved best for every circumstance, so IEEE 754 provides rounding towards zero or towards +∞ or towards −∞ at the programmer's option. And the same kinds of rounding are specified for Binary−Decimal Conversions, at least for magnitudes between roughly 1.0e−10 and 1.0e37.

Exceptions:

IEEE 754 recognizes five kinds of floating−point exceptions, listed below in declining order of probable importance.

Exception	Default Result
Invalid Operation	*NaN*, or FALSE
Overflow	±∞
Divide by Zero	±∞
Underflow	Gradual Underflow
Inexact	Rounded value

NOTE: An Exception is not an Error unless handled badly. What makes a class of exceptions exceptional is that no single default response can be satisfactory in every instance. On the other hand, if a default response will serve most instances satisfactorily, the unsatisfactory instances cannot justify aborting computation every time the exception occurs.

For each kind of floating−point exception, IEEE 754 provides a Flag that is raised each time its exception is signaled, and stays raised until the program resets it. Programs may also test, save and restore a flag. Thus, IEEE 754 provides three ways by which programs may cope with exceptions for which the default result might be unsatisfactory:

1)   Test for a condition that might cause an exception later, and branch to avoid the exception.

2)   Test a flag to see whether an exception has occurred since the program last reset its flag.

3) Test a result to see whether it is a value that only an exception could have produced. CAUTION: The only reliable ways to discover whether Underflow has occurred are to test whether products or quotients lie closer to zero than the underflow threshold, or to test the Underflow flag. (Sums and differences cannot underflow in IEEE 754; if $x \neq y$ then $x-y$ is correct to full precision and certainly nonzero regardless of how tiny it may be.) Products and quotients that underflow gradually can lose accuracy gradually without vanishing, so comparing them with zero (as one might on a VAX) will not reveal the loss. Fortunately, if a gradually underflowed value is destined to be added to something bigger than the underflow threshold, as is almost always the case, digits lost to gradual underflow will not be missed because they would have been rounded off anyway. So gradual underflows are usually *provably* ignorable. The same cannot be said of underflows flushed to 0.

At the option of an implementor conforming to IEEE 754, other ways to cope with exceptions may be provided:

4) ABORT. This mechanism classifies an exception in advance as an incident to be handled by means traditionally associated with error–handling statements like "ON ERROR GO TO ...". Different languages offer different forms of this statement, but most share the following characteristics:

— No means is provided to substitute a value for the offending operation's result and resume computation from what may be the middle of an expression. An exceptional result is abandoned.

— In a subprogram that lacks an error–handling statement, an exception causes the subprogram to abort within whatever program called it, and so on back up the chain of calling subprograms until an error–handling statement is encountered or the whole task is aborted and memory is dumped.

5) STOP. This mechanism, requiring an interactive debugging environment, is more for the programmer than the program. It classifies an exception in advance as a symptom of a programmer's error; the exception suspends execution as near as it can to the offending operation so that the programmer can look around to see how it happened. Quite often the first several exceptions turn out to be quite unexceptionable, so the programmer ought ideally to be able to resume execution after each one as if execution had not been stopped.

6) ... Other ways lie beyond the scope of this document.

The crucial problem for exception handling is the problem of Scope, and the problem's solution is understood, but not enough manpower was available to implement it fully in time to be distributed in 4.3 BSD's *libm*. Ideally, each elementary function should act as if it were indivisible, or atomic, in the sense that ...

i) No exception should be signaled that is not deserved by the data supplied to that function.

ii) Any exception signaled should be identified with that function rather than with one of its subroutines.

iii) The internal behavior of an atomic function should not be disrupted when a calling program changes from one to another of the five or so ways of handling exceptions listed above, although the definition of the function may be correlated intentionally with exception handling.

Ideally, every programmer should be able *conveniently* to turn a debugged subprogram into one that appears atomic to its users. But simulating all three characteristics of an atomic function is still a tedious affair, entailing hosts of tests and saves–restores; work is under way to ameliorate the inconvenience.

Meanwhile, the functions in *libm* are only approximately atomic. They signal no inappropriate exception except possibly ...
        Over/Underflow
            when a result, if properly computed, might have lain barely within range, and
       Inexact in *cabs, cbrt, hypot, log10* and *pow*
            when it happens to be exact, thanks to fortuitous cancellation of errors.

Otherwise, ...

Invalid Operation is signaled only when
any result but *NaN* would probably be misleading.

Overflow is signaled only when
the exact result would be finite but beyond the overflow threshold.

Divide–by–Zero is signaled only when
a function takes exactly infinite values at finite operands.

Underflow is signaled only when
the exact result would be nonzero but tinier than the underflow threshold.

Inexact is signaled only when
greater range or precision would be needed to represent the exact result.

3

BUGS

When signals are appropriate, they are emitted by certain operations within the codes, so a subroutine–trace may be needed to identify the function with its signal in case method 5) above is in use. And the codes all take the IEEE 754 defaults for granted; this means that a decision to trap all divisions by zero could disrupt a code that would otherwise get correct results despite division by zero.

SEE ALSO

An explanation of IEEE 754 and its proposed extension p854 was published in the IEEE magazine MICRO in August 1984 under the title "A Proposed Radix– and Word–length–independent Standard for Floating–point Arithmetic" by W. J. Cody et al. The manuals for Pascal, C and BASIC on the Apple Macintosh document the features of IEEE 754 pretty well. Articles in the IEEE magazine COMPUTER vol. 14 no. 3 (Mar. 1981), and in the ACM SIGNUM Newsletter Special Issue of Oct. 1979, may be helpful although they pertain to superseded drafts of the standard.

3

NAME

mbrune, mbrrune, mbmb – multibyte rune support for C

SYNOPSIS

```
#include <rune.h>
```

char *
mbrune(*const char *string, rune_t rune*);

char *
mbrrune(*const char *string, rune_t rune*);

char *
mbmb(*const char *string, char *pattern*);

DESCRIPTION

These routines provide the corresponding functionality of **strchr**(), **strrchr**() and **strstr**() for multi-byte strings.

The **mbrune**() function locates the first occurrence of **rune**() in the string pointed to by *string*. The terminating NULL character is considered part of the string. If *rune* is '\0', **mbrune**() locates the terminating '\0'.

The **mbrrune**() function locates the last occurrence of *rune* in the string *string*. If *rune* is '\0', **mbrune**() locates the terminating '\0'.

The **mbmb**() function locates the first occurrence of the null-terminated string *pattern* in the null-terminated string *string*. If *pattern* is the empty string, **mbmb**() returns *string*; if *pattern* occurs nowhere in *string*, **mbmb**() returns NULL; otherwise **mbmb**() returns a pointer to the first character of the first occurrence of *pattern*.

RETURN VALUES

The function **mbrune**() returns a pointer to the located character, or NULL if the character does not appear in the string.

The **mbrrune**() function returns a pointer to the character, or NULL if the character does not appear in the string.

The **mbmb**() function returns a pointer to the *pattern*, or NULL if the *pattern* does not appear in the string.

SEE ALSO

euc(4), mbrune(3), rune(3), setlocale(3), utf2(4)

HISTORY

The **mbrune**(), **mbrrune**(), and **mbmb**() functions first appeared in Plan 9 from Bell Labs as **utfrune**(), **utfrrune**(), and **utfutf**().

NAME

memccpy – copy string until character found

SYNOPSIS

#include <string.h>

void *
memccpy(*void *dst, const void *src, int c, size_t len*);

DESCRIPTION

The **memccpy**( ) function copies bytes from string *src* to string *dst*. If the character *c* (as converted to an unsigned char) occurs in the string *src*, the copy stops and a pointer to the byte after the copy of *c* in the string *dst* is returned. Otherwise, *len* bytes are copied, and a NULL pointer is returned.

SEE ALSO

bcopy(3), memcpy(3), memmove(3), strcpy(3)

HISTORY

The **memccpy**( ) function first appeared in 4.4BSD.

3

NAME
memchr – locate byte in byte string

SYNOPSIS
```
#include <string.h>
```

```
void *
memchr(const void *b, int c, size_t len);
```

DESCRIPTION
The memchr( ) function locates the first occurrence of c (converted to an unsigned char) in string b.

RETURN VALUES
The memchr( ) function returns a pointer to the byte located, or NULL if no such byte exists within *len* bytes.

SEE ALSO
index(3), rindex(3), strchr(3), strcspn(3), strpbrk(3), strrchr(3), strsep(3), strspn(3), strstr(3), strtok(3)

STANDARDS
The memchr( ) function conforms to ANSI C X3.159-1989 (''ANSI C '').

NAME

memcmp – compare byte string

SYNOPSIS

```
#include <string.h>
```

int
memcmp(*const void *b1, const void *b2, size_t len*);

DESCRIPTION

The memcmp( ) function compares byte string *b1* against byte string *b2*. Both strings are assumed to be *len* bytes long.

RETURN VALUES

The memcmp( ) function returns zero if the the two strings are identical, otherwise returns the difference between the first two differing bytes (treated as unsigned char values, so that '\200' is greater than '\0', for example). Zero-length strings are always identical.

SEE ALSO

bcmp(3), strcasecmp(3), strcmp(3), strcoll(3), strxfrm(3)

STANDARDS

The memcmp( ) function conforms to ANSI C X3.159-1989 (''ANSI C '').

NAME

memcpy – copy byte string

SYNOPSIS

#include <string.h>

void *
memcpy(void *dst, const void *src, size_t len);

DESCRIPTION

The memcpy( ) function copies len bytes from string src to string dst.

RETURN VALUES

The memcpy( ) function returns the original value of dst.

SEE ALSO

bcopy(3), memccpy(3), memmove(3), strcpy(3)

STANDARDS

The memcpy( ) function conforms to ANSI C X3.159-1989 (''ANSI C '').

BUGS

In this implementation memcpy( ) is implemented using bcopy(3), and therefore the strings may overlap. On other systems, copying overlapping strings may produce surprises. A simpler solution is to not use memcpy().

NAME
memmove – copy byte string

SYNOPSIS
#include <string.h>

void *
memmove(*void *dst, const void *src, size_t len*);

DESCRIPTION
The memmove() function copies *len* bytes from string *src* to string *dst*. The two strings may overlap; the copy is always done in a non-destructive manner.

RETURN VALUES
The memmove() function returns the original value of *dst*.

SEE ALSO
bcopy(3), memccpy(3), memcpy(3), strcpy(3)

STANDARDS
The memmove() function conforms to ANSI C X3.159-1989 (''ANSI C '').

3

3

NAME
malloc, free, realloc, calloc, alloca – general memory allocation operations

SYNOPSIS
```
#include <stdlib.h>
```

void *
malloc(*size_t size*);

void
free(*void *ptr*);

void *
realloc(*void *ptr, size_t size*);

void *
calloc(*size_t nelem, size_t elsize*);

void *
alloca(*size_t size*);

DESCRIPTION
These functions allocate and free memory for the calling process. They are described in the individual manual pages.

SEE ALSO
calloc(3), free(3), malloc(3), realloc(3), alloca(3),

STANDARDS
These functions, with the exception of **alloca**( ) conform to ANSI C X3.159-1989 (''ANSI C '').

NAME

memset – write a byte to byte string

SYNOPSIS

```
#include <string.h>
```

void *
memset(*void* *b*, *int* *c*, *size_t* *len*);

DESCRIPTION

The **memset**( ) function writes *len* bytes of value *c* (converted to an unsigned char) to the string *b*.

RETURNS

The **memset**( ) function returns its first argument.

SEE ALSO

bzero(3), swab(3)

STANDARDS

The **memset**( ) function conforms to ANSI C X3.159-1989 (''ANSI C '').

NAME

mktemp – make temporary file name (unique)

SYNOPSIS

#include ⟨unistd.h⟩

char *
mktemp(char *template);

int
mkstemp(char *template);

DESCRIPTION

The mktemp() function takes the given file name template and overwrites a portion of it to create a file name. This file name is unique and suitable for use by the application. The template may be any file name with some number of 'Xs' appended to it, for example /tmp/temp.XXXX. The trailing 'Xs' are replaced with the current process number and/or a unique letter combination. The number of unique file names mktemp() can return depends on the number of 'Xs' provided; six 'Xs' will result in mktemp() testing roughly 26 ** 6 combinations.

The mkstemp() function makes the same replacement to the template and creates the template file, mode 0600, returning a file descriptor opened for reading and writing. This avoids the race between testing for a file's existence and opening it for use.

RETURN VALUES

The mktemp() function returns a pointer to the template on success and NULL on failure. The mkstemp() function returns −1 if no suitable file could be created. If either call fails an error code is placed in the global variable *errno*.

ERRORS

The mktemp() and mkstemp() functions may set *errno* to one of the following values:

[ENOTDIR] The pathname portion of the template is not an existing directory.

The mktemp() and mkstemp() functions may also set *errno* to any value specified by the stat(2) function.

The mkstemp() function may also set *errno* to any value specified by the open(2) function.

SEE ALSO

chmod(2), getpid(2), open(2), stat(2)

HISTORY

A mktemp function appeared in Version 7 AT&T UNIX.

NAME

modf – extract signed integral and fractional values from floating-point number

SYNOPSIS

```
#include <math.h>
```

double
modf(*double value, double *iptr*);

DESCRIPTION

The **modf**() function breaks the argument *value* into integral and fractional parts, each of which has the same sign as the argument. It stores the integral part as a *double* in the object pointed to by *iptr*.

RETURN VALUES

The **modf**() function returns the signed fractional part of *value*.

SEE ALSO

frexp(3), ldexp(3), math(3)

STANDARDS

The **modf**() function conforms to ANSI C X3.159-1989 (''ANSI C '').

3

NAME
moncontrol, monstartup – control execution profile

SYNOPSIS
moncontrol(*int mode*);

monstartup(*u_long *lowpc, u_long *highpc*);

DESCRIPTION
An executable program compiled using the −**pg** option to cc(1) automatically includes calls to collect statistics for the gprof(1) call-graph execution profiler. In typical operation, profiling begins at program startup and ends when the program calls exit. When the program exits, the profiling data are written to the file *gmon.out*, then gprof(1) can be used to examine the results.

moncontrol( ) selectively controls profiling within a program. When the program starts, profiling begins. To stop the collection of histogram ticks and call counts use **moncontrol**(*0*); to resume the collection of histogram ticks and call counts use **moncontrol**(*1*). This feature allows the cost of particular operations to be measured. Note that an output file will be produced on program exit regardless of the state of **moncontrol**().

Programs that are not loaded with −**pg** may selectively collect profiling statistics by calling **monstartup**( ) with the range of addresses to be profiled. *lowpc* and *highpc* specify the address range that is to be sampled; the lowest address sampled is that of *lowpc* and the highest is just below *highpc*. Only functions in that range that have been compiled with the −**pg** option to cc(1) will appear in the call graph part of the output; however, all functions in that address range will have their execution time measured. Profiling begins on return from **monstartup**().

FILES
gmon.out   execution data file

SEE ALSO
cc(1), gprof(1), profil(2)

3

NAME

fmin, fmout, gcd, invert, itom m_in, m_out, madd, mcmp, mdiv, min, mout, move, msqrt, msub, mult, omin, omout, pow, rpow, sdiv, – multiple precision integer arithmetic

SYNOPSIS

```
#include <mp.h>
#include <stdio.h>
typedef struct mint { int len; short *val; } MINT;
```

madd(*MINT *a, MINT *b, MINT *c*);

msub(*MINT *a, MINT *b, MINT *c*);

mult(*MINT *a, MINT *b, MINT *c*);

mdiv(*MINT *a, MINT *b, MINT *q, short r*);

pow(*MINT *a, MINT *b, m, MINT *c*);

gcd(*MINT *a, MINT *b, MINT *c*);

invert(*MINT *a, MINT *b, MINT *c*);

rpow(*MINT *a, short n, MINT *c*);

msqrt(*MINT *a, MINT *b, short r*);

mcmp(*MINT *a, MINT *b*);

move(*MINT *a, MINT *b*);

min(*MINT *a*);

omin(*MINT *a*);

fmin(*MINT *a, FILE *f*);

m_in(*MINT *a, int n, FILE *f*);

mout(*MINT *a*);

omout(*MINT *a*);

fmout(*MINT *a, FILE *f*);

m_out(*MINT *a, int n, FILE *f*);

sdiv(*MINT *a, short n, MINT *q, short r*);

itom(*short n*);

DESCRIPTION

The interface for this library is expected to change.

These functions operate on integers of variable length. The function itom( ) allocates space for an integer of length *n* which may be accessed via the returned *MINT* pointer. The underlying storage scheme is transparent to the user.

fmin( )
fmout( ) Convert decimal input and output using file *f*.

gcd( )   Finds the greatest common denominator of *a* and *b*, storing the result in *c*.

invert( )
           Computes *c* such that $a * c \mod b = 1$, for *a* and *b* relatively prime.

m_in( )
m_out( )   I/O with arbitrary radix *n*.

madd( )   The sum of *a* and *b* is stored in *c*.

mcmp( )   Returns a negative, zero or positive integer value when *a* is less than, equal to or greater than *b*, respectively.

move( )   Copies *a* to *b*.

min( )
mout( )   Convert decimal input and output.

mdiv( )   Divides *a* by *b* and stores the quotient in *q* and the remainder in *r*.

msqrt( )   Calculates the integer square root of *a* in *b* and places the remainder in *r*.

msub( )   The difference of *a* and *b* is stored in *c*.

mult( )   The product of *a* and *b* is stored in *c*.

omin( )
omout( )   Convert octal input and output.

pow( )   Calculates the value of *a* raised to the full multiple precision exponent *b*, the result is reduced modulo *m* and stored in *c*.

rpow( )   Calculates the value of *a* raised to the ("regular" integral) power *n* and stores the result in *c*.

sdiv( )   (Short divisor.) Divides *a* by the short integer *b* and stores the quotient in *q* and the remainder in short integer *r*. On input, records should have the form of strings of digits terminated by a newline; output records have a similar form.

FILES
/usr/lib/libmp.a   object code library
/usr/include/mp.h include file

SEE ALSO
dc(1), bc(1)

HISTORY
A gcd(), itom(), madd(), mdiv(), min(), mout(), msqrt(), msub(), mult(), pow(), rpow(), and sdiv() function appeared in Version 7 AT&T UNIX.

BUGS
Bases for input and output should be <= 10.

The interpreters dc(1) and bc(1) don't use this library.

The input and output routines are a crock.

The function name pow( ) is also the name of a standard math library routine.

NAME

    mpool – shared memory buffer pool

SYNOPSIS

    #include <db.h>
    #include <mpool.h>

    MPOOL *
    mpool_open (DBT *key, int fd, pgno_t pagesize, pgno_t maxcache);

    void
    mpool_filter (MPOOL *mp, void (*pgin)(void *, pgno_t, void *),
          void (*pgout)(void *, pgno_t, void *), void *pgcookie);

    void *
    mpool_new (MPOOL *mp, pgno_t *pgnoaddr);

    void *
    mpool_get (MPOOL *mp, pgno_t pgno, u_int flags);

    int
    mpool_put (MPOOL *mp, void *pgaddr, u_int flags);

    int
    mpool_sync (MPOOL *mp);

    int
    mpool_close (MPOOL *mp);

DESCRIPTION

    Mpool is the library interface intended to provide page oriented buffer management of files. The buffers may be shared between processes.

    The function *mpool_open* initializes a memory pool. The *key* argument is the byte string used to negotiate between multiple processes wishing to share buffers. If the file buffers are mapped in shared memory, all processes using the same key will share the buffers. If *key* is NULL, the buffers are mapped into private memory. The *fd* argument is a file descriptor for the underlying file, which must be seekable. If *key* is non-NULL and matches a file already being mapped, the *fd* argument is ignored.

    The *pagesize* argument is the size, in bytes, of the pages into which the file is broken up. The *maxcache* argument is the maximum number of pages from the underlying file to cache at any one time. This value is not relative to the number of processes which share a file's buffers, but will be the largest value specified by any of the processes sharing the file.

    The *mpool_filter* function is intended to make transparent input and output processing of the pages possible. If the *pgin* function is specified, it is called each time a buffer is read into the memory pool from the backing file. If the *pgout* function is specified, it is called each time a buffer is written into the backing file. Both functions are are called with the *pgcookie* pointer, the page number and a pointer to the page to being read or written.

    The function *mpool_new* takes an MPOOL pointer and an address as arguments. If a new page can be allocated, a pointer to the page is returned and the page number is stored into the *pgnoaddr* address. Otherwise, NULL is returned and errno is set.

    The function *mpool_get* takes a MPOOL pointer and a page number as arguments. If the page exists, a pointer to the page is returned. Otherwise, NULL is returned and errno is set. The flags parameter is not currently used.

The function *mpool_put* unpins the page referenced by *pgaddr*. *Pgaddr* must be an address previously returned by *mpool_get* or *mpool_new*. The flag value is specified by *or*'ing any of the following values:

MPOOL_DIRTY
> The page has been modified and needs to be written to the backing file.

Mpool_put returns 0 on success and -1 if an error occurs.

The function *mpool_sync* writes all modified pages associated with the MPOOL pointer to the backing file. *Mpool_sync* returns 0 on success and -1 if an error occurs.

The *mpool_close* function free's up any allocated memory associated with the memory pool cookie. Modified pages are **not** written to the backing file. *Mpool_close* returns 0 on success and -1 if an error occurs.

ERRORS

The *mpool_open* function may fail and set *errno* for any of the errors specified for the library routine *malloc*(3).

The *mpool_get* function may fail and set *errno* for the following:

[EINVAL]   The requested record doesn't exist.

The *mpool_new* and *mpool_get* functions may fail and set *errno* for any of the errors specified for the library routines *read*(2), *write*(2), and *malloc*(3).

The *mpool_sync* function may fail and set *errno* for any of the errors specified for the library routine *write*(2).

The *mpool_close* function may fail and set *errno* for any of the errors specified for the library routine *free*(3).

SEE ALSO
dbopen(3), *btree*(3), *hash*(3), *recno*(3)

NAME

mblen, mbstowcs, mbtowc, wcstombs, wctomb – multibyte character support for C

SYNOPSIS

`#include <stdlib.h>`

int
mblen(*const char *mbchar, int nbytes*);

size_t
mbstowcs(*wchar_t *wcstring, const char *mbstring, size_t nwchars*);

int
mbtowc(*wchar_t *wcharp, const char *mbchar, size_t nbytes*);

size_t
wcstombs(*char *mbstring, const wchar_t *wcstring, size_t nbytes*);

int
wctomb(*char *mbchar, wchar_t wchar*);

DESCRIPTION

The basic elements of some written natural languages such as Chinese cannot be represented uniquely with single C *char*s. The C standard supports two different ways of dealing with extended natural language encodings, *wide* characters and *multibyte* characters. Wide characters are an internal representation which allows each basic element to map to a single object of type *wchar_t*. Multibyte characters are used for input and output and code each basic element as a sequence of C *char*s. Individual basic elements may map into one or more (up to MB_CHAR_MAX) bytes in a multibyte character.

The current locale (setlocale(3)) governs the interpretation of wide and multibyte characters. The locale category LC_CTYPE specifically controls this interpretation. The *wchar_t* type is wide enough to hold the largest value in the wide character representations for all locales.

Multibyte strings may contain 'shift' indicators to switch to and from particular modes within the given representation. If explicit bytes are used to signal shifting, these are not recognized as separate characters but are lumped with a neighboring character. There is always a distinguished 'initial' shift state. The **mbstowcs**() and **wcstombs**() functions assume that multibyte strings are interpreted starting from the initial shift state. The **mblen**(), **mbtowc**() and **wctomb**() functions maintain static shift state internally. A call with a null *mbchar* pointer returns nonzero if the current locale requires shift states, zero otherwise; if shift states are required, the shift state is reset to the initial state. The internal shift states are undefined after a call to **setlocale**() with the LC_CTYPE or LC_ALL categories.

For convenience in processing, the wide character with value 0 (the null wide character) is recognized as the wide character string terminator, and the character with value 0 (the null byte) is recognized as the multibyte character string terminator. Null bytes are not permitted within multibyte characters.

The **mblen**() function computes the length in bytes of a multibyte character *mbchar*. Up to *nbytes* bytes are examined.

The **mbtowc**() function converts a multibyte character *mbchar* into a wide character and stores the result in the object pointed to by *wcharp*. Up to *nbytes* bytes are examined.

The **wctomb**() function converts a wide character *wchar* into a multibyte character and stores the result in *mbchar*. The object pointed to by *mbchar* must be large enough to accommodate the multibyte character.

The **mbstowcs()** function converts a multibyte character string *mbstring* into a wide character string *wcstring*. No more than *nwchars* wide characters are stored. A terminating null wide character is appended if there is room.

The **wcstombs()** function converts a wide character string *wcstring* into a multibyte character string *mbstring*. Up to *nbytes* bytes are stored in *mbstring*. Partial multibyte characters at the end of the string are not stored. The multibyte character string is null terminated if there is room.

RETURN VALUES

If multibyte characters are not supported in the current locale, all of these functions will return −1 if characters can be processed, otherwise 0.

If *mbchar* is NULL, the **mblen()**, **mbtowc()** and **wctomb()** functions return nonzero if shift states are supported, zero otherwise. If *mbchar* is valid, then these functions return the number of bytes processed in *mbchar*, or −1 if no multibyte character could be recognized or converted.

The **mbstowcs()** function returns the number of wide characters converted, not counting any terminating null wide character. The **wcstombs()** function returns the number of bytes converted, not counting any terminating null byte. If any invalid multibyte characters are encountered, both functions return −1.

SEE ALSO

euc(4), mbrune(3), rune(3), setlocale(3), utf2(4)

STANDARDS

The **mblen()**, **mbstowcs()**, **mbtowc()**, **wcstombs()** and **wctomb()** functions conform to ANSI C X3.159-1989 (''ANSI C '').

BUGS

The current implementation does not support shift states.

NAME
`nice` – set program scheduling priority

SYNOPSIS
`nice`(*int incr*);

DESCRIPTION
This interface is obsoleted by setpriority(2).

The `nice`( ) function obtains the scheduling priority of the process from the system and sets it to the priority value specified in *incr*. The priority is a value in the range -20 to 20. The default priority is 0; lower priorities cause more favorable scheduling. Only the super-user may lower priorities.

Children inherit the priority of their parent processes via `fork`(2).

SEE ALSO
`nice`(1), `setpriority`(2), `fork`(2), `renice`(8)

HISTORY
A `nice`( ) syscall appeared in Version 6 AT&T UNIX.

NAME

`nlist` – retrieve symbol table name list from an executable file

SYNOPSIS

`#include <nlist.h>`

int
`nlist(const char *filename, struct nlist *nl);`

DESCRIPTION

The **nlist**() function retrieves name list entries from the symbol table of an executable file. (See a.out(5).) The argument *nl* is set to reference the beginning of the list. The list is preened of binary and invalid data; if an entry in the name list is valid, the *n_type* and *n_value* for the entry are copied into the list referenced by *nl*. No other data is copied. The last entry in the list is always NULL.

RETURN VALUES

The number of invalid entries is returned if successful; otherwise, if the file *filename* does not exist or is not executable, the returned value is –1.

SEE ALSO

a.out(5)

HISTORY

A **nlist**() function appeared in Version 6 AT&T UNIX.

3

NAME

ns_addr, ns_ntoa – Xerox NS(tm) address conversion routines

SYNOPSIS

```
#include <sys/types.h>
#include <netns/ns.h>
```

struct ns_addr
ns_addr(*char *cp*);

*char **
ns_ntoa(*struct ns_addr ns*);

DESCRIPTION

The routine **ns_addr**() interprets character strings representing XNS addresses, returning binary information suitable for use in system calls. The routine **ns_ntoa**() takes XNS addresses and returns ASCII strings representing the address in a notation in common use in the Xerox Development Environment:

        \<network number>.\<host number>.\<port number>

Trailing zero fields are suppressed, and each number is printed in hexadecimal, in a format suitable for input to **ns_addr**(). Any fields lacking super-decimal digits will have a trailing 'H' appended.

Unfortunately, no universal standard exists for representing XNS addresses. An effort has been made to insure that **ns_addr**() be compatible with most formats in common use. It will first separate an address into 1 to 3 fields using a single delimiter chosen from period '.', colon ':' or pound-sign '#'. Each field is then examined for byte separators (colon or period). If there are byte separators, each subfield separated is taken to be a small hexadecimal number, and the entirety is taken as a network-byte-ordered quantity to be zero extended in the high-network-order bytes. Next, the field is inspected for hyphens, in which case the field is assumed to be a number in decimal notation with hyphens separating the millenia. Next, the field is assumed to be a number: It is interpreted as hexadecimal if there is a leading '0x' (as in C), a trailing 'H' (as in Mesa), or there are any super-decimal digits present. It is interpreted as octal is there is a leading '0' and there are no super-octal digits. Otherwise, it is converted as a decimal number.

RETURN VALUES

None. (See BUGS.)

SEE ALSO

hosts(5), networks(5),

HISTORY

The **ns_addr**() and **ns_toa**() functions appeared in 4.3BSD.

BUGS

The string returned by **ns_ntoa**() resides in a static memory area. The function **ns_addr**() should diagnose improperly formed input, and there should be an unambiguous way to recognize this.

NAME
pause – stop until signal

SYNOPSIS
```
#include <unistd.h>

int
pause(void);
```

DESCRIPTION
Pause is made obsolete by sigpause(3).

The `pause()` function forces a process to pause until a signal is received from either the `kill(2)` function or an interval timer. (See `setitimer(2)`.) Upon termination of a signal handler started during a `pause()`, the `pause()` call will return.

RETURN VALUES
Always returns −1.

ERRORS
The `pause()` function always returns:

[`EINTR`] The call was interrupted.

SEE ALSO
`kill(2)`, `select(2)`, `sigpause(2)`

HISTORY
A `pause()` syscall appeared in Version 6 AT&T UNIX.

NAME

   plot: openpl, erase, label, line, circle, arc, move, cont, point, linemod, space, closepl – graphics interface

SYNOPSIS

   openpl()

   erase()

   label(s)
   char s[];

   line(x1, y1, x2, y2)

   circle(x, y, r)

   arc(x, y, x0, y0, x1, y1)

   move(x, y)

   cont(x, y)

   point(x, y)

   linemod(s)
   char s[];

   space(x0, y0, x1, y1)

   closepl()

DESCRIPTION

   These subroutines generate graphic output in a relatively device-independent manner. See *plot*(5) for a description of their effect. *Openpl* must be used before any of the others to open the device for writing. *Closepl* flushes the output.

   String arguments to *label* and *linemod* are null-terminated, and do not contain newlines.

   Various flavors of these functions exist for different output devices. They are obtained by the following *ld*(1) options:

   –lplot   device-independent graphics stream on standard output for *plot*(1) filters
   –l300   GSI 300 terminal
   –l300s   GSI 300S terminal
   –l450   GSI 450 terminal
   –l4013   Tektronix 4013 terminal
   –l4014   Tektronix 4014 and 4015 terminals with the Enhanced Graphics Module (Use **–l4013** for 4014's or 4015's without the Enhanced Graphics Module)
   –lplotaed
              AED 512 color graphics terminal
   –lplotbg BBN bitgraph graphics terminal
   –lplotdumb
              Dumb terminals without cursor addressing or line printers
   –lplotgigi
              DEC Gigi terminals
   –lvt0   DEC vt100 terminals
   –lplot2648
              Hewlett Packard 2648 graphics terminal
   –lplot7221
              Hewlett Packard 7221 graphics terminal
   –lplotimagen
              Imagen laser printer (default 240 dots-per-inch resolution).

On many devices, it is necessary to pause after *erase*(), otherwise plotting commands are lost. The pause is normally done by the tty driver if at login time, *tset* found a *df* field in the *termcap*(5) entry for the terminal. If a pause is needed but not automatically being generated, add

```
flush(stdout);
sleep(1);
```

after each *erase*().

SEE ALSO

plot(5), plot(1G), plot(3F), graph(1G)

NAME
popen, pclose – process I/O

SYNOPSIS
```
#include <stdio.h>
```

FILE *
popen(*const char *command, const char *type*);

int
pclose(*FILE *stream*);

DESCRIPTION
The popen() function "opens" a process by creating a pipe, forking, and invoking the shell. Since a pipe is by definition unidirectional, the *type* argument may specify only reading or writing, not both; the resulting stream is correspondingly read-only or write-only.

The *command* argument is a pointer to a null-terminated string containing a shell command line. This command is passed to /bin/sh using the −c flag; interpretation, if any, is performed by the shell. The *mode* argument is a pointer to a null-terminated string which must be either 'r' for reading or 'w' for writing.

The return value from popen() is a normal standard I/O stream in all respects save that it must be closed with pclose() rather than fclose(). Writing to such a stream writes to the standard input of the command; the command's standard output is the same as that of the process that called popen(), unless this is altered by the command itself. Conversely, reading from a "popened" stream reads the command's standard output, and the command's standard input is the same as that of the process that called popen().

Note that output popen() streams are fully buffered by default.

The pclose() function waits for the associated process to terminate and returns the exit status of the command as returned by wait4().

RETURN VALUE
The popen() function returns NULL if the fork(2) or pipe(2) calls fail, or if it cannot allocate memory.

The pclose() function returns −1 if *stream* is not associated with a "popened" command, if *stream* already "pclosed", or if wait4 returns an error.

ERRORS
The popen() function does not reliably set *errno*.

SEE ALSO
fork(2), sh(1), pipe(2), wait4(2), fflush(3), fclose(3), fopen(3), stdio(3), system(3)

BUGS
Since the standard input of a command opened for reading shares its seek offset with the process that called popen(), if the original process has done a buffered read, the command's input position may not be as expected. Similarly, the output from a command opened for writing may become intermingled with that of the original process. The latter can be avoided by calling fflush(3) before popen().

Failure to execute the shell is indistinguishable from the shell's failure to execute command, or an immediate exit of the command. The only hint is an exit status of 127.

The popen() argument always calls sh, never calls csh.

HISTORY

A **popen**( ) and a **pclose**( ) function appeared in Version 7 AT&T UNIX.

NAME

printf, fprintf, sprintf, snprintf, vprintf, vfprintf, vsprintf, vsnprintf – formatted output conversion

SYNOPSIS

```
#include <stdio.h>
```

int
printf(*const char *format, ...*);

int
fprintf(*FILE *stream, const char *format, ...*);

int
sprintf(*char *str, const char *format, ...*);

int
snprintf(*char *str, size_t size, const char *format, ...*);

```
#include <stdarg.h>
```

int
vprintf(*const char *format, va_list ap*);

int
vfprintf(*FILE *stream, const char *format, va_list ap*);

int
vsprintf(*char *str, char *format, va_list ap*);

int
vsnprintf(*char *str, size_t size, const char *format, va_list ap*);

DESCRIPTION

The **printf**( ) family of functions produces output according to a *format* as described below. **Printf**( ) and **vprintf**( ) write output to *stdout*, the standard output stream; **fprintf**( ) and **vfprintf**( ) write output to the given output *stream*; **sprintf**(), **snprintf**(), **vsprintf**(), and **vsnprintf**() write to the character string *str*. These functions write the output under the control of a *format* string that specifies how subsequent arguments (or arguments accessed via the variable-length argument facilities of stdarg(3)) are converted for output. These functions return the number of characters printed (not including the trailing '\0' used to end output to strings). **Snprintf**() and **vsnprintf**() will write at most *size*–1 of the characters printed into the output string (the *size*'th character then gets the terminating '\0'); if the return value is greater than or equal to the *size* argument, the string was too short and some of the printed characters were discarded. **Sprintf**( ) and **vsprintf**() effectively assume an infinite *size*.

The format string is composed of zero or more directives: ordinary characters (not %), which are copied unchanged to the output stream; and conversion specifications, each of which results in fetching zero or more subsequent arguments. Each conversion specification is introduced by the character %. The arguments must correspond properly (after type promotion) with the conversion specifier. After the %, the following appear in sequence:

- Zero or more of the following flags:

    - A # character specifying that the value should be converted to an "alternate form". For c, d, i, n, p, s, and u, conversions, this option has no effect. For o conversions, the precision of the number is increased to force the first character of the output string to a zero (except if a zero value is printed with an explicit precision of zero). For x and X conversions, a non-zero result has the string '0x' (or

'0X' for X conversions) prepended to it. For e, E, f, g, and G, conversions, the result will always contain a decimal point, even if no digits follow it (normally, a decimal point appears in the results of those conversions only if a digit follows). For g and G conversions, trailing zeros are not removed from the result as they would otherwise be.

- A zero '0' character specifying zero padding. For all conversions except n, the converted value is padded on the left with zeros rather than blanks. If a precision is given with a numeric conversion (Mc d, i, o, u, i, x, and X), the '0' flag is ignored.

- A negative field width flag '−' indicates the converted value is to be left adjusted on the field boundary. Except for n conversions, the converted value is padded on the right with blanks, rather than on the left with blanks or zeros. A '−' overrides a '0' if both are given.

- A space, specifying that a blank should be left before a positive number produced by a signed conversion (d, e, E, f, g, G, or i).

- A '+' character specifying that a sign always be placed before a number produced by a signed conversion. A '+' overrides a space if both are used.

● An optional decimal digit string specifying a minimum field width. If the converted value has fewer characters than the field width, it will be padded with spaces on the left (or right, if the left-adjustment flag has been given) to fill out the field width.

● An optional precision, in the form of a period '.' followed by an optional digit string. If the digit string is omitted, the precision is taken as zero. This gives the minimum number of digits to appear for d, i, o, u, x, and X conversions, the number of digits to appear after the decimal-point for e, E, and f conversions, the maximum number of significant digits for g and G conversions, or the maximum number of characters to be printed from a string for s conversions.

● The optional character h, specifying that a following d, i, o, u, x, or X conversion corresponds to a *short int* or *unsigned short int* argument, or that a following n conversion corresponds to a pointer to a *short int* argument.

● The optional character l (ell) specifying that a following d, i, o, u, x, or X conversion applies to a pointer to a *long int* or *unsigned long int* argument, or that a following n conversion corresponds to a pointer to a *long int* argument.

● The optional character q, specifying that a following d, i, o, u, x, or X conversion corresponds to a *quad int* or *unsigned quad int* argument, or that a following n conversion corresponds to a pointer to a *quad int* argument.

● The character L specifying that a following e, E, f, g, or G conversion corresponds to a *long double* argument (but note that long double values are not currently supported by the VAX and Tahoe compilers).

● A character that specifies the type of conversion to be applied.

A field width or precision, or both, may be indicated by an asterisk '*' instead of a digit string. In this case, an *int* argument supplies the field width or precision. A negative field width is treated as a left adjustment flag followed by a positive field width; a negative precision is treated as though it were missing.

The conversion specifiers and their meanings are:

diouxX The *int* (or appropriate variant) argument is converted to signed decimal (d and i), unsigned octal (o), unsigned decimal (u), or unsigned hexadecimal (x and X) notation. The letters abcdef are used for x conversions; the letters ABCDEF are used for conversions. The precision, if any, gives the minimum number of digits that must appear; if the converted value requires fewer digits, it is padded on the left with zeros.

DOU The *long int* argument is converted to signed decimal, unsigned octal, or unsigned decimal, as if the format had been ld, lo, or lu respectively. These conversion characters are deprecated, and will eventually disappear.

eE The *double* argument is rounded and converted in the style [-]d.ddde±dd where there is one digit before the decimal-point character and the number of digits after it is equal to the precision; if the precision is missing, it is taken as 6; if the precision is zero, no decimal-point character appears. An E conversion uses the letter E (rather than e) to introduce the exponent. The exponent always contains at least two digits; if the value is zero, the exponent is 00.

f The *double* argument is rounded and converted to decimal notation in the style [-]ddd.ddd, where the number of digits after the decimal-point character is equal to the precision specification. If the precision is missing, it is taken as 6; if the precision is explicitly zero, no decimal-point character appears. If a decimal point appears, at least one digit appears before it.

g The *double* argument is converted in style f or e (or E for G conversions). The precision specifies the number of significant digits. If the precision is missing, 6 digits are given; if the precision is zero, it is treated as 1. Style e is used if the exponent from its conversion is less than -4 or greater than or equal to the precision. Trailing zeros are removed from the fractional part of the result; a decimal point appears only if it is followed by at least one digit.

c The *int* argument is converted to an *unsigned char*, and the resulting character is written.

s The "*char ***" argument is expected to be a pointer to an array of character type (pointer to a string). Characters from the array are written up to (but not including) a terminating NUL character; if a precision is specified, no more than the number specified are written. If a precision is given, no null character need be present; if the precision is not specified, or is greater than the size of the array, the array must contain a terminating NUL character.

p The "*void ***" pointer argument is printed in hexadecimal (as if by %#x or %#lx).

n The number of characters written so far is stored into the integer indicated by the "*int ***" (or variant) pointer argument. No argument is converted.

% A '%' is written. No argument is converted. The complete conversion specification is '%%'.

In no case does a non-existent or small field width cause truncation of a field; if the result of a conversion is wider than the field width, the field is expanded to contain the conversion result.

EXAMPLES

To print a date and time in the form 'Sunday, July 3, 10:02', where *weekday* and *month* are pointers to strings:

```
#include <stdio.h>
fprintf(stdout, "%s, %s %d, %.2d:%.2d\n",
        weekday, month, day, hour, min);
```

To print π to five decimal places:

```
#include <math.h>
#include <stdio.h>
fprintf(stdout, "pi = %.5f\n", 4 * atan(1.0));
```

To allocate a 128 byte string and print into it:

```
#include <stdio.h>
#include <stdlib.h>
#include <stdarg.h>
char *newfmt(const char *fmt, ...)
{
                char *p;
                va_list ap;
                if ((p = malloc(128)) == NULL)
                        return (NULL);
                va_start(ap, fmt);
                (void) vsnprintf(p, 128, fmt, ap);
                va_end(ap);
                return (p);
}
```

SEE ALSO

printf(1), scanf(3)

STANDARDS

The fprintf(), printf(), sprintf(), vprintf(), vfprintf(), and vsprintf() functions conform to ANSI C X3.159-1989 (''ANSI C '').

HISTORY

The functions snprintf() and vsnprintf() are new to this release.

BUGS

The conversion formats %D, %O, and %U are not standard and are provided only for backward compatibility. The effect of padding the %p format with zeros (either by the '0' flag or by specifying a precision), and the benign effect (i.e., none) of the '#' flag on %n and %p conversions, as well as other nonsensical combinations such as %Ld, are not standard; such combinations should be avoided.

Because sprintf() and vsprintf() assume an infinitely long string, callers must be careful not to overflow the actual space; this is often impossible to assure. For safety, programmers should use the snprintf() interface instead. Unfortunately, this interface is not portable.

NAME

psignal, sys_siglist sys_signame – system signal messages

SYNOPSIS

#include ⟨sys/signal.h⟩

void
psignal(*unsigned sig, const char *s*);

*extern char *sys_siglist[];*
*extern char *sys_signame[];*

DESCRIPTION

The **psignal**() function locates the descriptive message string for the given signal number *sig* and writes it to the standard error.

If the argument *s* is non-NULL it is written to the standard error file descriptor prior to the message string, immediately followed by a colon and a space. If the signal number is not recognized (sigaction(2)), the string "Unknown signal" is produced.

The message strings can be accessed directly through the external array *sys_siglist*, indexed by recognized signal numbers. The external array *sys_signame* is used similarly and contains short, lower-case abbreviations for signals which are useful for recognizing signal names in user input. The defined variable NSIG contains a count of the strings in *sys_siglist* and *sys_signame*.

SEE ALSO

sigaction(2), perror(3)

HISTORY

The **psignal**() function appeared in 4.2BSD.

3

NAME

fputc, putc, putchar, putw – output a character or word to a stream

SYNOPSIS

```
#include <stdio.h>
```

int
fputc(*int c, FILE *stream*);

int
putc(*int c, FILE *stream*);

int
putchar(*int c*);

int
putw(*int w, FILE *stream*);

DESCRIPTION

The **fputc**( ) function writes the character *c* (converted to an "unsigned char") to the output stream pointed to by *stream*.

Putc( ) acts essentially identically to **fputc**(), but is a macro that expands in-line. It may evaluate *stream* more than once, so arguments given to **putc**( ) should not be expressions with potential side effects.

Putchar( ) is identical to **putc**( ) with an output stream of *stdout*.

The **putw**( ) function writes the specified *int* to the named output *stream*.

RETURN VALUES

The functions, **fputc**(), **putc**( ) and **putchar**( ) return the character written. If an error occurs, the value EOF is returned. The **putw**( ) function returns 0 on success; EOF is returned if a write error occurs, or if an attempt is made to write a read-only stream.

SEE ALSO

ferror(3), fopen(3), getc(3), stdio(3)

STANDARDS

The functions **fputc**(), **putc**(), and **putchar**(), conform to ANSI C X3.159-1989 ("ANSI C "). A function **putw**( ) function appeared in Version 6 AT&T UNIX.

BUGS

The size and byte order of an *int* varies from one machine to another, and **putw**( ) is not recommended for portable applications.

NAME

   pwcache – cache password and group entries

SYNOPSIS

   user_from_uid(*uid_t uid*, *int nouser*);

   group_from_gid(*gid_t gid*, *int nogroup*);

DESCRIPTION

   The **user_from_uid**( ) function returns the user name associated with the argument *uid*. The user name
   is cached so that multiple calls with the same *uid* do not require additional calls to getpwuid(3). If there
   is no user associated with the *uid*, a pointer is returned to a string representation of the *uid*, unless the argument *nouser* is non-zero, in which case a NULL pointer is returned.

   The **group_from_gid**( ) function returns the group name associated with the argument *gid*. The group
   name is cached so that multiple calls with the same *gid* do not require additional calls to getgrgid(3). If
   there is no group associated with the *gid*, a pointer is returned to a string representation of the *gid*, unless
   the argument *nogroup* is non-zero, in which case a NULL pointer is returned.

SEE ALSO

   getgrgid(3), getpwuid(3)

HISTORY

   The **user_from_id**( ) and **group_from_id**( ) functions first appeared in 4.4BSD.

3

NAME

qsort, heapsort, mergesort – sort functions

SYNOPSIS

#include <stdlib.h>

void
qsort(*void *base, size_t nmemb, size_t size,*
        *int (*compar)(const void *, const void *))*;

int
heapsort(*void *base, size_t nmemb, size_t size,*
        *int (*compar)(const void *, const void *))*;

int
mergesort(*void *base, size_t nmemb, size_t size,*
        *int (*compar)(const void *, const void *))*;

DESCRIPTION

The **qsort**() function is a modified partition-exchange sort, or quicksort. The **heapsort**() function is a modified selection sort. The **mergesort**() function is a modified merge sort with exponential search intended for sorting data with pre-existing order.

The **qsort**() and **heapsort**() functions sort an array of *nmemb* objects, the initial member of which is pointed to by *base*. The size of each object is specified by *size*. **Mergesort**() behaves similarly, but *requires* that *size* be greater than "sizeof(void *) / 2".

The contents of the array *base* are sorted in ascending order according to a comparison function pointed to by *compar*, which requires two arguments pointing to the objects being compared.

The comparison function must return an integer less than, equal to, or greater than zero if the first argument is considered to be respectively less than, equal to, or greater than the second.

The functions **qsort**() and **heapsort**() are *not* stable, that is, if two members compare as equal, their order in the sorted array is undefined. The function **mergesort**() is stable.

The **qsort**() function is an implementation of C.A.R. Hoare's "quicksort" algorithm, a variant of partition-exchange sorting; in particular, see D.E. Knuth's Algorithm Q. **Qsort**() takes O N lg N average time. This implementation uses median selection to avoid its O N**2 worst-case behavior.

The **heapsort**() function is an implementation of J.W.J. William's "heapsort" algorithm, a variant of selection sorting; in particular, see D.E. Knuth's Algorithm H. **Heapsort**() takes O N lg N worst-case time. Its *only* advantage over **qsort**() is that it uses almost no additional memory; while **qsort**() does not allocate memory, it is implemented using recursion.

The function **mergesort**() requires additional memory of size *nmemb* * *size* bytes; it should be used only when space is not at a premium. **Mergesort**() is optimized for data with pre-existing order; its worst case time is O N lg N; its best case is O N.

Normally, **qsort**() is faster than **mergesort**() is faster than **heapsort**(). Memory availability and pre-existing order in the data can make this untrue.

RETURN VALUES

The **qsort**() function returns no value.

Upon successful completion, **heapsort**( ) and **mergesort**( ) return 0. Otherwise, they return −1 and the global variable *errno* is set to indicate the error.

ERRORS

The **heapsort**( ) function succeeds unless:

[EINVAL] The *size* argument is zero, or, the *size* argument to **mergesort**( ) is less than "sizeof(void *) / 2".

[ENOMEM] **Heapsort**( ) or **mergesort**( ) were unable to allocate memory.

COMPATIBILITY

Previous versions of **qsort**( ) did not permit the comparison routine itself to call **qsort**(*3*). This is no longer true.

SEE ALSO

sort(1), radixsort(3)

Hoare, C.A.R., "Quicksort", *The Computer Journal*, 5:1, pp. 10-15, 1962.

Williams, J.W.J, "Heapsort", *Communications of the ACM*, 7:1, pp. 347-348, 1964.

Knuth, D.E., "Sorting and Searching", *The Art of Computer Programming*, Vol. 3, pp. 114-123, 145-149, 1968.

Mcilroy, P.M., "Optimistic Sorting and Information Theoretic Complexity", *Fourth Annual ACM-SIAM Symposium on Discrete Algorithms*, January 1992.

Bentley, J.L., "Engineering a Sort Function", *bentley@research.att.com*, January 1992.

STANDARDS

The **qsort**( ) function conforms to ANSI C X3.159-1989 ("ANSI C ").

3

NAME

LIST_ENTRY, LIST_HEAD, LIST_INIT, LIST_INSERT_AFTER, LIST_INSERT_HEAD, LIST_REMOVE, TAILQ_ENTRY, TAILQ_HEAD, TAILQ_INIT, TAILQ_INSERT_AFTER, TAILQ_INSERT_HEAD, TAILQ_INSERT_TAIL, TAILQ_REMOVE, CIRCLEQ_ENTRY, CIRCLEQ_HEAD, CIRCLEQ_INIT, CIRCLEQ_INSERT_AFTER, CIRCLEQ_INSERT_BEFORE, CIRCLEQ_INSERT_HEAD, CIRCLEQ_INSERT_TAIL, CIRCLEQ_REMOVE – implementations of lists, tail queues, and circular queues

SYNOPSIS

`#include <sys/queue.h>`

`LIST_ENTRY(`*TYPE*`);`

`LIST_HEAD(`*HEADNAME*`, `*TYPE*`);`

`LIST_INIT(`*LIST_HEAD *head*`);`

`LIST_INSERT_AFTER(`*LIST_ENTRY *listelm*`, `*TYPE *elm*`, `*LIST_ENTRY NAME*`);`

`LIST_INSERT_HEAD(`*LIST_HEAD *head*`, `*TYPE *elm*`, `*LIST_ENTRY NAME*`);`

`LIST_REMOVE(`*TYPE *elm*`, `*LIST_ENTRY NAME*`);`

`TAILQ_ENTRY(`*TYPE*`);`

`TAILQ_HEAD(`*HEADNAME*`, `*TYPE*`);`

`TAILQ_INIT(`*TAILQ_HEAD *head*`);`

`TAILQ_INSERT_AFTER(`*TAILQ_HEAD *head*`, `*TYPE *listelm*`, `*TYPE *elm*`, `*TAILQ_ENTRY NAME*`);`

`TAILQ_INSERT_HEAD(`*TAILQ_HEAD *head*`, `*TYPE *elm*`, `*TAILQ_ENTRY NAME*`);`

`TAILQ_INSERT_TAIL(`*TAILQ_HEAD *head*`, `*TYPE *elm*`, `*TAILQ_ENTRY NAME*`);`

`TAILQ_REMOVE(`*TAILQ_HEAD *head*`, `*TYPE *elm*`, `*TAILQ_ENTRY NAME*`);`

`CIRCLEQ_ENTRY(`*TYPE*`);`

`CIRCLEQ_HEAD(`*HEADNAME*`, `*TYPE*`);`

`CIRCLEQ_INIT(`*CIRCLEQ_HEAD *head*`);`

`CIRCLEQ_INSERT_AFTER(`*CIRCLEQ_HEAD *head*`, `*TYPE *listelm*`, `*TYPE *elm*`, `*CIRCLEQ_ENTRY NAME*`);`

`CIRCLEQ_INSERT_BEFORE(`*CIRCLEQ_HEAD *head*`, `*TYPE *listelm*`, `*TYPE *elm*`, `*CIRCLEQ_ENTRY NAME*`);`

`CIRCLEQ_INSERT_HEAD(`*CIRCLEQ_HEAD *head*`, `*TYPE *elm*`, `*CIRCLEQ_ENTRY NAME*`);`

`CIRCLEQ_INSERT_TAIL(`*CIRCLEQ_HEAD *head*`, `*TYPE *elm*`, `*CIRCLEQ_ENTRY NAME*`);`

`CIRCLEQ_REMOVE(`*CIRCLEQ_HEAD *head*`, `*TYPE *elm*`, `*CIRCLEQ_ENTRY NAME*`);`

DESCRIPTION

These macros define and operate on three types of data structures: lists, tail queues, and circular queues. All three structures support the following functionality:

1. Insertion of a new entry at the head of the list.
2. Insertion of a new entry after any element in the list.
3. Removal of any entry in the list.
4. Forward traversal through the list.

Lists are the simplest of the three data structures and support only the above functionality.

Tail queues add the following functionality:

1. Entries can be added at the end of a list.

However:

1. All list insertions and removals must specify the head of the list.
2. Each head entry requires two pointers rather than one.
3. Code size is about 15% greater and operations run about 20% slower than lists.

Circular queues add the following functionality:

1. Entries can be added at the end of a list.
2. Entries can be added before another entry.
3. They may be traversed backwards, from tail to head.

However:

1. All list insertions and removals must specify the head of the list.
2. Each head entry requires two pointers rather than one.
3. The termination condition for traversal is more complex.
4. Code size is about 40% greater and operations run about 45% slower than lists.

In the macro definitions, *TYPE* is the name of a user defined structure, that must contain a field of type LIST_ENTRY, TAILQ_ENTRY, or CIRCLEQ_ENTRY, named *NAME*. The argument *HEADNAME* is the name of a user defined structure that must be declared using the macros LIST_HEAD, TAILQ_HEAD, or CIRCLEQ_HEAD. See the examples below for further explanation of how these macros are used.

LISTS

A list is headed by a structure defined by the **LIST_HEAD** macro. This structure contains a single pointer to the first element on the list. The elements are doubly linked so that an arbitrary element can be removed without traversing the list. New elements can be added to the list after an existing element or at the head of the list. A *LIST_HEAD* structure is declared as follows:

```
LIST_HEAD(HEADNAME, TYPE) head;
```

where *HEADNAME* is the name of the structure to be defined, and *TYPE* is the type of the elements to be linked into the list. A pointer to the head of the list can later be declared as:

```
struct HEADNAME *headp;
```

(The names head and headp are user selectable.)

The macro **LIST_ENTRY** declares a structure that connects the elements in the list.

The macro **LIST_INIT** initializes the list referenced by *head*.

The macro **LIST_INSERT_HEAD** inserts the new element *elm* at the head of the list.

The macro **LIST_INSERT_AFTER** inserts the new element *elm* after the element *listelm*.

The macro **LIST_REMOVE** removes the element *elm* from the list.

LIST EXAMPLE

```
LIST_HEAD(listhead, entry) head;
struct listhead *headp;              /* List head. */
struct entry {
        ...
        LIST_ENTRY(entry) entries;   /* List. */
        ...
} *n1, *n2, *np;

LIST_INIT(&head);                    /* Initialize the list. */

n1 = malloc(sizeof(struct entry));   /* Insert at the head. */
LIST_INSERT_HEAD(&head, n1, entries);

n2 = malloc(sizeof(struct entry));   /* Insert after. */
LIST_INSERT_AFTER(n1, n2, entries);
                                     /* Forward traversal. */
for (np = head.lh_first; np != NULL; np = np->entries.le_next)
        np-> ...

while (head.lh_first != NULL)        /* Delete. */
        LIST_REMOVE(head.lh_first, entries);
```

TAIL QUEUES

A tail queue is headed by a structure defined by the **TAILQ_HEAD** macro. This structure contains a pair of pointers, one to the first element in the tail queue and the other to the last element in the tail queue. The elements are doubly linked so that an arbitrary element can be removed without traversing the tail queue. New elements can be added to the tail queue after an existing element, at the head of the tail queue, or at the end of the tail queue. A *TAILQ_HEAD* structure is declared as follows:

```
TAILQ_HEAD(HEADNAME, TYPE) head;
```

where HEADNAME is the name of the structure to be defined, and TYPE is the type of the elements to be linked into the tail queue. A pointer to the head of the tail queue can later be declared as:

```
struct HEADNAME *headp;
```

(The names head and headp are user selectable.)

The macro **TAILQ_ENTRY** declares a structure that connects the elements in the tail queue.

The macro **TAILQ_INIT** initializes the tail queue referenced by *head*.

The macro **TAILQ_INSERT_HEAD** inserts the new element *elm* at the head of the tail queue.

The macro **TAILQ_INSERT_TAIL** inserts the new element *elm* at the end of the tail queue.

The macro **TAILQ_INSERT_AFTER** inserts the new element *elm* after the element *listelm*.

The macro **TAILQ_REMOVE** removes the element *elm* from the tail queue.

TAIL QUEUE EXAMPLE

```
TAILQ_HEAD(tailhead, entry) head;
struct tailhead *headp;                 /* Tail queue head. */
struct entry {
        ...
        TAILQ_ENTRY(entry) entries;     /* Tail queue. */
        ...
} *n1, *n2, *np;

TAILQ_INIT(&head);                      /* Initialize the queue. */

n1 = malloc(sizeof(struct entry));   /* Insert at the head. */
TAILQ_INSERT_HEAD(&head, n1, entries);

n1 = malloc(sizeof(struct entry));   /* Insert at the tail. */
TAILQ_INSERT_TAIL(&head, n1, entries);

n2 = malloc(sizeof(struct entry));   /* Insert after. */
TAILQ_INSERT_AFTER(&head, n1, n2, entries);
                                        /* Forward traversal. */
for (np = head.tqh_first; np != NULL; np = np->entries.tqe_next)
        np-> ...
                                        /* Delete. */
while (head.tqh_first != NULL)
        TAILQ_REMOVE(&head, head.tqh_first, entries);
```

CIRCULAR QUEUES

A circular queue is headed by a structure defined by the **CIRCLEQ_HEAD** macro. This structure contains a pair of pointers, one to the first element in the circular queue and the other to the last element in the circular queue. The elements are doubly linked so that an arbitrary element can be removed without traversing the queue. New elements can be added to the queue after an existing element, before an existing element, at the head of the queue, or at the end of the queue. A *CIRCLEQ_HEAD* structure is declared as follows:

```
CIRCLEQ_HEAD(HEADNAME, TYPE) head;
```

where HEADNAME is the name of the structure to be defined, and TYPE is the type of the elements to be linked into the circular queue. A pointer to the head of the circular queue can later be declared as:

```
struct HEADNAME *headp;
```

(The names head and headp are user selectable.)

The macro **CIRCLEQ_ENTRY** declares a structure that connects the elements in the circular queue.

The macro **CIRCLEQ_INIT** initializes the circular queue referenced by *head*.

The macro **CIRCLEQ_INSERT_HEAD** inserts the new element *elm* at the head of the circular queue.

The macro **CIRCLEQ_INSERT_TAIL** inserts the new element *elm* at the end of the circular queue.

The macro **CIRCLEQ_INSERT_AFTER** inserts the new element *elm* after the element *listelm*.

The macro CIRCLEQ_INSERT_BEFORE inserts the new element *elm* before the element *listelm*.

The macro CIRCLEQ_REMOVE removes the element *elm* from the circular queue.

CIRCULAR QUEUE EXAMPLE

```
CIRCLEQ_HEAD(circleq, entry) head;
struct circleq *headp;              /* Circular queue head. */
struct entry {
       ...
       CIRCLEQ_ENTRY entries;       /* Circular queue. */
       ...
} *n1, *n2, *np;

CIRCLEQ_INIT(&head);                /* Initialize the circular queue. */

n1 = malloc(sizeof(struct entry));   /* Insert at the head. */
CIRCLEQ_INSERT_HEAD(&head, n1, entries);

n1 = malloc(sizeof(struct entry));   /* Insert at the tail. */
CIRCLEQ_INSERT_TAIL(&head, n1, entries);

n2 = malloc(sizeof(struct entry));   /* Insert after. */
CIRCLEQ_INSERT_AFTER(&head, n1, n2, entries);

n2 = malloc(sizeof(struct entry));   /* Insert before. */
CIRCLEQ_INSERT_BEFORE(&head, n1, n2, entries);
                                     /* Forward traversal. */
for (np = head.cqh_first; np != (void *)&head; np = np->entries.cqe_next)
       np-> ...
                                     /* Reverse traversal. */
for (np = head.cqh_last; np != (void *)&head; np = np->entries.cqe_prev)
       np-> ...
                                     /* Delete. */
while (head.cqh_first != (void *)&head)
       CIRCLEQ_REMOVE(&head, head.cqh_first, entries);
```

HISTORY
The queue functions first appeared in 4.4BSD.

NAME

`radixsort` – radix sort

SYNOPSIS

```
#include <limits.h>
#include <stdlib.h>

int
radixsort(u_char **base, int nmemb, u_char *table, u_int endbyte);

int
sradixsort(u_char **base, int nmemb, u_char *table, u_int endbyte);
```

DESCRIPTION

The `radixsort()` and `sradixsort()` functions are implementations of radix sort.

These functions sort an array of pointers to byte strings, the initial member of which is referenced by *base*. The byte strings may contain any values; the end of each string is denoted by the user-specified value *endbyte*.

Applications may specify a sort order by providing the *table* argument. If non-NULL, *table* must reference an array of UCHAR_MAX + 1 bytes which contains the sort weight of each possible byte value. The end-of-string byte must have a sort weight of 0 or 255 (for sorting in reverse order). More than one byte may have the same sort weight. The *table* argument is useful for applications which wish to sort different characters equally, for example, providing a table with the same weights for A-Z as for a-z will result in a case-insensitive sort. If *table* is NULL, the contents of the array are sorted in ascending order according to the ASCII order of the byte strings they reference and *endbyte* has a sorting weight of 0.

The `sradixsort()` function is stable, that is, if two elements compare as equal, their order in the sorted array is unchanged. The `sradixsort()` function uses additional memory sufficient to hold *nmemb* pointers.

The `radixsort()` function is not stable, but uses no additional memory.

These functions are variants of most-significant-byte radix sorting; in particular, see D.E. Knuth's Algorithm R and section 5.2.5, exercise 10. They take linear time relative to the number of bytes in the strings.

RETURN VALUES

Upon successful completion 0 is returned. Otherwise, −1 is returned and the global variable *errno* is set to indicate the error.

ERRORS

[EINVAL]   The value of the *endbyte* element of *table* is not 0 or 255.

Additionally, the `sradixsort()` function may fail and set *errno* for any of the errors specified for the library routine malloc(3).

SEE ALSO

sort(1), qsort(3)

Knuth, D.E., "Sorting and Searching", *The Art of Computer Programming*, Vol. 3, pp. 170-178, 1968.

Paige, R., "Three Partition Refinement Algorithms", *SIAM J. Comput.*, No. 6, Vol. 16, 1987.

McIlroy, P., "Computing Systems", *Engineering Radix Sort*, Vol. 6:1, pp. 5-27, 1993.

HISTORY

The `radixsort( )` function first appeared in 4.4BSD.

NAME

raise – send a signal to the current process

SYNOPSIS

#include ⟨signal.h⟩

int
raise(*int sig*);

DESCRIPTION

The **raise**( ) function sends the signal *sig* to the current process.

RETURN VALUES

Upon successful completion, a value of 0 is returned. Otherwise, a value of −1 is returned and the global variable *errno* is set to indicate the error.

ERRORS

The **raise**( ) function may fail and set *errno* for any of the errors specified for the library functions getpid(2) and kill(2).

SEE ALSO

kill(2)

STANDARDS

The **raise**( ) function conforms to ANSI C X3.159-1989 (''ANSI C '').

3

NAME

rand, srand – bad random number generator

SYNOPSIS

```
#include <stdlib.h>
```

void
srand(*unsigned seed*);

int
rand(*void*);

DESCRIPTION

These interfaces are obsoleted by random(3).

The **rand**( ) function computes a sequence of pseudo-random integers in the range of 0 to RAND_MAX (as defined by the header file <stdlib.h>).

The **srand**( ) function sets its argument as the seed for a new sequence of pseudo-random numbers to be returned by **rand**(). These sequences are repeatable by calling **srand**( ) with the same seed value.

If no seed value is provided, the functions are automatically seeded with a value of 1.

SEE ALSO

random(3)

STANDARDS

The **rand**( ) and **srand**( ) functions conform to ANSI C X3.159-1989 (''ANSI C '').

NAME

random, **srandom**, **initstate**, **setstate** – better random number generator; routines for changing generators

SYNOPSIS

```
#include <stdlib.h>
```

long
random(*void*);

void
srandom(*unsigned seed*);

char *
initstate(*unsigned seed*, *char *state*, *int n*);

char *
setstate(*char *state*);

DESCRIPTION

The **random**( ) function uses a non-linear additive feedback random number generator employing a default table of size 31 long integers to return successive pseudo-random numbers in the range from 0 to 2^{31}–1. The period of this random number generator is very large, approximately $16 \times (2^{31}$–1).

The **random**()/ **srandom**( ) have (almost) the same calling sequence and initialization properties as rand(3)/ srand(3). The difference is that rand produces a much less random sequence — in fact, the low dozen bits generated by rand go through a cyclic pattern. All the bits generated by **random**( ) are usable. For example, 'random( )&01' will produce a random binary value.

Unlike srand, **srandom**( ) does not return the old seed; the reason for this is that the amount of state information used is much more than a single word. (Two other routines are provided to deal with restarting/changing random number generators). Like rand(3), however, **random**( ) will by default produce a sequence of numbers that can be duplicated by calling **srandom**( ) with '1' as the seed.

The **initstate**( ) routine allows a state array, passed in as an argument, to be initialized for future use. The size of the state array (in bytes) is used by **initstate**( ) to decide how sophisticated a random number generator it should use — the more state, the better the random numbers will be. (Current "optimal" values for the amount of state information are 8, 32, 64, 128, and 256 bytes; other amounts will be rounded down to the nearest known amount. Using less than 8 bytes will cause an error.) The seed for the initialization (which specifies a starting point for the random number sequence, and provides for restarting at the same point) is also an argument. The **initstate**( ) function returns a pointer to the previous state information array.

Once a state has been initialized, the **setstate**( ) routine provides for rapid switching between states. The **setstate**( ) function returns a pointer to the previous state array; its argument state array is used for further random number generation until the next call to **initstate**( ) or **setstate**( ).

Once a state array has been initialized, it may be restarted at a different point either by calling **initstate**( ) (with the desired seed, the state array, and its size) or by calling both **setstate**( ) (with the state array) and **srandom**( ) (with the desired seed). The advantage of calling both **setstate**( ) and **srandom**( ) is that the size of the state array does not have to be remembered after it is initialized.

With 256 bytes of state information, the period of the random number generator is greater than 2^{69}, which should be sufficient for most purposes.

AUTHOR

Earl T. Cohen

DIAGNOSTICS

If `initstate`( ) is called with less than 8 bytes of state information, or if **setstate**( ) detects that the state information has been garbled, error messages are printed on the standard error output.

SEE ALSO

rand(3)

HISTORY

These functions appeared in 4.2BSD.

BUGS

About 2/3 the speed of rand(3).

NAME

rcmd, rresvport, ruserok – routines for returning a stream to a remote command

SYNOPSIS

```
#include <unistd.h>
```

```
int
rcmd(char **ahost, int inport, const char *locuser, const char *remuser,
        const char *cmd, int *fd2p);
```

```
int
rresvport(int *port);
```

```
int
iruserok(u_long raddr, int superuser, const char *ruser, const char *luser);
```

```
int
ruserok(const char *rhost, int superuser, const char *ruser,
        const char *luser);
```

DESCRIPTION

The rcmd( ) function is used by the super-user to execute a command on a remote machine using an authentication scheme based on reserved port numbers. The rresvport( ) function returns a descriptor to a socket with an address in the privileged port space. The ruserok( ) function is used by servers to authenticate clients requesting service with rcmd(). All three functions are present in the same file and are used by the rshd(8) server (among others).

The rcmd( ) function looks up the host *ahost* using gethostbyname(3), returning −1 if the host does not exist. Otherwise *ahost* is set to the standard name of the host and a connection is established to a server residing at the well-known Internet port *inport*.

If the connection succeeds, a socket in the Internet domain of type SOCK_STREAM is returned to the caller, and given to the remote command as *stdin* and *stdout*. If *fd2p* is non-zero, then an auxiliary channel to a control process will be set up, and a descriptor for it will be placed in *fd2p*. The control process will return diagnostic output from the command (unit 2) on this channel, and will also accept bytes on this channel as being UNIX signal numbers, to be forwarded to the process group of the command. If *fd2p* is 0, then the *stderr* (unit 2 of the remote command) will be made the same as the *stdout* and no provision is made for sending arbitrary signals to the remote process, although you may be able to get its attention by using out-of-band data.

The protocol is described in detail in rshd(8).

The rresvport( ) function is used to obtain a socket with a privileged address bound to it. This socket is suitable for use by rcmd( ) and several other functions. Privileged Internet ports are those in the range 0 to 1023. Only the super-user is allowed to bind an address of this sort to a socket.

The iruserok( ) and ruserok( ) functions take a remote host's IP address or name, as returned by the gethostbyname(3) routines, two user names and a flag indicating whether the local user's name is that of the super-user. Then, if the user is *NOT* the super-user, it checks the /etc/hosts.equiv file. If that lookup is not done, or is unsuccessful, the .rhosts in the local user's home directory is checked to see if the request for service is allowed.

If this file does not exist, is not a regular file, is owned by anyone other than the user or the super-user, or is writeable by anyone other than the owner, the check automatically fails. Zero is returned if the machine name is listed in the ''hosts.equiv'' file, or the host and remote user name are found in the ''.rhosts'' file; otherwise iruserok( ) and ruserok( ) return −1. If the local domain (as obtained from `gethostname(2)`) is the same as the remote domain, only the machine name need be specified.

The **iruserok**( ) function is strongly preferred for security reasons. It requires trusting the local DNS at most, while the **ruserok**( ) function requires trusting the entire DNS, which can be spoofed.

DIAGNOSTICS

The **rcmd**( ) function returns a valid socket descriptor on success. It returns −1 on error and prints a diagnostic message on the standard error.

The **rresvport**( ) function returns a valid, bound socket descriptor on success. It returns −1 on error with the global value *errno* set according to the reason for failure. The error code EAGAIN is overloaded to mean ''All network ports in use.''

SEE ALSO

rlogin(1), rsh(1), intro(2), rexec(3), rexecd(8), rlogind(8), rshd(8)

HISTORY

These functions appeared in 4.2BSD.

NAME
re_comp, re_exec – regular expression handler

SYNOPSIS
`#include <unistd.h>`

char *
`re_comp`(*const char *s*);

int
`re_exec`(*const char *s*);

DESCRIPTION
This interface is made obsolete by regex(3).

The `re_comp()` function compiles a string into an internal form suitable for pattern matching. The `re_exec()` function checks the argument string against the last string passed to `re_comp()`.

The `re_comp()` function returns 0 if the string *s* was compiled successfully; otherwise a string containing an error message is returned. If `re_comp()` is passed 0 or a null string, it returns without changing the currently compiled regular expression.

The `re_exec()` function returns 1 if the string *s* matches the last compiled regular expression, 0 if the string *s* failed to match the last compiled regular expression, and −1 if the compiled regular expression was invalid (indicating an internal error).

The strings passed to both `re_comp()` and `re_exec()` may have trailing or embedded newline characters; they are terminated by NULs. The regular expressions recognized are described in the manual entry for ed(1), given the above difference.

DIAGNOSTICS
The `re_exec()` function returns −1 for an internal error.

The `re_comp()` function returns one of the following strings if an error occurs:

No previous regular expression,
Regular expression too long,
unmatched \\(,
missing],
too many \\(\\) pairs,
unmatched \\).

SEE ALSO
ed(1), ex(1), egrep(1), fgrep(1), grep(1), regex(3)

HISTORY
The `re_comp()` and `re_exec()` functions appeared in 4.0BSD.

NAME
　　　　`realloc` – reallocation of memory function

SYNOPSIS
　　　　`#include <stdlib.h>`

　　　　*void **
　　　　`realloc(`*void *ptr, size_t size*`)`;

DESCRIPTION
　　　　The `realloc()` function changes the size of the object pointed to by *ptr* to the size specified by *size*.
　　　　The contents of the object are unchanged up to the lesser of the new and old sizes. If the new size is larger,
　　　　the value of the newly allocated portion of the object is indeterminate. If *ptr* is a null pointer, the `real-`
　　　　`loc()` function behaves like the `malloc(3)` function for the specified size. Otherwise, if *ptr* does not
　　　　match a pointer earlier returned by the `calloc(3)`, `malloc(3)`, or `realloc()` function, or if the space
　　　　has been deallocated by a call to the `free` or `realloc()` function, unpredictable and usually detrimental
　　　　behavior will occur. If the space cannot be allocated, the object pointed to by *ptr* is unchanged. If *size* is
　　　　zero and *ptr* is not a null pointer, the object it points to is freed.

　　　　The `realloc()` function returns either a null pointer or a pointer to the possibly moved allocated space.

SEE ALSO
　　　　`alloca(3)`, `calloc(3)`, `free(3)`, `malloc(3)`,

STANDARDS
　　　　The `realloc()` function conforms to ANSI C X3.159-1989 ("ANSI C").

NAME

 realpath – returns the canonicalized absolute pathname

SYNOPSIS

 `#include <sys/param.h>`
 `#include <stdlib.h>`

 char *
 realpath(*const char *pathname, char resolvedname[MAXPATHLEN]*);

DESCRIPTION

 The **realpath**( ) function resolves all symbolic links, extra ''/'' characters and references to `/./` and
`/../` in *pathname*, and copies the resulting absolute pathname into the memory referenced by
resolvedname. The *resolvedname* argument *must* refer to a buffer capable of storing at least
MAXPATHLEN characters.

 The **realpath**( ) function will resolve both absolute and relative paths and return the absolute pathname
corresponding to *pathname*. All but the last component of *pathname* must exist when **realpath**( ) is
called.

RETURN VALUES

 The **realpath**( ) function returns *resolved_name* on success. If an error occurs, **realpath**( ) returns
NULL, and *resolved_name* contains the pathname which caused the problem.

ERRORS

 The function **realpath**( ) may fail and set the external variable *errno* for any of the errors specified for the
library functions chdir(2), close(2), fchdir(2), lstat(2), open(2), readlink(2) and
getcwd(3).

CAVEATS

 This implementation of **realpath**( ) differs slightly from the Solaris implementation. The 4.4BSD version
always returns absolute pathnames, whereas the Solaris implementation will, under certain circumstances,
return a relative *resolved_path* when given a relative *pathname*.

SEE ALSO

 getcwd(3)

HISTORY

 The **realpath**( ) function call first appeared in 4.4BSD.

NAME

recno – record number database access method

SYNOPSIS

#include <sys/types.h>
#include <db.h>

DESCRIPTION

The routine *dbopen* is the library interface to database files. One of the supported file formats is record number files. The general description of the database access methods is in *dbopen*(3), this manual page describes only the recno specific information.

The record number data structure is either variable or fixed-length records stored in a flat-file format, accessed by the logical record number. The existence of record number five implies the existence of records one through four, and the deletion of record number one causes record number five to be renumbered to record number four, as well as the cursor, if positioned after record number one, to shift down one record.

The recno access method specific data structure provided to *dbopen* is defined in the <db.h> include file as follows:

```
typedef struct {
        u_long flags;
        u_int cachesize;
        u_int psize;
        int lorder;
        size_t reclen;
        u_char bval;
        char *bfname;
} RECNOINFO;
```

The elements of this structure are defined as follows:

flags   The flag value is specified by *or*'ing any of the following values:

R_FIXEDLEN

The records are fixed-length, not byte delimited. The structure element *reclen* specifies the length of the record, and the structure element *bval* is used as the pad character.

R_NOKEY

In the interface specified by *dbopen*, the sequential record retrieval fills in both the caller's key and data structures. If the R_NOKEY flag is specified, the *cursor* routines are not required to fill in the key structure. This permits applications to retrieve records at the end of files without reading all of the intervening records.

R_SNAPSHOT

This flag requires that a snapshot of the file be taken when *dbopen* is called, instead of permitting any unmodified records to be read from the original file.

cachesize

A suggested maximum size, in bytes, of the memory cache. This value is **only** advisory, and the access method will allocate more memory rather than fail. If *cachesize* is 0 (no size is specified) a default cache is used.

psize   The recno access method stores the in-memory copies of its records in a btree. This value is the size (in bytes) of the pages used for nodes in that tree. If *psize* is 0 (no page size is specified) a page size is chosen based on the underlying file system I/O block size. See *btree*(3) for more information.

lorder The byte order for integers in the stored database metadata. The number should represent the order as an integer; for example, big endian order would be the number 4,321. If *lorder* is 0 (no order is specified) the current host order is used.

reclen The length of a fixed-length record.

bval The delimiting byte to be used to mark the end of a record for variable-length records, and the pad character for fixed-length records. If no value is specified, newlines ("\n") are used to mark the end of variable-length records and fixed-length records are padded with spaces.

bfname The recno access method stores the in-memory copies of its records in a btree. If bfname is non-NULL, it specifies the name of the btree file, as if specified as the file name for a dbopen of a btree file.

The data part of the key/data pair used by the recno access method is the same as other access methods. The key is different. The *data* field of the key should be a pointer to a memory location of type *recno_t*, as defined in the <db.h> include file. This type is normally the largest unsigned integral type available to the implementation. The *size* field of the key should be the size of that type.

In the interface specified by *dbopen*, using the *put* interface to create a new record will cause the creation of multiple, empty records if the record number is more than one greater than the largest record currently in the database.

SEE ALSO

dbopen(3), *hash*(3), *mpool*(3), *recno*(3)

Document Processing in a Relational Database System, Michael Stonebraker, Heidi Stettner, Joseph Kalash, Antonin Guttman, Nadene Lynn, Memorandum No. UCB/ERL M82/32, May 1982.

BUGS

Only big and little endian byte order is supported.

NAME

 regcomp, regexec, regerror, regfree – regular-expression library

SYNOPSIS

 #include <sys/types.h>
 #include <regex.h>

 int regcomp(regex_t *preg, const char *pattern, int cflags);

 int regexec(const regex_t *preg, const char *string, size_t nmatch, regmatch_t pmatch[], int eflags);

 size_t regerror(int errcode, const regex_t *preg, char *errbuf, size_t errbuf_size);

 void regfree(regex_t *preg);

DESCRIPTION

 These routines implement POSIX 1003.2 regular expressions ("RE"s); see *re_format*(7). *Regcomp* compiles an RE written as a string into an internal form, *regexec* matches that internal form against a string and reports results, *regerror* transforms error codes from either into human-readable messages, and *regfree* frees any dynamically-allocated storage used by the internal form of an RE.

 The header *<regex.h>* declares two structure types, *regex_t* and *regmatch_t*, the former for compiled internal forms and the latter for match reporting. It also declares the four functions, a type *regoff_t*, and a number of constants with names starting with "REG_".

 Regcomp compiles the regular expression contained in the *pattern* string, subject to the flags in *cflags*, and places the results in the *regex_t* structure pointed to by *preg*. *Cflags* is the bitwise OR of zero or more of the following flags:

 REG_EXTENDED   Compile modern ("extended") REs, rather than the obsolete ("basic") REs that are the default.

 REG_BASIC   This is a synonym for 0, provided as a counterpart to REG_EXTENDED to improve readability.

 REG_NOSPEC   Compile with recognition of all special characters turned off. All characters are thus considered ordinary, so the "RE" is a literal string. This is an extension, compatible with but not specified by POSIX 1003.2, and should be used with caution in software intended to be portable to other systems. REG_EXTENDED and REG_NOSPEC may not be used in the same call to *regcomp*.

 REG_ICASE   Compile for matching that ignores upper/lower case distinctions. See *re_format*(7).

 REG_NOSUB   Compile for matching that need only report success or failure, not what was matched.

 REG_NEWLINE   Compile for newline-sensitive matching. By default, newline is a completely ordinary character with no special meaning in either REs or strings. With this flag, '[' bracket expressions and '.' never match newline, a '^' anchor matches the null string after any newline in the string in addition to its normal function, and the '$' anchor matches the null string before any newline in the string in addition to its normal function.

 REG_PEND   The regular expression ends, not at the first NUL, but just before the character pointed to by the *re_endp* member of the structure pointed to by *preg*. The *re_endp* member is of type *const char *. This flag permits inclusion of NULs in the RE; they are considered ordinary characters. This is an extension, compatible with but not specified by POSIX 1003.2, and should be used with caution in software intended to be portable to other systems.

 When successful, *regcomp* returns 0 and fills in the structure pointed to by *preg*. One member of that structure (other than *re_endp*) is publicized: *re_nsub*, of type *size_t*, contains the number of parenthesized subexpressions within the RE (except that the value of this member is undefined if the REG_NOSUB flag was used). If *regcomp* fails, it returns a non-zero error code; see DIAGNOSTICS.

Regexec matches the compiled RE pointed to by *preg* against the *string*, subject to the flags in *eflags*, and reports results using *nmatch*, *pmatch*, and the returned value. The RE must have been compiled by a previous invocation of *regcomp*. The compiled form is not altered during execution of *regexec*, so a single compiled RE can be used simultaneously by multiple threads.

By default, the NUL-terminated string pointed to by *string* is considered to be the text of an entire line, minus any terminating newline. The *eflags* argument is the bitwise OR of zero or more of the following flags:

REG_NOTBOL   The first character of the string is not the beginning of a line, so the '^' anchor should not match before it. This does not affect the behavior of newlines under REG_NEWLINE.

REG_NOTEOL   The NUL terminating the string does not end a line, so the '$' anchor should not match before it. This does not affect the behavior of newlines under REG_NEWLINE.

REG_STARTEND   The string is considered to start at *string* + *pmatch*[0].*rm_so* and to have a terminating NUL located at *string* + *pmatch*[0].*rm_eo* (there need not actually be a NUL at that location), regardless of the value of *nmatch*. See below for the definition of *pmatch* and *nmatch*. This is an extension, compatible with but not specified by POSIX 1003.2, and should be used with caution in software intended to be portable to other systems. Note that a non-zero *rm_so* does not imply REG_NOTBOL; REG_STARTEND affects only the location of the string, not how it is matched.

See *re_format*(7) for a discussion of what is matched in situations where an RE or a portion thereof could match any of several substrings of *string*.

Normally, *regexec* returns 0 for success and the non-zero code REG_NOMATCH for failure. Other non-zero error codes may be returned in exceptional situations; see DIAGNOSTICS.

If REG_NOSUB was specified in the compilation of the RE, or if *nmatch* is 0, *regexec* ignores the *pmatch* argument (but see below for the case where REG_STARTEND is specified). Otherwise, *pmatch* points to an array of *nmatch* structures of type *regmatch_t*. Such a structure has at least the members *rm_so* and *rm_eo*, both of type *regoff_t* (a signed arithmetic type at least as large as an *off_t* and a *ssize_t*), containing respectively the offset of the first character of a substring and the offset of the first character after the end of the substring. Offsets are measured from the beginning of the *string* argument given to *regexec*. An empty substring is denoted by equal offsets, both indicating the character following the empty substring.

The 0th member of the *pmatch* array is filled in to indicate what substring of *string* was matched by the entire RE. Remaining members report what substring was matched by parenthesized subexpressions within the RE; member *i* reports subexpression *i*, with subexpressions counted (starting at 1) by the order of their opening parentheses in the RE, left to right. Unused entries in the array—corresponding either to subexpressions that did not participate in the match at all, or to subexpressions that do not exist in the RE (that is, *i* > *preg*->*re_nsub*)—have both *rm_so* and *rm_eo* set to −1. If a subexpression participated in the match several times, the reported substring is the last one it matched. (Note, as an example in particular, that when the RE '(b*)+' matches 'bbb', the parenthesized subexpression matches each of the three 'b's and then an infinite number of empty strings following the last 'b', so the reported substring is one of the empties.)

If REG_STARTEND is specified, *pmatch* must point to at least one *regmatch_t* (even if *nmatch* is 0 or REG_NOSUB was specified), to hold the input offsets for REG_STARTEND. Use for output is still entirely controlled by *nmatch*; if *nmatch* is 0 or REG_NOSUB was specified, the value of *pmatch*[0] will not be changed by a successful *regexec*.

Regerror maps a non-zero *errcode* from either *regcomp* or *regexec* to a human-readable, printable message. If *preg* is non-NULL, the error code should have arisen from use of the *regex_t* pointed to by *preg*, and if the error code came from *regcomp*, it should have been the result from the most recent *regcomp* using that *regex_t*. (*Regerror* may be able to supply a more detailed message using information from the *regex_t*.) *Regerror* places the NUL-terminated message into the buffer pointed to by *errbuf*, limiting the length (including the NUL) to at most *errbuf_size* bytes. If the whole message won't fit, as much of it as will fit before the terminating NUL is supplied. In any case, the returned value is the size of buffer needed to hold the whole message (including terminating NUL). If *errbuf_size* is 0, *errbuf* is ignored but the return value is still correct.

If the *errcode* given to *regerror* is first ORed with REG_ITOA, the "message" that results is the printable name of the error code, e.g. "REG_NOMATCH", rather than an explanation thereof. If *errcode* is REG_ATOI, then *preg* shall be non-NULL and the *re_endp* member of the structure it points to must point to the printable name of an error code; in this case, the result in *errbuf* is the decimal digits of the numeric value of the error code (0 if the name is not recognized). REG_ITOA and REG_ATOI are intended primarily as debugging facilities; they are extensions, compatible with but not specified by POSIX 1003.2, and should be used with caution in software intended to be portable to other systems. Be warned also that they are considered experimental and changes are possible.

Regfree frees any dynamically-allocated storage associated with the compiled RE pointed to by *preg*. The remaining *regex_t* is no longer a valid compiled RE and the effect of supplying it to *regexec* or *regerror* is undefined.

None of these functions references global variables except for tables of constants; all are safe for use from multiple threads if the arguments are safe.

IMPLEMENTATION CHOICES

There are a number of decisions that 1003.2 leaves up to the implementor, either by explicitly saying "undefined" or by virtue of them being forbidden by the RE grammar. This implementation treats them as follows.

See *re_format*(7) for a discussion of the definition of case-independent matching.

There is no particular limit on the length of REs, except insofar as memory is limited. Memory usage is approximately linear in RE size, and largely insensitive to RE complexity, except for bounded repetitions. See BUGS for one short RE using them that will run almost any system out of memory.

A backslashed character other than one specifically given a magic meaning by 1003.2 (such magic meanings occur only in obsolete ["basic"] REs) is taken as an ordinary character.

Any unmatched [is a REG_EBRACK error.

Equivalence classes cannot begin or end bracket-expression ranges. The endpoint of one range cannot begin another.

RE_DUP_MAX, the limit on repetition counts in bounded repetitions, is 255.

A repetition operator (?, *, +, or bounds) cannot follow another repetition operator. A repetition operator cannot begin an expression or subexpression or follow '^' or '|'.

'|' cannot appear first or last in a (sub)expression or after another '|', i.e. an operand of '|' cannot be an empty subexpression. An empty parenthesized subexpression, '()', is legal and matches an empty (sub)string. An empty string is not a legal RE.

A '{' followed by a digit is considered the beginning of bounds for a bounded repetition, which must then follow the syntax for bounds. A '{' *not* followed by a digit is considered an ordinary character.

'^' and '$' beginning and ending subexpressions in obsolete ("basic") REs are anchors, not ordinary characters.

SEE ALSO

grep(1), re_format(7)

POSIX 1003.2, sections 2.8 (Regular Expression Notation) and B.5 (C Binding for Regular Expression Matching).

DIAGNOSTICS

Non-zero error codes from *regcomp* and *regexec* include the following:

REG_NOMATCH	regexec() failed to match
REG_BADPAT	invalid regular expression
REG_ECOLLATE	invalid collating element
REG_ECTYPE	invalid character class
REG_EESCAPE	\ applied to unescapable character
REG_ESUBREG	invalid backreference number
REG_EBRACK	brackets [ ] not balanced
REG_EPAREN	parentheses ( ) not balanced
REG_EBRACE	braces { } not balanced
REG_BADBR	invalid repetition count(s) in { }
REG_ERANGE	invalid character range in [ ]
REG_ESPACE	ran out of memory
REG_BADRPT	?, *, or + operand invalid
REG_EMPTY	empty (sub)expression
REG_ASSERT	"can't happen"—you found a bug
REG_INVARG	invalid argument, e.g. negative-length string

HISTORY

Originally written by Henry Spencer. Altered for inclusion in the 4.4BSD distribution.

BUGS

This is an alpha release with known defects. Please report problems.

There is one known functionality bug. The implementation of internationalization is incomplete: the locale is always assumed to be the default one of 1003.2, and only the collating elements etc. of that locale are available.

The back-reference code is subtle and doubts linger about its correctness in complex cases.

Regexec performance is poor. This will improve with later releases. *Nmatch* exceeding 0 is expensive; *nmatch* exceeding 1 is worse. *Regexec* is largely insensitive to RE complexity *except* that back references are massively expensive. RE length does matter; in particular, there is a strong speed bonus for keeping RE length under about 30 characters, with most special characters counting roughly double.

Regcomp implements bounded repetitions by macro expansion, which is costly in time and space if counts are large or bounded repetitions are nested. An RE like, say, '((((a{1,100}){1,100}){1,100}){1,100}){1,100}' will (eventually) run almost any existing machine out of swap space.

There are suspected problems with response to obscure error conditions. Notably, certain kinds of internal overflow, produced only by truly enormous REs or by multiply nested bounded repetitions, are probably not handled well.

Due to a mistake in 1003.2, things like 'a)b' are legal REs because ')' is a special character only in the presence of a previous unmatched '('. This can't be fixed until the spec is fixed.

The standard's definition of back references is vague. For example, does 'a\(\(b\)*\2\)*d' match 'abbbd'? Until the standard is clarified, behavior in such cases should not be relied on.

The implementation of word-boundary matching is a bit of a kludge, and bugs may lurk in combinations of word-boundary matching and anchoring.

NAME

regcomp, regexec, regsub, regerror – regular expression handlers

SYNOPSIS

#include <regexp.h>

regexp *
regcomp(*const char *exp*);

int
regexec(*const regexp *prog, const char *string*);

void
regsub(*const regexp *prog, const char *source, char *dest*);

DESCRIPTION

This interface is made obsolete by regex(3).

The **regcomp()**, **regexec()**, **regsub()**, and **regerror()** functions implement egrep(1)-style regular expressions and supporting facilities.

The **regcomp()** function compiles a regular expression into a structure of type regexp, and returns a pointer to it. The space has been allocated using malloc(3) and may be released by free.

The **regexec()** function matches a NUL-terminated *string* against the compiled regular expression in *prog*. It returns 1 for success and 0 for failure, and adjusts the contents of *prog*'s *startp* and *endp* (see below) accordingly.

The members of a regexp structure include at least the following (not necessarily in order):

```
char *startp[NSUBEXP];
char *endp[NSUBEXP];
```

where NSUBEXP is defined (as 10) in the header file. Once a successful **regexec()** has been done using the **regexp()**, each *startp- endp* pair describes one substring within the *string*, with the *startp* pointing to the first character of the substring and the *endp* pointing to the first character following the substring. The 0th substring is the substring of *string* that matched the whole regular expression. The others are those substrings that matched parenthesized expressions within the regular expression, with parenthesized expressions numbered in left-to-right order of their opening parentheses.

The **regsub()** function copies *source* to *dest*, making substitutions according to the most recent **regexec()** performed using *prog*. Each instance of '&' in *source* is replaced by the substring indicated by *startp*[ ] and *endp*[ ]. Each instance of '\n', where *n* is a digit, is replaced by the substring indicated by *startp*[*n*] and *endp*[*n*]. To get a literal '&' or '\n' into *dest*, prefix it with '\'; to get a literal '\' preceding '&' or '\n', prefix it with another '\'.

The **regerror()** function is called whenever an error is detected in **regcomp()**, **regexec()**, or **regsub()**. The default **regerror()** writes the string *msg*, with a suitable indicator of origin, on the standard error output and invokes exit(2). The **regerror()** function can be replaced by the user if other actions are desirable.

REGULAR EXPRESSION SYNTAX

A regular expression is zero or more *branches*, separated by '|'. It matches anything that matches one of the branches.

A branch is zero or more *pieces*, concatenated. It matches a match for the first, followed by a match for the second, etc.

A piece is an *atom* possibly followed by '*', '+', or '?'. An atom followed by '*' matches a sequence of 0 or more matches of the atom. An atom followed by '+' matches a sequence of 1 or more matches of the atom. An atom followed by '?' matches a match of the atom, or the null string.

An atom is a regular expression in parentheses (matching a match for the regular expression), a *range* (see below), '.' (matching any single character), '^' (matching the null string at the beginning of the input string), '$' (matching the null string at the end of the input string), a '\' followed by a single character (matching that character), or a single character with no other significance (matching that character).

A *range* is a sequence of characters enclosed in '[]'. It normally matches any single character from the sequence. If the sequence begins with '^', it matches any single character *not* from the rest of the sequence. If two characters in the sequence are separated by '−', this is shorthand for the full list of ASCII characters between them (e.g. '[0-9]' matches any decimal digit). To include a literal ']' in the sequence, make it the first character (following a possible '^'). To include a literal '−', make it the first or last character.

AMBIGUITY

If a regular expression could match two different parts of the input string, it will match the one which begins earliest. If both begin in the same place but match different lengths, or match the same length in different ways, life gets messier, as follows.

In general, the possibilities in a list of branches are considered in left-to-right order, the possibilities for '*', '+', and '?' are considered longest-first, nested constructs are considered from the outermost in, and concatenated constructs are considered leftmost-first. The match that will be chosen is the one that uses the earliest possibility in the first choice that has to be made. If there is more than one choice, the next will be made in the same manner (earliest possibility) subject to the decision on the first choice. And so forth.

For example, '(ab|a)b*c' could match 'abc' in one of two ways. The first choice is between 'ab' and 'a'; since 'ab' is earlier, and does lead to a successful overall match, it is chosen. Since the 'b' is already spoken for, the 'b*' must match its last possibility—the empty string—since it must respect the earlier choice.

In the particular case where no '|'s are present and there is only one '*', '+', or '?', the net effect is that the longest possible match will be chosen. So 'ab*', presented with 'xabbbby', will match 'abbbb'. Note that if 'ab*', is tried against 'xabyabbbz', it will match 'ab' just after 'x', due to the begins-earliest rule. (In effect, the decision on where to start the match is the first choice to be made, hence subsequent choices must respect it even if this leads them to less-preferred alternatives.)

RETURN VALUES

The **regcomp**( ) function returns NULL for a failure (**regerror**( ) permitting), where failures are syntax errors, exceeding implementation limits, or applying '+' or '*' to a possibly-null operand.

SEE ALSO

ed(1), ex(1), expr(1), egrep(1), fgrep(1), grep(1), regex(3)

HISTORY

Both code and manual page for **regcomp()**, **regexec()**, **regsub()**, and **regerror**( ) were written at the University of Toronto and appeared in 4.3BSD–Tahoe. They are intended to be compatible with the Bell V8 regexp(3), but are not derived from Bell code.

BUGS

Empty branches and empty regular expressions are not portable to V8.

The restriction against applying '*' or '+' to a possibly-null operand is an artifact of the simplistic implementation.

Does not support `egrep`'s newline-separated branches; neither does the V8 `regexp`(3), though.

Due to emphasis on compactness and simplicity, it's not strikingly fast. It does give special attention to handling simple cases quickly.

NAME
remove – remove directory entry

SYNOPSIS
`#include <stdio.h>`

int
remove(*const char *path*);

DESCRIPTION
The **remove**( ) function is an alias for the unlink(2) system call. It deletes the file referenced by *path.*

RETURN VALUES
Upon successful completion, **remove**( ) returns 0. Otherwise, −1 is returned and the global variable *errno* is set to indicate the error.

ERRORS
The **remove**( ) function may fail and set *errno* for any of the errors specified for the routine unlink(2).

SEE ALSO
unlink(2)

STANDARDS
The **remove**( ) function conforms to ANSI C X3.159-1989 (''ANSI C ''). ·

NAME

    res_query, res_search, res_mkquery, res_send, res_init, dn_comp, dn_expand –
    resolver routines

SYNOPSIS

    #include ⟨sys/types.h⟩
    #include ⟨netinet/in.h⟩
    #include ⟨arpa/nameser.h⟩
    #include ⟨resolv.h⟩

    res_query(*char *dname, int class, int type, u_char *answer, int anslen*);

    res_search(*char *dname, int class, int type, u_char *answer, int anslen*);

    res_mkquery(*int op, char *dname, int class, int type, char *data,
            int datalen, struct rrec *newrr, char *buf, int buflen*);

    res_send(*char *msg, int msglen, char *answer, int anslen*);

    res_init( );

    dn_comp(*char *exp_dn, char *comp_dn, int length, char **dnptrs,
            char **lastdnptr*);

    dn_expand(*u_char *msg, u_char *eomorig, u_char *comp_dn, u_char *exp_dn,
            int length*);

DESCRIPTION

These routines are used for making, sending and interpreting query and reply messages with Internet domain name servers.

Global configuration and state information that is used by the resolver routines is kept in the structure _res. Most of the values have reasonable defaults and can be ignored. Options stored in _res.options_ are defined in resolv.h and are as follows. Options are stored as a simple bit mask containing the bitwise "or" of the options enabled.

RES_INIT   True if the initial name server address and default domain name are initialized (i.e., **res_init**( ) has been called).

RES_DEBUG   Print debugging messages.

RES_AAONLY   Accept authoritative answers only. With this option, **res_send**( ) should continue until it finds an authoritative answer or finds an error. Currently this is not implemented.

RES_USEVC   Use TCP connections for queries instead of UDP datagrams.

RES_STAYOPEN   Used with RES_USEVC to keep the TCP connection open between queries. This is useful only in programs that regularly do many queries. UDP should be the normal mode used.

RES_IGNTC   Unused currently (ignore truncation errors, i.e., don't retry with TCP).

RES_RECURSE   Set the recursion-desired bit in queries. This is the default. (**res_send**( ) does not do iterative queries and expects the name server to handle recursion.)

RES_DEFNAMES   If set, **res_search**( ) will append the default domain name to single-component names (those that do not contain a dot). This option is enabled by default.

RES_DNSRCH   If this option is set, **res_search**( ) will search for host names in the current domain and in parent domains; see `hostname`(7). This is used by the standard host lookup routine `gethostbyname`(3). This option is enabled by default.

The **res_init**( ) routine reads the configuration file (if any; see `resolver`(5)) to get the default domain name, search list and the Internet address of the local name server(s). If no server is configured, the host running the resolver is tried. The current domain name is defined by the hostname if not specified in the configuration file; it can be overridden by the environment variable `LOCALDOMAIN`. Initialization normally occurs on the first call to one of the following routines.

The **res_query**( ) function provides an interface to the server query mechanism. It constructs a query, sends it to the local server, awaits a response, and makes preliminary checks on the reply. The query requests information of the specified *type* and *class* for the specified fully-qualified domain name *dname*. The reply message is left in the *answer* buffer with length *anslen* supplied by the caller.

The **res_search**( ) routine makes a query and awaits a response like **res_query**(), but in addition, it implements the default and search rules controlled by the RES_DEFNAMES and RES_DNSRCH options. It returns the first successful reply.

The remaining routines are lower-level routines used by **res_query**(). The **res_mkquery**( ) function constructs a standard query message and places it in *buf*. It returns the size of the query, or −1 if the query is larger than *buflen*. The query type *op* is usually QUERY, but can be any of the query types defined in `<arpa/nameser.h>`. The domain name for the query is given by *dname*. *Newrr* is currently unused but is intended for making update messages.

The **res_send**( ) routine sends a pre-formatted query and returns an answer. It will call **res_init**( ) if RES_INIT is not set, send the query to the local name server, and handle timeouts and retries. The length of the reply message is returned, or −1 if there were errors.

The **dn_comp**( ) function compresses the domain name *exp_dn* and stores it in *comp_dn*. The size of the compressed name is returned or −1 if there were errors. The size of the array pointed to by *comp_dn* is given by *length*. The compression uses an array of pointers *dnptrs* to previously-compressed names in the current message. The first pointer points to the beginning of the message and the list ends with NULL. The limit to the array is specified by *lastdnptr*. A side effect of **dn_comp**( ) is to update the list of pointers for labels inserted into the message as the name is compressed. If *dnptr* is NULL, `names are not compressed`. If *lastdnptr* is NULL, the list of labels is not updated.

The **dn_expand**( ) entry expands the compressed domain name *comp_dn* to a full domain name The compressed name is contained in a query or reply message; *msg* is a pointer to the beginning of the message. The uncompressed name is placed in the buffer indicated by *exp_dn* which is of size *length*. The size of compressed name is returned or −1 if there was an error.

FILES
/etc/resolv.conf The configuration file see `resolver`(5).

SEE ALSO
`gethostbyname`(3), `named`(8), `resolver`(5), `hostname`(7),

RFC1032, RFC1033, RFC1034, RFC1035, RFC974

Name Server Operations Guide for BIND.

HISTORY
The **res_query** function appeared in 4.3BSD.

NAME

`rexec` – return stream to a remote command

SYNOPSIS

`int`
`rexec(ahost, int inport, char *user, char *passwd, char *cmd, int *fd2p);`

DESCRIPTION

This interface is obsoleted by krcmd(3). It is available from the compatibility library, libcompat.

The `rexec()` function looks up the host *ahost* using `gethostbyname(3)`, returning −1 if the host does not exist. Otherwise *ahost* is set to the standard name of the host. If a username and password are both specified, then these are used to authenticate to the foreign host; otherwise the environment and then the user's `.netrc` file in his home directory are searched for appropriate information. If all this fails, the user is prompted for the information.

The port *inport* specifies which well-known DARPA Internet port to use for the connection; the call `getservbyname("exec", "tcp")` (see `getservent(3)`) will return a pointer to a structure, which contains the necessary port. The protocol for connection is described in detail in `rexecd(8)`.

If the connection succeeds, a socket in the Internet domain of type `SOCK_STREAM` is returned to the caller, and given to the remote command as *stdin* and *stdout*. If *fd2p* is non-zero, then an auxiliary channel to a control process will be setup, and a descriptor for it will be placed in *fd2p*. The control process will return diagnostic output from the command (unit 2) on this channel, and will also accept bytes on this channel as being UNIX signal numbers, to be forwarded to the process group of the command. The diagnostic information returned does not include remote authorization failure, as the secondary connection is set up after authorization has been verified. If *fd2p* is 0, then the *stderr* (unit 2 of the remote command) will be made the same as the *stdout* and no provision is made for sending arbitrary signals to the remote process, although you may be able to get its attention by using out-of-band data.

SEE ALSO

`rcmd(3)`, `rexecd(8)`

HISTORY

The `rexec()` function appeared in 4.2BSD.

NAME

rindex – locate character in string

SYNOPSIS

`#include <string.h>`

*char ***
rindex(*const char *s, int c*);

DESCRIPTION

The **rindex**( ) function locates the last character matching *c* (converted to a *char*) in the null-terminated string *s*.

RETURN VALUES

A pointer to the character is returned if it is found; otherwise NULL is returned. If *c* is '\0', **rindex**( ) locates the terminating '\0'.

SEE ALSO

index(3), memchr(3), strchr(3), strcspn(3), strpbrk(3), strrchr(3), strsep(3), strspn(3), strstr(3), strtok(3)

HISTORY

A **rindex**( ) function appeared in Version 6 AT&T UNIX.

NAME

`rint` – round-to-closest integer functions

SYNOPSIS

`#include <math.h>`

double
`rint(`*double x*`);`

DESCRIPTION

The `rint()` function finds the integer (represented as a double precision number) nearest to x in the direction of the prevailing rounding mode.

NOTES

On a VAX, `rint(`x`)` is equivalent to adding half to the magnitude and then rounding towards zero.

In the default rounding mode, to nearest, on a machine that conforms to IEEE 754, `rint(`x`)` is the integer nearest x with the additional stipulation that if $|\text{rint}(x)-x|=1/2$ then `rint(`x`)` is even. Other rounding modes can make `rint()` act like `floor()`, or like `ceil()`, or round towards zero.

Another way to obtain an integer near x is to declare (in C)

```
double x;     int k;     k = x;
```

Most C compilers round x towards 0 to get the integer k, but some do otherwise. If in doubt, use `floor()`, `ceil()`, or `rint()` first, whichever you intend. Also note that, if x is larger than k can accommodate, the value of k and the presence or absence of an integer overflow are hard to predict.

SEE ALSO

`abs(3)`, `fabs(3)`, `ceil(3)`, `floor(3)`, `ieee(3)`, `math(3)`

HISTORY

A `rint()` function appeared in Version 6 AT&T UNIX.

3

NAME

setrunelocale, setinvalidrune, sgetrune, sputrune – rune support for C

SYNOPSIS

```
#include <rune.h>
#include <errno.h>
```

int
setrunelocale(*char *locale*);

void
setinvalidrune(*rune_t rune*);

rune_t
sgetrune(*const char *string, size_t n, char const **result*);

int
sputrune(*rune_t rune, char *string, size_t n, char **result*);

```
#include <stdio.h>
```

long
fgetrune(*FILE *stream*);

int
fungetrune(*rune_t rune, FILE *stream*);

int
fputrune(*rune_t rune, FILE *stream*);

DESCRIPTION

The **setrunelocale**() controls the type of encoding used to represent runes as multibyte strings as well as the properties of the runes as defined in **<ctype.h>**. The *locale* argument indicates which locale to load. If the locale is successfully loaded, 0 is returned, otherwise an errno value is returned to indicate the type of error.

The **setinvalidrune**() function sets the value of the global value _INVALID_RUNE to be *rune*.

The **sgetrune**() function tries to read a single multibyte character from *string*, which is at most *n* bytes long. If **sgetrune**() is successful, the rune is returned. If *result* is not NULL, *result* will point to the first byte which was not converted in *string*. If the first *n* bytes of *string* do not describe a full multibyte character, _INVALID_RUNE is returned and *result* will point to *string*. If there is an encoding error at the start of *string*, _INVALID_RUNE is returned and *result* will point to the second character of *string*.

the **sputrune**() function tries to encode *rune* as a multibyte string and store it at *string*, but no more than *n* bytes will be stored. If *result* is not NULL, *result* will be set to point to the first byte in string following the new multibyte character. If *string* is NULL, *result* will point to (char *)0 + *x*, where *x* is the number of bytes that would be needed to store the multibyte value. If the multibyte character would consist of more than *n* bytes and *result* is not NULL, *result* will be set to NULL. In all cases, **sputrune**() will return the number of bytes which would be needed to store *rune* as a multibyte character.

The **fgetrune**() function operates the same as **sgetrune**() with the exception that it attempts to read enough bytes from *stream* to decode a single rune. It returns either EOF on end of file, _INVALID_RUNE on an encoding error, or the rune decoded if all went well.

The **fungetrune**( ) function pushes the multibyte encoding, as provided by **sputrune**(), of *rune* onto *stream* such that the next **fgetrune**( ) call will return *rune*. It returns EOF if it fails and 0 on success.

The **fputrune**( ) function writes the multibyte encoding of *rune*, as provided by **sputrune**(), onto *stream*. It returns EOF on failure and 0 on success.

RETURN VALUES

The **setrunelocale**( ) function returns one of the following values:

0   *setrunelocale was successful.*

EFAULT   *locale* was NULL.

ENOENT   The locale could not be found.

EFTYPE   The file found was not a valid file.

EINVAL   The encoding indicated by the locale was unknown.

The **sgetrune**( ) function either returns the rune read or _INVALID_RUNE. The **sputrune**( ) function returns the number of bytes needed to store *rune* as a multibyte string.

FILES

$PATH_LOCALE/*locale*/LC_CTYPE
/usr/share/locale/*locale*/LC_CTYPE   binary LC_CTYPE file for the locale *locale*.

SEE ALSO

euc(4), mbrune(3), setlocale(3), utf2(4)

NOTE

The ANSI C type wchar_t is the same as rune_t. Rune_t was chosen to accent the purposeful choice of not basing the system with the ANSI C primitives, which were, shall we say, less aesthetic.

HISTORY

These functions first appeared in 4.4BSD.

The **setrunelocale**( ) function and the other non-ANSI rune functions were inspired by **Plan 9 from Bell Labs** as a much more sane alternative to the ANSI multibyte and wide character support.

All of the ANSI multibyte and wide character support functions are built using the rune functions.

3

NAME
scandir, alphasort – scan a directory

SYNOPSIS
```
#include <sys/types.h>
#include <dirent.h>

int
scandir(const char *dirname, struct dirent ***namelist,
        int (*select)(struct dirent *),
        int (*compar)(const void *, const void *));

int
alphasort(const void *d1, const void *d2);
```

DESCRIPTION
The `scandir()` function reads the directory *dirname* and builds an array of pointers to directory entries using malloc(3). It returns the number of entries in the array. A pointer to the array of directory entries is stored in the location referenced by *namelist*.

The *select* parameter is a pointer to a user supplied subroutine which is called by `scandir()` to select which entries are to be included in the array. The select routine is passed a pointer to a directory entry and should return a non-zero value if the directory entry is to be included in the array. If *select* is null, then all the directory entries will be included.

The *compar* parameter is a pointer to a user supplied subroutine which is passed to qsort(3) to sort the completed array. If this pointer is null, the array is not sorted.

The `alphasort()` function is a routine which can be used for the *compar* parameter to sort the array alphabetically.

The memory allocated for the array can be deallocated with free(3), by freeing each pointer in the array and then the array itself.

DIAGNOSTICS
Returns −1 if the directory cannot be opened for reading or if malloc(3) cannot allocate enough memory to hold all the data structures.

SEE ALSO
directory(3), malloc(3), qsort(3), dir(5)

HISTORY
The `scandir()` and `alphasort()` functions appeared in 4.2BSD.

NAME
scanf, fscanf, sscanf, vscanf, vsscanf, vfscanf – input format conversion

SYNOPSIS
```
#include <stdio.h>
```

int
scanf(*const char *format, ...*);

int
fscanf(*FILE *stream, const char *format, ...*);

int
sscanf(*const char *str, const char *format, ...*);

```
#include <stdarg.h>
```

int
vscanf(*const char *format, va_list ap*);

int
vsscanf(*const char *str, const char *format, va_list ap*);

int
vfscanf(*FILE *stream, const char *format, va_list ap*);

DESCRIPTION
The scanf() family of functions scans input according to a *format* as described below. This format may contain *conversion specifiers*; the results from such conversions, if any, are stored through the *pointer* arguments. The scanf() function reads input from the standard input stream *stdin*, fscanf() reads input from the stream pointer *stream*, and sscanf() reads its input from the character string pointed to by *str*. The vfscanf() function is analogous to vfprintf(3) and reads input from the stream pointer *stream* using a variable argument list of pointers (see stdarg(3)). The vscanf() function scans a variable argument list from the standard input and the vsscanf() function scans it from a string; these are analogous to the vprintf() and vsprintf() functions respectively. Each successive *pointer* argument must correspond properly with each successive conversion specifier (but see 'suppression' below). All conversions are introduced by the % (percent sign) character. The *format* string may also contain other characters. White space (such as blanks, tabs, or newlines) in the *format* string match any amount of white space, including none, in the input. Everything else matches only itself. Scanning stops when an input character does not match such a format character. Scanning also stops when an input conversion cannot be made (see below).

CONVERSIONS
Following the % character introducing a conversion there may be a number of *flag* characters, as follows:

* Suppresses assignment. The conversion that follows occurs as usual, but no pointer is used; the result of the conversion is simply discarded.

h Indicates that the conversion will be one of dioux or n and the next pointer is a pointer to a *short int* (rather than *int*).

l Indicates either that the conversion will be one of dioux or n and the next pointer is a pointer to a *long int* (rather than *int*), or that the conversion will be one of efg and the next pointer is a pointer to *double* (rather than *float*).

L Indicates that the conversion will be efg and the next pointer is a pointer to *long double*. (This type is not implemented; the L flag is currently ignored.)

In addition to these flags, there may be an optional maximum field width, expressed as a decimal integer, between the **%** and the conversion. If no width is given, a default of 'infinity' is used (with one exception, below); otherwise at most this many characters are scanned in processing the conversion. Before conversion begins, most conversions skip white space; this white space is not counted against the field width.

The following conversions are available:

%   Matches a literal '%'. That is, '%%' in the format string matches a single input '%' character. No conversion is done, and assignment does not occur.

d   Matches an optionally signed decimal integer; the next pointer must be a pointer to *int*.

D   Equivalent to **ld**; this exists only for backwards compatibility.

i   Matches an optionally signed integer; the next pointer must be a pointer to *int*. The integer is read in base 16 if it begins with '0x' or '0X', in base 8 if it begins with '0', and in base 10 otherwise. Only characters that correspond to the base are used.

o   Matches an octal integer; the next pointer must be a pointer to *unsigned int*.

O   Equivalent to **lo**; this exists for backwards compatibility.

u   Matches an optionally signed decimal integer; the next pointer must be a pointer to *unsigned int*.

x   Matches an optionally signed hexadecimal integer; the next pointer must be a pointer to *unsigned int*.

X   Equivalent to **lx**; this violates the ANSI C X3.159-1989 ("ANSI C"), but is backwards compatible with previous UNIX systems.

f   Matches an optionally signed floating-point number; the next pointer must be a pointer to *float*.

e   Equivalent to **f**.

g   Equivalent to **f**.

E   Equivalent to **lf**; this violates the ANSI C X3.159-1989 ("ANSI C"), but is backwards compatible with previous UNIX systems.

F   Equivalent to **lf**; this exists only for backwards compatibility.

s   Matches a sequence of non-white-space characters; the next pointer must be a pointer to *char*, and the array must be large enough to accept all the sequence and the terminating NUL character. The input string stops at white space or at the maximum field width, whichever occurs first.

c   Matches a sequence of *width* count characters (default 1); the next pointer must be a pointer to *char*, and there must be enough room for all the characters (no terminating NUL is added). The usual skip of leading white space is suppressed. To skip white space first, use an explicit space in the format.

[Matches a nonempty sequence of characters from the specified set of accepted characters; the next
        pointer must be a pointer to *char*, and there must be enough room for all the characters in the string,
        plus a terminating NUL character. The usual skip of leading white space is suppressed. The string is
        to be made up of characters in (or not in) a particular set; the set is defined by the characters between
        the open bracket [character and a close bracket] character. The set *excludes* those characters if the
        first character after the open bracket is a circumflex ^. To include a close bracket in the set, make it
        the first character after the open bracket or the circumflex; any other position will end the set. The
        hyphen character - is also special; when placed between two other characters, it adds all intervening
        characters to the set. To include a hyphen, make it the last character before the final close bracket.
        For instance, [^]0-9-] means the set 'everything except close bracket, zero through nine, and hy-
        phen'. The string ends with the appearance of a character not in the (or, with a circumflex, in) set or
        when the field width runs out.

p   Matches a pointer value (as printed by '%p' in printf(3)); the next pointer must be a pointer to
        void.

n   Nothing is expected; instead, the number of characters consumed thus far from the input is stored
        through the next pointer, which must be a pointer to *int*. This is *not* a conversion, although it can be
        suppressed with the * flag.

For backwards compatibility, other conversion characters (except '\0') are taken as if they were '%d' or, if
uppercase, %ld, and a 'conversion' of %\0 causes an immediate return of EOF. The F and X conversions
will be changed in the future to conform to the ANSI C standard, after which they will act like f and x
respectively.

RETURN VALUES
These functions return the number of input items assigned, which can be fewer than provided for, or even
zero, in the event of a matching failure. Zero indicates that, while there was input available, no conversions
were assigned; typically this is due to an invalid input character, such as an alphabetic character for a '%d'
conversion. The value EOF is returned if an input failure occurs before any conversion such as an end-of-
file occurs. If an error or end-of-file occurs after conversion has begun, the number of conversions which
were successfully completed is returned.

SEE ALSO
strtol(3), strtoul(3), strtod(3), getc(3), printf(3)

STANDARDS
The functions **fscanf**(), **scanf**(), and **sscanf**() conform to ANSI C X3.159-1989 (''ANSI C '').

HISTORY
The functions **vscanf**(), **vsscanf**() and **vfscanf**() are new to this release.

BUGS
The current situation with %F and %X conversions is unfortunate.

All of the backwards compatibility formats will be removed in the future.

Numerical strings are truncated to 512 characters; for example, %f and %d are implicitly %512f and
%512d.

NAME

setbuf, setbuffer, setlinebuf, setvbuf – stream buffering operations

SYNOPSIS

```
#include <stdio.h>

void
setbuf(FILE *stream, char *buf);

void
setbuffer(FILE *stream, char *buf, size_t size);

int
setlinebuf(FILE *stream);

int
setvbuf(FILE *stream, char *buf, int mode, size_t size);
```

DESCRIPTION

The three types of buffering available are unbuffered, block buffered, and line buffered. When an output stream is unbuffered, information appears on the destination file or terminal as soon as written; when it is block buffered many characters are saved up and written as a block; when it is line buffered characters are saved up until a newline is output or input is read from any stream attached to a terminal device (typically stdin). The function fflush(3) may be used to force the block out early. (See fclose(3).)

Normally all files are block buffered. When the first I/O operation occurs on a file, malloc(3) is called, and an optimally-sized buffer is obtained. If a stream refers to a terminal (as *stdout* normally does) it is line buffered. The standard error stream *stderr* is always unbuffered.

The **setvbuf**() function may be used to alter the buffering behavior of a stream. The *mode* parameter must be one of the following three macros:

> _IONBF unbuffered

> _IOLBF line buffered

> _IOFBF fully buffered

The *size* parameter may be given as zero to obtain deferred optimal-size buffer allocation as usual. If it is not zero, then except for unbuffered files, the *buf* argument should point to a buffer at least *size* bytes long; this buffer will be used instead of the current buffer. (If the *size* argument is not zero but *buf* is NULL, a buffer of the given size will be allocated immediately, and released on close. This is an extension to ANSI C; portable code should use a size of 0 with any NULL buffer.)

The **setvbuf**() function may be used at any time, but may have peculiar side effects (such as discarding input or flushing output) if the stream is "active". Portable applications should call it only once on any given stream, and before any I/O is performed.

The other three calls are, in effect, simply aliases for calls to **setvbuf**(). Except for the lack of a return value, the **setbuf**() function is exactly equivalent to the call

```
setvbuf(stream, buf, buf ? _IOFBF : _IONBF, BUFSIZ);
```

The **setbuffer**() function is the same, except that the size of the buffer is up to the caller, rather than being determined by the default BUFSIZ. The **setlinebuf**() function is exactly equivalent to the call:

```
setvbuf(stream, (char *)NULL, _IOLBF, 0);
```

RETURN VALUES

The `setvbuf()` function returns 0 on success, or EOF if the request cannot be honored (note that the stream is still functional in this case).

The `setlinebuf()` function returns what the equivalent `setvbuf()` would have returned.

SEE ALSO

fopen(3), fclose(3), fread(3), malloc(3), puts(3), printf(3)

STANDARDS

The `setbuf()` and `setvbuf()` functions conform to ANSI C X3.159-1989 (''ANSI C '').

BUGS

The `setbuffer()` and `setlinebuf()` functions are not portable to versions of BSD before 4.2BSD. On 4.2BSD and 4.3BSD systems, `setbuf()` always uses a suboptimal buffer size and should be avoided.

3

NAME

sigsetjmp, siglongjmp, setjmp, longjmp, _setjmp, _longjmp longjmperror – non-local jumps

SYNOPSIS

```
#include <setjmp.h>
```

int
sigsetjmp(*sigjmp_buf env, int savemask*);

void
siglongjmp(*sigjmp_buf env, int val*);

int
setjmp(*jmp_buf env*);

void
longjmp(*jmp_buf env, int val*);

int
_setjmp(*jmp_buf env*);

void
_longjmp(*jmp_buf env, int val*);

void
longjmperror(*void*);

DESCRIPTION

The **sigsetjmp**(), **setjmp**(), and **_setjmp**() functions save their calling environment in *env*. Each of these functions returns 0.

The corresponding **longjmp**() functions restore the environment saved by their most recent respective invocations of the **setjmp**() function. They then return so that program execution continues as if the corresponding invocation of the **setjmp**() call had just returned the value specified by *val*, instead of 0.

Pairs of calls may be intermixed, i.e. both **sigsetjmp**() and **siglongjmp**() and **setjmp**() and **longjmp**() combinations may be used in the same program, however, individual calls may not, e.g. the *env* argument to **setjmp**() may not be passed to **siglongjmp**().

The **longjmp**() routines may not be called after the routine which called the **setjmp**() routines returns.

All accessible objects have values as of the time **longjmp**() routine was called, except that the values of objects of automatic storage invocation duration that do not have the *volatile* type and have been changed between the **setjmp**() invocation and **longjmp**() call are indeterminate.

The **setjmp**()/**longjmp**() pairs save and restore the signal mask while **_setjmp**()/**_longjmp**() pairs save and restore only the register set and the stack. (See **sigmask**(*2*).)

The **sigsetjmp**()/**siglongjmp**() function pairs save and restore the signal mask if the argument *savemask* is non-zero, otherwise only the register set and the stack are saved.

ERRORS

If the contents of the *env* are corrupted, or correspond to an environment that has already returned, the `longjmp()` routine calls the routine `longjmperror(3)`. If `longjmperror()` returns the program is aborted (see abort(2)). The default version of `longjmperror()` prints the message ''longjmp botch'' to standard error and returns. User programs wishing to exit more gracefully should write their own versions of `longjmperror()`.

SEE ALSO

sigaction(2), sigaltstack(2), signal(3)

STANDARDS

The `setjmp()` and `longjmp()` functions conform to ANSI C X3.159-1989 (''ANSI C ''). The `sigsetjmp()` and `siglongjmp()` functions conform to IEEE Std1003.1-1988 (''POSIX'').

NAME

setlocale, localeconv – natural language formatting for C

SYNOPSIS

```
#include <locale.h>
```

char *
setlocale(*int category*, *const char *locale*);

struct lconv *
localeconv(*void*);

DESCRIPTION

The setlocale() function sets the C library's notion of natural language formatting style for particular sets of routines. Each such style is called a 'locale' and is invoked using an appropriate name passed as a C string. The localeconv() routine returns the current locale's parameters for formatting numbers.

The setlocale() function recognizes several categories of routines. These are the categories and the sets of routines they select:

LC_ALL   Set the entire locale generically.

LC_COLLATE   Set a locale for string collation routines. This controls alphabetic ordering in strcoll() and strxfrm().

LC_CTYPE   Set a locale for the ctype(3), mbrune(3), multibyte(3) and rune(3) functions. This controls recognition of upper and lower case, alphabetic or non-alphabetic characters, and so on. The real work is done by the setrunelocale() function.

LC_MONETARY Set a locale for formatting monetary values; this affects the localeconv() function.

LC_NUMERIC Set a locale for formatting numbers. This controls the formatting of decimal points in input and output of floating point numbers in functions such as printf() and scanf(), as well as values returned by localeconv().

LC_TIME   Set a locale for formatting dates and times using the strftime() function.

Only three locales are defined by default, the empty string " " which denotes the native environment, and the "C" and locales, which denote the C language environment. A *locale* argument of NULL causes setlocale() to return the current locale. By default, C programs start in the "C" locale. The only function in the library that sets the locale is setlocale(); the locale is never changed as a side effect of some other routine.

The localeconv() function returns a pointer to a structure which provides parameters for formatting numbers, especially currency values:

```
struct lconv {
        char    *decimal_point;
        char    *thousands_sep;
        char    *grouping;
        char    *int_curr_symbol;
        char    *currency_symbol;
        char    *mon_decimal_point;
        char    *mon_thousands_sep;
        char    *mon_grouping;
        char    *positive_sign;
        char    *negative_sign;
```

```
        char    int_frac_digits;
        char    frac_digits;
        char    p_cs_precedes;
        char    p_sep_by_space;
        char    n_cs_precedes;
        char    n_sep_by_space;
        char    p_sign_posn;
        char    n_sign_posn;
    };
```

The individual fields have the following meanings:

decimal_point   The decimal point character, except for currency values.

thousands_sep   The separator between groups of digits before the decimal point, except for currency values.

grouping   The sizes of the groups of digits, except for currency values. This is a pointer to a vector of integers, each of size *char*, representing group size from low order digit groups to high order (right to left). The list may be terminated with 0 or CHAR_MAX. If the list is terminated with 0, the last group size before the 0 is repeated to account for all the digits. If the list is terminated with CHAR_MAX, no more grouping is performed.

int_curr_symbol   The standardized international currency symbol.

currency_symbol   The local currency symbol.

mon_decimal_point   The decimal point character for currency values.

mon_thousands_sep   The separator for digit groups in currency values.

mon_grouping   Like *grouping* but for currency values.

positive_sign   The character used to denote nonnegative currency values, usually the empty string.

negative_sign   The character used to denote negative currency values, usually a minus sign.

int_frac_digits   The number of digits after the decimal point in an international-style currency value.

frac_digits   The number of digits after the decimal point in the local style for currency values.

p_cs_precedes   1 if the currency symbol precedes the currency value for nonnegative values, 0 if it follows.

p_sep_by_space   1 if a space is inserted between the currency symbol and the currency value for nonnegative values, 0 otherwise.

n_cs_precedes   Like *p_cs_precedes* but for negative values.

n_sep_by_space   Like *p_sep_by_space* but for negative values.

p_sign_posn   The location of the *positive_sign* with respect to a nonnegative quantity and the *currency_symbol*, coded as follows:
                      0   Parentheses around the entire string.
                      1   Before the string.

2   After the string.
3   Just before *currency_symbol*.
4   Just after *currency_symbol*.

n_sign_posn   Like *p_sign_posn* but for negative currency values.

Unless mentioned above, an empty string as a value for a field indicates a zero length result or a value that is not in the current locale. A CHAR_MAX result similarly denotes an unavailable value.

RETURN VALUES

The **setlocale**( ) function returns NULL and fails to change the locale if the given combination of *category* and *locale* makes no sense. The **localeconv**( ) function returns a pointer to a static object which may be altered by later calls to **setlocale**() or **localeconv**().

FILES

$PATH_LOCALE/*locale/category*
/usr/share/locale/*locale/category*   locale file for the locale *locale* and the category *category*.

SEE ALSO

euc(4), mbrune(3), multibyte(3), rune(3), strcoll(3), strxfrm(3), utf2(4)

STANDARDS

The **setlocale**( ) and **localeconv**( ) functions conform to ANSI C X3.159-1989 (''ANSI C '').

HISTORY

The **setlocale**( ) and **localeconv**( ) functions first appeared in 4.4BSD.

BUGS

The current implementation supports only the "C" and "POSIX" locales for all but the LC_CTYPE locale.

In spite of the gnarly currency support in **localeconv**(), the standards don't include any functions for generalized currency formatting.

LC_COLLATE does not make sense for many languages. Use of LC_MONETARY could lead to misleading results until we have a real time currency conversion function. LC_NUMERIC and LC_TIME are personal choices and should not be wrapped up with the other categories.

NAME
getmode, setmode – modify mode bits

SYNOPSIS
mode_t
getmode(*const void *set, mode_t mode*);

void
setmode(*const char *mode_str*);

DESCRIPTION
The **getmode**( ) function returns a copy of the file permission bits *mode* as altered by the values pointed to by *set*. While only the mode bits are altered, other parts of the file mode may be examined.

The **setmode**( ) function takes an absolute (octal) or symbolic value, as described in chmod(1), as an argument and returns a pointer to mode values to be supplied to **getmode**(). Because some of the symbolic values are relative to the file creation mask, **setmode**( ) may call umask(2). If this occurs, the file creation mask will be restored before **setmode**( ) returns. If the calling program changes the value of its file creation mask after calling **setmode**(), **setmode**( ) must be called again if **getmode**( ) is to modify future file modes correctly.

If the mode passed to **setmode**( ) is invalid, **setmode**( ) returns NULL.

ERRORS
The **setmode**( ) function may fail and set errno for any of the errors specified for the library routine malloc(3).

SEE ALSO
chmod(1), stat(2), umask(2), malloc(3)

HISTORY
The **getmode**( ) and **setmode**( ) functions first appeared in 4.4BSD.

NAME

setruid, setrgid – set user and group ID

SYNOPSIS

```
#include <sys/types.h>

int
setruid(uid_t ruid);

int
setrgid(gid_t rgid);
```

DESCRIPTION

The setruid() function (setrgid()) sets the real user ID (group ID) of the current process.

RETURN VALUES

Upon success, these functions return 0; otherwise −1 is returned.

If the user is not the super user, or the uid specified is not the real or effective ID, these functions return −1.

The use of these calls is not portable. Their use is discouraged; they will be removed in the future.

SEE ALSO

setuid(2), setgid(2), seteuid(2), setegid(2), getuid(2), getgid(2)

HISTORY

The setruid() and setrgid() syscalls appeared in 4.2BSD and were dropped in 4.4BSD.

NAME

    `siginterrupt` – allow signals to interrupt system calls

SYNOPSIS

    `#include <signal.h>`

    int
    `siginterrupt(`*int sig*`,` *int flag*`)`;

DESCRIPTION

    The `siginterrupt()` function is used to change the system call restart behavior when a system call is interrupted by the specified signal. If the flag is false (0), then system calls will be restarted if they are interrupted by the specified signal and no data has been transferred yet. System call restart is the default behavior on 4.2BSD.

    If the flag is true (1), then restarting of system calls is disabled. If a system call is interrupted by the specified signal and no data has been transferred, the system call will return −1 with the global variable *errno* set to `EINTR`. Interrupted system calls that have started transferring data will return the amount of data actually transferred. System call interrupt is the signal behavior found on 4.1BSD and AT&T System V UNIX systems.

    Note that the new 4.2BSD signal handling semantics are not altered in any other way. Most notably, signal handlers always remain installed until explicitly changed by a subsequent `sigaction`(2) call, and the signal mask operates as documented in `sigaction`(2). Programs may switch between restartable and interruptible system call operation as often as desired in the execution of a program.

    Issuing a `siginterrupt`(3) call during the execution of a signal handler will cause the new action to take place on the next signal to be caught.

NOTES

    This library routine uses an extension of the `sigaction`(2) system call that is not available in 4.2BSD, hence it should not be used if backward compatibility is needed.

RETURN VALUES

    A 0 value indicates that the call succeeded. A −1 value indicates that an invalid signal number has been supplied.

SEE ALSO

    `sigaction`(2), `sigblock`(2), `sigpause`(2), `sigsetmask`(2).

HISTORY

    The `siginterrupt()` function appeared in 4.3BSD.

NAME
signal – simplified software signal facilities

SYNOPSIS
```
#include <signal.h>
```
void
***signal**(*sig*, *func*());

void
(*func)()

DESCRIPTION
This **signal**() facility is a simplified interface to the more general sigaction(2) facility.

Signals allow the manipulation of a process from outside its domain as well as allowing the process to manipulate itself or copies of itself (children). There are two general types of signals: those that cause termination of a process and those that do not. Signals which cause termination of a program might result from an irrecoverable error or might be the result of a user at a terminal typing the 'interrupt' character. Signals are used when a process is stopped because it wishes to access its control terminal while in the background (see tty(4)). Signals are optionally generated when a process resumes after being stopped, when the status of child processes changes, or when input is ready at the control terminal. Most signals result in the termination of the process receiving them if no action is taken; some signals instead cause the process receiving them to be stopped, or are simply discarded if the process has not requested otherwise. Except for the SIGKILL and SIGSTOP signals, the **signal**() function allows for a signal to be caught, to be ignored, or to generate an interrupt. These signals are defined in the file <signal.h>:

Name	Default Action	Description
SIGHUP	terminate process	terminal line hangup
SIGINT	terminate process	interrupt program
SIGQUIT	create core image	quit program
SIGILL	create core image	illegal instruction
SIGTRAP	create core image	trace trap
SIGABRT	create core image	abort(2) call (formerly SIGIOT)
SIGEMT	create core image	emulate instruction executed
SIGFPE	create core image	floating-point exception
SIGKILL	terminate process	kill program
SIGBUS	create core image	bus error
SIGSEGV	create core image	segmentation violation
SIGSYS	create core image	system call given invalid argument
SIGPIPE	terminate process	write on a pipe with no reader
SIGALRM	terminate process	real-time timer expired
SIGTERM	terminate process	software termination signal
SIGURG	discard signal	urgent condition present on socket
SIGSTOP	stop process	stop (cannot be caught or ignored)
SIGTSTP	stop process	stop signal generated from keyboard
SIGCONT	discard signal	continue after stop
SIGCHLD	discard signal	child status has changed
SIGTTIN	stop process	background read attempted from control terminal
SIGTTOU	stop process	background write attempted to control terminal

SIGIO	discard signal	I/O is possible on a descriptor (see fcntl(2))
SIGXCPU	terminate process	cpu time limit exceeded (see setrlimit(2))
SIGXFSZ	terminate process	file size limit exceeded (see setrlimit(2))
SIGVTALRM	terminate process	virtual time alarm (see setitimer(2))
SIGPROF	terminate process	profiling timer alarm (see setitimer(2))
SIGWINCH	discard signal	Window size change
SIGINFO	discard signal	status request from keyboard
SIGUSR1	terminate process	User defined signal 1
SIGUSR2	terminate process	User defined signal 2

The *func* procedure allows a user to choose the action upon receipt of a signal. To set the default action of the signal to occur as listed above, *func* should be SIG_DFL. A SIG_DFL resets the default action. To ignore the signal *func* should be SIG_IGN. This will cause subsequent instances of the signal to be ignored and pending instances to be discarded. If SIG_IGN is not used, further occurrences of the signal are automatically blocked and *func* is called.

The handled signal is unblocked with the function returns and the process continues from where it left off when the signal occurred. **Unlike previous signal facilities, the handler func() remains installed after a signal has been delivered.**

For some system calls, if a signal is caught while the call is executing and the call is prematurely terminated, the call is automatically restarted. (The handler is installed using the SA_RESTART flag with sigaction(2).) The affected system calls include read(2), write(2), sendto(2), recvfrom(2), sendmsg(2) and recvmsg(2) on a communications channel or a low speed device and during a ioctl(2) or wait(2). However, calls that have already committed are not restarted, but instead return a partial success (for example, a short read count).

When a process which has installed signal handlers forks, the child process inherits the signals. All caught signals may be reset to their default action by a call to the execve(2) function; ignored signals remain ignored.

RETURN VALUES
The previous action is returned on a successful call. Otherwise, −1 is returned and the global variable *errno* is set to indicate the error.

ERRORS
Signal will fail and no action will take place if one of the following occur:

[EINVAL] *Sig* is not a valid signal number.

[EINVAL] An attempt is made to ignore or supply a handler for SIGKILL or SIGSTOP.

SEE ALSO
kill(1), ptrace(2), kill(2), sigaction(2), sigaltstack(2), sigprocmask(2), sigsuspend(2), setjmp(3), tty(4)

HISTORY
This signal facility appeared in 4.0BSD.

NAME

sigemptyset, sigfillset, sigaddset, sigdelset, sigismember – manipulate signal sets

SYNOPSIS

#include <signal.h>

sigemptyset(*sigset_t *set*);

sigfillset(*sigset_t *set*);

sigaddset(*sigset_t *set*, *int signo*);

sigdelset(*sigset_t *set*, *int signo*);

sigismember(*sigset_t *set*, *int signo*);

DESCRIPTION

These functions manipulate signal sets stored in a *sigset_t*. Either sigemptyset() or sigfillset() must be called for every object of type *sigset_t* before any other use of the object.

The sigemptyset() function initializes a signal set to be empty.

The sigfillset() function initializes a signal set to contain all signals.

The sigaddset() function adds the specified signal *signo* to the signal set.

The sigdelset() function deletes the specified signal *signo* from the signal set.

The sigismember() function returns whether a specified signal *signo* is contained in the signal set.

These functions are provided as macros in the include file <signal.h>. Actual functions are available if their names are undefined (with #undef *name*).

RETURN VALUES

The sigismember() function returns 1 if the signal is a member of the set, 0 otherwise. The other functions return 0.

ERRORS

Currently no errors are detected.

SEE ALSO

kill(2), sigaction(2), sigsuspend(2)

STANDARDS

These functions are defined by IEEE Std1003.1-1988 (''POSIX'').

3

NAME
sin – sine function

SYNOPSIS
```
#include <math.h>
```
double
sin(*double x*);

DESCRIPTION
The sin() function computes the sine of x (measured in radians). A large magnitude argument may yield a result with little or no significance.

RETURN VALUES
The sin() function returns the sine value.

SEE ALSO
acos(3), asin(3), atan(3), atan2(3), cos(3), cosh(3), sinh(3), tan(3), tanh(3), math(3),

STANDARDS
The sin() function conforms to ANSI C X3.159-1989 (''ANSI C '').

NAME

sinh – hyperbolic sine function

SYNOPSIS

```
#include <math.h>
```

double
sinh(*double x*);

DESCRIPTION

The sinh( ) function computes the hyperbolic sine of x.

RETURN VALUES

The sinh( ) function returns the hyperbolic sine value unless the magnitude of x is too large; in this event, the global variable *errno* is set to ERANGE.

SEE ALSO

acos(3), asin(3), atan(3), atan2(3), cos(3), cosh(3), sin(3), tan(3), tanh(3), math(3),

STANDARDS

The sinh( ) function conforms to ANSI C X3.159-1989 (''ANSI C '').

3

NAME

`sleep` – suspend process execution for interval of seconds

SYNOPSIS

`#include <unistd.h>`

u_int
`sleep(`*u_int seconds*`)`;

DESCRIPTION

The `sleep()` function suspends execution of the calling process for *seconds* of time. System activity or time spent in processing the call may lengthen the sleep by a second.

If a timer is already running on the process its state is saved. If the value *seconds* is more than or equal to the remaining clock time for the saved timer, the sleep time is set to the remaining clock time. The state of the previous timer is restored after *seconds* has passed.

This function is implemented using `setitimer(2)`; it requires eight system calls each time it is invoked. A similar but less compatible function can be obtained with a single `select(2)`; such a function would not restart after signals, but would not interfere with other uses of `setitimer`.

RETURN VALUES
SEE ALSO

`setitimer(2)`, `sigpause(2)`, `usleep(3)`

HISTORY

A `sleep()` function appeared in Version 7 AT&T UNIX.

NAME

cbrt, sqrt – cube root and square root functions

SYNOPSIS

`#include <math.h>`

double
cbrt(*double* x);

double
sqrt(*double* x);

DESCRIPTION

The cbrt( ) function computes the cube root of x.

The sqrt( ) computes the non-negative square root of x.

RETURN VALUES

The cbrt( ) function returns the requested cube root. The sqrt( ) function returns the requested square root unless an error occurs. On the VAX or Tahoe processor an attempt to take the sqrt( ) of negative x causes an error; in this event, the global variable *errno* is set to EDOM and a reserved operand fault is generated.

ERROR (due to Roundoff etc.)

The cbrt( ) function is accurate to within 0.7 *ulps*.

The sqrt( ) function on a VAX is accurate to within 0.501 *ulps*. Sqrt on a machine that conforms to IEEE 754 is correctly rounded in accordance with the rounding mode in force; the error is less than half an *ulp* in the default mode (round–to–nearest). An *ulp* is one *U*nit in the *L*ast *P*lace carried.

SEE ALSO

math(3), infnan(3)

STANDARDS

The sqrt function conforms to ANSI C X3.159-1989 (''ANSI C '').

HISTORY

The cbrt function appeared in 4.3BSD.

3

NAME
`stdarg` – variable argument lists

SYNOPSIS
`#include <stdarg.h>`

void
`va_start(`*va_list ap*`, `*last*`)`;

type
`va_arg(`*va_list ap*`, `*type*`)`;

void
`va_end(`*va_list ap*`)`;

DESCRIPTION
A function may be called with a varying number of arguments of varying types. The include file `<stdarg.h>` declares a type (*va_list*) and defines three macros for stepping through a list of arguments whose number and types are not known to the called function.

The called function must declare an object of type *va_list* which is used by the macros **va_start**(), **va_arg**(), and **va_end**().

The **va_start**() macro initializes *ap* for subsequent use by **va_arg**() and **va_end**(), and must be called first.

The parameter *last* is the name of the last parameter before the variable argument list, i.e. the last parameter of which the calling function knows the type.

Because the address of this parameter is used in the **va_start**() macro, it should not be declared as a register variable, or as a function or an array type.

The **va_start**() macro returns no value.

The **va_arg**() macro expands to an expression that has the type and value of the next argument in the call. The parameter *ap* is the *va_list ap* initialized by **va_start**(). Each call to **va_arg**() modifies *ap* so that the next call returns the next argument. The parameter *type* is a type name specified so that the type of a pointer to an object that has the specified type can be obtained simply by adding a * to *type*.

If there is no next argument, or if *type* is not compatible with the type of the actual next argument (as promoted according to the default argument promotions), random errors will occur.

The first use of the **va_arg**() macro after that of the **va_start**() macro returns the argument after *last*. Successive invocations return the values of the remaining arguments.

The **va_end**() macro handles a normal return from the function whose variable argument list was initialized by **va_start**().

The **va_end**() macro returns no value.

EXAMPLES
The function *foo* takes a string of format characters and prints out the argument associated with each format character based on the type.

```
void foo(char *fmt, ...)
{
        va_list ap;
        int d;
```

```
        char c, *p, *s;

        va_start(ap, fmt);
        while (*fmt)
               switch(*fmt++) {
               case 's':                              /* string */
                      s = va_arg(ap, char *);
                      printf("string %s\n", s);
                      break;
               case 'd':                              /* int */
                      d = va_arg(ap, int);
                      printf("int %d\n", d);
                      break;
               case 'c':                              /* char */
                      c = va_arg(ap, char);
                      printf("char %c\n", c);
                      break;
               }
        va_end(ap);
}
```

STANDARDS

The **va_start**(), **va_arg**(), and **va_end**( ) macros conform to ANSI C X3.159-1989 ("ANSI C ").

COMPATIBILITY

These macros are *not* compatible with the historic macros they replace. A backward compatible version can be found in the include file <varargs.h>.

BUGS

Unlike the *varargs* macros, the **stdarg** macros do not permit programmers to code a function with no fixed arguments. This problem generates work mainly when converting *varargs* code to **stdarg** code, but it also creates difficulties for variadic functions that wish to pass all of their arguments on to a function that takes a *va_list* argument, such as vfprintf(3).

NAME

    `stdio` – standard input/output library functions

SYNOPSIS

    `#include <stdio.h>`
    `FILE *stdin;`
    `FILE *stdout;`
    `FILE *stderr;`

DESCRIPTION

The standard I/O library provides a simple and efficient buffered stream I/O interface. Input and ouput is mapped into logical data streams and the physical I/O characteristics are concealed. The functions and macros are listed below; more information is available from the individual man pages.

A stream is associated with an external file (which may be a physical device) by *opening* a file, which may involve creating a new file. Creating an existing file causes its former contents to be discarded. If a file can support positioning requests (such as a disk file, as opposed to a terminal) then a *file position indicator* associated with the stream is positioned at the start of the file (byte zero), unless the file is opened with appended mode. If append mode is used, the position indicator will be placed the end-of-file. The position indicator is maintained by subsequent reads, writes and positioning requests. All input occurs as if the characters were read by successive calls to the `fgetc`(3) function; all ouput takes place as if all characters were read by successive calls to the `fputc`(3) function.

A file is disassociated from a stream by *closing* the file. Ouput streams are flushed (any unwritten buffer contents are transferred to the host environment) before the stream is disassociated from the file. The value of a pointer to a `FILE` object is indeterminate after a file is closed (garbage).

A file may be subsequently reopened, by the same or another program execution, and its contents reclaimed or modified (if it can be repositioned at the start). If the main function returns to its original caller, or the `exit`(3) function is called, all open files are closed (hence all output streams are flushed) before program termination. Other methods of program termination, such as `abort`(3) do not bother about closing files properly.

This implementation needs and makes no distinction between ''text'' and ''binary'' streams. In effect, all streams are binary. No translation is performed and no extra padding appears on any stream.

At program startup, three streams are predefined and need not be opened explicitly:

- *standard input* (for reading conventional input),
- *standard output* (for writing conventional input), and
- *standard error* (for writing diagnostic output).

These streams are abbreviated *stdin*, *stdout* and *stderr*. Initially, the standard error stream is unbuffered; the standard input and output streams are fully buffered if and only if the streams do not refer to an interactive or ''terminal'' device, as determined by the `isatty`(3) function. In fact, *all* freshly-opened streams that refer to terminal devices default to line buffering, and pending output to such streams is written automatically whenever an such an input stream is read. Note that this applies only to ''true reads''; if the read request can be satisfied by existing buffered data, no automatic flush will occur. In these cases, or when a large amount of computation is done after printing part of a line on an output terminal, it is necessary to `fflush`(3) the standard output before going off and computing so that the output will appear. Alternatively, these defaults may be modified via the `setvbuf`(3) function.

The `stdio` library is a part of the library `libc` and routines are automatically loaded as needed by the compilers `cc`(1) and `pc`(1). The SYNOPSIS sections of the following manual pages indicate which include files are to be used, what the compiler declaration for the function looks like and which external variables are of interest.

The following are defined as macros; these names may not be re-used without first removing their current definitions with #undef: BUFSIZ, EOF, FILENAME_MAX, L_cuserid, L_ctermid, L_tmpnam, NULL, SEEK_END, SEEK_SET, SEE_CUR, TMP_MAX, clearerr, feof, ferror, fileno, freopen, fwopen, getc, getchar, putc, putchar, stderr, stdin, stdout. Function versions of the macro functions feof, ferror, clearerr, fileno, getc, getchar, putc, and putchar exist and will be used if the macros definitions are explicitly removed.

SEE ALSO
open(2), close(2), read(2), write(2)

BUGS
The standard buffered functions do not interact well with certain other library and system functions, especially vfork and abort.

STANDARDS
The stdio library conforms to ANSI C X3.159-1989 (''ANSI C '').

LIST OF FUNCTIONS

Function	Description
clearerr	check and reset stream status
fclose	close a stream
fdopen	stream open functions
feof	check and reset stream status
ferror	check and reset stream status
fflush	flush a stream
fgetc	get next character or word from input stream
fgetline	get a line from a stream
fgetpos	reposition a stream
fgets	get a line from a stream
fileno	check and reset stream status
fopen	stream open functions
fprintf	formatted output conversion
fpurge	flush a stream
fputc	output a character or word to a stream
fputs	output a line to a stream
fread	binary stream input/output
freopen	stream open functions
fropen	open a stream
fscanf	input format conversion
fseek	reposition a stream
fsetpos	reposition a stream
ftell	reposition a stream
funopen	open a stream
fwopen	open a stream
fwrite	binary stream input/output
getc	get next character or word from input stream
getchar	get next character or word from input stream
gets	get a line from a stream
getw	get next character or word from input stream
mkstemp	create unique temporary file
mktemp	create unique temporary file
perror	system error messages

3

printf	formatted output conversion
putc	output a character or word to a stream
putchar	output a character or word to a stream
puts	output a line to a stream
putw	output a character or word to a stream
remove	remove directory entry
rewind	reposition a stream
scanf	input format conversion
setbuf	stream buffering operations
setbuffer	stream buffering operations
setlinebuf	stream buffering operations
setvbuf	stream buffering operations
snprintf	formatted output conversion
sprintf	formatted output conversion
sscanf	input format conversion
strerror	system error messages
sys_errlist	system error messages
sys_nerr	system error messages
tempnam	temporary file routines
tmpfile	temporary file routines
tmpnam	temporary file routines
ungetc	un-get character from input stream
vfprintf	formatted output conversion
vfscanf	input format conversion
vprintf	formatted output conversion
vscanf	input format conversion
vsnprintf	formatted output conversion
vsprintf	formatted output conversion
vsscanf	input format conversion

3

NAME
strcasecmp – compare strings, ignoring case

SYNOPSIS
```
#include <string.h>
```
int
strcasecmp(*const char *s1, const char *s2*);

int
strncasecmp(*const char *s1, const char *s2, size_t len*);

DESCRIPTION
The **strcasecmp**( ) and **strncasecmp**( ) functions compare the null-terminated strings *s1* and *s2* and return an integer greater than, equal to, or less than 0, according as *s1* is lexicographically greater than, equal to, or less than *s2* after translation of each corresponding character to lower-case. The strings themselves are not modified. The comparison is done using unsigned characters, so that '\200' is greater than '\0'.

The **strncasecmp**( ) compares at most *len* characters.

SEE ALSO
bcmp(3), memcmp(3), strcmp(3), strcoll(3), strxfrm(3)

HISTORY
The **strcasecmp**( ) and **strncasecmp**( ) functions first appeared in 4.4BSD.

3

NAME
strcat – concatenate strings

SYNOPSIS
`#include <string.h>`

`char *`
`strcat(char *s, const char *append);`

`char *`
`strncat(char *s, const char *append, size_t count);`

DESCRIPTION
The `strcat()` and `strncat()` functions append a copy of the null-terminated string *append* to the end of the null-terminated string *s*, then add a terminating '\0'. The string *s* must have sufficient space to hold the result.

The `strncat()` function appends not more than *count* characters.

RETURN VALUES
The `strcat()` and `strncat()` functions return the pointer *s*.

SEE ALSO
bcopy(3), memccpy(3), memcpy(3), memmove(3), strcpy(3)

STANDARDS
The `strcat()` and `strncat()` functions conform to ANSI C X3.159-1989 ("ANSI C").

NAME

strchr – locate character in string

SYNOPSIS

```
#include <string.h>
```

*char ***
strchr(*const char *s, int c*);

DESCRIPTION

The **strchr**() function locates the first occurrence of c in the string pointed to by s. The terminating NULL character is considered part of the string. If c is '\0', **strchr**() locates the terminating '\0'.

RETURN VALUES

The function **strchr**() returns a pointer to the located character, or NULL if the character does not appear in the string.

SEE ALSO

index(3), memchr(3), rindex(3), strcspn(3), strpbrk(3), strrchr(3), strsep(3), strspn(3), strstr(3), strtok(3)

STANDARDS

The **strchr**() function conforms to ANSI C X3.159-1989 (''ANSI C '').

NAME

strcmp – compare strings

SYNOPSIS

#include <string.h>

int
strcmp(const char *s1, const char *s2);

int
strncmp(const char *s1, const char *s2, size_t len);

DESCRIPTION

The strcmp() and strncmp() functions lexicographically compare the null-terminated strings s1 and s2.

RETURN VALUES

The strcmp() and strncmp() return an integer greater than, equal to, or less than 0, according as the string s1 is greater than, equal to, or less than the string s2. The comparison is done using unsigned characters, so that \200 is greater than '\0'.

The strncmp() compares not more than len characters.

SEE ALSO

bcmp(3), memcmp(3), strcasecmp(3), strcoll(3), strxfrm(3)

STANDARDS

The strcmp() and strncmp() functions conform to ANSI C X3.159-1989 ("ANSI C").

NAME

strcoll – compare strings according to current collation

SYNOPSIS

#include <string.h>

int
strcoll(*const char *s1, const char *s2*);

DESCRIPTION

The **strcoll**() function lexicographically compares the null-terminated strings *s1* and *s2* according to the current locale collation and returns an integer greater than, equal to, or less than 0, according as *s1* is greater than, equal to, or less than *s2*.

SEE ALSO

bcmp(3), memcmp(3), setlocale(3), strcasecmp(3), strcmp(3), strxfrm(3)

STANDARDS

The **strcoll**() function conforms to ANSI C X3.159-1989 (''ANSI C '').

3

NAME
strcpy – copy strings

SYNOPSIS
```
#include <string.h>
```

```
char *
strcpy(char *dst, const char *src);
```

```
char *
strncpy(char *dst, const char *src, size_t len);
```

DESCRIPTION
The strcpy() and strncpy() functions copy the string *src* to *dst* (including the terminating '\0' character).

The strncpy() copies not more than *len* characters into *dst*, appending '\0' characters if *src* is less than *len* characters long, and *not* terminating *dst* if *src* is more than *len* characters long.

RETURN VALUES
The strcpy() and strncpy() functions return *dst*.

EXAMPLES
The following sets "chararray" to "abc\0\0\0":

```
(void)strncpy(chararray, "abc", 6).
```

The following sets "chararray" to "abcdef":

```
(void)strncpy(chararray, "abcdefgh", 6);
```

SEE ALSO
bcopy(3), memccpy(3), memcpy(3), memmove(3)

STANDARDS
The strcpy() and strncpy() functions conform to ANSI C X3.159-1989 ("ANSI C ").

NAME

strcspn – span the complement of a string

SYNOPSIS

#include <string.h>

size_t
strcspn(*const char *s, const char *charset*);

DESCRIPTION

The **strcspn**() function spans the initial part of the null-terminated string *s* as long as the characters from *s* do not occur in string *charset* (it spans the *complement* of *charset*).

RETURN VALUES

The **strcspn**() function returns the number of characters spanned.

SEE ALSO

index(3), memchr(3), rindex(3), strchr(3), strpbrk(3), strrchr(3), strsep(3), strspn(3), strstr(3), strtok(3)

STANDARDS

The **strcspn**() function conforms to ANSI C X3.159-1989 ("ANSI C").

3

NAME
strdup – save a copy of a string

SYNOPSIS
`#include <string.h>`

`char *`
`strdup(const char *str);`

DESCRIPTION
The `strdup()` function allocates sufficient memory for a copy of the string *str*, does the copy, and returns a pointer to it. The pointer may subsequently be used as an argument to the function `free(3)`.

If insufficient memory is available, NULL is returned.

SEE ALSO
`malloc(3) free(3)`

HISTORY
The `strdup()` function first appeared in 4.4BSD.

3

NAME
perror, strerror, sys_errlist, sys_nerr – system error messages

SYNOPSIS
```
#include <stdio.h>

void
perror(const char *string);

extern char *sys_errlist[];
extern int sys_nerr;

#include <string.h>

char *
strerror(int errnum);
```

DESCRIPTION
The **strerror()** and **perror()** functions look up the error message string corresponding to an error number.

The **strerror()** function accepts an error number argument *errnum* and returns a pointer to the corresponding message string.

The **perror()** function finds the error message corresponding to the current value of the global variable *errno* (intro(2)) and writes it, followed by a newline, to the standard error file descriptor. If the argument *string* is non-NULL, it is prepended to the message string and separated from it by a colon and space (': '). If *string* is NULL, only the error message string is printed.

If *errnum* is not a recognized error number, the error message string will contain "Unknown error: " followed by the error number in decimal.

The message strings can be accessed directly using the external array *sys_errlist*. The external value *sys_nerr* contains a count of the messages in *sys_errlist*. The use of these variables is deprecated; **strerror()** should be used instead.

SEE ALSO
intro(2), psignal(3)

HISTORY
The **strerror()** and **perror()** functions first appeared in 4.4BSD.

BUGS
For unknown error numbers, the **strerror()** function will return its result in a static buffer which may be overwritten by subsequent calls.

NAME
strftime – format date and time

SYNOPSIS
```
#include <sys/types.h>
#include <time.h>
#include <string.h>

size_t
strftime(char *buf, size_t maxsize, const char *format,
        const struct tm *timeptr);
```

DESCRIPTION

The **strftime()** function formats the information from *timeptr* into the buffer *buf* according to the string pointed to by *format*.

The *format* string consists of zero or more conversion specifications and ordinary characters. All ordinary characters are copied directly into the buffer. A conversion specification consists of a percent sign ''"%"'' and one other character.

No more than *maxsize* characters will be placed into the array. If the total number of resulting characters, including the terminating null character, is not more than *maxsize*, **strftime()** returns the number of characters in the array, not counting the terminating null. Otherwise, zero is returned.

Each conversion specification is replaced by the characters as follows which are then copied into the buffer.

%A   is replaced by the full weekday name.

%a   is replaced by the abbreviated weekday name, where the abbreviation is the first three characters.

%B   is replaced by the full month name.

%b or %h
        is replaced by the abbreviated month name, where the abbreviation is the first three characters.

%C   is equivalent to ''%a %b %e %H:%M:%S %Y'' (the format produced by asctime(3).

%c   is equivalent to ''%m/%d/%y''.

%D   is replaced by the date in the format ''mm/dd/yy''.

%d   is replaced by the day of the month as a decimal number (01-31).

%e   is replaced by the day of month as a decimal number (1-31); single digits are preceded by a blank.

%H   is replaced by the hour (24-hour clock) as a decimal number (00-23).

%I   is replaced by the hour (12-hour clock) as a decimal number (01-12).

%j   is replaced by the day of the year as a decimal number (001-366).

%k   is replaced by the hour (24-hour clock) as a decimal number (0-23); single digits are preceded by a blank.

%l   is replaced by the hour (12-hour clock) as a decimal number (1-12); single digits are preceded by a blank.

%M   is replaced by the minute as a decimal number (00-59).

%m   is replaced by the month as a decimal number (01-12).

%n   is replaced by a newline.

%p   is replaced by either ''AM'' or ''PM'' as appropriate.

%R   is equivalent to ''`%H:%M`''

%r   is equivalent to ''`%I:%M:%S %p`''.

%t   is replaced by a tab.

%S   is replaced by the second as a decimal number (00-60).

%s   is replaced by the number of seconds since the Epoch, UCT (see mktime(3)).

%T or **%X**
    is equivalent to ''`%H:%M:%S`''.

%U   is replaced by the week number of the year (Sunday as the first day of the week) as a decimal number (00-53).

%W   is replaced by the week number of the year (Monday as the first day of the week) as a decimal number (00-53).

%w   is replaced by the weekday (Sunday as the first day of the week) as a decimal number (0-6).

%x   is equivalent to ''`%m/%d/%y %H:%M:%S`''.

%Y   is replaced by the year with century as a decimal number.

%y   is replaced by the year without century as a decimal number (00-99).

%Z   is replaced by the time zone name.

%%   is replaced by '%'.

SEE ALSO

date(1), ctime(3), printf(1), printf(3)

STANDARDS

The **strftime**() function conforms to ANSI C X3.159-1989 (''ANSI C ''). The '%s' conversion specification is an extension.

BUGS

There is no conversion specification for the phase of the moon.

NAME

strcat, strncat, strchr, strrchr, strcmp, strncmp, strcasecmp, strncasecmp, strcpy, strncpy, strerror, strlen, strpbrk, strsep, strspn, strcspn, strstr, strtok, index, rindex – string specific functions

SYNOPSIS

```
#include <string.h>
```

char *
strcat(*char *s, const char * append*);

char *
strncat(*char *s, const char *append, size_t count*);

char *
strchr(*const char *s, int c*);

char *
strrchr(*const char *s, int c*);

int
strcmp(*const char *s1, const char *s2*);

int
strncmp(*const char *s1, const char *s2, size_t count*);

int
strcasecmp(*const char *s1, const char *s2*);

int
strncasecmp(*const char *s1, const char *s2, size_t count*);

char *
strcpy(*char *dst, const char *src*);

char *
strncpy(*char *dst, const char *src, size_t count*);

char *
strerror(*int errno*);

size_t
strlen(*const char *s*);

char *
strpbrk(*const char *s, const char *charset*);

char *
strsep(*char **stringp, const char *delim*);

size_t
strspn(*const char *s, const char *charset*);

size_t
strcspn(*const char *s, const char *charset*);

char *
strstr(*const char *big, const char *little*);

```
char *
strtok(char *s, const char *delim);

char *
index(const char *s, int c);

char *
rindex(const char *s, int c);
```

DESCRIPTION

The string functions manipulate strings terminated by a null byte.

See the specific manual pages for more information. For manipulating variable length generic objects as byte strings (without the null byte check), see `bstring(3)`.

Except as noted in their specific manual pages, the string functions do not test the destination for size limitations.

SEE ALSO

index(3), strcat(3), strchr(3), strrchr(3), strcmp(3), strcasecmp(3), strcpy(3), strerror(3), strlen(3), strpbrk(3), strsep(3), strspn(3), strcspn(3), strstr(3), strtok(3), rindex(3) bstring(3)

STANDARDS

The **strcat()**, **strncat()**, **strchr()**, **strrchr()**, **strcmp()**, **strncmp()**, **strcpy()**, **strncpy()**, **strerror()**, **strlen()**, **strpbrk()**, **strsep()**, **strspn()**, **strcspn()**, **strstr()**, and strtok() functions conform to ANSI C X3.159-1989 (''ANSI C '').

NAME

strlen – find length of string

SYNOPSIS

```
#include <string.h>
```

size_t
strlen(*const char *s*);

DESCRIPTION

The **strlen**( ) function computes the length of the string *s*.

RETURN VALUES

The **strlen**( ) function returns the number of characters that precede the terminating NUL character.

SEE ALSO

string(3)

STANDARDS

The **strlen**( ) function conforms to ANSI C X3.159-1989 (''ANSI C '').

NAME
strmode – convert inode status information into a symbolic string

SYNOPSIS
```
#include <string.h>
```
void
strmode(*mode_t mode, char *bp*);

DESCRIPTION
The **strmode**( ) function converts a file *mode* (the type and permission information associated with an inode, see stat(2)) into a symbolic string which is stored in the location referenced by *bp*. This stored string is eleven characters in length plus a trailing NULL.

The first character is the inode type, and will be one of the following:

–	regular file
b	block special
c	character special
d	directory
l	symbolic link
p	fifo
s	socket
?	unknown inode type

The next nine characters encode three sets of permissions, in three characters each. The first three characters are the permissions for the owner of the file, the second three for the group the file belongs to, and the third for the "other", or default, set of users.

Permission checking is done as specifically as possible. If read permission is denied to the owner of a file in the first set of permissions, the owner of the file will not be able to read the file. This is true even if the owner is in the file's group and the group permissions allow reading or the "other" permissions allow reading.

If the first character of the three character set is an "r", the file is readable for that set of users; if a dash "–", it is not readable.

If the second character of the three character set is a "w", the file is writable for that set of users; if a dash "–", it is not writable.

The third character is the first of the following characters that apply:

S　　If the character is part of the owner permissions and the file is not executable or the directory is not searchable by the owner, and the set-user-id bit is set.

S　　If the character is part of the group permissions and the file is not executable or the directory is not searchable by the group, and the set-group-id bit is set.

T　　If the character is part of the other permissions and the file is not executable or the directory is not searchable by others, and the "sticky" (S_ISVTX) bit is set.

s　　If the character is part of the owner permissions and the file is executable or the directory searchable by the owner, and the set-user-id bit is set.

s　　If the character is part of the group permissions and the file is executable or the directory searchable by the group, and the set-group-id bit is set.

t   If the character is part of the other permissions and the file is executable or the directory searchable by others, and the "sticky" (S_ISVTX) bit is set.

x   The file is executable or the directory is searchable.

−   None of the above apply.

The last character is a plus sign "+" if any there are any alternate or additional access control methods associated with the inode, otherwise it will be a space.

RETURN VALUES

The strmode( ) function always returns 0.

SEE ALSO

chmod(1), find(1), stat(2), getmode(3), setmode(3)

HISTORY

The strmode( ) function first appeared in 4.4BSD.

NAME
strpbrk – locate multiple characters in string

SYNOPSIS
#include <string.h>

char *
strpbrk(const char *s, const char *charset);

DESCRIPTION
The strpbrk() function locates in the null-terminated string *s* the first occurrence of any character in the string *charset* and returns a pointer to this character. If no characters from *charset* occur anywhere in *s* strpbrk() returns NULL.

SEE ALSO
index(3), memchr(3), rindex(3), strchr(3), strcspn(3), strrchr(3), strsep(3), strspn(3), strstr(3), strtok(3)

STANDARDS
The strpbrk() function conforms to ANSI C X3.159-1989 (''ANSI C '').

NAME
strrchr – locate character in string

SYNOPSIS
`#include <string.h>`

`char *`
`strrchr(const char *s, int c);`

DESCRIPTION
The `strrchr()` function locates the last occurrence of c (converted to a char) in the string s. If c is '\0', `strrchr()` locates the terminating '\0'.

RETURN VALUES
The `strrchr()` function returns a pointer to the character, or a null pointer if c does not occur anywhere in s.

SEE ALSO
index(3), memchr(3), rindex(3), strchr(3), strcspn(3), strpbrk(3), strsep(3), strspn(3), strstr(3), strtok(3)

STANDARDS
The `strrchr()` function conforms to ANSI C X3.159-1989 (''ANSI C '').

NAME

strsep – separate strings

SYNOPSIS

```
#include <string.h>
```

char *
strsep(*char **stringp, char *delim*);

DESCRIPTION

The **strsep**( ) function locates, in the string referenced by *stringp, the first occurrence of any character in the string *delim* (or the terminating '\0' character) and replaces it with a '\0'. The location of the next character after the delimiter character (or NULL, if the end of the string was reached) is stored in *stringp. The original value of *stringp is returned.

An "empty" field, i.e. one caused by two adjacent delimiter characters, can be detected by comparing the location referenced by the pointer returned in *stringp to '\0'.

If *stringp is initially NULL, **strsep**( ) returns NULL.

EXAMPLES

The following uses **strsep**( ) to parse a string, containing tokens delimited by white space, into an argument vector:

```
char **ap, *argv[10], *inputstring;

for (ap = argv; (*ap = strsep(&inputstring, " \t")) != NULL;)
        if (**ap != '\0')
                ++ap;
```

HISTORY

The **strsep**( ) function is intended as a replacement for the **strtok**( ) function. While the **strtok**( ) function should be preferred for portability reasons (it conforms to ANSI C X3.159-1989 ("ANSI C ")) it is unable to handle empty fields, i.e. detect fields delimited by two adjacent delimiter characters, or to be used for more than a single string at a time. The **strsep**( ) function first appeared in 4.4BSD.

NAME

   strspn – span a string

SYNOPSIS

   `#include <string.h>`

   `size_t`
   `strspn(const char *s, const char *charset);`

DESCRIPTION

   The **strcspn()** function spans the initial part of the null-terminated string *s* as long as the characters from *s* occur in string *charset*.

RETURN VALUES

   The **strspn()** function returns the number of characters spanned.

SEE ALSO

   index(3), memchr(3), rindex(3), strchr(3), strcspn(3), strpbrk(3), strrchr(3),
   strsep(3), strstr(3), strtok(3)

STANDARDS

   The **strspn()** function conforms to ANSI C X3.159-1989 (''ANSI C '').

NAME
strstr – locate a substring in a string

SYNOPSIS
`#include <string.h>`

```
char *
strstr(const char *big, const char *little);
```

DESCRIPTION
The **strstr**() function locates the first occurrence of the null-terminated string *little* in the null-terminated string *big*. If *little* is the empty string, **strstr**() returns *big*; if *little* occurs nowhere in *big*, **strstr**() returns NULL; otherwise **strstr**() returns a pointer to the first character of the first occurrence of *little*.

SEE ALSO
index(3), memchr(3), rindex(3), strchr(3), strcspn(3), strpbrk(3), strrchr(3), strsep(3), strspn(3), strtok(3)

STANDARDS
The **strstr**() function conforms to ANSI C X3.159-1989 ("ANSI C ").

NAME

`strtod` – convert ASCII string to double

SYNOPSIS

`#include <stdlib.h>`

double
`strtod`(*const char *nptr, char **endptr*);

DESCRIPTION

The `strtod`() function converts the initial portion of the string pointed to by *nptr* to *double* representation.

The expected form of the string is an optional plus ("+") or minus sign ("–") followed by a sequence of digits optionally containing a decimal-point character, optionally followed by an exponent. An exponent consists of an "E" or "e", followed by an optional plus or minus sign, followed by a sequence of digits.

Leading white-space characters in the string (as defined by the `isspace`(3) function) are skipped.

RETURN VALUES

The `strtod`() function returns the converted value, if any.

If *endptr* is not NULL, a pointer to the character after the last character used in the conversion is stored in the location referenced by *endptr*.

If no conversion is performed, zero is returned and the value of *nptr* is stored in the location referenced by *endptr*.

If the correct value would cause overflow, plus or minus HUGE_VAL is returned (according to the sign of the value), and ERANGE is stored in *errno*. If the correct value would cause underflow, zero is returned and ERANGE is stored in *errno*.

ERRORS

[ERANGE] Overflow or underflow occurred.

SEE ALSO

`atof`(3), `atoi`(3), `atol`(3), `strtol`(3), `strtoul`(3)

STANDARDS

The `strtod`() function conforms to ANSI C X3.159-1989 (''ANSI C '').

AUTHORS

The author of this software is David M. Gay.

Copyright (c) 1991 by AT&T.

Permission to use, copy, modify, and distribute this software for any purpose without fee is hereby granted, provided that this entire notice is included in all copies of any software which is or includes a copy or modification of this software and in all copies of the supporting documentation for such software.

THIS SOFTWARE IS BEING PROVIDED "AS IS", WITHOUT ANY EXPRESS OR IMPLIED WARRANTY. IN PARTICULAR, NEITHER THE AUTHOR NOR AT&T MAKES ANY REPRESENTATION OR WARRANTY OF ANY KIND CONCERNING THE MERCHANTABILITY OF THIS SOFTWARE OR ITS FITNESS FOR ANY PARTICULAR PURPOSE.

Contact your vendor for a free copy of the source code to **strtod**() and accompanying functions.

NAME
　　　　strtok – string tokens

SYNOPSIS
　　　　#include <string.h>

　　　　char *
　　　　strtok(char *str, const char *sep);

DESCRIPTION
　　　　This interface is obsoleted by strsep(3).

　　　　The strtok() function is used to isolate sequential tokens in a null-terminated string, str. These tokens
　　　　are separated in the string by at least one of the characters in sep. The first time that strtok() is called,
　　　　str should be specified; subsequent calls, wishing to obtain further tokens from the same string, should pass
　　　　a null pointer instead. The separator string, sep, must be supplied each time, and may change between
　　　　calls.

　　　　The strtok() function returns a pointer to the beginning of each subsequent token in the string, after re-
　　　　placing the token itself with a NUL character. When no more tokens remain, a null pointer is returned.

SEE ALSO
　　　　index(3), memchr(3), rindex(3), strchr(3), strcspn(3), strpbrk(3), strrchr(3),
　　　　strsep(3), strspn(3), strstr(3)

STANDARDS
　　　　The strtok() function conforms to ANSI C X3.159-1989 (''ANSI C '').

BUGS
　　　　There is no way to get tokens from multiple strings simultaneously.

　　　　The System V strtok(), if handed a string containing only delimiter characters, will not alter the next
　　　　starting point, so that a call to strtok() with a different (or empty) delimiter string may return a non-NULL
　　　　value. Since this implementation always alters the next starting point, such a sequence of calls would always
　　　　return NULL.

NAME

strtol, strtoq – convert string value to a long or quad_t integer

SYNOPSIS

```
#include <stdlib.h>
#include <limits.h>
```

long
strtol(*char *nptr, char **endptr, int base*);

```
#include <sys/types.h>
#include <stdlib.h>
#include <limits.h>
```

quad_t
strtoq(*char *nptr, char **endptr, int base*);

DESCRIPTION

The **strtol**() function converts the string in *nptr* to a *long* value. The **strtoq**() function converts the string in *nptr* to a *quad_t* value. The conversion is done according to the given *base*, which must be between 2 and 36 inclusive, or be the special value 0.

The string may begin with an arbitrary amount of white space (as determined by isspace(3)) followed by a single optional '+' or '-' sign. If *base* is zero or 16, the string may then include a '0x' prefix, and the number will be read in base 16; otherwise, a zero *base* is taken as 10 (decimal) unless the next character is '0', in which case it is taken as 8 (octal).

The remainder of the string is converted to a *long* value in the obvious manner, stopping at the first character which is not a valid digit in the given base. (In bases above 10, the letter 'A' in either upper or lower case represents 10, 'B' represents 11, and so forth, with 'Z' representing 35.)

If *endptr* is non nil, **strtol**() stores the address of the first invalid character in *endptr*. If there were no digits at all, however, **strtol**() stores the original value of *nptr* in *endptr*. (Thus, if *nptr* is not '\0' but **endptr* is '\0' on return, the entire string was valid.)

RETURN VALUES

The **strtol**() function returns the result of the conversion, unless the value would underflow or overflow. If an underflow occurs, **strtol**() returns LONG_MIN. If an overflow occurs, **strtol**() returns LONG_MAX. In both cases, *errno* is set to ERANGE.

ERRORS

[ERANGE]   The given string was out of range; the value converted has been clamped.

SEE ALSO

atof(3), atoi(3), atol(3), strtod(3), strtoul(3)

STANDARDS

The **strtol**() function conforms to ANSI C X3.159-1989 ("ANSI C").

BUGS

Ignores the current locale.

3

NAME

strtoul, strtouq – convert a string to an unsigned long or uquad_t

SYNOPSIS

```
#include <stdlib.h>
#include <limits.h>
```

unsigned long
strtoul(*const char *nptr, char **endptr, int base*);

```
#include <sys/types.h>
#include <stdlib.h>
#include <limits.h>
```

u_quad_t
strtouq(*const char *nptr, char **endptr, int base*);

DESCRIPTION

The **strtoul( )** function converts the string in *nptr* to an *unsigned long* value. The **strtouq( )** function converts the string in *nptr* to a *u_quad_t* value. The conversion is done according to the given *base*, which must be between 2 and 36 inclusive, or be the special value 0.

The string may begin with an arbitrary amount of white space (as determined by isspace(3)) followed by a single optional '+' or '-' sign. If *base* is zero or 16, the string may then include a '0x' prefix, and the number will be read in base 16; otherwise, a zero *base* is taken as 10 (decimal) unless the next character is '0', in which case it is taken as 8 (octal).

The remainder of the string is converted to an *unsigned long* value in the obvious manner, stopping at the end of the string or at the first character that does not produce a valid digit in the given base. (In bases above 10, the letter 'A' in either upper or lower case represents 10, 'B' represents 11, and so forth, with 'Z' representing 35.)

If *endptr* is non nil, **strtoul( )** stores the address of the first invalid character in *endptr*. If there were no digits at all, however, **strtoul( )** stores the original value of *nptr* in *endptr*. (Thus, if *nptr* is not '\0' but **endptr* is '\0' on return, the entire string was valid.)

RETURN VALUES

The **strtoul( )** function returns either the result of the conversion or, if there was a leading minus sign, the negation of the result of the conversion, unless the original (non-negated) value would overflow; in the latter case, **strtoul( )** returns ULONG_MAX and sets the global variable *errno* to ERANGE.

ERRORS

[ERANGE]   The given string was out of range; the value converted has been clamped.

SEE ALSO

strtol(3)

STANDARDS

The **strtoul( )** function conforms to ANSI C X3.159-1989 ("ANSI C ").

BUGS

    Ignores the current locale.

NAME

strxfrm – transform a string under locale

SYNOPSIS

#include ⟨string.h⟩

size_t
strxfrm(*char *dst, const char *src, size_t n*);

DESCRIPTION

The strxfrm( ) function does something horrible (see ANSI standard). In this implementation it just copies.

SEE ALSO

bcmp(3), memcmp(3), strcasecmp(3), strcmp(3), strcoll(3)

STANDARDS

The strxfrm( ) function conforms to ANSI C X3.159-1989 (''ANSI C '').

NAME
stty, gtty – set and get terminal state (defunct)

SYNOPSIS
#include <sgtty.h>

stty(int fd, struct sgttyb *buf);

gtty(int fd, struct sgttyb *buf);

DESCRIPTION
These interfaces are obsoleted by ioctl(2). They are available from the compatibility library, libcompat.

The **stty**() function sets the state of the terminal associated with fd. The **gtty**() function retrieves the state of the terminal associated with fd. To set the state of a terminal the call must have write permission.

The **stty**() call is actually ioctl(fd, TIOCSETP, buf), while the **gtty**() call is ioctl(fd, TIOCGETP, buf). See ioctl(2) and tty(4) for an explanation.

DIAGNOSTICS
If the call is successful 0 is returned, otherwise –1 is returned and the global variable *errno* contains the reason for the failure.

SEE ALSO
ioctl(2), tty(4)

HISTORY
The **stty**() and **gtty**() functions appeared in 4.2BSD.

3

NAME

swab – swap adjacent bytes

SYNOPSIS

```
#include <string.h>
```

void
swab(*const void *src*, *void *dst*, *size_t len*);

DESCRIPTION

The function **swab**( ) copies *len* bytes from the location referenced by *src* to the location referenced by *dst*, swapping adjacent bytes.

The argument *len* must be even number.

SEE ALSO

bzero(3), memset(3)

HISTORY

A **swab**( ) function appeared in Version 7 AT&T UNIX.

NAME

sysconf – get configurable system variables

SYNOPSIS

#include <unistd.h>

long
sysconf(*int name*);

DESCRIPTION

This interface is defined by IEEE Std1003.1-1988 ("POSIX"). A far more complete interface is available using sysctl(3).

The **sysconf**() function provides a method for applications to determine the current value of a configurable system limit or option variable. The *name* argument specifies the system variable to be queried. Symbolic constants for each name value are found in the include file <unistd.h>.

The available values are as follows:

_SC_ARG_MAX
> The maximum bytes of argument to exec(2).

_SC_CHILD_MAX
> The maximum number of simultaneous processes per user id.

_SC_CLK_TCK
> Number of micro-seconds per hz tick.

_SC_NGROUPS_MAX
> The maximum number of supplemental groups.

_SC_OPEN_MAX
> The maximum number of open files per user id.

_SC_STREAM_MAX
> The minimum maximum number of streams that a process may have open at any one time.

_SC_TZNAME_MAX
> The minimum maximum number of types supported for the name of a timezone.

_SC_JOB_CONTROL
> Return 1 if job control is available on this system, otherwise –1.

_SC_SAVED_IDS
> Returns 1 if saved set-group and saved set-user ID is available, otherwise –1.

_SC_VERSION
> The version of ISO/IEC 9945 (POSIX 1003.1) with which the system attempts to comply.

_SC_BC_BASE_MAX
> The maximum ibase/obase values in the bc(1) utility.

_SC_BC_DIM_MAX
> The maximum array size in the bc(1) utility.

3

_SC_BC_SCALE_MAX
> The maximum scale value in the bc(1) utility.

_SC_BC_STRING_MAX
> The maximum string length in the bc(1) utility.

_SC_COLL_WEIGHTS_MAX
> The maximum number of weights that can be assigned to any entry of the LC_COLLATE order keyword in the locale definition file.

_SC_EXPR_NEST_MAX
> The maximum number of expressions that can be nested within parenthesis by the expr(1) utility.

_SC_LINE_MAX
> The maximum length in bytes of a text-processing utility's input line.

_SC_RE_DUP_MAX
> The maximum number of repeated occurrences of a regular expression permitted when using interval notation.

_SC_2_VERSION
> The version of POSIX 1003.2 with which the system attempts to comply.

_SC_2_C_BIND
> Return 1 if the system's C-language development facilities support the C-Language Bindings Option, otherwise −1.

_SC_2_C_DEV
> Return 1 if the system supports the C-Language Development Utilities Option, otherwise −1.

_SC_2_CHAR_TERM
> Return 1 if the system supports at least one terminal type capable of all operations described in POSIX 1003.2, otherwise −1.

_SC_2_FORT_DEV
> Return 1 if the system supports the FORTRAN Development Utilities Option, otherwise −1.

_SC_2_FORT_RUN
> Return 1 if the system supports the FORTRAN Runtime Utilities Option, otherwise −1.

_SC_2_LOCALEDEF
> Return 1 if the system supports the creation of locales, otherwise −1.

_SC_2_SW_DEV
> Return 1 if the system supports the Software Development Utilities Option, otherwise −1.

_SC_2_UPE
> Return 1 if the system supports the User Portability Utilities Option, otherwise −1.

RETURN VALUES

If the call to sysconf is not successful, −1 is returned and *errno* is set appropriately. Otherwise, if the variable is associated with functionality that is not supported, −1 is returned and *errno* is not modified. Otherwise, the current variable value is returned.

ERRORS

The **sysconf**() function may fail and set *errno* for any of the errors specified for the library functions sysctl(3). In addition, the following error may be reported:

[EINVAL]   The value of the *name* argument is invalid.

SEE ALSO

sysctl(3)

BUGS

The value for _SC_STREAM_MAX is a minimum maximum, and required to be the same as ANSI C's FOPEN_MAX, so the returned value is a ridiculously small and misleading number.

STANDARDS

The **sysconf**() function conforms to IEEE Std1003.1-1988 ("POSIX").

HISTORY

The **sysconf** function first appeared in 4.4BSD.

NAME

`sysctl` – get or set system information

SYNOPSIS

```
#include <sys/sysctl.h>
```

```
int
sysctl(int *name, u_int namelen, void *oldp, size_t *oldlenp, void *newp,
     size_t newlen);
```

DESCRIPTION

The `sysctl` function retrieves system information and allows processes with appropriate privileges to set system information. The information available from `sysctl` consists of integers, strings, and tables. Information may be retrieved and set from the command interface using the `sysctl`(1) utility.

Unless explicitly noted below, `sysctl` returns a consistent snapshot of the data requested. Consistency is obtained by locking the destination buffer into memory so that the data may be copied out without blocking. Calls to `sysctl` are serialized to avoid deadlock.

The state is described using a ''Management Information Base'' (MIB) style name, listed in *name*, which is a *namelen* length array of integers.

The information is copied into the buffer specified by *oldp*. The size of the buffer is given by the location specified by *oldlenp* before the call, and that location gives the amount of data copied after a successful call. If the amount of data available is greater than the size of the buffer supplied, the call supplies as much data as fits in the buffer provided and returns with the error code ENOMEM. If the old value is not desired, *oldp* and *oldlenp* should be set to NULL.

The size of the available data can be determined by calling `sysctl` with a NULL parameter for *oldp*. The size of the available data will be returned in the location pointed to by *oldlenp*. For some operations, the amount of space may change often. For these operations, the system attempts to round up so that the returned size is large enough for a call to return the data shortly thereafter.

To set a new value, *newp* is set to point to a buffer of length *newlen* from which the requested value is to be taken. If a new value is not to be set, *newp* should be set to NULL and *newlen* set to 0.

The top level names are defined with a CTL_ prefix in <sys/sysctl.h>, and are as follows. The next and subsequent levels down are found in the include files listed here, and described in separate sections below.

Name	Next level names	Description
CTL_DEBUG	sys/sysctl.h	Debugging
CTL_FS	sys/sysctl.h	File system
CTL_HW	sys/sysctl.h	Generic CPU, I/O
CTL_KERN	sys/sysctl.h	High kernel limits
CTL_MACHDEP	sys/sysctl.h	Machine dependent
CTL_NET	sys/socket.h	Networking
CTL_USER	sys/sysctl.h	User-level
CTL_VM	vm/vm_param.h	Virtual memory

For example, the following retrieves the maximum number of processes allowed in the system:

```
int mib[2], maxproc;
size_t len;

mib[0] = CTL_KERN;
```

```
        mib[1] = KERN_MAXPROC;
        len = sizeof(maxproc);
        sysctl(mib, 2, &maxproc, &len, NULL, 0);
```

To retrieve the standard search path for the system utilities:

```
        int mib[2];
        size_t len;
        char *p;

        mib[0] = CTL_USER;
        mib[1] = USER_CS_PATH;
        sysctl(mib, 2, NULL, &len, NULL, 0);
        p = malloc(len);
        sysctl(mib, 2, p, &len, NULL, 0);
```

CTL_DEBUG

The debugging variables vary from system to system. A debugging variable may be added or deleted without need to recompile **sysctl** to know about it. Each time it runs, **sysctl** gets the list of debugging variables from the kernel and displays their current values. The system defines twenty (*struct ctldebug*) variables named **debug0** through **debug19**. They are declared as separate variables so that they can be individually initialized at the location of their associated variable. The loader prevents multiple use of the same variable by issuing errors if a variable is initialized in more than one place. For example, to export the variable **dospecialcheck** as a debugging variable, the following declaration would be used:

```
        int dospecialcheck = 1;
        struct ctldebug debug5 = { "dospecialcheck", &dospecialcheck };
```

CTL_FS

There are currently no second level names for the file system.

CTL_HW

The string and integer information available for the CTL_HW level is detailed below. The changeable column shows whether a process with appropriate privilege may change the value.

Second level name	Type	Changeable
HW_MACHINE	string	no
HW_MODEL	string	no
HW_NCPU	integer	no
HW_BYTEORDER	integer	no
HW_PHYSMEM	integer	no
HW_USERMEM	integer	no
HW_PAGESIZE	integer	no

HW_MACHINE
        The machine class.

HW_MODEL
        The machine model

HW_NCPU
        The number of cpus.

HW_BYTEORDER
:   The byteorder (4,321, or 1,234).

HW_PHYSMEM
:   The bytes of physical memory.

HW_USERMEM
:   The bytes of non-kernel memory.

HW_PAGESIZE
:   The software page size.

CTL_KERN

The string and integer information available for the CTL_KERN level is detailed below. The changeable column shows whether a process with appropriate privilege may change the value. The types of data currently available are process information, system vnodes, the open file entries, routing table entries, virtual memory statistics, load average history, and clock rate information.

Second level name	Type	Changeable
KERN_ARGMAX	integer	no
KERN_BOOTTIME	struct timeval	no
KERN_CHOWN_RESTRICTED	integer	no
KERN_CLOCKRATE	struct clockinfo	no
KERN_FILE	struct file	no
KERN_HOSTID	integer	yes
KERN_HOSTNAME	string	yes
KERN_JOB_CONTROL	integer	no
KERN_LINK_MAX	integer	no
KERN_MAXFILES	integer	yes
KERN_MAXPROC	integer	yes
KERN_MAXVNODES	integer	yes
KERN_MAX_CANON	integer	no
KERN_MAX_INPUT	integer	no
KERN_NAME_MAX	integer	no
KERN_NGROUPS	integer	no
KERN_NO_TRUNC	integer	no
KERN_OSRELEASE	string	no
KERN_OSREV	integer	no
KERN_OSTYPE	string	no
KERN_PATH_MAX	integer	no
KERN_PIPE_BUF	integer	no
KERN_POSIX1	integer	no
KERN_PROC	struct proc	no
KERN_PROF	node	not applicable
KERN_SAVED_IDS	integer	no
KERN_SECURELVL	integer	raise only
KERN_VDISABLE	integer	no
KERN_VERSION	string	no
KERN_VNODE	struct vnode	no

KERN_ARGMAX
> The maximum bytes of argument to exec(2).

KERN_BOOTTIME
> A *struct timeval* structure is returned. This structure contains the time that the system was booted.

KERN_CHOWN_RESTRICTED
> Return 1 if appropriate privileges are required for the chown(2) system call, otherwise 0.

KERN_CLOCKRATE
> A *struct clockinfo* structure is returned. This structure contains the clock, statistics clock and profiling clock frequencies, and the number of micro-seconds per hz tick.

KERN_FILE
> Return the entire file table. The returned data consists of a single *struct filehead* followed by an array of *struct file*, whose size depends on the current number of such objects in the system.

KERN_HOSTID
> Get or set the host id.

KERN_HOSTNAME
> Get or set the hostname.

KERN_JOB_CONTROL
> Return 1 if job control is available on this system, otherwise 0.

KERN_LINK_MAX
> The maximum file link count.

KERN_MAXFILES
> The maximum number of open files that may be open in the system.

KERN_MAXPROC
> The maximum number of simultaneous processes the system will allow.

KERN_MAXVNODES
> The maximum number of vnodes available on the system.

KERN_MAX_CANON
> The maximum number of bytes in terminal canonical input line.

KERN_MAX_INPUT
> The minimum maximum number of bytes for which space is available in a terminal input queue.

KERN_NAME_MAX
> The maximum number of bytes in a file name.

KERN_NGROUPS
> The maximum number of supplemental groups.

KERN_NO_TRUNC
> Return 1 if file names longer than KERN_NAME_MAX are truncated.

KERN_OSRELEASE
> The system release string.

KERN_OSREV
> The system revision string.

KERN_OSTYPE
>   The system type string.

KERN_PATH_MAX
>   The maximum number of bytes in a pathname.

KERN_PIPE_BUF
>   The maximum number of bytes which will be written atomically to a pipe.

KERN_POSIX1
>   The version of ISO/IEC 9945 (POSIX 1003.1) with which the system attempts to comply.

KERN_PROC
>   Return the entire process table, or a subset of it. An array of *struct kinfo_proc* structures is returned, whose size depends on the current number of such objects in the system. The third and fourth level names are as follows:

Third level name	Fourth level is:
KERN_PROC_ALL	None
KERN_PROC_PID	A process ID
KERN_PROC_PGRP	A process group
KERN_PROC_TTY	A tty device
KERN_PROC_UID	A user ID
KERN_PROC_RUID	A real user ID

KERN_PROF
>   Return profiling information about the kernel. If the kernel is not compiled for profiling, attempts to retrieve any of the KERN_PROF values will fail with EOPNOTSUPP. The third level names for the string and integer profiling information is detailed below. The changeable column shows whether a process with appropriate privilege may change the value.

Third level name	Type	Changeable
GPROF_STATE	integer	yes
GPROF_COUNT	u_short[ ]	yes
GPROF_FROMS	u_short[ ]	yes
GPROF_TOS	struct tostruct	yes
GPROF_GMONPARAM	struct gmonparam	no

The variables are as follows:

GPROF_STATE
>   Returns GMON_PROF_ON or GMON_PROF_OFF to show that profiling is running or stopped.

GPROF_COUNT
>   Array of statistical program counter counts.

GPROF_FROMS
>   Array indexed by program counter of call-from points.

GPROF_TOS
>   Array of *struct tostruct* describing destination of calls and their counts.

GPROF_GMONPARAM
>   Structure giving the sizes of the above arrays.

KERN_SAVED_IDS
>   Returns 1 if saved set-group and saved set-user ID is available.

KERN_SECURELVL
>   The system security level. This level may be raised by processes with appropriate privilege. It may only be lowered by process 1.

KERN_VDISABLE
>   Returns the terminal character disabling value.

KERN_VERSION
>   The system version string.

KERN_VNODE
>   Return the entire vnode table. Note, the vnode table is not necessarily a consistent snapshot of the system. The returned data consists of an array whose size depends on the current number of such objects in the system. Each element of the array contains the kernel address of a vnode *struct vnode** followed by the vnode itself *struct vnode*.

CTL_MACHDEP

The set of variables defined is architecture dependent. Most architectures define at least the following variables.

Second level name	Type	Changeable
CPU_CONSDEV	dev_t	no

CTL_NET

The string and integer information available for the CTL_NET level is detailed below. The changeable column shows whether a process with appropriate privilege may change the value.

Second level name	Type	Changeable
PF_ROUTE	routing messages	no
PF_INET	internet values	yes

PF_ROUTE
>   Return the entire routing table or a subset of it. The data is returned as a sequence of routing messages (see route(4) for the header file, format and meaning). The length of each message is contained in the message header.
>
>   The third level name is a protocol number, which is currently always 0. The fourth level name is an address family, which may be set to 0 to select all address families. The fifth and sixth level names are as follows:

Fifth level name	Sixth level is:
NET_RT_FLAGS	rtflags
NET_RT_DUMP	None
NET_RT_IFLIST	None

PF_INET
>   Get or set various global information about the internet protocols. The third level name is the protocol. The fourth level name is the variable name. The currently defined protocols and names are:

Protocol name	Variable name	Type	Changeable
ip	forwarding	integer	yes
ip	redirect	integer	yes
ip	ttl	integer	yes
icmp	maskrepl	integer	yes
udp	checksum	integer	yes

The variables are as follows:

ip.forwarding
> Returns 1 when IP forwarding is enabled for the host, meaning that the host is acting as a router.

ip.redirect
> Returns 1 when ICMP redirects may be sent by the host. This option is ignored unless the host is routing IP packets, and should normally be enabled on all systems.

ip.ttl The maximum time-to-live (hop count) value for an IP packet sourced by the system. This value applies to normal transport protocols, not to ICMP.

icmp.maskrepl
> Returns 1 if ICMP network mask requests are to be answered.

udp.checksum
> Returns 1 when UDP checksums are being computed and checked. Disabling UDP checksums is strongly discouraged.

CTL_USER

The string and integer information available for the CTL_USER level is detailed below. The changeable column shows whether a process with appropriate privilege may change the value.

Second level name	Type	Changeable
USER_BC_BASE_MAX	integer	no
USER_BC_DIM_MAX	integer	no
USER_BC_SCALE_MAX	integer	no
USER_BC_STRING_MAX	integer	no
USER_COLL_WEIGHTS_MAX	integer	no
USER_CS_PATH	string	no
USER_EXPR_NEST_MAX	integer	no
USER_LINE_MAX	integer	no
USER_POSIX2_CHAR_TERM	integer	no
USER_POSIX2_C_BIND	integer	no
USER_POSIX2_C_DEV	integer	no
USER_POSIX2_FORT_DEV	integer	no
USER_POSIX2_FORT_RUN	integer	no
USER_POSIX2_LOCALEDEF	integer	no
USER_POSIX2_SW_DEV	integer	no
USER_POSIX2_UPE	integer	no
USER_POSIX2_VERSION	integer	no
USER_RE_DUP_MAX	integer	no
USER_STREAM_MAX	integer	no
USER_TZNAME_MAX	integer	no

USER_BC_BASE_MAX
> The maximum ibase/obase values in the bc(1) utility.

USER_BC_DIM_MAX
> The maximum array size in the bc(1) utility.

USER_BC_SCALE_MAX
> The maximum scale value in the bc(1) utility.

USER_BC_STRING_MAX
> The maximum string length in the bc(1) utility.

USER_COLL_WEIGHTS_MAX
> The maximum number of weights that can be assigned to any entry of the LC_COLLATE order keyword in the locale definition file.

USER_CS_PATH
> Return a value for the PATH environment variable that finds all the standard utilities.

USER_EXPR_NEST_MAX
> The maximum number of expressions that can be nested within parenthesis by the expr(1) utility.

USER_LINE_MAX
> The maximum length in bytes of a text-processing utility's input line.

USER_POSIX2_CHAR_TERM
> Return 1 if the system supports at least one terminal type capable of all operations described in POSIX 1003.2, otherwise 0.

USER_POSIX2_C_BIND
> Return 1 if the system's C-language development facilities support the C-Language Bindings Option, otherwise 0.

USER_POSIX2_C_DEV
> Return 1 if the system supports the C-Language Development Utilities Option, otherwise 0.

USER_POSIX2_FORT_DEV
> Return 1 if the system supports the FORTRAN Development Utilities Option, otherwise 0.

USER_POSIX2_FORT_RUN
> Return 1 if the system supports the FORTRAN Runtime Utilities Option, otherwise 0.

USER_POSIX2_LOCALEDEF
> Return 1 if the system supports the creation of locales, otherwise 0.

USER_POSIX2_SW_DEV
> Return 1 if the system supports the Software Development Utilities Option, otherwise 0.

USER_POSIX2_UPE
> Return 1 if the system supports the User Portability Utilities Option, otherwise 0.

USER_POSIX2_VERSION
> The version of POSIX 1003.2 with which the system attempts to comply.

USER_RE_DUP_MAX
> The maximum number of repeated occurrences of a regular expression permitted when using interval notation.

USER_STREAM_MAX
> The minimum maximum number of streams that a process may have open at any one time.

USER_TZNAME_MAX
> The minimum maximum number of types supported for the name of a timezone.

CTL_VM

The string and integer information available for the CTL_VM level is detailed below. The changeable column shows whether a process with appropriate privilege may change the value.

Second level name	Type	Changeable
VM_LOADAVG	struct loadavg	no
VM_METER	struct vmtotal	no

VM_LOADAVG
> Return the load average history. The returned data consists of a *struct loadavg*.

VM_METER
> Return the system wide virtual memory statistics. The returned data consists of a *struct vmtotal*.

RETURN VALUES

If the call to **sysctl** is successful, 0 is returned. Otherwise −1 is returned and *errno* is set appropriately.

ERRORS

The following errors may be reported:

[EFAULT]   The buffer *name*, *oldp*, *newp*, or length pointer *oldlenp* contains an invalid address.

[EINVAL]   The *name* array is less than two or greater than CTL_MAXNAME.

[EINVAL]   A non-null *newp* is given and its specified length in *newlen* is too large or too small.

[ENOMEM]   The length pointed to by *oldlenp* is too short to hold the requested value.

[ENOTDIR]   The *name* array specifies an intermediate rather than terminal name.

[EOPNOTSUPP]
> The *name* array specifies a value that is unknown.

[EPERM]   An attempt is made to set a read-only value.

[EPERM]   A process without appropriate privilege attempts to set a value.

FILES

<sys/sysctl.h>	definitions for top level identifiers, second level kernel and hardware identifiers, and user level identifiers
<sys/socket.h>	definitions for second level network identifiers
<sys/gmon.h>	definitions for third level profiling identifiers
<vm/vm_param.h>	definitions for second level virtual memory identifiers
<netinet/in.h>	definitions for third level Internet identifiers and fourth level IP identifiers
<netinet/icmp_var.h>	definitions for fourth level ICMP identifiers
<netinet/udp_var.h>	definitions for fourth level UDP identifiers

SEE ALSO

sysctl(8)

HISTORY
　　　The **sysctl** function first appeared in 4.4BSD.

3

NAME
syslog, vsyslog, openlog, closelog, setlogmask – control system log

SYNOPSIS
```
#include <syslog.h>
#include <varargs.h>
```

void
syslog(*int priority, const char *message, . . .*);

void
vsyslog(*int priority, const char *message, va_list args*);

void
openlog(*const char *ident, int logopt, int facility*);

void
closelog(*void*);

int
setlogmask(*int maskpri*);

DESCRIPTION
The **syslog**( ) function writes *message* to the system message logger. The message is then written to the system console, log files, logged-in users, or forwarded to other machines as appropriate. (See syslogd(8).)

The message is identical to a printf(3) format string, except that '%m' is replaced by the current error message. (As denoted by the global variable *errno*; see strerror(3).) A trailing newline is added if none is present.

The **vsyslog**( ) function is an alternate form in which the arguments have already been captured using the variable-length argument facilities of varargs(3).

The message is tagged with *priority*. Priorities are encoded as a *facility* and a *level*. The facility describes the part of the system generating the message. The level is selected from the following *ordered* (high to low) list:

LOG_EMERG   A panic condition. This is normally broadcast to all users.

LOG_ALERT   A condition that should be corrected immediately, such as a corrupted system database.

LOG_CRIT   Critical conditions, e.g., hard device errors.

LOG_ERR   Errors.

LOG_WARNING   Warning messages.

LOG_NOTICE   Conditions that are not error conditions, but should possibly be handled specially.

LOG_INFO   Informational messages.

LOG_DEBUG   Messages that contain information normally of use only when debugging a program.

The **openlog**( ) function provides for more specialized processing of the messages sent by **syslog**( ) and **vsyslog**(). The parameter *ident* is a string that will be prepended to every message. The *logopt* argument is a bit field specifying logging options, which is formed by OR'ing one or more of the following values:

LOG_CONS   If **syslog**( ) cannot pass the message to syslogd it will attempt to write the message to the console (''/dev/console.'')

LOG_NDELAY   Open the connection to syslogd immediately. Normally the open is delayed until the first message is logged. Useful for programs that need to manage the order in which file descriptors are allocated.

LOG_PERROR   Write the message to standard error output as well to the system log.

LOG_PID   Log the process id with each message: useful for identifying instantiations of daemons.

The *facility* parameter encodes a default facility to be assigned to all messages that do not have an explicit facility encoded:

LOG_AUTH   The authorization system: login(1), su(1), getty(8), etc.

LOG_AUTHPRIV The same as LOG_AUTH, but logged to a file readable only by selected individuals.

LOG_CRON   The clock daemon.

LOG_DAEMON   System daemons, such as routed(8), that are not provided for explicitly by other facilities.

LOG_KERN   Messages generated by the kernel. These cannot be generated by any user processes.

LOG_LPR   The line printer spooling system: lpr(1), lpc(8), lpd(8), etc.

LOG_MAIL   The mail system.

LOG_NEWS   The network news system.

LOG_SYSLOG   Messages generated internally by syslogd(8).

LOG_USER   Messages generated by random user processes. This is the default facility identifier if none is specified.

LOG_UUCP   The uucp system.

LOG_LOCAL0   Reserved for local use. Similarly for LOG_LOCAL1 through LOG_LOCAL7.

The **closelog**( ) function can be used to close the log file.

The **setlogmask**( ) function sets the log priority mask to *maskpri* and returns the previous mask. Calls to **syslog**( ) with a priority not set in *maskpri* are rejected. The mask for an individual priority *pri* is calculated by the macro **LOG_MASK**(*pri*); the mask for all priorities up to and including *toppri* is given by the macro **LOG_UPTO**(*toppri*);. The default allows all priorities to be logged.

RETURN VALUES

The routines **closelog**(), **openlog**(), **syslog**( ) and **vsyslog**( ) return no value.

The routine **setlogmask**( ) always returns the previous log mask level.

EXAMPLES

```
syslog(LOG_ALERT, "who: internal error 23");
```

```
openlog("ftpd", LOG_PID, LOG_DAEMON);
setlogmask(LOG_UPTO(LOG_ERR));
syslog(LOG_INFO, "Connection from host %d", CallingHost);

syslog(LOG_INFO|LOG_LOCAL2, "foobar error: %m");
```

SEE ALSO

logger(1), syslogd(8)

HISTORY

These functions appeared in 4.2BSD.

NAME

system – pass a command to the shell

SYNOPSIS

#include <stdlib.h>

int
system(*const char *string*);

DESCRIPTION

The **system**( ) function hands the argument *string* to the command interpreter sh(1). The calling process waits for the shell to finish executing the command, ignoring SIGINT and SIGQUIT, and blocking SIGCHLD.

If *string* is a NULL pointer, **system**( ) will return non-zero if the command interpreter sh(1) is available, and zero if it is not.

The **system**( ) function returns the exit status of the shell, or −1 if the wait(3) for the shell failed. A return value of 127 means the execution of the shell failed.

SEE ALSO

sh(1), execve(2), wait(2), popen(3)

STANDARDS

The **system**( ) function conforms to ANSI C X3.159-1989 (''ANSI C '').

NAME
   tan – tangent function

SYNOPSIS
   #include <math.h>

   double
   tan(*double x*);

DESCRIPTION
   The tan() function computes the tangent of *x* (measured in radians). A large magnitude argument may yield a result with little or no significance. For a discussion of error due to roundoff, see math(3).

RETURN VALUES
   The tan() function returns the tangent value.

SEE ALSO
   acos(3), asin(3), atan(3), atan2(3), cos(3), cosh(3), sin(3), sinh(3), tanh(3), math(3),

STANDARDS
   The tan() function conforms to ANSI C X3.159-1989 ("ANSI C ").

NAME

tanh – hyperbolic tangent function

SYNOPSIS

```
#include <math.h>
```

double
tanh(*double x*);

DESCRIPTION

The **tanh**( ) function computes the hyperbolic tangent of *x*. For a discussion of error due to roundoff, see math(3).

RETURN VALUES

The **tanh**( ) function returns the hyperbolic tangent value.

SEE ALSO

acos(3), asin(3), atan(3), atan2(3), cos(3), cosh(3), sin(3), sinh(3), tan(3), math(3),

STANDARDS

The **tanh**( ) function conforms to ANSI C X3.159-1989 (''ANSI C '').

3

NAME
   tcgetpgrp – get foreground process group ID

SYNOPSIS
   #include <sys/types.h>
   #include <unistd.h>

   pid_t
   tcgetpgrp(*int fd*);

DESCRIPTION
   The **tcgetpgrp** function returns the value of the process group ID of the foreground process group associated with the terminal device. If there is no foreground process group, **tcgetpgrp** returns an invalid process ID.

ERRORS
   If an error occurs, **tcgetpgrp** returns -1 and the global variable *errno* is set to indicate the error, as follows:

   [EBADF]   The *fd* argument is not a valid file descriptor.

   [ENOTTY]   The calling process does not have a controlling terminal or the underlying terminal device represented by *fd* is not the controlling terminal.

SEE ALSO
   setpgid(3), setsid(2), tcsetpgrp(3)

STANDARDS
   The **tcgetpgrp** function is expected to be compliant with the IEEE Std1003.1-1988 ("POSIX") specification.

3

NAME

tcsendbreak, tcdrain, tcflush, tcflow – line control functions

SYNOPSIS

```
#include <termios.h>
```

int
tcdrain(*int fd*);

int
tcflow(*int fd, int action*);

int
tcflush(*int fd, int action*);

int
tcsendbreak(*int fd, int len*);

DESCRIPTION

The **tcdrain** function waits until all output written to the terminal referenced by *fd* has been transmitted to the terminal.

The **tcflow** function suspends transmission of data to or the reception of data from the terminal referenced by *fd* depending on the value of *action*. The value of *action* must be one of the following:

TCOOFF　Suspend output.

TCOON　　Restart suspended output.

TCIOFF　Transmit a STOP character, which is intended to cause the terminal to stop transmitting data to the system. (See the description of IXOFF in the Input Modes section of termios(4)).

TCION　　Transmit a START character, which is intended to cause the terminal to start transmitting data to the system. (See the description of IXOFF in the Input Modes section of termios(4)).

The **tcflush** function discards any data written to the terminal referenced by *fd* which has not been transmitted to the terminal, or any data received from the terminal but not yet read, depending on the value of *action*. The value of *action* must be one of the following:

TCIFLUSH　　Flush data received but not read.

TCOFLUSH　　Flush data written but not transmitted.

TCIOFLUSH　Flush both data received but not read and data written but not transmitted.

The **tcsendbreak** function transmits a continuous stream of zero-valued bits for four-tenths of a second to the terminal referenced by *fd*. The *len* parameter is ignored in this implementation.

RETURN VALUES

Upon successful completion, all of these functions return a value of zero.

ERRORS

If any error occurs, a value of -1 is returned and the global variable *errno* is set to indicate the error, as follows:

[EBADF]　　　The *fd* argument is not a valid file descriptor.

[EINVAL]　　　The *action* argument is not a proper value.

[ENOTTY]　　　The file associated with *fd* is not a terminal.

[EINTR]　　　A signal interrupted the **tcdrain** function.

SEE ALSO
tcsetattr(3), termios(4)

STANDARDS
The **tcsendbreak**, **tcdrain**, **tcflush** and **tcflow** functions are expected to be compliant with the IEEE Std1003.1-1988 (''POSIX'') specification.

NAME

cfgetispeed, **cfsetispeed**, **cfgetospeed**, **cfsetospeed**, **cfsetspeed**, **cfmakeraw**, **tcgetattr**, **tcsetattr** – manipulating the termios structure

SYNOPSIS

#include <termios.h>

speed_t
cfgetispeed(*struct termios *t*);

int
cfsetispeed(*struct termios *t, speed_t speed*);

speed_t
cfgetospeed(*struct termios *t*);

int
cfsetospeed(*struct termios *t, speed_t speed*);

int
cfsetspeed(*struct termios *t, speed_t speed*);

void
cfmakeraw(*struct termios *t*);

int
tcgetattr(*int fd, struct termios *t*);

int
tcsetattr(*int fd, int action, struct termios *t*);

DESCRIPTION

The **cfmakeraw**, **tcgetattr** and **tcsetattr** functions are provided for getting and setting the termios structure.

The **cfgetispeed**, **cfsetispeed**, **cfgetospeed**, **cfsetospeed** and **cfsetspeed** functions are provided for getting and setting the baud rate values in the termios structure. The effects of the functions on the terminal as described below do not become effective, nor are all errors detected, until the **tcsetattr** function is called. Certain values for baud rates set in the termios structure and passed to **tcsetattr** have special meanings. These are discussed in the portion of the manual page that describes the **tcsetattr** function.

GETTING AND SETTING THE BAUD RATE

The input and output baud rates are found in the termios structure. The unsigned integer speed_t is typdef'd in the include file <termios.h>. The value of the integer corresponds directly to the baud rate being represented, however, the following symbolic values are defined.

```
#define B0      0
#define B50     50
#define B75     75
#define B110    110
#define B134    134
#define B150    150
#define B200    200
#define B300    300
#define B600    600
```

```
#define B1200   1200
#define B1800   1800
#define B2400   2400
#define B4800   4800
#define B9600   9600
#define B19200  19200
#define B38400  38400
#ifndef _POSIX_SOURCE
#define EXTA    19200
#define EXTB    38400
#endif  /*_POSIX_SOURCE */
```

The cfgetispeed function returns the input baud rate in the termios structure referenced by tp.

The cfsetispeed function sets the input baud rate in the termios structure referenced by tp to speed.

The cfgetospeed function returns the output baud rate in the termios structure referenced by tp.

The cfsetospeed function sets the output baud rate in the termios structure referenced by tp to speed.

The cfsetspeed function sets both the input and output baud rate in the termios structure referenced by tp to speed.

Upon successful completion, the functions cfsetispeed, cfsetospeed, and cfsetspeed return a value of 0. Otherwise, a value of -1 is returned and the global variable errno is set to indicate the error.

GETTING AND SETTING THE TERMIOS STATE

This section describes the functions that are used to control the general terminal interface. Unless otherwise noted for a specific command, these functions are restricted from use by background processes. Attempts to perform these operations shall cause the process group to be sent a SIGTTOU signal. If the calling process is blocking or ignoring SIGTTOU signals, the process is allowed to perform the operation and the SIGTTOU signal is not sent.

In all the functions, although fd is an open file descriptor, the functions affect the underlying terminal file, not just the open file description associated with the particular file descriptor.

The cfmakeraw function sets the flags stored in the termios structure to a state disabling all input and output processing, giving a "raw I/O path." It should be noted that there is no function to reverse this effect. This is because there are a variety of processing options that could be re-enabled and the correct method is for an application to snapshot the current terminal state using the function tcgetattr, setting raw mode with cfmakeraw and the subsequent tcsetattr, and then using another tcsetattr with the saved state to revert to the previous terminal state.

The tcgetattr function copies the parameters associated with the terminal referenced by fd in the termios structure referenced by tp. This function is allowed from a background process, however, the terminal attributes may be subsequently changed by a foreground process.

The tcsetattr function sets the parameters associated with the terminal from the termios structure referenced by tp. The action field is created by or'ing the following values, as specified in the include file <termios.h>.

TCSANOW   The change occurs immediately.

TCSADRAIN   The change occurs after all output written to fd has been transmitted to the terminal. This value of action should be used when changing parameters that affect output.

TCSAFLUSH The change occurs after all output written to *fd* has been transmitted to the terminal. Additionally, any input that has been received but not read is discarded.

TCSASOFT If this value is *or*'ed into the *action* value, the values of the *c_cflag*, *c_ispeed*, and *c_ospeed* fields are ignored.

The 0 baud rate is used to terminate the connection. If 0 is specified as the output speed to the function **tcsetattr**, modem control will no longer be asserted on the terminal, disconnecting the terminal.

If zero is specified as the input speed to the function **tcsetattr**, the input baud rate will be set to the same value as that specified by the output baud rate.

If **tcsetattr** is unable to make any of the requested changes, it returns -1 and sets errno. Otherwise, it makes all of the requested changes it can. If the specified input and output baud rates differ and are a combination that is not supported, neither baud rate is changed.

Upon successful completion, the functions **tcgetattr** and **tcsetattr** return a value of 0. Otherwise, they return -1 and the global variable *errno* is set to indicate the error, as follows:

[EBADF]   The *fd* argument to **tcgetattr** or **tcsetattr** was not a valid file descriptor.

[EINTR]   The **tcsetattr** function was interrupted by a signal.

[EINVAL]   The *action* argument to the **tcsetattr** function was not valid, or an attempt was made to change an attribute represented in the termios structure to an unsupported value.

[ENOTTY]   The file associated with the *fd* argument to **tcgetattr** or **tcsetattr** is not a terminal.

SEE ALSO
tcsendbreak(3), termios(4)

STANDARDS
The **cfgetispeed**, **cfsetispeed**, **cfgetospeed**, **cfsetospeed**, **tcgetattr** and **tcsetattr** functions are expected to be compliant with the IEEE Std1003.1-1988 ("POSIX") specification. The **cfmakeraw** and **cfsetspeed** functions, as well as the TCSASOFT option to the **tcsetattr** function are extensions to the IEEE Std1003.1-1988 ("POSIX") specification.

3

NAME
tcsetpgrp – set foreground process group ID

SYNOPSIS
```
#include <sys/types.h>
#include <unistd.h>

int
tcsetpgrp(int fd, pid_t pgrp_id);
```

DESCRIPTION
If the process has a controlling terminal, the **tcsetpgrp** function sets the foreground process group ID associated with the terminal device to *pgrp_id*. The terminal device associated with *fd* must be the controlling terminal of the calling process and the controlling terminal must be currently associated with the session of the calling process. The value of *pgrp_id* must be the same as the process group ID of a process in the same session as the calling process.

Upon successful completion, **tcsetpgrp** returns a value of zero.

ERRORS
If an error occurs, **tcgetpgrp** returns -1 and the global variable *errno* is set to indicate the error, as follows:

[EBADF]   The *fd* argument is not a valid file descriptor.

[EINVAL]   An invalid value of *pgrp_id* was specified.

[ENOTTY]   The calling process does not have a controlling terminal, or the file represented by *fd* is not the controlling terminal, or the controlling terminal is no longer associated with the session of the calling process.

[EPERM]   The *pgrp_id* argument does not match the process group ID of a process in the same session as the calling process.

SEE ALSO
setpgid(3), setsid(2), tcgetpgrp(3)

STANDARDS
The **tcsetpgprp** function is expected to be compliant with the IEEE Std1003.1-1988 ("POSIX") specification.

NAME

tgetent, tgetnum, tgetflag, tgetstr, tgoto, tputs – terminal independent operation routines

SYNOPSIS

```
char PC;
char *BC;
char *UP;
short ospeed;
```

tgetent(*char *bp*, *char *name*);

tgetnum(*char *id*);

tgetflag(*char *id*);

```
char *
```
tgetstr(*char *id*, *char **area*);

```
char *
```
tgoto(*char *cm*, *destcol*, *destline*);

tputs(*register char *cp*, *int affcnt*, *int (*outc)()*);

DESCRIPTION

These functions extract and use capabilities from a terminal capability data base, usually /usr/share/misc/termcap, the format of which is described in termcap(5). These are low level routines; see curses(3) for a higher level package.

The **tgetent**( ) function extracts the entry for terminal *name* into the buffer at *bp*. The *bp* argument should be a character buffer of size 1024 and must be retained through all subsequent calls to **tgetnum**(), **tgetflag**(), and **tgetstr**(). The **tgetent**( ) function returns −1 if none of the **termcap** data base files could be opened, 0 if the terminal name given does not have an entry, and 1 if all goes well. It will look in the environment for a TERMCAP variable. If found, and the value does not begin with a slash, and the terminal type *name* is the same as the environment string TERM, the TERMCAP string is used instead of reading a **termcap** file. If it does begin with a slash, the string is used as a path name of the **termcap** file to search. If TERMCAP does not begin with a slash and *name* is different from TERM, **tgetent**( ) searches the files $HOME/.termcap and /usr/share/misc/termcap, in that order, unless the environment variable TERMPATH exists, in which case it specifies a list of file pathnames (separated by spaces or colons) to be searched instead. Whenever multiple files are searched and a **tc** field occurs in the requested entry, the entry it names must be found in the same file or one of the succeeding files. This can speed up entry into programs that call **tgetent**(), as well as help debug new terminal descriptions or make one for your terminal if you can't write the file /usr/share/misc/termcap.

The **tgetnum**( ) function gets the numeric value of capability *id*, returning −1 if it is not given for the terminal. The **tgetflag**( ) function returns 1 if the specified capability is present in the terminal's entry, 0 if it is not. The **tgetstr**( ) function returns the string value of the capability *id*, places it in the buffer at *area*, and advances the *area* pointer. It decodes the abbreviations for this field described in termcap(5), except for cursor addressing and padding information. The **tgetstr**( ) function returns NULL if the capability was not found.

The **tgoto**( ) function returns a cursor addressing string decoded from *cm* to go to column *destcol* in line *destline*. It uses the external variables *UP* (from the **up** capability) and *BC* (if **bc** is given rather than **bs**) if necessary to avoid placing \n, ^D or ^@ in the returned string. (Programs which call **tgoto**( ) should be sure to turn off the XTABS bit(s), since **tgoto**( ) may now output a tab. Note that programs using termcap should in general turn off XTABS anyway since some terminals use control-I for other functions, such as nondestructive space.) If a **%** sequence is given which is not understood, then **tgoto**( ) returns (OOPS).

The **tputs**( ) function decodes the leading padding information of the string *cp*; *affcnt* gives the number of lines affected by the operation, or 1 if this is not applicable, *outc* is a routine which is called with each character in turn. The external variable *ospeed* should contain the output speed of the terminal as encoded by stty(3). The external variable *PC* should contain a pad character to be used (from the capability) if a null (**^@**) is inappropriate.

FILES

/usr/lib/libtermcap.a	**−l** *ltermcap* library (also known as **−l** *ltermlib*)
/usr/share/misc/termcap	standard terminal capability data base
$HOME/.termcap	user's terminal capability data base

SEE ALSO
ex(1), curses(3), termcap(5)

HISTORY
The **tgetent** functions appeared in 4.0BSD.

NAME

      tf_init, tf_get_pname, tf_get_pinst, tf_get_cred, tf_close – routines for manipulating a Kerberos ticket file

SYNOPSIS

      #include <kerberosIV/krb.h>

      extern char *krb_err_txt[];

      tf_init(tf_name, rw)
      char *tf_name;
      int rw;

      tf_get_pname(pname)
      char *pname;

      tf_get_pinst(pinst)
      char *pinst;

      tf_get_cred(c)
      CREDENTIALS *c;

      tf_close()

DESCRIPTION

      This group of routines are provided to manipulate the Kerberos tickets file. A ticket file has the following format:

principal's name	(null-terminated string)
principal's instance	(null-terminated string)
CREDENTIAL_1	
CREDENTIAL_2	
...	
CREDENTIAL_n	
EOF	

      Where "CREDENTIAL_x" consists of the following fixed-length
fields from the CREDENTIALS structure (defined in <kerberosIV/krb.h>):

char	service[ANAME_SZ]
char	instance[INST_SZ]
char	realm[REALM_SZ]
des_cblock	session
int	lifetime
int	kvno
KTEXT_ST	ticket_st
long	issue_date

      tf_init must be called before the other ticket file routines. It takes the name of the ticket file to use, and a read/write flag as arguments. It tries to open the ticket file, checks the mode and if everything is okay, locks the file. If it's opened for reading, the lock is shared. If it's opened for writing, the lock is exclusive. KSUCCESS is returned if all went well, otherwise one of the following:

NO_TKT_FIL   - file wasn't there
TKT_FIL_ACC - file was in wrong mode, etc.
TKT_FIL_LCK - couldn't lock the file, even after a retry

The *tf_get_pname* reads the principal's name from a ticket file. It should only be called after tf_init has been called. The principal's name is filled into the *pname* parameter. If all goes well, KSUCCESS is returned. If tf_init wasn't called, TKT_FIL_INI is returned. If the principal's name was null, or EOF was encountered, or the name was longer than ANAME_SZ, TKT_FIL_FMT is returned.

The *tf_get_pinst* reads the principal's instance from a ticket file. It should only be called after tf_init and tf_get_pname have been called. The principal's instance is filled into the *pinst* parameter. If all goes well, KSUCCESS is returned. If tf_init wasn't called, TKT_FIL_INI is returned. If EOF was encountered, or the name was longer than INST_SZ, TKT_FIL_FMT is returned. Note that, unlike the principal name, the instance name may be null.

The *tf_get_cred* routine reads a CREDENTIALS record from a ticket file and fills in the given structure. It should only be called after tf_init, tf_get_pname, and tf_get_pinst have been called. If all goes well, KSUCCESS is returned. Possible error codes are:

```
TKT_FIL_INI    - tf_init wasn't called first
TKT_FIL_FMT    - bad format
EOF            - end of file encountered
```

tf_close closes the ticket file and releases the lock on it.

SEE ALSO
> krb(3)

DIAGNOSTICS
BUGS
> The ticket file routines have to be called in a certain order.

AUTHORS
> Jennifer Steiner, MIT Project Athena
> Bill Bryant, MIT Project Athena

RESTRICTIONS
> Copyright 1987 Massachusetts Institute of Technology

NAME

    time – get time of day

SYNOPSIS

    `#include <sys/types.h>`

    time_t
    time(*time_t *tloc*);

DESCRIPTION

    The **time**( ) function returns the value of time in seconds since 0 hours, 0 minutes, 0 seconds, January 1, 1970, Coordinated Universal Time.

    A copy of the time value may be saved to the area indicated by the pointer *tloc*. If *tloc* is a NULL pointer, no value is stored.

    Upon successful completion, **time**( ) returns the value of time. Otherwise a value of $((time\_t) - 1)$ is returned and the global variable *errno* is set to indicate the error.

ERRORS

    The following error codes may be set in *errno*:

    `[EFAULT]` An argument address referenced invalid memory.

SEE ALSO

    gettimeofday(2), ctime(3)

HISTORY

    A **time**( ) function appeared in Version 6 AT&T UNIX.

3

NAME
       times – process times

SYNOPSIS
       #include <sys/times.h>

       clock_t
       times(*struct tms *tp*);

DESCRIPTION
       This interface is obsoleted by getrusage(2) and gettimeofday(3).

       The **times**() function returns the value of time in CLK_TCK's of a second since 0 hours, 0 minutes, 0
       seconds, January 1, 1970, Coordinated Universal Time.

       It also fills in the structure pointed to by *tp* with time-accounting information.

       The *tms* structure is defined as follows:

```
typedef struct {
        clock_t tms_utime;
        clock_t tms_stime;
        clock_t tms_cutime;
        clock_t tms_cstime;
}
```

       The elements of this structure are defined as follows:

       tms_utime   The CPU time charged for the execution of user instructions.

       tms_stime   The CPU time charged for execution by the system on behalf of the process.

       tms_cutime The sum of the *tms_utime* s and *tms_cutime* s of the child processes.

       tms_cstime The sum of the *tms_stime*s and *tms_cstime*s of the child processes.

       All times are in CLK_TCK's of a second.

       The times of a terminated child process are included in the *tms_cutime* and *tms_cstime* elements of
       the parent when one of the wait(2) functions returns the process ID of the terminated child to the parent. If
       an error occurs, **times**() returns the value ((clock_t)−1), and sets errno to indicate the error.

ERRORS
       The **times**() function may fail and set the global variable *errno* for any of the errors specified for the li-
       brary routines getrusage(2) and gettimeofday(2).

# SEE ALSO
       time(1), getrusage(2), gettimeofday(2), wait(2)

STANDARDS
       The **times**() function conforms to IEEE Std1003.1-1988 ("POSIX").

NAME

timezone – return the timezone abbreviation

SYNOPSIS

char *
timezone(*int zone, int dst*);

DESCRIPTION

This interface is for compatibility only; it is impossible to reliably map timezone's arguments to a time zone abbreviation. See ctime(3).

The **timezone**( ) function returns a pointer to a time zone abbreviation for the specified *zone* and *dst* values. *Zone* is the number of minutes west of GMT and *dst* is non-zero if daylight savings time is in effect.

SEE ALSO

ctime(3)

HISTORY

A **timezone**( ) function appeared in Version 7 AT&T UNIX.

NAME

tempnam, tmpfile, tmpnam – temporary file routines

SYNOPSIS

```
#include <stdio.h>
```

FILE *
tmpfile(*void*);

char *
tmpnam(*char *str*);

char *
tempnam(*const char *tmpdir, const char *prefix*);

DESCRIPTION

The **tmpfile**( ) function returns a pointer to a stream associated with a file descriptor returned by the routine mkstemp(3). The created file is unlinked before **tmpfile**( ) returns, causing the file to be automatically deleted when the last reference to it is closed. The file is opened with the access value 'w+'.

The **tmpnam**( ) function returns a pointer to a file name, in the P_tmpdir directory, which did not reference an existing file at some indeterminate point in the past. P_tmpdir is defined in the include file <stdio.h>. If the argument *s* is non-NULL, the file name is copied to the buffer it references. Otherwise, the file name is copied to a static buffer. In either case, **tmpnam**( ) returns a pointer to the file name.

The buffer referenced by *s* is expected to be at least L_tmpnam bytes in length. L_tmpnam is defined in the include file <stdio.h>.

The **tempnam**( ) function is similar to **tmpnam**(), but provides the ability to specify the directory which will contain the temporary file and the file name prefix.

The environment variable TMPDIR (if set), the argument *tmpdir* (if non-NULL), the directory P_tmpdir, and the directory /tmp are tried, in the listed order, as directories in which to store the temporary file.

The argument *prefix*, if non-NULL, is used to specify a file name prefix, which will be the first part of the created file name. **Tempnam**( ) allocates memory in which to store the file name; the returned pointer may be used as a subsequent argument to free(3).

RETURN VALUES

The **tmpfile**( ) function returns a pointer to an open file stream on success, and a NULL pointer on error.

The **tmpnam**( ) and **tempfile**( ) functions return a pointer to a file name on success, and a NULL pointer on error.

ERRORS

The **tmpfile**( ) function may fail and set the global variable *errno* for any of the errors specified for the library functions fdopen(3) or mkstemp(3).

The **tmpnam**( ) function may fail and set *errno* for any of the errors specified for the library function mktemp(3).

The **tempnam**( ) function may fail and set *errno* for any of the errors specified for the library functions malloc(3) or mktemp(3).

SEE ALSO

mkstemp(3), mktemp(3)

STANDARDS

The **tmpfile**( ) and **tmpnam**( ) functions conform to ANSI C X3.159-1989 (''ANSI C '').

BUGS

These interfaces are provided for System V and ANSI compatibility only. The mkstemp(3) interface is strongly preferred.

There are four important problems with these interfaces (as well as with the historic mktemp(3) interface). First, there is an obvious race between file name selection and file creation and deletion. Second, most historic implementations provide only a limited number of possible temporary file names (usually 26) before file names will start being recycled. Third, the System V implementations of these functions (and of mktemp) use the access(2) function to determine whether or not the temporary file may be created. This has obvious ramifications for setuid or setgid programs, complicating the portable use of these interfaces in such programs. Finally, there is no specification of the permissions with which the temporary files are created.

This implementation does not have these flaws, but portable software cannot depend on that. In particular, the **tmpfile**( ) interface should not be used in software expected to be used on other systems if there is any possibility that the user does not wish the temporary file to be publicly readable and writable.

3

NAME
toascii – convert a byte to 7-bit ASCII

SYNOPSIS
#include <ctype.h>

int
toascii(int c);

DESCRIPTION
The toascii() function strips all but the low 7 bits from a letter, including parity or other marker bits.

RETURN VALUES
The toascii() function always returns a valid ASCII character.

SEE ALSO
isascii(3), isalnum(3), isalpha(3), iscntrl(3), isdigit(3), isgraph(3), islower(3), isprint(3), ispunct(3), isspace(3), isupper(3), isxdigit(3), tolower(3), toupper(3), stdio(3), ascii(7)

NAME

tolower – upper case to lower case letter conversion

SYNOPSIS

#include <ctype.h>

int
tolower(*int c*);

DESCRIPTION

The **tolower**( ) function converts an upper-case letter to the corresponding lower-case letter.

RETURN VALUES

If the argument is an upper-case letter, the **tolower**( ) function returns the corresponding lower-case letter if there is one; otherwise the argument is returned unchanged.

SEE ALSO

isascii(3), isalnum(3), isalpha(3), iscntrl(3), isdigit(3), isgraph(3), islower(3), isprint(3), ispunct(3), isspace(3), isupper(3), isxdigit(3), toascii(3), toupper(3), stdio(3) ascii(7)

STANDARDS

The **tolower**( ) function conforms to ANSI C X3.159-1989 (''ANSI C '').

NAME

`toupper` – lower case to upper case letter conversion

SYNOPSIS

`#include <ctype.h>`

int
`toupper(`*int c*`);`

DESCRIPTION

The `toupper()` function converts a lower-case letter to the corresponding upper-case letter. If the argument is a lower-case letter, the `toupper()` function returns the corresponding upper-case letter if there is one; otherwise the argument is returned unchanged.

SEE ALSO

isascii(3), isalnum(3), isalpha(3), iscntrl(3), isdigit(3), isgraph(3), islower(3), isprint(3), ispunct(3), isspace(3), isupper(3), isxdigit(3), toascii(3), toupper(3), stdio(3) ascii(7)

STANDARDS

The `tolower()` function conforms to ANSI C X3.159-1989 (''ANSI C '').

NAME

ttyname, isatty, ttyslot – get name of associated terminal (tty) from file descriptor

SYNOPSIS

```
#include <unistd.h>
```

char *
ttyname(*int fd*);

int
isatty(*int fd*);

int
ttyslot();

DESCRIPTION

These functions operate on the system file descriptors for terminal type devices. These descriptors are not related to the standard I/O FILE typedef, but refer to the special device files found in /dev and named /dev/tty*xx* and for which an entry exists in the initialization file /etc/ttys. (See ttys(5).)

The isatty() function determines if the file descriptor *fd* refers to a valid terminal type device.

The ttyname() function gets the related device name of a file descriptor for which isatty() is true

The ttyslot() function fetches the current process' control terminal number from the ttys(5) file entry.

RETURN VALUES

The ttyname() function returns the null terminated name if the device is found and isatty() is true; otherwise a NULL pointer is returned.

The ttyslot() function returns the unit number of the device file if found; otherwise the value zero is returned.

FILES

/dev/*
/etc/ttys

SEE ALSO

ioctl(2), ttys(5)

HISTORY

A isatty(), ttyname(), and ttyslot() function appeared in Version 7 AT&T UNIX.

BUGS

The ttyname() function leaves its result in an internal static object and returns a pointer to that object. Subsequent calls to ttyname() will modify the same object.

3

NAME
tzset, tzsetwall – initialize time conversion information

SYNOPSIS
`#include <time.h>`

void
tzset(*void*);

void
tzsetwall(*void*);

DESCRIPTION
The `tzset()` function initializes time conversion information used by the library routine `localtime`(3). The environment variable TZ specifies how this is done.

If TZ does not appear in the environment, the best available approximation to local wall clock time, as specified by the `tzfile`(5)-format file /etc/localtime is used.

If TZ appears in the environment but its value is a null string, Coordinated Universal Time (UTC) is used (without leap second correction).

If TZ appears in the environment and its value begins with a colon ( ) :, the rest of its value is used as a path-name of a `tzfile`(5)-format file from which to read the time conversion information. If the first character of the pathname is a slash ('/') it is used as an absolute pathname; otherwise, it is used as a pathname rela-tive to the system time conversion information directory.

If its value does not begin with a colon, it is first used as the pathname of a file (as described above) from which to read the time conversion information. If that file cannot be read, the value is then interpreted as a direct specification (the format is described below) of the time conversion information.

If the TZ environment variable does not specify a `tzfile`(5)-format file and cannot be interpreted as a direct specification, UTC is used.

The `tzsetwall()` function sets things up so that `localtime` returns the best available approximation of local wall clock time.

SPECIFICATION FORMAT
When TZ is used directly as a specification of the time conversion information, it must have the following syntax (spaces inserted for clarity):

    std offset [*dst* [*offset*] [, *rule*]]

Where:

std and *dst*	Three or more bytes that are the designation for the standard (*std*) or summer (*dst*) time zone. Only *std* is required; if *dst* is missing, then summer time does not apply in this locale. Upper and lowercase letters are explicitly allowed. Any char-acters except a leading colon ( ) :, digits, comma (','), minus ('−'), plus ('+'), and ASCII NUL are allowed.
offset	Indicates the value one must add to the local time to arrive at Coordinated Univer-sal Time. The *offset* has the form:

        hh [:*mm*[: *ss*]]

The minutes (*mm*) and seconds (*ss*) are optional. The hour (*hh*) is required and may be a single digit. The *offset* following *std* is required. If no *offset* follows *dst*, summer time is assumed to be one hour ahead of standard time. One or more digits may be used; the value is always interpreted as a decimal number. The hour must be between zero and 24, and the minutes (and seconds) — if present — between zero and 59. If preceded by a ('−') the time zone shall be east of the Prime Meridian; otherwise it shall be west (which may be indicated by an optional preceding ('+')).

rule   Indicates when to change to and back from summer time. The *rule* has the form:

> *date/time,date/time*

where the first *date* describes when the change from standard to summer time occurs and the second *date* describes when the change back happens. Each *time* field describes when, in current local time, the change to the other time is made.

The format of *date* is one of the following:

J *n*   The Julian day *n* ($1 \le n \le 365$). Leap days are not counted; that is, in all years — including leap years — February 28 is day 59 and March 1 is day 60. It is impossible to explicitly refer to the occasional February 29.

n   The zero-based Julian day ($0 \le n \le 365$). Leap days are counted, and it is possible to refer to February 29.

M *m.n.d*   The *d*'th day ($0 \le d \le 6$) of week *n* of month *m* of the year ($1 \le n \le 5$), ($1 \le m \le 12$), where week 5 means "the last *d* day in month *m*" which may occur in either the fourth or the fifth week). Week 1 is the first week in which the *d*'th day occurs. Day zero is Sunday.

The *time* has the same format as *offset* except that no leading sign ('−') or ('+') is allowed. The default, if *time* is not given, is **02:00:00**.

If no *rule* is present in the TZ specification, the rules specified by the `tzfile`(5)-format file *posixrules* in the system time conversion information directory are used, with the standard and summer time offsets from UTC replaced by those specified by the *offset* values in TZ.

For compatibility with System V Release 3.1, a semicolon ( ); may be used to separate the *rule* from the rest of the specification.

FILES

/etc/localtime	local time zone file
/usr/share/zoneinfo	time zone directory
/usr/share/zoneinfo/posixrules	rules for POSIX-style TZ's
/usr/share/zoneinfo/GMT for	UTC leap seconds

If the file `/usr/share/zoneinfo/GMT` does not exist, UTC leap seconds are loaded from `/usr/share/zoneinfo/posixrules`.

SEE ALSO

date(1), gettimeofday(2), ctime(3), getenv(3), time(3), tzfile(5)

HISTORY
    The `tzset` and `tzsetwall` functions first appeared in 4.4BSD.

NAME

ualarm – schedule signal after specified time

SYNOPSIS

#include <unistd.h>

u_int
ualarm(*u_int microseconds*, *u_int interval*);

DESCRIPTION

This is a simplified interface to setitimer(2).

The **ualarm()** function waits a count of *microseconds* before asserting the terminating signal SIGALRM. System activity or time used in processing the call may cause a slight delay.

If the *interval* argument is non-zero, the SIGALRM signal will be sent to the process every *interval* microseconds after the timer expires (e.g. after *value* microseconds have passed).

RETURN VALUES

When the signal has successfully been caught, **alarm()** returns the amount of time left on the clock. The maximum number of *microseconds* allowed is 2147483647.

SEE ALSO

getitimer(2), setitimer(2), sigpause(2), sigvec(2), signal(3), sleep(3), alarm(3), usleep(3)

HISTORY

The **ualarm()** function appeared in 4.3BSD.

NAME

     uname – get system identification

SYNOPSIS

     #include <sys/utsname.h>

     int
     uname(*struct utsname *name*);

DESCRIPTION

     The uname( ) function stores nul-terminated strings of information identifying the current system into the
     structure referenced by *name*.

     The utsname structure is defined in the <sys/utsname.h> header file, and contains the following
     members:

sysname	Name of the operating system implementation.
nodename	Network name of this machine.
release	Release level of the operating system.
version	Version level of the operating system.
machine	Machine hardware platform.

RETURN VALUES

     If uname is successful, 0 is returned, otherwise, -1 is returned and *errno* is set appropriately.

ERRORS

     The uname( ) function may fail and set *errno* for any of the errors specified for the library functions
     sysctl(3).

SEE ALSO

     uname(1), sysctl(3)

STANDARDS

     The uname( ) function conforms to IEEE Std1003.1-1988 ("POSIX").

HISTORY

     The uname function first appeared in 4.4BSD.

NAME

ungetc – un-get character from input stream

SYNOPSIS

#include <stdio.h>

int
ungetc(*int c, FILE *stream*);

DESCRIPTION

The **ungetc**( ) function pushes the character *c* (converted to an unsigned char) back onto the input stream pointed to by *stream*. The pushed-backed characters will be returned by subsequent reads on the stream (in reverse order). A successful intervening call, using the same stream, to one of the file positioning functions (fseek(3), fsetpos(3), or rewind(3)) will discard the pushed back characters.

One character of push-back is guaranteed, but as long as there is sufficient memory, an effectively infinite amount of pushback is allowed.

If a character is successfully pushed-back, the end-of-file indicator for the stream is cleared.

RETURN VALUES

The **ungetc**( ) function returns the character pushed-back after the conversion, or EOF if the operation fails. If the value of the argument *c* character equals EOF, the operation will fail and the stream will remain unchanged.

SEE ALSO

getc(3), fseek(3), setvbuf(3)

STANDARDS

The **ungetc**( ) function conforms to ANSI C X3.159-1989 (''ANSI C '').

3

NAME
unvis, strunvis – decode a visual representation of characters

SYNOPSIS
```
#include <vis.h>
```
```
int
unvis(u_char *cp, u_char c, int *astate, int flag);
```
```
int
strunvis(char *dst, char *src);
```

DESCRIPTION
The **unvis**( ) and **strunvis**( ) functions are used to decode a visual representation of characters, as produced by the vis(3) function, back into the original form. Unvis is called with successive characters in *c* until a valid sequence is recognized, at which time the decoded character is available at the character pointed to by *cp*. Strunvis decodes the characters pointed to by *src* into the buffer pointed to by *dst*.

The **strunvis**( ) function simply copies *src* to *dst*, decoding any escape sequences along the way, and returns the number of characters placed into *dst*, or −1 if an invalid escape sequence was detected. The size of *dst* should be equal to the size of *src* (that is, no expansion takes place during decoding).

The **unvis**( ) function implements a state machine that can be used to decode an arbitrary stream of bytes. All state associated with the bytes being decoded is stored outside the **unvis**( ) function (that is, a pointer to the state is passed in), so calls decoding different streams can be freely intermixed. To start decoding a stream of bytes, first initialize an integer to zero. Call **unvis**( ) with each successive byte, along with a pointer to this integer, and a pointer to a destination character. The unvis function has several return codes that must be handled properly. They are:

0 (zero)	Another character is necessary; nothing has been recognized yet.
UNVIS_VALID	A valid character has been recognized and is available at the location pointed to by cp.
UNVIS_VALIDPUSH	A valid character has been recognized and is available at the location pointed to by cp; however, the character currently passed in should be passed in again.
UNVIS_NOCHAR	A valid sequence was detected, but no character was produced. This return code is necessary to indicate a logical break between characters.
UNVIS_SYNBAD	An invalid escape sequence was detected, or the decoder is in an unknown state. The decoder is placed into the starting state.

When all bytes in the stream have been processed, call **unvis**( ) one more time with flag set to UNVIS_END to extract any remaining character (the character passed in is ignored).

The following code fragment illustrates a proper use of **unvis**( ).

```
        int state = 0;
        char out;

        while ((ch = getchar()) != EOF) {
        again:
                switch(unvis(&out, ch, &state, 0)) {
                case 0:
                case UNVIS_NOCHAR:
                        break;
```

```
        case UNVIS_VALID:
                (void) putchar(out);
                break;
        case UNVIS_VALIDPUSH:
                (void) putchar(out);
                goto again;
        case UNVIS_SYNBAD:
                (void)fprintf(stderr, "bad sequence!0);
        exit(1);
        }
    }
    if (unvis(&out, (char)0, &state, UNVIS_END) == UNVIS_VALID)
        (void) putchar(out);
```

SEE ALSO

    vis(1)

HISTORY

    The unvis function first appeared in 4.4BSD.

NAME

usleep – suspend execution for interval of microseconds

SYNOPSIS

`#include <unistd.h>`

void
`usleep(`*u_int microseconds*`);`

DESCRIPTION

The `usleep()` function suspends execution of the calling process for *microseconds* of time. System activity or time spent in processing the call may lengthen the sleep slightly.

If a timer is already running on the process its state is saved. If the value *microseconds* is more than or equal to the remaining clock time for the saved timer, the sleep time is set to the remaining clock time. The state of the previous timer is restored after *microseconds* has passed.

This routine is implemented using `setitimer(2)`; it requires eight system calls each time it is invoked. A similar but less compatible function can be obtained with a single `select(2)`; such a function would not restart after signals, but would not interfere with other uses of `setitimer`.

SEE ALSO

setitimer(2), getitimer(2), sigpause(2), ualarm(3), sleep(3), alarm(3)

HISTORY

The `usleep()` function appeared in 4.3BSD.

NAME
utime – set file times

SYNOPSIS
```
#include <sys/types.h>
#include <utime.h>
```

int
utime(*const char *file, const struct utimbuf *timep*);

DESCRIPTION
This interface is obsoleted by utimes(2) .

The **utime**( ) function sets the access and modification times of the named file from the structures in the argument array *timep*.

If the times are specified (the *timep* argument is non-NULL) the caller must be the owner of the file or be the super-user.

If the times are not specified (the *timep* argument is NULL) the caller must be the owner of the file, have permission to write the file, or be the super-user.

ERRORS
The **utime**( ) function may fail and set *errno* for any of the errors specified for the library function utimes(2).

SEE ALSO
utimes(2), stat(2)

HISTORY
A **utime**( ) function appeared in Version 7 AT&T UNIX.

STANDARDS
The **utime** function conforms to IEEE Std1003.1-1988 ("POSIX").

NAME
valloc – aligned memory allocation function

SYNOPSIS
#include <unistd.h>

char *
valloc(*unsigned size*);

DESCRIPTION
Valloc is obsoleted by the current version of malloc(3), which aligns page-sized and larger allocations.

The valloc() function allocates *size* bytes aligned on a page boundary. It is implemented by calling malloc(3) with a slightly larger request, saving the true beginning of the block allocated, and returning a properly aligned pointer.

RETURN VALUES
The valloc() function returns a pointer to the allocated space if successful; otherwise a null pointer is returned

HISTORY
The valloc() function appeared in 3.0BSD.

BUGS
A *vfree* function has not been implemented.

3

NAME

vis – visually encode characters

SYNOPSIS

```
#include <vis.h>

char *
vis(char *dst, char c, int flag, char nextc);

int
strvis(char *dst, char *src, int flag);

int
strvisx(char *dst, char *src, int len, int flag);
```

DESCRIPTION

The **vis()** function copies into *dst* a string which represents the character *c*. If *c* needs no encoding, it is copied in unaltered. The string is null terminated, and a pointer to the end of the string is returned. The maximum length of any encoding is four characters (not including the trailing NULL); thus, when encoding a set of characters into a buffer, the size of the buffer should be four times the number of characters encoded, plus one for the trailing NULL. The flag parameter is used for altering the default range of characters considered for encoding and for altering the visual representation. The additional character, *nextc*, is only used when selecting the VIS_CSTYLE encoding format (explained below).

The **strvis()** and **strvisx()** functions copy into *dst* a visual representation of the string *src*. The **strvis()** function encodes characters from *src* up to the first NULL. The **strvisx()** function encodes exactly *len* characters from *src* (this is useful for encoding a block of data that may contain NULL's). Both forms NULL terminate *dst*. The size of *dst* must be four times the number of characters encoded from *src* (plus one for the NULL). Both forms return the number of characters in dst (not including the trailing NULL).

The encoding is a unique, invertible representation comprised entirely of graphic characters; it can be decoded back into the original form using the unvis(3) or strunvis(3) functions.

There are two parameters that can be controlled: the range of characters that are encoded, and the type of representation used. By default, all non-graphic characters. except space, tab, and newline are encoded. (See isgraph(3).) The following flags alter this:

VIS_SP　　　　Also encode space.

VIS_TAB

　　　　　　　Also encode tab.

VIS_NL　　　　Also encode newline.

VIS_WHITE

　　　　　　　Synonym for VIS_SP | VIS_TAB | VIS_NL.

VIS_SAFE

　　　　　　　Only encode "unsafe" characters. Unsafe means control characters which may cause common terminals to perform unexpected functions. Currently this form allows space, tab, newline, backspace, bell, and return - in addition to all graphic characters - unencoded.

There are three forms of encoding. All forms use the backslash character '\' to introduce a special sequence; two backslashes are used to represent a real backslash. These are the visual formats:

(default)   Use an 'M' to represent meta characters (characters with the 8th bit set), and use carat '^' to represent control characters see (iscntrl(3)). The following formats are used:

\^C   Represents the control character 'C'. Spans characters \000 through \037, and \177 (as \^?).

\M-C   Represents character 'C' with the 8th bit set. Spans characters \241 through \376.

\M^C   Represents control character 'C' with the 8th bit set. Spans characters \200 through \237, and \377 (as \M^?).

\040   Represents ASCII space.

\240   Represents Meta-space.

VIS_CSTYLE   Use C-style backslash sequences to represent standard non-printable characters. The following sequences are used to represent the indicated characters:

> \a - BEL (007)
> \b - BS (010)
> \f - NP (014)
> \n - NL (012)
> \r - CR (015)
> \t - HT (011)
> \v - VT (013)
> \0 - NUL (000)

When using this format, the nextc parameter is looked at to determine if a NULL character can be encoded as '\0' instead of \000. If *nextc* is an octal digit, the latter representation is used to avoid ambiguity.

VIS_OCTAL   Use a three digit octal sequence. The form is \ddd where *d* represents an octal digit.

There is one additional flag, VIS_NOSLASH, which inhibits the doubling of backslashes and the backslash before the default format (that is, control characters are represented by '^C' and meta characters as M-C). With this flag set, the encoding is ambiguous and non-invertible.

SEE ALSO
unvis(1), unvis(3) strunvis(3)

HISTORY
These functions first appeared in 4.4BSD.

NAME

vlimit – control maximum system resource consumption

SYNOPSIS

```
#include <sys/vlimit.h>
```

vlimit(*resource*, *value*);

DESCRIPTION

This interface is obsoleted by getrlimit(2). It is available from the compatibility library, libcompat.

Limits the consumption by the current process and each process it creates to not individually exceed *value* on the specified *resource*. If *value* is specified as −1, then the current limit is returned and the limit is unchanged. The resources which are currently controllable are:

LIM_NORAISE   A pseudo-limit; if set non-zero then the limits may not be raised. Only the super-user may remove the *noraise* restriction.

LIM_CPU   the maximum number of cpu-seconds to be used by each process

LIM_FSIZE   the largest single file which can be created

LIM_DATA   the maximum growth of the data+stack region via sbrk(2) beyond the end of the program text

LIM_STACK   the maximum size of the automatically-extended stack region

LIM_CORE   the size of the largest core dump that will be created.

LIM_MAXRSS   a soft limit for the amount of physical memory (in bytes) to be given to the program. If memory is tight, the system will prefer to take memory from processes which are exceeding their declared LIM_MAXRSS.

Because this information is stored in the per-process information this system call must be executed directly by the shell if it is to affect all future processes created by the shell; limit is thus a built-in command to csh(1).

The system refuses to extend the data or stack space when the limits would be exceeded in the normal way; a break(2) call fails if the data space limit is reached, or the process is killed when the stack limit is reached (since the stack cannot be extended, there is no way to send a signal!).

A file I/O operation which would create a file which is too large will cause a signal SIGXFSZ to be generated, this normally terminates the process, but may be caught. When the cpu time limit is exceeded, a signal SIGXCPU is sent to the offending process; to allow it time to process the signal it is given 5 seconds grace by raising the CPU time limit.

SEE ALSO

csh(1)

HISTORY

The vlimit() function appeared in 4.2BSD.

BUGS

LIM_NORAISE no longer exists.

NAME
vtimes – get information about resource utilization

SYNOPSIS
`#include <sys/vtimes.h>`

`vtimes(struct vtimes *par_vm, struct vtimes *ch_vm);`

DESCRIPTION
This interface is obsoleted by getrusage(2). It is available from the compatibility library, libcompat.

The **vtimes**() function returns accounting information for the current process and for the terminated child processes of the current process. Either *par_vm* or *ch_vm* or both may be 0, in which case only the information for the pointers which are non-zero is returned.

After the call, each buffer contains information as defined by the contents of the include file /usr/include/sys/vtimes.h:

```
struct vtimes {
        int     vm_utime;       /* user time (*HZ) */
        int     vm_stime;       /* system time (*HZ) */
        /* divide next two by utime+stime to get averages */
        unsigned vm_idsrss;     /* integral of d+s rss */
        unsigned vm_ixrss;      /* integral of text rss */
        int     vm_maxrss;      /* maximum rss */
        int     vm_majflt;      /* major page faults */
        int     vm_minflt;      /* minor page faults */
        int     vm_nswap;       /* number of swaps */
        int     vm_inblk;       /* block reads */
        int     vm_oublk;       /* block writes */
};
```

The *vm_utime* and *vm_stime* fields give the user and system time respectively in 60ths of a second (or 50ths if that is the frequency of wall current in your locality.) The *vm_idrss* and *vm_ixrss* measure memory usage. They are computed by integrating the number of memory pages in use each over CPU time. They are reported as though computed discretely, adding the current memory usage (in 512 byte pages) each time the clock ticks. If a process used 5 core pages over 1 cpu-second for its data and stack, then *vm_idsrss* would have the value 5*60, where *vm_utime+vm_stime* would be the 60. The *Vm_idsrss* argument integrates data and stack segment usage, while *vm_ixrss* integrates text segment usage. The *Vm_maxrss* function reports the maximum instantaneous sum of the text+data+stack core-resident page count.

The *vm_majflt* field gives the number of page faults which resulted in disk activity; the *vm_minflt* field gives the number of page faults incurred in simulation of reference bits; *vm_nswap* is the number of swaps which occurred. The number of file system input/output events are reported in *vm_inblk* and *vm_oublk* These numbers account only for real I/O; data supplied by the caching mechanism is charged only to the first process to read or write the data.

SEE ALSO
time(2), wait3(2), getrusage(2)

HISTORY

The **vlimit**( ) function appeared in 4.2BSD.

4

Section 4

Special
Files

4

NAME

intro – introduction to special files and hardware support

DESCRIPTION

This section describes the special files, related driver functions, and networking support available in the system. In this part of the manual, the SYNOPSIS section of each configurable device gives a sample specification for use in constructing a system description for the config(8) program. The DIAGNOSTICS section lists messages which may appear on the console and/or in the system error log /usr/adm/messages due to errors in device operation; see syslogd(8) for more information.

This section contains both devices which may be configured into the system and network related information. The networking support is introduced in netintro(4).

HP DEVICE SUPPORT

This section describes the hardware supported on the HP 9000/300 series. Software support for these devices comes in two forms. A hardware device may be supported with a character or block *device driver*, or it may be used within the networking subsystem and have a *network interface driver*. Block and character devices are accessed through files in the file system of a special type; see mknod(8). Network interfaces are indirectly accessed through the interprocess communication facilities provided by the system; see socket(2).

A hardware device is identified to the system at configuration time and the appropriate device or network interface driver is then compiled into the system. When the resultant system is booted, the autoconfiguration facilities in the system probe for the device and, if found, enable the software support for it. If a device does not respond at autoconfiguration time it is not accessible at any time afterwards. To enable a device which did not autoconfigure, the system will have to be rebooted.

The autoconfiguration system is described in autoconf(4). A list of the supported devices is given below.

SEE ALSO

intro(4), intro(4), autoconf(4), config(8).

Building 4.3 BSD UNIX Systems with Config (SMM:2).

LIST OF DEVICES

The devices listed below are supported in this incarnation of the system. Pseudo-devices are not listed. Devices are indicated by their functional interface. Occasionally, new devices of a similar type may be added simply by creating appropriate table entries in the driver; for example, new CS/80 drives.

ct	7946/9144 CS/80 cartridge tape
dca	98644 built-in serial interface
dcl	HP 98628A communications link
dcm	HP 98642A communications multiplexer
dma	98620B DMA controller
dv	HP98730 ''DaVinci'' device interface
gb	HP98700 ''Gatorbox'' device interface
grf/ite	Topcat/Gatorbox/Renaissance frame buffer
hil	HIL interface
hpib	Built-in and 98625 HP-IB interface
ite	HP Internal Terminal Emulator
le	98643 Lance-based ethernet interface
mem	main memory
ppi	HP-IB printer/plotter interface

rb	HP98720 ''Renaissance'' device interface
rd	CS/80 disk interface
rmp	HP Remote Maintenance Protocol family
st	CCS SCSI tape drive
tc	HP98544-98550 ''Topcat'' and ''Catseye'' device interface

HISTORY
The HP300 `intro` appeared in 4.3BSD–Reno.

NAME
networking – introduction to networking facilities

SYNOPSIS
```
#include <sys/socket.h>
#include <net/route.h>
#include <net/if.h>
```

DESCRIPTION
This section is a general introduction to the networking facilities available in the system. Documentation in this part of section 4 is broken up into three areas: *protocol families* (domains), *protocols*, and *network interfaces*.

All network protocols are associated with a specific *protocol family*. A protocol family provides basic services to the protocol implementation to allow it to function within a specific network environment. These services may include packet fragmentation and reassembly, routing, addressing, and basic transport. A protocol family may support multiple methods of addressing, though the current protocol implementations do not. A protocol family is normally comprised of a number of protocols, one per socket(2) type. It is not required that a protocol family support all socket types. A protocol family may contain multiple protocols supporting the same socket abstraction.

A protocol supports one of the socket abstractions detailed in socket(2). A specific protocol may be accessed either by creating a socket of the appropriate type and protocol family, or by requesting the protocol explicitly when creating a socket. Protocols normally accept only one type of address format, usually determined by the addressing structure inherent in the design of the protocol family/network architecture. Certain semantics of the basic socket abstractions are protocol specific. All protocols are expected to support the basic model for their particular socket type, but may, in addition, provide non-standard facilities or extensions to a mechanism. For example, a protocol supporting the SOCK_STREAM abstraction may allow more than one byte of out-of-band data to be transmitted per out-of-band message.

A network interface is similar to a device interface. Network interfaces comprise the lowest layer of the networking subsystem, interacting with the actual transport hardware. An interface may support one or more protocol families and/or address formats. The SYNOPSIS section of each network interface entry gives a sample specification of the related drivers for use in providing a system description to the config(8) program. The DIAGNOSTICS section lists messages which may appear on the console and/or in the system error log, /var/log/messages (see syslogd(8)), due to errors in device operation.

PROTOCOLS
The system currently supports the Internet protocols, the Xerox Network Systems(tm) protocols, and some of the ISO OSI protocols. Raw socket interfaces are provided to the IP protocol layer of the Internet, and to the IDP protocol of Xerox NS. Consult the appropriate manual pages in this section for more information regarding the support for each protocol family.

ADDRESSING
Associated with each protocol family is an address format. All network address adhere to a general structure, called a sockaddr, described below. However, each protocol imposes finer and more specific structure, generally renaming the variant, which is discussed in the protocol family manual page alluded to above.

```
struct sockaddr {
    u_char  sa_len;
    u_char  sa_family;
    char    sa_data[14];
};
```

The field *sa_len* contains the total length of the of the structure, which may exceed 16 bytes. The following address values for *sa_family* are known to the system (and additional formats are defined for possible future implementation):

```
#define     AF_UNIX      1     /* local to host (pipes, portals) */
#define     AF_INET      2     /* internetwork: UDP, TCP, etc. */
#define     AF_NS        6     /* Xerox NS protocols */
#define     AF_CCITT     10    /* CCITT protocols, X.25 etc */
#define     AF_HYLINK    15    /* NSC Hyperchannel */
#define     AF_ISO       18    /* ISO protocols */
```

ROUTING

UNIX provides some packet routing facilities. The kernel maintains a routing information database, which is used in selecting the appropriate network interface when transmitting packets.

A user process (or possibly multiple co-operating processes) maintains this database by sending messages over a special kind of socket. This supplants fixed size ioctl(2) used in earlier releases.

This facility is described in route(4).

INTERFACES

Each network interface in a system corresponds to a path through which messages may be sent and received. A network interface usually has a hardware device associated with it, though certain interfaces such as the loopback interface, lo(4), do not.

The following ioctl calls may be used to manipulate network interfaces. The ioctl is made on a socket (typically of type SOCK_DGRAM) in the desired domain. Most of the requests supported in earlier releases take an *ifreq* structure as its parameter. This structure has the form

```
struct ifreq {
#define     IFNAMSIZ    16
    char    ifr_name[IFNAMSIZE];        /* if name, e.g. "en0" */
    union {
        struct    sockaddr ifru_addr;
        struct    sockaddr ifru_dstaddr;
        struct    sockaddr ifru_broadaddr;
        short     ifru_flags;
        int       ifru_metric;
        caddr_t   ifru_data;
    } ifr_ifru;
#define ifr_addr        ifr_ifru.ifru_addr      /* address */
#define ifr_dstaddr     ifr_ifru.ifru_dstaddr /* other end of p-to-p link */
#define ifr_broadaddr   ifr_ifru.ifru_broadaddr /* broadcast address */
#define ifr_flags       ifr_ifru.ifru_flags   /* flags */
#define ifr_metric      ifr_ifru.ifru_metric  /* metric */
#define ifr_data        ifr_ifru.ifru_data    /* for use by interface */
};
```

Calls which are now deprecated are:

SIOCSIFADDR　　　Set interface address for protocol family. Following the address assignment, the "initialization" routine for the interface is called.

SIOCSIFDSTADDR Set point to point address for protocol family and interface.

SIOCSIFBRDADDR Set broadcast address for protocol family and interface.

Ioctl requests to obtain addresses and requests both to set and retrieve other data are still fully supported and use the *ifreq* structure:

SIOCGIFADDR   Get interface address for protocol family.

SIOCGIFDSTADDR Get point to point address for protocol family and interface.

SIOCGIFBRDADDR Get broadcast address for protocol family and interface.

SIOCSIFFLAGS   Set interface flags field. If the interface is marked down, any processes currently routing packets through the interface are notified; some interfaces may be reset so that incoming packets are no longer received. When marked up again, the interface is reinitialized.

SIOCGIFFLAGS   Get interface flags.

SIOCSIFMETRIC   Set interface routing metric. The metric is used only by user-level routers.

SIOCGIFMETRIC   Get interface metric.

There are two requests that make use of a new structure:

SIOCAIFADDR   An interface may have more than one address associated with it in some protocols. This request provides a means to add additional addresses (or modify characteristics of the primary address if the default address for the address family is specified). Rather than making separate calls to set destination or broadcast addresses, or network masks (now an integral feature of multiple protocols) a separate structure is used to specify all three facets simultaneously (see below). One would use a slightly tailored version of this struct specific to each family (replacing each sockaddr by one of the family-specific type). Where the sockaddr itself is larger than the default size, one needs to modify the ioctl identifier itself to include the total size, as described in ioctl.

SIOCDIFADDR   This requests deletes the specified address from the list associated with an interface. It also uses the *if_aliasreq* structure to allow for the possibility of protocols allowing multiple masks or destination addresses, and also adopts the convention that specification of the default address means to delete the first address for the interface belonging to the address family in which the original socket was opened.

SIOCGIFCONF   Get interface configuration list. This request takes an *ifconf* structure (see below) as a value-result parameter. The *ifc_len* field should be initially set to the size of the buffer pointed to by *ifc_buf*. On return it will contain the length, in bytes, of the configuration list.

```
/*
 * Structure used in SIOCAIFCONF request.
 */
struct ifaliasreq {
        char    ifra_name[IFNAMSIZ];   /* if name, e.g. "en0" */
        struct  sockaddr      ifra_addr;
        struct  sockaddr      ifra_broadaddr;
        struct  sockaddr      ifra_mask;
};
```

```
/*
 * Structure used in SIOCGIFCONF request.
 * Used to retrieve interface configuration
 * for machine (useful for programs which
 * must know all networks accessible).
 */
struct ifconf {
    int    ifc_len;                /* size of associated buffer */
    union {
        caddr_t    ifcu_buf;
        struct     ifreq *ifcu_req;
    } ifc_ifcu;
#define ifc_buf ifc_ifcu.ifcu_buf /* buffer address */
#define ifc_req ifc_ifcu.ifcu_req /* array of structures returned */
};
```

SEE ALSO

socket(2), ioctl(2), intro(4), config(8), routed(8)

HISTORY

The **netintro** manual appeared in 4.3BSD–Tahoe.

NAME

`autoconf` – diagnostics from the autoconfiguration code

DESCRIPTION

When UNIX bootstraps it probes the innards of the machine on which it is running and locates controllers, drives, and other devices, printing out what it finds on the console. This procedure is driven by a system configuration table which is processed by `config`(8) and compiled into each kernel.

Autoconfiguration on the HP300s is similar to that on the VAX, the primary difference is in the naming conventions. On the HP300, if devices exist which are not configured they will be ignored; if devices exist of unsupported type they will be ignored.

Normally, the system uses the disk from which it was loaded as the root filesystem. If that is not possible, a generic system will use 'rd0' if it exists. If such a system is booted with the `RB_ASKNAME` option (see `reboot`(2)), then the name of the root device is read from the console terminal at boot time, and any available device may be used.

DIAGNOSTICS

CPU type not configured. You tried to boot UNIX on a CPU type which it doesn't (or at least this compiled version of UNIX doesn't) understand.

hpib%d at sc%d, ipl %d. An HP-IB was found at sc%d (the select code) with ipl%d (interrupt priority level). UNIX will call it hpib%d.

%s%d: %s.
%s%d at hpib%d, slave %d. An HP-IB disk or tape controller was found. For disks %s%d will look like 'rd0', for tapes like 'ct0'. The '%s' in the first line will be a product type like "7945A" or "9144". The slave number comes from the address select switches on the drive.

grf0 csr 0x560000
grf%d at sc%d A bit mapped display was found either at the "internal" address (first case) or at some "external" select code (second case). If it exists, the internal display will always be unit 0.

%s%d at sc%d, ipl %d flags %d Another peripheral controller was found at the indicated select code and with indicated interrupt priority level. '%s' will be one of dca(4) (single-port serial interfaces), dcm(4) (four-port serial interfaces), or le(4) (LAN cards). The slave number comes from the address select switches on the interface card.

SEE ALSO

intro(4), boot(8), config(8)

4.3BSD for the HP300, in the distribution documentation package.

NAME

   bwtwo – monochromatic frame buffer

SYNOPSIS

   bwtwo* at sbus? slot ? offset ?

DESCRIPTION

   The **bwtwo** is a memory based black and white frame buffer. It supports the minimal ioctl's needed to run
   X11.

SEE ALSO

   cgsix(4), cgthree(4)

NAME

cgsix – accelerated 8-bit color frame buffer

SYNOPSIS

cgsix* at sbus? slot ? offset ?

DESCRIPTION

The cgsix is a memory based color frame buffer. It supports the minimal ioctl's needed to run X11.

SEE ALSO

bwtwo(4), cgthree(4)

NAME

  `cgthree` – 8-bit color frame buffer

SYNOPSIS

  `cgthree* at sbus? slot ? offset ?`

DESCRIPTION

  The `cgthree` is a memory based color frame buffer. It supports the minimal ioctl's needed to run X11.

SEE ALSO

  bwtwo(4), cgsix(4)

NAME

clnp – Connectionless-Mode Network Protocol

SYNOPSIS

```
#include <sys/socket.h>
#include <netiso/iso.h>
#include <netiso/clnp.h>
```

int
socket(AF_ISO, SOCK_RAW, 0);

DESCRIPTION

CLNP is the connectionless-mode network protocol used by the connectionless-mode network service. This protocol is specified in ISO 8473. It may be accessed through a "raw socket" for debugging purposes only. CLNP sockets are connectionless, and are normally used with the sendto and recvfrom calls, though the connect(2) call may also be used to fix the destination for future packets (in which case the read(2) or recv(2) and write(2) or send(2) system calls may be used).

Outgoing packets automatically have a CLNP header prepended to them. Incoming packets received by the user contain the full CLNP header. The following setsockopt options apply to CLNP:

CLNPOPT_FLAGS   Sets the flags which are passed to clnp when sending a datagram. Valid flags are:

CLNP_NO_SEG	Do not allow segmentation
CLNP_NO_ER	Suppress ER pdus
CLNP_NO_CKSUM	Do not generate the CLNP checksum

CLNPOPT_OPTS   Sets CLNP options. The options must be formatted exactly as specified by ISO 8473, section 7.5 "Options Part." Once an option has been set, it will be sent on all packets until a different option is set.

CONGESTION EXPERIENCE BIT

Whenever a packet is transmitted, the globally unique quality of service option is added to the packet. The sequencing preferred bit and the low transit delay bit are set in this option.

If a packet is forwarded containing the globally unique quality of service option, and the interface through which the packet will be transmitted has a queue length greater than *congest_threshold*, then the congestion experienced bit is set in the quality of service option.

The threshold value stored in *congest_threshold* may be tuned.

When a packet is received with the globally unique quality of service option present, and the congestion experienced bit is set, then the transport congestion control function is called.

DIAGNOSTICS

A socket operation may fail with one of the following errors returned:

[EISCONN]   When trying to establish a connection on a socket which already has one, or when trying to send a datagram with the destination address specified and the socket is already connected;

[ENOTCONN]   When trying to send a datagram, but no destination address is specified, and the socket hasn't been connected;

[ENOBUFS]   When the system runs out of memory for an internal data structure;

[EADDRNOTAVAIL]   When an attempt is made to create a socket with a network address for which no net-
                       work interface exists;

[EHOSTUNREACH]   When trying to send a datagram, but no route to the destination address exists.

[EINVAL]   When specifying unsupported options.

SEE ALSO
send(2), recv(2), intro(4), iso(4)

BUGS
Packets are sent with the type code of 0x1d (technically an invalid packet type) for lack of a better way to
identify raw CLNP packets.

No more than MLEN bytes of options can be specified.

4

NAME

`cltp` – ISO Connectionless Transport Protocol

SYNOPSIS

```
#include <sys/socket.h>
#include <netiso/iso.h>

int
socket(AF_ISO, SOCK_DGRAM, 0);
```

DESCRIPTION

CLTP is a simple, unreliable datagram protocol which is accessed via the SOCK_DGRAM abstraction for the ISO protocol family. CLTP sockets are connectionless, and are normally used with the `sendto` and `recvfrom` calls, though the connect(2) call may also be used to fix the destination for future packets (in which case the `recv`(2) or read(2) and send(2) or `write`(2) system calls may be used).

CLTP address formats are identical to those used by TP. In particular CLTP provides a service selector in addition to the normal ISO NSAP. Note that the CLTP selector space is separate from the TP selector space (i.e. a CLTP selector may not be ''connected'' to a TP selector).

Options at the CLNP network level may be used with CLTP; see `clnp`(4).

DIAGNOSTICS

A socket operation may fail with one of the following errors returned:

[EISCONN]　　　　　　when trying to establish a connection on a socket which already has one, or when trying to send a datagram with the destination address specified and the socket is already connected;

[ENOTCONN]　　　　　when trying to send a datagram, but no destination address is specified, and the socket hasn't been connected;

[ENOBUFS]　　　　　　when the system runs out of memory for an internal data structure;

[EADDRINUSE]　　　　when an attempt is made to create a socket with a selector which has already been allocated;

[EADDRNOTAVAIL]　when an attempt is made to create a socket with a network address for which no network interface exists.

SEE ALSO

getsockopt(2), recv(2), send(2), socket(2), intro(4), iso(4), clnp(4)

NAME

cons – HP300 console interface

DESCRIPTION

This release supports a "virtual" console device used for *kernel printf* messages and accessed in user mode via /dev/console. It is virtual in the sense that it is attached to a hardware interface at boot time. Currently the choices are limited to: a bit-mapped display acting as an *internal terminal emulator* "ITE", the builtin serial interface dca(4), or a null(4) console in that order.

FILES

/dev/console

SEE ALSO

tty(4), reboot(8)

BUGS

You should be able to specify potential console devices at config(8) time.

NAME

    ct – CS/80 cartridge tape interface

SYNOPSIS

    tape ct0 at hpib? slave ?

DESCRIPTION

    The cartridge tape interface as found in the 7946 and 9144 products provides a standard tape drive interface
    as described in mtio(4) with the following exceptions:

    1.   There is only one density.

    2.   Only the "raw" interface is supported.

    3.   The MTIOCTOP ioctl(2) is limited. In particular, the command, MTFSR is not supported.

    4.   The MTIOCGET ioctl is not supported.

    5.   The record size for read and write operations must be between 1K and 64K inclusive.

    Special files rct0 through rct3 refer to rewind on close interfaces to drives 0 to 3. Files rct4 through
    rct7 refer to no-rewind interfaces. Files rct8 through rct11 refer to streaming rewind on close inter-
    faces. (Only 9144 type devices can stream.) Lastly, rct12 through rct15 refer to streaming no-rewind in-
    terfaces.

SEE ALSO

    mt(1), tar(1), tp(1), mtio(4).

BUGS

    Read and writes of less than 1024 bytes will not behave as expected.

NAME

dca – HP 98644A communications interface

SYNOPSIS

`device dca0 at scode9 flags 0x1`

DESCRIPTION

The 98644A is a single port EIA RS-232C (CCITT V.28) communications interface with a single character buffer. Such an interface is built-in to all series 300 machines.

Input and output for each line may set to one of following baud rates; 50, 75, 110, 134.5, 150, 300, 600, 1200, 1800, 2400, 4800, 9600 or 19200.

An optional argument *flags* may be set to 1 if the line should be treated as hard-wired with carrier always present or 0 if modem control is desired.

FILES

`/dev/tty0`

DIAGNOSTICS

dca%d: silo overflow. The single-character input "silo" has overflowed and incoming data has been lost.

SEE ALSO

`tty(4)`

BUGS

Data loss is possible on busy systems with baud rates greater than 300. The dca has never been tested with modem control enabled or on anything but the built-in interface.

NAME
dcl – HP 98628A communications link

SYNOPSIS
`device dcl0 at scode? flags 0x1`

DESCRIPTION
The 98628A is a buffered EIA RS-232C (CCITT V.28) communications interface. It has one port with full modem control.

Input and output for each line may set to one of following baud rates; 0, 50, 75, 110, 134.5, 150, 200, 300, 600, 1200, 1800, 2400, 4800, 9600, 19200.

An optional argument *flags* may be set to 1 if the line should be treated as hard-wired with carrier always present, or to 0 if modem control is desired.

Use HP cable "98626 & 98628 opts.002, RS232-C DCE CABLE, 5061-4216" to attach non-modem devices.
Use HP cable "98626 & 98628 opts.001, RS232-C DTE CABLE, 5061-4215" to attach modems.

The 98628A has a 256 byte input silo and a 256 output silo. Input interrupts happen on a per character basis.

The high water and low water marks in the kernel tty routines are completely inappropriate for a device like this with a large input buffer. Don't use tandem mode if possible. A fast system can handle input at 19.2K baud without receive overflow.

For output to devices that make heavy use of XON/XOFF a write size of less then 256 will improve performance marginally.

FILES
`/dev/ttyl[0-9]`

DIAGNOSTICS
dcl%d: error 0x%x RESET CARD. Where the errors are encoded:

    0x06 card failure
    0x0d uart receive overflow
    0x0e receive overflow
    0x0f missing external clock
    0x10 cts false too long
    0x11 lost carrier
    0x12 activity timeout
    0x13 connection not established
    0x19 illegal databits/parity
    0x1a register address out of range
    0x1b register value out of range
    0x-- unknown error

SEE ALSO
tty(4)

BUGS
Breaks received at a faster rate then 1 break every second will be recognized as a single break.

Console use is not supported.

The RS-422/423/499, MTS-DSN/DL modes of the card are not supported.

NAME

dcm – HP 98642A communications multiplexer

SYNOPSIS

```
device dcm0 at scode? flags 0xe
```

DESCRIPTION

The 98642A is a four port EIA RS-232C (CCITT V.28) communications multiplexer. The 98642A has three direct-connect ports and one port with full modem control.

Input and output for each line may set to one of following baud rates; 50, 75, 110, 134.5, 150, 300, 600, 1200, 1800, 2400, 4800, 9600, 19200, 38400.

Flags is usually specified as 0xe since 3 of the 4 ports (1-3) do not support modem control and should be treated as hard-wired with carrier always present. If port 0 does not have the need for modem control then flags can be specified as 0xf.

Each port on the 98642A has a 128 byte input silo and a 16 byte output silo. Interrupts happen on a per character basis unless the interrupt rate for the card reaches 70 interrupts per second at which time the driver changes to a 16.7ms (60 interrupts per second) polling scheme until the interrupt rate drops.

FILES

```
/dev/tty0[0-9a-f]
```

DIAGNOSTICS

dcm %d port %d: silo overflow Input Silo has overflowed and incoming data has been lost.

dcm %d port %d: uart overflow The 3 character buffer in the uart has overflowed.

SEE ALSO

tty(4)

BUGS

Total throughput per card, all ports together, is limited to 76800 bits per second continuous input rate.

NAME

drum – paging device

DESCRIPTION

This file refers to the paging device in use by the system. This may actually be a subdevice of one of the disk drivers, but in a system with paging interleaved across multiple disk drives it provides an indirect driver for the multiple drives.

FILES

/dev/drum

HISTORY

The **drum** special file appeared in 3.0BSD.

BUGS

Reads from the drum are not allowed across the interleaving boundaries. Since these only occur every .5Mbytes or so, and since the system never allocates blocks across the boundary, this is usually not a problem.

NAME

    dv – HP98730 "DaVinci" device interface

DESCRIPTION

This driver is for the HP98730 and 98731 graphics device, also known as the DaVinci. This driver has not been tested with all possible combinations of frame buffer boards and scan boards installed in the device. The driver merely checks for the existence of the device and does minimal set up.

The DaVinci can be configured at either the "internal" address (frame buffer address 0x200000, control register space address 0x560000) or at an external select code less than 32. At the internal address it will be the "preferred" console device (see cons(4)). The hardware installation manual describes the procedure for setting these values.

A user process communicates to the device initially by means of ioctl(2) calls. For the HP-UX ioctl calls supported, refer to HP-UX manuals. The BSD calls supported are:

GRFIOCGINFO

> Get Graphics Info

> Get info about device, setting the entries in the *grfinfo* structure, as defined in <hpdev/grfioctl.h>. For the standard 98730, the number of planes should be 4. The number of colors would therefore be 15, excluding black. If one 98732A frame buffer board is installed, there will still be 4 planes, with the 4 planes on the colormap board becoming overlay planes. With each additional 98732 frame buffer board 4 planes will be added up to a maximum of 32 planes total.

GRFIOCON

> Graphics On

> Turn graphics on by enabling CRT output. The screen will come on, displaying whatever is in the frame buffer, using whatever colormap is in place.

GRFIOCOFF

> Graphics Off

> Turn graphics off by disabling output to the CRT. The frame buffer contents are not affected.

GRFIOCMAP

> Map Device to user space

> Map in control registers and frame buffer space. Once the device file is mapped, the frame buffer structure is accessible. The structure describing the 98730 is defined in <hpdev/grf_dvreg.h>.

EXAMPLE

This is a short segment of code showing how the device is opened and mapped into user process address space assuming that it is grf0:

```
struct dvboxfb *dvbox;
u_char *Addr, frame_buffer;
struct grfinfo gi;
int disp_fd;

disp_fd = open("/dev/grf0",1);

if (ioctl (disp_fd, GRFIOCGINFO, &gi) < 0) return -1;
```

```
    (void) ioctl (disp_fd, GRFIOCON, 0);

    Addr = (u_char *) 0;
    if (ioctl (disp_fd, GRFIOCMAP, &Addr) < 0) {
    (void) ioctl (disp_fd, GRFIOCOFF, 0);
    return -1;
    }
    dvbox = (dvboxfb *) Addr;                    /* Control Registers  */
    frame_buffer=(u_char *)Addr+gi.gd_regsize; /* Frame buffer memory */
```

FILES

/dev/grf?   BSD special file
/dev/crt98730
/dev/ocrt98730   HP-UX *starbase* special files
/dev/MAKEDEV.hpux script for creating HP-UX special files

DIAGNOSTICS

None under BSD. HP-UX CE.utilities must be used.

ERRORS

[ENODEV] no such device.

[EBUSY]   Another process has the device open.

[EINVAL] Invalid ioctl specification.

SEE ALSO

ioctl(2), grf(4).

BUGS

Not tested for all configurations of scan board and frame buffer memory boards.

NAME

`es-is` – End System to Intermediate System Routing Protocol

SYNOPSIS

pseudo-device
ether

DESCRIPTION

The `ES-IS` routing protocol is used to dynamically map between ISO NSAP addresses and ISO SNPA addresses; to permit End and Intermediate Systems to learn of each other's existence; and to allow Intermediate Systems to inform End Systems of (potentially) better routes to use when forwarding NPDUs to a particular destination.

The mapping between NSAP addresses and SNPA addresses is accomplished by transmitting hello PDUs between the cooperating Systems. These PDUs are transmitted whenever the *configuration* timer expires. When a hello PDU is received, the SNPA address that it conveys is stored in the routing table for as long as the *holding time* in the PDU suggests. The default *holding time* (120 seconds) placed in the hello PDU, the configuration timer value, and the system type (End System or Intermediate System) may be changed by issuing an `SIOCSSTYPE ioctl(2)`, which is defined in `/sys/netiso/iso_snpac.h`.

The protocol behaves differently depending on whether the System is configured as an End System or an Intermediate System.

END SYSTEM OPERATION

When an interface requests a mapping for an address not in the cache, the SNPA of any known Intermediate System is returned. If an Intermediate System is not known, then the *all end systems* multicast address is returned. It is assumed that the intended recipient of the NPDU will immediately transmit a hello PDU back to the originator of the NPDU.

If an NPDU is forwarded by the End System, a redirect PDU will not be generated. However, redirect PDUs received will be processed. This processing consists of adding an entry in the routing table. If the redirect is towards an Intermediate System, then an entry is made in the routing table as well. The entry in the routing table will mark the NSAP address contained in the redirect PDU as the gateway for the destination system (if an NET is supplied), or will create a route with the NSAP address as the destination and the SNPA address (embodied as a link-level sockaddr) as the gateway.

If the System is configured as an End System, it will report all the NSAPs that have been configured using the ifconfig command, and no others. It is possible to have more than one NSAP assigned to a given interface, and it is also possible to have the same NSAP assigned to multiple interfaces. However, any NSAP containing an NSEL that is consistent with the nsellength option (default one) of any interface will be accepted as an NSAP for this System.

INTERMEDIATE SYSTEM OPERATION

When an interface requests a mapping for an address not in the routing table, an error is returned.

When an NPDU is forwarded out on the same interface that the NPDU arrived upon, a redirect PDU is generated.

MANUAL ROUTING TABLE MODIFICATION

To facilitate communications with systems which do not use ES-IS, one may add a route whose destination is a sockaddr_iso containing the NSAP in question, and the gateway being a link-level sockaddr, either by writing a special purpose program, or using the route(8) command e.g.:

```
route add -iface -osi 49.0.4.8.0.2b.b.83.bf  -link qe0:8.0.2b.b.83.bf
```

If the System is configured as an End System and has a single network interface which does not support multicast reception, it is necessary to manually configure the location of an IS, using the route command in a similar way. There, the destination address should be "default" (spelled out literally as 7 ASCII characters), and the gateway should be once again be a link-level sockaddr specifying the SNPA of the IS.

SEE ALSO

un(4), iso(4), route(8), ifconfig(8)

End system to Intermediate system routing exchange protocol for use in conjunction with the Protocol for providing the connectionless-mode network service, ISO, 9542.

BUGS

Redirect PDUs do not contain options from the forwarded NPDU which generated the redirect. The multicast address used on the 802.3 network is taken from the NBS December 1987 agreements. This multicast address is not compatible with the 802.5 (Token Ring) multicast addresses format. Therefore, broadcast addresses are used on the 802.5 subnetwork. Researchers at the University of Wisconsin are constructing an implementation of the IS-IS routing protocol.

4

NAME

  EUC – EUC encoding of runes

SYNOPSIS

  ENCODING "EUC"
  VARIABLE *len1 mask1 len2 mask2 len3 mask3 len4 mask4 mask*

DESCRIPTION

  The EUC encoding is provided for compatibility with UNIX based systems. See mklocale(1) for a complete description of the LC_CTYPE source file format.

  EUC implements a system of 4 multibyte codesets. A multibyte character in the first codeset consists of *len1* bytes starting with a byte in the range of 0x00 to 0x7f. To allow use of ASCII, *len1* is always 1. A multibyte character in the second codeset consists of *len2* bytes starting with a byte in the range of 0x80-0xff excluding 0x8e and 0x8f. A multibyte character in the third codeset consists of *len3* bytes starting with the byte 0x8e. A multibyte character in the fourth codeset consists of *len4* bytes starting with the byte 0x8f.

  The rune_t encoding of EUC multibyte characters is dependent on the *len* and *mask* arguments. First, the bytes are moved into a rune_t as follows:

  byte0 << ((*len*N-1) * 8) | byte1 << ((*len*N-2) * 8) | ... | byte*len*N-1

  The result is then ANDed with ~*mask* and ORed with *mask*N. Codesets 2 and 3 are special in that the leading byte (0x8e or 0x8f) is first removed and the *len*N argument is reduced by 1.

  For example, the Japanese locale has the following VARIABLE line:

  VARIABLE   1 0x0000 2 0x8080 2 0x0080 3 0x8000 0x8080

  Codeset 1 consists of the values 0x0000 - 0x007f.

  Codeset 2 consists of the values who have the bits 0x8080 set.

  Codeset 3 consists of the values 0x0080 - 0x00ff.

  Codeset 4 consists of the values 0x8000 - 0xff7f excluding the values which have the 0x0080 bit set.

  Notice that the global *mask* is set to 0x8080, this implies that from those 2 bits the codeset can be determined.

EXAMPLE - Japanese Locale

  This is a complete example of an LC_CTYPE source file for the Japanese locale

```
/*
 * Japanese LOCALE_CTYPE definitions using EUC of JIS character sets
 */

ENCODING        "EUC"

/*              JIS     JIS     JIS             */
/*              X201    X208    X201            */
/*              00-7f           84-fe           */
```

```
VARIABLE        1 0x0000 2 0x8080 2 0x0080 3 0x8000 0x8080

/*
 * Code Set 1
 */
ALPHA           'A' - 'Z' 'a' - 'z'
CONTROL         0x00 - 0x1f 0x7f
DIGIT           '0' - '9'
GRAPH           0x21 - 0x7e
LOWER           'a' - 'z'
PUNCT           0x21 - 0x2f 0x3a - 0x40 0x5b - 0x60 0x7b - 0x7e
SPACE           0x09 - 0x0d 0x20
UPPER           'A' - 'Z'
XDIGIT          'a' - 'f' 'A' - 'F'
BLANK           ' ' ''
PRINT           0x20 - 0x7e

MAPLOWER        < 'A' - 'Z' : 'a' > < 'a' - 'z' : 'a' >
MAPUPPER        < 'A' - 'Z' : 'A' > < 'a' - 'z' : 'A' >
TODIGIT         < '0' - '9' : 0 >
TODIGIT         < 'A' - 'F' : 10 > < 'a' - 'f' : 10 >

/*
 * Code Set 2
 */

SPACE           0xa1a1
PHONOGRAM       0xa1bc
SPECIAL         0xa1a2 - 0xa1fe
PUNCT           0xa1a2 - 0xa1f8                  /* A few too many in here... */

SPECIAL         0xa2a1 - 0xa2ae 0xa2ba - 0xa2c1 0xa2ca - 0xa2d0 0xa2dc - 0xa2ea
SPECIAL         0xa2f2 - 0xa2f9 0xa2fe

DIGIT           0xa3b0 - 0xa3b9
UPPER           0xa3c1 - 0xa3da                  /* Romaji */
LOWER           0xa3e1 - 0xa3fa                  /* Romaji */
MAPLOWER        < 0xa3c1 - 0xa3da : 0xa3e1 >     /* English */
MAPLOWER        < 0xa3e1 - 0xa3fa : 0xa3e1 >     /* English */
MAPUPPER        < 0xa3c1 - 0xa3da : 0xa3c1 >
MAPUPPER        < 0xa3e1 - 0xa3fa : 0xa3c1 >

XDIGIT          0xa3c1 - 0xa3c6 0xa3e1 - 0xa3e6

TODIGIT         < 0xa3b0 - 0xa3b9 : 0 >
TODIGIT         < 0xa3c1 - 0xa3c6 : 10 > < 0xa3e1 - 0xa3e6 : 10 >

PHONOGRAM       0xa4a1 - 0xa4f3
PHONOGRAM       0xa5a1 - 0xa5f6

UPPER           0xa6a1 - 0xa6b8                  /* Greek */
```

4

```
       LOWER         0xa6c1 - 0xa6d8                                  /* Greek */
       MAPLOWER      < 0xa6a1 - 0xa6b8 : 0xa6c1 > < 0xa6c1 - 0xa6d8 : 0xa6c1 >
       MAPUPPER      < 0xa6a1 - 0xa6b8 : 0xa6a1 > < 0xa6c1 - 0xa6d8 : 0xa6a1 >


       UPPER         0xa7a1 - 0xa7c1                                  /* Cyrillic */
       LOWER         0xa7d1 - 0xa7f1                                  /* Cyrillic */
       MAPLOWER      < 0xa7a1 - 0xa7c1 : 0xa7d1 > < 0xa7d1 - 0xa7f1 : 0xa7d1 >
       MAPUPPER      < 0xa7a1 - 0xa7c1 : 0xa7a1 > < 0xa7d1 - 0xa7f1 : 0xa7a1 >


       SPECIAL       0xa8a1 - 0xa8c0


       IDEOGRAM      0xb0a1 - 0xb0fe 0xb1a1 - 0xb1fe 0xb2a1 - 0xb2fe
       IDEOGRAM      0xb3a1 - 0xb3fe 0xb4a1 - 0xb4fe 0xb5a1 - 0xb5fe
       IDEOGRAM      0xb6a1 - 0xb6fe 0xb7a1 - 0xb7fe 0xb8a1 - 0xb8fe
       IDEOGRAM      0xb9a1 - 0xb9fe 0xbaa1 - 0xbafe 0xbba1 - 0xbbfe
       IDEOGRAM      0xbca1 - 0xbcfe 0xbda1 - 0xbdfe 0xbea1 - 0xbefe
       IDEOGRAM      0xbfa1 - 0xbffe 0xc0a1 - 0xc0fe 0xc1a1 - 0xc1fe
       IDEOGRAM      0xc2a1 - 0xc2fe 0xc3a1 - 0xc3fe 0xc4a1 - 0xc4fe
       IDEOGRAM      0xc5a1 - 0xc5fe 0xc6a1 - 0xc6fe 0xc7a1 - 0xc7fe
       IDEOGRAM      0xc8a1 - 0xc8fe 0xc9a1 - 0xc9fe 0xcaa1 - 0xcafe
       IDEOGRAM      0xcba1 - 0xcbfe 0xcca1 - 0xccfe 0xcda1 - 0xcdfe
       IDEOGRAM      0xcea1 - 0xcefe 0xcfa1 - 0xcfd3 0xd0a1 - 0xd0fe
       IDEOGRAM      0xd1a1 - 0xd1fe 0xd2a1 - 0xd2fe 0xd3a1 - 0xd3fe
       IDEOGRAM      0xd4a1 - 0xd4fe 0xd5a1 - 0xd5fe 0xd6a1 - 0xd6fe
       IDEOGRAM      0xd7a1 - 0xd7fe 0xd8a1 - 0xd8fe 0xd9a1 - 0xd9fe
       IDEOGRAM      0xdaa1 - 0xdafe 0xdba1 - 0xdbfe 0xdca1 - 0xdcfe
       IDEOGRAM      0xdda1 - 0xddfe 0xdea1 - 0xdefe 0xdfa1 - 0xdffe
       IDEOGRAM      0xe0a1 - 0xe0fe 0xe1a1 - 0xe1fe 0xe2a1 - 0xe2fe
       IDEOGRAM      0xe3a1 - 0xe3fe 0xe4a1 - 0xe4fe 0xe5a1 - 0xe5fe
       IDEOGRAM      0xe6a1 - 0xe6fe 0xe7a1 - 0xe7fe 0xe8a1 - 0xe8fe
       IDEOGRAM      0xe9a1 - 0xe9fe 0xeaa1 - 0xeafe 0xeba1 - 0xebfe
       IDEOGRAM      0xeca1 - 0xecfe 0xeda1 - 0xedfe 0xeea1 - 0xeefe
       IDEOGRAM      0xefa1 - 0xeffe 0xf0a1 - 0xf0fe 0xf1a1 - 0xf1fe
       IDEOGRAM      0xf2a1 - 0xf2fe 0xf3a1 - 0xf3fe 0xf4a1 - 0xf4a4
       /*
        * This is for Code Set 3, half-width kana
        */
       SPECIAL       0xa1 - 0xdf
       PHONOGRAM     0xa1 - 0xdf
       CONTROL       0x84 - 0x97 0x9b - 0x9f 0xe0 - 0xfe
```

SEE ALSO

       mklocale(1), setlocale(3)

NAME

fd, stdin, stdout, stderr – file descriptor files

DESCRIPTION

The files `/dev/fd/0` through `/dev/fd/#` refer to file descriptors which can be accessed through the file system. If the file descriptor is open and the mode the file is being opened with is a subset of the mode of the existing descriptor, the call:

        fd = open("/dev/fd/0", mode);

and the call:

        fd = fcntl(0, F_DUPFD, 0);

are equivalent.

Opening the files `/dev/stdin`, `/dev/stdout` and `/dev/stderr` is equivalent to the following calls:

        fd = fcntl(STDIN_FILENO, F_DUPFD, 0);
        fd = fcntl(STDOUT_FILENO, F_DUPFD, 0);
        fd = fcntl(STDERR_FILENO, F_DUPFD, 0);

Flags to the open(2) call other than O_RDONLY, O_WRONLY and O_RDWR are ignored.

FILES

        /dev/fd/#
        /dev/stdin
        /dev/stdout
        /dev/stderr

SEE ALSO

tty(4)

NAME

gb – HP98700 "Gatorbox" device interface

DESCRIPTION

This driver is for the HP98700 and 98710 graphics devices, also known as the Gatorbox. The term "Gator" will often be used, and it is not to be confused with "Gator" used in reference to an HP 9837 or 200/237 machine. Also, the term Gatorbox is used for the 98700 alone, with the 98701 frame buffer memory or with the 98710 accelerator installed. This driver merely checks for the existence of the device and does minimal set up, as it is expected the applications will initialize the device to their requirements.

The 98700 can be used as the only graphics device on a system, in which case it will be used as the system console. It can also be installed as a secondary display device. For the first case, the HP 98287A M.A.D. interface card should be set to internal control space. This will put the frame buffer at the DIO address 0x200000 and the control registers at 0x560000. At this address it will be the "preferred" console device (see cons(4)). For use as a secondary device, the 98287A should be set to frame buffer address 0x300000, and to an external select code.

It should be noted that this configuration will conflict with the 98547 display card which has a 2 megabyte frame buffer starting at address 0x200000. The 98700 should only be installed as a secondary device in a machine with a 1 bit 98544 display card or 4 bit 98545 card. The *98700H Installation Guide* contains further configuration information.

The ioctl(2) calls supported by the BSD system for the Gatorbox are:

GRFIOCGINFO

Get Graphics Info

Get info about device, setting the entries in the *grfinfo* structure, as defined in `<hpdev/grfioctl.h>`. For the standard 98700, the number of planes should be 4. The number of colors would therefore be 15, excluding black. With the 98701 option installed there will be another 4 planes for a total of 8, giving 255 colors.

GRFIOCON

Graphics On

Turn graphics on by enabling CRT output. The screen will come on, displaying whatever is in the frame buffer, using whatever colormap is in place.

GRFIOCOFF

Graphics Off

Turn graphics off by disabling output to the CRT. The frame buffer contents are not affected.

GRFIOCMAP

Map Device to user space

Map in control registers and framebuffer space. Once the device file is mapped, the frame buffer structure is accessible. The frame buffer structure describing the 98700 is given in `<hpdev/grf_gbreg.h>`.

GRFIOCUNMAP

Unmap Device

Unmap control registers and framebuffer space.

For further information about the use of ioctl see the man page.

EXAMPLE

A small example of opening, mapping and using the device is given below. For more examples of the details on the behavior of the device, see the device dependent source files for the X Window System, in the /usr/src/new/X/libhp.fb directory.

```
struct gboxfb *gbox;
u_char *Addr, frame_buffer;
struct grfinfo gi;
int disp_fd;

disp_fd = open("/dev/grf0",1);

if (ioctl (disp_fd, GRFIOCGINFO, &gi) < 0) return -1;

(void) ioctl (disp_fd, GRFIOCON, 0);

Addr = (u_char *) 0;
if (ioctl (disp_fd, GRFIOCMAP, &Addr) < 0) {
(void) ioctl (disp_fd, GRFIOCOFF, 0);
return -1;
}
gbox = (gboxfb *) Addr;                        /* Control Registers  */
frame_buffer = (u_char *) Addr + gi.gd_regsize; /* Frame buffer memory */
```

FILES

/dev/grf?　　　BSD special file
/dev/crt98700　HP-UX *starbase* special file

DIAGNOSTICS

None under BSD. HP-UX The CE.utilities/Crtadjust programs must be used.

ERRORS

[ENODEV]　no such device.

[EBUSY]　Another process has the device open.

[EINVAL]　Invalid ioctl specification.

SEE ALSO

ioctl(2), grf(4)

NAME

`grf` – HP graphics frame buffer device interface

DESCRIPTION

This is a generic description of the frame buffer device interface. The devices to which this applies are the 98544, 98545 and 98547 Topcat display cards (also known as HP300H devices), the 98548, 98549 and 98550 Catseye display cards, the 98700 Gatorbox graphics box, the 98720 Renaissance graphics box, and the 98730 DaVinci graphics box.

Use of the devices can be effectively approached from two directions. The first is through HP-UX *Starbase* routines, the second is by direct control in the BSD environment. In order to use the Starbase libraries, code must be compiled in an HP-UX environment, either by doing so on an HP-UX machine and transferring the binaries to the BSD machine, or by compilation with the use of the hpux(1) command. Applications using Starbase libraries have been run successfully on BSD machines using both of these compilation techniques.

Direct compilation, such as that used for the X Window System servers, has also been successful. Examples of some frame buffer operations can be found in the device dependent X Window system sources, for example the /usr/src/new/X/libhp.fb directory. These files contain examples of device dependent color map initialization, frame buffer operations, bit moving routines etc.

The basic programming of the `grf`? devices involves opening the device file, mapping the control registers and frame buffer addresses into user space, and then manipulating the device as the application requires. The address mapping is controlled by an ioctl(2) call to map the device into user space, and an unmap call when finished. The ioctls supported by BSD are:

GRFIOCGINFO

    Get Graphics Info

    Get info about device, setting the entries in the *grfinfo* structure, as defined in <hpdev/grfioctl.h>:

```
struct  grfinfo {
        int      gd_id;          /* HPUX identifier */
        caddr_t gd_regaddr;      /* control registers physaddr */
        int      gd_regsize;     /* control registers size */
        caddr_t gd_fbaddr;       /* frame buffer physaddr */
        int      gd_fbsize;      /* frame buffer size */
        short    gd_colors;      /* number of colors */
        short    gd_planes;      /* number of planes */
/* new stuff */
        int      gd_fbwidth;     /* frame buffer width */
        int      gd_fbheight;    /* frame buffer height */
        int      gd_dwidth;      /* displayed part width */
        int      gd_dheight;     /* displayed part height */
        int      gd_pad[6];      /* for future expansion */
};
```

GRFIOCON

    Graphics On

    Turn graphics on by enabling CRT output. The screen will come on, displaying whatever is in the frame buffer, using whatever colormap is in place.

GRFIOCOFF

    Graphics Off

Turn graphics off by disabling output to the CRT. The frame buffer contents are not affected.

GRFIOCMAP
> Map Device to user space

> Map in control registers and framebuffer space. Once the device file is mapped, the frame buffer structure is accessible.

GRFIOCUNMAP
> Unmap Device

> Unmap control registers and framebuffer space.

For further information about the use of ioctl see the man page.

EXAMPLE

This short code fragment is an example of opening some graphics device and mapping in the control and frame buffer space:

```
#define GRF_DEV <some_graphics_device>  /* /dev/grfN */
{
        struct fbstruct *regs;  /*  fbstruct = gboxfb, rboxfb, etc. */
        u_char *Addr, frame_buffer;
        struct grfinfo gi;
        int disp_fd;

        disp_fd = open(GRF_DEV,1);
        if (ioctl (disp_fd, GRFIOCGINFO, &gi) < 0) return -1;
        (void) ioctl (disp_fd, GRFIOCON, 0);

        Addr = (u_char *) 0;
        if (ioctl (disp_fd, GRFIOCMAP, &Addr) < 0) {
                (void) ioctl (disp_fd, GRFIOCOFF, 0);
                return -1;
        }
        regs = (fbstruct *) Addr;                 /* Control Registers   */
        frame_buffer = (u_char *) Addr + gi.gd_regsize; /* Frame buffer mem */
}
```

FILES

/dev/grf?   BSD interface special files
/dev/*crt* HP-UX *starbase* interface special files

DIAGNOSTICS

None under BSD. HP-UX The CE.utilities/Crtadjust programs must be used for each specific device.

ERRORS

[ENODEV] no such device.

[EBUSY]   Another process has the device open.

[EINVAL] Invalid ioctl specification.

SEE ALSO
    ioctl(2), dv(4), gb(4), rb(4), tc(4), hil(4)

NAME

hil – Human Interface Link device driver

DESCRIPTION

The Human Interface Link (HIL) is the interface used by the Series 300 computers to connect devices such as keyboards, mice, control knobs, and ID modules to the machine.

Special files /dev/hil[1-7] refer to physical HIL devices 1 through 7. /dev/hil0 refers to the "loop" pseudo-device and is used for the queue allocation commands described below. In the current implementation, there can only be one keyboard and it must be the first device (hil1).

The device file that corresponds to a particular HIL device is determined by the order of the devices on the loop. For instance, if the ID module is the second physical device on the loop, then /dev/hil2 is the special file that should be used for communication with the module.

Communication with an HIL device is begun with an *open* system call. A process may open a device already opened by another process unless the process is operating in HP-UX compatibility mode in which case it requires exclusive use of the device, or another process has the device open and is using HP-UX style device access (see HILIOCHPUX below).

Input data from a device are obtained in one of two ways. Processes may use an HP-UX style interface in which the read(2) system call is used to get fixed-size input packets, or they can use a *shared-queue* interface. The shared-queue interface avoids the system call overhead associated with the HP-UX read interface by sharing a region of memory between the system and a user process. This region consists of a circular list of 255 event packets, and a header containing the size of the queue, and its head and tail indices. The system deposits event data at the tail of the queue, a process extracts it from the head. Extracting an event is done by copying it from the queue and then updating the head appropriately (i.e. head = (head + 1) % qsize). It is up to the process to ensure that packets are removed from the queue quickly enough to prevent the queue from filling. The system, when it determines that the queue is full, will ignore future packets from the device. Devices are *mapped* to queues via an ioctl(2.) More than one device can be mapped to a single queue and one device can be mapped to several queues. Queues are implicitly unmapped by a fork(2) and thus, cannot be shared between processes.

Choosing the type of interface is done on a per device basis using an ioctl, but each device can only have one interface at any given time.

Select may be used with either interface to detect when input data are present. With the read interface, selecting indicates when there is input for a given device. With the shared-queue interface, selecting on the loop pseudo-device (hil0) indicates when data are present from any device on any queue while selecting on an individual device indicates when data are present for that device on any queue.

Close shuts down the file descriptor associated with the HIL device. The last close (system-wide) of any device removes that device from all queues it was mapped to while the last close of the loop pseudo-device unmaps all devices and deallocates all queues.

Ioctl(2) is used to control the HIL device. The ioctl commands (see <hpdev/hilioctl.h>) listed below are separated into two groups. The first are those which provide functions identical to HP-UX. Refer to hil(7) in the HP-UX documentation for more complete descriptions of these ioctls. The second set of ioctls are specific to this implementation and are primarily related to the shared-queue interface.

HILIOCID   Identify and Describe

The device will return up to 11 bytes of information describing the type and characteristics of the device. At the very least, 2 bytes of information, the device ID, and the Describe Record Header will be returned. Identical to the HP-UX HILID ioctl.

HILIOCSC   Report Security Code

Request the security code record from a device. The security code can vary from 1 byte to 15, and is only supported by some HIL devices. Identical to the HP-UX HILSC ioctl.

HILIOCRN   Report Name

An ascii string of up to 15 bytes in length that describes the device is returned. Identical to the HP-UX HILRN ioctl.

HILIOCRS   Report Status

An ascii string of up to 15 bytes in length that describes the current status of the device is returned. Identical to the HP-UX HILRS ioctl.

HILIOCED   Extended Describe

Additional information of up to 15 bytes is returned describing the device. This ioctl is similar to HILIOCID, which must be used first to determine if the device supports extended describe. Identical to the HP-UX HILED ioctl.

HILIOCAROFF

Disable Auto Repeat

Turn off auto repeat on the keyboard while it is in cooked mode. Identical to the HP-UX HILDKR ioctl.

HILIOCAR1   Enable Auto Repeat

Turn on auto repeat on the keyboard while it is in raw mode. The repeat rate is set to 1/30th of a second. Identical to the HP-UX HILER1 ioctl.

HILIOCAR2   Enable Auto Repeat

Turn on auto repeat on the keyboard while it is in raw mode. The repeat rate is set to 1/60th of a second. Identical to the HP-UX HILER2 ioctl.

The following ioctls are specific to this implementation:

HILIOCBEEP

Beep

Generate a keyboard beep as defined by *arg*. *Arg* is a pointer to two bytes of information, the first is the duration of the beep (microseconds), the second is the frequency of the beep.

HILIOCALLOCQ

Allocate Queue

Allocate and map into user space, an HILQ structure as defined in <hpdev/hilioctl.h>. *Arg* is a pointer to a *hilqinfo* structure (also described in <hpdev/hilioctl.h>) consisting of a qid and an addr. If addr is non-zero it specifies where in the address space to map the queue. If zero, the system will select a convenient location and fill in addr. Qid is filled in by the system and is a small integer used to uniquely identify this queue. This ioctl can only be issued to the loop pseudo-device.

HILIOCFREEQ
        Free Queue

Release a previously allocated HIL event queue, unmapping it from the user's address space. *Arg* should point to a *hilqinfo* structure which contains the qid of the queue to be released. All devices that are currently mapped to the queue are unmapped. This ioctl can only be issued to the loop pseudo-device.

HILIOCMAPQ
        Map Device to Queue

Maps this device to a previously allocated HIL event queue. *Arg* is a pointer to an integer containing the qid of the queue. Once a device is mapped to a queue, all event information generated by the device will be placed into the event queue at the tail.

HILIOCUNMAPQ
        Unmap Device from Queue

Unmap this device from a previously allocated HIL event queue. *Arg* is a pointer to an integer containing the qid for the queue. Future events from the device are no longer placed on the event queue.

HILIOCHPUX
        Use HP-UX Read Interface

Use HP-UX semantics for gathering data from this device. Instead of placing input events for the device on a queue, they are placed, in HP-UX format, into a buffer from which they can be obtained via read(2). This interface is provided for backwards compatibility. Refer to the HP-UX documentation for a description of the event packet.

FILES
    /dev/hil0   HIL loop pseudo device.
    /dev/hil1   HIL keyboard device.
    /dev/hil[2-7]   Individual HIL loop devices.

ERRORS
    [ENODEV]   no such HIL loop device.

    [ENXIO]   HIL loop is inoperative.

    [EBUSY]   Another HP-UX process has the device open, or another BSD process has the device open, and is using it in HP-UX mode.

    [EINVAL]   Invalid ioctl specification.

    [EMFILE]   No more shared queues available.

NAME
icmp – Internet Control Message Protocol

SYNOPSIS
```
#include <sys/socket.h>
#include <netinet/in.h>

int
socket(AF_INET, SOCK_RAW, proto);
```

DESCRIPTION
ICMP is the error and control message protocol used by IP and the Internet protocol family. It may be accessed through a "raw socket" for network monitoring and diagnostic functions. The *proto* parameter to the socket call to create an ICMP socket is obtained from getprotobyname(3). ICMP sockets are connectionless, and are normally used with the sendto and recvfrom calls, though the connect(2) call may also be used to fix the destination for future packets (in which case the read(2) or recv(2) and write(2) or send(2) system calls may be used).

Outgoing packets automatically have an IP header prepended to them (based on the destination address). Incoming packets are received with the IP header and options intact.

DIAGNOSTICS
A socket operation may fail with one of the following errors returned:

[EISCONN]   when trying to establish a connection on a socket which already has one, or when trying to send a datagram with the destination address specified and the socket is already connected;

[ENOTCONN]   when trying to send a datagram, but no destination address is specified, and the socket hasn't been connected;

[ENOBUFS]   when the system runs out of memory for an internal data structure;

[EADDRNOTAVAIL]   when an attempt is made to create a socket with a network address for which no network interface exists.

SEE ALSO
send(2), recv(2), intro(4), inet(4), ip(4)

HISTORY
The icmp protocol appeared in 4.3BSD.

NAME

idp – Xerox Internet Datagram Protocol

SYNOPSIS

```
#include <sys/socket.h>
#include <netns/ns.h>
#include <netns/idp.h>

int
socket(AF_NS, SOCK_DGRAM, 0);
```

DESCRIPTION

IDP is a simple, unreliable datagram protocol which is used to support the SOCK_DGRAM abstraction for the Internet protocol family. IDP sockets are connectionless, and are normally used with the sendto and recvfrom calls, though the connect(2) call may also be used to fix the destination for future packets (in which case the recv(2) or read(2) and send(2) or write(2) system calls may be used).

Xerox protocols are built vertically on top of IDP. Thus, IDP address formats are identical to those used by SPP. Note that the IDP port space is the same as the SPP port space (i.e. a IDP port may be "connected" to a SPP port, with certain options enabled below). In addition broadcast packets may be sent (assuming the underlying network supports this) by using a reserved "broadcast address"; this address is network interface dependent.

DIAGNOSTICS

A socket operation may fail with one of the following errors returned:

[EISCONN]   when trying to establish a connection on a socket which already has one, or when trying to send a datagram with the destination address specified and the socket is already connected;

[ENOTCONN]   when trying to send a datagram, but no destination address is specified, and the socket hasn't been connected;

[ENOBUFS]   when the system runs out of memory for an internal data structure;

[EADDRINUSE]   when an attempt is made to create a socket with a port which has already been allocated;

[EADDRNOTAVAIL]   when an attempt is made to create a socket with a network address for which no network interface exists.

SOCKET OPTIONS

[SO_ALL_PACKETS]   When set, this option defeats automatic processing of Error packets, and Sequence Protocol packets.

[SO_DEFAULT_HEADERS]   The user provides the kernel an IDP header, from which it gleans the Packet Type. When requested, the kernel will provide an IDP header, showing the default packet type, and local and foreign addresses, if connected.

[SO_HEADERS_ON_INPUT] When set, the first 30 bytes of any data returned from a read or recv from will be the initial 30 bytes of the IDP packet, as described by

```
                   struct idp {
                           u_short         idp_sum;
                           u_short         idp_len;
                           u_char          idp_tc;
```

```
                    u_char         idp_pt;
                    struct ns_addr idp_dna;
                    struct ns_addr idp_sna;
            };
```

This allows the user to determine the packet type, and whether the packet was a multi-cast packet or directed specifically at the local host. When requested, gives the current state of the option, (NSP_RAWIN or 0).

[SO_HEADERS_ON_OUTPUT] When set, the first 30 bytes of any data sent will be the initial 30 bytes of the IDP packet. This allows the user to determine the packet type, and whether the packet should be multi-cast packet or directed specifically at the local host. You can also misrepresent the sender of the packet. When requested, gives the current state of the option. (NSP_RAWOUT or 0).

[SO_SEQNO] When requested, this returns a sequence number which is not likely to be repeated until the machine crashes or a very long time has passed. It is useful in constructing Packet Exchange Protocol packets.

SEE ALSO
       send(2), recv(2), intro(4), ns(4)

HISTORY
       The idp protocol appeared in 4.3BSD.

NAME

inet – Internet protocol family

SYNOPSIS

```
#include <sys/types.h>
#include <netinet/in.h>
```

DESCRIPTION

The Internet protocol family is a collection of protocols layered atop the *Internet Protocol* (IP) transport layer, and utilizing the Internet address format. The Internet family provides protocol support for the SOCK_STREAM, SOCK_DGRAM, and SOCK_RAW socket types; the SOCK_RAW interface provides access to the IP protocol.

ADDRESSING

Internet addresses are four byte quantities, stored in network standard format (on the VAX these are word and byte reversed). The include file <netinet/in.h> defines this address as a discriminated union.

Sockets bound to the Internet protocol family utilize the following addressing structure,

```
struct sockaddr_in {
        short   sin_family;
        u_short sin_port;
        struct  in_addr sin_addr;
        char    sin_zero[8];
};
```

Sockets may be created with the local address INADDR_ANY to effect "wildcard" matching on incoming messages. The address in a connect(2) or sendto(2) call may be given as INADDR_ANY to mean "this host". The distinguished address INADDR_BROADCAST is allowed as a shorthand for the broadcast address on the primary network if the first network configured supports broadcast.

PROTOCOLS

The Internet protocol family is comprised of the IP transport protocol, Internet Control Message Protocol (ICMP), Transmission Control Protocol (TCP), and User Datagram Protocol (UDP). TCP is used to support the SOCK_STREAM abstraction while UDP is used to support the SOCK_DGRAM abstraction. A raw interface to IP is available by creating an Internet socket of type SOCK_RAW. The ICMP message protocol is accessible from a raw socket.

The 32-bit Internet address contains both network and host parts. It is frequency-encoded; the most-significant bit is clear in Class A addresses, in which the high-order 8 bits are the network number. Class B addresses use the high-order 16 bits as the network field, and Class C addresses have a 24-bit network part. Sites with a cluster of local networks and a connection to the Internet may chose to use a single network number for the cluster; this is done by using subnet addressing. The local (host) portion of the address is further subdivided into subnet and host parts. Within a subnet, each subnet appears to be an individual network; externally, the entire cluster appears to be a single, uniform network requiring only a single routing entry. Subnet addressing is enabled and examined by the following ioctl(2) commands on a datagram socket in the Internet domain; they have the same form as the SIOCIFADDR command (see intro(4)).

SIOCSIFNETMASK Set interface network mask. The network mask defines the network part of the address; if it contains more of the address than the address type would indicate, then subnets are in use.

SIOCGIFNETMASK Get interface network mask.

SEE ALSO

ioctl(2), socket(2), intro(4), tcp(4), udp(4), ip(4), icmp(4)

"An Introductory 4.3 BSD Interprocess Communication Tutorial", *PS1*, 7.

"An Advanced 4.3 BSD Interprocess Communication Tutorial", *PS1*, 8.

CAVEAT

The Internet protocol support is subject to change as the Internet protocols develop. Users should not depend on details of the current implementation, but rather the services exported.

HISTORY

The inet protocol interface appeared in 4.2BSD.

4

NAME

ip – Internet Protocol

SYNOPSIS

```
#include <sys/socket.h>
#include <netinet/in.h>

int
socket(AF_INET, SOCK_RAW, proto);
```

DESCRIPTION

IP is the transport layer protocol used by the Internet protocol family. Options may be set at the IP level when using higher-level protocols that are based on IP (such as TCP and UDP). It may also be accessed through a "raw socket" when developing new protocols, or special-purpose applications.

There are several IP-level setsockopt(2)/ getsockopt(2) options. IP_OPTIONS may be used to provide IP options to be transmitted in the IP header of each outgoing packet or to examine the header options on incoming packets. IP options may be used with any socket type in the Internet family. The format of IP options to be sent is that specified by the IP protocol specification (RFC-791), with one exception: the list of addresses for Source Route options must include the first-hop gateway at the beginning of the list of gateways. The first-hop gateway address will be extracted from the option list and the size adjusted accordingly before use. To disable previously specified options, use a zero-length buffer:

```
setsockopt(s, IPPROTO_IP, IP_OPTIONS, NULL, 0);
```

IP_TOS and IP_TTL may be used to set the type-of-service and time-to-live fields in the IP header for SOCK_STREAM and SOCK_DGRAM sockets. For example,

```
int tos = IPTOS_LOWDELAY;          /* see <netinet/in.h> */
setsockopt(s, IPPROTO_IP, IP_TOS, &tos, sizeof(tos));

int ttl = 60;                      /* max = 255 */
setsockopt(s, IPPROTO_IP, IP_TTL, &ttl, sizeof(ttl));
```

If the IP_RECVDSTADDR option is enabled on a SOCK_DGRAM socket, the recvmsg call will return the destination IP address for a UDP datagram. The msg_control field in the msghdr structure points to a buffer that contains a cmsghdr structure followed by the IP address. The cmsghdr fields have the following values:

```
cmsg_len = sizeof(struct in_addr)
cmsg_level = IPPROTO_IP
cmsg_type = IP_RECVDSTADDR
```

Multicast Options

IP multicasting is supported only on AF_INET sockets of type SOCK_DGRAM and SOCK_RAW, and only on networks where the interface driver supports multicasting.

The IP_MULTICAST_TTL option changes the time-to-live (TTL) for outgoing multicast datagrams in order to control the scope of the multicasts:

```
u_char ttl;    /* range: 0 to 255, default = 1 */
setsockopt(s, IPPROTO_IP, IP_MULTICAST_TTL, &ttl, sizeof(ttl));
```

Datagrams with a TTL of 1 are not forwarded beyond the local network. Multicast datagrams with a TTL of 0 will not be transmitted on any network, but may be delivered locally if the sending host belongs to the destination group and if multicast loopback has not been disabled on the sending socket (see below). Multicast datagrams with TTL greater than 1 may be forwarded to other networks if a multicast router is attached to the local network.

For hosts with multiple interfaces, each multicast transmission is sent from the primary network interface. The IP_MULTICAST_IF option overrides the default for subsequent transmissions from a given socket:

```
struct in_addr addr;
setsockopt(s, IPPROTO_IP, IP_MULTICAST_IF, &addr, sizeof(addr));
```

where "addr" is the local IP address of the desired interface or INADDR_ANY to specify the default interface. An interface's local IP address and multicast capability can be obtained via the SIOCGIFCONF and SIOCGIFFLAGS ioctls. Normal applications should not need to use this option.

If a multicast datagram is sent to a group to which the sending host itself belongs (on the outgoing interface), a copy of the datagram is, by default, looped back by the IP layer for local delivery. The IP_MULTICAST_LOOP option gives the sender explicit control over whether or not subsequent datagrams are looped back:

```
u_char loop;    /* 0 = disable, 1 = enable (default) */
setsockopt(s, IPPROTO_IP, IP_MULTICAST_LOOP, &loop, sizeof(loop));
```

This option improves performance for applications that may have no more than one instance on a single host (such as a router demon), by eliminating the overhead of receiving their own transmissions. It should generally not be used by applications for which there may be more than one instance on a single host (such as a conferencing program) or for which the sender does not belong to the destination group (such as a time querying program).

A multicast datagram sent with an initial TTL greater than 1 may be delivered to the sending host on a different interface from that on which it was sent, if the host belongs to the destination group on that other interface. The loopback control option has no effect on such delivery.

A host must become a member of a multicast group before it can receive datagrams sent to the group. To join a multicast group, use the IP_ADD_MEMBERSHIP option:

```
struct ip_mreq mreq;
setsockopt(s, IPPROTO_IP, IP_ADD_MEMBERSHIP, &mreq, sizeof(mreq));
```

where mreq is the following structure:

```
struct ip_mreq {
    struct in_addr imr_multiaddr; /* multicast group to join */
    struct in_addr imr_interface; /* interface to join on */
}
```

imr_interface should be INADDR_ANY to choose the default multicast interface, or the IP address of a particular multicast-capable interface if the host is multihomed. Membership is associated with a single interface; programs running on multihomed hosts may need to join the same group on more than one interface. Up to IP_MAX_MEMBERSHIPS (currently 20) memberships may be added on a single socket.

To drop a membership, use:

```
struct ip_mreq mreq;
setsockopt(s, IPPROTO_IP, IP_DROP_MEMBERSHIP, &mreq, sizeof(mreq));
```

where mreq contains the same values as used to add the membership. Memberships are dropped when the socket is closed or the process exits.

Raw IP Sockets

Raw IP sockets are connectionless, and are normally used with the sendto and recvfrom calls, though the connect(2) call may also be used to fix the destination for future packets (in which case the read(2) or recv(2) and write(2) or send(2) system calls may be used).

If *proto* is 0, the default protocol IPPROTO_RAW is used for outgoing packets, and only incoming packets destined for that protocol are received. If *proto* is non-zero, that protocol number will be used on outgoing packets and to filter incoming packets.

Outgoing packets automatically have an IP header prepended to them (based on the destination address and the protocol number the socket is created with), unless the IP_HDRINCL option has been set. Incoming packets are received with IP header and options intact.

IP_HDRINCL indicates the complete IP header is included with the data and may be used only with the SOCK_RAW type.

```
#include <netinet/ip.h>

int hincl = 1;                          /* 1 = on, 0 = off */
setsockopt(s, IPPROTO_IP, IP_HDRINCL, &hincl, sizeof(hincl));
```

Unlike previous BSD releases, the program must set all the fields of the IP header, including the following:

```
ip->ip_v = IPVERSION;
ip->ip_hl = hlen >> 2;
ip->ip_id = 0;   /* 0 means kernel set appropriate value */
ip->ip_off = offset;
```

If the header source address is set to INADDR_ANY, the kernel will choose an appropriate address.

DIAGNOSTICS

A socket operation may fail with one of the following errors returned:

[EISCONN]   when trying to establish a connection on a socket which already has one, or when trying to send a datagram with the destination address specified and the socket is already connected;

[ENOTCONN]   when trying to send a datagram, but no destination address is specified, and the socket hasn't been connected;

[ENOBUFS]   when the system runs out of memory for an internal data structure;

[EADDRNOTAVAIL]   when an attempt is made to create a socket with a network address for which no network interface exists.

[EACESS]   when an attempt is made to create a raw IP socket by a non-privileged process.

The following errors specific to IP may occur when setting or getting IP options:

[EINVAL]   An unknown socket option name was given.

[EINVAL]   The IP option field was improperly formed; an option field was shorter than the minimum value or longer than the option buffer provided.

SEE ALSO

getsockopt(2), send(2), recv(2), intro(4), icmp(4), inet(4)

HISTORY

  The ip protocol appeared in 4.2BSD.

NAME

iso – ISO protocol family

SYNOPSIS

```
#include <sys/types.h>
#include <netiso/iso.h>
```

DESCRIPTION

The ISO protocol family is a collection of protocols that uses the ISO address format. The ISO family provides protocol support for the SOCK_SEQPACKET abstraction through the TP protocol (ISO 8073), for the SOCK_DGRAM abstraction through the connectionless transport protocol (ISO 8602), and for the SOCK_RAW abstraction by providing direct access (for debugging) to the CLNP (ISO 8473) network layer protocol.

ADDRESSING

ISO addresses are based upon ISO 8348/AD2, *Addendum to the Network Service Definition Covering Network Layer Addressing.*

Sockets bound to the OSI protocol family use the following address structure:

```
struct iso_addr {
      u_char    isoa_len;  /* length, not including this byte */
      char      isoa_genaddr[20];  /* general opaque address */
};

struct sockaddr_iso {
      u_char    siso_len;       /* size of this sockaddr */
      u_char    siso_family;    /* addressing domain, AF_ISO */
      u_char    siso_plen;      /* presentation selector length */
      u_char    siso_slen;      /* session selector length */
      u_char    siso_tlen;      /* transport selector length */
      struct    iso_addr siso_addr; /* network address */
      u_char    siso_pad[6];    /* space for gosip v2 SELs */
};
#define siso_nlen siso_addr.isoa_len
#define siso_data siso_addr.isoa_genaddr
```

The fields of this structure are:

siso_len:
    Length of the entire address structure, in bytes, which may grow to be longer than the 32 bytes shown above.

siso_family:
    Identifies the domain: AF_ISO.

siso_tlen:
    Length of the transport selector.

siso_slen:
    Length of the session selector. This is not currently supported by the kernel and is provided as a convenience for user level programs.

siso_plen:
> Length of the presentation selector. This is not currently supported by the kernel and is provided as a convenience for user level programs.

siso_addr:
> The network part of the address, described below.

TRANSPORT ADDRESSING

An ISO transport address is similar to an Internet address in that it contains a network-address portion and a portion that the transport layer uses to multiplex its services among clients. In the Internet domain, this portion of the address is called a *port*. In the ISO domain, this is called a *transport selector* (also known at one time as a *transport suffix*). While ports are always 16 bits, transport selectors may be of (almost) arbitrary size.

Since the C language does not provide convenient variable length structures, we have separated the selector lengths from the data themselves. The network address and various selectors are stored contiguously, with the network address first, then the transport selector, and so on. Thus, if you had a nework address of less then 20 bytes, the transport selector would encroach on space normally reserved for the network address.

NETWORK ADDRESSING.

ISO network addresses are limited to 20 bytes in length. ISO network addresses can take any format.

PROTOCOLS

The ARGO 1.0 implementation of the ISO protocol family comprises the Connectionless-Mode Network Protocol (CLNP), and the Transport Protocol (TP), classes 4 and 0, and X.25. TP is used to support the SOCK_SEQPACKET abstraction. A raw interface to CLNP is available by creating an ISO socket of type SOCK_RAW. This is used for CLNP debugging only.

SEE ALSO

tp(4), clnp(4), cltp(4)

NAME

`ite` – HP Internal Terminal Emulator

DESCRIPTION

TTY special files of the form "ttye?" are interfaces to the HP ITE for bit-mapped displays as implemented under BSD. An ITE is the main system console on most HP300 workstations and is the mechanism through which a user communicates with the machine. If more than one display exists on a system, any or all can be used as ITEs with the limitation that only the first one opened will have a keyboard (since only one keyboard is supported).

ITE devices use the HP-UX '300h' termcap(5) or `terminfo`(5) entries. However, as currently implemented, the ITE does not support the full range of HP-UX capabilities for this device. Missing are multiple colors, underlining, blinking, softkeys, programmable tabs, scrolling memory and keyboard arrow keys. The keyboard does not have any of the international character support of HP's NLS system. It does use the left and right *extend char* keys as meta keys, in that it will set the eighth bit of the character code.

Upon booting, the kernel will first look for an ITE device to use as the system console (`/dev/console`). If a display exists at any hardware address, it will be the console. The kernel looks for, in order: a 98544, 98545, or 98547 Topcat display, a 98700 Gatorbox at a supported address (see gb(4)), or a 98720 Renaissance at a supported address (see rb(4)). Currently there is no ITE support for the 98548, 98549, 98550 and 98556 boards.

When activated as an ITE (special file opened), all displays go through a standard initialization sequence. The frame buffer is cleared, the ROM fonts are unpacked and loaded into off-screen storage and a cursor appears. The ITE initialization routine also sets the colormap entry used to white. Variable colors are not used, mainly for reasons of simplicity. The font pixels are all set to 0xff and the colormap entry corresponding to all planes is set to R=255, G=255 and B=255. The actual number of planes used to display the characters depends on the hardware installed. Finally, if the keyboard HIL device is not already assigned to another ITE device, it is placed in "cooked" mode and assigned to this ITE.

On most systems, a display is used both as an ITE (`/dev/ttye?` aka `/dev/console`) and as a graphics device (`/dev/grf?`). In this environment, there is some interaction between the two uses that should be noted. For example, opening `/dev/grf0` will deactivate the ITE, that is, write over whatever may be on the ITE display. When the graphics application is finished and `/dev/grf0` closed, the ITE will be reinitialized with the frame buffer cleared and the ITE colormap installed.

DIAGNOSTICS

None under BSD.

SEE ALSO

grf(4), hil(4), gb(4), rb(4), tc(4)

NAME

le – HP AMD 7990 LANCE Ethernet interface

SYNOPSIS

`device le0 at scode?`

DESCRIPTION

The `le` interface provides access to a 10 Mb/s Ethernet network via the AMD 7990 LANCE Ethernet chip set.

Each of the host's network addresses is specified at boot time with an `SIOCSIFADDR` ioctl. The `le` interface employs the address resolution protocol described in `arp`(4) to dynamically map between Internet and Ethernet addresses on the local network.

The use of "trailer" encapsulation to minimize copying data on input and output is supported by the interface but offers no advantage due to the large HP page size. The use of trailers is negotiated with ARP. This negotiation may be disabled, on a per-interface basis, by setting the `IFF_NOTRAILERS` flag with an `SIOCSIFFLAGS` ioctl.

DIAGNOSTICS

le%d: hardware address %s. This is a normal autoconfiguration message noting the 6 byte physical ethernet address of the adapter.

de%d: can't handle af%d. The interface was handed a message with addresses formatted in an unsuitable address family; the packet was dropped.

The following message indicates a possible hardware error performing the indicated operation during autoconfiguration or initialization.

le%d: init timeout, stat = 0x%x. The hardware did not respond to an initialize command during reset. The reset procedure continues anyway.

SEE ALSO

intro(4), inet(4), arp(4)

NAME

    le – SPARC AMD 7990 LANCE ethernet interface

SYNOPSIS

    le* at sbus? slot ? offset ?

DESCRIPTION

The `le` interface provides access to the 10 Mb/s Ethernet network via the AMD 7990 LANCE Ethernet chip set.

Each of the host's network addresses is specified at boot time with an `SIOCSIFADDR ioctl`. The `le` interface employs the address resolution protocol described in `arp`(4) to dynamically map between Internet and Ethernet addresses on the local network.

SEE ALSO

    intro(4), inet(4), arp(4)

NAME
lo – software loopback network interface

SYNOPSIS
pseudo-device
loop

DESCRIPTION
The loop interface is a software loopback mechanism which may be used for performance analysis, software testing, and/or local communication. As with other network interfaces, the loopback interface must have network addresses assigned for each address family with which it is to be used. These addresses may be set or changed with the SIOCSIFADDR ioctl(2). The loopback interface should be the last interface configured, as protocols may use the order of configuration as an indication of priority. The loopback should *never* be configured first unless no hardware interfaces exist.

DIAGNOSTICS
lo%d: can't handle af%d. The interface was handed a message with addresses formatted in an unsuitable address family; the packet was dropped.

SEE ALSO
intro(4), inet(4), ns(4)

HISTORY
The lo device appeared in 4.2BSD.

BUGS
Previous versions of the system enabled the loopback interface automatically, using a nonstandard Internet address (127.1). Use of that address is now discouraged; a reserved host address for the local network should be used instead.

NAME

mem, **kmem** – main memory

DESCRIPTION

The file **/dev/mem** is an interface to the physical memory of the computer. Byte offsets in this file are interpreted as physical memory addresses. Reading and writing this file is equivalent to reading and writing memory itself. An error will be returned if an attempt is made to reference an offset outside of **/dev/mem**.

Kernel virtual memory is accessed via the file **/dev/kmem** in the same manner as **/dev/mem**. Only kernel virtual addresses that are currently mapped to memory are allowed.

HP300

On the HP300, the last byte of physical memory is always $0xFFFFFFFF$. Therefore, on an HP300 with 8Mb of memory, physical memory would start at $0xFF800000$. On the HP300, kernel virtual memory runs from 0 to about $0x2400000$.

FILES

/dev/mem
/dev/kmem

HISTORY

The files **mem** and **kmem** appeared in Version 6 AT&T UNIX.

NAME

mem, kmem – main memory

DESCRIPTION

The file /dev/mem is an interface to the physical memory of the computer. Byte offsets in this file are interpreted as physical memory addresses. Reading and writing this file is equivalent to reading and writing memory itself. An error will be returned if an attempt is made to reference an offset outside of /dev/mem.

Kernel virtual memory is accessed via the file /dev/kmem in the same manner as /dev/mem. Only kernel virtual addresses that are currently mapped to memory are allowed.

SPARC

On the SPARC, physical memory may be discontiguous; kernel virtual memory begins at 0xf8000000.

FILES

/dev/mem
/dev/kmem

HISTORY

The files mem and kmem appeared in Version 6 AT&T UNIX.

NAME

ns – Xerox Network Systems(tm) protocol family

SYNOPSIS

```
options NS
options NSIP
pseudo-device ns
```

DESCRIPTION

The NS protocol family is a collection of protocols layered atop the *Internet Datagram Protocol* (IDP) transport layer, and using the Xerox NS address formats. The NS family provides protocol support for the SOCK_STREAM, SOCK_DGRAM, SOCK_SEQPACKET, and SOCK_RAW socket types; the SOCK_RAW interface is a debugging tool, allowing you to trace all packets entering, (or with toggling kernel variable, additionally leaving) the local host.

ADDRESSING

NS addresses are 12 byte quantities, consisting of a 4 byte Network number, a 6 byte Host number and a 2 byte port number, all stored in network standard format. (on the VAX these are word and byte reversed; on the SUN they are not reversed). The include file <netns/ns.h> defines the NS address as a structure containing unions (for quicker comparisons).

Sockets in the Internet protocol family use the following addressing structure:

```
struct sockaddr_ns {
        short           sns_family;
        struct ns_addr  sns_addr;
        char            sns_zero[2];
};
```

where an *ns_addr* is composed as follows:

```
union ns_host {
        u_char          c_host[6];
        u_short         s_host[3];
};

union ns_net {
        u_char          c_net[4];
        u_short         s_net[2];
};

struct ns_addr {
        union ns_net    x_net;
        union ns_host   x_host;
        u_short x_port;
};
```

Sockets may be created with an address of all zeroes to effect "wildcard" matching on incoming messages. The local port address specified in a bind(2) call is restricted to be greater than NSPORT_RESERVED (=3000, in <netns/ns.h>) unless the creating process is running as the super-user, providing a space of protected port numbers.

PROTOCOLS

The NS protocol family supported by the operating system is comprised of the Internet Datagram Protocol (IDP) idp(4), Error Protocol (available through IDP), and Sequenced Packet Protocol (SPP) spp(4).

SPP is used to support the SOCK_STREAM and SOCK_SEQPACKET abstraction, while IDP is used to support the SOCK_DGRAM abstraction. The Error protocol is responded to by the kernel to handle and report errors in protocol processing; it is, however, only accessible to user programs through heroic actions.

SEE ALSO

intro(3), byteorder(3), gethostbyname(3), getnetent(3), getprotoent(3), getservent(3), ns(3), intro(4), spp(4), idp(4), nsip(4)

Internet Transport Protocols, Xerox Corporation document XSIS, 028112.

An Advanced 4.3 BSD Interprocess Communication Tutorial.

HISTORY

The ns protocol family appeared in 4.3BSD.

4

NAME

nsip – software network interface encapsulating NS packets in IP packets

SYNOPSIS

options NSIP
#include <netns/ns_if.h>

DESCRIPTION

The **nsip** interface is a software mechanism which may be used to transmit Xerox NS(tm) packets through otherwise uncooperative networks. It functions by prepending an IP header, and resubmitting the packet through the UNIX IP machinery.

The super-user can advise the operating system of a willing partner by naming an IP address to be associated with an NS address. Presently, only specific hosts pairs are allowed, and for each host pair, an artificial point-to-point interface is constructed. At some future date, IP broadcast addresses or hosts may be paired with NS networks or hosts.

Specifically, a socket option of SO_NSIP_ROUTE is set on a socket of family AF_NS, type SOCK_DGRAM, passing the following structure:

```
struct nsip_req {
        struct sockaddr rq_ns; /* must be ns format destination */
        struct sockaddr rq_ip; /* must be ip format gateway */
        short rq_flags;
};
```

DIAGNOSTICS

nsip%d: can't handle af%d. The interface was handed a message with addresses formatted in an unsuitable address family; the packet was dropped.

SEE ALSO

intro(4), ns(4)

HISTORY

The **nsip** interface appeared in 4.3BSD.

BUGS

It is absurd to have a separate pseudo-device for each pt-to-pt link. There is no way to change the IP address for an NS host once the encapsulation interface is set up. The request should honor flags of RTF_GATEWAY to indicate remote networks, and the absence of RTF_UP should be a clue to remove that partner. This was intended to postpone the necessity of rewriting reverse ARP for the en(4) device, and to allow passing XNS packets through an Arpanet-Milnet gateway, to facilitate testing between some co-operating universities.

NAME

null – the null device

DESCRIPTION

The null device accepts and reads data as any ordinary (and willing) file – but throws it away. The length of the null device is always zero.

FILES

/dev/null

HISTORY

A null device appeared in Version 7 AT&T UNIX.

4

NAME

openprom – OPENPROM and EEPROM interface

SYNOPSIS

`#include <machine/openpromio.h>`

DESCRIPTION

The file /dev/openprom is an interface to the SPARC OPENPROM, including the EEPROM area. This interface is highly stylized; ioctls are used for all operations. These ioctls refer to "nodes", which are simply "magic" integer values describing data areas. Occasionally the number 0 may be used or returned instead, as described below. A special distinguished "options" node holds the EEPROM settings.

The calls that take and/or return a node use a pointer to an `int` variable for this purpose; others use a pointer to an `struct opiocdesc` descriptor, which contains a node and two counted strings. The first string is comprised of the fields op_namelen (an int) and op_name (a char *), giving the name of a field. The second string is comprised of the fields op_buflen and op_buf, used analogously. These two counted strings work in a "value-result" fashion. At entry to the ioctl, the counts are expected to reflect the buffer size; on return, the counts are updated to reflect the buffer contents.

The following ioctls are supported:

OPIOCGETOPTNODE Takes nothing, and fills in the options node number.

OPIOCGETNEXT   Takes a node number and returns the number of the following node. The node following the last node is number 0; the node following number 0 is the first node.

OPIOCGETCHILD   Takes a node number and returns the number of the first "child" of that node. This child may have siblings; these can be discovered by using OPIOCGETNEXT.

OPIOCGET   Fills in the value of the named property for the given node. If no such property is associated with that node, the value length is set to -1. If the named property exists but has no value, the value length is set to 0.

OPIOCSET   Writes the given value under the given name. The OPENPROM may refuse this operation; in this case EINVAL is returned.

OPIOCNEXTPROP   Finds the property whose name follows the given name in OPENPROM internal order. The resulting name is returned in the value field. If the named property is the last, the "next" name is the empty string. As with OPIOCGETNEXT, the next name after the empty string is the first name.

FILES

/dev/openprom

ERRORS

The following may result in rejection of an operation:

[EINVAL]   The given node number is not zero and does not correspond to any valid node, or is zero where zero is not allowed.

[EBADF]   The requested operation requires permissions not specified at the call to open().

[ENAMETOOLONG]
        The given name or value field exceeds the maximum allowed length (8191 bytes).

SEE ALSO

    ioctl(2)

BUGS

Due to limitations within the OPENPROM itself, these functions run at elevated priority and may adversely affect system performance.

NAME

ppi – HP-IB printer/plotter interface

SYNOPSIS

`device ppi0 at hpib0 slave 5`

DESCRIPTION

The `ppi` interface provides a means of communication with HP-IB printers and plotters.

Special files `ppi0` through `ppi7` are used to access the devices, with the digit at the end of the filename referring to the bus address of the device. Current versions of the autoconf code can not probe for these devices, so the device entry in the configuration file must be fully qualified.

The device files appear as follows:

```
"crw-rw-rw-  1 root       11,   0 Dec 21 11:22 /dev/ppi"
```

DIAGNOSTICS

None.

SEE ALSO

hpib(4).

BUGS

This driver is very primitive, it handshakes data out byte by byte. It should use DMA if possible.

4

NAME
      pty – pseudo terminal driver

SYNOPSIS
      `pseudo-device pty` [*count*]

DESCRIPTION
      The `pty` driver provides support for a device-pair termed a *pseudo terminal*. A pseudo terminal is a pair of
      character devices, a *master* device and a *slave* device. The slave device provides to a process an interface
      identical to that described in `tty`(4). However, whereas all other devices which provide the interface
      described in `tty`(4) have a hardware device of some sort behind them, the slave device has, instead, another
      process manipulating it through the master half of the pseudo terminal. That is, anything written on the mas-
      ter device is given to the slave device as input and anything written on the slave device is presented as input
      on the master device.

      In configuring, if an optional *count* is given in the specification, that number of pseudo terminal pairs are
      configured; the default count is 32.

      The following `ioctl`(2) calls apply only to pseudo terminals:

      TIOCSTOP   Stops output to a terminal (e.g. like typing '^S'). Takes no parameter.

      TIOCSTART   Restarts output (stopped by TIOCSTOP or by typing '^S'). Takes no parameter.

      TIOCPKT   Enable/disable *packet* mode. Packet mode is enabled by specifying (by reference) a nonzero
                     parameter and disabled by specifying (by reference) a zero parameter. When applied to the
                     master side of a pseudo terminal, each subsequent `read` from the terminal will return data
                     written on the slave part of the pseudo terminal preceded by a zero byte (symbolically
                     defined as TIOCPKT_DATA), or a single byte reflecting control status information. In the
                     latter case, the byte is an inclusive-or of zero or more of the bits:

                     TIOCPKT_FLUSHREAD   whenever the read queue for the terminal is flushed.

                     TIOCPKT_FLUSHWRITE   whenever the write queue for the terminal is flushed.

                     TIOCPKT_STOP   whenever output to the terminal is stopped a la '^S'.

                     TIOCPKT_START   whenever output to the terminal is restarted.

                     TIOCPKT_DOSTOP   whenever *t_stopc* is '^S' and *t_startc* is '^Q'.

                     TIOCPKT_NOSTOP   whenever the start and stop characters are not ^S/^Q.

                                          While this mode is in use, the presence of control status infor-
                                          mation to be read from the master side may be detected by a
                                          `select`(2) for exceptional conditions.

                                          This mode is used by `rlogin`(1) and `rlogind`(8) to imple-
                                          ment a remote-echoed, locally ^S/^Q flow-controlled remote
                                          login with proper back-flushing of output; it can be used by oth-
                                          er similar programs.

      TIOCUCNTL   Enable/disable a mode that allows a small number of simple user `ioctl` commands to be
                     passed through the pseudo-terminal, using a protocol similar to that of TIOCPKT. The
                     TIOCUCNTL and TIOCPKT modes are mutually exclusive. This mode is enabled from the
                     master side of a pseudo terminal by specifying (by reference) a nonzero parameter and dis-
                     abled by specifying (by reference) a zero parameter. Each subsequent `read` from the mas-
                     ter side will return data written on the slave part of the pseudo terminal preceded by a zero

byte, or a single byte reflecting a user control operation on the slave side. A user control command consists of a special ioctl operation with no data; the command is given as UIOCCMD(n), where n is a number in the range 1-255. The operation value n will be received as a single byte on the next read from the master side. The ioctl UIOCCMD(0) is a no-op that may be used to probe for the existence of this facility. As with TIOCPKT mode, command operations may be detected with a select for exceptional conditions.

TIOCREMOTE A mode for the master half of a pseudo terminal, independent of TIOCPKT. This mode causes input to the pseudo terminal to be flow controlled and not input edited (regardless of the terminal mode). Each write to the control terminal produces a record boundary for the process reading the terminal. In normal usage, a write of data is like the data typed as a line on the terminal; a write of 0 bytes is like typing an end-of-file character. TIOCREMOTE can be used when doing remote line editing in a window manager, or whenever flow controlled input is required.

FILES

```
/dev/pty[p-r][0-9a-f]     master pseudo terminals
/dev/tty[p-r][0-9a-f]     slave pseudo terminals
```

DIAGNOSTICS

None.

HISTORY

The **pty** driver appeared in 4.2BSD.

4

NAME
  rb – HP98720 "Renaissance" device interface

DESCRIPTION
  This driver is for the HP98720 and 98721 graphics device, also known as the Renaissance. This driver has not been tested with all possible combinations of frame buffer boards and scan boards installed in the device. The driver merely checks for the existence of the device and does minimal set up.

  The Renaissance can be configured at either the "internal" address (frame buffer address 0x200000, control register space address 0x560000) or at an external select code less than 32. At the internal address it will be the "preferred" console device (see cons(4)). The hardware installation manual describes the procedure for setting these values.

  A user process communicates to the device initially by means of ioctl(2) calls. For the HP-UX ioctl(2) calls supported, refer to HP-UX manuals. The BSD calls supported are:

GRFIOCGINFO
    Get Graphics Info

    Get info about device, setting the entries in the *grfinfo* structure, as defined in <hpdev/grfioctl.h>. For the standard 98720, the number of planes should be 4. The number of colors would therefore be 15, excluding black. If one 98722A frame buffer board is installed, there will still be 4 planes, with the 4 planes on the colormap board becoming overlay planes. With each additional 98722 frame buffer board 4 planes will be added up to a maximum of 32 planes total.

GRFIOCON
    Graphics On

    Turn graphics on by enabling CRT output. The screen will come on, displaying whatever is in the frame buffer, using whatever colormap is in place.

GRFIOCOFF
    Graphics Off

    Turn graphics off by disabling output to the CRT. The frame buffer contents are not affected.

GRFIOCMAP
    Map Device to user space

    Map in control registers and framebuffer space. Once the device file is mapped, the frame buffer structure is accessible. The structure describing the 98720 is defined in hpdev/grf_rbreg.h.

EXAMPLE
  This is a short segment of code showing how the device is opened and mapped into user process address space assuming that it is grf0:

```
struct rboxfb *rbox;
u_char *Addr, frame_buffer;
struct grfinfo gi;
int disp_fd;

disp_fd = open("/dev/grf0",1);

if (ioctl (disp_fd, GRFIOCGINFO, &gi) < 0) return -1;
```

```
(void) ioctl (disp_fd, GRFIOCON, 0);

Addr = (u_char *) 0;
if (ioctl (disp_fd, GRFIOCMAP, &Addr) < 0) {
        (void) ioctl (disp_fd, GRFIOCOFF, 0);
        return -1;
}
rbox = (rboxfb *) Addr;                              /* Control Registers  */
frame_buffer = (u_char *) Addr + gi.gd_regsize; /* Frame buffer memory */
```

FILES
/dev/grf?   BSD special file
/dev/crt98720
/dev/ocrt98720   HP-UX *starbase* special files
/dev/MAKEDEV.hpux script for creating HP-UX special files

DIAGNOSTICS
None under BSD. The HP-UX CE.utilities must be used.

ERRORS
[ENODEV] no such device.

[EBUSY]   Another process has the device open.

[EINVAL] Invalid ioctl specification.

SEE ALSO
ioctl(2), grf(4).

For extensive code examples using the Renaissance, see the X device dependent source.

BUGS
Not tested for all configurations of scan board and frame buffer memory boards.

NAME

rd – CS/80 disk interface

SYNOPSIS

```
master hpib? at scode?
disk rd? at hpib? slave?
```

DESCRIPTION

This is a generic CS/80 disk driver. Only a small number of possible CS/80 drives are supported, but others can easily be added by adding tables to the driver. It is a typical block-device driver; see physio(4).

The script MAKEDEV(8) should be used to create the **rd** special files; consult mknod(8) if a special file needs to be made manually.

DISK SUPPORT

The driver interrogates the controller to determine the type of drive attached. The driver recognizes the following drives: 7912, 7914, 7933, 7936, 7937, 7945, 757A/B, 7958A/B, 7959B, 7962, 7963, 9122, 9134, 7912, 7936, and 9122, not all of which have been tested. Special file names begin with 'rd' and 'rrd' for the block and character files respectively. The second component of the name, a drive unit number in the range of zero to seven, is represented by a '?' in the disk layouts below. The last component of the name is the file system partition and is designated by a letter from 'a' to 'h' which also corresponds to a minor device number sets: zero to seven, eight to 15, 16 to 23 and so forth for drive zero, drive two and drive three respectively (see physio 4) . The location and size (in sectors) of the partitions for these drives:

7945/7946 partitions:

disk	start	length	cyls
rd?a	112	15904	1-142
rd?b	16016	20160	143-322
rd?c	0	108416	0-967
rd?d	16016	40320	143-502
rd?e	undefined		
rd?f	undefined		
rd?g	36176	72240	323-967
rd?h	56336	52080	503-967

9134D partitions:

disk	start	length	cyls
rd?a	96	15936	1-166
rd?b	16032	13056	167-302
rd?c	0	29088	0-302
rd?d	undefined		
rd?e	undefined		
rd?f	undefined		
rd?g	undefined		
rd?h	undefined		

9122S partitions:

disk	start	length	cyls
rd?a	undefined		
rd?b	undefined		
rd?c	0	1232	0-76
rd?d	undefined		

```
                    rd?e    undefined
                    rd?f    undefined
                    rd?g    undefined
                    rd?h    undefined

            7912P partitions:
                    disk    start      length   cyls
                    rd?a    0          15904    0-70
                    rd?b    16128      22400    72-171
                    rd?c    0          128128   0-571
                    rd?d    16128      42560    72-261
                    rd?e    undefined
                    rd?f    undefined
                    rd?g    38528      89600    172-571
                    rd?h    58688      69440    262-571

            7914CT/P partitions:
                    disk    start      length   cyls
                    rd?a    224        15904    1-71
                    rd?b    16128      40320    72-251
                    rd?c    0          258048   0-1151
                    rd?d    16128      64960    72-361
                    rd?e    81088      98560    362-801
                    rd?f    179648     78400    802-1151
                    rd?g    56448      201600   252-1151
                    rd?h    81088      176960   362-1151

            7958A partitions:
                    disk    start      length   cyls
                    rd?a    252        16128    1-64
                    rd?b    16380      32256    65-192
                    rd?c    0          255276   0-1012
                    rd?d    16380      48384    65-256
                    rd?e    64764      100800   257-656
                    rd?f    165564     89712    657-1012
                    rd?g    48636      206640   193-1012
                    rd?h    64764      190512   257-1012

            7957A partitions:
                    disk    start      length   cyls
                    rd?a    154        16016    1-104
                    rd?b    16170      24640    105-264
                    rd?c    0          159544   0-1035
                    rd?d    16170      42350    105-379
                    rd?e    58520      54824    380-735
                    rd?f    113344     46200    736-1035
                    rd?g    40810      118734   265-1035
                    rd?h    58520      101024   380-1035

            7933H partitions:
                    disk    start      length   cyls
                    rd?a    598        16146    1-27
```

rd?b	16744	66976	28-139
rd?c	0	789958	0-1320
rd?d	83720	16146	140-166
rd?e	99866	165646	167-443
rd?f	265512	165646	444-720
rd?g	83720	706238	140-1320
rd?h	431158	358800	721-1320

9134L partitions:

disk	start	length	cyls
rd?a	80	15920	1-199
rd?b	16000	20000	200-449
rd?c	0	77840	0-972
rd?d	16000	32000	200-599
rd?e	undefined		
rd?f	undefined		
rd?g	36000	41840	450-972
rd?h	48000	29840	600-972

7936H partitions:

disk	start	length	cyls
rd?a	861	16359	1-19
rd?b	17220	67158	20-97
rd?c	0	600978	0-697
rd?d	84378	16359	98-116
rd?e	100737	120540	117-256
rd?f	220416	120540	256-395
rd?g	84378	516600	98-697
rd?h	341817	259161	397-697

7937H partitions:

disk	start	length	cyls
rd?a	1599	15990	1-10
rd?b	17589	67158	11-52
rd?c	0	1116102	0-697
rd?d	84747	15990	53-62
rd?e	100737	246246	63-216
rd?f	346983	246246	217-370
rd?g	84747	1031355	53-697
rd?h	593229	522873	371-697

7957B/7961B partitions:

disk	start	length	cyls
rd?a	126	16002	1-127
rd?b	16128	32760	128-387
rd?c	0	159894	0-1268
rd?d	16128	49140	128-517
rd?e	65268	50400	518-917
rd?f	115668	44226	918-1268
rd?g	48888	111006	388-1268
rd?h	65268	94626	518-1268

7958B/7962B partitions:

disk	start	length	cyls
rd?a	378	16254	1-43
rd?b	16632	32886	44-130
rd?c	0	297108	0-785
rd?d	16632	49140	44-173
rd?e	65772	121716	174-495
rd?f	187488	109620	496-785
rd?g	49518	247590	131-785
rd?h	65772	231336	174-785

7959B/7963B partitions:

disk	start	length	cyls
rd?a	378	16254	1-43
rd?b	16632	49140	44-173
rd?c	0	594216	0-1571
rd?d	16632	65772	44-217
rd?e	82404	303912	218-1021
rd?f	386316	207900	1022-1571
rd?g	65772	528444	174-1571
rd?h	82404	511812	218-1571

The eight partitions as given support four basic, non-overlapping layouts, though not all partitions exist on all drive types.

In the first layout there are three partitions and a "bootblock" area. The bootblock area is at the beginning of the disk and holds the standalone disk boot program. The rd?a partition is for the root file system, rd?b is a paging/swapping area, and rd?g is for everything else.

The second layout is the same idea, but has a larger paging/swapping partition (rd?d) and a smaller "everything else" partition (rd?h). This layout is better for environments which run many large processes.

The third layout is a variation of the second, but breaks the rd?h partition into two partitions, rd?e and rd?f.

The final layout is intended for a large, single file system second disk. It is also used when writing out the boot program since it is the only partition mapping the bootblock area.

FILES

```
/dev/rd[0-7][a-h]    block files
/dev/rrd[0-7][a-h]   raw files
```

DIAGNOSTICS

rd%d err: v%d u%d, R0x%x F0x%x A0x%x I0x%x, block %d An unrecoverable data error occurred during transfer of the specified block on the specified disk.

BUGS

The current disk partitioning is totally bogus. CS/80 drives have 256 byte sectors which are mapped to 512 byte "sectors" by the driver. Since some CS/80 drives have an odd number of sectors per cylinder, the disk geometry used is not always accurate.

The partition tables for the file systems should be read off of each pack, as they are never quite what any single installation would prefer, and this would make packs more portable.

A program to analyze the logged error information (even in its present reduced form) is needed.

NAME

`route` – kernel packet forwarding database

SYNOPSIS

```
#include <sys/socket.h>
#include <net/if.h>
#include <net/route.h>
```

int
socket(*PF_ROUTE, SOCK_RAW, int family*);

DESCRIPTION

UNIX provides some packet routing facilities. The kernel maintains a routing information database, which is used in selecting the appropriate network interface when transmitting packets.

A user process (or possibly multiple co-operating processes) maintains this database by sending messages over a special kind of socket. This supplants fixed size `ioctl(2)`'s used in earlier releases. Routing table changes may only be carried out by the super user.

The operating system may spontaneously emit routing messages in response to external events, such as receipt of a re-direct, or failure to locate a suitable route for a request. The message types are described in greater detail below.

Routing database entries come in two flavors: for a specific host, or for all hosts on a generic subnetwork (as specified by a bit mask and value under the mask. The effect of wildcard or default route may be achieved by using a mask of all zeros, and there may be hierarchical routes.

When the system is booted and addresses are assigned to the network interfaces, each protocol family installs a routing table entry for each interface when it is ready for traffic. Normally the protocol specifies the route through each interface as a "direct" connection to the destination host or network. If the route is direct, the transport layer of a protocol family usually requests the packet be sent to the same host specified in the packet. Otherwise, the interface is requested to address the packet to the gateway listed in the routing entry (i.e. the packet is forwarded).

When routing a packet, the kernel will attempt to find the most specific route matching the destination. (If there are two different mask and value-under-the-mask pairs that match, the more specific is the one with more bits in the mask. A route to a host is regarded as being supplied with a mask of as many ones as there are bits in the destination). If no entry is found, the destination is declared to be unreachable, and a routing–miss message is generated if there are any listers on the routing control socket described below.

A wildcard routing entry is specified with a zero destination address value, and a mask of all zeroes. Wildcard routes will be used when the system fails to find other routes matching the destination. The combination of wildcard routes and routing redirects can provide an economical mechanism for routing traffic.

One opens the channel for passing routing control messages by using the socket call shown in the synopsis above:

The *family* parameter may be `AF_UNSPEC` which will provide routing information for all address families, or can be restricted to a specific address family by specifying which one is desired. There can be more than one routing socket open per system.

Messages are formed by a header followed by a small number of sockadders (now variable length particularly in the ISO case), interpreted by position, and delimited by the new length entry in the sockaddr. An example of a message with four addresses might be an ISO redirect: Destination, Netmask, Gateway, and Author of the redirect. The interpretation of which address are present is given by a bit mask within the header, and the sequence is least significant to most significant bit within the vector.

Any messages sent to the kernel are returned, and copies are sent to all interested listeners. The kernel will provide the process id. for the sender, and the sender may use an additional sequence field to distinguish between outstanding messages. However, message replies may be lost when kernel buffers are exhausted.

The kernel may reject certain messages, and will indicate this by filling in the *rtm_errno* field. The routing code returns EEXIST if requested to duplicate an existing entry, ESRCH if requested to delete a non-existent entry, or ENOBUFS if insufficient resources were available to install a new route. In the current implementation, all routing process run locally, and the values for *rtm_errno* are available through the normal *errno* mechanism, even if the routing reply message is lost.

A process may avoid the expense of reading replies to its own messages by issuing a setsockopt(2) call indicating that the SO_USELOOPBACK option at the SOL_SOCKET level is to be turned off. A process may ignore all messages from the routing socket by doing a shutdown(2) system call for further input.

If a route is in use when it is deleted, the routing entry will be marked down and removed from the routing table, but the resources associated with it will not be reclaimed until all references to it are released. User processes can obtain information about the routing entry to a specific destination by using a RTM_GET message, or by reading the /dev/kmem device, or by issuing a getkerninfo(2) system call.

Messages include:

```
#define RTM_ADD        0x1    /* Add Route */
#define RTM_DELETE     0x2    /* Delete Route */
#define RTM_CHANGE     0x3    /* Change Metrics, Flags, or Gateway */
#define RTM_GET        0x4    /* Report Information */
#define RTM_LOOSING    0x5    /* Kernel Suspects Partitioning */
#define RTM_REDIRECT   0x6    /* Told to use different route */
#define RTM_MISS       0x7    /* Lookup failed on this address */
#define RTM_RESOLVE    0xb    /* request to resolve dst to LL addr */
```

A message header consists of:

```
struct rt_msghdr {
    u_short rmt_msglen;   /* to skip over non-understood messages */
    u_char  rtm_version;  /* future binary compatibility */
    u_char  rtm_type;     /* message type */
    u_short rmt_index;    /* index for associated ifp */
    pid_t   rmt_pid;      /* identify sender */
    int     rtm_addrs;    /* bitmask identifying sockaddrs in msg */
    int     rtm_seq;      /* for sender to identify action */
    int     rtm_errno;    /* why failed */
    int     rtm_flags;    /* flags, incl kern & message, e.g. DONE */
    int     rtm_use;      /* from rtentry */
    u_long  rtm_inits;    /* which values we are initializing */
    struct  rt_metrics rtm_rmx;     /* metrics themselves */
};
```

where

```
struct rt_metrics {
    u_long rmx_locks;     /* Kernel must leave these values alone */
    u_long rmx_mtu;       /* MTU for this path */
    u_long rmx_hopcount;  /* max hops expected */
    u_long rmx_expire;    /* lifetime for route, e.g. redirect */
    u_long rmx_recvpipe;  /* inbound delay-bandwith product */
    u_long rmx_sendpipe;  /* outbound delay-bandwith product */
```

```
        u_long rmx_ssthresh;    /* outbound gateway buffer limit */
        u_long rmx_rtt;         /* estimated round trip time */
        u_long rmx_rttvar;      /* estimated rtt variance */
};
```

Flags include the values:

```
#define RTF_UP          0x1         /* route usable */
#define RTF_GATEWAY     0x2         /* destination is a gateway */
#define RTF_HOST        0x4         /* host entry (net otherwise) */
#define RTF_REJECT      0x8         /* host or net unreachable */
#define RTF_DYNAMIC     0x10        /* created dynamically (by redirect) */
#define RTF_MODIFIED    0x20        /* modified dynamically (by redirect) */
#define RTF_DONE        0x40        /* message confirmed */
#define RTF_MASK        0x80        /* subnet mask present */
#define RTF_CLONING     0x100       /* generate new routes on use */
#define RTF_XRESOLVE    0x200       /* external daemon resolves name */
#define RTF_LLINFO      0x400       /* generated by ARP or ESIS */
#define RTF_STATIC      0x800       /* manually added */
#define RTF_BLACKHOLE   0x1000      /* just discard pkts (during updates) */
#define RTF_PROTO2      0x4000      /* protocol specific routing flag #1 */
#define RTF_PROTO1      0x8000      /* protocol specific routing flag #2 */
```

Specifiers for metric values in rmx_locks and rtm_inits are:

```
#define RTV_SSTHRESH    0x1         /* init or lock _ssthresh */
#define RTV_RPIPE       0x2         /* init or lock _recvpipe */
#define RTV_SPIPE       0x4         /* init or lock _sendpipe */
#define RTV_HOPCOUNT    0x8         /* init or lock _hopcount */
#define RTV_RTT         0x10        /* init or lock _rtt */
#define RTV_RTTVAR      0x20        /* init or lock _rttvar */
#define RTV_MTU         0x40        /* init or lock _mtu */
```

Specifiers for which addresses are present in the messages are:

```
#define RTA_DST         0x1         /* destination sockaddr present */
#define RTA_GATEWAY     0x2         /* gateway sockaddr present */
#define RTA_NETMASK     0x4         /* netmask sockaddr present */
#define RTA_GENMASK     0x8         /* cloning mask sockaddr present */
#define RTA_IFP         0x10        /* interface name sockaddr present */
#define RTA_IFA         0x20        /* interface addr sockaddr present */
#define RTA_AUTHOR      0x40        /* sockaddr for author of redirect */
```

4

NAME
spp – Xerox Sequenced Packet Protocol

SYNOPSIS
```
#include <sys/socket.h>
#include <netns/ns.h>
#include <netns/sp.h>

int
socket(AF_NS, SOCK_STREAM, 0);

int
socket(AF_NS, SOCK_SEQPACKET, 0);
```

DESCRIPTION
The SPP protocol provides reliable, flow-controlled, two-way transmission of data. It is a byte-stream proto-col used to support the SOCK_STREAM abstraction. SPP uses the standard NS(tm) address formats.

Sockets utilizing the SPP protocol are either "active" or "passive". Active sockets initiate connections to passive sockets. By default SPP sockets are created active; to create a passive socket the listen(2) system call must be used after binding the socket with the bind(2) system call. Only passive sockets may use the accept(2) call to accept incoming connections. Only active sockets may use the connect(2) call to ini-tiate connections.

Passive sockets may "underspecify" their location to match incoming connection requests from multiple networks. This technique, termed "wildcard addressing", allows a single server to provide service to clients on multiple networks. To create a socket which listens on all networks, the NS address of all zeroes must be bound. The SPP port may still be specified at this time; if the port is not specified the system will assign one. Once a connection has been established the socket's address is fixed by the peer entity's location. The ad-dress assigned the socket is the address associated with the network interface through which packets are be-ing transmitted and received. Normally this address corresponds to the peer entity's network.

If the SOCK_SEQPACKET socket type is specified, each packet received has the actual 12 byte sequenced packet header left for the user to inspect:

```
struct sphdr {
        u_char      sp_cc;  /* connection control */
#define SP_EM   0x10        /* end of message */
        u_char      sp_dt;  /* datastream type */
        u_short     sp_sid;
        u_short     sp_did;
        u_short     sp_seq;
        u_short     sp_ack;
        u_short     sp_alo;
};
```

This facilitates the implementation of higher level Xerox protocols which make use of the data stream type field and the end of message bit. Conversely, the user is required to supply a 12 byte header, the only part of which inspected is the data stream type and end of message fields.

For either socket type, packets received with the Attention bit sent are interpreted as out of band data. Data sent with "send(..., ..., ..., MSG_OOB)" cause the attention bit to be set.

DIAGNOSTICS

A socket operation may fail with one of the following errors returned:

[EISCONN]   when trying to establish a connection on a socket which already has one;

[ENOBUFS]   when the system runs out of memory for an internal data structure;

[ETIMEDOUT]   when a connection was dropped due to excessive retransmissions;

[ECONNRESET]   when the remote peer forces the connection to be closed;

[ECONNREFUSED]   when the remote peer actively refuses connection establishment (usually because no process is listening to the port);

[EADDRINUSE]   when an attempt is made to create a socket with a port which has already been allocated;

[EADDRNOTAVAIL]   when an attempt is made to create a socket with a network address for which no network interface exists.

SOCKET OPTIONS

SO_DEFAULT_HEADERS when set, this determines the data stream type and whether the end of message bit is to be set on every ensuing packet.

SO_MTU   This specifies the maximum amount of user data in a single packet. The default is 576 bytes - sizeof(struct spidp). This quantity affects windowing – increasing it without increasing the amount of buffering in the socket will lower the number of unread packets accepted. Anything larger than the default will not be forwarded by a bona fide XEROX product internetwork router. The data argument for the setsockopt call must be an unsigned short.

SEE ALSO

intro(4), ns(4)

HISTORY

The **spp** protocol appeared in 4.3BSD.

BUGS

There should be some way to reflect record boundaries in a stream. For stream mode, there should be an option to get the data stream type of the record the user process is about to receive.

NAME

st – CCS SCSI tape driver

SYNOPSIS

```
tape st0 at scsi? slave ?
```

DESCRIPTION

The st driver was written especially to support the Exabyte EXB-8200 8MM Cartridge Tape Subsystem. It has several extensions specific to the Exabyte, but should support other tape drives as long has they follow the ANSI SCSI-I specification. Besides extensive use with an Exabyte, the driver has been tested with an Archive QIC-24 tape drive. The st tape interface provides a standard tape drive interface as described in mtio(4) with the following exceptions:

1. Density is dependent on device type. Current Exabyte hardware has only one density. The EXB-8500 drive, when released, will have a high density format of 5.6GB. On an Archive QIC-24 drive the driver reads both QIC-11 and QIC-24 formats but writes only QIC-24.

2. Only the "raw" interface is supported.

Special Exabyte Support:

The MTIOCGET ioctl(2) call on an Exabyte returns this structure:

```
struct mtget {
        short mt_type;    /* type of magtape device */
        short mt_dsreg;   /* sc_flags */
        short mt_erreg;   /* high 8 bytes error status */
        /* low  8 bytes percentage of Rewrites
        if writing, ECC errors if reading */
        short mt_resid;   /* Mbyte until end of tape */
};
```

Bit 4 in the minor device number is used to select long filemarks or short filemarks. A long filemark occupies 2.12 MBytes of space on the tape, while a short filemark occupies 488 KBytes. A long filemark includes an erase gap while the short filemark does not. The tape can be positioned on the BOT side of a long filemark allowing data to be appended with a write operation. Since the short filemark does not contain an erase gap which would allow writing it is considered to be non-erasable. If either type of filemark is followed by blank tape, data may be appended on its EOT side.

Bit 5 in the minor device number selects fixed block mode with a block size of 1K. Variable length records are the default if bit 5 is not set.

For unit 0 here are the effects of minor device bits 2,3,4,5. For other units add the *unit#* to each of the device names.

	norewind	high density	short filemarks	fixed block mode
rst0				
nrst0	X			
rst8			X	
nrst8	X		X	
rst16				X
nrst16	X			X
rst24			X	X
nrst24	X		X	X

rst32			X
nrst32	X		X
rst40		X	X
nrst40	X	X	X
rst48			XX
nrst48	X		XX
rst56		X	XX
nrst56	X	X	XX

SEE ALSO

mt(1), tar(1), mtio(4),

EXB-8200 8MM Cartridge Tape Subsystem Interface User Manual..

BUGS

The HP 98268 SCSI controller hardware can not do odd length DMA transfers. If odd length DMA I/O is requested the driver will use the "Program Transfer Mode" of the Fujitsu MB87030 chip. Read requests are normally even length for which a DMA transfer is used. If, however, the driver detects that a odd length read has happened (when a even length was requested) it will issue the EIO error and the last byte of the read data will be 0x00. Odd length read requests must match the size of the requested data block on tape.

The following only applies when using long filemarks. Short filemarks can not be overwritten.

Due to the helical scan and the erase mechanism, there is a writing limitation on Exabyte drives. "tar r" or "tar u" will not work ("tar c" is ok). One can only start writing at 1) beginning of tape, 2) on the end of what was last written, 3) "front" side of a regular (long) filemark. For example, you have a tape with 3 tar files. If you want to save the first file, but overwrite the second two files with new data, on a normal 1/4" or 1/2" drive you would do:

mt fsf 1; tar cf /dev/nrst0 ...

but for an Exabyte you need to do:

mt fsf 1; mt bsf 1; mt weof 1; tar cf /dev/nrst0 ...

The regular long filemark consists of an erased zone 3.8" long (needed to begin a write). In this case, the first filemark is rewritten in place, which creates an erased zone *after* it, clearing the way to write more on the tape. The erase head is not helical.

One can position a tape to the end of what was last written by reading until a "BLANK CHECK" error is returned. Writing can be started at this point. (This applies to both long and short filemarks.) The tape does not become positioned somewhere down the "erased" area as does a conventional magtape. One can issue multiple reads at the "BLANK CHECK" error, but the Exabyte stays positioned at the beginning of the blank area, ready to accept write commands. File skip operations do not stop at blank tape and will run into old data or run to the end of the tape, so you have to be careful not to "mt fsf too_many".

Archive support gets confused if asked to moved more filemarks than there are on the tape.

This man page needs some work. Some of these are not really bugs, just unavoidable consequences of the hardware.

NAME

tc – HP98544 98550 ''Topcat'' and ''Catseye'' device interface

DESCRIPTION

This driver is for the HP98544, 98545 and 98547 ''Topcat'' and HP98548, 98549, and 98550 ''Catseye'' display cards. This driver merely checks for the existence of the device and does minimal set up, as it is expected the applications will initialize the device to their requirements. The Topcat and Catseye are nearly identical in common usage and only the Topcat will be referred to from now on.

The Topcat display cards are not user configurable. If one is present on a system, it will always have a frame buffer address of 0x200000 and a control register address of 0x560000. These are the HP series 300 ITE (Internal Terminal Emulator) defaults. The device can also be used as a graphics output device.

The ioctl(2) calls supported by the BSD system for the Topcat are:

GRFIOCGINFO   Get Graphics Info

> Get info about device, setting the entries in the *grfinfo* structure, as defined in <hpdev/grfioctl.h>. For the 98544 or 98549, the number of planes should be 1, as they are monochrome devices. The number of planes for a 98545 is 4, translating to 15 colors, excluding black. The 98547 and 98548 cards have 6 planes, yielding 63 colors and black. The 98550 has 8 planes, yielding 255 colors and black. The displayed frame buffer size for the 98549 and 98550 is 2048 x 1024, for the others it is 1024 x 768.

GRFIOCON   Graphics On

> Turn graphics on by enabling CRT output. The screen will come on, displaying whatever is in the frame buffer, using whatever colormap is in place.

GRFIOCOFF   Graphics Off

> Turn graphics off by disabling output to the CRT. The frame buffer contents are not affected.

GRFIOCMAP   Map Device to user space

> Map in control registers and framebuffer space. Once the device file is mapped, the frame buffer structure is accessible. The frame buffer structure describing Topcat/Catseye devices is defined in <hpdev/grf_tcreg.h>.

For further information about the use of ioctl see the man page.

EXAMPLE

A small example of opening, mapping and using the device is given below. For more examples of the details on the behavior of the device, see the device dependent source files for the X Window System, in the /usr/src/new/X/libhp directory.

```
struct tcboxfb *tc;
u_char *Addr, frame_buffer;
struct grfinfo gi;
int disp_fd;

disp_fd = open("/dev/grf0",1);

if (ioctl (disp_fd, GRFIOCGINFO, &gi) < 0) return -1;

(void) ioctl (disp_fd, GRFIOCON, 0);
```

```
Addr = (u_char *) 0;
if (ioctl (disp_fd, GRFIOCMAP, &Addr) < 0) {
        (void) ioctl (disp_fd, GRFIOCOFF, 0);
        return -1;
}
tc = (tcboxfb *) Addr;                          /* Control Registers  */
frame_buffer = (u_char *) Addr + gi.gd_regsize; /* Frame buffer memory */
```

FILES

/dev/grf?	BSD special file
/dev/crt9837	
/dev/crt98550	HP-UX *starbase* special files
/dev/MAKEDEV.hpux	script for creating HP-UX special files

DIAGNOSTICS

None under BSD. HP-UX /usr/CE.utilities/Crtadjust programs must be used.

ERRORS

[ENODEV]   no such device.

[EBUSY]   Another process has the device open.

[EINVAL]   Invalid ioctl specification.

SEE ALSO

ioctl(2), grf(4)

NAME
tcp – Internet Transmission Control Protocol

SYNOPSIS
```
#include <sys/socket.h>
#include <netinet/in.h>

int
socket(AF_INET, SOCK_STREAM, 0);
```

DESCRIPTION
The TCP protocol provides reliable, flow-controlled, two-way transmission of data. It is a byte-stream protocol used to support the SOCK_STREAM abstraction. TCP uses the standard Internet address format and, in addition, provides a per-host collection of "port addresses". Thus, each address is composed of an Internet address specifying the host and network, with a specific TCP port on the host identifying the peer entity.

Sockets utilizing the tcp protocol are either "active" or "passive". Active sockets initiate connections to passive sockets. By default TCP sockets are created active; to create a passive socket the listen(2) system call must be used after binding the socket with the bind(2) system call. Only passive sockets may use the accept(2) call to accept incoming connections. Only active sockets may use the connect(2) call to initiate connections.

Passive sockets may "underspecify" their location to match incoming connection requests from multiple networks. This technique, termed "wildcard addressing", allows a single server to provide service to clients on multiple networks. To create a socket which listens on all networks, the Internet address INADDR_ANY must be bound. The TCP port may still be specified at this time; if the port is not specified the system will assign one. Once a connection has been established the socket's address is fixed by the peer entity's location. The address assigned the socket is the address associated with the network interface through which packets are being transmitted and received. Normally this address corresponds to the peer entity's network.

TCP supports one socket option which is set with setsockopt(2) and tested with getsockopt(2). Under most circumstances, TCP sends data when it is presented; when outstanding data has not yet been acknowledged, it gathers small amounts of output to be sent in a single packet once an acknowledgement is received. For a small number of clients, such as window systems that send a stream of mouse events which receive no replies, this packetization may cause significant delays. Therefore, TCP provides a boolean option, TCP_NODELAY (from <netinet/tcp.h>, to defeat this algorithm. The option level for the setsockopt call is the protocol number for TCP, available from getprotobyname(3).

Options at the IP transport level may be used with TCP; see ip(4). Incoming connection requests that are source-routed are noted, and the reverse source route is used in responding.

DIAGNOSTICS
A socket operation may fail with one of the following errors returned:

[EISCONN]   when trying to establish a connection on a socket which already has one;

[ENOBUFS]   when the system runs out of memory for an internal data structure;

[ETIMEDOUT]   when a connection was dropped due to excessive retransmissions;

[ECONNRESET]   when the remote peer forces the connection to be closed;

[ECONNREFUSED]   when the remote peer actively refuses connection establishment (usually because no process is listening to the port);

[EADDRINUSE]   when an attempt is made to create a socket with a port which has already been allocated;

[EADDRNOTAVAIL]   when an attempt is made to create a socket with a network address for which no network interface exists.

SEE ALSO

getsockopt(2), socket(2), intro(4), inet(4), ip(4)

HISTORY

The **tcp** protocol stack appeared in 4.2BSD.

4

NAME
　　　`termios` – general terminal line discipline

SYNOPSIS
　　　`#include <termios.h>`

DESCRIPTION
　　　This describes a general terminal line discipline that is supported on tty asynchronous communication ports.

Opening a Terminal Device File
　　　When a terminal file is opened, it normally causes the process to wait until a connection is established. For most hardware, the presence of a connection is indicated by the assertion of the hardware CARRIER line. If the termios structure associated with the terminal file has the CLOCAL flag set in the cflag, or if the O_NONBLOCK flag is set in the open(2) call, then the open will succeed even without a connection being present. In practice, applications seldom open these files; they are opened by special programs, such as getty(2) or rlogind(2), and become an application's standard input, output, and error files.

Job Control in a Nutshell
　　　Every process is associated with a particular process group and session. The grouping is hierarchical: every member of a particular process group is a member of the same session. This structuring is used in managing groups of related processes for purposes of *job control*; that is, the ability from the keyboard (or from program control) to simultaneously stop or restart a complex command (a command composed of one or more related processes). The grouping into process groups allows delivering of signals that stop or start the group as a whole, along with arbitrating which process group has access to the single controlling terminal. The grouping at a higher layer into sessions is to restrict the job control related signals and system calls to within processes resulting from a particular instance of a "login". Typically, a session is created when a user logs in, and the login terminal is setup to be the controlling terminal; all processes spawned from that login shell are in the same session, and inherit the controlling terminal. A job control shell operating interactively (that is, reading commands from a terminal) normally groups related processes together by placing them into the same process group. A set of processes in the same process group is collectively referred to as a "job". When the foreground process group of the terminal is the same as the process group of a particular job, that job is said to be in the "foreground". When the process group of the terminal is different than the process group of a job (but is still the controlling terminal), that job is said to be in the "background". Normally the shell reads a command and starts the job that implements that command. If the command is to be started in the foreground (typical), it sets the process group of the terminal to the process group of the started job, waits for the job to complete, and then sets the process group of the terminal back to its own process group (it puts itself into the foreground). If the job is to be started in the background (as denoted by the shell operator "&"), it never changes the process group of the terminal and doesn't wait for the job to complete (that is, it immediately attempts to read the next command). If the job is started in the foreground, the user may type a key (usually '^Z') which generates the terminal stop signal (SIGTSTP) and has the affect of stopping the entire job. The shell will notice that the job stopped, and will resume running after placing itself in the foreground. The shell also has commands for placing stopped jobs in the background, and for placing stopped or background jobs into the foreground.

Orphaned Process Groups
　　　An orphaned process group is a process group that has no process whose parent is in a different process group, yet is in the same session. Conceptually it means a process group that doesn't have a parent that could do anything if it were to be stopped. For example, the initial login shell is typically in an orphaned process group. Orphaned process groups are immune to keyboard generated stop signals and job control signals resulting from reads or writes to the controlling terminal.

The Controlling Terminal

A terminal may belong to a process as its controlling terminal. Each process of a session that has a controlling terminal has the same controlling terminal. A terminal may be the controlling terminal for at most one session. The controlling terminal for a session is allocated by the session leader by issuing the TIOCSCTTY ioctl. A controlling terminal is never acquired by merely opening a terminal device file. When a controlling terminal becomes associated with a session, its foreground process group is set to the process group of the session leader.

The controlling terminal is inherited by a child process during a fork(2) function call. A process relinquishes its controlling terminal when it creates a new session with the function; other processes remaining in the old session that had this terminal as their controlling terminal continue to have it. A process does not relinquish its controlling terminal simply by closing all of its file descriptors associated with the controlling terminal if other processes continue to have it open.

When a controlling process terminates, the controlling terminal is disassociated from the current session, allowing it to be acquired by a new session leader. Subsequent access to the terminal by other processes in the earlier session will be denied, with attempts to access the terminal treated as if modem disconnect had been sensed.

Terminal Access Control

If a process is in the foreground process group of its controlling terminal, read operations are allowed. Any attempts by a process in a background process group to read from its controlling terminal causes a SIGTTIN signal to be sent to the process's group unless one of the following special cases apply: If the reading process is ignoring or blocking the SIGTTIN signal, or if the process group of the process is orphaned, the read(2) returns -1 with *errno set to* EIO and no signal is sent. The default action of the SIGTTIN signal is to stop the process to which it is sent.

If a process is in the foreground process group of its controlling terminal, write operations are allowed. Attempts by a process in a background process group to write to its controlling terminal will cause the process group to be sent a SIGTTOU signal unless one of the following special cases apply: If TOSTOP is not set, or if TOSTOP is set and the process is ignoring or blocking the SIGTTOU signal, the process is allowed to write to the terminal and the SIGTTOU signal is not sent. If TOSTOP is set, and the process group of the writing process is orphaned, and the writing process is not ignoring or blocking SIGTTOU, the write returns -1 with errno set to EIO and no signal is sent.

Certain calls that set terminal parameters are treated in the same fashion as write, except that TOSTOP is ignored; that is, the effect is identical to that of terminal writes when TOSTOP is set.

Input Processing and Reading Data

A terminal device associated with a terminal device file may operate in full-duplex mode, so that data may arrive even while output is occurring. Each terminal device file has associated with it an input queue, into which incoming data is stored by the system before being read by a process. The system imposes a limit, {MAX_INPUT}, on the number of bytes that may be stored in the input queue. The behavior of the system when this limit is exceeded depends on the setting of the IMAXBEL flag in the termios c_iflag. If this flag is set, the terminal is sent an ASCII BEL character each time a character is received while the input queue is full. Otherwise, the input queue is flushed upon receiving the character.

Two general kinds of input processing are available, determined by whether the terminal device file is in canonical mode or noncanonical mode. Additionally, input characters are processed according to the c_iflag and c_lflag fields. Such processing can include echoing, which in general means transmitting input characters immediately back to the terminal when they are received from the terminal. This is useful for terminals that can operate in full-duplex mode.

The manner in which data is provided to a process reading from a terminal device file is dependent on whether the terminal device file is in canonical or noncanonical mode.

Another dependency is whether the O_NONBLOCK flag is set by open() or fcntl(). If the O_NONBLOCK flag is clear, then the read request is blocked until data is available or a signal has been received. If the O_NONBLOCK flag is set, then the read request is completed, without blocking, in one of three ways:

1. If there is enough data available to satisfy the entire request, and the read completes successfully the number of bytes read is returned.

2. If there is not enough data available to satisfy the entire request, and the read completes successfully, having read as much data as possible, the number of bytes read is returned.

3. If there is no data available, the read returns -1, with errno set to EAGAIN.

When data is available depends on whether the input processing mode is canonical or noncanonical.

Canonical Mode Input Processing

In canonical mode input processing, terminal input is processed in units of lines. A line is delimited by a newline '\n' character, an end-of-file (EOF) character, or an end-of-line (EOL) character. See the Special Characters section for more information on EOF and EOL. This means that a read request will not return until an entire line has been typed, or a signal has been received. Also, no matter how many bytes are requested in the read call, at most one line is returned. It is not, however, necessary to read a whole line at once; any number of bytes, even one, may be requested in a read without losing information.

{MAX_CANON} is a limit on the number of bytes in a line. The behavior of the system when this limit is exceeded is the same as when the input queue limit {MAX_INPUT}, is exceeded.

Erase and kill processing occur when either of two special characters, the ERASE and KILL characters (see the Special Characters section), is received. This processing affects data in the input queue that has not yet been delimited by a newline NL, EOF, or EOL character. This un-delimited data makes up the current line. The ERASE character deletes the last character in the current line, if there is any. The KILL character deletes all data in the current line, if there is any. The ERASE and KILL characters have no effect if there is no data in the current line. The ERASE and KILL characters themselves are not placed in the input queue.

Noncanonical Mode Input Processing

In noncanonical mode input processing, input bytes are not assembled into lines, and erase and kill processing does not occur. The values of the MIN and TIME members of the c_cc array are used to determine how to process the bytes received.

MIN represents the minimum number of bytes that should be received when the read function successfully returns. TIME is a timer of 0.1 second granularity that is used to time out bursty and short term data transmissions. If MIN is greater than { MAX_INPUT}, the response to the request is undefined. The four possible values for MIN and TIME and their interactions are described below.

Case A: MIN > 0, TIME > 0

In this case TIME serves as an inter-byte timer and is activated after the first byte is received. Since it is an inter-byte timer, it is reset after a byte is received. The interaction between MIN and TIME is as follows: as soon as one byte is received, the inter-byte timer is started. If MIN bytes are received before the inter-byte timer expires (remember that the timer is reset upon receipt of each byte), the read is satisfied. If the timer expires before MIN bytes are received, the characters received to that point are returned to the user. Note that if TIME expires at least one byte is returned because the timer would not have been enabled unless a byte was received. In this case (MIN > 0, TIME > 0) the read blocks until the MIN and TIME mechanisms are activated by the receipt of the first byte, or a signal is received. If data is in the buffer at the time of the read(), the result is as if data had been received immediately after the read().

Case B: MIN > 0, TIME = 0

In this case, since the value of TIME is zero, the timer plays no role and only MIN is significant. A pending read is not satisfied until MIN bytes are received (i.e., the pending read blocks until MIN bytes are received), or a signal is received. A program that uses this case to read record-based terminal I/O may block indefinitely in the read operation.

Case C: MIN = 0, TIME > 0

In this case, since MIN = 0, TIME no longer represents an inter-byte timer. It now serves as a read timer that is activated as soon as the read function is processed. A read is satisfied as soon as a single byte is received or the read timer expires. Note that in this case if the timer expires, no bytes are returned. If the timer does not expire, the only way the read can be satisfied is if a byte is received. In this case the read will not block indefinitely waiting for a byte; if no byte is received within TIME*0.1 seconds after the read is initiated, the read returns a value of zero, having read no data. If data is in the buffer at the time of the read, the timer is started as if data had been received immediately after the read.

Case D: MIN = 0, TIME = 0

The minimum of either the number of bytes requested or the number of bytes currently available is returned without waiting for more bytes to be input. If no characters are available, read returns a value of zero, having read no data.

Writing Data and Output Processing

When a process writes one or more bytes to a terminal device file, they are processed according to the *c_oflag* field (see the Output Modes section). The implementation may provide a buffering mechanism; as such, when a call to write() completes, all of the bytes written have been scheduled for transmission to the device, but the transmission will not necessarily have been completed.

Special Characters

Certain characters have special functions on input or output or both. These functions are summarized as follows:

INTR   Special character on input and is recognized if the ISIG flag (see the Local Modes section) is enabled. Generates a SIGINT signal which is sent to all processes in the foreground process group for which the terminal is the controlling terminal. If ISIG is set, the INTR character is discarded when processed.

QUIT   Special character on input and is recognized if the ISIG flag is enabled. Generates a SIGQUIT signal which is sent to all processes in the foreground process group for which the terminal is the controlling terminal. If ISIG is set, the QUIT character is discarded when processed.

ERASE   Special character on input and is recognized if the ICANON flag is set. Erases the last character in the current line; see Canonical Mode Input Processing. It does not erase beyond the start of a line, as delimited by an NL, EOF, or EOL character. If ICANON is set, the ERASE character is discarded when processed.

KILL   Special character on input and is recognized if the ICANON flag is set. Deletes the entire line, as delimited by a NL, EOF, or EOL character. If ICANON is set, the KILL character is discarded when processed.

EOF   Special character on input and is recognized if the ICANON flag is set. When received, all the bytes waiting to be read are immediately passed to the process, without waiting for a newline, and the EOF is discarded. Thus, if there are no bytes waiting (that is, the EOF occurred at the beginning of a line), a byte count of zero is returned from the read(), representing an end-of-file indication. If ICANON is set, the EOF character is discarded when processed. NL Special character on input and is recognized if the ICANON flag is set. It is the line delimiter '\n'.

EOL   Special character on input and is recognized if the ICANON flag is set. Is an additional line delimiter, like NL.

SUSP   If the ISIG flag is enabled, receipt of the SUSP character causes a SIGTSTP signal to be sent to all processes in the foreground process group for which the terminal is the controlling terminal, and the SUSP character is discarded when processed.

STOP   Special character on both input and output and is recognized if the IXON (output control) or IXOFF (input control) flag is set. Can be used to temporarily suspend output. It is useful with fast terminals to prevent output from disappearing before it can be read. If IXON is set, the STOP character is discarded when processed.

START   Special character on both input and output and is recognized if the IXON (output control) or IXOFF (input control) flag is set. Can be used to resume output that has been suspended by a STOP character. If IXON is set, the START character is discarded when processed. CR Special character on input and is recognized if the ICANON flag is set; it is the '\r', as denoted in the C Standard {2}. When ICANON and ICRNL are set and IGNCR is not set, this character is translated into a NL, and has the same effect as a NL character.

The following special characters are extensions defined by this system and are not a part of 1003.1 termios.

EOL2   Secondary EOL character. Same function as EOL .

WERASE Special character on input and is recognized if the ICANON flag is set. Erases the last word in the current line according to one of two algorithms. If the ALTWERASE flag is not set, first any preceding whitespace is erased, and then the maximal sequence of non-whitespace characters. If ALTWERASE is set, first any preceding whitespace is erased, and then the maximal sequence of alphabetic/underscores or non alphabetic/underscores. As a special case in this second algorithm, the first previous non-whitespace character is skipped in determining whether the preceding word is a sequence of alphabetic/undercores. This sounds confusing but turns out to be quite practical.

REPRINT
      Special character on input and is recognized if the ICANON flag is set. Causes the current input edit line to be retyped.

DSUSP   Has similar actions to the SUSP character, except that the SIGTSTP signal is delivered when one of the processes in the foreground process group issues a read() to the controlling terminal.

LNEXT   Special character on input and is recognized if the IEXTEN flag is set. Receipt of this character causes the next character to be taken literally.

DISCARD
      Special character on input and is recognized if the IEXTEN flag is set. Receipt of this character toggles the flushing of terminal output.

STATUS   Special character on input and is recognized if the ICANON flag is set. Receipt of this character causes a SIGINFO signal to be sent to the foreground process group of the terminal. Also, if the NOKERNINFO flag is not set, it causes the kernel to write a status message to the terminal that displays the current load average, the name of the command in the foreground, its process ID, the symbolic wait channel, the number of user and system seconds used, the percentage of cpu the process is getting, and the resident set size of the process.

The NL and CR characters cannot be changed. The values for all the remaining characters can be set and are described later in the document under Special Control Characters.

Special character functions associated with changeable special control characters can be disabled individually by setting their value to {_POSIX_VDISABLE}; see Special Control Characters.

If two or more special characters have the same value, the function performed when that character is received is undefined.

Modem Disconnect

If a modem disconnect is detected by the terminal interface for a controlling terminal, and if CLOCAL is not set in the c_cflag field for the terminal, the SIGHUP signal is sent to the controlling process associated with the terminal. Unless other arrangements have been made, this causes the controlling process to terminate. Any subsequent call to the read() function returns the value zero, indicating end of file. Thus, processes that read a terminal file and test for end-of-file can terminate appropriately after a disconnect. Any subsequent write() to the terminal device returns -1, with *errno* set to EIO, until the device is closed.

General Terminal Interface

Closing a Terminal Device File

The last process to close a terminal device file causes any output to be sent to the device and any input to be discarded. Then, if HUPCL is set in the control modes, and the communications port supports a disconnect function, the terminal device performs a disconnect.

Parameters That Can Be Set

Routines that need to control certain terminal I/O characteristics do so by using the termios structure as defined in the header <termios.h>. This structure contains minimally four scalar elements of bit flags and one array of special characters. The scalar flag elements are named: c_iflag, c_oflag, c_cflag, and c_lflag. The character array is named c_cc, and its maximum index is NCCS.

Input Modes

Values of the c_iflag field describe the basic terminal input control, and are composed of following masks:

```
IGNBRK   /* ignore BREAK condition */
BRKINT   /* map BREAK to SIGINTR */
IGNPAR   /* ignore (discard) parity errors */
PARMRK   /* mark parity and framing errors */
INPCK    /* enable checking of parity errors */
ISTRIP   /* strip 8th bit off chars */
INLCR    /* map NL into CR */
IGNCR    /* ignore CR */
ICRNL    /* map CR to NL (ala CRMOD) */
IXON     /* enable output flow control */
IXOFF    /* enable input flow control */
```

```
IXANY    /* any char will restart after stop */
IMAXBEL  /* ring bell on input queue full */
```

In the context of asynchronous serial data transmission, a break condition is defined as a sequence of zero-valued bits that continues for more than the time to send one byte. The entire sequence of zero-valued bits is interpreted as a single break condition, even if it continues for a time equivalent to more than one byte. In contexts other than asynchronous serial data transmission the definition of a break condition is implementation defined.

If IGNBRK is set, a break condition detected on input is ignored, that is, not put on the input queue and therefore not read by any process. If IGNBRK is not set and BRKINT is set, the break condition flushes the input and output queues and if the terminal is the controlling terminal of a foreground process group, the break condition generates a single SIGINT signal to that foreground process group. If neither IGNBRK nor BRKINT is set, a break condition is read as a single '\0', or if PARMRK is set, as \377, '\0', '\0'.

If IGNPAR is set, a byte with a framing or parity error (other than break) is ignored.

If PARMRK is set, and IGNPAR is not set, a byte with a framing or parity error (other than break) is given to the application as the three-character sequence \377, '\0', X, where \377, '\0' is a two-character flag preceding each sequence and X is the data of the character received in error. To avoid ambiguity in this case, if ISTRIP is not set, a valid character of \377 is given to the application as \377, \377. If neither PARMRK nor IGNPAR is set, a framing or parity error (other than break) is given to the application as a single character '\0'.

If INPCK is set, input parity checking is enabled. If INPCK is not set, input parity checking is disabled, allowing output parity generation without input parity errors. Note that whether input parity checking is enabled or disabled is independent of whether parity detection is enabled or disabled (see Control Modes). If parity detection is enabled but input parity checking is disabled, the hardware to which the terminal is connected recognizes the parity bit, but the terminal special file does not check whether this bit is set correctly or not.

If ISTRIP is set, valid input bytes are first stripped to seven bits, otherwise all eight bits are processed.

If INLCR is set, a received NL character is translated into a CR character. If IGNCR is set, a received CR character is ignored (not read). If IGNCR is not set and ICRNL is set, a received CR character is translated into a NL character.

If IXON is set, start/stop output control is enabled. A received STOP character suspends output and a received START character restarts output. If IXANY is also set, then any character may restart output. When IXON is set, START and STOP characters are not read, but merely perform flow control functions. When IXON is not set, the START and STOP characters are read.

If IXOFF is set, start/stop input control is enabled. The system shall transmit one or more STOP characters, which are intended to cause the terminal device to stop transmitting data, as needed to prevent the input queue from overflowing and causing the undefined behavior described in Input Processing and Reading Data, and shall transmit one or more START characters, which are intended to cause the terminal device to resume transmitting data, as soon as the device can continue transmitting data without risk of overflowing the input queue. The precise conditions under which STOP and START characters are transmitted are implementation defined.

If IMAXBEL is set and the input queue is full, subsequent input shall cause an ASCII BEL character to be transmitted to the the output queue.

The initial input control value after open() is implementation defined.

Output Modes

Values of the *c_oflag* field describe the basic terminal output control, and are composed of the following masks:

    OPOST   /* enable following output processing */
    ONLCR   /* map NL to CR-NL (ala CRMOD) */
    OXTABS /* expand tabs to spaces */
    ONOEOT /* discard EOT's '^D' on output) */

If OPOST is set, the remaining flag masks are interpreted as follows; otherwise characters are transmitted without change.

If ONLCR is set, newlines are translated to carriage return, linefeeds.

If OXTABS is set, tabs are expanded to the appropriate number of spaces (assuming 8 column tab stops).

If ONOEOT is set, ASCII EOT NS ' s are discarded on output.

Control Modes

Values of the *c_cflag* field describe the basic terminal hardware control, and are composed of the following masks. Not all values specified are supported by all hardware.

    CSIZE   /* character size mask */
    CS5   /* 5 bits (pseudo) */
    CS6   /* 6 bits */
    CS7   /* 7 bits */
    CS8   /* 8 bits */
    CSTOPB   /* send 2 stop bits */
    CREAD   /* enable receiver */
    PARENB   /* parity enable */
    PARODD   /* odd parity, else even */
    HUPCL   /* hang up on last close */
    CLOCAL   /* ignore modem status lines */
    CCTS_OFLOW   /* CTS flow control of output */
    CRTSCTS   /* same as CCTS_OFLOW */
    CRTS_IFLOW   /* RTS flow control of input */
    MDMBUF   /* flow control output via Carrier */

The CSIZE bits specify the byte size in bits for both transmission and reception. The *c_cflag* is masked with CSIZE and compared with the values CS5, CS6, CS7, or CS8. This size does not include the parity bit, if any. If CSTOPB is set, two stop bits are used, otherwise one stop bit. For example, at 110 baud, two stop bits are normally used.

If CREAD is set, the receiver is enabled. Otherwise, no character is received. Not all hardware supports this bit. In fact, this flag is pretty silly and if it were not part of the **termios** specification it would be omitted.

If PARENB is set, parity generation and detection are enabled and a parity bit is added to each character. If parity is enabled, PARODD specifies odd parity if set, otherwise even parity is used.

If HUPCL is set, the modem control lines for the port are lowered when the last process with the port open closes the port or the process terminates. The modem connection is broken.

If CLOCAL is set, a connection does not depend on the state of the modem status lines. If CLOCAL is clear, the modem status lines are monitored.

Under normal circumstances, a call to the open() function waits for the modem connection to complete. However, if the O_NONBLOCK flag is set or if CLOCAL has been set, the open() function returns immediately without waiting for the connection.

The CCTS_OFLOW (CRTSCTS) flag is currently unused.

If MDMBUF is set then output flow control is controlled by the state of Carrier Detect.

If the object for which the control modes are set is not an asynchronous serial connection, some of the modes may be ignored; for example, if an attempt is made to set the baud rate on a network connection to a terminal on another host, the baud rate may or may not be set on the connection between that terminal and the machine it is directly connected to.

Local Modes

Values of the *c_lflag* field describe the control of various functions, and are composed of the following masks.

```
ECHOKE      /* visual erase for line kill */
ECHOE       /* visually erase chars */
ECHO        /* enable echoing */
ECHONL      /* echo NL even if ECHO is off */
ECHOPRT     /* visual erase mode for hardcopy */
ECHOCTL     /* echo control chars as ^(Char) */
ISIG        /* enable signals INTR, QUIT, [D]SUSP */
ICANON      /* canonicalize input lines */
ALTWERASE   /* use alternate WERASE algorithm */
IEXTEN      /* enable DISCARD and LNEXT */
EXTPROC     /* external processing */
TOSTOP      /* stop background jobs from output */
FLUSHO      /* output being flushed (state) */
NOKERNINFO  /* no kernel output from VSTATUS */
PENDIN      /* XXX retype pending input (state) */
NOFLSH      /* don't flush after interrupt */
```

If ECHO is set, input characters are echoed back to the terminal. If ECHO is not set, input characters are not echoed.

If ECHOE and ICANON are set, the ERASE character causes the terminal to erase the last character in the current line from the display, if possible. If there is no character to erase, an implementation may echo an indication that this was the case or do nothing.

If ECHOK and ICANON are set, the KILL character causes the current line to be discarded and the system echoes the '\n' character after the KILL character.

If ECHOKE and ICANON are set, the KILL character causes the current line to be discarded and the system causes the terminal to erase the line from the display.

If ECHOPRT and ICANON are set, the system assumes that the display is a printing device and prints a backslash and the erased characters when processing ERASE characters, followed by a forward slash.

If ECHOCTL is set, the system echoes control characters in a visible fashion using a caret followed by the control character.

If ALTWERASE is set, the system uses an alternative algorithm for determining what constitutes a word when processing WERASE characters (see WERASE).

If ECHONL and ICANON are set, the '\n' character echoes even if ECHO is not set.

If ICANON is set, canonical processing is enabled. This enables the erase and kill edit functions, and the assembly of input characters into lines delimited by NL, EOF, and EOL, as described in Canonical Mode Input Processing.

If ICANON is not set, read requests are satisfied directly from the input queue. A read is not satisfied until at least MIN bytes have been received or the timeout value TIME expired between bytes. The time value represents tenths of seconds. See Noncanonical Mode Input Processing for more details.

If ISIG is set, each input character is checked against the special control characters INTR, QUIT, and SUSP (job control only). If an input character matches one of these control characters, the function associated with that character is performed. If ISIG is not set, no checking is done. Thus these special input functions are possible only if ISIG is set.

If IEXTEN is set, implementation-defined functions are recognized from the input data. How IEXTEN being set interacts with ICANON, ISIG, IXON, or IXOFF is implementation defined. If IEXTEN is not set, then implementation-defined functions are not recognized, and the corresponding input characters are not processed as described for ICANON, ISIG, IXON, and IXOFF.

If NOFLSH is set, the normal flush of the input and output queues associated with the INTR, QUIT, and SUSP characters are not be done.

If TOSTOP is set, the signal SIGTTOU is sent to the process group of a process that tries to write to its controlling terminal if it is not in the foreground process group for that terminal. This signal, by default, stops the members of the process group. Otherwise, the output generated by that process is output to the current output stream. Processes that are blocking or ignoring SIGTTOU signals are excepted and allowed to produce output and the SIGTTOU signal is not sent.

If NOKERNINFO is set, the kernel does not produce a status message when processing STATUS characters (see STATUS).

Special Control Characters

The special control characters values are defined by the array c_cc. This table lists the array index, the corresponding special character, and the system default value. For an accurate list of the system defaults, consult the header file <ttydefaults.h>.

Index Name	Special Character	Default Value
VEOF	EOF	^D
VEOL	EOL	_POSIX_VDISABLE
VEOL2	EOL2	_POSIX_VDISABLE
VERASE	ERASE	^? \177
VWERASE	WERASE	^W
VKILL	KILL	^U
VREPRINT	REPRINT	^R
VINTR	INTR	^C
VQUIT	QUIT	^\ \34
VSUSP	SUSP	^Z
VDSUSP	DSUSP	^Y
VSTART	START	^Q
VSTOP	STOP	^S
VLNEXT	LNEXT	^V
VDISCARD	DISCARD	^O

```
VMIN       ---        1
VTIME      ---        0
VSTATUS    STATUS     ^T
```

If the value of one of the changeable special control characters (see Special Characters) is {_POSIX_VDISABLE}, that function is disabled; that is, no input data is recognized as the disabled special character. If ICANON is not set, the value of {_POSIX_VDISABLE} has no special meaning for the VMIN and VTIME entries of the *c_cc* array.

The initial values of the flags and control characters after open() is set according to the values in the header <sys/ttydefaults.h>.

4

NAME
TP – ISO Transport Protocol

SYNOPSIS
```
#include <sys/socket.h>
#include <netiso/iso_errno.h>
#include <netiso/tp_param.h>
#include <netiso/tp_user.h>
```

int
socket(*[AF_INET, AF_ISO]*, *SOCK_SEQPACKET, 0*);

DESCRIPTION
The TP protocol provides reliable, flow-controlled, two-way transmission of data and record boundaries. It is a byte-stream protocol and is accessed according to the SOCK_SEQPACKET abstraction. The TP protocol makes use of a standard ISO address format, including a Network Service Access Point, and a Transport Service Entity Selector. Subclass 4 may make use of the internet Internet address format.

Sockets utilizing the tp protocol are either "active" or "passive". Active sockets initiate connections to passive sockets. By default TCP sockets are created active; to create a passive socket the listen(2) system call must be used after binding the socket with the bind(2) system call. Only passive sockets may use the accept(2) call to accept incoming connections. Only active sockets may use the connect(2) call to initiate connections.

Passive sockets may "underspecify" their location to match incoming connection requests from multiple networks. This technique, termed "wildcard addressing", allows a single server to provide service to clients on multiple networks. To create a socket which listens on all networks, the NSAP portion of the bound address must be void (of length zero). The Transport Selector may still be specified at this time; if the port is not specified the system will assign one. Once a connection has been established the socket's address is fixed by the peer entity's location. The address assigned the socket is the address associated with the network interface through which packets are being transmitted and received.

The ISO Transport Protocol implemented for AOS R2 at the University of Wisconsin - Madison, and modified for inclusion in the Berkeley Software Distribution, includes classes 0 and 4 of the ISO transport protocols as specified in the June 1986 version of IS 8073. Class 4 of the protocol provides reliable, sequenced, flow-controlled, two-way transmission of data packets with an alternate stop-and-wait data path called the "expedited data" service. Class 0 is essentially a null transport protocol, which is used when the underlying network service provides reliable, sequenced, flow-controlled, two-way data transmission. Class 0 does not provide the expedited data service. The protocols are implemented as a single transport layer entity that coexists with the Internet protocol suite. Class 0 may be used only in the ISO domain. Class 4 may be used in the Internet domain as well as in the ISO domain.

Two system calls were modified from the previous release of the Berkeley Software Distribution to permit the support of the end-of-transport-service-data-unit (EOTSDU) indication, and for the receipt and transmission of user connect, confirm, and disconnect data. See sendmsg(2) and recvmsg(2), and further discussion below for the formats of the data in the ancillary data buffer. If the EOTSDU is not needed, the normal read(2), and write(2) system calls may be used.

Through the getsockopt and setsockopt system calls, TP supports several options to control such things as negotiable options in the protocol and protocol strategies. The options are defined in <netiso/tp_user.h>, and are described below.

In the tables below, the options marked with a pound sign '#' may be used with setsockopt after a connection is established. Others must be used before the connection is established, in other words, before calling connect or accept. All options may be used with getsockopt before or after a connection is established.

TPOPT_CONN_DATA   (char *) [none]
                     Data to send on connect. The passive user may issue a getsockopt call to
                     retrieve a connection request's user data, after having done the accept system
                     call without implying confirmation of the connection.

                     The data may also be retrieved by issuing a recvmsg request for ancillary data
                     only, without implying confirmation of the connection. The returned *cmsghdr*
                     will contain SOL_TRANSPORT for the *csmg_level* and TPOPT_CONN_DATA for
                     cmsg_type.

TPOPT_DISC_DATA #   (char *) [none]
                     Data to send on close. Disconnect data may be sent by the side initiating the
                     close but not by the passive side ("passive" with respect to the closing of the connection), so there is no need to read disconnect data after calling close. This
                     may be sent by a setsockopt system call, or by issuing a sendmsg request
                     specifying ancillary data only. The user-provided *cmsghdr* must contain
                     SOL_TRANSPORT for *csmg_level* and TPOPT_DISC_DATA for *cmsg_type*.
                     Sending of disconnect data will in of itself tear down (or reject) the connection.

TPOPT_CFRM_DATA #   (char *) [none]
                     Data to send when confirming a connection. This may also be sent by a set-
                     sockopt system call, or by issuing a sendmsg request, as above. Sending of
                     connect confirm data will cause the connection to be confirmed rather than reject-
                     ed.

TPOPT_PERF_MEAS #   Boolean.
                     When true, performance measurements will be kept for this connection. When
                     set before a connection is established, the active side will use a locally defined
                     parameter on the connect request packet; if the peer is another ARGO implementation, this will cause performance measurement to be turned on on the passive side
                     as well. See tpperf(8).

TPOPT_PSTATISTICS   No associated value on input. On output, *struct tp_pmeas*.

                     This command is used to read the performance statistics accumulated during a
                     connection's lifetime. It can only be used with getsockopt. The structure it
                     returns is described in <netiso/tp_stat.h>. See tpperf(8).

TPOPT_FLAGS   unsigned integer. [0x0]
                     This command can only be used with getsockopt. See the description of the
                     flags below.

TPOPT_PARAMS   *struct tp_conn_param*
                     Used to get or set a group parameters for a connection. The *struct*
                     tp_conn_param is the argument used with the getsockopt or set-
                     sockopt system call. It is described in <netiso/tp_user.h>.

                     The fields of the *tp_conn_param* structure are described below.

Values for TPOPT_PARAMS:

p_Nretrans   nonzero short integer [1]
                    Number of times a TPDU will be retransmitted before the local TP entity closes a
                    connection.

p_dr_ticks   nonzero short integer [various]
                    Number of clock ticks between retransmissions of disconnect request TPDUs.

p_dt_ticks   nonzero short integer [various]
                    Number of clock ticks between retransmissions of data TPDUs. This parameter ap-
                    plies only to class 4.

p_cr_ticks   nonzero short integer [various]
                    Number of clock ticks between retransmissions of connection request TPDUs.

p_cc_ticks   nonzero short integer [various]
                    Number of clock ticks between retransmissions of connection confirm TPDUs. This
                    parameter applies only to class 4.

p_x_ticks   nonzero short integer [various]
                    Number of clock ticks between retransmissions of expedited data TPDUs. This
                    parameter applies only to class 4.

p_sendack_ticks   nonzero short integer [various]
                    Number of clock ticks that the local TP entity will wait before sending an ack-
                    nowledgment for normal data (not applicable if the acknowledgement strategy is
                    TPACK_EACH). This parameter applies only to class 4.

p_ref_ticks   nonzero short integer [various]
                    Number of clock ticks for which a reference will be considered frozen after the con-
                    nection to which it applied is closed. This parameter applies to classes 4 and 0 in the
                    ARGO implementation, despite the fact that the frozen reference function is required
                    only for class 4.

p_inact_ticks   nonzero short integer [various]
                    Number of clock ticks without an incoming packet from the peer after which TP
                    close the connection. This parameter applies only to class 4.

p_keepalive_ticks
                    nonzero short integer [various]
                    Number of clock ticks between acknowledgments that are sent to keep an inactive
                    connection open (to prevent the peer's inactivity control function from closing the
                    connection). This parameter applies only to class 4.

p_winsize   short integer between 128 and 16384. [4096 bytes]
                    The buffer space limits in bytes for incoming and outgoing data. There is no way to
                    specify different limits for incoming and outgoing paths. The actual window size at
                    any time during the lifetime of a connection is a function of the buffer size limit, the
                    negotiated maximum TPDU size, and the rate at which the user program receives
                    data. This parameter applies only to class 4.

p_tpdusize   unsigned char between 0x7 and 0xd. [0xc for class 4] [0xb for class 0]
Log 2 of the maximum TPDU size to be negotiated. The TP standard (ISO 8473) gives an upper bound of 0xd for class 4 and 0xb for class 0. The ARGO implementation places upper bounds of 0xc on class 4 and 0xb on class 0.

p_ack_strat   TPACK_EACH or TPACK_WINDOW. [TPACK_WINDOW]
This parameter applies only to class 4. Two acknowledgment strategies are supported:

TPACK_EACH means that each data TPDU is acknowledged with an AK TPDU.

TPACK_WINDOW means that upon receipt of the packet that represents the high edge of the last window advertised, an AK TPDU is generated.

p_rx_strat   4 bit mask [TPRX_USE_CW | TPRX_FASTSTART] over connectionless network protocols] [TPRX_USE_CW over connection-oriented network protocols]
This parameter applies only to class 4. The bit mask may include the following values:

TPRX_EACH: When a retransmission timer expires, retransmit each packet in the send window rather than just the first unacknowledged packet.

TPRX_USE_CW: Use a "congestion window" strategy borrowed from Van Jacobson's congestion window strategy for TCP. The congestion window size is set to one whenever a retransmission occurs.

TPRX_FASTSTART: Begin sending the maximum amount of data permitted by the peer (subject to availability). The alternative is to start sending slowly by pretending the peer's window is smaller than it is, and letting it slowly grow up to the peer window's real size. This is to smooth the effect of new connections on a congested network by preventing a transport connection from suddenly overloading the network with a burst of packets. This strategy is also due to Van Jacobson.

p_class   5 bit mask [TP_CLASS_4 | TP_CLASS_0]
Bit mask including one or both of the values TP_CLASS_4 and TP_CLASS_0. The higher class indicated is the preferred class. If only one class is indicated, negotiation will not occur during connection establishment.

p_xtd_format   Boolean. [false]
Boolean indicating that extended format is negotiated. This parameter applies only to class 4.

p_xpd_service   Boolean. [true]
Boolean indicating that the expedited data transport service will be negotiated. This parameter applies only to class 4.

p_use_checksum Boolean. [true]
Boolean indicating the the use of checksums will be negotiated. This parameter applies only to class 4.

p_use_nxpd   Reserved for future use.

p_use_rcc   Reserved for future use.

p_use_efc   Reserved for future use.

p_no_disc_indications

> Boolean. [false]
>
> Boolean indicating that the local TP entity will not issue indications (signals) when a TP connection is disconnected.

p_dont_change_params

> Boolean. [false]
>
> If *true* the TP entity will not override any of the other values given in this structure. If the values cannot be used, the TP entity will drop, disconnect, or refuse to establish the connection to which this structure pertains.

p_netservice　　　One of { ISO_CLNS, ISO_CONS, ISO_COSNS, IN_CLNS }. [ISO_CLNS] Indicates which network service is to be used.

> ISO_CLNS indicates the connectionless network service provided by CLNP (ISO 8473).
>
> ISO_CONS indicates the connection-oriented network service provided by X.25 (ISO 8208) and ISO 8878.
>
> ISO_COSNS indicates the connectionless network service running over a connection-oriented subnetwork service: CLNP (ISO 8473) over X.25 (ISO 8208).
>
> IN_CLNS indicates the DARPA Internet connectionless network service provided by IP (RFC 791).

p_dummy　　　　　Reserved for future use.

The TPOPT_FLAGS option is used for obtaining various boolean-valued options. Its meaning is as follows. The bit numbering used is that of the RT PC, which means that bit 0 is the most significant bit, while bit 8 is the least significant bit.

Values for TPOPT_FLAGS:

Bits　**Description [Default]**

0　　　TPFLAG_NLQOS_PDN: set when the quality of the network service is similar to that of a public data network.

1　　　TPFLAG_PEER_ON_SAMENET: set when the peer TP entity is considered to be on the same network as the local TP entity.

2　　　Not used.

3　　　TPFLAG_XPD_PRES: set when expedited data are present [0]

4..7　　Reserved.

ERROR VALUES

The TP entity returns *errno* error values as defined in <sys/errno.h> and <netiso/iso_errno.h>. User programs may print messages associated with these value by using an expanded version of perror found in the ISO library, libisodir.a.

If the TP entity encounters asynchronous events that will cause a transport connection to be closed, such as timing out while retransmitting a connect request TPDU, or receiving a DR TPDU, the TP entity issues a SIGURG signal, indicating that disconnection has occurred. If the signal is issued during a a system call, the system call may be interrupted, in which case the *errno* value upon return from the system call is EINTR. If the signal SIGURG is being handled by reading from the socket, and it was an accept(2) that timed out, the read may result in ENOTSOCK, because the accept call had not yet returned a legitimate socket descriptor when the signal was handled. ETIMEDOUT (or a some other errno value appropriate to the type of error) is returned if SIGURG is blocked for the duration of the system call. A user program should take one of the following approaches:

Block SIGURG

If the program is servicing only one connection, it can block or ignore SIGURG during connection establishment. The advantage of this is that the *errno* value returned is somewhat meaningful. The disadvantage of this is that if ignored, disconnection and expedited data indications could be missed. For some programs this is not a problem.

Handle SIGURG

If the program is servicing more than one connection at a time or expedited data may arrive or both, the program may elect to service SIGURG. It can use the **getsockopt(**...*TPOPT_FLAGS*...**)** system call to see if the signal was due to the arrival of expedited data or due to a disconnection. In the latter case, getsockopt will return ENOTCONN.

SEE ALSO

tcp(4), netstat(1), iso(4), clnp(4), cltp(4), ifconfig(8).

BUGS

The protocol definition of expedited data is slightly problematic, in a way that renders expedited data almost useless, if two or more packets of expedited data are send within time ε, where ε depends on the application. The problem is not of major significance since most applications do not use transport expedited data. The problem is this: the expedited data acknowledgment TPDU has no field for conveying credit, thus it is not possible for a TP entity to inform its peer that "I received your expedited data but have no room to receive more." The TP entity has the choice of acknowledging receipt of the XPD TPDU:

when the user receives the XPD TSDU

which may be a fairly long time, which may cause the sending TP entity to retransmit the packet, and possibly to close the connection after retransmission, or

when the TP entity receives it

so the sending entity does not retransmit or close the connection. If the sending user then tries to send more expedited data "soon", the expedited data will not be acknowledged (until the receiving user receives the first XPD TSDU).

The ARGO implementation acknowledges XPD TPDUs immediately, in the hope that most users will not use expedited data frequently enough for this to be a problem.

NAME
tty – general terminal interface

SYNOPSIS
`#include <sys/ioctl.h>`

DESCRIPTION
This section describes the interface to the terminal drivers in the system.

Terminal Special Files
Each hardware terminal port on the system usually has a terminal special device file associated with it in the directory "/dev/" (for example, "/dev/tty03"). When a user logs into the system on one of these hardware terminal ports, the system has already opened the associated device and prepared the line for normal interactive use (see getty(8).) There is also a special case of a terminal file that connects not to a hardware terminal port, but to another program on the other side. These special terminal devices are called *ptys* and provide the mechanism necessary to give users the same interface to the system when logging in over a network (using rlogin(1), or telnet(1) for example.) Even in these cases the details of how the terminal file was opened and set up is already handled by special software in the system. Thus, users do not normally need to worry about the details of how these lines are opened or used. Also, these lines are often used for dialing out of a system (through an out-calling modem), but again the system provides programs that hide the details of accessing these terminal special files (see tip(2).)

When an interactive user logs in, the system prepares the line to behave in a certain way (called a *line discipline*), the particular details of which is described in stty(1) at the command level, and in termios(4) at the programming level. A user may be concerned with changing settings associated with his particular login terminal and should refer to the preceding man pages for the common cases. The remainder of this man page is concerned with describing details of using and controlling terminal devices at a low level, such as that possibly required by a program wishing to provide features similar to those provided by the system.

Line disciplines
A terminal file is used like any other file in the system in that it can be opened, read, and written to using standard system calls. For each existing terminal file, there is a software processing module called a *line discipline* is associated with it. The *line discipline* essentially glues the low level device driver code with the high level generic interface routines (such as read(2) and write(2)), and is responsible for implementing the semantics associated with the device. When a terminal file is first opened by a program, the default *line discipline* called the termios line discipline is associated with the file. This is the primary line discipline that is used in most cases and provides the semantics that users normally associate with a terminal. When the termios line discipline is in effect, the terminal file behaves and is operated according to the rules described in termios(4). Please refer to that man page for a full description of the terminal semantics. The operations described here generally represent features common across all *line disciplines*, however some of these calls may not make sense in conjunction with a line discipline other than termios, and some may not be supported by the underlying hardware (or lack thereof, as in the case of ptys).

Terminal File Operations
All of the following operations are invoked using the ioctl(2) system call. Refer to that man page for a description of the *request* and *argp* parameters. In addition to the ioctl *requests* defined here, the specific line discipline in effect will define other *requests* specific to it (actually termios(4) defines them as function calls, not ioctl *requests*.) The following section lists the available ioctl requests. The name of the request, a description of its purpose, and the typed *argp* parameter (if any) are listed. For example, the first entry says

TIOCSETD int *ldisc

and would be called on the terminal associated with file descriptor zero by the following code fragment:

```
int ldisc;

ldisc = TTYDISC;
ioctl(0, TIOCSETD, &ldisc);
```

Terminal File Request Descriptions

TIOCSETD *int *ldisc*

Change to the new line discipline pointed to by *ldisc*. The available line disciplines are listed in <sys/termios.h> and currently are:

TTYDISC	Termios interactive line discipline.
TABLDISC	Tablet line discipline.
SLIPDISC	Serial IP line discipline.

TIOCGETD *int *ldisc*

Return the current line discipline in the integer pointed to by *ldisc*.

TIOCSBRK *void*

Set the terminal hardware into BREAK condition.

TIOCCBRK *void*

Clear the terminal hardware BREAK condition.

TIOCSDTR *void*

Assert data terminal ready (DTR).

TIOCCDTR *void*

Clear data terminal ready (DTR).

TIOCGPGRP *int *tpgrp*

Return the current process group the terminal is associated with in the integer pointed to by *tpgrp*. This is the underlying call that implements the termios(4) **tcgetattr**( ) call.

TIOCSPGRP *int *tpgrp*

Associate the terminal with the process group (as an integer) pointed to by *tpgrp*. This is the underlying call that implements the termios(4) **tcsetattr**( ) call.

TIOCGETA *struct termios *term*

Place the current value of the termios state associated with the device in the termios structure pointed to by *term*. This is the underlying call that implements the termios(4) **tcgetattr**( ) call.

TIOCSETA *struct termios *term*

Set the termios state associated with the device immediately. This is the underlying call that implements the termios(4) **tcsetattr**( ) call with the TCSANOW option.

TIOCSETAW *struct termios *term*

First wait for any output to complete, then set the termios state associated with the device. This is the underlying call that implements the termios(4) **tcsetattr**( ) call with the TCSADRAIN option.

TIOCSETAF *struct termios *term*
> First wait for any output to complete, clear any pending input, then set the termios state associated with the device. This is the underlying call that implements the termios(4) **tcsetattr**( ) call with the TCSAFLUSH option.

TIOCOUTQ *int *num*
> Place the current number of characters in the output queue in the integer pointed to by *num*.

TIOCSTI *char *cp*
> Simulate typed input. Pretend as if the terminal received the character pointed to by *cp*.

TIOCNOTTY *void*
> This call is obsolete but left for compatibility. In the past, when a process that didn't have a controlling terminal (see *The Controlling Terminal* in termios(4)) first opened a terminal device, it acquired that terminal as its controlling terminal. For some programs this was a hazard as they didn't want a controlling terminal in the first place, and this provided a mechanism to disassociate the controlling terminal from the calling process. It *must* be called by opening the file /dev/tty and calling TIOCNOTTY on that file descriptor.
>
> The current system does not allocate a controlling terminal to a process on an **open**( ) call: there is a specific ioctl called TIOSCTTY to make a terminal the controlling terminal. In addition, a program can **fork**( ) and call the **setsid**( ) system call which will place the process into its own session - which has the effect of disassociating it from the controlling terminal. This is the new and preferred method for programs to lose their controlling terminal.

TIOCSTOP *void*
> Stop output on the terminal (like typing ^S at the keyboard).

TIOCSTART *void*
> Start output on the terminal (like typing ^Q at the keyboard).

TIOCSCTTY *void*
> Make the terminal the controlling terminal for the process (the process must not currently have a controlling terminal).

TIOCDRAIN *void*
> Wait until all output is drained.

TIOCEXCL *void*
> Set exclusive use on the terminal. No further opens are permitted except by root. Of course, this means that programs that are run by root (or setuid) will not obey the exclusive setting - which limits the usefulness of this feature.

TIOCNXCL *void*
> Clear exclusive use of the terminal. Further opens are permitted.

TIOCFLUSH *int *what*

    If the value of the int pointed to by *what* contains the FREAD bit as defined in <sys/file.h>, then all characters in the input queue are cleared. If it contains the FWRITE bit, then all characters in the output queue are cleared. If the value of the integer is zero, then it behaves as if both the FREAD and FWRITE bits were set (i.e. clears both queues).

TIOCGWINSZ *struct winsize *ws*

    Put the window size information associated with the terminal in the *winsize* structure pointed to by *ws*. The window size structure contains the number of rows and columns (and pixels if appropriate) of the devices attached to the terminal. It is set by user software and is the means by which most full-screen oriented programs determine the screen size. The *winsize* structure is defined in <sys/ioctl.h>.

TIOCSWINSZ *struct winsize *ws*

    Set the window size associated with the terminal to be the value in the *winsize* structure pointed to by *ws* (see above).

TIOCCONS *int *on*

    If *on* points to a non-zero integer, redirect kernel console output (kernel printf's) to this terminal. If *on* points to a zero integer, redirect kernel console output back to the normal console. This is usually used on workstations to redirect kernel messages to a particular window.

TIOCMSET *int *state*

    The integer pointed to by *state* contains bits that correspond to modem state. Following is a list of defined variables and the modem state they represent:

    TIOCM_LE   Line Enable.
    TIOCM_DTR
                Data Terminal Ready.
    TIOCM_RTS
                Request To Send.
    TIOCM_ST   Secondary Transmit.
    TIOCM_SR   Secondary Receive.
    TIOCM_CTS
                Clear To Send.
    TIOCM_CAR
                Carrier Detect.
    TIOCM_CD   Carier Detect (synonym).
    TIOCM_RNG
                Ring Indication.
    TIOCM_RI   Ring Indication (synonym).
    TIOCM_DSR
                Data Set Ready.

    This call sets the terminal modem state to that represented by *state*. Not all terminals may support this.

TIOCMGET *int *state*

    Return the current state of the terminal modem lines as represented above in the integer pointed to by *state*.

TIOCMBIS *int *state*
> The bits in the integer pointed to by *state* represent modem state as described above, however the state is OR-ed in with the current state.

TIOCMBIC *int *state*
> The bits in the integer pointed to by *state* represent modem state as described above, however each bit which is on in *state* is cleared in the terminal.

SEE ALSO
getty(8), ioctl(2), pty(4), stty(1), termios(4)

NAME
udp – Internet User Datagram Protocol

SYNOPSIS
```
#include <sys/socket.h>
#include <netinet/in.h>

int
socket(AF_INET, SOCK_DGRAM, 0);
```

DESCRIPTION
UDP is a simple, unreliable datagram protocol which is used to support the SOCK_DGRAM abstraction for the
Internet protocol family. UDP sockets are connectionless, and are normally used with the sendto and
recvfrom calls, though the connect(2) call may also be used to fix the destination for future packets (in
which case the recv(2) or read(2) and send(2) or write(2) system calls may be used).

UDP address formats are identical to those used by TCP. In particular UDP provides a port identifier in addition to the normal Internet address format. Note that the UDP port space is separate from the TCP port space
(i.e. a UDP port may not be "connected" to a TCP port). In addition broadcast packets may be sent (assuming the underlying network supports this) by using a reserved "broadcast address"; this address is network
interface dependent.

Options at the IP transport level may be used with UDP; see ip(4).

DIAGNOSTICS
A socket operation may fail with one of the following errors returned:

[EISCONN]   when trying to establish a connection on a socket which already has one, or when
                    trying to send a datagram with the destination address specified and the socket is al-
                    ready connected;

[ENOTCONN]   when trying to send a datagram, but no destination address is specified, and the sock-
                    et hasn't been connected;

[ENOBUFS]   when the system runs out of memory for an internal data structure;

[EADDRINUSE]   when an attempt is made to create a socket with a port which has already been allo-
                    cated;

[EADDRNOTAVAIL]   when an attempt is made to create a socket with a network address for which no net-
                    work interface exists.

SEE ALSO
getsockopt(2), recv(2), send(2), socket(2), intro(4), inet(4), ip(4)

HISTORY
The udp protocol appeared in 4.2BSD.

NAME

unix – UNIX-domain protocol family

SYNOPSIS

```
#include <sys/types.h>
#include <sys/un.h>
```

DESCRIPTION

The UNIX-domain protocol family is a collection of protocols that provides local (on-machine) interprocess communication through the normal socket(2) mechanisms. The UNIX-domain family supports the SOCK_STREAM and SOCK_DGRAM socket types and uses filesystem pathnames for addressing.

ADDRESSING

UNIX-domain addresses are variable-length filesystem pathnames of at most 104 characters. The include file <sys/un.h> defines this address:

```
struct sockaddr_un {
u_char  sun_len;
u_char  sun_family;
char    sun_path[104];
};
```

Binding a name to a UNIX-domain socket with bind(2) causes a socket file to be created in the filesystem. This file is *not* removed when the socket is closed—unlink(2) must be used to remove the file.

The UNIX-domain protocol family does not support broadcast addressing or any form of "wildcard" matching on incoming messages. All addresses are absolute- or relative-pathnames of other UNIX-domain sockets. Normal filesystem access-control mechanisms are also applied when referencing pathnames; e.g., the destination of a connect(2) or sendto(2) must be writable.

PROTOCOLS

The UNIX-domain protocol family is comprised of simple transport protocols that support the SOCK_STREAM and SOCK_DGRAM abstractions. SOCK_STREAM sockets also support the communication of UNIX file descriptors through the use of the *msg_control* field in the *msg* argument to sendmsg(2) and recvmsg(2).

Any valid descriptor may be sent in a message. The file descriptor(s) to be passed are described using a *struct cmsghdr* that is defined in the include file <sys/socket.h>. The type of the message is SCM_RIGHTS, and the data portion of the messages is an array of integers representing the file descriptors to be passed. The number of descriptors being passed is defined by the length field of the message; the length field is the sum of the size of the header plus the size of the array of file descriptors.

The received descriptor is a *duplicate* of the sender's descriptor, as if it were created with a call to dup(2). Per-process descriptor flags, set with fcntl(2), are *not* passed to a receiver. Descriptors that are awaiting delivery, or that are purposely not received, are automatically closed by the system when the destination socket is closed.

SEE ALSO

socket(2), intro(4)

"An Introductory 4.3 BSD Interprocess Communication Tutorial", *PSI*, 7.

"An Advanced 4.3 BSD Interprocess Communication Tutorial", *PSI*, 8.

NAME

UTF2 – Universal character set Transformation Format encoding of runes

SYNOPSIS

ENCODING "UTF2"

DESCRIPTION

The UTF2 encoding is based on a proposed X-Open multibyte FSS-UCS-TF (File System Safe Universal Character Set Transformation Format) encoding as used in **Plan 9 from Bell Labs.** Although it is capable of representing more than 16 bits, the current implementation is limited to 16 bits as defined by the Unicode Standard.

UTF2 representation is backwards compatible with ASCII, so 0x00-0x7f refer to the ASCII character set. The multibyte encoding of runes between 0x0080 and 0xffff consist entirely of bytes whose high order bit is set. The actual encoding is represented by the following table:

```
[0x0000 - 0x007f] [00000000.0bbbbbbb] -> 0bbbbbbb
[0x0080 - 0x03ff] [00000bbb.bbbbbbbb] -> 110bbbbb, 10bbbbbb
[0x0400 - 0xffff] [bbbbbbbb.bbbbbbbb] -> 1110bbbb, 10bbbbbb, 10bbbbbb
```

If more than a single representation of a value exists (for example, 0x00; 0xC0 0x80; 0xE0 0x80 0x80) the shortest representation is always used (but the longer ones will be correctly decoded).

The final three encodings provided by X-Open:

```
[00000000.000bbbbb.bbbbbbbb.bbbbbbbb] ->
        11110bbb, 10bbbbbb, 10bbbbbb, 10bbbbbb

[000000bb.bbbbbbbb.bbbbbbbb.bbbbbbbb] ->
        111110bb, 10bbbbbb, 10bbbbbb, 10bbbbbb, 10bbbbbb

[0bbbbbbb.bbbbbbbb.bbbbbbbb.bbbbbbbb] ->
        1111110b, 10bbbbbb, 10bbbbbb, 10bbbbbb, 10bbbbbb, 10bbbbbb
```

which provides for the entire proposed ISO-10646 31 bit standard are currently not implemented.

SEE ALSO

mklocale(1), setlocale(3)

Section 5

File
Formats

5

NAME
>   a.out – format of executable binary files

SYNOPSIS
>   #include <a.out.h>

DESCRIPTION
>   The include file <a.out.h> declares three structures and several macros. The structures describe the format of executable machine code files ('binaries') on the system.
>
>   A binary file consists of up to 7 sections. In order, these sections are:
>
>   exec header   Contains parameters used by the kernel to load a binary file into memory and execute it, and by the link editor ld(1) to combine a binary file with other binary files. This section is the only mandatory one.
>
>   text segment   Contains machine code and related data that are loaded into memory when a program executes. May be loaded read-only.
>
>   data segment   Contains initialized data; always loaded into writable memory.
>
>   text relocations   Contains records used by the link editor to update pointers in the text segment when combining binary files.
>
>   data relocations   Like the text relocation section, but for data segment pointers.
>
>   symbol table   Contains records used by the link editor to cross reference the addresses of named variables and functions ('symbols') between binary files.
>
>   string table   Contains the character strings corresponding to the symbol names.
>
>   Every binary file begins with an *exec* structure:

```
        struct exec {
                unsigned short a_mid;
                unsigned short a_magic;
                unsigned long  a_text;
                unsigned long  a_data;
                unsigned long  a_bss;
                unsigned long  a_syms;
                unsigned long  a_entry;
                unsigned long  a_trsize;
                unsigned long  a_drsize;
        };
```

>   The fields have the following functions:
>
>   *a_mid*   Contains a bit pattern that identifies binaries that were built for certain sub-classes of an architecture ('machine IDs') or variants of the operating system on a given architecture. The kernel may not support all machine IDs on a given architecture. The *a_mid* field is not present on some architectures; in this case, the *a_magic* field has type *unsigned long*.
>
>   *a_magic*   Contains a bit pattern ('magic number') that uniquely identifies binary files and distinguishes different loading conventions. The field must contain one of the following values:

OMAGIC   The text and data segments immediately follow the header and are contiguous. The kernel loads both text and data segments into writable memory.

NMAGIC   As with OMAGIC, text and data segments immediately follow the header and are contiguous. However, the kernel loads the text into read-only memory and loads the data into writable memory at the next page boundary after the text.

ZMAGIC   The kernel loads individual pages on demand from the binary. The header, text segment and data segment are all padded by the link editor to a multiple of the page size. Pages that the kernel loads from the text segment are read-only, while pages from the data segment are writable.

a_text   Contains the size of the text segment in bytes.

a_data   Contains the size of the data segment in bytes.

a_bss   Contains the number of bytes in the 'bss segment' and is used by the kernel to set the initial break (brk(2)) after the data segment. The kernel loads the program so that this amount of writable memory appears to follow the data segment and initially reads as zeroes.

a_syms   Contains the size in bytes of the symbol table section.

a_entry   Contains the address in memory of the entry point of the program after the kernel has loaded it; the kernel starts the execution of the program from the machine instruction at this address.

a_trsize Contains the size in bytes of the text relocation table.

a_drsize Contains the size in bytes of the data relocation table.

The a.out.h include file defines several macros which use an *exec* structure to test consistency or to locate section offsets in the binary file.

N_BADMAG(*exec*)   Nonzero if the *a_magic* field does not contain a recognized value.

N_TXTOFF(*exec*)   The byte offset in the binary file of the beginning of the text segment.

N_SYMOFF(*exec*)   The byte offset of the beginning of the symbol table.

N_STROFF(*exec*)   The byte offset of the beginning of the string table.

Relocation records have a standard format which is described by the *relocation_info* structure:

```
struct relocation_info {
        int             r_address;
        unsigned int    r_symbolnum : 24,
                        r_pcrel : 1,
                        r_length : 2,
                        r_extern : 1,
                        : 4;
};
```

The *relocation_info* fields are used as follows:

r_address   Contains the byte offset of a pointer that needs to be link-edited. Text relocation offsets are reckoned from the start of the text segment, and data relocation offsets from the start of the data segment. The link editor adds the value that is already stored at this offset into the new value that it computes using this relocation record.

r_symbolnum　Contains the ordinal number of a symbol structure in the symbol table (it is *not* a byte offset). After the link editor resolves the absolute address for this symbol, it adds that address to the pointer that is undergoing relocation. (If the r_extern bit is clear, the situation is different; see below.)

r_pcrel　If this is set, the link editor assumes that it is updating a pointer that is part of a machine code instruction using pc-relative addressing. The address of the relocated pointer is implicitly added to its value when the running program uses it.

r_length　Contains the log base 2 of the length of the pointer in bytes; 0 for 1-byte displacements, 1 for 2-byte displacements, 2 for 4-byte displacements.

r_extern　Set if this relocation requires an external reference; the link editor must use a symbol address to update the pointer. When the r_extern bit is clear, the relocation is 'local'; the link editor updates the pointer to reflect changes in the load addresses of the various segments, rather than changes in the value of a symbol. In this case, the content of the r_symbolnum field is an n_type value (see below); this type field tells the link editor what segment the relocated pointer points into.

Symbols map names to addresses (or more generally, strings to values). Since the link-editor adjusts addresses, a symbol's name must be used to stand for its address until an absolute value has been assigned. Symbols consist of a fixed-length record in the symbol table and a variable-length name in the string table. The symbol table is an array of nlist structures:

```
struct nlist {
        union {
                char    *n_name;
                long    n_strx;
        } n_un;
        unsigned char   n_type;
        char            n_other;
        short           n_desc;
        unsigned long   n_value;
};
```

The fields are used as follows:

n_un.n_strx　Contains a byte offset into the string table for the name of this symbol. When a program accesses a symbol table with the nlist(3) function, this field is replaced with the n_un.n_name field, which is a pointer to the string in memory.

n_type　Used by the link editor to determine how to update the symbol's value. The n_type field is broken down into three sub-fields using bitmasks. The link editor treats symbols with the N_EXT type bit set as 'external' symbols and permits references to them from other binary files. The N_TYPE mask selects bits of interest to the link editor:

N_UNDF　An undefined symbol. The link editor must locate an external symbol with the same name in another binary file to determine the absolute value of this symbol. As a special case, if the n_value field is nonzero and no binary file in the link-edit defines this symbol, the link-editor will resolve this symbol to an address in the bss segment, reserving an amount of bytes equal to n_value. If this symbol is undefined in more than one binary file and the binary files do not agree on the size, the link editor chooses the greatest size found across all binaries.

N_ABS   An absolute symbol. The link editor does not update an absolute symbol.

N_TEXT   A text symbol. This symbol's value is a text address and the link editor will up-
          date it when it merges binary files.

N_DATA   A data symbol; similar to N_TEXT but for data addresses. The values for text
          and data symbols are not file offsets but addresses; to recover the file offsets, it is
          necessary to identify the loaded address of the beginning of the corresponding
          section and subtract it, then add the offset of the section.

N_BSS   A bss symbol; like text or data symbols but has no corresponding offset in the
          binary file.

N_FN   A filename symbol. The link editor inserts this symbol before the other symbols
          from a binary file when merging binary files. The name of the symbol is the
          filename given to the link editor, and its value is the first text address from that
          binary file. Filename symbols are not needed for link-editing or loading, but are
          useful for debuggers.

The N_STAB mask selects bits of interest to symbolic debuggers such as gdb(1); the
values are described in stab(5).

n_other   This field is currently unused.

n_desc   Reserved for use by debuggers; passed untouched by the link editor. Different debuggers
              use this field for different purposes.

n_value   Contains the value of the symbol. For text, data and bss symbols, this is an address; for
              other symbols (such as debugger symbols), the value may be arbitrary.

The string table consists of an *unsigned long* length followed by null-terminated symbol strings. The length
represents the size of the entire table in bytes, so its minimum value (or the offset of the first string) is always
4 on 32-bit machines.

SEE ALSO
ld(1), execve(2), nlist(3), core(5), dbx(5), stab(5)

HISTORY
The a.out.h include file appeared in Version 7 AT&T UNIX.

BUGS
Since not all of the supported architectures use the *a_mid* field, it can be difficult to determine what architecture a binary will execute on without examining its actual machine code. Even with a machine identifier,
the byte order of the *exec* header is machine-dependent.

Nobody seems to agree on what *bss* stands for.

New binary file formats may be supported in the future, and they probably will not be compatible at any level with this ancient format.

NAME

acct – execution accounting file

SYNOPSIS

#include <sys/acct.h>

DESCRIPTION

The kernel maintains the following *acct* information structure for all processes. If a process terminates, and accounting is enabled, the kernel calls the acct(2) function call to prepare and append the record to the accounting file.

```
/*
 * Accounting structures; these use a comp_t type which is a 3 bits base 8
 * exponent, 13 bit fraction ''floating point'' number.  Units are 1/AHZ
 * seconds.
 */
typedef u_short comp_t;

struct acct {
        char    ac_comm[10];    /* name of command */
        comp_t  ac_utime;       /* user time */
        comp_t  ac_stime;       /* system time */
        comp_t  ac_etime;       /* elapsed time */
        time_t  ac_btime;       /* starting time */
        uid_t   ac_uid;         /* user id */
        gid_t   ac_gid;         /* group id */
        short   ac_mem;         /* memory usage average */
        comp_t  ac_io;          /* count of IO blocks */
        dev_t   ac_tty;         /* controlling tty */
#define AFORK   0x01            /* forked but not execed */
#define ASU     0x02            /* used super-user permissions */
#define ACOMPAT 0x04            /* used compatibility mode */
#define ACORE   0x08            /* dumped core */
#define AXSIG   0x10            /* killed by a signal */
        char    ac_flag;        /* accounting flags */
};

/*
 * 1/AHZ is the granularity of the data encoded in the comp_t fields.
 * This is not necessarily equal to hz.
 */
#define AHZ     64

#ifdef KERNEL
struct vnode    *acctp;
#endif
```

If a terminated process was created by an execve(2), the name of the executed file (at most ten characters of it) is saved in the field *ac_comm* and its status is saved by setting one of more of the following flags in *ac_flag*: AFORK, ASU, ACOMPAT, ACORE and ASIG.

SEE ALSO
> acct(2), execve(2), sa(8)

HISTORY
> A acct file format appeared in Version 7 AT&T UNIX.

5

NAME
`aliases` – aliases file for sendmail

SYNOPSIS
`aliases`

DESCRIPTION
This file describes user ID aliases used by `/usr/sbin/sendmail`. The file resides in `/etc` and is formatted as a series of lines of the form

> name: name_1, name2, name_3, . . .

The *name* is the name to alias, and the *name_n* are the aliases for that name. Lines beginning with white space are continuation lines. Lines beginning with '#' are comments.

Aliasing occurs only on local names. Loops can not occur, since no message will be sent to any person more than once.

After aliasing has been done, local and valid recipients who have a ''`.forward`'' file in their home directory have messages forwarded to the list of users defined in that file.

This is only the raw data file; the actual aliasing information is placed into a binary format in the file `/etc/aliases.db` using the program `newaliases(1)`. A `newaliases` command should be executed each time the aliases file is changed for the change to take effect.

SEE ALSO
`newaliases(1)`, `dbopen(3)`, `dbm(3)`, `sendmail(8)`

SENDMAIL Installation and Operation Guide.

SENDMAIL An Internetwork Mail Router.

BUGS
If you have compiled `sendmail` with DBM support instead of NEWDB, you may have encountered problems in dbm(3) restricting a single alias to about 1000 bytes of information. You can get longer aliases by ''chaining''; that is, make the last name in the alias be a dummy name which is a continuation alias.

HISTORY
The `aliases` file format appeared in 4.0BSD.

NAME
ar – archive (library) file format

SYNOPSIS
#include <ar.h>

DESCRIPTION
The archive command **ar** combines several files into one. Archives are mainly used as libraries of object files intended to be loaded using the link-editor ld(1).

A file created with **ar** begins with the ''magic'' string "!<arch>\n". The rest of the archive is made up of objects, each of which is composed of a header for a file, a possible file name, and the file contents. The header is portable between machine architectures, and, if the file contents are printable, the archive is itself printable.

The header is made up of six variable length ASCII fields, followed by a two character trailer. The fields are the object name (16 characters), the file last modification time (12 characters), the user and group id's (each 6 characters), the file mode (8 characters) and the file size (10 characters). All numeric fields are in decimal, except for the file mode which is in octal.

The modification time is the file st_mtime field, i.e., CUT seconds since the epoch. The user and group id's are the file st_uid and st_gid fields. The file mode is the file st_mode field. The file size is the file st_size field. The two-byte trailer is the string "'\n".

Only the name field has any provision for overflow. If any file name is more than 16 characters in length or contains an embedded space, the string "#1/" followed by the ASCII length of the name is written in the name field. The file size (stored in the archive header) is incremented by the length of the name. The name is then written immediately following the archive header.

Any unused characters in any of these fields are written as space characters. If any fields are their particular maximum number of characters in length, there will be no separation between the fields.

Objects in the archive are always an even number of bytes long; files which are an odd number of bytes long are padded with a newline (''\n'') character, although the size in the header does not reflect this.

SEE ALSO
ar(1), stat(2)

HISTORY
There have been at least four **ar** formats. The first was denoted by the leading ''magic'' number 0177555 (stored as type int). These archives were almost certainly created on a 16-bit machine, and contain headers made up of five fields. The fields are the object name (8 characters), the file last modification time (type long), the user id (type char), the file mode (type char) and the file size (type unsigned int). Files were padded to an even number of bytes.

The second was denoted by the leading ''magic'' number 0177545 (stored as type int). These archives may have been created on either 16 or 32-bit machines, and contain headers made up of six fields. The fields are the object name (14 characters), the file last modification time (type long), the user and group id's (each type char), the file mode (type int) and the file size (type long). Files were padded to an even number of bytes. For more information on converting from this format see arcv(8).

The current archive format (without support for long character names and names with embedded spaces) was introduced in 4.0BSD. The headers were the same as the current format, with the exception that names longer than 16 characters were truncated, and names with embedded spaces (and often trailing spaces) were not supported. It has been extended for these reasons, as described above. This format first appeared in 4.4BSD.

COMPATIBILITY

No archive format is currently specified by any standard. AT&T System V UNIX has historically distributed archives in a different format from all of the above.

5

NAME
core – memory image file format

SYNOPSIS
`#include <sys/param.h>`

DESCRIPTION
A small number of signals which cause abnormal termination of a process also cause a record of the process's in-core state to be written to disk for later examination by one of the available debuggers. (See sigaction(2).) This memory image is written to a file named **programname.core** in the working directory; provided the terminated process had write permission in the directory, and provided the abnormality did not cause a system crash. (In this event, the decision to save the core file is arbitrary, see savecore(8).)

The maximum size of a **programname.core** file is limited by setrlimit(2). Files which would be larger than the limit are not created.

The **programname.core** file consists of the $u.$ area, whose size (in pages) is defined by the UPAGES manifest in the `<sys/param.h>` file. The $u.$ area starts with a *user* structure as given in `<sys/user.h>`. The remainder of the **programname.core** file consists of the data pages followed by the stack pages of the process image. The amount of data space image in the **programname.core** file is given (in pages) by the variable u_dsize in the $u.$ area. The amount of stack image in the core file is given (in pages) by the variable u_ssize in the $u.$ area. The size of a "page" is given by the constant NBPG (also from `<sys/param.h>`).

SEE ALSO
adb(1), dbx(1), gdb(1), kgdb(1), sigaction(2), setrlimit(2)

HISTORY
A **core** file format appeared in Version 6 AT&T UNIX.

NAME
crontab – chronological services schedule file

SYNOPSIS
crontab

DESCRIPTION
The crontab file contains the schedules used by the cron(8) daemon. Each line in the schedule gives a time of execution and the command to be executed.

A line consists of two fields giving the time, three fields giving the day, a user name field, and lastly the command to be executed. The first five fields are space or tab separated and may consist of a number, a comma separated list of numbers, or an asterisk meaning any or all possible values. The last field (the command field) may contain spaces. A field containing two hyphen separated numbers is treated as an inclusive range.

The fields are:

1. The minute of the hour, a number from 0 to 59.

2. The hour, a number from 0 to 23.

3. The day in terms of the month, a number from 1 to 31.

4. The month in terms of the year, a number from 1 to 12.

5. The day in terms of the week, a number from 1 to 7. Monday is considered day one, Sunday is day seven.

6. The name of a user: the command will be run with the user's uid and permissions.

7. The command to execute. This field may be terminated with a newline or the '%' character.

An optional file crontab.local may be created and used for additional scheduling.

EXAMPLES
In the example below, the first field indicates the command should be executed at the hour, a quarter past the hour, on the half hour and at a quarter to the hour. The next four fields indicate the command should be run every hour, every day. The sixth field indicates the command is to be run with root privileges.

```
0,15,30,45 * * * *     root /usr/libexec/atrun
```

In this next example, the first field indicates this command should be executed on the half hour. The second field constrains the hour to 3 A.M. The third and fourth fields indicate any day of the month and any month of the year, but are constrained by the fifth field to the sixth day of the week (Saturday). The command is to be executed with root privileges. The example shown here has been folded (spread across two lines) to make it readable. It must not be folded in the the crontab file.

```
30 3 * * 6     root    /bin/sh /etc/weekly 2>&1 | tee
          /var/log/weekly.out | mail -s "weekly output" root
```

SEE ALSO
cron(8) rc(8)

FILES

    /etc/crontab   General system tasks.
    /etc/crontab.local   Optional local tasks.
    /etc/rc   System initialization script (normally, **cron** is executed from this script.)

HISTORY

A **crontab** file appeared in Version 6 AT&T UNIX.

NAME
dir, dirent – directory file format

SYNOPSIS
```
#include <sys/types.h>
#include <sys/dir.h>
```

DESCRIPTION
Directories provide a convenient hierarchical method of grouping files while obscuring the underlying details of the storage medium. A directory file is differentiated from a plain file by a flag in its inode(5) entry. It consists of records (directory entries) each of which contains information about a file and a pointer to the file itself. Directory entries may contain other directories as well as plain files; such nested directories are refered to as subdirectories. A hierarchy of directories and files is formed in this manner and is called a file system (or referred to as a file system tree).

Each directory file contains two special directory entries; one is a pointer to the directory itself called dot '.' and the other a pointer to its parent directory called dot-dot '..'. Dot and dot-dot are valid pathnames, however, the system root directory '/', has no parent and dot-dot points to itself like dot.

File system nodes are ordinary directory files on which has been grafted a file system object, such as a physical disk or a partitioned area of such a disk. (See mount(1) and mount(8).)

The directory entry format is defined in the file <dirent.h>:

```
#ifndef _DIRENT_H_
#define _DIRENT_H_

/*
 * A directory entry has a struct dirent at the front of it, containing its
 * inode number, the length of the entry, and the length of the name
 * contained in the entry.  These are followed by the name padded to a 4
 * byte boundary with null bytes.  All names are guaranteed null terminated.
 * The maximum length of a name in a directory is MAXNAMLEN.
 */

struct dirent {
        u_long  d_fileno;       /* file number of entry */
        u_short d_reclen;       /* length of this record */
        u_short d_namlen;       /* length of string in d_name */
#ifdef _POSIX_SOURCE
        char    d_name[MAXNAMLEN + 1]; /* maximum name length */
#else
#define MAXNAMLEN       255
        char    d_name[MAXNAMLEN + 1];  /* maximum name length */
#endif

};

#ifdef _POSIX_SOURCE
typedef void * DIR;
#else

#define d_ino           d_fileno        /* backward compatibility */
```

```
/* definitions for library routines operating on directories. */
#define DIRBLKSIZ      1024

/* structure describing an open directory. */
typedef struct _dirdesc {
        int     dd_fd;    /* file descriptor associated with directory */
        long    dd_loc;   /* offset in current buffer */
        long    dd_size;  /* amount of data returned by getdirentries */
        char    *dd_buf;  /* data buffer */
        int     dd_len;   /* size of data buffer */
        long    dd_seek;  /* magic cookie returned by getdirentries */
} DIR;

#define dirfd(dirp)      ((dirp)->dd_fd)

#ifndef NULL
#define NULL    0
#endif

#endif /* _POSIX_SOURCE */

#ifndef KERNEL

#include <sys/cdefs.h>

#endif /* !KERNEL */

#endif /* !_DIRENT_H_ */
```

SEE ALSO

fs(5) inode(5)

HISTORY

A dir file format appeared in Version 7 AT&T UNIX.

NAME
disklabel – disk pack label

SYNOPSIS
```
#include <sys/disklabel.h>
```

DESCRIPTION
Each disk or disk pack on a system may contain a disk label which provides detailed information about the geometry of the disk and the partitions into which the disk is divided. It should be initialized when the disk is formatted, and may be changed later with the disklabel(8) program. This information is used by the system disk driver and by the bootstrap program to determine how to program the drive and where to find the filesystems on the disk partitions. Additional information is used by the filesystem in order to use the disk most efficiently and to locate important filesystem information. The description of each partition contains an identifier for the partition type (standard filesystem, swap area, etc.). The filesystem updates the in-core copy of the label if it contains incomplete information about the filesystem.

The label is located in sector number LABELSECTOR of the drive, usually sector 0 where it may be found without any information about the disk geometry. It is at an offset LABELOFFSET from the beginning of the sector, to allow room for the initial bootstrap. The disk sector containing the label is normally made read-only so that it is not accidentally overwritten by pack-to-pack copies or swap operations; the DIOCWLABEL ioctl(2), which is done as needed by the disklabel program.

A copy of the in-core label for a disk can be obtained with the DIOCGDINFO ioctl; this works with a file descriptor for a block or character ("raw") device for any partition of the disk. The in-core copy of the label is set by the DIOCSDINFO ioctl. The offset of a partition cannot generally be changed while it is open, nor can it be made smaller while it is open. One exception is that any change is allowed if no label was found on the disk, and the driver was able to construct only a skeletal label without partition information. Finally, the DIOCWDINFO ioctl operation sets the in-core label and then updates the on-disk label; there must be an existing label on the disk for this operation to succeed. Thus, the initial label for a disk or disk pack must be installed by writing to the raw disk. All of these operations are normally done using disklabel.

The format of the disk label, as specified in is

```
/*
 * Disk description table, see disktab(5)
 */
#define DISKTAB        "/etc/disktab"


/*
 * Each disk has a label which includes information about the hardware
 * disk geometry, filesystem partitions, and drive specific information.
 * The label is in block 0 or 1, possibly offset from the beginning
 * to leave room for a bootstrap, etc.
 */

#ifndef LABELSECTOR
#define LABELSECTOR    0                        /* sector containing label */
#endif

#ifndef LABELOFFSET
#define LABELOFFSET    64                       /* offset of label in sector */
#endif
```

```
#define DISKMAGIC      ((u_long) 0x82564557)  /* The disk magic number */
#ifndef MAXPARTITIONS
#define MAXPARTITIONS  8
#endif

#ifndef LOCORE
struct disklabel {
        u_long  d_magic;        /* the magic number */
        short   d_type;         /* drive type */
        short   d_subtype;      /* controller/d_type specific */
        char    d_typename[16];         /* type name, e.g. "eagle" */
        /*
         * d_packname contains the pack identifier and is returned when
         * the disklabel is read off the disk or in-core copy.
         * d_boot0 and d_boot1 are the (optional) names of the
         * primary (block 0) and secondary (block 1-15) bootstraps
         * as found in /usr/mdec.  These are returned when using
         * getdiskbyname(3)
        to retrieve the values from /etc/disktab.
         */
#if defined(KERNEL) || defined(STANDALONE)
        char    d_packname[16];                 /* pack identifier */
#else
        union {
                char    un_d_packname[16];      /* pack identifier */
                struct {
                        char *un_d_boot0;       /* primary bootstrap name */
                        char *un_d_boot1;       /* secondary bootstrap name */
                } un_b;
        } d_un;

#define d_packname      d_un.un_d_packname
#define d_boot0                 d_un.un_b.un_d_boot0
#define d_boot1                 d_un.un_b.un_d_boot1
#endif /* ! KERNEL or STANDALONE */

        /* disk geometry: */
        u_long  d_secsize;      /* # of bytes per sector */
        u_long  d_nsectors;     /* # of data sectors per track */
        u_long  d_ntracks;      /* # of tracks per cylinder */
        u_long  d_ncylinders;   /* # of data cylinders per unit */
        u_long  d_secpercyl;    /* # of data sectors per cylinder */
        u_long  d_secperunit;   /* # of data sectors per unit */
        /*
         * Spares (bad sector replacements) below
         * are not counted in d_nsectors or d_secpercyl.
         * Spare sectors are assumed to be physical sectors
         * which occupy space at the end of each track and/or cylinder.
         */
        u_short d_sparespertrack;       /* # of spare sectors per track */
        u_short d_sparespercyl;         /* # of spare sectors per cylinder */
```

```
        /*
         * Alternate cylinders include maintenance, replacement,
         * configuration description areas, etc.
         */
        u_long d_acylinders;    /* # of alt. cylinders per unit */

                /* hardware characteristics: */
        /*
         * d_interleave, d_trackskew and d_cylskew describe perturbations
         * in the media format used to compensate for a slow controller.
         * Interleave is physical sector interleave, set up by the formatter
         * or controller when formatting.  When interleaving is in use,
         * logically adjacent sectors are not physically contiguous,
         * but instead are separated by some number of sectors.
         * It is specified as the ratio of physical sectors traversed
         * per logical sector.  Thus an interleave of 1:1 implies contiguous
         * layout, while 2:1 implies that logical sector 0 is separated
         * by one sector from logical sector 1.
         * d_trackskew is the offset of sector 0 on track N
         * relative to sector 0 on track N-1 on the same cylinder.
         * Finally, d_cylskew is the offset of sector 0 on cylinder N
         * relative to sector 0 on cylinder N-1.
         */
        u_short d_rpm;  /* rotational speed */
        u_short d_interleave;   /* hardware sector interleave */
        u_short d_trackskew;    /* sector 0 skew, per track */
        u_short d_cylskew;     - /* sector 0 skew, per cylinder */
        u_long d_headswitch;   /* head switch time, usec */
        u_long d_trkseek;      /* track-to-track seek, usec */
        u_long d_flags;        /* generic flags */
#define NDDATA 5
        u_long d_drivedata[NDDATA];   /* drive-type specific information */
#define NSPARE 5
        u_long d_spare[NSPARE];      /* reserved for future use */
        u_long d_magic2;       /* the magic number (again) */
        u_short d_checksum;    /* xor of data incl. partitions */

        /* filesystem and partition information: */
        u_short d_npartitions; /* number of partitions in following */
        u_long d_bbsize;       /* size of boot area at sn0, bytes */
        u_long d_sbsize;       /* max size of fs superblock, bytes */
        struct  partition {    /* the partition table */
                u_long p_size; /* number of sectors in partition */
                u_long p_offset;       /* starting sector */
                u_long p_fsize;        /* filesystem basic fragment size */
                u_char p_fstype;       /* filesystem type, see below */
                u_char p_frag; /* filesystem fragments per block */
                union {
                        u_short cpg;    /* UFS: FS cylinders per group */
                        u_short sgs;    /* LFS: FS segment shift */
                } __partition_u1;
#define p_cpg   __partition_u1.cpg
```

```
#define p_sgs    __partition_u1.sgs
                 u_short p_cpg;  /* filesystem cylinders per group */
         } d_partitions[MAXPARTITIONS];         /* actually may be more */
};

/* d_type values: */
#define DTYPE_SMD      1        /* SMD, XSMD; VAX hp/up */
#define DTYPE_MSCP     2        /* MSCP */
#define DTYPE_DEC      3        /* other DEC (rk, rl) */
#define DTYPE_SCSI     4        /* SCSI */
#define DTYPE_ESDI     5        /* ESDI interface */
#define DTYPE_ST506    6        /* ST506 etc. */
#define DTYPE_HPIB     7        /* CS/80 on HP-IB */
#define DTYPE_HPFL     8        /* HP Fiber-link */
#define DTYPE_FLOPPY   10       /* floppy */

#ifdef DKTYPENAMES
static char *dktypenames[] = {
        "unknown",
        "SMD",
        "MSCP",
        "old DEC",
        "SCSI",
        "ESDI",
        "ST506",
        "HP-IB",
        "HP-FL",
        "type 9",
        "floppy",
        0
};
#define DKMAXTYPES      (sizeof(dktypenames) / sizeof(dktypenames[0]) - 1)
#endif

/*
 * Filesystem type and version.
 * Used to interpret other filesystem-specific
 * per-partition information.
 */
#define FS_UNUSED      0        /* unused */
#define FS_SWAP        1        /* swap */
#define FS_V6          2        /* Sixth Edition */
#define FS_V7          3        /* Seventh Edition */
#define FS_SYSV        4        /* System V */
#define FS_V71K        5        /* V7 with 1K blocks (4.1, 2.9) */
#define FS_V8          6        /* Eighth Edition, 4K blocks */
#define FS_BSDFFS      7        /* 4.2BSD fast file system */
#define FS_MSDOS       8        /* MSDOS file system */
#define FS_BSDLFS      9        /* 4.4BSD log-structured file system */
#define FS_OTHER       10       /* in use, but unknown/unsupported */
#define FS_HPFS        11       /* OS/2 high-performance file system */
#define FS_ISO9660     12       /* ISO 9660, normally CD-ROM */
```

```
#define FS_BOOT          13        /* partition contains bootstrap */

#ifdef  DKTYPENAMES
static char *fstypenames[] = {
        "unused",
        "swap",
        "Version 6",
        "Version 7",
        "System V",
        "4.1BSD",
        "Eighth Edition",
        "4.2BSD",
        "MSDOS",
        "4.4LFS",
        "unknown",
        "HPFS",
        "ISO9660",
        "boot",
        0
};
#define FSMAXTYPES      (sizeof(fstypenames) / sizeof(fstypenames[0]) - 1)
#endif

/*
* flags shared by various drives:
*/
#define D_REMOVABLE     0x01      /* removable media */
#define D_ECC           0x02      /* supports ECC */
#define D_BADSECT       0x04      /* supports bad sector forw. */
#define D_RAMDISK       0x08      /* disk emulator */
#define D_CHAIN         0x10      /* can do back-back transfers */

/*
* Drive data for SMD.
*/

#define d_smdflags      d_drivedata[0]
#define D_SSE           0x1       /* supports skip sectoring */
#define d_mindist       d_drivedata[1]
#define d_maxdist       d_drivedata[2]
#define d_sdist         d_drivedata[3]

/*
* Drive data for ST506.
*/
#define d_precompcyl    d_drivedata[0]
#define d_gap3          d_drivedata[1] /* used only when formatting */

/*
 * Drive data for SCSI.
 */
#define d_blind         d_drivedata[0]
```

```
#ifndef LOCORE
/*
 * Structure used to perform a format
 * or other raw operation, returning data
 * and/or register values.
 * Register identification and format
 * are device- and driver-dependent.
 */
struct format_op {
        char    *df_buf;
        int     df_count;       /* value-result */
        daddr_t df_startblk;
        int     df_reg[8];      /* result */
};

/*
 * Structure used internally to retrieve
 * information about a partition on a disk.
 */
struct partinfo {
        struct disklabel *disklab;
        struct partition *part;
};

/*
 * Disk-specific ioctls.
 */
        /* get and set disklabel; DIOCGPART used internally */
#define DIOCGDINFO   _IOR('d', 101, struct disklabel) /* get */
#define DIOCSDINFO   _IOW('d', 102, struct disklabel) /* set */
#define DIOCWDINFO   _IOW('d', 103, struct disklabel) /* set, update disk */
#define DIOCGPART    _IOW('d', 104, struct partinfo)  /* get partition */

/* do format operation, read or write */
#define DIOCRFORMAT  _IOWR('d', 105, struct format_op)
#define DIOCWFORMAT  _IOWR('d', 106, struct format_op)

#define DIOCSSTEP    _IOW('d', 107, int) /* set step rate */
#define DIOCSRETRIES _IOW('d', 108, int) /* set # of retries */
#define DIOCWLABEL   _IOW('d', 109, int) /* write en/disable label */

#define DIOCSBAD     _IOW('d', 110, struct dkbad) /* set kernel dkbad */

#endif LOCORE
```

SEE ALSO

disktab(5), disklabel(8)

HISTORY

The **disklabel** function was introduced in 4.3BSD–Tahoe.

NAME
disktab – disk description file

SYNOPSIS
#include <disktab.h>

DESCRIPTION
Disktab is a simple database which describes disk geometries and disk partition characteristics. It is used
to initialize the disk label on the disk. The format is patterned after the termcap(5) terminal data base.
Entries in disktab consist of a number of ':' separated fields. The first entry for each disk gives the names
which are known for the disk, separated by 'l' characters. The last name given should be a long name fully
identifying the disk.

The following list indicates the normal values stored for each disk entry.

Name	Type	Description
ty	str	Type of disk (e.g. removable, winchester)
dt	str	Type of controller (e.g. SMD, ESDI, floppy)
ns	num	Number of sectors per track
nt	num	Number of tracks per cylinder
nc	num	Total number of cylinders on the disk
sc	num	Number of sectors per cylinder, nc*nt default
su	num	Number of sectors per unit, sc*nc default
se	num	Sector size in bytes, DEV_BSIZE default
sf	bool	Controller supports bad144-style bad sector forwarding
rm	num	Rotation speed, rpm, 3600 default
sk	num	Sector skew per track, default 0
cs	num	Sector skew per cylinder, default 0
hs	num	Headswitch time, usec, default 0
ts	num	One-cylinder seek time, usec, default 0
il	num	Sector interleave (n:1), 1 default
d[0-4]	num	Drive-type-dependent parameters
bs	num	Boot block size, default BBSIZE
sb	num	Superblock size, default SBSIZE
ba	num	Block size for partition 'a' (bytes)
bd	num	Block size for partition 'd' (bytes)
be	num	Block size for partition 'e' (bytes)
bf	num	Block size for partition 'f' (bytes)
bg	num	Block size for partition 'g' (bytes)
bh	num	Block size for partition 'h' (bytes)
fa	num	Fragment size for partition 'a' (bytes)
fd	num	Fragment size for partition 'd' (bytes)
fe	num	Fragment size or partition 'e' (bytes)
ff	num	Fragment size for partition 'f' (bytes)
fg	num	Fragment size for partition 'g' (bytes)
fh	num	Fragment size for partition 'h' (bytes)
oa	num	Offset of partition 'a' in sectors
ob	num	Offset of partition 'b' in sectors
oc	num	Offset of partition 'c' in sectors

od	num	Offset of partition 'd' in sectors
oe	num	Offset of partition 'e' in sectors
of	num	Offset of partition 'f' in sectors
og	num	Offset of partition 'g' in sectors
oh	num	Offset of partition 'h' in sectors
pa	num	Size of partition 'a' in sectors
pb	num	Size of partition 'b' in sectors
pc	num	Size of partition 'c' in sectors
pd	num	Size of partition 'd' in sectors
pe	num	Size of partition 'e' in sectors
pf	num	Size of partition 'f' in sectors
pg	num	Size of partition 'g' in sectors
ph	num	Size of partition 'h' in sectors
ta	str	Partition type of partition 'a' (Bx 4.2 filesystem, swap, etc)
tb	str	Partition type of partition 'b'
tc	str	Partition type of partition 'c'
td	str	Partition type of partition 'd'
te	str	Partition type of partition 'e'
tf	str	Partition type of partition 'f'
tg	str	Partition type of partition 'g'
th	str	Partition type of partition 'h'

FILES
    /etc/disktab

SEE ALSO
    getdiskbyname(3), disklabel(5), disklabel(8), newfs(8)

HISTORY
    The **disktab** description file appeared in 4.2BSD.

NAME

dm.conf – dm configuration file

DESCRIPTION

The `dm.conf` file is the configuration file for the dm(8) program. It consists of lines beginning with one of three keywords, ''badtty'', ''game'', and ''time''. All other lines are ignored.

Any tty listed after the keyword ''badtty'' may not have games played on it. Entries consist of two white-space separated fields: the string ''badtty'' and the ttyname as returned by `ttyname`(3). For example, to keep the uucp dialout, ''tty19'', from being used for games, the entry would be:

```
badtty  /dev/tty19
```

Any day/hour combination listed after the keyword ''time'' will disallow games during those hours. Entries consist of four white-space separated fields: the string ''time'', the unabbreviated day of the week and the beginning and ending time of a period of the day when games may not be played. The time fields are in a 0 based, 24-hour clock. For example, the following entry allows games playing before 8AM and after 5PM on Mondays.

```
time        Monday  8       17
```

Any game listed after the keyword ''game'' will set parameters for a specific game. Entries consist of five white-space separated fields: the keyword ''game'', the name of a game, the highest system load average at which the game may be played, the maximum users allowed if the game is to be played, and the priority at which the game is to be run. Any of these fields may start with a non-numeric character, resulting in no game limitation or priority based on that field. The game "default" controls the settings for any game not otherwise listed, and must be the last ''game'' entry in the file. Priorities may not be negative. For example, the following entries limits the game ''hack'' to running only when the system has 10 or less users and a load average of 5 or less; all other games may be run any time the system has 15 or less users.

```
game        hack        5       10      *
game        default *   15      *
```

FILES

`/etc/dm.conf` The dm(8) configuration file.

SEE ALSO

`setpriority`(2), `ttyname`(3), dm(8)

NAME

dump, dumpdates – incremental dump format

SYNOPSIS

#include <sys/types.h>
#include <sys/inode.h>
#include <protocols/dumprestore.h>

DESCRIPTION

Tapes used by *dump* and *restore*(8) contain:

    a header record
    two groups of bit map records
    a group of records describing directories
    a group of records describing files

The format of the header record and of the first record of each description as given in the include file
<protocols/dumprestore.h> is:

```
#define NTREC          10
#define MLEN    16
#define MSIZ    4096

#define TS_TAPE      1
#define TS_INODE     2
#define TS_BITS      3
#define TS_ADDR      4
#define TS_END       5
#define TS_CLRI      6
#define MAGIC        (int) 60011
#define CHECKSUM     (int) 84446

struct   spcl {
         int          c_type;
         time_t       c_date;
         time_t       c_ddate;
         int          c_volume;
         daddr_t      c_tapea;
         ino_t        c_inumber;
         int          c_magic;
         int          c_checksum;
         struct       dinode          c_dinode;
         int          c_count;
         char         c_addr[BSIZE];
} spcl;

struct   idates {
         char         id_name[16];
         char         id_incno;
         time_t       id_ddate;
};

#define  DUMPOUTFMT "%-16s %c %s"        /* for printf */
                                         /* name, incno, ctime(date) */
#define  DUMPINFMT   "%16s %c %[^\n]\n"  /* inverse for scanf */
```

NTREC is the number of 1024 byte records in a physical tape block. MLEN is the number of bits in a bit map word. MSIZ is the number of bit map words.

The TS_ entries are used in the *c_type* field to indicate what sort of header this is. The types and their meanings are as follows:

TS_TAPE	Tape volume label
TS_INODE	A file or directory follows. The *c_dinode* field is a copy of the disk inode and contains bits telling what sort of file this is.
TS_BITS	A bit map follows. This bit map has a one bit for each inode that was dumped.
TS_ADDR	A subrecord of a file description. See *c_addr* below.
TS_END	End of tape record.
TS_CLRI	A bit map follows. This bit map contains a zero bit for all inodes that were empty on the file system when dumped.
MAGIC	All header records have this number in *c_magic*.
CHECKSUM	Header records checksum to this value.

The fields of the header structure are as follows:

c_type	The type of the header.
c_date	The date the dump was taken.
c_ddate	The date the file system was dumped from.
c_volume	The current volume number of the dump.
c_tapea	The current number of this (1024-byte) record.
c_inumber	The number of the inode being dumped if this is of type TS_INODE.
c_magic	This contains the value MAGIC above, truncated as needed.
c_checksum	This contains whatever value is needed to make the record sum to CHECKSUM.
c_dinode	This is a copy of the inode as it appears on the file system; see *fs*(5).
c_count	The count of characters in *c_addr*.
c_addr	An array of characters describing the blocks of the dumped file. A character is zero if the block associated with that character was not present on the file system, otherwise the character is non-zero. If the block was not present on the file system, no block was dumped; the block will be restored as a hole in the file. If there is not sufficient space in this record to describe all of the blocks in a file, TS_ADDR records will be scattered through the file, each one picking up where the last left off.

Each volume except the last ends with a tapemark (read as an end of file). The last volume ends with a TS_END record and then the tapemark.

The structure *idates* describes an entry in the file */etc/dumpdates* where dump history is kept. The fields of the structure are:

id_name	The dumped filesystem is '/dev/*id_nam*'.
id_incno	The level number of the dump tape; see *dump*(8).
id_ddate	The date of the incremental dump in system format see *types*(5).

FILES

/etc/dumpdates

SEE ALSO

dump(8), restore(8), fs(5), types(5)

NAME

`exports` – define remote mount points for NFS mount requests

SYNOPSIS

`exports`

DESCRIPTION

The `exports` file specifies remote mount points for the NFS mount protocol per the NFS server specification; see *Network File System Protocol Specification RFC 1094, Appendix A.*

Each line in the file (other than comment lines that begin with a #) specifies the mount point(s) and export flags within one local server filesystem for one or more hosts. A host may be specified only once for each local filesystem on the server and there may be only one default entry for each server filesystem that applies to all other hosts. The latter exports the filesystem to the "world" and should be used only when the filesystem contains public information.

In a mount entry, the first field(s) specify the directory path(s) within a server filesystem that can be mounted on by the corresponding client(s). There are two forms of this specification. The first is to list all mount points as absolute directory paths separated by whitespace. The second is to specify the pathname of the root of the filesystem followed by the `−alldirs` flag; this form allows the host(s) to mount any directory within the filesystem. The pathnames must not have any symbolic links in them and should not have any "." or ".." components. Mount points for a filesystem may appear on multiple lines each with different sets of hosts and export options.

The second component of a line specifies how the filesystem is to be exported to the host set. The option flags specify whether the filesystem is exported read-only or read-write and how the client uid is mapped to user credentials on the server.

Export options are specified as follows:

−maproot=user The credential of the specified user is used for remote access by root. The credential includes all the groups to which the user is a member on the local machine (see `id(1)`). The user may be specified by name or number.

−maproot=user:group1:group2:... The colon separated list is used to specify the precise credential to be used for remote access by root. The elements of the list may be either names or numbers. Note that user: should be used to distinguish a credential containing no groups from a complete credential for that user.

−mapall=user or **−mapall=user:group1:group2:...** specifies a mapping for all client uids (including root) using the same semantics as **−maproot**.

The option **−r** is a synonym for **−maproot** in an effort to be backward compatible with older export file formats.

In the absence of **−maproot** and **−mapall** options, remote accesses by root will result in using a credential of -2:-2. All other users will be mapped to their remote credential. If a **−maproot** option is given, remote access by root will be mapped to that credential instead of -2:-2. If a **−mapall** option is given, all users (including root) will be mapped to that credential in place of their own.

The **−kerb** option specifies that the Kerberos authentication server should be used to authenticate and map client credentials. (Note that this is NOT Sun NFS compatible and is supported for TCP transport only.)

The **−ro** option specifies that the filesystem should be exported read-only (default read/write). The option **−o** is a synonym for **−ro** in an effort to be backward compatible with older export file formats.

The third component of a line specifies the host set to which the line applies. The set may be specified in three ways. The first way is to list the host name(s) separated by white space. (Standard internet "dot" addresses may be used in place of names.) The second way is to specify a "netgroup" as defined in the netgroup file (see `netgroup`(5)). The third way is to specify an internet subnetwork using a network and network mask that is defined as the set of all hosts with addresses within the subnetwork. This latter approach requires less overhead within the kernel and is recommended for cases where the export line refers to a large number of clients within an administrative subnet.

The first two cases are specified by simply listing the name(s) separated by whitespace. All names are checked to see if they are "netgroup" names first and are assumed to be hostnames otherwise. Using the full domain specification for a hostname can normally circumvent the problem of a host that has the same name as a netgroup. The third case is specified by the flag **−network=netname** and optionally **−mask=netmask**. If the mask is not specified, it will default to the mask for that network class (A, B or C; see `inet`(5)).

For example:

```
/usr /usr/local -maproot=0:10 friends
/usr -maproot=daemon grumpy.cis.uoguelph.ca 131.104.48.16
/usr -ro -mapall=nobody
/u -maproot=bin: -network 131.104.48 -mask 255.255.255.0
/u2 -maproot=root friends
/u2 -alldirs -kerb -network cis-net -mask cis-mask
```

Given that **/usr**, **/u** and **/u2** are local filesystem mount points, the above example specifies the following: **/usr** is exported to hosts *friends* where friends is specified in the netgroup file with users mapped to their remote credentials and root mapped to uid 0 and group 10. It is exported read-write and the hosts in "friends" can mount either /usr or /usr/local. It is exported to *131.104.48.16* and *grumpy.cis.uoguelph.ca* with users mapped to their remote credentials and root mapped to the user and groups associated with "daemon"; it is exported to the rest of the world as read-only with all users mapped to the user and groups associated with "nobody".

/u is exported to all hosts on the subnetwork *131.104.48* with root mapped to the uid for "bin" and with no group access.

/u2 is exported to the hosts in "friends" with root mapped to uid and groups associated with "root"; it is exported to all hosts on network "cis-net" allowing mounts at any directory within /u2 and mapping all uids to credentials for the principal that is authenticated by a Kerberos ticket.

FILES
`/etc/exports` The default remote mount-point file.

SEE ALSO
`netgroup`(5), `mountd`(8), `nfsd`(8), `showmount`(8)

BUGS
The export options are tied to the local mount points in the kernel and must be non-contradictory for any exported subdirectory of the local server mount point. It is recommended that all exported directories within the same server filesystem be specified on adjacent lines going down the tree. You cannot specify a hostname that is also the name of a netgroup. Specifying the full domain specification for a hostname can normally circumvent the problem.

NAME

fs, inode – format of file system volume

SYNOPSIS

```
#include <sys/types.h>
#include <ufs/fs.h>
#include <ufs/inode.h>
```

DESCRIPTION

The files <fs.h> and <inode.h> declare several structures, defined variables and macros which are used to create and manage the underlying format of file system objects on random access devices (disks).

The block size and number of blocks which comprise a file system are parameters of the file system. Sectors beginning at BBLOCK and continuing for BBSIZE are used for a disklabel and for some hardware primary and secondary bootstrapping programs.

The actual file system begins at sector SBLOCK with the *super-block* that is of size SBSIZE. The following structure described the super-block and is from the file <ufs/fs.h>:

```
#define FS_MAGIC 0x011954
struct fs {
        struct  fs *fs_link;    /* linked list of file systems */
        struct  fs *fs_rlink;   /*     used for incore super blocks */
        daddr_t fs_sblkno;      /* addr of super-block in filesys */
        daddr_t fs_cblkno;      /* offset of cyl-block in filesys */
        daddr_t fs_iblkno;      /* offset of inode-blocks in filesys */
        daddr_t fs_dblkno;      /* offset of first data after cg */
        long    fs_cgoffset;    /* cylinder group offset in cylinder */
        long    fs_cgmask;      /* used to calc mod fs_ntrak */
        time_t  fs_time;        /* last time written */
        long    fs_size;        /* number of blocks in fs */
        long    fs_dsize;       /* number of data blocks in fs */
        long    fs_ncg; /* number of cylinder groups */
        long    fs_bsize;       /* size of basic blocks in fs */
        long    fs_fsize;       /* size of frag blocks in fs */
        long    fs_frag;        /* number of frags in a block in fs */
/* these are configuration parameters */
        long    fs_minfree;     /* minimum percentage of free blocks */
        long    fs_rotdelay;    /* num of ms for optimal next block */
        long    fs_rps; /* disk revolutions per second */
/* these fields can be computed from the others */
        long    fs_bmask;       /* ''blkoff'' calc of blk offsets */
        long    fs_fmask;       /* ''fragoff'' calc of frag offsets */
        long    fs_bshift;      /* ''lblkno'' calc of logical blkno */
        long    fs_fshift;      /* ''numfrags'' calc number of frags */
/* these are configuration parameters */
        long    fs_maxcontig;   /* max number of contiguous blks */
        long    fs_maxbpg;      /* max number of blks per cyl group */
/* these fields can be computed from the others */
        long    fs_fragshift;   /* block to frag shift */
        long    fs_fsbtodb;     /* fsbtodb and dbtofsb shift constant */
        long    fs_sbsize;      /* actual size of super block */
```

```
            long    fs_csmask;      /* csum block offset */
            long    fs_csshift;     /* csum block number */
            long    fs_nindir;      /* value of NINDIR */
            long    fs_inopb;       /* value of INOPB */
            long    fs_nspf;        /* value of NSPF */
/* yet another configuration parameter */
            long    fs_optim;       /* optimization preference, see below */
/* these fields are derived from the hardware */
            long    fs_npsect;      /* # sectors/track including spares */
            long    fs_interleave;  /* hardware sector interleave */
            long    fs_trackskew;   /* sector 0 skew, per track */
            long    fs_headswitch;  /* head switch time, usec */
            long    fs_trkseek;     /* track-to-track seek, usec */
/* sizes determined by number of cylinder groups and their sizes */
            daddr_t fs_csaddr;      /* blk addr of cyl grp summary area */
            long    fs_cssize;      /* size of cyl grp summary area */
            long    fs_cgsize;      /* cylinder group size */
/* these fields are derived from the hardware */
            long    fs_ntrak;       /* tracks per cylinder */
            long    fs_nsect;       /* sectors per track */
            long    fs_spc;         /* sectors per cylinder */
/* this comes from the disk driver partitioning */
            long    fs_ncyl;        /* cylinders in file system */
/* these fields can be computed from the others */
            long    fs_cpg; /* cylinders per group */
            long    fs_ipg; /* inodes per group */
            long    fs_fpg; /* blocks per group * fs_frag */
/* this data must be re-computed after crashes */
            struct  csum fs_cstotal;        /* cylinder summary information */
/* these fields are cleared at mount time */
            char    fs_fmod;        /* super block modified flag */
            char    fs_clean;       /* file system is clean flag */
            char    fs_ronly;       /* mounted read-only flag */
            char    fs_flags;       /* currently unused flag */
            char    fs_fsmnt[MAXMNTLEN];    /* name mounted on */
/* these fields retain the current block allocation info */
            long    fs_cgrotor;     /* last cg searched */
            struct  csum *fs_csp[MAXCSBUFS]; /* list of fs_cs info buffers */
            long    fs_cpc; /* cyl per cycle in postbl */
            short   fs_opostbl[16][8];      /* old rotation block list head */
            long    fs_sparecon[56];        /* reserved for future constants */
            quad    fs_qbmask;      /* ~fs_bmask - for use with quad size */
            quad    fs_qfmask;      /* ~fs_fmask - for use with quad size */
            long    fs_postblformat; /* format of positional layout tables */
            long    fs_nrpos;       /* number of rotational positions */
            long    fs_postbloff;   /* (short) rotation block list head */
            long    fs_rotbloff;    /* (u_char) blocks for each rotation */
            long    fs_magic;       /* magic number */
            u_char  fs_space[1];    /* list of blocks for each rotation */
/* actually longer */
};
```

Each disk drive contains some number of file systems. A file system consists of a number of cylinder groups. Each cylinder group has inodes and data.

A file system is described by its super-block, which in turn describes the cylinder groups. The super-block is critical data and is replicated in each cylinder group to protect against catastrophic loss. This is done at file system creation time and the critical super-block data does not change, so the copies need not be referenced further unless disaster strikes.

Addresses stored in inodes are capable of addressing fragments of 'blocks'. File system blocks of at most size MAXBSIZE can be optionally broken into 2, 4, or 8 pieces, each of which is addressable; these pieces may be DEV_BSIZE, or some multiple of a DEV_BSIZE unit.

Large files consist of exclusively large data blocks. To avoid undue wasted disk space, the last data block of a small file is allocated as only as many fragments of a large block as are necessary. The file system format retains only a single pointer to such a fragment, which is a piece of a single large block that has been divided. The size of such a fragment is determinable from information in the inode, using the blksize(*fs*, *ip*, *lbn*) macro.

The file system records space availability at the fragment level; to determine block availability, aligned fragments are examined.

The root inode is the root of the file system. Inode 0 can't be used for normal purposes and historically bad blocks were linked to inode 1, thus the root inode is 2 (inode 1 is no longer used for this purpose, however numerous dump tapes make this assumption, so we are stuck with it).

The *fs_minfree* element gives the minimum acceptable percentage of file system blocks that may be free. If the freelist drops below this level only the super-user may continue to allocate blocks. The *fs_minfree* element may be set to 0 if no reserve of free blocks is deemed necessary, however severe performance degradations will be observed if the file system is run at greater than 90% full; thus the default value of *fs_minfree* is 10%.

Empirically the best trade-off between block fragmentation and overall disk utilization at a loading of 90% comes with a fragmentation of 8, thus the default fragment size is an eighth of the block size.

The element *fs_optim* specifies whether the file system should try to minimize the time spent allocating blocks, or if it should attempt to minimize the space fragmentation on the disk. If the value of fs_minfree (see above) is less than 10%, then the file system defaults to optimizing for space to avoid running out of full sized blocks. If the value of minfree is greater than or equal to 10%, fragmentation is unlikely to be problematical, and the file system defaults to optimizing for time.

Cylinder group related limits: Each cylinder keeps track of the availability of blocks at different rotational positions, so that sequential blocks can be laid out with minimum rotational latency. With the default of 8 distinguished rotational positions, the resolution of the summary information is 2ms for a typical 3600 rpm drive.

The element *fs_rotdelay* gives the minimum number of milliseconds to initiate another disk transfer on the same cylinder. It is used in determining the rotationally optimal layout for disk blocks within a file; the default value for *fs_rotdelay* is 2ms.

Each file system has a statically allocated number of inodes. An inode is allocated for each NBPI bytes of disk space. The inode allocation strategy is extremely conservative.

MINBSIZE is the smallest allowable block size. With a MINBSIZE of 4096 it is possible to create files of size 2^{32} with only two levels of indirection. MINBSIZE must be big enough to hold a cylinder group block, thus changes to (*struct cg*) must keep its size within MINBSIZE. Note that super-blocks are never more than size SBSIZE.

The path name on which the file system is mounted is maintained in *fs_fsmnt*. MAXMNTLEN defines the amount of space allocated in the super-block for this name. The limit on the amount of summary information per file system is defined by MAXCSBUFS. For a 4096 byte block size, it is currently parameterized for a maximum of two million cylinders.

Per cylinder group information is summarized in blocks allocated from the first cylinder group's data blocks. These blocks are read in from *fs_csaddr* (size *fs_cssize*) in addition to the super-block.

N.B.: sizeof(*struct csum*) must be a power of two in order for the **fs_cs**() macro to work.

The *Super-block for a file system*: The size of the rotational layout tables is limited by the fact that the super-block is of size SBSIZE. The size of these tables is *inversely* proportional to the block size of the file system. The size of the tables is increased when sector sizes are not powers of two, as this increases the number of cylinders included before the rotational pattern repeats (*fs_cpc*). The size of the rotational layout tables is derived from the number of bytes remaining in (*struct fs*).

The number of blocks of data per cylinder group is limited because cylinder groups are at most one block. The inode and free block tables must fit into a single block after deducting space for the cylinder group structure (*struct cg*).

The *Inode*: The inode is the focus of all file activity in the UNIX file system. There is a unique inode allocated for each active file, each current directory, each mounted-on file, text file, and the root. An inode is 'named' by its device/i-number pair. For further information, see the include file <sys/inode.h>.

HISTORY

A super-block structure named filsys appeared in Version 6 AT&T UNIX. The file system described in this manual appeared in 4.2BSD.

5

NAME

`fstab` – static information about the filesystems

SYNOPSIS

`#include <fstab.h>`

DESCRIPTION

The file `fstab` contains descriptive information about the various file systems. `fstab` is only read by programs, and not written; it is the duty of the system administrator to properly create and maintain this file. Each filesystem is described on a separate line; fields on each line are separated by tabs or spaces. The order of records in `fstab` is important because fsck(8), mount(8), and umount(8) sequentially iterate through `fstab` doing their thing.

The first field, (*fs_spec*), describes the block special device or remote filesystem to be mounted. For filesystems of type *ufs*, the special file name is the block special file name, and not the character special file name. If a program needs the character special file name, the program must create it by appending a "r" after the last "/" in the special file name.

The second field, (*fs_file*), describes the mount point for the filesystem. For swap partitions, this field should be specified as "none".

The third field, (*fs_vfstype*), describes the type of the filesystem. The system currently supports four types of filesystems:

 ufs   a local UNIX filesystem

 mfs   a local memory-based UNIX filesystem

 nfs   a Sun Microsystems compatible "Network File System"

 swap a disk partition to be used for swapping

The fourth field, (*fs_mntops*), describes the mount options associated with the filesystem. It is formatted as a comma separated list of options. It contains at least the type of mount (see *fs_type* below) plus any additional options appropriate to the filesystem type.

If the options "userquota" and/or "groupquota" are specified, the filesystem is automatically processed by the quotacheck(8) command, and user and/or group disk quotas are enabled with quotaon(8). By default, filesystem quotas are maintained in files named quota.user and quota.group which are located at the root of the associated filesystem. These defaults may be overridden by putting an equal sign and an alternative absolute pathname following the quota option. Thus, if the user quota file for /tmp is stored in /var/quotas/tmp.user, this location can be specified as:

 userquota=/var/quotas/tmp.user

The type of the mount is extracted from the *fs_mntops* field and stored separately in the *fs_type* field (it is not deleted from the *fs_mntops* field). If *fs_type* is "rw" or "ro" then the filesystem whose name is given in the *fs_file* field is normally mounted read-write or read-only on the specified special file. If *fs_type* is "sw" then the special file is made available as a piece of swap space by the swapon(8) command at the end of the system reboot procedure. The fields other than *fs_spec* and *fs_type* are unused. If *fs_type* is specified as "xx" the entry is ignored. This is useful to show disk partitions which are currently unused.

The fifth field, (*fs_freq*), is used for these filesystems by the dump(8) command to determine which filesystems need to be dumped. If the fifth field is not present, a value of zero is returned and dump will assume that the filesystem does not need to be dumped.

The sixth field, (fs_passno), is used by the fsck(8) program to determine the order in which filesystem checks are done at reboot time. The root filesystem should be specified with a fs_passno of 1, and other filesystems should have a fs_passno of 2. Filesystems within a drive will be checked sequentially, but filesystems on different drives will be checked at the same time to utilize parallelism available in the hardware. If the sixth field is not present or zero, a value of zero is returned and fsck will assume that the filesystem does not need to be checked.

```
#define FSTAB_RW        "rw"    /* read-write device */
#define FSTAB_RO        "ro"    /* read-only device */
#define FSTAB_SW        "sw"    /* swap device */
#define FSTAB_XX        "xx"    /* ignore totally */

struct fstab {
        char    *fs_spec;       /* block special device name */
        char    *fs_file;       /* filesystem path prefix */
        char    *fs_vfstype;    /* type of filesystem */
        char    *fs_mntops;     /* comma separated mount options */
        char    *fs_type;       /* rw, ro, sw, or xx */
        int     fs_freq;        /* dump frequency, in days */
        int     fs_passno;      /* pass number on parallel dump */
};
```

The proper way to read records from fstab is to use the routines getfsent(3), getfsspec(3), getfstype(3), and getfsfile(3).

FILES
/etc/fstab The file **fstab** resides in /etc.

SEE ALSO
getfsent(3)

HISTORY
The **fstab** file format appeared in 4.0BSD.

NAME

gettytab – terminal configuration data base

SYNOPSIS

gettytab

DESCRIPTION

The **gettytab** file is a simplified version of the termcap(5) data base used to describe terminal lines. The initial terminal login process getty(8) accesses the **gettytab** file each time it starts, allowing simpler reconfiguration of terminal characteristics. Each entry in the data base is used to describe one class of terminals.

There is a default terminal class, *default*, that is used to set global defaults for all other classes. (That is, the *default* entry is read, then the entry for the class required is used to override particular settings.)

CAPABILITIES

Refer to termcap(5) for a description of the file layout. The *default* column below lists defaults obtained if there is no entry in the table obtained, nor one in the special *default* table.

Name	Type	Default	Description
ap	bool	false	terminal uses any parity
bd	num	0	backspace delay
bk	str	0377	alternate end of line character (input break)
cb	bool	false	use crt backspace mode
cd	num	0	carriage-return delay
ce	bool	false	use crt erase algorithm
ck	bool	false	use crt kill algorithm
cl	str	NULL	Ta screen clear sequence
co	bool	false	console - add '\n' after login prompt
ds	str	'^Y'	delayed suspend character
dx	bool	false	set DECCTLQ
ec	bool	false	leave echo OFF
ep	bool	false	terminal uses even parity
er	str	'^?'	erase character
et	str	'^D'	end of text (EOF) character
ev	str	NULL	Ta initial environment
f0	num	unused	tty mode flags to write messages
f1	num	unused	tty mode flags to read login name
f2	num	unused	tty mode flags to leave terminal as
fd	num	0	form-feed (vertical motion) delay
fl	str	'^O'	output flush character
hc	bool	false	do NOT hangup line on last close
he	str	NULL	Ta hostname editing string
hn	str	hostname	hostname
ht	bool	false	terminal has real tabs
ig	bool	false	ignore garbage characters in login name
im	str	NULL	initial (banner) message
in	str	'^C'	interrupt character
is	num	unused	input speed

kl	str	'^U'	kill character
lc	bool	false	terminal has lower case
lm	str	login:	login prompt
ln	str	'^V'	"literal next" character
lo	str	/usr/bin/login	program to exec when name obtained
nd	num	0	newline (line-feed) delay
nl	bool	false	terminal has (or might have) a newline character
np	bool	false	terminal uses no parity (i.e. 8-bit characters)
nx	str	default	next table (for auto speed selection)
op	bool	false	terminal uses odd parity
os	num	unused	output speed
pc	str	'\0'	pad character
pe	bool	false	use printer (hard copy) erase algorithm
pf	num	0	delay between first prompt and following flush (seconds)
ps	bool	false	line connected to a MICOM port selector
qu	str	'^\'	quit character
rp	str	'^R'	line retype character
rw	bool	false	do NOT use raw for input, use cbreak
sp	num	unused	line speed (input and output)
su	str	'^Z'	suspend character
tc	str	none	table continuation
to	num	0	timeout (seconds)
tt	str	NULL	terminal type (for environment)
ub	bool	false	do unbuffered output (of prompts etc)
uc	bool	false	terminal is known upper case only
we	str	'^W'	word erase character
xc	bool	false	do NOT echo control chars as '^X'
xf	str	'^S'	XOFF (stop output) character
xn	str	'^Q'	XON (start output) character

If no line speed is specified, speed will not be altered from that which prevails when getty is entered. Specifying an input or output speed will override line speed for stated direction only.

Terminal modes to be used for the output of the message, for input of the login name, and to leave the terminal set as upon completion, are derived from the boolean flags specified. If the derivation should prove inadequate, any (or all) of these three may be overridden with one of the *f0*, or , numeric specifications, which can be used to specify (usually in octal, with a leading '0') the exact values of the flags. Local (new tty) flags are set in the top 16 bits of this (32 bit) value.

Should getty receive a null character (presumed to indicate a line break) it will restart using the table indicated by the *nx* entry. If there is none, it will re-use its original table.

Delays are specified in milliseconds, the nearest possible delay available in the tty driver will be used. Should greater certainty be desired, delays with values 0, 1, 2, and 3 are interpreted as choosing that particular delay algorithm from the driver.

The *cl* screen clear string may be preceded by a (decimal) number of milliseconds of delay required (a la termcap). This delay is simulated by repeated use of the pad character *pc*.

The initial message, and login message, *im* and *lm* may include the character sequence %h or %t to obtain the hostname or tty name respectively. (%% obtains a single '%' character.) The hostname is normally obtained from the system, but may be set by the *hn* table entry. In either case it may be edited with *he*. The *he* string is a sequence of characters, each character that is neither '@' nor '#' is copied into the final hostname. A '@' in the *he* string, causes one character from the real hostname to be copied to the final hostname. A '#'

in the *he* string, causes the next character of the real hostname to be skipped. Surplus '@' and '#' characters are ignored.

When getty execs the login process, given in the *lo* string (usually "/usr/bin/login"), it will have set the environment to include the terminal type, as indicated by the *tt* string (if it exists). The *ev* string, can be used to enter additional data into the environment. It is a list of comma separated strings, each of which will presumably be of the form *name=value*.

If a non-zero timeout is specified, with *to*, then getty will exit within the indicated number of seconds, either having received a login name and passed control to login, or having received an alarm signal, and exited. This may be useful to hangup dial in lines.

Output from getty is even parity unless *op* is specified. The *op* string may be specified with *ap* to allow any parity on input, but generate odd parity output. Note: this only applies while getty is being run, terminal driver limitations prevent a more complete implementation. Getty does not check parity of input characters in RAW mode.

SEE ALSO
login(1), termcap(5), getty(8).

BUGS
The special characters (erase, kill, etc.) are reset to system defaults by login(1). In *all* cases, '#' or '^H' typed in a login name will be treated as an erase character, and '@' will be treated as a kill character.

The delay stuff is a real crock. Apart form its general lack of flexibility, some of the delay algorithms are not implemented. The terminal driver should support sane delay settings.

The *he* capability is stupid.

The termcap format is horrid, something more rational should have been chosen.

HISTORY
The gettytab file format appeared in 4.2BSD.

NAME

groff_font – format of groff device and font description files

DESCRIPTION

The groff font format is roughly a superset of the ditroff font format. Unlike the ditroff font format, there is no associated binary format. The font files for device *name* are stored in a directory **dev***name*. There are two types of file: a device description file called **DESC** and for each font *F* a font file called *F*. These are text files; there is no associated binary format.

DESC file format

The DESC file can contain the following types of line:

res *n*   There are *n* machine units per inch.

hor *n*   The horizontal resolution is *n* machine units.

vert *n*   The vertical resolution is *n* machine units.

sizescale *n*

> The scale factor for pointsizes. By default this has a value of 1. One *scaled point* is equal to one point/*n*. The arguments to the **unitwidth** and **sizes** commands are given in scaled points.

unitwidth *n*

> Quantities in the font files are given in machine units for fonts whose point size is *n* scaled points.

tcommand

> This means that the postprocessor can handle the **t** and **u** output commands.

sizes *s1 s2 ... sn* **0**

> This means that the device has fonts at *s1*, *s2*, ... *sn* scaled points. The list of sizes must be terminated by a **0**. Each *si* can also be a range of sizes *m−n*. The list can extend over more than one line.

styles *S1 S2 ... Sm*

> The first *m* font positions will be associated with styles *S1 ... Sm*.

fonts *n F1 F2 F3 ... Fn*

> Fonts *F1 ... Fn* will be mounted in the font positions *m+1,...,m+n* where *m* is the number of styles. This command may extend over more than one line. A font name of **0** will cause no font to be mounted on the corresponding font position.

family *fam*

> The default font family is *fam*.

charset   This line and everything following in the file are ignored. It is allowed for the sake of backwards compatibility.

The res, unitwidth, fonts and sizes lines are compulsory. Other commands are ignored by **troff** but may be used by postprocessors to store arbitrary information about the device in the DESC file.

Font file format

A font file has two sections. The first section is a sequence of lines each containing a sequence of blank delimited words; the first word in the line is a key, and subsequent words give a value for that key.

name *F*   The name of the font is *F*.

spacewidth *n*

> The normal width of a space is *n*.

slant *n*   The characters of the font have a slant of *n* degrees. (Positive means forward.)

ligatures *lig1 lig2 ... lign* **[0]**

> Characters *lig1*, *lig2*,...,*lign* are ligatures; possible ligatures are **ff**, **fi**, **fl** and **ffl**. For backwards compatibiliy, the list of ligatures may be terminated with a **0**. The list of ligatures may not extend over more than one line.

special The font is *special*; this means that when a character is requested that is not present in the current font, it will be searched for in any special fonts that are mounted.

Other commands are ignored by **troff** but may be used by postprocessors to store arbitrary information about the font in the font file.

The first section can contain comments which start with the # character and extend to the end of a line.

The second section contains one or two subsections. It must contain a *charset* subsection and it may also contain a *kernpairs* subsection. These subsections can appear in any order. Each subsection starts with a word on a line by itself.

The word **charset** starts the charset subsection. The **charset** line is followed by a sequence of lines. Each line gives information for one character. A line comprises a number of fields separated by blanks or tabs. The format is

    name metrics type code comment

name identifies the character: if *name* is a single character *c* then it corresponds to the groff input character *c*; if it is of the form \c where c is a single character, then it corresponds to the groff input character \c; otherwise it corresponds to the groff input character \[*name*] (if it is exactly two characters *xx* it can be entered as \(*xx*.) Groff supports eight bit characters; however some utilities has difficulties with eight bit characters. For this reason, there is a convention that the name **char***n* is equivalent to the single character whose code is *n* . For example, **char163** would be equivalent to the character with code 163 which is the pounds sterling sign in ISO Latin-1. The name —— is special and indicates that the character is unnamed; such characters can only be used by means of the \N escape sequence in **troff**.

The *type* field gives the character type:

1   means the character has an descender, for example, p;

2   means the character has an ascender, for example, b;

3   means the character has both an ascender and a descender, for example, (.

The *code* field gives the code which the postprocessor uses to print the character. The character can also be input to groff using this code by means of the \N escape sequence. The code can be any integer. If it starts with a **0** it will be interpreted as octal; if it starts with **0x** or **0X** it will be intepreted as hexdecimal.

Anything on the line after the code field will be ignored.

The *metrics* field has the form:

    width[,*height*[,*depth*[,

There must not be any spaces between these subfields. Missing subfields are assumed to be 0. The subfields are all decimal integers. Since there is no associated binary format, these values are not required to fit into a variable of type **char** as they are in ditroff. The *width* subfields gives the width of the character. The *height* subfield gives the height of the character (upwards is positive); if a character does not extend above the baseline, it should be given a zero height, rather than a negative height. The *depth* subfield gives the depth of the character, that is, the distance below the lowest point below the baseline to which the character extends (downwards is positive); if a character does not extend below above the baseline, it should be given a zero depth, rather than a negative depth. The *italic_correction* subfield gives the amount of space that should be added after the character when it is immediately to be followed by a character from a roman font. The *left_italic_correction* subfield gives the amount of space that should be added before the character when it is immediately to be preceded by a character from a roman font. The *subscript_correction* gives the amount of space that should be added after a character before adding a subscript. This should be less than the italic correction.

A line in the charset section can also have the format

    name "

This indicates that *name* is just another name for the character mentioned in the preceding line.

The word **kernpairs** starts the kernpairs section. This contains a sequence of lines of the form:

> *c1 c2 n*

This means that when character *c1* appears next to character *c2* the space between them should be increased by *n*. Most entries in kernpairs section will have a negative value for *n*.

FILES

> **/usr/share/groff_font/dev***name***/DESC**　　Device description file for device *name*.
>
> **/usr/share/groff_font/dev***name***/***F*　　　　　Font file for font *F* of device *name*.

SEE ALSO

> **groff_out**(5), **troff**(1).

NAME

groff_out – groff intermediate output format

DESCRIPTION

This manual page describes the format output by GNU troff. The output format used by GNU troff is very similar to that used by Unix device-independent troff. Only the differences are documented here.

The argument to the **s** command is in scaled points (units of *points*/n, where *n* is the argument to the **sizescale** command in the DESC file.) The argument to the **x Height** command is also in scaled points.

The first three output commands are guaranteed to be:

> **x T** *device*
> **x res** *n h v*
> **x init**

If the **tcommand** line is present in the DESC file, troff will use the following two commands

t*xxx*   *xxx* is any sequence of characters terminated by a space or a newline; the first character should be printed at the current position, the current horizontal position should be increased by the width of the first character, and so on for each character. The width of the character is that given in the font file, appropriately scaled for the current point size, and rounded so that it is a multiple of the horizontal resolution. Special characters cannot be printed using this command.

u*n xxx* This is same as the **t** command except that after printing each character, the current horizontal position is increased by the sum of the width of that character and *n*.

Note that single characters can have the eighth bit set, as can the names of fonts and special characters.

The names of characters and fonts can be of arbitrary length; drivers should not assume that they will be only two characters long.

When a character is to be printed, that character will always be in the current font. Unlike device-independent troff, it is not necessary for drivers to search special fonts to find a character.

The **D** drawing command has been extended. These extensions will only be used by GNU pic if the −x option is given.

Df *n*\n   Set the shade of gray to be used for filling solid objects to *n*; *n* must be an integer between 0 and 1000, where 0 corresponds solid white and 1000 to solid black, and values in between correspond to intermediate shades of gray. This applies only to solid circles, solid ellipses and solid polygons. By default, a level of 1000 will be used. Whatever color a solid object has, it should completely obscure everything beneath it. A value greater than 1000 or less than 0 can also be used: this means fill with the shade of gray that is currently being used for lines and text. Normally this will be black, but some drivers may provide a way of changing this.

DC *d*\n Draw a solid circle with a diameter of *d* with the leftmost point at the current position.

DE *dx dy*\n
Draw a solid ellipse with a horizontal diameter of *dx* and a vertical diameter of *dy* with the leftmost point at the current position. delim $$

Dp \$dx sub 1\$ \$dy sub 1\$ \$dx sub 2\$ \$dy sub 2\$ \$...\$ \$dx sub n\$ \$dy sub n\$\n
Draw a polygon with, for \$i = 1 ,..., n+1\$, the *i*-th vertex at the current position \$+ sum from j=1 to i-1 (dx sub j , dy sub j)\$. At the moment, GNU pic only uses this command to generate triangles and rectangles.

DP \$dx sub 1\$ \$dy sub 1\$ \$dx sub 2\$ \$dy sub 2\$ \$...\$ \$dx sub n\$ \$dy sub n\$\n
Like **Dp** but draw a solid rather than outlined polygon.

Dt *n*\n   Set the current line thickness to *n* machine units. Traditionally Unix troff drivers use a line thickness proportional to the current point size; drivers should continue to do this if no **Dt** command has been given, or if a **Dt** command has been given with a negative value of *n*. A zero value of *n* selects the smallest available line thickness.

A difficulty arises in how the current position should be changed after the execution of these commands. This is not of great importance since the code generated by GNU pic does not depend on this. Given a drawing command of the form

$$\backslash\mathbf{D}'c\ \$x\ sub\ 1\$\ \$y\ sub\ 1\$\ \$x\ sub\ 2\$\ \$y\ sub\ 2\$\ \$...\$\ \$x\ sub\ n\$\ \$y\ sub\ n\$'$$

where c is not one of **c, e, l, a** or ˜, Unix troff will treat each of the $x\ sub\ i\$ as a horizontal quantity, and each of the $y\ sub\ i\$ as a vertical quantity and will assume that the width of the drawn object is $sum\ from\ i=1\ to\ n\ x\ sub\ i\$, and that the height is $sum\ from\ i=1\ to\ n\ y\ sub\ i\$. (The assumption about the height can be seen by examining the **st** and **sb** registers after using such a **D** command in a \w escape sequence.) This rule also holds for all the original drawing commands with the exception of **De**. For the sake of compatibility GNU troff also follows this rule, even though it produces an ugly result in the case of the **Df, Dt**, and, to a lesser extent, **DE** commands. Thus after executing a **D** command of the form

$$\mathbf{D}c\ \$x\ sub\ 1\$\ \$y\ sub\ 1\$\ \$x\ sub\ 2\$\ \$y\ sub\ 2\$\ \$...\$\ \$x\ sub\ n\$\ \$y\ sub\ n\$\backslash n$$

the current position should be increased by $(\ sum\ from\ i=1\ to\ n\ x\ sub\ i\ ,\ sum\ from\ i=1\ to\ n\ y\ sub\ i\ )\$.

There is a continuation convention which permits the argument to the **x X** command to contain newlines: when outputting the argument to the **x X** command, GNU troff will follow each newline in the argument with a + character (as usual, it will terminate the entire argument with a newline); thus if the line after the line containing the **x X** command starts with +, then the newline ending the line containing the **x X** command should be treated as part of the argument to the **x X** command, the + should be ignored, and the part of the line following the + should be treated like the part of the line following the **x X** command.

SEE ALSO
> **groff_font**(5)

NAME
group – format of the group permissions file

DESCRIPTION
The file </etc/group> consists of newline separated ASCII records, one per group, containing four colon ': ' separated fields. These fields are as follows:

group	Name of the group.
passwd	Group's *encrypted* password.
gid	The group's decimal ID.
member	Group members.

The *group* field is the group name used for granting file access to users who are members of the group. The *gid* field is the number associated with the group name. They should both be unique across the system (and often across a group of systems) since they control file access. The *passwd* field is an optional *encrypted* password. This field is rarely used and an asterisk is normally placed in it rather than leaving it blank. The *member* field contains the names of users granted the privileges of *group*. The member names are separated by commas without spaces or newlines. A user is automatically in a group if that group was specified in their /etc/passwd entry and does not need to be added to that group in the /etc/group file.

FILES
/etc/group

SEE ALSO
setgroups(2), initgroups(3), crypt(3), passwd(1), passwd(5)

BUGS
The passwd(1) command does not change the **group** passwords.

HISTORY
A **group** file format appeared in Version 6 AT&T UNIX.

NAME
hosts – host name data base

DESCRIPTION
The **hosts** file contains information regarding the known hosts on the network. For each host a single line should be present with the following information:

> official host name
> Internet address
> aliases

Items are separated by any number of blanks and/or tab characters. A ''#'' indicates the beginning of a comment; characters up to the end of the line are not interpreted by routines which search the file.

When using the name server named(8), this file provides a backup when the name server is not running. For the name server, it is suggested that only a few addresses be included in this file. These include address for the local interfaces that ifconfig(8) needs at boot time and a few machines on the local network.

This file may be created from the official host data base maintained at the Network Information Control Center (NIC), though local changes may be required to bring it up to date regarding unofficial aliases and/or unknown hosts. As the data base maintained at NIC is incomplete, use of the name server is recommended for sites on the DARPA Internet.

Network addresses are specified in the conventional ''.'' (dot) notation using the inet_addr(3) routine from the Internet address manipulation library, inet(3). Host names may contain any printable character other than a field delimiter, newline, or comment character.

FILES
/etc/hosts The **hosts** file resides in /etc.

SEE ALSO
gethostbyname(3), ifconfig(8), named(8)

Name Server Operations Guide for BIND.

HISTORY
The **hosts** file format appeared in 4.2BSD.

NAME

/etc/kerberosIV/krb.conf – Kerberos configuration file

DESCRIPTION

krb.conf contains configuration information describing the Kerberos realm and the Kerberos key distribution center (KDC) servers for known realms.

krb.conf contains the name of the local realm in the first line, followed by lines indicating realm/host entries. The first token is a realm name, and the second is the hostname of a host running a KDC for that realm. The words "admin server" following the hostname indicate that the host also provides an administrative database server. For example:

    ATHENA.MIT.EDU
    ATHENA.MIT.EDU kerberos-1.mit.edu admin server
    ATHENA.MIT.EDU kerberos-2.mit.edu
    LCS.MIT.EDU kerberos.lcs.mit.edu admin server

SEE ALSO

krb.realms(5), krb_get_krbhst(3), krb_get_lrealm(3)

NAME

/etc/kerberosIV/krb.realms – host to Kerberos realm translation file

DESCRIPTION

krb.realms provides a translation from a hostname to the Kerberos realm name for the services provided by that host.

Each line of the translation file is in one of the following forms (domain_name should be of the form .XXX.YYY, e.g. .LCS.MIT.EDU):

    host_name kerberos_realm
    domain_name kerberos_realm

If a hostname exactly matches the *host_name* field in a line of the first form, the corresponding realm is the realm of the host. If a hostname does not match any *host_name* in the file, but its domain exactly matches the *domain_name* field in a line of the second form, the corresponding realm is the realm of the host.

If no translation entry applies, the host's realm is considered to be the hostname's domain portion converted to upper case.

SEE ALSO

krb_realmofhost(3)

NAME

L-devices – UUCP device description file

DESCRIPTION

The L-devices file is consulted by the UUCP daemon *uucico*(8C) under the direction of *L.sys*(5) for information on the devices that it may use. Each line describes exactly one device.

A line in *L-devices* has the form:

Caller Device Call_Unit Class Dialer [Expect Send]....

Each item can be separated by any number of blanks or tabs. Lines beginning with a '#' character are comments; long lines can be continued by appending a '\' character to the end of the line.

Caller denotes the type of connection, and must be one of the following:

ACU   Automatic call unit, e.g., autodialing modems such as the Hayes Smartmodem 1200 or Novation "Smart Cat".

DIR   Direct connect; hardwired line (usually RS-232) to a remote system.

DK   AT&T Datakit.

MICOM
            Micom Terminal switch.

PAD   X.25 PAD connection.

PCP   GTE Telenet PC Pursuit.

SYTEK   Sytek high-speed dedicated modem port connection.

TCP   Berkeley TCP/IP or 3Com UNET connection. These are mutually exclusive. Note that listing TCP connections in *L-devices* is superfluous; *uucico* does not even bother to look here since it has all the information it needs in *L.sys*(5).

Device is a device file in /dev/ that is opened to use the device. The device file must be owned by UUCP, with access modes of 0600 or better. (See *chmod*(2)).

Call_Unit is an optional second device file name. True automatic call units use a separate device file for data and for dialing; the *Device* field specifies the data port, while the *Call_unit* field specifies the dialing port. If the *Call_unit* field is unused, it must not be left empty. Insert a dummy entry as a placeholder, such as "0" or "unused."

Class is an integer number that specifies the line baud (for dialers and direct lines) or the port number (for network connections).

The *Class* may be preceded by a non-numeric prefix. This is to differentiate among devices that have identical *Caller* and baud, but are distinctly different. For example, "1200" could refer to all Bell 212-compatible modems, "V1200" to Racal-Vadic modems, and "C1200" to CCITT modems, all at 1200 baud. Similarly, "W1200" could denote long distance lines, while "L1200" could refer to local phone lines.

Dialer applies only to ACU devices. This is the "brand" or type of the ACU or modem.

DF02   DEC DF02 or DF03 modems.

DF112   Dec DF112 modems. Use a *Dialer* field of **DF112T** to use tone dialing, or **DF112P** for pulse dialing.

att   AT&T 2224 2400 baud modem.

cds224 Concord Data Systems 224 2400 baud modem.

dn11   DEC DN11 Unibus dialer.

hayes   Hayes Smartmodem 1200 and compatible autodialing modems. Use a *Dialer* field of **hayestone** to use tone dialing, or **hayespulse** for pulse dialing. It is also permissible to include the letters

'T' and 'P' in the phone number (in *L.sys*) to change to tone or pulse midway through dialing. (Note that a leading 'T' or 'P' will be interpreted as a dialcode!)

hayes2400

Hayes Smartmodem 2400 and compatible modems. Use a *Dialer* field of **hayes2400tone** to use tone dialing, or **hayes2400pulse** for pulse dialing.

novation

Novation "Smart Cat" autodialing modem.

penril   Penril Corp "Hayes compatible" modems (they really aren't or they would use the **hayes** entry.)

rvmacs   Racal-Vadic 820 dialer with 831 adapter in a MACS configuration.

va212   Racal-Vadic 212 autodialing modem.

va811s   Racal-Vadic 811s dialer with 831 adapter.

va820   Racal-Vadic 820 dialer with 831 adapter.

vadic   Racal-Vadic 3450 and 3451 series autodialing modems.

ventel   Ventel 212+ autodialing modem.

vmacs   Racal-Vadic 811 dialer with 831 adapter in a MACS configuration.

Expect/Send is an optional *Expect/Send* script for getting through a smart port selector, or for issuing special commands to the modem. The syntax is identical to that of the Expect/Send script of *L.sys*. The difference is that the *L-devices* script is used *before* the connection is made, while the *L.sys* script is used *after*.

FILES

/usr/lib/uucp/L-devices
/usr/lib/uucp/UUAIDS/L-devices   L-devices example

SEE ALSO

uucp(1C), uux(1C), L.sys(5), uucico(8C)

5

NAME

L-dialcodes – UUCP phone number index file

DESCRIPTION

The *L-dialcodes* file defines the mapping of strings from the phone number field of *L.sys*(5) to actual phone numbers.

Each line in L-dialcodes has the form:

        alpha_string phone_number

The two items can be separated by any number of blanks or tabs. Lines beginning with a '#' character are comments.

A phone number in *L.sys* can be preceded by an arbitrary alphabetic character string; the string is matched against the list of *alpha_string*s in *L-dialcodes*. If a match is found, *phone_number* is substituted for it. If no match is found, the string is discarded.

L-dialcodes is commonly used either of two ways:

(1)   The alphabetic strings are used as prefixes to denote area codes, zones, and other commonly used sequences. For example, if *L-dialcodes* included the following lines:

        chi   1312
        mv   1415

In *L.sys* you could enter:

        chivax Any ACU 1200 chi5551234 ogin:--ogin: nuucp
        mvpyr Any ACU 1200 mv5556001   ogin:--ogin: Uuucp

instead of

        chivax Any ACU 1200 13125551234 ogin:--ogin: nuucp
        mvpyr Any ACU 1200 14155556001 ogin:--ogin: Uuucp

(2)   All phone numbers are placed in *L-dialcodes*, one for each remote site. *L.sys* then refers to these by name. For example, if *L-dialcodes* contains the following lines:

        chivax   13125551234
        mvpyr   14155556601

then *L.sys* could have:

        chivax Any ACU 1200 chivax ogin:--ogin: nuucp
        mvpyr Any ACU 1200 mvpyr   ogin:--ogin: Uuucp

This scheme allows a site administrator to give users read access to the table of phone numbers, while still protecting the login/password sequences in *L.sys*.

FILES

/usr/lib/uucp/L-dialcodes
/usr/lib/uucp/UUAIDS/L-dialcodes   L-dialcodes example

SEE ALSO

uucp(1C), uux(1C), L.sys(5), uucico(8C).

NAME

L.aliases – UUCP hostname alias file

DESCRIPTION

The *L.aliases* file defines mapping (aliasing) of system names for uucp. This is intended for compensating for systems that have changed names, or do not provide their entire machine name (like most USG systems). It is also useful when a machine's name is not obvious or commonly misspelled.

Each line in *L.aliases* is of the form:

real_name alias_name

Any amount of whitespace may separate the two items. Lines beginning with a '#' character are comments.

All occurrences of *alias_name* are mapped to *real_name* by *uucico*(8C), *uucp*(1), and *uux*(1). The mapping occurs regardless of whether the name was typed in by a user or provided by a remote site. An exception is the **-s** option of *uucico*; only the site's real hostname (the name in *L.sys*(5)) will be accepted there.

Aliased system names should not be placed in *L.sys*; they will not be used.

FILES

/usr/lib/uucp/L.aliases /usr/lib/uucp/UUAIDS/L.aliases   L.aliases example

SEE ALSO

uucp(1C), uux(1C), L.sys(5), uucico(8C)

NAME

L.cmds – UUCP remote command permissions file

DESCRIPTION

The *L.cmds* file contains a list of commands, one per line, that are permitted for remote execution via *uux*(1C).

The default search path is /bin:/usr/bin:/usr/ucb. To change the path, include anywhere in the file a line of the form:

PATH=/bin:/usr/bin:/usr/ucb

Normally, an acknowledgment is mailed back to the requesting site after the command completes. If a command name is suffixed with **,Error**, then an acknowledgment will be mailed only if the command fails. If the command is suffixed with **,No**, then no acknowledgment will ever be sent. (These correspond with the −**z** and −**n** options of *uux*, respectively.)

For most sites, *L.cmds* should only include the lines:

rmail
ruusend

News sites should add:

PATH=/bin:/usr/bin:/usr/ucb:/usr/new
rnews,Error

While file names supplied as arguments to *uux* commands will be checked against the list of accessible directory trees in *USERFILE*(5), this check can be easily circumvented and should not be depended upon. In other words, it is unwise to include any commands in *L.cmds* that accept local file names. In particular, *sh*(1) and *csh*(1) are extreme risks.

It is common (but hazardous) to include *uucp*(1C) in *L.cmds*; see the NOTES section of *USERFILE*.

FILES

/usr/lib/uucp/L.cmds
/usr/lib/uucp/UUAIDS/L.cmds   L.cmds example.

SEE ALSO

uucp(1C), uux(1C), USERFILE(5), uucico(8C), uuxqt(8C)

NAME

L.sys – UUCP remote host description file

DESCRIPTION

The *L.sys* file is consulted by the UUCP daemon *uucico*(8C) for information on remote systems. *L.sys* includes the system name, appropriate times to call, phone numbers, and a login and password for the remote system. *L.sys* is thus a privileged file, owned by the UUCP Administrator; it is accessible only to the Administrator and to the superuser.

Each line in *L.sys* describes one connection to one remote host, and has the form:

System Times Caller Class Device/Phone_Number [Expect Send]....

Fields can be separated by any number of blanks or tabs. Lines beginning with a '#' character are comments; long lines can be continued by appending a '\' character to the end of the line.

The first five fields (*System* through *Device/Phone_Number*) specify the hardware mechanism that is necessary to make a connection to a remote host, such as a modem or network. *Uucico* searches from the top down through *L.sys* to find the desired *System*; it then opens the *L-devices*(5) file and searches for the first available device with the same *Caller*, *Class*, and (possibly) *Device*. ("Available" means that the device is ready and not being used for something else.) *Uucico* attempts a connection using that device; if the connection cannot be made (for example, a dialer gets a busy signal), *uucico* tries the next available device. If this also fails, it returns to *L.sys* to look for another line for the same *System*. If none is found, *uucico* gives up.

System is the hostname of the remote system. Every machine with which this system communicates via UUCP should be listed, regardless of who calls whom. Systems not listed in *L.sys* will not be permitted a connection. The local hostname should **not** appear here for security reasons.

Times is a comma-separated list of the times of the day and week that calls are permitted to this *System*. *Times* is most commonly used to restrict long distance telephone calls to those times when rates are lower. List items are constructed as:

keyword*hhmm-hhmm/grade*;*retry_time*

Keyword is required, and must be one of:

Any   Any time, any day of the week.

Wk   Any weekday. In addition, **Mo, Tu, We, Th, Fr, Sa**, and **Su** can be used for Monday through Sunday, respectively.

Evening When evening telephone rates are in effect, from 1700 to 0800 Monday through Friday, and all day Saturday and Sunday. **Evening** is the same as **Wk1700-0800,Sa,Su**.

Night   When nighttime telephone rates are in effect, from 2300 to 0800 Monday through Friday, all day Saturday, and from 2300 to 1700 Sunday. **Night** is the same as **Any2300-0800,Sa,Su0800-1700**.

NonPeak

This is a slight modification of **Evening**. It matches when the USA X.25 carriers have their lower rate period. This is 1800 to 0700 Monday through Friday, and all day Saturday and Sunday. **NonPeak** is the same as **Any1800-0700,Sa,Su**.

Never   Never call; calling into this *System* is forbidden or impossible. This is intended for polled connections, where the remote system calls into the local machine periodically. This is necessary when one of the machines is lacking either dial-in or dial-out modems.

The optional *hhmm-hhmm* subfield provides a time range that modifies the keyword. *hhmm* refers to *hours* and *minutes* in 24-hour time (from 0000 to 2359). The time range is permitted to "wrap" around midnight, and will behave in the obvious way. It is invalid to follow the **Evening**, **NonPeak**, and **Night** keywords with a time range.

The *grade* subfield is optional; if present, it is composed of a '/' (slash) and single character denoting the *grade* of the connection, from **0** to **9**, **A** to **Z**, or **a** to **z**. This specifies that only requests of grade *grade* or better will be transferred during this time. (The grade of a request or job is specified when it is queued by *uucp* or *uux*.) By convention, mail is sent at grade **C**, news is sent at grade **d**, and uucp copies are sent at grade **n**. Unfortunately, some sites do not follow these conventions, so it is not 100% reliable.

The *retry_time* subfield is optional; it must be preceded by a ';' (semicolon) and specifies the time, in minutes, before a failed connection may be tried again. (This restriction is in addition to any constraints imposed by the rest of the *Time* field.) By default, the retry time starts at 10 minutes and gradually increases at each failure, until after 26 tries *uucico* gives up completely (MAX RETRIES). If the retry time is too small, *uucico* may run into MAX RETRIES too soon.

Caller is the type of device used:

ACU   Automatic call unit or auto-dialing modem such as the Hayes Smartmodem 1200 or Novation "Smart Cat". See *L-devices* for a list of supported modems.

DIR   Direct connect; hardwired line (usually RS-232) to a remote system.

MICOM
            Micom Terminal Switch.

PAD   X.25 PAD connection.

PCP   GTE Telenet PC Pursuit. See *L-devices* for configuration details.

SYTEK   Sytek high-speed dedicated modem port connection.

TCP   Berkeley TCP/IP or 3Com UNET connection. These are mutually exclusive. TCP ports do **not** need entries in *L-devices* since all the necessary information is contained in *L.sys*. If several alternate ports or network connections should be tried, use multiple *L.sys* entries.

Class is usually the speed (baud) of the device, typically 300, 1200, or 2400 for ACU devices and 9600 for direct lines. Valid values are device dependent, and are specified in the *L–devices* file.

On some devices, the baud may be preceded by a non-numeric prefix. This is used in *L–devices* to distinguish among devices that have identical *Caller* and baud, but yet are distinctly different. For example, 1200 could refer to all Bell 212-compatible modems, V1200 to Racal-Vadic modems, and C1200 to CCITT modems, all at 1200 baud.

On TCP connections, *Class* is the port number (an integer number) or a port name from */etc/services* that is used to make the connection. For standard Berkeley TCP/IP, UUCP normally uses port number 540.

Device/Phone_Number varies based on the *Caller* field. For ACU devices, this is the phone number to dial. The number may include: digits **0** through **9**; **#** and ***** for dialing those symbols on tone telephone lines; **-** (hyphen) to pause for a moment, typically two to four seconds; **=** (equal sign) to wait for a second dial tone (implemented as a pause on many modems). Other characters are modem dependent; generally standard telephone punctuation characters (such as the slash and parentheses) are ignored, although *uucico* does not guarantee this.

The phone number can be preceded by an alphabetic string; the string is indexed and converted through the *L–dialcodes*(5) file.

For DIR devices, the *Device/Phone_Number* field contains the name of the device in */dev* that is used to make the connection. There must be a corresponding line in *L–devices* with identical *Caller*, *Class*, and *Device* fields.

For TCP and other network devices, *Device/Phone_Number* holds the true network name of the remote system, which may be different from its UUCP name (although one would hope not).

Expect and *Send* refer to an arbitrarily long set of strings that alternately specify what to *expect* and what to *send* to login to the remote system once a physical connection has been established. A complete set of expect/send strings is referred to as an *expect/send script*. The same syntax is used in the *L–devices* file to interact with the dialer prior to making a connection; there it is referred to as a *chat script*. The complete format for one *expect/send* pair is:

   expect-timeout-send-expect-timeout   send

Expect and *Send* are character strings. *Expect* is compared against incoming text from the remote host; *send* is sent back when *expect* is matched. By default, the *send* is followed by a '\r' (carriage return). If the *expect* string is not matched within *timeout* seconds (default 45), then it is assumed that the match failed. The '*expect-send-expect*' notation provides a limited loop mechanism; if the first *expect* string fails to match, then the *send* string between the hyphens is transmitted, and *uucico* waits for the second *expect* string. This can be repeated indefinitely. When the last *expect* string fails, *uucico* hangs up and logs that the connection failed.

The timeout can (optionally) be specified by appending the parameter '~*nn*' to the expect string, when *nn* is the timeout time in seconds.

Backslash escapes that may be imbedded in the *expect* or *send* strings include:

\b	Generate a 3/10 second BREAK.
\b*n*	Where *n* is a single-digit number;
	generate an *n*/10 second BREAK.
\c	Suppress the \r at the end of a *send* string.
\d	Delay; pause for 1 second. (*Send* only.)
\r	Carriage Return.
\s	Space.
\n	Newline.
\xxx	Where *xxx* is an octal constant;
	denotes the corresponding ASCII character.

As a special case, an empty pair of double-quotes " " in the *expect* string is interpreted as "expect nothing"; that is, transmit the *send* string regardless of what is received. Empty double-quotes in the *send* string cause a lone '\r' (carriage return) to be sent.

One of the following keywords may be substituted for the *send* string:

BREAK	Generate a 3/10 second BREAK
BREAK*n*	Generate an *n*/10 second BREAK
CR	Send a Carriage Return (same as "").
EOT	Send an End-Of-Transmission character, ASCII \004.
	Note that this will cause most hosts to hang up.
NL	Send a Newline.
PAUSE	Pause for 3 seconds.
PAUSE*n*	Pause for *n* seconds.
P_ODD	Use odd parity on future send strings.
P_ONE	Use parity one on future send strings.
P_EVEN	Use even parity on future send strings. (Default)
P_ZERO	Use parity zero on future send strings.

Finally, if the *expect* string consists of the keyword **ABORT**, then the string following is used to arm an abort trap. If that string is subsequently received any time prior to the completion of the entire *expect/send* script, then *uucico* will abort, just as if the script had timed out. This is useful for trapping error messages from port selectors or front-end processors such as "Host Unavailable" or "System is Down."

For example:

   "" "" ogin:--ogin: nuucp ssword: ufeedme

This is executed as, "When the remote system answers, *expect* nothing. *Send* a carriage return. *Expect* the remote to transmit the string 'ogin:'. If it doesn't within 45 seconds, send another carriage return. When it finally does, *send* it the string 'nuucp'. Then *expect* the string 'ssword:'; when that is received, *send* 'ufeedme'."

FILES

     /usr/lib/uucp/L.sys

     /usr/lib/uucp/UUAIDS/L.sys   L.sys example

SEE ALSO

     uucp(1C), uux(1C), L-devices(5), services(5), uucico(8C)

BUGS

     "ABORT" in the send/expect script is expressed "backwards," that is, it should be written " *expect* **ABORT**" but instead it is " **ABORT** *expect*".

     Several of the backslash escapes in the send/expect strings are confusing and/or different from those used by AT&T and Honey-Danber UUCP. For example, '\b' requests a BREAK, while practically everywhere else '\b' means backspace. '\t' for tab and '\f' for formfeed are not implemented. '\s' is a kludge; it would be more sensible to be able to delimit strings with quotation marks.

5

NAME

`man.conf` – configuration file for man(1)

DESCRIPTION

The man(1), apropos(1), and whatis(1) commands search for manual pages or their database files as specified by the **man.conf** file. Manual pages are normally expected to be preformatted (see nroff(1)) and named with a trailing ".0".

The **man.conf** file contains two types of lines.

The first type of line is a "section" line, which contains a section name followed by one or more directory paths. The directory paths may contain the normal shell globbing characters, including curly braces ("{}"); to escape a shell globbing character, precede it with a backslash ("\"). Lines in this format specify that manual pages for the section may be found in the following directories.

Directories named with a trailing slash character ("/") are expected to contain subdirectories of manual pages, (see the keyword "_subdir" below) instead of manual pages. These subdirectories are searched instead of the directory.

Before searching any directory for a manual page, the man(1) command always searches the subdirectory with the same name as the current machine type, if it exists. No specification of these subdirectories is necessary in the **man.conf** file.

Section names are unrestricted except for the reserved words specified below; in general, you should avoid anything with a leading underscore ("_") to avoid future incompatibilities.

The section named "_default" is the list of directories that will be searched if no section is specified by the user.

The second type of line is preceded with a "keyword". The possible keywords and their meanings are as follows:

_build   Man file names, regardless of their format, are expected to end in a ".*" pattern, i.e. a "." followed by some suffix. The first field of a _build line lists a suffix which indicates files which need to be reformated or manipulated in some way before being displayed to the user. The suffix may contain the normal shell globbing characters (NOT including curly braces ("{}")). The rest of the line must be a shell command line, the standard output of which is the manual page in a format which may be directly displayed to the user. Any occurrences of the string "%s" in the shell command line will be replaced by the name of the file which is being reformatted.

_subdir   The list (in search order) of subdirectories which will be searched in any directory named with a trailing slash ("/") character. This list is also used when a path is specified to the man(1) utility by the user, using the MANPATH environment variable or the −M and −m options.

_suffix   Man file names, regardless of their format are expected to end in a ".*" pattern, i.e. a "." followed by some suffix. Each field of a _suffix line is a suffix which indicates files which do not need to be reformatted or manipulated in any way, but which may be directly displayed to the user. Each suffix may contain the normal shell globbing characters (NOT including curly braces ("{}")).

_version   The version of the configuration file.

_whatdb   The full pathname (not just a directory path) for a database to be used by the apropos(1) and whatis(1) commands.

Multiple specifications for all types of lines are cumulative and the entries are used in the order listed in the file; multiple entries may be listed per line, as well.

Empty lines or lines whose first non-whitespace character is a hash mark ("#") are ignored.

EXAMPLES

Given the following `man.conf` file:

```
_version    BSD.2
_subdir     cat[123]
_suffix     .0
_build      .[1-9]  nroff -man %s
_build      .tbl    tbl %s | nroff -man
_default    /usr/share/man/
sect3       /usr/share/man/{old/,}cat3
```

By default, the command "man mktemp" will search for "mktemp.<any_digit>" and "mktemp.tbl" in the directories "/usr/share/man/cat1", "/usr/share/man/cat2", and "/usr/share/man/cat3". If on a machine of type "vax", the subdirectory "vax" in each directory would be searched as well, before the directory was searched.

If "mktemp.tbl" was found first, the command "tbl <manual page> nroff -man" would be run to build a man page for display to the user.

The command "man sect3 mktemp" would search the directories "/usr/share/man/old/cat3" and "/usr/share/man/cat3", in that order, for the mktemp manual page. If a subdirectory with the same name as the current machine type existed in any of them, it would be searched as well, before each of them were searched.

FILES

`/etc/man.conf` Standard manual directory search path.

SEE ALSO

apropos(1), machine(1), man(1), whatis(1), whereis(1), fnmatch(3), glob(3)

5

NAME

map3270 – database for mapping ascii keystrokes into IBM 3270 keys

SYNOPSIS

map3270

DESCRIPTION

When emulating IBM-style 3270 terminals under UNIX (see *tn3270*(1)), a mapping must be performed between sequences of keys hit on a user's (ascii) keyboard, and the keys that are available on a 3270. For example, a 3270 has a key labeled **EEOF** which erases the contents of the current field from the location of the cursor to the end. In order to accomplish this function, the terminal user and a program emulating a 3270 must agree on what keys will be typed to invoke the **EEOF** function.

The requirements for these sequences are:

    1)   that the first character of the sequence be outside of the standard ascii printable characters;

    2)   that no sequence *be* an initial part of another (although sequences may *share* initial parts).

FORMAT

The file consists of entries for various keyboards. The first part of an entry lists the names of the keyboards which use that entry. These names will often be the same as in */etc/termcap* (see *termcap*(5)); however, note that often the terminals from various termcap entries will all use the same *map3270* entry; for example, both 925 and 925vb (for 925 with visual bells) would probably use the same *map3270* entry. Additionally, there are occasions when the terminal type defines a window manager, and it will then be necessary to specify a keyboard name (via the **KEYBD** environment variable) as the name of the entry. After the names, separated by vertical bars ('I'), comes a left brace ('{'); the definitions; and, finally, a right brace ('}').

Each definition consists of a reserved keyword (see list below) which identifies the 3270 function (extended as defined below), followed by an equal sign ('='), followed by the various ways to generate this particular function, followed by a semi-colon (';'). Each way is a sequence of strings of *printable* ascii characters enclosed inside single quotes ('''); various ways (alternatives) are separated by vertical bars ('I').

Inside the single quotes, a few characters are special. A caret (''') specifies that the next character is the "control" character of whatever the character is. So, '^a' represents control-a, ie: hexadecimal 1 (note that '^A' would generate the same code). To generate **rubout** (DEL), one enters '^?'. To represent a control character inside a file requires using the caret to represent a control sequence; simply typing control-A will not work. Note: the ctrl-caret sequence (to generate a hexadecimal 1E) is represented as '^^' (not '^\').

In addition to the caret, a letter may be preceded by a backslash ('\'). Since this has little effect for most characters, its use is usually not recommended. For the case of a single quote ('''), the backslash prevents that single quote from terminating the string. For the case of a caret (''''), the backslash prevents the caret from having its special meaning. To have the backslash be part of the string, it is necessary to place two backslashes ('\\') in the file.

In addition, the following characters are special:

    '\E'   means an escape character;
    '\n'   means newline;
    '\t'   means tab;
    '\r'   means carriage return.

MAP3270(5)   UNIX Programmer's Manual   MAP3270(5)

It is not necessary for each character in a string to be enclosed within single quotes. '\E\E\E' means three escape characters.

Comments, which may appear anywhere on a line, begin with a hash mark ('#'), and terminate at the end of that line. However, comments cannot begin inside a quoted string; a hash mark inside a quoted string has no special meaning.

3270 KEYS SUPPORTED

The following is the list of 3270 key names that are supported in this file. Note that some of the keys don't really exist on a 3270. In particular, the developers of this file have relied extensively on the work at the Yale University Computer Center with their 3270 emulator which runs in an IBM Series/1 front end. The following list corresponds closely to the functions that the developers of the Yale code offer in their product.

In the following list, the starred ("*") functions are not supported by *tn3270*(1). An unsupported function will cause *tn3270(1)* to send a (possibly visual) bell sequence to the user's terminal.

3270 Key Name   Functional description

(*)LPRT	local print
DP	dup character
FM	field mark character
CURSEL	cursor select
CENTSIGN	EBCDIC cent sign
RESHOW	redisplay the screen
EINP	erase input
EEOF	erase end of field
DELETE	delete character
INSRT	toggle insert mode
TAB	field tab
BTAB	field back tab
COLTAB	column tab
COLBAK	column back tab
INDENT	indent one tab stop
UNDENT	undent one tab stop
NL	new line
HOME	home the cursor
UP	up cursor
DOWN	down cursor
RIGHT	right cursor
LEFT	left cursor
SETTAB	set a column tab
DELTAB	delete a columntab
SETMRG	set left margin
SETHOM	set home position
CLRTAB	clear all column tabs
(*)APLON	apl on
(*)APLOFF	apl off
(*)APLEND	treat input as ascii
(*)PCON	xon/xoff on
(*)PCOFF	xon/xoff off
DISC	disconnect (suspend)
(*)INIT	new terminal type
(*)ALTK	alternate keyboard dvorak
FLINP	flush input

```
    ERASE          erase last character
    WERASE          erase last word
    FERASE          erase field
    SYNCH          we are in synch with the user
    RESET          reset key-unlock keyboard
    MASTER_RESET   reset, unlock and redisplay
 (*)XOFF           please hold output
 (*)XON            please give me output
    ESCAPE          enter telnet command mode
    WORDTAB          tab to beginning of next word
    WORDBACKTAB     tab to beginning of current/last word
    WORDEND          tab to end of current/next word
    FIELDEND          tab to last non-blank of current/next
               unprotected (writable) field.


    PA1            program attention 1
    PA2            program attention 2
    PA3            program attention 3


    CLEAR          local clear of the 3270 screen
    TREQ           test request
    ENTER          enter key


    PFK1           program function key 1
    PFK2           program function key 2
    etc.           etc.
    PFK36          program function key 36
```

A SAMPLE ENTRY

The following entry is used by tn3270(1) when unable to locate a reasonable version in the user's environment and in /etc/map3270:

```
    name {        # actual name comes from TERM variable
    clear = '^z';
    flinp = '^x';
    enter = '^m';
    delete = '^d' | '^?';   # note that '^?' is delete (rubout)
    synch = '^r';
    reshow = '^v';
    eeof = '^e';
    tab = '^i';
    btab = '^b';
    nl = '^n';
    left = '^h';
    right = '^l';
    up = '^k';
    down = '^j';
    einp = '^w';
    reset = '^t';
    xoff = '^s';
    xon = '^q';
    escape = '^c';
    ferase = '^u';
    insrt = 'E ';
```

MAP3270(5)   UNIX Programmer's Manual   MAP3270(5)

```
# program attention keys
pa1 = '^p1'; pa2 = '^p2'; pa3 = '^p3';
# program function keys
pfk1 = '\E1'; pfk2 = '\E2'; pfk3 = '\E3'; pfk4 = '\E4';
pfk5 = '\E5'; pfk6 = '\E6'; pfk7 = '\E7'; pfk8 = '\E8';
pfk9 = '\E9'; pfk10 = '\E0'; pfk11 = '\E-'; pfk12 = '\E=';
pfk13 = '\E!'; pfk14 = '\E@'; pfk15 = '\E#'; pfk16 = '\E$';
pfk17 = '\E%'; pfk18 = '\E'; pfk19 = '\E&'; pfk20 = '\E*';
pfk21 = '\E('; pfk22 = '\E)'; pfk23 = '\E_'; pfk24 = '\E+';
}
```

IBM 3270 KEY DEFINITONS FOR AN ABOVE DEFINITION

The charts below show the proper keys to emulate each 3270 function when using the default key mapping supplied with *tn3270*(1) and *mset*(1).

Command Keys	IBM 3270 Key	Default Key(s)
Enter	RETURN	
Clear	control-z	
Cursor Movement Keys		
New Line	control-n or	
	Home	
Tab	control-i	
Back Tab	control-b	
Cursor Left	control-h	
Cursor Right	control-l	
Cursor Up	control-k	
Cursor Down	control-j or	
	LINE FEED	
Edit Control Keys		
Delete Char	control-d or	
	RUB	
Erase EOF	control-e	
Erase Input	control-w	
Insert Mode	ESC Space	
End Insert	ESC Space	
Program Function Keys		
PF1	ESC 1	
PF2	ESC 2	
...	...	
PF10	ESC 0	
PF11	ESC -	
PF12	ESC =	
PF13	ESC !	
PF14	ESC @	
...	...	
PF24	ESC +	
Program Attention Keys		
PA1	control-p 1	
PA2	control-p 2	
PA3	control-p 3	
Local Control Keys		
Reset After Error	control-r	
Purge Input Buffer	control-x	

MAP3270(5)   UNIX Programmer's Manual   MAP3270(5)

	Keyboard Unlock	control-t
	Redisplay Screen	control-v
Other Keys		
	Erase current field	control-u

FILES

/etc/map3270

SEE ALSO

tn3270(1), mset(1), *Yale ASCII Terminal Communication System II Program Description/Operator's Manual* (IBM SB30-1911)

AUTHOR

Greg Minshall

BUGS

Tn3270 doesn't yet understand how to process all the functions available in *map3270;* when such a function is requested *tn3270* will beep at you.

The definition of "word" (for "word erase", "word tab") should be a run-time option. Currently it is defined as the kernel tty driver defines it (strings of non-whitespace); more than one person would rather use the "vi" definition (strings of specials, strings of alphanumeric).

5

NAME
   `netgroup` – defines network groups

SYNOPSIS
   `netgroup`

DESCRIPTION
   The `netgroup` file specifies ''netgroups'', which are sets of (**host, user, domain**) tuples that are to be given similar network access.

   Each line in the file consists of a netgroup name followed by a list of the members of the netgroup. Each member can be either the name of another netgroup or a specification of a tuple as follows:

   `(host, user, domain)`

   where the **host**, **user**, and **domain** are character string names for the corresponding component. Any of the comma separated fields may be empty to specify a ''wildcard'' value or may consist of the string ''-'' to specify ''no valid value''. The members of the list may be separated by whitespace and/or commas; the ''\'' character may be used at the end of a line to specify line continuation. The functions specified in `getnetgrent`(3) should normally be used to access the **netgroup** database.

   Lines that begin with a # are treated as comments.

FILES
   `/etc/netgroup` the netgroup database.

SEE ALSO
   getnetgrent(3), exports(5)

COMPATIBILITY
   The file format is compatible with that of various vendors, however it appears that not all vendors use an identical format.

BUGS
   The interpretation of access restrictions based on the member tuples of a netgroup is left up to the various network applications. Also, it is not obvious how the domain specification applies to the BSD environment.

NAME

`networks` – network name data base

DESCRIPTION

The `networks` file contains information regarding the known networks which comprise the DARPA Internet. For each network a single line should be present with the following information:

official network name
network number
aliases

Items are separated by any number of blanks and/or tab characters. A "#" indicates the beginning of a comment; characters up to the end of the line are not interpreted by routines which search the file. This file is normally created from the official network data base maintained at the Network Information Control Center (NIC), though local changes may be required to bring it up to date regarding unofficial aliases and/or unknown networks.

Network number may be specified in the conventional "." (dot) notation using the `inet_network`(3) routine from the Internet address manipulation library, `inet`(3). Network names may contain any printable character other than a field delimiter, newline, or comment character.

FILES

`/etc/networks`   The **networks** file resides in `/etc`.

SEE ALSO

`getnetent`(3)

BUGS

A name server should be used instead of a static file.

HISTORY

The **networks** file format appeared in 4.2BSD.

NAME

`passwd` – format of the password file

DESCRIPTION

The `passwd` files are files consisting of newline separated records, one per user, containing ten colon ("`:`") separated fields. These fields are as follows:

name	User's login name.
password	User's *encrypted* password.
uid	User's id.
gid	User's login group id.
class	User's general classification (unused).
change	Password change time.
expire	Account expiration time.
gecos	General information about the user.
home_dir	User's home directory.
shell	User's login shell.

The *name* field is the login used to access the computer account, and the *uid* field is the number associated with it. They should both be unique across the system (and often across a group of systems) since they control file access.

While it is possible to have multiple entries with identical login names and/or identical user id's, it is usually a mistake to do so. Routines that manipulate these files will often return only one of the multiple entries, and that one by random selection.

The login name must never begin with a hyphen ("`-`"); also, it is strongly suggested that neither upper-case characters or dots ("`.`") be part of the name, as this tends to confuse mailers. No field may contain a colon ("`:`") as this has been used historically to separate the fields in the user database.

The password field is the *encrypted* form of the password. If the *password* field is empty, no password will be required to gain access to the machine. This is almost invariably a mistake. Because these files contain the encrypted user passwords, they should not be readable by anyone without appropriate privileges.

The group field is the group that the user will be placed in upon login. Since this system supports multiple groups (see `groups`(1)) this field currently has little special meaning.

The *class* field is currently unused. In the near future it will be a key to a `termcap`(5) style database of user attributes.

The *change* field is the number in seconds, GMT, from the epoch, until the password for the account must be changed. This field may be left empty to turn off the password aging feature.

The *expire* field is the number in seconds, GMT, from the epoch, until the account expires. This field may be left empty to turn off the account aging feature.

The *gecos* field normally contains comma ("`,`") separated subfields as follows:

name	user's full name
office	user's office number
wphone	user's work phone number
hphone	user's home phone number

This information is used by the finger(1) program.

The user's home directory is the full UNIX path name where the user will be placed on login.

The shell field is the command interpreter the user prefers. If there is nothing in the *shell* field, the Bourne shell (/bin/sh) is assumed.

SEE ALSO
chpass(1), login(1), passwd(1), getpwent(3), adduser(8), pwd_mkdb(8), vipw(8)

BUGS
User information should (and eventually will) be stored elsewhere.

COMPATIBILITY
The password file format has changed since 4.3BSD. The following awk script can be used to convert your old-style password file into a new style password file. The additional fields "class", "change" and "expire" are added, but are turned off by default. Class is currently not implemented, but change and expire are; to set them, use the current day in seconds from the epoch + whatever number of seconds of offset you want.

```
BEGIN { FS = ":"}
{ print $1 ":" $2 ":" $3 ":" $4 "::0:0:" $5 ":" $6 ":" $7 }
```

HISTORY
A **passwd** file format appeared in Version 6 AT&T UNIX.

NAME

phones – remote host phone number data base

DESCRIPTION

The file /etc/phones contains the system-wide private phone numbers for the tip(1) program. This file is normally unreadable, and so may contain privileged information. The format of the file is a series of lines of the form: <system-name>[\t]*<phone-number>. The system name is one of those defined in the remote(5) file and the phone number is constructed from any sequence of characters terminated only by ",'' or the end of the line. The "=" and "*" characters are indicators to the auto call units to pause and wait for a second dial tone (when going through an exchange). The "=" is required by the DF02-AC and the "*" is required by the BIZCOMP 1030.

Only one phone number per line is permitted. However, if more than one line in the file contains the same system name tip(1) will attempt to dial each one in turn, until it establishes a connection.

FILES

/etc/phones

SEE ALSO

tip(1), remote(5)

HISTORY

The **phones** file appeared in 4.2BSD.

5

NAME

plot – graphics interface

DESCRIPTION

Files of this format are produced by routines described in *plot*(3X) and *plot*(3F), and are interpreted for various devices by commands described in *plot*(1G). A graphics file is a stream of plotting instructions. Each instruction consists of an ASCII letter usually followed by bytes of binary information. The instructions are executed in order. A point is designated by four bytes representing the x and y values; each value is a signed integer. The last designated point in an **l, m, n, a,** or **p** instruction becomes the 'current point' for the next instruction. The **a** and **c** instructions change the current point in a manner dependent upon the specific device.

Each of the following descriptions begins with the name of the corresponding routine in *plot*(3X).

m move: The next four bytes give a new current point.

n cont: Draw a line from the current point to the point given by the next four bytes.

p point: Plot the point given by the next four bytes.

l line: Draw a line from the point given by the next four bytes to the point given by the following four bytes.

t label: Place the following ASCII string so that its first character falls on the current point. The string is terminated by a newline.

a arc: The first four bytes give the center, the next four give the starting point, and the last four give the end point of a circular arc. The least significant coordinate of the end point is used only to determine the quadrant. The arc is drawn counter-clockwise.

c circle: The first four bytes give the center of the circle, the next two the radius.

e erase: Start another frame of output.

f linemod: Take the following string, up to a newline, as the style for drawing further lines. The styles are 'dotted,' 'solid,' 'longdashed,' 'shortdashed,' and 'dotdashed.' Effective only in *plot 4014* and *plot ver*.

s space: The next four bytes give the lower left corner of the plotting area; the following four give the upper right corner. The plot will be magnified or reduced to fit the device as closely as possible.

Space settings that exactly fill the plotting area with unity scaling appear below for devices supported by the filters of *plot*(1G). The upper limit is just outside the plotting area. In every case the plotting area is taken to be square; points outside may be displayable on devices whose face isn't square.

4013	space(0, 0, 780, 780);
4014	space(0, 0, 3120, 3120);
ver	space(0, 0, 2048, 2048);
300, 300s	space(0, 0, 4096, 4096);
450	space(0, 0, 4096, 4096);

SEE ALSO

plot(1G), plot(3X), plot(3F), graph(1G)

BUGS

A *label* instruction immediately followed by a *cont* instruction does the wrong thing on a 4014.

NAME
　　　　printcap – printer capability data base

SYNOPSIS
　　　　printcap

DESCRIPTION
　　　　The **Printcap** function is a simplified version of the termcap(5) data base used to describe line printers.
　　　　The spooling system accesses the **printcap** file every time it is used, allowing dynamic addition and dele-
　　　　tion of printers. Each entry in the data base is used to describe one printer. This data base may not be sub-
　　　　stituted for, as is possible for termcap, because it may allow accounting to be bypassed.

　　　　The default printer is normally *lp*, though the environment variable PRINTER may be used to override this.
　　　　Each spooling utility supports an option, **-P** *printer*, to allow explicit naming of a destination printer.

　　　　Refer to the *4.3 BSD Line Printer Spooler Manual* for a complete discussion on how to setup the database
　　　　for a given printer.

CAPABILITIES
　　　　Refer to termcap(5) for a description of the file layout.

Name	Type	Description	
af	str	NULL	name of accounting file
br	num	none	if lp is a tty, set the baud rate (ioctl(2) call)
cf	str	NULL	cifplot data filter
df	str	NULL	tex data filter (DVI format)
fc	num	0	if lp is a tty, clear flag bits (sgtty.h)
ff	str	'\f'	string to send for a form feed
fo	bool	false	print a form feed when device is opened
fs	num	0	like 'fc' but set bits
gf	str	NULL	graph data filter (plot(3) format)
hl	bool	false	print the burst header page last
ic	bool	false	driver supports (non standard) ioctl to indent printout
if	str	NULL	name of text filter which does accounting
lf	str	/dev/console	error logging file name
lo	str	lock	name of lock file
lp	str	/dev/lp	device name to open for output
mx	num	1000	maximum file size (in BUFSIZ blocks), zero = unlimited
nd	str	NULL	next directory for list of queues (unimplemented)
nf	str	NULL	ditroff data filter (device independent troff)
of	str	NULL	name of output filtering program
pc	num	200	price per foot or page in hundredths of cents
pl	num	66	page length (in lines)
pw	num	132	page width (in characters)
px	num	0	page width in pixels (horizontal)
py	num	0	page length in pixels (vertical)
rf	str	NULL	filter for printing FORTRAN style text files
rg	str	NULL	restricted group. Only members of group allowed access
rm	str	NULL	machine name for remote printer
rp	str	"lp"	remote printer name argument

rs	bool	false	restrict remote users to those with local accounts
rw	bool	false	open the printer device for reading and writing
sb	bool	false	short banner (one line only)
sc	bool	false	suppress multiple copies
sd	str	/var/spool/lpd	spool directory
sf	bool	false	suppress form feeds
sh	bool	false	suppress printing of burst page header
st	str	status	status file name
tf	str	NULL	troff data filter (cat phototypesetter)
tr	str	NULL	trailer string to print when queue empties
vf	str	NULL	raster image filter
xc	num	0	if lp is a tty, clear local mode bits (tty(4))
xs	num	0	like 'xc' but set bits

If the local line printer driver supports indentation, the daemon must understand how to invoke it.

FILTERS

The lpd(8) daemon creates a pipeline of *filters* to process files for various printer types. The filters selected depend on the flags passed to lpr(1). The pipeline set up is:

```
p       pr | if regular text + pr(1)
none    if       regular text
c       cf       cifplot
d       df       DVI (tex)
g       gf       plot(3)
n       nf       ditroff
f       rf       Fortran
t       tf       troff
v       vf       raster image
```

The **if** filter is invoked with arguments:

    if [−c] −w*width* −l*length* −i*indent* −n *login* −h *host acct-file*

The −c flag is passed only if the −l flag (pass control characters literally) is specified to lpr. The *Width* function and *length* specify the page width and length (from **pw** and **pl** respectively) in characters. The −n and −h parameters specify the login name and host name of the owner of the job respectively. The *Acct-file* function is passed from the **af printcap** entry.

If no **if** is specified, **of** is used instead, with the distinction that **of** is opened only once, while **if** is opened for every individual job. Thus, **if** is better suited to performing accounting. The **of** is only given the *width* and *length* flags.

All other filters are called as:

    filter −x*width* −y*length* −n *login* −h *host acct-file*

where *width* and *length* are represented in pixels, specified by the **px** and **py** entries respectively.

All filters take *stdin* as the file, *stdout* as the printer, may log either to *stderr* or using syslog(3), and must not ignore SIGINT.

LOGGING

Error messages generated by the line printer programs themselves (that is, the lp* programs) are logged by syslog(3) using the LPR facility. Messages printed on *stderr* of one of the filters are sent to the corresponding **lf** file. The filters may, of course, use syslog themselves.

Error messages sent to the console have a carriage return and a line feed appended to them, rather than just a line feed.

SEE ALSO

termcap(5), lpc(8), lpd(8), pac(8), lpr(1), lpq(1), lprm(1)

4.3 BSD Line Printer Spooler Manual.

HISTORY

The printcap file format appeared in 4.2BSD..

NAME

`protocols` – protocol name data base

DESCRIPTION

The **protocols** file contains information regarding the known protocols used in the DARPA Internet. For each protocol a single line should be present with the following information:

        official protocol name
        protocol number
        aliases

Items are separated by any number of blanks and/or tab characters. A "#" indicates the beginning of a comment; characters up to the end of the line are not interpreted by routines which search the file.

Protocol names may contain any printable character other than a field delimiter, newline, or comment character.

FILES

`/etc/protocols` The **protocols** file resides in `/etc`.

SEE ALSO

`getprotoent`(3)

BUGS

A name server should be used instead of a static file.

HISTORY

The **protocols** file format appeared in 4.2BSD.

5

NAME

publickey – public key database

SYNOPSIS

/etc/publickey

DESCRIPTION

/etc/publickey is the public key database used for secure networking. Each entry in the database consists of a network user name (which may either refer to a user or a hostname), followed by the user's public key (in hex notation), a colon, and then the user's secret key encrypted with its login password (also in hex notation).

This file is altered either by the user through the **chkey**(1) command or by the system administrator through the **newkey**(8) command. The file **/etc/publickey** should only contain data on the Yellow Pages master machine, where it is converted into the YP database **publickey.byname**.

SEE ALSO

chkey(1), **publickey**(3R), **newkey**(8), **ypupdated**(8C)

NAME

ranlib – archive (library) table-of-contents format

SYNOPSIS

```
#include <ranlib.h>
```

DESCRIPTION

The archive table-of-contents command **ranlib** creates a table of contents for archives, containing object files, to be used by the link-editor ld(1). It operates on archives created with the utility ar(1).

The **Ranlib** function prepends a new file to the archive which has three separate parts. The first part is a standard archive header, which has a special name field, "__.SYMDEF".

The second part is a ''long'' followed by a list of ranlib structures. The long is the size, in bytes, of the list of ranlib structures. Each of the ranlib structures consists of a zero based offset into the next section (a string table of symbols) and an offset from the beginning of the archive to the start of the archive file which defines the symbol. The actual number of ranlib structures is this number divided by the size of an individual ranlib structure.

The third part is a ''long'' followed by a string table. The long is the size, in bytes of the string table.

SEE ALSO

ar(1), ranlib(1)

NAME

    rcsfile – format of RCS file

DESCRIPTION

    An RCS file's contents are described by the grammar below.

    The text is free format: space, backspace, tab, newline, vertical tab, form feed, and carriage return (collectively, *white space*) have no significance except in strings. However, an RCS file must end in a newline character.

    Strings are enclosed by **@**. If a string contains a **@**, it must be doubled; otherwise, strings may contain arbitrary binary data.

    The meta syntax uses the following conventions: 'l' (bar) separates alternatives; '{' and '}' enclose optional phrases; '{' and '}*' enclose phrases that may be repeated zero or more times; '{' and '}+' enclose phrases that must appear at least once and may be repeated; Terminal symbols are in **boldface**; nonterminal symbols are in *italics*.

rcstext	::=	*admin {delta}* desc {deltatext}**	
admin	::=	**head**	*{num}*;
		{ branch	*{num}*; **}**
		access	*{id}**;
		symbols	*{id : num}**;
		locks	*{id : num}**; **{strict ;}**
		{ comment	*{string}*; **}**
		{ expand	*{string}*; **}**
		{ *newphrase* **}***	
delta	::=	*num*	
		date	*num*;
		author	*id*;
		state	*{id}*;
		branches	*{num}**;
		next	*{num}*;
		{ *newphrase* **}***	
desc	::=	**desc**	*string*
deltatext	::=	*num*	
		log	*string*
		{ *newphrase* **}***	
		text	*string*
num	::=	*{digit{.}}+*	
digit	::=	**0** l **1** l ... l **9**	
id	::=	*letter{idchar}**	
letter	::=	any letter	
idchar	::=	any visible graphic character except *special*	
special	::=	**$** l **,** l **.** l **:** l **;** l **@**	
string	::=	**@**{any character, with **@** doubled}***@**	
newphrase	::=	*id word** ;	
word	::=	*id* l *num* l *string* l **:**	

    Identifiers are case sensitive. Keywords are in lower case only. The sets of keywords and identifiers may overlap. In most environments RCS uses the ISO 8859/1 encoding: letters are octal codes 101–132, 141–172, 300–326, 330–366 and 370–377, visible graphic characters are codes 041–176 and 240–377, and white space characters are codes 010–015 and 040.

The *newphrase* productions in the grammar are reserved for future extensions to the format of RCS files. No *newphrase* will begin with any keyword already in use.

The *delta* nodes form a tree. All nodes whose numbers consist of a single pair (e.g., 2.3, 2.1, 1.3, etc.) are on the trunk, and are linked through the **next** field in order of decreasing numbers. The **head** field in the *admin* node points to the head of that sequence (i.e., contains the highest pair). The **branch** node in the admin node indicates the default branch (or revision) for most RCS operations. If empty, the default branch is the highest branch on the trunk.

All *delta* nodes whose numbers consist of $2n$ fields (n) (e.g., 3.1.1.1, 2.1.2.2, etc.) are linked as follows. All nodes whose first $2n-1$ number fields are identical are linked through the **next** field in order of increasing numbers. For each such sequence, the *delta* node whose number is identical to the first $2n-2$ number fields of the deltas on that sequence is called the branchpoint. The **branches** field of a node contains a list of the numbers of the first nodes of all sequences for which it is a branchpoint. This list is ordered in increasing numbers.

Example:

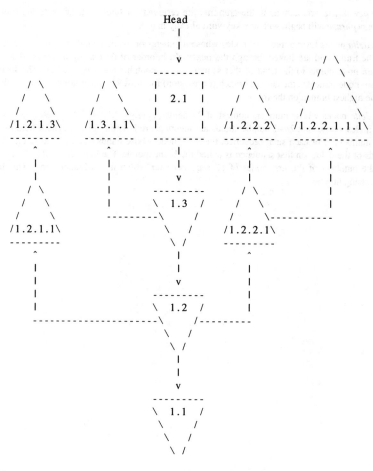

Fig. 1: A revision tree

IDENTIFICATION

Author: Walter F. Tichy, Purdue University, West Lafayette, IN, 47907.
Revision Number: 5.1; Release Date: 1991/08/19.
Copyright © 1982, 1988, 1989 by Walter F. Tichy.
Copyright © 1990, 1991 by Paul Eggert.

SEE ALSO

ci(1), co(1), ident(1), rcs(1), rcsdiff(1), rcsmerge(1), rlog(1),
Walter F. Tichy, RCS—A System for Version Control, *Software—Practice & Experience* **15**, 7 (July 1985), 637-654.

NAME

`remote` – remote host description file

DESCRIPTION

The systems known by `tip(1)` and their attributes are stored in an ASCII file which is structured somewhat like the `termcap`(5) file. Each line in the file provides a description for a single `system`. Fields are separated by a colon ("`:`"). Lines ending in a `\` character with an immediately following newline are continued on the next line.

The first entry is the name(s) of the host system. If there is more than one name for a system, the names are separated by vertical bars. After the name of the system comes the fields of the description. A field name followed by an '`=`' sign indicates a string value follows. A field name followed by a '#' sign indicates a following numeric value.

Entries named "tip*" and "cu*" are used as default entries by `tip`, and the `cu` interface to `tip`, as follows. When `tip` is invoked with only a phone number, it looks for an entry of the form "tip300", where 300 is the baud rate with which the connection is to be made. When the `cu` interface is used, entries of the form "cu300" are used.

CAPABILITIES

Capabilities are either strings (str), numbers (num), or boolean flags (bool). A string capability is specified by *capability=value*; for example, "dv=/dev/harris". A numeric capability is specified by *capability#value*; for example, "xa#99". A boolean capability is specified by simply listing the capability.

at	(str) Auto call unit type.
br	(num) The baud rate used in establishing a connection to the remote host. This is a decimal number. The default baud rate is 300 baud.
cm	(str) An initial connection message to be sent to the remote host. For example, if a host is reached through port selector, this might be set to the appropriate sequence required to switch to the host.
cu	(str) Call unit if making a phone call. Default is the same as the 'dv' field.
di	(str) Disconnect message sent to the host when a disconnect is requested by the user.
du	(bool) This host is on a dial-up line.
dv	(str) UNIX device(s) to open to establish a connection. If this file refers to a terminal line, `tip`(1) attempts to perform an exclusive open on the device to insure only one user at a time has access to the port.
el	(str) Characters marking an end-of-line. The default is NULL. '˜' escapes are only recognized by `tip` after one of the characters in 'el', or after a carriage-return.
fs	(str) Frame size for transfers. The default frame size is equal to BUFSIZ.
hd	(bool) The host uses half-duplex communication, local echo should be performed.
ie	(str) Input end-of-file marks. The default is NULL.
oe	(str) Output end-of-file string. The default is NULL. When `tip` is transferring a file, this string is sent at end-of-file.

pa   (str) The type of parity to use when sending data to the host. This may be one of "even", "odd", "none", "zero" (always set bit 8 to zero), "one" (always set bit 8 to 1). The default is even parity.

pn   (str) Telephone number(s) for this host. If the telephone number field contains an @ sign, tip searches the file /etc/phones file for a list of telephone numbers; (See phones(5).)

tc   (str) Indicates that the list of capabilities is continued in the named description. This is used primarily to share common capability information.

Here is a short example showing the use of the capability continuation feature:

```
UNIX-1200:\
	:dv=/dev/cau0:el=^D^U^C^S^Q^O@:du:at=ventel:ie=#$%:oe=^D:br#1200:
arpavax|ax:\
	:pn=7654321%:tc=UNIX-1200
```

FILES
/etc/remote The **remote** host description file resides in /etc.

SEE ALSO
tip(1), phones(5)

HISTORY
The **remote** file format appeared in 4.2BSD.

5

NAME

`resolver` – resolver configuration file

SYNOPSIS

`resolv.conf`

DESCRIPTION

The `resolver`(3) is a set of routines in the C library which provide access to the Internet Domain Name System. The resolver configuration file contains information that is read by the resolver routines the first time they are invoked by a process. The file is designed to be human readable and contains a list of keywords with values that provide various types of resolver information.

On a normally configured system this file should not be necessary. The only name server to be queried will be on the local machine, the domain name is determined from the host name, and the domain search path is constructed from the domain name.

The different configuration options are:

nameserver   Internet address (in dot notation) of a name server that the resolver should query. Up to MAXNS (currently 3) name servers may be listed, one per keyword. If there are multiple servers, the resolver library queries them in the order listed. If no **nameserver** entries are present, the default is to use the name server on the local machine. (The algorithm used is to try a name server, and if the query times out, try the next, until out of name servers, then repeat trying all the name servers until a maximum number of retries are made).

domain   Local domain name. Most queries for names within this domain can use short names relative to the local domain. If no **domain** entry is present, the domain is determined from the local host name returned by `gethostname`(2); the domain part is taken to be everything after the first '.'. Finally, if the host name does not contain a domain part, the root domain is assumed.

search   Search list for host-name lookup. The search list is normally determined from the local domain name; by default, it begins with the local domain name, then successive parent domains that have at least two components in their names. This may be changed by listing the desired domain search path following the **search** keyword with spaces or tabs separating the names. Most resolver queries will be attempted using each component of the search path in turn until a match is found. Note that this process may be slow and will generate a lot of network traffic if the servers for the listed domains are not local, and that queries will time out if no server is available for one of the domains.

The search list is currently limited to six domains with a total of 256 characters.

The **domain** and **search** keywords are mutually exclusive. If more than one instance of these keywords is present, the last instance will override.

The keyword and value must appear on a single line, and the keyword (e.g. **nameserver**) must start the line. The value follows the keyword, separated by white space.

FILES

`/etc/resolv.conf` The file **resolv.conf** resides in `/etc`.

SEE ALSO

`gethostbyname`(3), `resolver`(3), `hostname`(7), `named`(8)

Name Server Operations Guide for BIND.

HISTORY

The `resolv.conf` file format appeared in 4.3BSD.

NAME

rpc – rpc program number data base

SYNOPSIS

/etc/rpc

DESCRIPTION

The *rpc* file contains user readable names that can be used in place of rpc program numbers. Each line has the following information:

name of server for the rpc program
rpc program number
aliases

Items are separated by any number of blanks and/or tab characters. A "#" indicates the beginning of a comment; characters up to the end of the line are not interpreted by routines which search the file.

Here is an example of the */etc/rpc* file from the Sun RPC Source distribution.

```
#
# rpc 88/08/01 4.0 RPCSRC; from 1.12   88/02/07 SMI
#
portmapper       100000    portmap sunrpc
rstatd           100001    rstat rstat_svc rup perfmeter
rusersd          100002    rusers
nfs              100003    nfsprog
ypserv           100004    ypprog
mountd           100005    mount showmount
ypbind           100007
walld            100008    rwall shutdown
yppasswdd        100009    yppasswd
etherstatd       100010    etherstat
rquotad          100011    rquotaprog quota rquota
sprayd           100012    spray
3270_mapper      100013
rje_mapper       100014
selection_svc    100015    selnsvc
database_svc     100016
rexd             100017    rex
alis             100018
sched            100019
llockmgr         100020
nlockmgr         100021
x25.inr          100022
statmon          100023
status           100024
bootparam        100026
ypupdated        100028    ypupdate
keyserv          100029    keyserver
tfsd             100037
nsed             100038
nsemntd          100039
```

FILES

/etc/rpc

SEE ALSO

getrpcent(3N)

NAME

`services` – service name data base

DESCRIPTION

The **services** file contains information regarding the known services available in the DARPA Internet. For each service a single line should be present with the following information:

> official service name
> port number
> protocol name
> aliases

Items are separated by any number of blanks and/or tab characters. The port number and protocol name are considered a single *item*; a "/" is used to separate the port and protocol (e.g. "512/tcp"). A "#" indicates the beginning of a comment; subsequent characters up to the end of the line are not interpreted by the routines which search the file.

Service names may contain any printable character other than a field delimiter, newline, or comment character.

FILES

`/etc/services` The **services** file resides in `/etc`.

SEE ALSO

`getservent`(3)

BUGS

A name server should be used instead of a static file.

HISTORY

The **services** file format appeared in 4.2BSD.

NAME

    shells – shell database

DESCRIPTION

    The **shells** file contains a list of the shells on the system. For each shell a single line should be present, consisting of the shell's path, relative to root.

    A hash mark ("#") indicates the beginning of a comment; subsequent characters up to the end of the line are not interpreted by the routines which search the file. Blank lines are also ignored.

FILES

    /etc/shells The **shells** file resides in /etc.

SEE ALSO

    getusershell(3)

HISTORY

    The **shells** file format appeared in 4.3BSD–Tahoe.

5

NAME

stab – symbol table types

SYNOPSIS

`#include <stab.h>`

DESCRIPTION

The file <stab.h> defines some of the symbol table *n_type* field values for a.out files. These are the types for permanent symbols (i.e. not local labels, etc.) used by the old debugger *sdb* and the Berkeley Pascal compiler pc(1). Symbol table entries can be produced by the .stabs assembler directive. This allows one to specify a double-quote delimited name, a symbol type, one char and one short of information about the symbol, and an unsigned long (usually an address). To avoid having to produce an explicit label for the address field, the .stabd directive can be used to implicitly address the current location. If no name is needed, symbol table entries can be generated using the .stabn directive. The loader promises to preserve the order of symbol table entries produced by .stab directives. As described in a.out(5), an element of the symbol table consists of the following structure:

```
/*
 * Format of a symbol table entry.
 */

struct nlist {
        union {
                char    *n_name;        /* for use when in-core */
                long    n_strx;         /* index into file string table */
        } n_un;
        unsigned char   n_type;         /* type flag */
        char            n_other;        /* unused */
        short           n_desc;         /* see struct desc, below */
        unsigned        n_value;        /* address or offset or line */
};
```

The low bits of the *n_type* field are used to place a symbol into at most one segment, according to the following masks, defined in <a.out.h>. A symbol can be in none of these segments by having none of these segment bits set.

```
/*
 * Simple values for n_type.
 */

#define N_UNDF  0x0     /* undefined */
#define N_ABS   0x2     /* absolute */
#define N_TEXT  0x4     /* text */
#define N_DATA  0x6     /* data */
#define N_BSS   0x8     /* bss */

#define N_EXT   01      /* external bit, or'ed in */
```

The *n_value* field of a symbol is relocated by the linker, ld(1) as an address within the appropriate segment. *N_value* fields of symbols not in any segment are unchanged by the linker. In addition, the linker will discard certain symbols, according to rules of its own, unless the *n_type* field has one of the following bits set:

```
/*
 * Other permanent symbol table entries have some of the N_STAB bits set.
 * These are given in <stab.h>
 */
```

```
#define N_STAB 0xe0     /* if any of these bits set, don't discard */
```

This allows up to 112 (7 * 16) symbol types, split between the various segments. Some of these have already been claimed. The old symbolic debugger, *sdb*, uses the following n_type values:

```
#define N_GSYM  0x20    /* global symbol: name,,0,type,0 */
#define N_FNAME 0x22    /* procedure name (f77 kludge): name,,0 */
#define N_FUN   0x24    /* procedure: name,,0,linenumber,address */
#define N_STSYM 0x26    /* static symbol: name,,0,type,address */
#define N_LCSYM 0x28    /* .lcomm symbol: name,,0,type,address */
#define N_RSYM  0x40    /* register sym: name,,0,type,register */
#define N_SLINE 0x44    /* src line: 0,,0,linenumber,address */
#define N_SSYM  0x60    /* structure elt: name,,0,type,struct_offset */
#define N_SO    0x64    /* source file name: name,,0,0,address */
#define N_LSYM  0x80    /* local sym: name,,0,type,offset */
#define N_SOL   0x84    /* #included file name: name,,0,0,address */
#define N_PSYM  0xa0    /* parameter: name,,0,type,offset */
#define N_ENTRY 0xa4    /* alternate entry: name,linenumber,address */
#define N_LBRAC 0xc0    /* left bracket: 0,,0,nesting level,address */
#define N_RBRAC 0xe0    /* right bracket: 0,,0,nesting level,address */
#define N_BCOMM 0xe2    /* begin common: name,, */
#define N_ECOMM 0xe4    /* end common: name,, */
#define N_ECOML 0xe8    /* end common (local name): ,,address */
#define N_LENG  0xfe    /* second stab entry with length information */
```

where the comments give *sdb* conventional use for .stab s and the *n_name*, *n_other*, *n_desc*, and *n_value* fields of the given *n_type*. *Sdb* uses the *n_desc* field to hold a type specifier in the form used by the Portable C Compiler, cc(1); see the header file pcc.h for details on the format of these type values.

The Berkeley Pascal compiler, pc(1), uses the following *n_type* value:

```
#define N_PC    0x30    /* global pascal symbol: name,,0,subtype,line */
```

and uses the following subtypes to do type checking across separately compiled files:

1	source file name
2	included file name
3	global label
4	global constant
5	global type
6	global variable
7	global function
8	global procedure
9	external function
10	external procedure
11	library variable
12	library routine

5

SEE ALSO

as(1), ld(1), dbx(1), a.out(5)

BUGS

More basic types are needed.

HISTORY

The **stab** file appeared in 4.0BSD.

NAME

syslog.conf – syslogd(8) configuration file

DESCRIPTION

The **syslog.conf** file is the configuration file for the syslogd(8) program. It consists of lines with two fields: the *selector* field which specifies the types of messages and priorities to which the line applies, and an *action* field which specifies the action to be taken if a message syslogd receives matches the selection criteria. The *selector* field is separated from the *action* field by one or more tab characters.

The *Selectors* function are encoded as a *facility*, a period ("."), and a *level*, with no intervening white-space. Both the *facility* and the *level* are case insensitive.

The *facility* describes the part of the system generating the message, and is one of the following keywords: auth, authpriv, cron, daemon, kern, lpr, mail, mark, news, syslog, user, uucp and local0 through local7. These keywords (with the exception of mark) correspond to the similar "LOG_" values specified to the openlog(3) and syslog(3) library routines.

The *level* describes the severity of the message, and is a keyword from the following ordered list (higher to lower): emerg, alert, crit, err, warning, notice and debug. These keywords correspond to the similar (LOG_) values specified to the syslog library routine.

See syslog(3) for a further descriptions of both the *facility* and *level* keywords and their significance.

If a received message matches the specified *facility* and is of the specified *level (or a higher level)*, the action specified in the *action* field will be taken.

Multiple *selectors* may be specified for a single *action* by separating them with semicolon (";") characters. It is important to note, however, that each *selector* can modify the ones preceding it.

Multiple *facilities* may be specified for a single *level* by separating them with comma (",") characters.

An asterisk ("*") can be used to specify all *facilities* or all *levels*.

The special *facility* "mark" receives a message at priority "info" every 20 minutes (see syslogd(8)). This is not enabled by a *facility* field containing an asterisk.

The special *level* "none" disables a particular *facility*.

The *action* field of each line specifies the action to be taken when the *selector* field selects a message. There are four forms:

- A pathname (beginning with a leading slash). Selected messages are appended to the file.

- A hostname (preceded by an at ("@") sign). Selected messages are forwarded to the syslogd program on the named host.

- A comma separated list of users. Selected messages are written to those users if they are logged in.

- An asterisk. Selected messages are written to all logged-in users.

Blank lines and lines whose first non-blank character is a hash ("#") character are ignored.

EXAMPLES

A configuration file might appear as follows:

```
# Log all kernel messages, authentication messages of
# level notice or higher and anything of level err or
# higher to the console.
# Don't log private authentication messages!
```

```
*.err;kern.*;auth.notice;authpriv.none          /dev/console

# Log anything (except mail) of level info or higher.
# Don't log private authentication messages!
*.info;mail.none;authpriv.none           /var/log/messages

# The authpriv file has restricted access.
authpriv.*                               /var/log/secure

# Log all the mail messages in one place.
mail.*                                   /var/log/maillog

# Everybody gets emergency messages, plus log them on another
# machine.
*.emerg                                  *
*.emerg                                  @arpa.berkeley.edu

# Root and Eric get alert and higher messages.
*.alert                                  root,eric

# Save mail and news errors of level err and higher in a
# special file.
uucp,news.crit                           /var/log/spoolerr
```

FILES

    /etc/syslog.conf The syslogd(8) configuration file.

BUGS

    The effects of multiple selectors are sometimes not intuitive. For example ''mail.crit,*.err'' will select
    ''mail'' facility messages at the level of ''err'' or higher, not at the level of ''crit'' or higher.

SEE ALSO

    syslog(3), syslogd(8)

NAME

tar – tape archive file format

DESCRIPTION

The **tar** tape archive command dumps several files into one, in a medium suitable for transportation.

A "tar tape" or file is a series of blocks. Each block is of size TBLOCK. A file on the tape is represented by a header block which describes the file, followed by zero or more blocks which give the contents of the file. At the end of the tape are two blocks filled with binary zeros, as an end-of-file indicator.

The blocks are grouped for physical I/O operations. Each group of *n* functions blocks (where *n* is set by the **b** keyletter on the tar(1) command line — default is 20 blocks) is written with a single system call; on nine-track tapes, the result of this write is a single tape record. The last group is always written at the full size, so blocks after the two zero blocks contain random data. On reading, the specified or default group size is used for the first read, but if that read returns less than a full tape block, the reduced block size is used for further reads.

The header block looks like:

```
#define TBLOCK 512
#define NBLOCK 20
#define NAMSIZ 100

union hblock {
        char dummy[TBLOCK];
        struct header {
                char name[NAMSIZ];
                char mode[8];
                char uid[8];
                char gid[8];
                char size[12];
                char mtime[12];
                char chksum[8];
                char linkflag;
                char linkname[NAMSIZ];
        } dbuf;
};
```

The *name* field is a null-terminated string. The other fields are zero-filled octal numbers in ASCII. Each field (of width w) contains w−2 digits, a space, and a null, except *size* and *mtime*, which do not contain the trailing null and *chksum* which has a null followed by a space. *Name* is the name of the file, as specified on the **tar** command line. Files dumped because they were in a directory which was named in the command line have the directory name as prefix and /filename as suffix. *Mode* is the file mode, with the top bit masked off. *Uid* and *gid* are the user and group numbers which own the file. *Size* is the size of the file in bytes. Links and symbolic links are dumped with this field specified as zero. *Mtime* is the modification time of the file at the time it was dumped. *Chksum* is an octal ASCII value which represents the sum of all the bytes in the header block. When calculating the checksum, the *chksum* field is treated as if it were all blanks. *Linkflag* is NULL if the file is "normal" or a special file, ASCII '1' if it is a hard link, and ASCII '2' if it is a symbolic link. The name linked-to, if any, is in *linkname*, with a trailing null. Unused fields of the header are binary zeros (and are included in the checksum).

The first time a given i-node number is dumped, it is dumped as a regular file. The second and subsequent times, it is dumped as a link instead. Upon retrieval, if a link entry is retrieved, but not the file it was linked to, an error message is printed and the tape must be manually re-scanned to retrieve the linked-to file.

The encoding of the header is designed to be portable across machines.

SEE ALSO
tar(1)

BUGS
Names or linknames longer than NAMSIZ produce error reports and cannot be dumped.

HISTORY
The **tar** file format manual appeared in 4.2BSD.

NAME

termcap – terminal capability data base

SYNOPSIS

termcap

DESCRIPTION

The **Termcap** file is a data base describing terminals, used, for example, by vi(1) and curses(3). Terminals are described in **termcap** by giving a set of capabilities that they have and by describing how operations are performed. Padding requirements and initialization sequences are included in **termcap**.

Entries in **termcap** consist of a number of ':'-separated fields. The first entry for each terminal gives the names that are known for the terminal, separated by 'I' characters. The first name given is the most common abbreviation for the terminal. The last name given should be a long name fully identifying the terminal, and all others are understood as synonyms for the terminal name. All names but the last should be in lower case and contain no blanks; the last name may well contain upper case characters and blanks for readability.

Terminal names (except for the last, verbose entry) should be chosen using the following conventions. The particular piece of hardware making up the terminal should have a root name chosen, thus ''hp2621'' This name should not contain hyphens. Modes that the hardware can be in or user preferences should be indicated by appending a hyphen and an indicator of the mode. Therefore, a ''vt100'' in 132-column mode would be ''vt100-w''. The following suffixes should be used where possible:

Suffix	Meaning	Example
-w	Wide mode (more than 80 columns)	vt100-w
-am	With automatic margins (usually default)	vt100-am
-nam	Without automatic margins	vt100-nam
$-n$	Number of lines on screen	aaa-60
-na	No arrow keys (leave them in local)	concept100-na
$-np$	Number of pages of memory	concept100-4p
-rv	Reverse video	concept100-rv

CAPABILITIES

The characters in the *Notes* function field in the table have the following meanings (more than one may apply to a capability):

N	indicates numeric parameter(s)
P	indicates that padding may be specified
*	indicates that padding may be based on the number of lines affected
o	indicates capability is obsolete

''Obsolete'' capabilities have no *terminfo* equivalents, since they were considered useless, or are subsumed by other capabilities. New software should not rely on them at all.

Name	Type	Notes	Description
functions			
ae	str	(P)	End alternate character set.
AL	str	(NP*)	Add" *n* new blank lines
al	str	(P*)	Add new blank line.
am	bool		Terminal has automatic margins.
as	str	(P)	Start alternate character set.

bc	str	(o)	Backspace if not. **^H**.
bl	str	(P)	Audible signal (bell).
bs	bool	(o)	Terminal can backspace with **^H**.
bt	str	(P)	Back tab.
bw	bool		**le** (backspace) wraps from column 0 to last column.
CC	str		Terminal settable command character in prototype.
cd	str	(P*)	Clear to end of display.
ce	str	(P)	Clear to end of line.
ch	str	(NP)	Set cursor column (horizontal position).
cl	str	(P*)	Clear screen and home cursor.
CM	str	(NP)	Memory-relative cursor addressing.
cm	str	(NP)	Screen-relative cursor motion.
co	num		Number of columns in a line (See BUGS section below).
cr	str	(P)	Carriage return.
cs	str	(NP)	Change scrolling region (VT100).
ct	str	(P)	Clear all tab stops.
cv	str	(NP)	Set cursor row (vertical position).
da	bool		Display may be retained above the screen.
dB	num	(o)	Milliseconds of **bs** delay needed (default 0).
db	bool		Display may be retained below the screen.
DC	str	(NP*)	Delete n characters.
dC	num	(o)	Milliseconds of **cr** delay needed (default 0).
dc	str	(P*)	Delete character.
dF	num	(o)	Milliseconds of **ff** delay needed (default 0).
DL	str	(NP*)	Delete n lines.
dl	str	(P*)	Delete line.
dm	str		Enter delete mode.
dN	num	(o)	Milliseconds of **nl** delay needed (default 0).
DO	str	(NP*)	Move cursor down: n lines.
do	str		Down one line.
ds	str		Disable status line.
dT	num	(o)	Milliseconds of horizontal tab delay needed (default 0).
dV	num	(o)	Milliseconds of vertical tab delay needed (default 0).
ec	str	(NP)	Erase n characters.
ed	str		End delete mode.
ei	str		End insert mode.
eo	bool		Can erase overstrikes with a blank.
EP	bool	(o)	Even parity.
es	bool		Escape can be used on the status line.
ff	str	(P*)	Hardcopy terminal page eject.
fs	str		Return from status line.
gn	bool		Generic line type, for example dialup, switch).
hc	bool		Hardcopy terminal.
HD	bool	(o)	Half-duplex.
hd	str		Half-line down (forward 1/2 linefeed).
ho	str	(P)	Home cursor.
hs	bool		Has extra "status line".
hu	str		Half-line up (reverse 1/2 linefeed).
hz	bool		Cannot print "~" (Hazeltine).

i1-i3	str		Terminal initialization strings (`terminfo` only)
IC	str	(NP*)	Insert *n* blank characters.
ic	str	(P*)	Insert character.
if	str		Name of file containing initialization string.
im	str		Enter insert mode.
in	bool		Insert mode distinguishes nulls.
iP	str		Pathname of program for initialization (`terminfo` only).
ip	str	(P*)	Insert pad after character inserted.
is	str		Terminal initialization string (`termcap` only).
it	num		Tabs initially every *n* positions.
K1	str		Sent by keypad upper left.
K2	str		Sent by keypad upper right.
K3	str		Sent by keypad center.
K4	str		Sent by keypad lower left.
K5	str		Sent by keypad lower right.
k0-k9	str		Sent by function keys 0-9.
kA	str		Sent by insert-line key.
ka	str		Sent by clear-all-tabs key.
kb	str		Sent by backspace key.
kC	str		Sent by clear-screen or erase key.
kD	str		Sent by delete-character key.
kd	str		Sent by down-arrow key.
kE	str		Sent by clear-to-end-of-line key.
ke	str		Out of "keypad transmit" mode.
kF	str		Sent by scroll-forward/down key.
kH	str		Sent by home-down key.
kh	str		Sent by home key.
kI	str		Sent by insert-character or enter-insert-mode key.
kL	str		Sent by delete-line key.
kl	str		Sent by left-arrow key.
kM	str		Sent by insert key while in insert mode.
km	bool		Has a "meta" key (shift, sets parity bit).
kN	str		Sent by next-page key.
kn	num	(o)	Number of function (**k0**– **k9**) keys (default 0).
ko	str	(o)	Termcap entries for other non-function keys.
kP	str		Sent by previous-page key.
kR	str		Sent by scroll-backward/up key.
kr	str		Sent by right-arrow key.
kS	str		Sent by clear-to-end-of-screen key.
ks	str		Put terminal in "keypad transmit" mode.
kT	str		Sent by set-tab key.
kt	str		Sent by clear-tab key.
ku	str		Sent by up-arrow key.
l0-l9	str		Labels on function keys if not "f*n*".
LC	bool	(o)	Lower-case only.
LE	str	(NP)	Move cursor left *n* positions.
le	str	(P)	Move cursor left one position.
li	num		Number of lines on screen or page (See BUGS section below)
ll	str		Last line, first column

lm	num		Lines of memory if > **li** (0 means varies).
ma	str	(o)	Arrow key map (used by vi version 2 only).
mb	str		Turn on blinking attribute.
md	str		Turn on bold (extra bright) attribute.
me	str		Turn off all attributes.
mh	str		Turn on half-bright attribute.
mi	bool		Safe to move while in insert mode.
mk	str		Turn on blank attribute (characters invisible).
ml	str	(o)	Memory lock on above cursor.
mm	str		Turn on ''meta mode'' (8th bit).
mo	str		Turn off ''meta mode''.
mp	str		Turn on protected attribute.
mr	str		Turn on reverse-video attribute.
ms	bool		Safe to move in standout modes.
mu	str	(o)	Memory unlock (turn off memory lock).
nc	bool	(o)	No correctly-working **cr** (Datamedia 2500, Hazeltine 2000).
nd	str		Non-destructive space (cursor right).
NL	bool	(o)	**\n** is newline, not line feed.
nl	str	(o)	Newline character if not **\n**.
ns	bool	(o)	Terminal is a CRT but doesn't scroll.
nw	str	(P)	Newline (behaves like **cr** followed by **do**).
OP	bool	(o)	Odd parity.
os	bool		Terminal overstrikes.
pb	num		Lowest baud where delays are required.
pc	str		Pad character (default NUL).
pf	str		Turn off the printer.
pk	str		Program function key n to type string s (terminfo only).
pl	str		Program function key n to execute string s (terminfo only).
pO	str	(N)	Turn on the printer for n bytes.
po	str		Turn on the printer.
ps	str		Print contents of the screen.
pt	bool	(o)	Has hardware tabs (may need to be set with **is**).
px	str		Program function key n to transmit string s (terminfo only).
r1-r3	str		Reset terminal completely to sane modes (terminfo only).
rc	str	(P)	Restore cursor to position of last **sc**.
rf	str		Name of file containing reset codes.
RI	str	(NP)	Move cursor right n positions.
rp	str	(NP*)	Repeat character c n times.
rs	str		Reset terminal completely to sane modes (**termcap** only).
sa	str	(NP)	Define the video attributes.
sc	str	(P)	Save cursor position.
se	str		End standout mode.
SF	str	(NP*)	Scroll forward n lines.
sf	str	(P)	Scroll text up.
sg	num		Number of garbage chars left by **so** or **se** (default 0).
so	str		Begin standout mode.
SR	str	(NP*)	Scroll backward n lines.
sr	str	(P)	Scroll text down.
st	str		Set a tab in all rows, current column.

5

ta	str	(P)	Tab to next 8-position hardware tab stop.
tc	str		Entry of similar terminal – must be last.
te	str		String to end programs that use **termcap**.
ti	str		String to begin programs that use **termcap**.
ts	str	(N)	Go to status line, column *n*.
UC	bool	(o)	Upper-case only.
uc	str		Underscore one character and move past it.
ue	str		End underscore mode.
ug	num		Number of garbage chars left by **us** or **ue** (default 0).
ul	bool		Underline character overstrikes.
UP	str	(NP∗)	Move cursor up *n* lines.
up	str		Upline (cursor up).
us	str		Start underscore mode.
vb	str		Visible bell (must not move cursor).
ve	str		Make cursor appear normal (undo **vs**/ **vi**).
vi	str		Make cursor invisible.
vs	str		Make cursor very visible.
vt	num		Virtual terminal number (not supported on all systems).
wi	str	(N)	Set current window.
ws	num		Number of columns in status line.
xb	bool		Beehive (f1= ESC, f2=^**C**).
xn	bool		Newline ignored after 80 cols (Concept).
xo	bool		Terminal uses xoff/xon (DC3/DC1) handshaking.
xr	bool	(o)	Return acts like **ce cr nl** (Delta Data).
xs	bool		Standout not erased by overwriting (Hewlett-Packard).
xt	bool		Tabs ruin, magic char (Teleray 1061).
xx	bool	(o)	Tektronix 4025 insert-line.

A Sample Entry

The following entry, which describes the Concept–100, is among the more complex entries in the **termcap** file as of this writing.

```
ca | concept100 | c100 | concept | c104 | concept100-4p | HDS Concept-100:\
        :al=3*\E^R:am:bl=^G:cd=16*\E^C:ce=16\E^U:cl=2*^L:cm=\Ea%+ %+ :\
        :co#80:.cr=9^M:db:dc=16\E^A:dl=3*\E^B:do=^J:ei=\E\200:eo:im=\E^P:in:\
        :ip=16*:is=\EU\Ef\E7\E5\E8\El\ENH\EK\E\200\Eo&\200\Eo\47\E:k1=\E5:\
        :k2=\E6:k3=\E7:kb=^h:kd=\E<:ke=\Ex:kh=\E?:kl=\E>:kr=\E=:ks=\EX:\
        :ku=\E;:le=^H:li#24:mb=\EC:me=\EN\200:mh=\EE:mi:mk=\EH:mp=\EI:\
        :mr=\ED:nd=\E=:pb#9600:rp=0.2*\Er%.%+ :se=\Ed\Ee:sf=^J:so=\EE\ED:\
        :.ta=8\t:te=\Ev    \200\200\200\200\200\200\Ep\r\n:\
        :ti=\EU\Ev  8p\Ep\r:ue=\Eg:ul:up=\E;:us=\EG:\
        :vb=\Ek\200\200\200\200\200\200\200\200\200\200\200\200\EK:\
        :ve=\Ew:vs=\EW:vt#8:xn:\
        :bs:cr=^M:dC#9:dT#8:nl=^J:ta=^I:pt:
```

Entries may continue onto multiple lines by giving a \ as the last character of a line, and empty fields may be included for readability (here between the last field on a line and the first field on the next). Comments may be included on lines beginning with "#".

Types of Capabilities

Capabilities in **termcap** are of three types: Boolean capabilities, which indicate particular features that the terminal has; numeric capabilities, giving the size of the display or the size of other attributes; and string capabilities, which give character sequences that can be used to perform particular terminal operations. All capabilities have two-letter codes. For instance, the fact that the Concept has *automatic margins* (an automatic return and linefeed when the end of a line is reached) is indicated by the Boolean capability **am**. Hence the description of the Concept includes **am**.

Numeric capabilities are followed by the character '#' then the value. In the example above **co**, which indicates the number of columns the display has, gives the value '80' for the Concept.

Finally, string-valued capabilities, such as **ce** (clear-to-end-of-line sequence) are given by the two-letter code, an '=', then a string ending at the next following ':'. A delay in milliseconds may appear after the '=' in such a capability, which causes padding characters to be supplied by tputs after the remainder of the string is sent to provide this delay. The delay can be either a number, such as '20', or a number followed by an '*', such as '3*'. An '*' indicates that the padding required is proportional to the number of lines affected by the operation, and the amount given is the per-affected-line padding required. (In the case of insert-character, the factor is still the number of *lines* affected; this is always 1 unless the terminal has **in** and the software uses it.) When an '*' is specified, it is sometimes useful to give a delay of the form '3.5' to specify a delay per line to tenths of milliseconds. (Only one decimal place is allowed.)

A number of escape sequences are provided in the string-valued capabilities for easy encoding of control characters there. \E maps to an ESC character, ^X maps to a control-X for any appropriate X, and the sequences \n \r \t \b \f map to linefeed, return, tab, backspace, and formfeed, respectively. Finally, characters may be given as three octal digits after a \, and the characters ^ and \ may be given as \^ and \\. If it is necessary to place a : in a capability it must be escaped in octal as \072. If it is necessary to place a NUL character in a string capability it must be encoded as \200. (The routines that deal with **termcap** use C strings and strip the high bits of the output very late, so that a \200 comes out as a \000 would.)

Sometimes individual capabilities must be commented out. To do this, put a period before the capability name. For example, see the first **cr** and **ta** in the example above.

Preparing Descriptions

The most effective way to prepare a terminal description is by imitating the description of a similar terminal in **termcap** and to build up a description gradually, using partial descriptions with vi to check that they are correct. Be aware that a very unusual terminal may expose deficiencies in the ability of the **termcap** file to describe it or bugs in vi. To easily test a new terminal description you are working on you can put it in your home directory in a file called .termcap and programs will look there before looking in /usr/share/misc/termcap. You can also set the environment variable TERMPATH to a list of absolute file pathnames (separated by spaces or colons), one of which contains the description you are working on, and programs will search them in the order listed, and nowhere else. See termcap(3). The TERMCAP environment variable is usually set to the **termcap** entry itself to avoid reading files when starting up a program.

To get the padding for insert-line right (if the terminal manufacturer did not document it), a severe test is to use vi to edit /etc/passwd at 9600 baud, delete roughly 16 lines from the middle of the screen, then hit the 'u' key several times quickly. If the display messes up, more padding is usually needed. A similar test can be used for insert-character.

Basic Capabilities

The number of columns on each line of the display is given by the **co** numeric capability. If the display is a CRT, then the number of lines on the screen is given by the **li** capability. If the display wraps around to the beginning of the next line when the cursor reaches the right margin, then it should have the **am** capability. If the terminal can clear its screen, the code to do this is given by the **cl** string capability. If the terminal overstrikes (rather than clearing the position when a character is overwritten), it should have the **os** capability. If the terminal is a printing terminal, with no soft copy unit, give it both **hc** and **os**. (**os** applies to storage scope terminals, such as the Tektronix 4010 series, as well as to hard copy and APL terminals.) If there is a code to move the cursor to the left edge of the current row, give this as **cr**. (Normally this will be carriage-return, ^M.) If there is a code to produce an audible signal (bell, beep, etc.) , give this as **bl**.

If there is a code (such as backspace) to move the cursor one position to the left, that capability should be given as **le**. Similarly, codes to move to the right, up, and down should be given as **nd**, **up**, and **do**, respectively. These *local cursor motions* should not alter the text they pass over; for example, you would not normally use "nd=" unless the terminal has the **os** capability, because the space would erase the character moved over.

A very important point here is that the local cursor motions encoded in `termcap` have undefined behavior at the left and top edges of a CRT display. Programs should never attempt to backspace around the left edge, unless **bw** is given, and never attempt to go up off the top using local cursor motions.

In order to scroll text up, a program goes to the bottom left corner of the screen and sends the **sf** (index) string. To scroll text down, a program goes to the top left corner of the screen and sends the **sr** (reverse index) string. The strings **sf** and **sr** have undefined behavior when not on their respective corners of the screen. Parameterized versions of the scrolling sequences are **SF** and **SR**, which have the same semantics as **sf** and **sr** except that they take one parameter and scroll that many lines. They also have undefined behavior except at the appropriate corner of the screen.

The **am** capability tells whether the cursor sticks at the right edge of the screen when text is output there, but this does not necessarily apply to **nd** from the last column. Leftward local motion is defined from the left edge only when **bw** is given; then an **le** from the left edge will move to the right edge of the previous row. This is useful for drawing a box around the edge of the screen, for example. If the terminal has switch-selectable automatic margins, the `termcap` description usually assumes that this feature is on, *i.e.*, **am**. If the terminal has a command that moves to the first column of the next line, that command can be given as **nw** (newline). It is permissible for this to clear the remainder of the current line, so if the terminal has no correctly-working CR and LF it may still be possible to craft a working **nw** out of one or both of them.

These capabilities suffice to describe hardcopy and "glass-tty" terminals. Thus the Teletype model 33 is described as

```
T3 | tty33 | 33 | tty | Teletype model 33:\
        :bl=^G:co#72:cr=^M:do=^J:hc:os:
```

and the Lear Siegler ADM–3 is described as

```
l3 | adm3 | 3 | LSI ADM-3:\
        :am:bl=^G:cl=^Z:co#80:cr=^M:do=^J:le=^H:li#24:sf=^J:
```

Parameterized Strings

Cursor addressing and other strings requiring parameters are described by a parameterized string capability, with `printf(3)`–like escapes **%x** in it, while other characters are passed through unchanged. For example, to address the cursor the **cm** capability is given, using two parameters: the row and column to move to. (Rows and columns are numbered from zero and refer to the physical screen visible to the user, not to any unseen memory. If the terminal has memory-relative cursor addressing, that can be indicated by an analogous **CM** capability.)

The **%** encodings have the following meanings:

%%	output '%'
%d	output value as in `printf` %d
%2	output value as in `printf` %2d

%3	output value as in `printf %3d`
%.	output value as in `printf %c`
%+x	add x to value, then do %
%>xy	if value > x then add y, no output
%r	reverse order of two parameters, no output
%i	increment by one, no output
%n	exclusive-or all parameters with 0140 (Datamedia 2500)
%B	BCD (16*(value/10)) + (value%10), no output
%D	Reverse coding (value − 2*(value%16)), no output (Delta Data).

Consider the Hewlett-Packard 2645, which, to get to row 3 and column 12, needs to be sent "\E&a12c03Y" padded for 6 milliseconds. Note that the order of the row and column coordinates is reversed here and that the row and column are sent as two-digit integers. Thus its **cm** capability is "cm=6\E&%r%2c%2Y".

The Datamedia 2500 needs the current row and column sent encoded in binary using "%.". Terminals that use "%." need to be able to backspace the cursor (**le**) and to move the cursor up one line on the screen (**up**). This is necessary because it is not always safe to transmit \n, ^D, and \r, as the system may change or discard them. (Programs using `termcap` must set terminal modes so that tabs are not expanded, so \t is safe to send. This turns out to be essential for the Ann Arbor 4080.)

A final example is the Lear Siegler ADM–3a, which offsets row and column by a blank character, thus "cm=\E=%+ %+ ".

Row or column absolute cursor addressing can be given as single parameter capabilities **ch** (horizontal position absolute) and **cv** (vertical position absolute). Sometimes these are shorter than the more general two-parameter sequence (as with the Hewlett-Packard 2645) and can be used in preference to **cm**. If there are parameterized local motions (*e.g.*, move *n* positions to the right) these can be given as **DO, LE, RI,** and **UP** with a single parameter indicating how many positions to move. These are primarily useful if the terminal does not have **cm**, such as the Tektronix 4025.

Cursor Motions

If the terminal has a fast way to home the cursor (to the very upper left corner of the screen), this can be given as **ho**. Similarly, a fast way of getting to the lower left-hand corner can be given as **ll**; this may involve going up with **up** from the home position, but a program should never do this itself (unless **ll** does), because it can make no assumption about the effect of moving up from the home position. Note that the home position is the same as cursor address (0,0): to the top left corner of the screen, not of memory. (Therefore, the "\EH" sequence on Hewlett-Packard terminals cannot be used for **ho**.)

Area Clears

If the terminal can clear from the current position to the end of the line, leaving the cursor where it is, this should be given as **ce**. If the terminal can clear from the current position to the end of the display, this should be given as **cd**. **cd** must only be invoked from the first column of a line. (Therefore, it can be simulated by a request to delete a large number of lines, if a true **cd** is not available.)

Insert/Delete Line

If the terminal can open a new blank line before the line containing the cursor, this should be given as **al**; this must be invoked only from the first position of a line. The cursor must then appear at the left of the newly blank line. If the terminal can delete the line that the cursor is on, this should be given as **dl**; this must only be used from the first position on the line to be deleted. Versions of **al** and **dl** which take a single parameter and insert or delete that many lines can be given as **AL** and **DL**. If the terminal has a settable scrolling region (like the VT100), the command to set this can be described with the **cs** capability, which takes two parameters: the top and bottom lines of the scrolling region. The cursor position is, alas, undefined after using this command. It is possible to get the effect of insert or delete line using this command — the **sc** and **rc** (save and restore cursor) commands are also useful. Inserting lines at the top or bottom of the screen can also be done using **sr** or **sf** on many terminals without a true insert/delete line, and is often faster even on terminals with those features.

If the terminal has the ability to define a window as part of memory which all commands affect, it should be given as the parameterized string **wi**. The four parameters are the starting and ending lines in memory and the starting and ending columns in memory, in that order. (This `terminfo` capability is described for completeness. It is unlikely that any `termcap`– using program will support it.)

If the terminal can retain display memory above the screen, then the **da** capability should be given; if display memory can be retained below, then **db** should be given. These indicate that deleting a line or scrolling may bring non-blank lines up from below or that scrolling back with **sr** may bring down non-blank lines.

Insert/Delete Character

There are two basic kinds of intelligent terminals with respect to insert/delete character that can be described using `termcap`. The most common insert/delete character operations affect only the characters on the current line and shift characters off the end of the line rigidly. Other terminals, such as the Concept–100 and the Perkin Elmer Owl, make a distinction between typed and untyped blanks on the screen, shifting upon an insert or delete only to an untyped blank on the screen which is either eliminated or expanded to two untyped blanks. You can determine the kind of terminal you have by clearing the screen then typing text separated by cursor motions. Type "`abc     def`" using local cursor motions (not spaces) between the "`abc`" and the "`def`". Then position the cursor before the "`abc`" and put the terminal in insert mode. If typing characters causes the rest of the line to shift rigidly and characters to fall off the end, then your terminal does not distinguish between blanks and untyped positions. If the "`abc`" shifts over to the "`def`" which then move together around the end of the current line and onto the next as you insert, then you have the second type of terminal and should give the capability **in**, which stands for "insert null". While these are two logically separate attributes (one line *vs.* multi-line insert mode, and special treatment of untyped spaces), we have seen no terminals whose insert mode cannot be described with the single attribute.

`Termcap` can describe both terminals that have an insert mode and terminals that send a simple sequence to open a blank position on the current line. Give as **im** the sequence to get into insert mode. Give as **ei** the sequence to leave insert mode. Now give as **ic** any sequence that needs to be sent just before each character to be inserted. Most terminals with a true insert mode will not give **ic**; terminals that use a sequence to open a screen position should give it here. (If your terminal has both, insert mode is usually preferable to **ic**. Do not give both unless the terminal actually requires both to be used in combination.) If post-insert padding is needed, give this as a number of milliseconds in **ip** (a string option). Any other sequence that may need to be sent after insertion of a single character can also be given in **ip**. If your terminal needs to be placed into an 'insert mode' and needs a special code preceding each inserted character, then both **im/ ei** and **ic** can be given, and both will be used. The **IC** capability, with one parameter *n*, will repeat the effects of **ic** *n* times.

It is occasionally necessary to move around while in insert mode to delete characters on the same line (*e.g.*, if there is a tab after the insertion position). If your terminal allows motion while in insert mode, you can give the capability **mi** to speed up inserting in this case. Omitting **mi** will affect only speed. Some terminals (notably Datamedia's) must not have **mi** because of the way their insert mode works.

Finally, you can specify **dc** to delete a single character, **DC** with one parameter *n* to delete *n* characters, and delete mode by giving **dm** and **ed** to enter and exit delete mode (which is any mode the terminal needs to be placed in for **dc** to work).

Highlighting, Underlining, and Visible Bells

If your terminal has one or more kinds of display attributes, these can be represented in a number of different ways. You should choose one display form as *standout mode*, representing a good high-contrast, easy-on-the-eyes format for highlighting error messages and other attention getters. (If you have a choice, reverse video plus half-bright is good, or reverse video alone.) The sequences to enter and exit standout mode are given as **so** and **se**, respectively. If the code to change into or out of standout mode leaves one or even two blank spaces or garbage characters on the screen, as the TVI 912 and Teleray 1061 do, then **sg** should be given to tell how many characters are left.

Codes to begin underlining and end underlining can be given as **us** and **ue**, respectively. Underline mode change garbage is specified by **ug**, similar to **sg**. If the terminal has a code to underline the current character and move the cursor one position to the right, such as the Microterm Mime, this can be given as **uc**.

Other capabilities to enter various highlighting modes include **mb** (blinking), **md** (bold or extra bright), **mh** (dim or half-bright), **mk** (blanking or invisible text), **mp** (protected), **mr** (reverse video), **me** (turn off *all* attribute modes), **as** (enter alternate character set mode), and **ae** (exit alternate character set mode). Turning on any of these modes singly may or may not turn off other modes.

If there is a sequence to set arbitrary combinations of mode, this should be given as **sa** (set attributes), taking 9 parameters. Each parameter is either 0 or 1, as the corresponding attributes is on or off. The 9 parameters are, in order: standout, underline, reverse, blink, dim, bold, blank, protect, and alternate character set. Not all modes need be supported by **sa**, only those for which corresponding attribute commands exist. (It is unlikely that a `termcap`–using program will support this capability, which is defined for compatibility with `terminfo`.)

Terminals with the "magic cookie" glitches (**sg** and **ug**), rather than maintaining extra attribute bits for each character cell, instead deposit special "cookies", or "garbage characters „" when they receive mode-setting sequences, which affect the display algorithm.

Some terminals, such as the Hewlett-Packard 2621, automatically leave standout mode when they move to a new line or when the cursor is addressed. Programs using standout mode should exit standout mode on such terminals before moving the cursor or sending a newline. On terminals where this is not a problem, the **ms** capability should be present to say that this overhead is unnecessary.

If the terminal has a way of flashing the screen to indicate an error quietly (a bell replacement), this can be given as **vb**; it must not move the cursor.

If the cursor needs to be made more visible than normal when it is not on the bottom line (to change, for example, a non-blinking underline into an easier-to-find block or blinking underline), give this sequence as **vs**. If there is a way to make the cursor completely invisible, give that as **vi**. The capability **ve**, which undoes the effects of both of these modes, should also be given.

If your terminal correctly displays underlined characters (with no special codes needed) even though it does not overstrike, then you should give the capability **ul**. If overstrikes are erasable with a blank, this should be indicated by giving **eo**.

Keypad

If the terminal has a keypad that transmits codes when the keys are pressed, this information can be given. Note that it is not possible to handle terminals where the keypad only works in local mode (this applies, for example, to the unshifted Hewlett-Packard 2621 keys). If the keypad can be set to transmit or not transmit, give these codes as **ks** and **ke**. Otherwise the keypad is assumed to always transmit. The codes sent by the left-arrow, right-arrow, up-arrow, down-arrow, and home keys can be given as **kl**, **kr**, **ku**, **kd**, and **kh**, respectively. If there are function keys such as f0, f1, ..., f9, the codes they send can be given as **k0**, , If these keys have labels other than the default f0 through f9, the labels can be given as **l0**, , The codes transmitted by certain other special keys can be given: **kH** (home down), **kb** (backspace), **ka** (clear all tabs), **kt** (clear the tab stop in this column), **kC** (clear screen or erase), **kD** (delete character), **kL** (delete line), **kM** (exit insert mode), **kE** (clear to end of line), **kS** (clear to end of screen), **kI** (insert character or enter insert mode), **kA** (insert line), **kN** (next page), **kP** (previous page), **kF** (scroll forward/down), **kR** (scroll backward/up), and **kT** (set a tab stop in this column). In addition, if the keypad has a 3 by 3 array of keys including the four arrow keys, then the other five keys can be given as , , and These keys are useful when the effects of a 3 by 3 directional pad are needed. The obsolete . capability formerly used to describe "other" function keys has been completely supplanted by the above capabilities.

The **ma** entry is also used to indicate arrow keys on terminals that have single-character arrow keys. It is obsolete but still in use in version 2 of **vi** which must be run on some minicomputers due to memory limitations. This field is redundant with **kl**, **kr**, **ku**, **kd**, and **kh**. It consists of groups of two characters. In each group, the first character is what an arrow key sends, and the second character is the corresponding **vi** command. These commands are *h* for **kl**, *j* for **kd**, *k* for **ku**, *l* for **kr**, and *H* for **kh**. For example, the Mime would have ''ma=^Hh^Kj^Zk^Xl'' indicating arrow keys left (^H), down (^K), up (^Z), and right (^X). (There is no home key on the Mime.)

Tabs and Initialization

If the terminal needs to be in a special mode when running a program that uses these capabilities, the codes to enter and exit this mode can be given as **ti** and **te**. This arises, for example, from terminals like the Concept with more than one page of memory. If the terminal has only memory-relative cursor addressing and not screen-relative cursor addressing, a screen-sized window must be fixed into the display for cursor addressing to work properly. This is also used for the Tektronix 4025, where **ti** sets the command character to be the one used by **termcap**.

Other capabilities include **is**, an initialization string for the terminal, and **if**, the name of a file containing long initialization strings. These strings are expected to set the terminal into modes consistent with the rest of the **termcap** description. They are normally sent to the terminal by the **tset** program each time the user logs in. They will be printed in the following order: **is**; setting tabs using **ct** and **st**; and finally **if**. (Terminfo uses **i1-i2** instead of **is** and runs the program **iP** and prints **i3** after the other initializations.) A pair of sequences that does a harder reset from a totally unknown state can be analogously given as **rs** and **if**. These strings are output by the **reset** program, which is used when the terminal gets into a wedged state. (Terminfo uses **r1-r3** instead of **rs**.) Commands are normally placed in **rs** and **rf** only if they produce annoying effects on the screen and are not necessary when logging in. For example, the command to set the VT100 into 80-column mode would normally be part of **is**, but it causes an annoying glitch of the screen and is not normally needed since the terminal is usually already in 80-column mode.

If the terminal has hardware tabs, the command to advance to the next tab stop can be given as **ta** (usually ^I). A ''backtab'' command which moves leftward to the previous tab stop can be given as **bt**. By convention, if the terminal driver modes indicate that tab stops are being expanded by the computer rather than being sent to the terminal, programs should not use **ta** or **bt** even if they are present, since the user may not have the tab stops properly set. If the terminal has hardware tabs that are initially set every *n* positions when the terminal is powered up, then the numeric parameter **it** is given, showing the number of positions between tab stops. This is normally used by the **tset** command to determine whether to set the driver mode for hardware tab expansion, and whether to set the tab stops. If the terminal has tab stops that can be saved in nonvolatile memory, the **termcap** description can assume that they are properly set.

If there are commands to set and clear tab stops, they can be given as **ct** (clear all tab stops) and **st** (set a tab stop in the current column of every row). If a more complex sequence is needed to set the tabs than can be described by this, the sequence can be placed in **is** or **if**.

Delays

Certain capabilities control padding in the terminal driver. These are primarily needed by hardcopy terminals and are used by the **tset** program to set terminal driver modes appropriately. Delays embedded in the capabilities **cr**, **sf**, **le**, **ff**, and **ta** will cause the appropriate delay bits to be set in the terminal driver. If **pb** (padding baud rate) is given, these values can be ignored at baud rates below the value of **pb**. For 4.2BSD **tset**, the delays are given as numeric capabilities **dC**, **dN**, **dB**, **dF**, and **dT** instead.

Miscellaneous

If the terminal requires other than a NUL (zero) character as a pad, this can be given as **pc**. Only the first character of the **pc** string is used.

If the terminal has commands to save and restore the position of the cursor, give them as **sc** and **rc**.

If the terminal has an extra "status line" that is not normally used by software, this fact can be indicated. If the status line is viewed as an extra line below the bottom line, then the capability **hs** should be given. Special strings to go to a position in the status line and to return from the status line can be given as **ts** and **fs**. (fs must leave the cursor position in the same place that it was before **ts**. If necessary, the **sc** and **rc** strings can be included in **ts** and **fs** to get this effect.) The capability **ts** takes one parameter, which is the column number of the status line to which the cursor is to be moved. If escape sequences and other special commands such as tab work while in the status line, the flag **es** can be given. A string that turns off the status line (or otherwise erases its contents) should be given as **ds**. The status line is normally assumed to be the same width as the rest of the screen, *i.e.*, **co**. If the status line is a different width (possibly because the terminal does not allow an entire line to be loaded), then its width in columns can be indicated with the numeric parameter **ws**.

If the terminal can move up or down half a line, this can be indicated with **hu** (half-line up) and **hd** (half-line down). This is primarily useful for superscripts and subscripts on hardcopy terminals. If a hardcopy terminal can eject to the next page (form feed), give this as **ff** (usually ^L).

If there is a command to repeat a given character a given number of times (to save time transmitting a large number of identical characters), this can be indicated with the parameterized string **rp**. The first parameter is the character to be repeated and the second is the number of times to repeat it. (This is a `terminfo` feature that is unlikely to be supported by a program that uses `termcap`.)

If the terminal has a settable command character, such as the Tektronix 4025, this can be indicated with **CC**. A prototype command character is chosen which is used in all capabilities. This character is given in the **CC** capability to identify it. The following convention is supported on some UNIX systems: The environment is to be searched for a CC variable, and if found, all occurrences of the prototype character are replaced by the character in the environment variable. This use of the CC environment variable is a very bad idea, as it conflicts with make(1).

Terminal descriptions that do not represent a specific kind of known terminal, such as *switch*, *dialup*, *patch*, and `network`, should include the **gn** (generic) capability so that programs can complain that they do not know how to talk to the terminal. (This capability does not apply to *virtual* terminal descriptions for which the escape sequences are known.)

If the terminal uses xoff/xon (DC3/DC1) handshaking for flow control, give **xo**. Padding information should still be included so that routines can make better decisions about costs, but actual pad characters will not be transmitted.

If the terminal has a "meta key" which acts as a shift key, setting the 8th bit of any character transmitted, then this fact can be indicated with **km**. Otherwise, software will assume that the 8th bit is parity and it will usually be cleared. If strings exist to turn this "meta mode" on and off, they can be given as **mm** and **mo**.

If the terminal has more lines of memory than will fit on the screen at once, the number of lines of memory can be indicated with **lm**. An explicit value of 0 indicates that the number of lines is not fixed, but that there is still more memory than fits on the screen.

If the terminal is one of those supported by the UNIX system virtual terminal protocol, the terminal number can be given as **vt**.

Media copy strings which control an auxiliary printer connected to the terminal can be given as **ps**: print the contents of the screen; **pf**: turn off the printer; and **po**: turn on the printer. When the printer is on, all text sent to the terminal will be sent to the printer. It is undefined whether the text is also displayed on the terminal screen when the printer is on. A variation **pO** takes one parameter and leaves the printer on for as many characters as the value of the parameter, then turns the printer off. The parameter should not exceed 255. All text, including **pf**, is transparently passed to the printer while **pO** is in effect.

Strings to program function keys can be given as **pk**, **pl**, and **px**. Each of these strings takes two parameters: the function key number to program (from 0 to 9) and the string to program it with. Function key numbers out of this range may program undefined keys in a terminal-dependent manner. The differences among the capabilities are that **pk** causes pressing the given key to be the same as the user typing the given string; **pl** causes the string to be executed by the terminal in local mode; and **px** causes the string to be transmitted to the computer. Unfortunately, due to lack of a definition for string parameters in `termcap`, only `terminfo` supports these capabilities.

Glitches and Braindamage

Hazeltine terminals, which do not allow '˜' characters to be displayed, should indicate **hz**.

The **nc** capability, now obsolete, formerly indicated Datamedia terminals, which echo \r \n for carriage return then ignore a following linefeed.

Terminals that ignore a linefeed immediately after an **am** wrap, such as the Concept, should indicate **xn**.

If **ce** is required to get rid of standout (instead of merely writing normal text on top of it), **xs** should be given.

Teleray terminals, where tabs turn all characters moved over to blanks, should indicate **xt** (destructive tabs). This glitch is also taken to mean that it is not possible to position the cursor on top of a magic cookie, and that to erase standout mode it is necessary to use delete and insert line.

The Beehive Superbee, which is unable to correctly transmit the ESC or ^C characters, has **xb**, indicating that the "f1" key is used for ESC and "f2" for ^C. (Only certain Superbees have this problem, depending on the ROM.)

Other specific terminal problems may be corrected by adding more capabilities of the form x *x*.

Similar Terminals

If there are two very similar terminals, one can be defined as being just like the other with certain exceptions. The string capability **tc** can be given with the name of the similar terminal. This capability must be *last*, and the combined length of the entries must not exceed 1024. The capabilities given before **tc** override those in the terminal type invoked by **tc**. A capability can be canceled by placing **xx@** to the left of the **tc** invocation, where **xx** is the capability. For example, the entry

```
hn | 2621-nl:ks@:ke@:tc=2621:
```

defines a "2621-nl" that does not have the **ks** or **ke** capabilities, hence does not turn on the function key labels when in visual mode. This is useful for different modes for a terminal, or for different user preferences.

FILES
```
/usr/share/misc/termcap       File containing terminal descriptions.
/usr/share/misc/termcap.db    Hash  database  file  containing  terminal  descriptions  (see
                              cap_mkdb(1)).
```

SEE ALSO
ex(1), cap_mkdb(1), more(1), tset(1), ul(1), vi(1), curses(3), printf(3), termcap(3), term(7)

CAVEATS AND BUGS
The *Note*: `termcap` functions were replaced by `terminfo` in AT&T System V UNIX Release 2.0. The transition will be relatively painless if capabilities flagged as "obsolete" are avoided.

Lines and columns are now stored by the kernel as well as in the termcap entry. Most programs now use the kernel information primarily; the information in this file is used only if the kernel does not have any information.

Vi allows only 256 characters for string capabilities, and the routines in `termlib`(3) do not check for overflow of this buffer. The total length of a single entry (excluding only escaped newlines) may not exceed 1024.

Not all programs support all entries.

HISTORY

The `termcap` file format appeared in 3BSD.

NAME

ttys – terminal initialization information

DESCRIPTION

The file **ttys** contains information that is used by various routines to initialize and control the use of terminal special files. This information is read with the getttyent(3) library routines. There is one line in the **ttys** file per special device file. Fields are separated by tabs and/or spaces. Fields comprised of more than one word should be enclosed in double quotes ("''"). Blank lines and comments may appear anywhere in the file; comments are delimited by hash marks ("#") and new lines. Any unspecified fields will default to null.

The first field is the name of the terminal special file as it is found in /dev.

The second field of the file is the command to execute for the line, usually getty(8), which initializes and opens the line, setting the speed, waiting for a user name and executing the login(1) program. It can be, however, any desired command, for example the start up for a window system terminal emulator or some other daemon process, and can contain multiple words if quoted.

The third field is the type of terminal usually connected to that tty line, normally the one found in the termcap(5) data base file. The environment variable TERM is initialized with the value by either getty(8) or login(1).

The remaining fields set flags in the *ty_status* entry (see getttyent(3)) or specify a window system process that init(8) will maintain for the terminal line.

As flag values, the strings "on" and "off" specify that init should (should not) execute the command given in the second field, while "secure" (if "on" is also specified) allows users with a uid of 0 to login on this line. These flag fields should not be quoted.

The string "window=" may be followed by a quoted command string which init will execute *before* starting the command specified by the second field.

EXAMPLES

```
# root login on console at 1200 baud
console "/usr/libexec/getty std.1200" vt100   on secure
# dialup at 1200 baud, no root logins
ttyd0   "/usr/libexec/getty d1200"    dialup on      # 555-1234
# Mike's terminal: hp2621
ttyh0   "/usr/libexec/getty std.9600" hp2621-nl      on      # 457 Evans
# John's terminal: vt100
ttyh1   "/usr/libexec/getty std.9600" vt100     on           # 459 Evans
# terminal emulate/window system
ttyv0   "/usr/new/xterm -L :0"        vs100   on window="/usr/new/Xvs100 0"
# Network pseudo ttys -- don't enable getty
ttyp0   none    network
ttyp1   none    network off
```

FILES

/etc/ttys

SEE ALSO

login(1), getttyent(3), ttyslot(3), gettytab(5), termcap(5), getty(8), init(8)

HISTORY

A **ttys** file appeared in Version 6 AT&T UNIX.

NAME

types – system data types

SYNOPSIS

#include <sys/types.h>

DESCRIPTION

The file sys/types.h contains the defined data types used in the kernel (most are used through out the system).

```
#ifndef _TYPES_H_
#define _TYPES_H_

typedef short   dev_t;
#ifndef _POSIX_SOURCE
                                  /* major part of a device */
#define major(x)       ((int)(((unsigned)(x)>>8)&0377))
                                  /* minor part of a device */
#define minor(x)       ((int)((x)&0377))
                                  /* make a device number */
#define makedev(x,y)   ((dev_t)(((x)<<8) | (y)))
#endif

typedef unsigned char  u_char;
typedef unsigned short u_short;
typedef unsigned int   u_int;
typedef unsigned long  u_long;
typedef unsigned short ushort;        /* Sys V compatibility */

#include <machine/ansi.h>
#if !defined(_ANSI_SOURCE) && !defined(_POSIX_SOURCE)
#include <machine/types.h>
#endif

#ifdef  _CLOCK_T_
typedef _CLOCK_T_        clock_t;
#undef  _CLOCK_T_
#endif

#ifdef _SIZE_T_
typedef _SIZE_T_        size_t;
#undef _SIZE_T_
#endif

#ifdef _TIME_T_
typedef _TIME_T_        time_t;
#undef _TIME_T_
#endif

#ifndef _POSIX_SOURCE
typedef struct _uquad { unsigned long val[2]; } u_quad;
```

```
        typedef struct _quad { long val[2]; } quad;
        #endif
        typedef long * qaddr_t;             /* should be typedef quad * qaddr_t; */

        typedef long    daddr_t;
        typedef char *  caddr_t;
        typedef u_long  ino_t;
        typedef long    swblk_t;
        typedef long    segsz_t;
        typedef long    off_t;
        typedef u_short uid_t;
        typedef u_short gid_t;
        typedef short   pid_t;
        typedef u_short nlink_t;
        typedef u_short mode_t;
        typedef u_long  fixpt_t;

        #ifndef _POSIX_SOURCE
        #define NBBY    8               /* number of bits in a byte */

        /*
         * Select uses bit masks of file descriptors in longs.  These macros
         * manipulate such bit fields (the filesystem macros use chars).
         * FD_SETSIZE may be defined by the user, but the default here should
         * be >= NOFILE (param.h).
         */
        #ifndef FD_SETSIZE
        #define FD_SETSIZE      256
        #endif

        typedef long    fd_mask;
        #define NFDBITS         (sizeof(fd_mask) * NBBY)        /* bits per mask */

        #ifndef howmany
        #define howmany(x, y)   (((x)+((y)-1))/(y))
        #endif

        typedef struct fd_set {
                fd_mask fds_bits[howmany(FD_SETSIZE, NFDBITS)];
        } fd_set;

        #define FD_SET(n, p)    ((p)->fds_bits[(n)/NFDBITS] |= (1 << ((n) % NFDBITS)))
        #define FD_CLR(n, p)    ((p)->fds_bits[(n)/NFDBITS] &= ~(1 << ((n) % NFDBITS)))
        #define FD_ISSET(n, p)  ((p)->fds_bits[(n)/NFDBITS] & (1 << ((n) % NFDBITS)))
        #define FD_ZERO(p)      bzero((char *)(p), sizeof(*(p)))

        #endif /* !_POSIX_SOURCE */
        #endif /* !_TYPES_H_ */
```

SEE ALSO

    fs(5), time(3), lseek(2), adb(1)

HISTORY

    A **types** file appeared in Version 7 AT&T UNIX.

NAME
　　`tzfile` – time zone information

SYNOPSIS
　　`#include ⟨tzfile.h⟩`

DESCRIPTION
The time zone information files used by `tzset`(3) begin with bytes reserved for future use, followed by four four-byte values of type *long*, written in a "standard" byte order (the high-order byte of the value is written first). These values are, in order:

`tzh_ttisstdcnt`　The number of standard/wall indicators stored in the file.

`tzh_leapcnt`　　The number of leap seconds for which data is stored in the file.

`tzh_timecnt`　　The number of "transition times" for which data is stored in the file.

`tzh_typecnt`　　The number of "local time types" for which data is stored in the file (must not be zero).

`tzh_charcnt`　　The number of characters of "time zone abbreviation strings" stored in the file.

The above header is followed by `tzh_timecnt` four-byte values of type *long*, sorted in ascending order. These values are written in "standard" byte order. Each is used as a transition time (as returned by `time`(2)) at which the rules for computing local time change. Next come `tzh_timecnt` one-byte values of type *unsigned char*; each one tells which of the different types of "local time" types described in the file is associated with the same-indexed transition time. These values serve as indices into an array of `ttinfo` structures that appears next in the file; these structures are defined as follows:

```
struct ttinfo {
        long     tt_gmtoff;
        int      tt_isdst;
        unsigned int    tt_abbrind;
};
```

Each structure is written as a four-byte value for `tt_gmtoff` of type *long*, in a standard byte order, followed by a one-byte value for `tt_isdst` and a one-byte value for `tt_abbrind`. In each structure, `tt_gmtoff` gives the number of seconds to be added to GMT, `tt_isdst` tells whether `tm_isdst` should be set by `localtime`(3) and `tt_abbrind` serves as an index into the array of time zone abbreviation characters that follow the `ttinfo` structure(s) in the file.

Then there are `tzh_leapcnt` pairs of four-byte values, written in standard byte order; the first value of each pair gives the time (as returned by `time`(2)) at which a leap second occurs; the second gives the *total* number of leap seconds to be applied after the given time. The pairs of values are sorted in ascending order by time.

Finally there are `tzh_ttisstdcnt` standard/wall indicators, each stored as a one-byte value; they tell whether the transition times associated with local time types were specified as standard time or wall clock time, and are used when a time zone file is used in handling POSIX-style time zone environment variables.

Localtime uses the first standard-time `ttinfo` structure in the file (or simply the first `ttinfo` structure in the absence of a standard-time structure) if either `tzh_timecnt` is zero or the time argument is less than the first transition time recorded in the file.

SEE ALSO
　　`ctime`(3)

HISTORY

　　The **tzfile** file format appeared in 4.3BSDtahoe.

NAME

USERFILE – UUCP pathname permissions file

DESCRIPTION

The *USERFILE* file specifies the file system directory trees that are accessible to local users and to remote systems via UUCP.

Each line in *USERFILE* is of the form:

[*loginname*],[*system*] [**c**] *pathname* [*pathname*] [*pathname*]

The first two items are separated by a comma; any number of spaces or tabs may separate the remaining items. Lines beginning with a '#' character are comments. A trailing '\' indicates that the next line is a continuation of the current line.

Loginname is a login (from */etc/passwd*) on the local machine.

System is the name of a remote machine, the same name used in *L.sys*(5).

c denotes the optional *callback* field. If a **c** appears here, a remote machine that calls in will be told that callback is requested, and the conversation will be terminated. The local system will then immediately call the remote host back.

Pathname is a pathname prefix that is permissible for this *login* and/or *system*.

When *uucico*(8C) runs in master role or *uucp*(1C) or *uux*(1C) are run by local users, the permitted pathnames are those on the first line with a *loginname* that matches the name of the user who executed the command. If no such line exists, then the first line with a null (missing) *loginname* field is used. (Beware: *uucico* is often run by the superuser or the UUCP administrator through *cron*(8).)

When *uucico* runs in slave role, the permitted pathnames are those on the first line with a *system* field that matches the hostname of the remote machine. If no such line exists, then the first line with a null (missing) *system* field is used.

Uuxqt(8) works differently; it knows neither a login name nor a hostname. It accepts the pathnames on the first line that has a null *system* field. (This is the same line that is used by *uucico* when it cannot match the remote machine's hostname.)

A line with both *loginname* and *system* null, for example

, /var/spool/uucppublic

can be used to conveniently specify the paths for both "no match" cases if lines earlier in *USERFILE* did not define them. (This differs from older Berkeley and all USG versions, where each case must be individually specified. If neither case is defined earlier, a "null" line only defines the "unknown login" case.)

To correctly process *loginname* on systems that assign several logins per UID, the following strategy is used to determine the current *loginname*:

1)   If the process is attached to a terminal, a login entry exists in */var/run/utmp*, and the UID for the *utmp* name matches the current real UID, then *loginname* is set to the *utmp* name.

2)   If the **USER** environment variable is defined and the UID for this name matches the current real UID, then *loginname* is set to the name in **USER**.

3)   If both of the above fail, call *getpwuid*(3) to fetch the first name in */etc/passwd* that matches the real UID.

4)   If all of the above fail, the utility aborts.

FILES

/usr/lib/uucp/USERFILE
/usr/lib/uucp/UUAIDS/USERFILE   USERFILE example

SEE ALSO

uucp(1C), uux(1C), L.cmds(5), L.sys(5), uucico(8C), uuxqt(8C)

NOTES

The UUCP utilities (*uucico*, *uucp*, *uux*, and *uuxqt*) always have access to the UUCP spool files in */var/spool/uucp*, regardless of pathnames in *USERFILE*.

If **uucp** is listed in *L.cmds*(5), then a remote system will execute *uucp* on the local system with the *USERFILE* privileges for its *login*, not its hostname.

Uucico freely switches between master and slave roles during the course of a conversation, regardless of the role it was started with. This affects how *USERFILE* is interpreted.

WARNING

USERFILE restricts access only on strings that the UUCP utilities identify as being pathnames. If the wrong holes are left in other UUCP control files (notably *L.cmds*), it can be easy for an intruder to open files anywhere in the file system. Arguments to *uucp*(1C) are safe, since it assumes all of its non-option arguments are files. *Uux*(1C) cannot make such assumptions; hence, it is more dangerous.

BUGS

The *UUCP Implementation Description* explicitly states that all remote login names must be listed in *USERFILE*. This requirement is not enforced by Berkeley UUCP, although it is by USG UUCP.

Early versions of 4.2BSD *uuxqt*(8) erroneously check UUCP spool files against the *USERFILE* pathname permissions. Hence, on these systems it is necessary to specify */var/spool/uucp* as a valid path on the *USERFILE* line used by *uuxqt*. Otherwise, all *uux*(1C) requests are rejected with a "PERMISSION DENIED" message.

5

NAME

utmp, wtmp, lastlog – login records

SYNOPSIS

#include ⟨utmp.h⟩

DESCRIPTION

The file <utmp.h> declares the structures used to record information about current users in the file **utmp**, logins and logouts in the file **wtmp**, and last logins in the file **lastlog**. The time stamps of date changes, shutdowns and reboots are also logged in the **wtmp** file.

These files can grow rapidly on busy systems, daily or weekly rotation is recommended. If any of these files do not exist, it is not created. These files must be created manually and are normally maintained in either the script /etc/daily or the script /etc/weekly. (See cron(8).)

```
#define _PATH_UTMP       "/var/run/utmp"
#define _PATH_WTMP       "/var/log/wtmp"
#define _PATH_LASTLOG    "/var/log/lastlog"

#define UT_NAMESIZE      8
#define UT_LINESIZE      8
#define UT_HOSTSIZE      16

struct lastlog {
        time_t  ll_time;
        char    ll_line[UT_LINESIZE];
        char    ll_host[UT_HOSTSIZE];
};

struct utmp {
        char    ut_line[UT_LINESIZE];
        char    ut_name[UT_NAMESIZE];
        char    ut_host[UT_HOSTSIZE];
        long    ut_time;
};
```

Each time a user logs in, the login program looks up the user's UID in the file **lastlog.** If it is found, the timestamp of the last time the user logged in, the terminal line and the hostname are written to the standard output. (Providing the login is not *quiet*, see login(1).) The login program then records the new login time in the file **lastlog.**

After the new *lastlog* record is written , the file **utmp** is opened and the *utmp* record for the user inserted. This record remains there until the user logs out at which time it is deleted. The **utmp** file is used by the programs rwho(1), users(1), w(1), and who(1).

Next, the login program opens the file **wtmp,** and appends the user's *utmp* record. The same *utmp* record, with an updated time stamp is later appended to the file when the user logs out. (See init(8).) The **wtmp** file is used by the programs last(1) and ac(8).

In the event of a date change, a shutdown or reboot, the following items are logged in the **wtmp** file.

reboot
shutdown   A system reboot or shutdown has been initiated. The character '~' is placed in the field
              ut_line, and reboot or shutdown in the field ut_name. (See shutdown(8) and
              reboot(8).)

date   The system time has been manually or automatically updated. (See date(1).) The com-
              mand name date is recorded in the field ut_name. In the field ut_line, the character '|'
              indicates the time prior to the change, and the character '{' indicates the new time.

FILES
    /var/run/utmp   The **utmp file.**
    /var/log/wtmp   The **wtmp file.**
    /var/log/lastlog The **lastlog file.**

SEE ALSO
    last(1), login(1), who(1), ac(8), init(8)

HISTORY
    A **utmp** and **wtmp** file format appeared in Version 6 AT&T UNIX. The **lastlog** file format appeared in
    3.0BSD.

NAME

uuencode – format of an encoded uuencode file

DESCRIPTION

Files output by uuencode(1) consist of a header line, followed by a number of body lines, and a trailer line. The uudecode(1) command will ignore any lines preceding the header or following the trailer. Lines preceding a header must not, of course, look like a header.

The header line is distinguished by having the first 6 characters ''begin '' (note the trailing space). The word *begin* is followed by a mode (in octal), and a string which names the remote file. A space separates the three items in the header line.

The body consists of a number of lines, each at most 62 characters long (including the trailing newline). These consist of a character count, followed by encoded characters, followed by a newline. The character count is a single printing character, and represents an integer, the number of bytes the rest of the line represents. Such integers are always in the range from 0 to 63 and can be determined by subtracting the character space (octal 40) from the character.

Groups of 3 bytes are stored in 4 characters, 6 bits per character. All are offset by a space to make the characters printing. The last line may be shorter than the normal 45 bytes. If the size is not a multiple of 3, this fact can be determined by the value of the count on the last line. Extra garbage will be included to make the character count a multiple of 4. The body is terminated by a line with a count of zero. This line consists of one ASCII space.

The trailer line consists of ''end'' on a line by itself.

SEE ALSO

uuencode(1), uudecode(1), uusend(1), uucp(1), mail(1)

HISTORY

The uuencode file format appeared in 4.0BSD.

NAME
vgrindefs – language definition data base for vgrind(1)

SYNOPSIS
vgrindefs

DESCRIPTION
The **vgrindefs** file contains all language definitions for vgrind(1). The data base is very similar to termcap(5).

FIELDS
The following table names and describes each field.

Name	Type	Description
pb	str	regular expression for start of a procedure
bb	str	regular expression for start of a lexical block
be	str	regular expression for the end of a lexical block
cb	str	regular expression for the start of a comment
ce	str	regular expression for the end of a comment
sb	str	regular expression for the start of a string
se	str	regular expression for the end of a string
lb	str	regular expression for the start of a character constant
le	str	regular expression for the end of a character constant
tl	bool	present means procedures are only defined at the top lexical level
oc	bool	present means upper and lower case are equivalent
kw	str	a list of keywords separated by spaces

EXAMPLES
The following entry, which describes the C language, is typical of a language entry.

```
C|c::pb=^\d?*?\d?\p\d?\(\a?\):bb={:be=}:cb=/*:ce=*/:sb=":se=\e":\
:lb=':le=\e':tl:\
:kw=asm auto break case char continue default do double else enum\
extern float for fortran goto if int long register return short\
sizeof static struct switch typedef union unsigned while #define\
#else #endif #if #ifdef #ifndef #include #undef # define else endif\
if ifdef ifndef include undef:
```

Note that the first field is just the language name (and any variants of it). Thus the C language could be specified to vgrind(1) as "c" or "C".

Entries may continue onto multiple lines by giving a \ as the last character of a line. Capabilities in **vgrindefs** are of two types: Boolean capabilities which indicate that the language has some particular feature and string capabilities which give a regular expression or keyword list.

REGULAR EXPRESSIONS
Vgrindefs uses regular expression which are very similar to those of ex(1) and lex(1). The characters '^', '$', ':' and '\' are reserved characters and must be "quoted" with a preceding '\' if they are to be included as normal characters. The metasymbols and their meanings are:

$ the end of a line

^	the beginning of a line
\d	a delimiter (space, tab, newline, start of line)
\a	matches any string of symbols (like .* in lex)
\p	matches any alphanumeric name. In a procedure definition (pb) the string that matches this symbol is used as the procedure name.
()	grouping
|	alternation
?	last item is optional
\e	preceding any string means that the string will not match an input string if the input string is preceded by an escape character (\). This is typically used for languages (like C) which can include the string delimiter in a string by escaping it.

Unlike other regular expressions in the system, these match words and not characters. Hence something like "(tramp|steamer)flies?" would match "tramp", "steamer", "trampflies", or "steamerflies".

KEYWORD LIST

The keyword list is just a list of keywords in the language separated by spaces. If the "oc" boolean is specified, indicating that upper and lower case are equivalent, then all the keywords should be specified in lower case.

FILES

/usr/share/misc/vgrindefs File containing terminal descriptions.

SEE ALSO

vgrind(1), troff(1)

HISTORY

The **vgrindefs** file format appeared in 4.2BSD.

BERKELEY 4.4 SOFTWARE DISTRIBUTION

4.4BSD is the final release of what may be one of the most significant research projects in the history of computing. When Bell Labs originally released UNIX source code to the R&D community, brilliant researchers wrote their own software and added it to UNIX in a spree of creative anarchy that hasn't been equaled since. The Berkeley Software Distribution became the repository of much of that work.

In those years of creative ferment, source code was widely available, so programmers could build on the work of others. As UNIX became commercialized, access to source became increasingly curtailed and original development more difficult.

With this release of 4.4BSD-Lite, you need no longer work at a university or UNIX system development house to have access to UNIX source. The source code included on the 4.4BSD-Lite CD-ROM Companion will provide invaluable information on the design of any modern UNIX or UNIX-like system, and the source code for the utilities and support libraries will greatly enhance any programmer's toolkit. (Note that the 4.4BSD-Lite distribution does not include sources for the complete 4.4BSD system.

The source code for a small number of utilities and files, including a few from the operating system, were removed so that the system could be freely distributed.)

In addition to source code, the CD includes the manual pages, other documentation, and research papers from the University of California, Berkeley's 4.4BSD-Lite distribution.

This documentation is also available in printed form as a five-volume set.

—*Tim O'Reilly*

4.4BSD-Lite CD Companion

112 pages plus CD-ROM
CD Domestic ISBN 1-56592-081-3
CD International ISBN 1-56592-092-9

This CD is a copy of the University of California, Berkeley's 4.4BSD-Lite release, with additional documentation and enhancements. Access to the source code included here will provide invaluable information on the design of a modern UNIX-like system, and the source code for the utilities and support libraries will greatly enhance any programmer's toolkit. The CD is a source distribution, and does not contain program binaries for any architecture. It will not be possible to compile or run this software without a pre-existing system that is already installed and running. The 4.4BSD-Lite distribution did not include sources for the complete 4.4BSD system. The source code for a small number of utilities and files (including a few from the operating system) were removed so that the system could be freely distributed.

4.4BSD System Manager's Manual

646(est.) pages, ISBN 1-56592-080-5

Man pages for system administration commands and files, plus papers on system administration.

4.4BSD User's Reference Manual

909 pages, ISBN 1-56592-075-9

The famous "man pages" for over 500 utilities.

4.4BSD User's Supplementary Documents

686(est.) pages, ISBN 1-56592-076-7

Papers providing in-depth documentation of complex programs such as the shell, editors, and word processing utilities.

4.4BSD Programmer's Reference Manual

884 pages, ISBN 1-56592-078-3

Man pages for system calls, libraries, and file formats.

4.4BSD Programmer's Supplementary Documents

606(est.) pages, ISBN 1-56592-079-1

The original Bell and BSD research papers providing in-depth documentation of the programming environment.

TO ORDER: **800-889-8969** (CREDIT CARD ORDERS ONLY); **ORDER@ORA.COM**

GLOBAL NETWORK NAVIGATOR

The Global Network Navigator™ (GNN) is a unique kind of information service that makes the Internet easy and enjoyable to use. We organize access to the vast information resources of the Internet so that you can find what you want. We also help you understand the Internet and the many ways you can explore it.

Charting the Internet, the Ultimate Online Service

In GNN you'll find:

- *The Online Whole Internet Catalog*, an interactive card catalog for Internet resources that expands on the catalog in Ed Krol's bestselling book, *The Whole Internet User's Guide & Catalog*.

- *Newsnet*, a news service that keeps you up to date on what's happening on the Net.

- *The Netheads department*, which features profiles of interesting people on the Internet and commentary by Internet experts.

- *GNN Metacenters*, special-interest online magazines aimed at serving the needs of particular audiences. GNN Metacenters not only gather the best Internet resources together in one convenient place, they also introduce new material from a variety of sources. Each Metacenter contains new feature articles, as well as columns, subject-oriented reference guides for using the Internet, and topic-oriented discussion groups. Travel, music, education, and computers are some of the areas that we cover.

All in all, GNN helps you get more value for the time you spend on the Internet.

Subscribe Today

GNN is available over the Internet as a subscription service. To get complete information about subscribing to GNN, send email to **info@gnn.com**. If you have access to a World Wide Web browser such as Mosaic or Lynx, you can use the following URL to register online: `http://gnn.com/`

If you use a browser that does not support online forms, you can retrieve an email version of the registration form automatically by sending email to **form@gnn.com**. Fill this form out and send it back to us by email, and we will confirm your registration.

BOOK INFORMATION AT YOUR FINGERTIPS

O'Reilly & Associates offers extensive online information through a Gopher server (*gopher.ora.com*). Here you can find detailed information on our entire catalog of books, tapes, and much more.

The O'Reilly Online Catalog

Gopher is basically a hierarchy of menus and files that can easily lead you to a wealth of information. Gopher is also easy to navigate; helpful instructions appear at the bottom of each screen (notice the three prompts in the sample screen below). Another nice feature is that Gopher files can be downloaded, saved, or printed out for future reference. You can also search Gopher files and even email them.

To give you an idea of our Gopher, here's a look at the top, or root, menu:

```
O'Reilly & Associates (The public gopher server)

   1.  News Flash! -- New Products and Projects/

   2.  Feature Articles/

   3.  Product Descriptions/

   4.  Ordering Information/

   5.  Complete Listing of Titles

   6.  Errata for "Learning Perl"

   7.  FTP Archive and Email Information/

   8.  Bibliographies/


   Press ? for Help, q to Quit, u to go up a menu
```

The heart of the O'Reilly Gopher service is the extensive information provided on all ORA products in menu item three, "Product Descriptions." For most books this usually includes title information, a long description, a short author bio, the table of contents, quotes and reviews, a gif image of the book's cover, and even some interesting information about the animal featured on the cover (one of the benefits of a Gopher database is the ability to pack a lot of information in an organized, easy-to-find place).

How to Order

Another important listing is "Ordering Information," where we supply information to those interested in buying our books. Here, you'll find instructions and an application for ordering O'Reilly products online, a listing of distributors (local and international), a listing of bookstores that carry our titles, and much more.

The item that follows, "Complete Listing of Titles," is helpful when it's time to order. This single file, with short one-line listings of all ORA products, quickly provides the essentials for easy ordering: title, ISBN, and price.

And More

One of the most widely read areas of the O'Reilly Gopher is "News Flash!," which focuses on important new products and projects of ORA. Here, you'll find entries on newly published books and audiotapes; announcements of exciting new projects and product lines from ORA; upcoming tradeshows, conferences, and exhibitions of interest; author appearances; contest winners; job openings; and anything else that's timely and topical.

"Feature Articles" contains just that—many of the articles and interviews found here are excerpted from the O'Reilly magazine/catalog *ora.com*.

The "Bibliographies" entries are also very popular with readers, providing critical, objective reviews on the important literature in the field.

"FTP Archive and Email Information" contains helpful ORA email addresses, information about our "ora-news" listproc server, and detailed instructions on how to download ORA book examples via FTP.

Other menu listings are often available. "Errata for 'Learning Perl,'" for example, apprised readers of errata found in the first edition of our book, and responses to this file greatly aided our campaign to ferret out errors and typos for the upcoming corrected edition (a nice example of the mutual benefits of online interactivity).

Come and Explore

Our Gopher is vibrant and constantly in flux. By the time you actually log onto this Gopher, the root menu may well have changed. The goal is to always improve, and to that end we welcome your input (email: **gopher@ora.com**). We invite you to come and explore.

Here are four basic ways to call up our Gopher online.

1) If you have a local Gopher client, type:
   ```
   gopher gopher.ora.com
   ```

2) For Xgopher:
   ```
   xgopher -xrm "xgopher.root\
   Server: gopher.ora.com"
   ```

3) To use telnet (for those without a Gopher client):
   ```
   telnet gopher.ora.com
   ```
   login: **gopher** (no password)

4) For a World Wide Web browser, use this URL:
   ```
   http://gopher.ora.com:70/
   ```

COMPLETE LISTING OF TITLES
from O'Reilly & Associates, Inc.

INTERNET
The Whole Internet User's Guide & Catalog
Connecting to the Internet: An O'Reilly Buyer's Guide
!%@:: A Directory of Electronic Mail Addressing & Networks
Smileys

USING UNIX AND X
UNIX Power Tools (with CD-ROM)
UNIX in a Nutshell: System V Edition
UNIX in a Nutshell: Berkeley Edition
SCO UNIX in a Nutshell
Learning the UNIX Operating System
Learning the vi Editor
Learning GNU Emacs
Learning the Korn Shell
Making TeX Work
sed & awk
MH & xmh: E-mail for Users & Programmers
Using UUCP and Usenet
X Window System User's Guide: Volume 3
X Window System User's Guide, Motif Edition: Volume 3M

SYSTEM ADMINISTRATION
Essential System Administration
sendmail
Computer Security Basics
Practical UNIX Security
System Performance Tuning
TCP/IP Network Administration
Learning Perl
Programming perl
Managing NFS and NIS
Managing UUCP and Usenet
DNS and BIND
termcap & terminfo
X Window System Administrator's Guide: Volume 8
   (available with or without CD-ROM)

UNIX AND C PROGRAMMING
ORACLE Performance Tuning
High Performance Computing
lex & yacc
POSIX Programmer's Guide
Power Programming with RPC
Programming with curses
Managing Projects with make
Software Portability with imake
Understanding and Using COFF
Migrating to Fortran 90
UNIX for FORTRAN Programmers
Using C on the UNIX System
Checking C Programs with lint
Practical C Programming
Understanding Japanese Information Processing

DCE (DISTRIBUTED COMPUTING ENVIRONMENT)
Distributing Applications Across DCE and Windows NT
Guide to Writing DCE Applications
Understanding DCE

BERKELEY 4.4 SOFTWARE DISTRIBUTION
4.4BSD System Manager's Manual
4.4BSD User's Reference Manual
4.4BSD User's Supplementary Documents
4.4BSD Programmer's Reference Manual
4.4BSD Programmer's Supplementary Documents
4.4BSD-Lite CD Companion

X PROGRAMMING
The X Window System in a Nutshell
X Protocol Reference Manual: Volume 0
Xlib Programming Manual: Volume 1
Xlib Reference Manual: Volume 2
X Toolkit Intrinsics Programming Manual: Volume 4
X Toolkit Intrinsics Programming Manual, Motif Edition: Volume 4M
X Toolkit Intrinsics Reference Manual: Volume 5
Motif Programming Manual: Volume 6A
Motif Reference Manual: Volume 6B
XView Programming Manual: Volume 7A
XView Reference Manual: Volume 7B
PEXlib Programming Manual
PEXlib Reference Manual
PHIGS Programming Manual (softcover or hardcover)
PHIGS Reference Manual
Programmer's Supplement for R5 of the X Window System

THE X RESOURCE
A quarterly working journal for X programmers
The X Resource: Issues 0 through 10

OTHER
Building a Successful Software Business
Love Your Job!

TRAVEL
Travelers' Tales Thailand

AUDIOTAPES
Internet Talk Radio's "Geek of the Week" Interviews

The Future of the Internet Protocol, 4 hours
Global Network Operations, 2 hours
Mobile IP Networking, 1 hour
Networked Information and Online Libraries, 1 hour
Security and Networks, 1 hour
European Networking, 1 hour

Notable Speeches of the Information Age

John Perry Barlow, 1.5 hours

INTERNATIONAL DISTRIBUTORS

Customers outside North America can now order O'Reilly & Associates' books through the following distributors. They offer our international customers faster order processing, more bookstores, increased representation at tradeshows worldwide, and the high-quality, responsive service our customers have come to expect.

EUROPE, MIDDLE EAST, AND AFRICA
except Germany, Switzerland, and Austria

INQUIRIES
International Thomson Publishing Europe
Berkshire House
168-173 High Holborn
London WC1V 7AA
United Kingdom
Telephone: 44-71-497-1422
Fax: 44-71-497-1426
Email: danni.dolbear@itpuk.co.uk

ORDERS
International Thomson Publishing Services, Ltd.
Cheriton House, North Way
Andover, Hampshire SP10 5BE
United Kingdom
Telephone: 44-264-342-832 (UK orders)
Telephone: 44-264-342-806 (outside UK)
Fax: 44-264-364418 (UK orders)
Fax: 44-264-342761 (outside UK)

GERMANY, SWITZERLAND, AND AUSTRIA
International Thomson Publishing GmbH
O'Reilly-International Thomson Verlag
Königswinterer Strasse 418
53227 Bonn
Germany
Telephone: 49-228-445171
Fax: 49-228-441342
Email (CompuServe): 100272,2422
Email (Internet): 100272.2422@compuserve.com

ASIA
except Japan

INQUIRIES
International Thomson Publishing Asia
221 Henderson Road
#05 10 Henderson Building
Singapore 0315
Telephone: 65-272-6496
Fax: 65-272-6498

ORDERS
Telephone: 65-268-7867
Fax: 65-268-6727

AUSTRALIA
WoodsLane Pty. Ltd.
Unit 8, 101 Darley Street (P.O. Box 935)
Mona Vale NSW 2103
Australia
Telephone: 61-2-9795944
Fax: 61-2-9973348
Email: woods@tmx.mhs.oz.au

NEW ZEALAND
WoodsLane New Zealand Ltd.
7 Purnell Street (P.O. Box 575)
Wanganui, New Zealand
Telephone: 64-6-3476543
Fax: 64-6-3454840
Email: woods@tmx.mhs.oz.au

THE AMERICAS, JAPAN, AND OCEANIA
O'Reilly & Associates, Inc.
103A Morris Street
Sebastopol, CA 95472 U.S.A.
Telephone: 707-829-0515
Telephone: 800-998-9938 (U.S. & Canada)
Fax: 707-829-0104
Email: order@ora.com

WE WOULD LIKE TO TELL YOU MORE ABOUT

USENIX is the Unix and advanced computing systems technical and professional membership association founded in 1975. We would like to send you information about our major conferences and frequent symposia held throughout the United States and Canada, about our important technical documentation and other publications, and about the benefits of becoming a member of USENIX and or SAGE, the System Administrators Guild.

Please send me information about:

❏ Joining the USENIX Association

❏ Joining the System Administrators Guild, dedicated to the advancement of system administration as a profession

❏ The bimonthly newsletter *;login:*, featuring technical articles, a worldwide calendar of events, SAGE News, media reviews, reports from USENIX representatives on various ANSI, IEEE, and ISO standards and much more

❏ The refereed technical quarterly *Computing Systems*, published with The MIT Press

❏ Proceedings from USENIX conferences and symposia and other technical publications

❏ The USENIX Association book series published by The MIT Press. First in the series: *The Evolution of C++: Language Design in the Marketplace of Ideas*, edited by Jim Waldo of Sun Microsystems Laboratories

Name/Title

Company/Institution

Mail Address

City   State   Zip/Postal Code   Country

Telephone   FAX   Internet Address

You may receive the catalog of available conference information for the USENIX Winter multi-topic technical conference, the annual Systems Administration (LISA) conference, and the frequent symposia addressing topics such as Operating System Design, High Speed Networking, Security, Object-Oriented Technologies, and Mobile Computing, by telephoning the USENIX conference office at 1-714-588-8649 or sending e-mail to: **info@usenix.org**. In the body of your mail message, send the line: **send conferences catalog**.

O'REILLY WOULD LIKE TO HEAR FROM YOU

Please send me the following:

❏ *ora.com*
O'Reilly's magazine/catalog, containing behind-the-scenes articles, interviews on the technology we write about, and a complete listing of O'Reilly books and products.

❏ *Global Network Navigator*™
Subscription information.

Please print legibly

Thank you for purchasing a *Berkeley 4.4 Software Distribution* document.

Where did you buy this book? ❏ Bookstore ❏ Class/seminar
   ❏ Direct from O'Reilly ❏ Bundled with hardware/software

What computer system do you use? ❏ UNIX ❏ PC(DOS/Windows)
   ❏ MAC ❏ SUN ❏ Other _____

How do you use computers? ❏ Programmer ❏ SysAdmin
   ❏ End user ❏ Other _____

Do you have a modem? ❏ yes ❏ no What speed?_____

Name   Company/Organization

Address

City   State   Zip/Postal Code   Country

Telephone   Internet or other email address (specify network)

The UNIX AND ADVANCED COMPUTING SYSTEMS PROFESSIONAL AND TECHNICAL ASSOCIATION

2560 Ninth Street, Suite 215, Berkeley, CA USA 94710
Telephone 1-510-528-8649, FAX: 1-510-548-5738
Internet: office@usenix.org

NO POSTAGE
NECESSARY IF
MAILED IN THE
UNITED STATES

BUSINESS REPLY MAIL
FIRST CLASS MAIL   PERMIT NO. 80   SEBASTOPOL, CA
Postage will be paid by addressee

O'Reilly & Associates, Inc.
103A Morris Street
Sebastopol, CA 95472-9902

NO POSTAGE
NECESSARY IF
MAILED IN THE
UNITED STATES

BUSINESS REPLY MAIL
FIRST CLASS MAIL   PERMIT NO. 80   SEBASTOPOL, CA
Postage will be paid by addressee

O'Reilly & Associates, Inc.
103A Morris Street
Sebastopol, CA 95472-9902